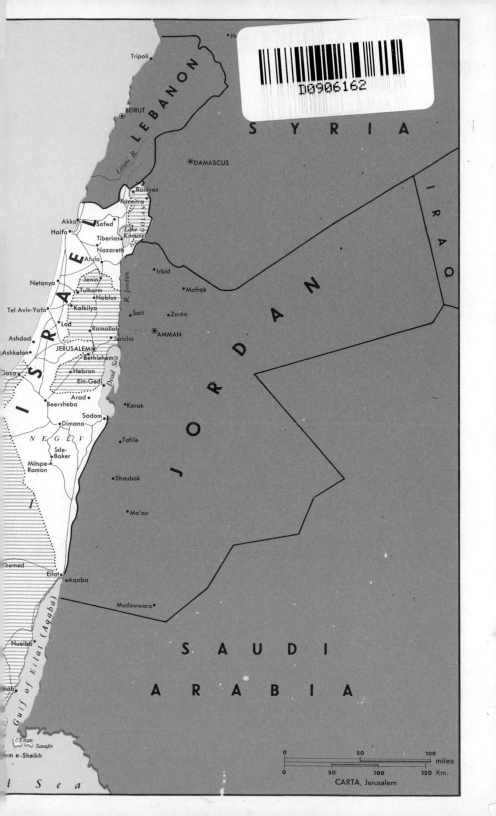

Tripoli

LEBANON

BEIRUT

Litani R.

SYRIA

DAMASCUS

Baniyas
Kuneitra
Akko
Safed
Haifa
Tiberias
Lake
Kinneret
GOLAN
Nazareth
Afula

Irbid

Netanya
Jenin
Tulkarm
Nablus
Mafrak
R. Jordan

Tel Aviv-Yafo
Kalkilya
Lod
Ramallah
Salt
Zarka

Ashdod
Jericho
AMMAN

Ashkelon
JERUSALEM
Bethlehem

Gaza
Hebron
Ein-Gedi

Dead Sea

Arad
Beersheba
Karak
Sodom
Dimona

N E G E V
Tafile

Sde-
Boker

Mitspe-
Ramon
Shaubak

I

Ma'an

Themed
Eilat
Aqaba

Mudawwara

Nueiba

S A U D I

A R A B I A

Gulf of Eilat (Aqaba)

Tiran
Sanafir
rm e-Sheikh

I S R A E L

J O R D A N

I R A Q

l Sea

0   50   100
                              miles
0   50   100
         50   100   150 Km.

CARTA, Jerusalem

DECISIONS IN
ISRAEL'S
FOREIGN POLICY

Books by Michael Brecher
THE STRUGGLE FOR KASHMIR
1953

NEHRU
A Political Biography 1959
(Abridged Edition 1961)

THE NEW STATES OF ASIA
A Political Analysis
1963

SUCCESSION IN INDIA
A Study in Decision-Making
1966

INDIA AND WORLD POLITICS
Krishna Menon's View of the World
1968

POLITICAL LEADERSHIP IN INDIA
An Analysis of Élite Attitudes
1969

THE FOREIGN POLICY SYSTEM OF ISRAEL
Setting, Images, Process
1972

DECISIONS IN ISRAEL'S FOREIGN POLICY
1974

DECISIONS IN ISRAEL'S FOREIGN POLICY

MICHAEL BRECHER

NEW HAVEN
YALE UNIVERSITY PRESS
1975

Published with assistance from the foundation established in memory of Calvin Chapin of the Class of 1788, Yale College.

Library of Congress catalog card number: 73-77143

International standard book number: 0-300-01660-3

Printed in Great Britain

TO THOSE WHO FELL
IN THE YOM KIPPUR WAR OF
1973

PREFACE

This book is consciously directed to bridging the gap between research and theory in the study of foreign policy. Its rationale is the value of the case study, both to illuminate a particular issue and to build a data base for theory-building about how states behave. Its origins lie in dissent from traditional, as well as some modern, methods of analysing foreign policy. Historians have long engaged in the chronicling of relations between states during specific time periods, with an emphasis on diplomacy, alliances, and conflicts culminating in wars. Political scientists carried their analysis a step further by analysing policy, as well as relations, and in some cases behaviour, using multiple indices of how states in the contemporary international system act. Yet even they, for the most part, conducted their research 'at home', through simulation, the application of game theoretic models, or the analysis of event data, with a heavy reliance on secondary sources. Where theory was the explicit objective, field research was conspicuously absent or the benefits of multiple streams of evidence were ignored. Where case studies were conducted, rarely were the findings used as a basis for generalization or prediction.

The precursor to this volume, *The Foreign Policy System of Israel* (1972), offered a *macro* analysis of a system in action over a twenty-year time span: it explored, separately, all components of the environment for decision, the changing composition of the decision-making élite, their attitudes and perceptions, and the formulation and implementation of policy choices and acts of a new Middle East state—for a period of two decades as a whole. *Decisions in Israel's Foreign Policy* provides a complementary *micro* analysis. It applies the same research design to seven case studies, using a wide range of issue-areas, issues (cases), and decisions in the behaviour of one of the most controversial—but not atypical—among contemporary international actors, the state of Israel, from 1948 to 1970. In terms of the framework elaborated in its companion volume, the case studies relate to all four issue-areas: Military-Security (Sinai Campaign, 1956, Six Day War, 1967, and Rogers Proposals, 1970); Political-Diplomatic (Korean War and China, 1950–5); Economic-Developmental (German Reparations, 1950–2, and Jordan Waters, 1953–5); and Cultural-Status (Jerusalem, 1949, 1967). They involve conflict and non-conflict situations, pre-crisis, crisis, and post-crisis phases of a foreign policy decision process, and all three major types of decision—strategic, tactical, and implementing.

The two Israel volumes together constitute a stage in an on-going project which is designed to make the study of foreign policy more scientific and more relevant. The several stages in the intellectual history of this project may be of interest to the reader. The first was the construction of a universally applicable research design. It emerged from a McGill University seminar on the comparative analysis of foreign policy from 1961 to 1964 and, again, in a more refined form, from 1966 to 1968. Two former students and, at present, McGill colleagues, Professors Blema Steinberg and Janice Stein, played important roles in the crystallization of the design, which was presented as 'A Framework for Research on Foreign Policy Behavior' in the *Journal of Conflict Resolution* in 1969. Long before, when the essentials of the design were already clear, I felt the need to test its utility and viability—in the conviction that models, designs, or frameworks which cannot be, or are not, operationalized are of little value in the growth of a discipline.

The second stage became unexpectedly long: field research in India and Israel from 1964 to 1966 and the writing of the two Israel volumes between 1968 and 1973. The parallel India studies in foreign policy are now in process. The choice of these two *new, middle powers*, one developing and one developed, was not by chance. Related projects on Asian and international politics had led to extensive field research since 1951, including three years each in India and Israel, a cumulative body of data, and ready access to decision-makers, bureaucrats, moulders of opinion, and academicians in these new states. At the same time, it became increasingly apparent that they are representative of a large number of Asian and African states in the contemporary international system, those which became independent during the two decades following the Second World War.

The present volume marks the essential completion of the task allotted for Stage 2 of the project. The India studies, apart from the inherent interest in the case studies themselves—for example, India's policy towards China culminating in the 1962 border war, or towards Pakistan, leading to the 1965 war and the conflict over Bangladesh in 1971—will enrich the data base for comparative analysis and generalization.

The third stage concentrates on theory-building in foreign policy, based upon empirical findings. One result is the concluding chapter of the present volume, which tests the validity of some fifty hypotheses drawn from the literature on international relations, using the evidence of Israel's behaviour. Those propositions deal with general as well as crisis behaviour and indicate the extent and clusters of support to be found in the Israeli experience. (The general reader, with a primary interest in the actual behaviour of Israel on seven major issues, may readily dispense with that academic exercise.) A further development of Stage 3 is the generation of new hypotheses, based upon a combined quantitative–qualitative analysis of the Military–Security (or war–peace) issue area of foreign policy. About twenty such propositions are contained in a paper prepared for the IXth Congress of the International Political Science Association in 1973. Closely related to this is the attempt to integrate the research framework underlying these studies with general facet design.

Completion of the India studies will provide fresh data to test both the hypotheses on state behaviour proposed by other scholars and those which emerged from the Israel volumes. Stage 4 will take the form of several parallel volumes on foreign policy systems in action, using a typology which is amplified in the concluding pages of this book, namely: power—super, great, middle, and small; economic development—developed and developing; culture—Western and non-Western; and location—geographic distribution among the continents. From this interaction of systematic and systemic case studies on the one hand, and the testing of a cumulative body of hypotheses on the other, there will emerge building blocks for a general theory of foreign policy behaviour.

The preparation of this book, as well as the research for this foreign policy project as a whole, was made possible by an exceptionally generous Izaak Walton Killam Senior Research Fellowship from the Canada Council from 1970 to 1974. McGill University displayed imaginative understanding of a scholar's long-term research plan by granting a five-year leave of absence. The Hebrew University of Jerusalem provided a congenial and stimulating atmosphere from 1970 to 1973, as well as high-quality graduate students, with whom a fruitful dialogue has taken place over theory and methods, as well as over the substance of Israel's foreign policy.

Several persons have contributed to the quality of the analysis and the accuracy of the data: my McGill colleagues, Professors Blema Steinberg and Janice Stein; my Hebrew University colleague, Professor Raymond Tanter; the two Israel Foreign Office specialists who were so helpful with their comments on the companion volume—Ya'acov Shimoni and Dr. Haim Yahil; and other readers of one or more chapters of the manuscript—Professors D. Avni-Segre and Shaul Friedlander, Michael Elizur, Benjamin Geist, and Ya'acov Vardi.

Valuable research assistance was rendered by Benjamin Geist, Avigdor Hazelkorn, Reudor Manor, Avraham Uliell, and Shimon Wainer, all graduate students at the Hebrew University; Howard Stanislawsky, a former McGill student; and Sheila Moser, who has worked devotedly on both Israel volumes. Hazelkorn also contributed the splendidly helpful indexes for both volumes. And Moser prepared the drafts of the decision flow and feedback charts, which Pirhia Cohen of Carta, Jerusalem, completed under the skilled direction of E. Hausman. René Anug and Evelyn Nadler deciphered illegible drafts and prepared versions which Ena Sheen of Oxford University Press, London, as often in the past, edited with meticulous care.

My wife, Eva, contributed more than she knows, as always. She also displayed understanding, good spirits, and fortitude over the years during which this seemingly endless project has preoccupied me and continues to demand so much time more than a decade after it was set in motion.

Jerusalem   MICHAEL BRECHER
June 1973

The writing of this book was completed a year before the Yom Kippur War of October 1973.

December 1973   M.B.

CONTENTS

Preface   vii

List of Figures   xii

List of Tables   xiii

1 INTRODUCTION   1

2 JERUSALEM   9

3 GERMAN REPARATIONS   56

4 KOREAN WAR AND CHINA   111

5 JORDAN WATERS   173

6 SINAI CAMPAIGN   225

7 SIX DAY WAR   318

8 ROGERS PROPOSALS   454

9 THEORY-BUILDING AND RESEARCH FINDINGS   518

Appendix: Ministers of the Governments of Israel, May 1948–
   May 1973   582

Bibliography   590

Glossary   618

Name Index   625

Subject Index   633

MAPS

Middle East Core   *front endpaper*

Jerusalem: Boundaries 1949–73   *page 36*

The National Water Carrier of Israel   *page 177*

Competing Israeli Territorial Solutions: June 1973   *back endpaper*

FIGURES

Page

1   The Research Design   6–7
2   Decision Flow: Jerusalem   44–5
3   Feedback: Jerusalem   54–5
4   Decision Flow: German Reparations   100–1
5   Feedback: German Reparations   108–9
6   Decision Flow: Korean War and China   162–3
7   Feedback: Korean War and China   170–1
8   Decision Flow: Jordan Waters   216–17
9   Feedback: Jordan Waters   222–3
10 Advocacy Position of Israeli Decision-Makers:
    March–October 1956   251
11 Decision Flow: Sinai Campaign   306–7
12 Feedback: Sinai Campaign   316–17
13 Advocacy Position of Israeli Decision-Makers:
    May–June 1967   353
14 Decision Flow: Six Day War   438–9
15 Post-June 1967 Dual Alliance System   445
16 Feedback: Six Day War   450–2
17 Advocacy Position of Israeli Decision-Makers:
    April–September 1970   477
18 Decision Flow: Rogers Proposals   502–3
19 Feedback: Rogers Proposals   512–13
20 Policy Spectrum on Conditions for Peace: Spring 1973   517
21 Foreign Policy Analytic Model   524
22 Degree of Support for Selected Hypotheses Applied to
    Israeli Foreign Policy Decisions: General Behaviour   572
23 Degree of Support for Selected Hypotheses Applied to
    Israeli Foreign Policy Decisions: Crisis Behaviour   578

TABLES

		Page
1	Jerusalem: Distribution of Population 1922–46	21
2	UN General Assembly Voting Record on Jerusalem: 1947–52	28
3	Diplomatic Representation to Israel: 1949–72 *following*	55
4	Ranking of Ben Gurion's Image-Components Relating to German Reparations: 1951–52	67
5	Comparison of Jordan Valley Regional Water Plans: 1953–55	204
6	Decision-Makers' Images of the Global System: March–October 1956	237
7	Decision-Makers' Images of Near-Neighbours: March–October 1956	
	(a) Actors	244
	(b) Leaders	244
8	Decision-Makers' Images of Israel's Relative Military Capability: March–October 1956	246
9	Distribution of Advocacy of Decision-Makers, Frequency and Intensity: March–October 1956	250
10	Median Value of Advocacy Statements by Decision-Makers: March–October 1956	250
11	Correlation of Decision-Makers' Advocacy: March–October 1956	252
12	Arab–Israel Military Capability: May 1967	325
13	Decision-Makers' Images of the Global System and Dominant–Bilateral Relations: May–June 1967	342
14	Decision-Makers' Images of Near-Neighbours: May–June 1967	
	(a) Actors	346
	(b) Leaders	346
15	Decision-Makers' Images of Israel's Relative Military Capability: May–June 1967	349
16	Distribution of Advocacy of Decision-Makers, Frequency and Intensity: May–early June 1967	352
17	Median Value of Advocacy Statements by Decision-Makers: May–early June 1967	352

18   Correlation of Decision-Makers' Advocacy: May–June 1967   354
19   Chronology of Crisis: I
      The Period of Innocence: 14–18 May 1967   368–71
20   Chronology of Crisis: II
      The Period of Apprehension: 19–22 May 1967   375–7
21   Chronology of Crisis: III
      The Period of Diplomacy: 23–28 May 1967   402–9
22   Chronology of Crisis: IV
      The Period of Resolution: 29 May–4 June 1967   423–31
23   Soviet Military Aid and Presence in Egypt:
      January–June 1970   458
24   Israel's Military Imports: 1968–70   459
25   Decision-Makers' Images of Dominant–Bilateral
      Relations: April–September 1970   472
26   Decision-Makers' Images of Israel's Relative
      Military Capability: April–September 1970   473
27   Decision-Makers' Images of Near-Neighbours:
      April–September 1970
      (a) Actors   473
      (b) Leaders   474
28   Distribution of Advocacy of Decision-Makers, Frequency
      and Intensity: April–September 1970   476
29   Median Value of Advocacy Statements by Decision-Makers:
      April–September 1970   476
30   Correlation of Decision-Makers' Advocacy:
      April–September 1970   478
31   Policy of United States and Israel on Settlement of Arab–
      Israel Conflict: 1969–73   482
32   Rogers 'C' and the Conflicting Parties' Stand:
      October 1971–3   507
33   Hypothesis-Testing of Israeli Foreign Policy Decisions:
      General Behaviour   570
34   Support for Selected Hypotheses Applied to Israeli
      Foreign Policy Decisions: General Behaviour   571
35   Hypothesis-Testing of Israeli Foreign Policy Decisions:
      Crisis Behaviour   575
36   Support for Selected Hypotheses Applied to Israeli
      Foreign Policy Decisions: Crisis Behaviour   576–7

      APPENDIX TABLE: Composition of the Government of
      Israel: March 1949–May 1973   *following* 589

CHAPTER 1

Introduction

The focus of this book is foreign policy decisions. It ranges over a period of more than two decades of permanent conflict (1948–70) and seven clusters of decisions. By consensus, they provide significant indicators of Israel's behaviour in international relations. The issues to be analysed are:

Jerusalem	—the decisions to make it the seat of government (1949) and to unify the City (1967);
German Reparations	—the decisions to seek and accept reparations from the successor to the Nazi regime (1950–2);
Korean War and China	—the decisions to support UN and US actions in response to the Korean War (1950–1), to recognize the People's Republic of China (1950), and to decline overtures for diplomatic relations (1950–5);
Jordan Waters	—the decisions to divert the Jordan River (1953), to accept the Johnston Unified Plan (1955), and to construct the National Water Carrier (1959–64);
Sinai Campaign	—the decisions to align with France, to launch the Campaign, and to withdraw from occupied territory (Gaza Strip, Sinai Peninsula, and Sharm-e-Sheikh, 1956–7);
Six Day War	—the decisions culminating in the War (May–June 1967); and
Rogers Proposals	—the decisions relating to the US peace initiatives leading to the end of the War of Attrition and the three-year Cease-Fire with Egypt (1969–1970).

It is important at the outset to clarify the concept of decision and to indicate the types of decisions to be analysed. A foreign policy decision may be defined as the selection, among perceived alternatives, of one option leading to a course of action in the International System. Contrary to conventional wisdom or myth, a decision is made by identifiable persons authorized by a state's political system to act within a prescribed sphere of external behaviour. In the Israeli system the Foreign Minister or Prime Minister or Defence Minister, or the Cabinet or its Ministerial Committee on Defence, or on rare occasions the *Knesset*, or a Foreign Office Committee or official(s) select(s) option *x* at point *y* in time, which leads to an action towards another state or states, international organization, etc. In short, *a decision is an explicit act of choice, which can be located precisely in time and space. It has definable sources within a setting*. These are related perceptions which predispose decision-makers to select a particular option. And it is aimed at a specific target or targets—state(s), bloc(s), organization(s), and/or region(s). A decision, therefore, can be described and explained: that is, it is researchable. Moreover, consequences can be identified. The resultant data can be collated to test hypotheses about foreign policy behaviour, providing a potential for prediction—the ultimate goal of International Relations.

The classification of foreign policy decisions is based upon a combination of three indicators—time, a spectrum of initiation–reaction, and a scale of importance. There appears to be a meaningful correlation between time-span, initiation–reaction 'mix', and the importance of foreign policy decisions. They may be scaled into three categories.

Strategic decisions are irrevocable policy acts, measured by significance for a foreign policy system as a whole. 'Significance', a concept to be operationalized in the concluding chapter, refers to the number of environmental components which receive feedback from the decision, the intensity of those consequences, and the length of time in which the 'fall out' from the decision affects the behaviour of decision-makers or institutions; that is, the scope and duration of impact. The time dimension in this context may extend from the immediate future to many years, as the decision studies will reveal.

Tactical decisions are indissolubly linked to strategic (high-policy) decisions and are almost always of lesser significance. They may precede, and serve as pre-decisional stages for, a strategic decision: for example, Sinai Campaign (alignment with France—20 September 1956—preparatory to launching the Campaign—29 October); and the Six Day War (mobilization of reserves, delay in military action, and formation of the National Unity Government—16 May–1 June 1967—and the decision to go to war—4 June). They may also follow strategic decisions, from which they logically derive and *without which they could not have occurred*: for example, Jerusalem (the annexation of East Jerusalem in June 1967, more than seventeen years after the decision to make the City Israel's capital); and Reparations (acceptance of direct negotiations with Bonn—in January 1951—after the strategic decision to seek and accept German Reparations—in January 1950—could not be fulfilled through an indirect approach to the four Occupying Powers).

The continuous flow of day-to-day foreign policy choices to execute strategic and tactical decisions may be designated *implementing* decisions. They comprise the bulk of behaviour-creating choices in the on-going process of action–reaction–interaction which, in its totality, constitutes Foreign Policy for any designated period.

The framework of analysis used in this volume has been elaborated elsewhere.[1] It is sufficient here to emphasize the two principal characteristics—*systemic* and *dynamic*.

1. *Systems Approach*: This book applies the universal concept of system and gives it form and substance in an international relations context. The pivotal concepts which infuse the framework may be restated briefly:

a *foreign policy system* comprises a set of components which are classified as inputs, process, and outputs;

the two key clusters of *inputs* are the operational and psychological environments; the *operational environment* refers to ten potentially relevant factors which may affect a state's external behaviour and which define the setting within which decision-makers must choose; the *communication network* is the screen through which reality (the operational environment) is conveyed to those who are authorized to make decisions;

decision-makers are the individuals or groups with authority to decide in the sphere of external behaviour;

the *psychological environment* comprises an *attitudinal prism* and *images*; the prism, product of societal factors (ideology, tradition, and historical legacy) and personality, serves as the lens through which élite perceptions of the operational environment are filtered; élite image is the decisive input into a foreign policy system—because decision-makers act in accordance with their perception of reality, not in response to reality itself;

the *decision*, or *output*, as noted, is an identifiable choice among foreign policy options;

the *issue-areas* of foreign policy are the categories into which all data may be classified—Military–Security, Political–Diplomatic, Economic–Developmental, and Cultural–Status;

the *formulation* process refers to the making of policy, the methods through which environmental stimuli act as inputs and lead to decisions;

implementation is the process of converting decisions into acts; and

feedback designates the consequences of the implemented decisions for various segments of the foreign policy system.

[1] See Brecher, Steinberg and Stein, and Brecher, ch. 1 (*a*). The complete source citations, to which all names in the notes refer, are to be found in the Bibliography, pp. 590 ff.

2. *Dynamic Interaction*: The concept of feedback[1] is crucial to this inquiry, among other reasons because it points up the dynamic character of state behaviour. More generally, the framework emphasizes the dimension of on-going interrelations: from inputs to perceptions, to the formulation of decisions, to their implementation, and to the feedback effects on various environmental components—operational and psychological—in the future. The flow and the concept of dynamic interaction reveal that, like life itself, foreign policy is a ceaseless process; it therefore requires a dynamic model to absorb changes in 'the state of the system'.

This systemic, dynamic framework permits an inquiry into cause–effect relations, as well as into the search for patterns of regularity in state behaviour. Therein lies the basis for probabilistic prediction of choices among foreign policy options: the interplay among different image-components can be assessed, and their influence on decision-makers measured. The framework is schematically presented on pages 6–7 below.

The technique of research combines qualitative and quantitative elements. It derives from a working assumption, which was clearly supported in the course of this inquiry: that every foreign policy issue can be dissected through time and within the context of the system of which it is a part; further, that there are universal categories to classify foreign policy data; and, thirdly, that comparable data can be used to test and to generate hypotheses, as a fruitful path towards theory in international relations.

The method may be termed *structured empiricism*.[2] It denotes the amassing of empirical data on a foreign policy issue and their integration into a structured analytic framework. There are several operational steps in this method, which is applied to all seven decision clusters in this volume.

(*a*) A question is first posed—which components of the operational environment are relevant to the issue under investigation? Theoreti-

---

[1] See Deutsch, ch. 11, for a sophisticated application of the feedback concept, especially to political systems.

[2] A relevant distinction may be drawn between empirical and hypothetical constructs. The former provide a convenient shorthand summary of facts and contain variables whose value can be measured from empirical observations. The latter, further removed from reality, *assume* the existence of an object, agent, process, or occurrence which cannot be directly observed. Whereas empirical constructs are derived from observed data, hypothetical constructs are inferred from reasoning.

The distinction between empirical and hypothetical approaches to knowledge must be viewed along a spectrum. Structured empiricism acknowledges the *sine qua non* role of describable and measurable data; but it also emphasizes the need to order, classify, and integrate data with a conscious objective of testing hypotheses and, therefore, building theory. The two components of the method—structure and empiricism—are, in short, complementary and equally important to productive research.

cally, any or all ten may impinge on the setting for decision. Once these are determined, the nature of their relevance is briefly indicated: for example, the United Nations, the universal actor of the global system (G), had a profound direct effect on Israel's strategic decision of December 1949 to make Jerusalem the seat of government; and intensely hostile Arab actions—*Feda'iyun* raids, closure of the Straits, massing of troops in Sinai (S)—shaped the decision process culminating in the Six Day War.

(*b*) The second step is to designate the high-policy decision-makers. Theoretically, the group may vary from 1 to *n* persons. In the Israeli experience the spectrum was broad: Ben Gurion alone made the decision to launch the Sinai Campaign (25 October 1956); the decision to accept the Revised Unified Plan on Jordan Waters was taken by 3 persons, Ben Gurion, Eshkol, and Sharett; and the entire Cabinet of 21 made the strategic decision of 4 June 1967 leading to the Six Day War.

The psychological environment of the decision-makers is then dissected—both their perceptions of the setting and their articulated goals. Image-advocacy data are emphasized because of the underlying thesis that they provide the foundation for probabilistic prediction of decisions. Images may be partial or general. They may be conscious or sub-conscious. They may be based upon carefully thought-out judgements about the world or they may flow from instinctive perceptions and assumptions. In any event, every decision-maker may be said to possess a set of images and to be conditioned by them in his behaviour on foreign policy (as well as on domestic) issues.

Two techniques are used to uncover the relevant psychological environment—qualitative analysis of an array of documents, and quantitative analysis of the content of speeches, statements, letters, diary entries, etc., during a period of days, weeks, or, at most, a few months preceding the decision. Three of Israel's strategic decisions—to launch the Sinai Campaign, to go to war in June 1967, and to accept the US (Rogers) peace initiative in 1970—were subjected to frequency count and advocacy analysis, with the purpose of producing a scale of importance of environmental components in the image of each decision-maker. The results are collated and compared, facilitating an assessment of the linkage between image-advocacy data and decisions.

(*c*) Analysis of the psychological environment is followed by an inquiry into the decision process through time. This step, which most closely resembles traditional foreign policy research, is not, however, mere chronological survey. Rather, a decision process is explored in terms of the three systemic phases—input, process, and output, that is, within a framework of structured empiricism. It begins with the relevant pre-decisional events and proceeds to decisive inputs: the distinction is between occurrences which impinge upon the decisional setting, and

FIGURE I: THE RESEARCH DESIGN

INPUTS

OPERATIONAL ENVIRONMENT

EXTERNAL	—Global System	(G)
	Subordinate System	(S)
	Other Subordinate Systems	(SO)
	Dominant Bilateral Relations	(DB)
	Bilateral Relations	(B)
INTERNAL	—Military Capability	(M)
	Economic Capability	(E)
	Political Structure	(PS)
	Interest Groups	(IG)
	Competing Élites	(CE)
COMMUNICATIONS	—The transmission of data about the operational environment by mass media, internal bureaucratic reports, face-to-face contact, etc.	

PSYCHOLOGICAL ENVIRONMENT

| ATTITUDINAL PRISM | —Ideology, Historical Legacy, Personality Predispositions |
| ÉLITE IMAGES | —of the operational environment including competing élites' advocacy and pressure potential |

PROCESS

FORMULATION	—of strategic and tactical decisions in 4 ISSUE AREAS:	
	Military–Security	(M–S)
	Political–Diplomatic	(P–D)
	Economic–Developmental	(E–D)
	Cultural–Status	(C–S)
IMPLEMENTATION	—of decisions by various structures: Head of State, Head of Government, Foreign Office, etc.	

OUTPUTS   —The substance of acts or decisions

FIGURE I: THE RESEARCH DESIGN

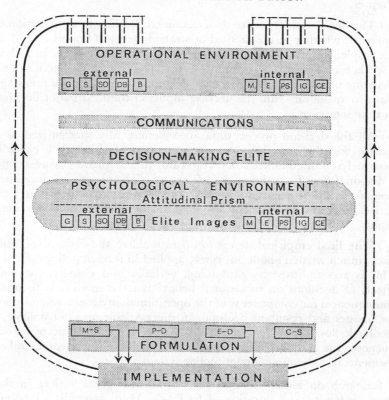

the direct environmental stimuli or pressures leading to a decision. The number of pre-decisional events was found to vary from many (Jerusalem, German Reparations, Jordan Waters) to very few (Rogers Proposals) to none at all, as in the decision to recognize China. The number and intensity of decisive inputs also vary, from super power demands (DB) affecting the Sinai withdrawal decision in 1956, at one extreme of the spectrum, to interest group advocacy (IG) on reparations, at the other extreme. This will be documented in the concluding chapter.

(d) The decisional stages are then examined, leading to the selection of option x, whether at the tactical or strategic level of importance. And the implementation of the decision—by word and/or deed, in a day, a week, a month, a year, or more—is traced. If the issue contains more than one tactical (T) or strategic (S) decision, the implementation stage leads to an inquiry into the decisive inputs of the next major decision in time sequence.

(e) All the decision process data are schematically summarized as a *decision flow* through time. An accompanying decision flow chart is designed as a three-dimensional visual aid: time sequence, expressed by a diagonal flow from the upper-left corner of the chart (pre-decisional events) to the lower-right corner (implementation of decisions); an action flow; and the concept of system linkage and interaction among inputs, process, and outputs.

(f) The final empirical step is to operationalize the concept of feedback, much written about but rarely applied in foreign policy analysis. This is accomplished by explaining, verbally and visually, the flow effects of decisions on subsequent behaviour: the method is to trace consequences for components of the operational environment and then for images and resultant decisions in diverse issue-areas of policy. A feedback flow chart demonstrates the direction and scope of consequences, the spillover from change in any one component to other segments of a dynamic foreign policy system.

Research on Israel's foreign policy indicates great variety in the scope, intensity and duration of feedback. More generally, it points to many linkages: between decision-making groups on different issues; between foreign policy issues in several issue-areas, and their related decision-making processes; between the strategies pursued by decision-makers in different periods and on diverse types of issue; and, most important, the mutual interaction between images and choices. All of these findings make possible the use of knowledge about an individual state to test hypotheses about the behaviour of international actors in general. This jump, from empirical analysis to theory-building, will be attempted in the concluding chapter.

CHAPTER 2

Jerusalem

One issue—Jerusalem—dominates the cultural–status area of Israel's foreign policy. Its role as a uniquely unifying symbol of the Jewish People during the past three millennia is universally acknowledged. Its associations—national, religious, and cultural—are deeply rooted in the consciousness of Jews everywhere. Thus not without reason was Jerusalem perceived by the Zionists and others as an inseparable part of the revived Jewish State.

In the last phase of the struggle for independence the *Yishuv* made a seemingly intolerable concession, namely, acceptance of the UN proposal for the territorial internationalization of Jerusalem. That commitment was nullified, in the Israeli view, by the Arab states' rejection of the UN Partition Resolution, their military assault on the new state, the siege of Jerusalem, and the impotence of the universal organization in the Holy City's hour of need. By the beginning of 1949 the physical link between Jerusalem and Israel's heartland on the coastal plain was secure. Yet almost another year passed before the first of the crucial decisions concerning Jerusalem was taken:

on 11 December 1949   the Government of Israel decided to make Jerusalem the seat of Government. (S)

There was a series of implementing decisions in December 1949 and January 1950, and, after a hiatus of three years, the transfer of the Foreign Office to Jerusalem. After a much longer interval the even more controversial tactical decision was made:

on 18 June 1967   the Government of Israel decided to annex East Jerusalem and surrounding areas. (T)

The dual focus of this inquiry will be the process and feedback consequences of the December 1949 and June 1967 decisions.[1] The research framework of a Foreign Policy System, however, requires a prior exploration of the operational environment, the decision-making group, and the prism-cum-perceptions which induced their decisions.

(A) OPERATIONAL ENVIRONMENT

Few components of Israel's foreign policy setting were relevant to her high-policy and tactical decisions on Jerusalem.

[1] All those events will be analysed in sections (c) and (D) below. A summary and diagrammatic presentation of the decision flow is provided in section (E).

The road to bipolarity was well-advanced by the autumn of 1949, especially after the prolonged crisis over the Berlin blockade. Yet the post-Korean War rigidity was not yet evident. And Israel's relations with the two super powers (DB) continued to be amiable, following the pattern just before and after independence. Indeed they were such as to permit, even to encourage, her policy of *Ee-hizdahut* (non-identification).

The only aspect of the *global system* (G) to impinge upon the Jerusalem issue was the behaviour of the United Nations. On two occasions, in November 1947 and December 1948, the General Assembly had approved resolutions calling for territorial internationalization. Few acts could be—and were—perceived by Israeli decision-makers and their publics as more inimical to Israeli interests. The second was even more offensive, for it was proclaimed soon after *Tzahal* had broken the Arab siege of the New City and thereby liberated the 100,000 Jerusalem Jews from what Israelis were convinced would have been a genocidal fate.

Soon after the General Assembly convened in the autumn of 1949, the evidence mounted that another diplomatic assault on Israel's claim to Jerusalem was in the making. Not only did internationalization have the support of the US and the USSR: more perilous was the massive pressure being brought to bear on Catholic member-states by the Vatican. Thus even without formal relations the Holy See was a crucial *bilateral* component: papal diplomacy was to forge a victorious (and un-usual) coalition of Catholic, Muslim, and Communist states in favour of territorial internationalization once more, on 9 December 1949.[1]

The Middle East Core (S) was more tranquil than at any other period during the protracted conflict: Armistice Agreements had just been formalized between Israel and her four contiguous Arab adversaries—Egypt, Lebanon, Jordan, and Syria (February to July 1949).[2] They remained resentfully hostile; and all Arab states except Jordan actively supported internationalization. But Jordan's posture amply counterbalanced the rest; she was, in reality, an informal ally of Israel in the struggle against the Vatican–Arab alliance—because, like Israel, she opposed any physical international presence in Jerusalem.[3] As such, Jordan was a second important *bilateral* component.

Only two internal components of the operational environment had a bearing on the Jerusalem issue. One was an *interest group* of Jerusalem residents who urged the Government of Israel to take decisive steps to ensure the safety and well-being of Jerusalem Jewry—and the effective

[1] Unbemused Israelis with a sense of history referred to it as 'The Unholy Alliance'.

[2] For an instructive juridical interpretation of those Agreements see Rosenne, *passim*. Iraq, the fifth active Arab participant in the 1948 War, never concluded an Armistice Agreement with Israel.

[3] Eban, who was then Permanent Representative of Israel to the UN, noted this co-operative Israel–Jordan relationship during the battle to negate internationalization in 1950–1. Interview, 1965.

incorporation of the City into the new state. Led by Jerusalem Cabinet Ministers Dov Joseph and Rabbi Fishman (Maimon), it was vocally supported by a small group of parliamentarians, at first in the Provisional State Council and, from February 1949, in the *Knesset*.[1] The decision of 29 July 1948 to appoint a Military Governor of Jerusalem (Dov Joseph) was a partial response to that pressure. Once the siege was broken, delegations of prominent Jerusalemites began to lobby for official action to confirm Israeli sovereignty over Jerusalem.[2]

Among the *competing élites* there was considerable diversity of views. All the secular Zionist parties, from the Nationalist Right (*Herut*) to the Marxist Left (*Mapam*), insisted throughout that Jerusalem be territorially integrated into Israel. The ultra-Orthodox *Agudat Yisrael* and the Communist Party (*Maki*) opposed Israeli sovereignty over the Holy City.[3] And *Mizrahi* was prepared to accept internationalization in the summer of 1948—as preferable to the imminent danger of damage to the holy shrines. By September it advocated Israeli control and never wavered thereafter.[4] On the related issue of Jerusalem as the capital of Israel, *Herut* was relentless in urging the Government to act, from the earliest days of independence to the eve of the high-policy decision.[5] In other parties many persons had doubts, for several reasons—a perceived intolerable security burden, the certain drain on economic resources, etc. As Ben Gurion recalled: 'In almost all parties—all but *Herut*—there were those who opposed the transfer of the Government to Jerusalem. [Among other things,] they were concerned about international repercussions.'[6]

The two types of pressure (IG and CE) reinforced each other as

---

[1] See, especially, the debate on 24 June 1948. RPSC, 6th Sitting, Tel Aviv, 1948, pp. 9–21. Participating were Yitzhak Ben-Zvi, later the second President of Israel; Rabbi M. Berlin, a respected leader of the World *Mizrahi* Movement, who complained bitterly of Government indifference—and expressed regret that, when Israel's independence was proclaimed, Jerusalem was not internationalized; Granofsky; Katznelson of *Mapai*, who also criticized the state leadership's isolation from Jerusalem; *Mizrahi*'s Warhaftig; *Maki's* Wilner; *Mapam*'s (*Ahdut Ha'avoda*'s) Zisling, and others. Ben Gurion's sympathetic yet critical response is elaborated in section (B) below.

[2] Joseph interview, 1960.

[3] There was a brief lapse in the pro-Soviet advocacy of *Maki*: its daily, *Kol Ha'am* (20 December), contained a confession that support of internationalization was 'an opportunistic mistake'. It returned to the path of Stalinist orthodoxy soon afterwards.

[4] See the editorials in *Ha-tzofeh*, 26 and 30 June 1948. On 29 September 1948 it wrote: 'There can be no *further* justification for the internationalization of the eternal capital of Israel. Jewish Jerusalem wants to come under the state.' (Emphasis added.) As an Orthodox civil servant observed: '*Mizrahi*, like all parties, had a deep commitment to Jerusalem, though for tactical reasons only, during the siege of 1948, there was some wavering.' Herzog interview, 1966.

[5] See *Ha-mashkif*, 30 June 1948: 'The Jews of Jerusalem want Jerusalem to be the capital of the State.' On several occasions, as late as 22 November 1949, Begin moved a motion in the *Knesset* to discuss a bill to proclaim Jerusalem the capital.

[6] Ben Gurion interview, 1966.

agents of advocacy. Yet their demand for government action was resisted until eighteen months after independence, when far more dangerous external pressure (the UN) was bluntly reaffirmed. Whether internal advocacy influenced decision-makers' images and then their behaviour is subject to controversy. Suffice it to note the assessment of one careful student of Israeli politics: 'While the question was being considered in the General Assembly's *Ad Hoc* Political Committee [early December 1949] . . . The Prime Minister intervened, under pressure of public opinion and of the opposition parties.'[1] Other internal components—military and economic capability, and political structure —were irrelevant to the issue.

(B) DECISION-MAKERS AND THEIR IMAGES

The decision to make Jerusalem the seat of government was taken by Israel's Cabinet on 11 December 1949: it was less than thirty-six hours after the UN General Assembly had reaffirmed its recommendation for a *corpus separatum*, that is, the territorial internationalization of Jerusalem. At that time the (first) Coalition comprised the following parties and persons:[2]

Mapai

David Ben Gurion	Prime Minister and Defence
Dov Joseph	Agriculture, and Supply and Rationing
Eliezer Kaplan	Finance, and Commerce and Industry
Golda Meyerson (Meir)	Labour and National Insurance
David Remez	Communications and Transport
Moshe Sharett	Foreign Affairs
Zalman Shazar	Education and Culture
Behor-Shalom Shitreet (*Sepharadim*)	Police

Progressives

Pinhas Rosen	Justice

Religious Front
  Agudat Yisrael

Rabbi Yitzhak Meir Levin	Welfare

  Ha-po'el Ha-mizrahi

Moshe Shapira	Immigration and Health, and Interior

[1] Halpern, p. 387.
[2] This Government took office on 7 March 1949, following the First *Knesset* elections, and remained unchanged in composition until 31 October 1950, that is, throughout the period of strategic decision and all related implementing acts except the transfer of the Foreign Ministry to Jerusalem.

Mizrahi
Rabbi Yehuda Leib Fishman   Religious Affairs and War Victims
(Maimon)

Mapai held a decisive majority (8 of 12 Ministers, including the *Sepharadi* representative, Shitreet, who was later to join the party).[1] This assured Government approval for any *Mapai*-initiated or -supported foreign policy proposal unless the Prime Minister and Foreign Minister were in open disagreement. Throughout that early period of Israel's statehood an informal triumvirate held sway in *Mapai* councils —Ben Gurion, Sharett, and Kaplan. In this issue, however, the Finance Minister did not play an active role. Joseph, an articulate spokesman of the Jerusalem Jewish community, filled that void with a forceful advocacy. So too did Rabbi Maimon, the senior Minister from the Religious Front; and his judgement, especially on an issue like Jerusalem, was highly respected by the Prime Minister.

How did these central figures perceive the setting for a high-policy decision fraught with controversy? What was the nature of the attitudinal prism governing their image, and which image-components did they emphasize? There were, in fact, two critical decision points on Jerusalem, one before independence, relating to the UN Partition Resolution, passed on 29 November 1947, the other to make Jerusalem the seat of government, two years later. Both merit attention. Before examining those specific images, however, it is essential to lay bare the profound attachment to Jerusalem of the Jewish People as a whole.

In terms of Israeli thought and action that feeling was poignantly expressed by Israel's most influential decision-maker, David Ben Gurion, on the eve of a crucial UN General Assembly debate.

'Our membership [in the UN]', he began, 'obliges us to say here . . . what lies in the hearts of the Israeli people . . . on Jerusalem as a Holy City and on its relationship to the sanctity of all religions.' He reaffirmed that 'Jewish Jerusalem is an organic part, and cannot be separated from, the State of Israel'.[2] And in that context he laid bare the prismatic core of his image:

as it is an integral part of Israeli history, in her faith and in the depths of her soul. Jerusalem is the 'heart of hearts' of Israel. . . .

---

[1] It did so in all Governments from May 1948 to the end of 1965. In 1966, after the Alignment (*Ma'arakh*) was formed, *Mapai* and *Ahdut Ha'avoda* held a combined majority of 11 out of 18 ministers. From the beginning of June 1967 they comprised 12 of 21 members of the 'National Unity Government'. In the 16th Government, formed after the Seventh *Knesset* election in October 1969, the Labour Alignment (including 2 from *Mapam*) comprised 14 of 24. And in August 1970, with the departure of *Gahal* from the Government, 13 of the 18 ministers represented the Labour Alignment.

[2] Ben Gurion made similar declarations to parliament, notably on 10 March and 8 Nov. 1949. *Divrei Ha-knesset*, i, p. 135, and iii, p. 15.

A nation which over 2,500 years has always maintained the pledge vowed by the banished people on the rivers of Babylon, not to forget Jerusalem—this nation will never sanction its separation. [Moreover,] Jewish Jerusalem will never accept foreign rule after thousands of her sons and daughters have freed, for the third time, their historic homeland and delivered Jerusalem from destruction.... [Finally, lest the commitment be undervalued,] Israelis are ready to sacrifice themselves for Jerusalem no less than the English for London, the Russians for Moscow, and the Americans for Washington.[1]

The Executive of the Jewish Agency, by agreeing to the Partition plan, gave the *Yishuv*'s sanction to the proposal of *corpus separatum*, which placed Jerusalem's 100,000 Jews under an international administration, at least for a period of ten years. Why was Jerusalem 'sacrificed'? Reflections of many Israeli decision-makers after the event illuminate their perceptions and the ensuing decision.

Ben Gurion recalled, a few years after leaving the Government: 'It was *the price to be paid for statehood*. We accepted the UN decision, everything. If the Arabs had accepted it fully, we would have carried it out fully.'[2]

Sharett, who conducted the Jewish case at the UN, together with American Zionist leader Abba Hillel Silver, recorded a few years after the diplomatic battle his explanation for the acceptance of internationalization: 'As regards Jerusalem. . . . It became evident that *the requisite majority for the Partition plan could not be mustered if the internationalization of the Holy City was omitted from it*. . . . The Vatican regarded the latter measure [as one which would] ". . . vest the Catholic Church with predominant influence . . . [and thus] warranting acquiescence in the elevation of the Jewish People to the level of sovereign statehood. . . ."'[3]

This perception of a necessary 'trade-off' was articulated by other decision-makers as well. Dov Joseph, writing about the 'faithful city', observed: 'In particular, the proposal that Jewish Jerusalem should be detached from the Jewish state evoked resentment. . . . In spite of all [their] misgivings, the partition settlement was accepted by the bulk of the Jewish community as *offering the only practicable way out from the untenable White Paper [1939] regime* . . . which had played havoc with Jewish immigration and reconstruction.'[4] Many years later he put the issue more bluntly: 'We had no alternative; we wanted a Jewish state;

---

[1] On 5 Dec. 1949, *Divrei Ha-knesset*, iii, p. 221.

[2] Ben Gurion interview, 1966 (emphasis added). Five years later he elaborated on this without hesitation, emphasizing the same rationale—'the price of statehood': 'In November 1947 I was of the belief that we have the right to the entire Land of Israel. But if the UN passed the Resolution, by a large majority, and if the Arabs would concede [Israel's independence], the issue would be settled totally, and it shall be so.'

[3] As quoted in Sharef, pp. 111–12 (emphasis added).

[4] Joseph, p. 18 (emphasis added).

we weren't prepared to oppose an independent state without Jerusalem. And so, on a provisional basis, we *acquiesced* in the plan for a *corpus separatum*. But we didn't *accept* it—voluntarily. In a word, we yielded to the facts. But we never ceased to protest against the setting up of an internationalized Jerusalem.'[1]

Mrs. Meir, too, recalled: 'We went along with the 1947 UN Resolution, as painful as the idea was that Jerusalem would be internationalized. Had the Arabs gone along with the Resolution, Jerusalem would not have been the capital.'[2] The image of *'ein breira'*, 'bitter sacrifice', 'the price to be paid', is also noted by Israeli civil servants, UN aides, and scholars, who have offered an explanation of the *Yishuv*'s response to the Partition Resolution.[3]

Only one divergent perception was encountered in the course of this inquiry. Abba Eban, then a promising young member of the Jewish Agency's Political Department with direct access to high-policy decision-makers, recalled: 'This question has to be seen against the background of the Peel Commission's recommendation for the internationalization of Jerusalem in 1937. Moreover, the *Yishuv* had developed in the Galil and the coastal plain, with Jerusalem a mixed population centre surrounded by Arab areas. I do not recall any discussion among the leadership in that period suggesting Jerusalem as part of a Jewish state. *The best that could be imagined* was internationalization—to prevent it from being incorporated into an Arab state.'[4]

At first glance this appears to contradict the widespread consensus; but it does not negate the sense of loss and sacrifice felt by Palestine Jewry. Rather, it draws attention to their pragmatic image of the Partition plan and their decision *at the time*: in November 1947 internationalization was perceived as a tactical concession to political necessity. Moreover, it was regarded as a temporary acquiescence, for the attachment to Jerusalem was deep.

According to Ze'ev Sharef, the idea of Jerusalem as a *corpus separatum*

---

[1] Joseph interview, 1971. David Horowitz, then Director-General of the Finance Ministry, also differentiated between acquiescence and positive acceptance. Interview, 1965.

[2] Meir interview, 1966.

[3] These include the first Director-General of the Israel Foreign Office (Eytan, p. 69—'. . . the establishment of an independent Jewish state outweighed the bitter sacrifice . . .'); the Adviser on Jerusalem Affairs (Herzog interview, 1966—'the price of internationalization was worth paying—if necessary—for independence'); a personal consultant to the UN Mediator and, later, Personal Representative to the Acting Mediator, Dr. Ralph Bunche, in Tel Aviv (Mohn, p. 453—'. . . was finally accepted as the price to be paid for the coming into being of a Jewish state'); a group of Israeli scholars (*Israel and the United Nations*, p. 130—'. . . a very serious national and spiritual sacrifice . . .'); and Halpern (pp. 373–4—'in order to gain the most essential sovereign rights needed to solve the post-war problems of the Jews . . .').

[4] Eban interview, 1965.

began to fade among *Yishuv* leaders as early as January–February 1948.[1] This is certainly true of Ben Gurion at the dawn of independence, as is evident in his reply to the tense debate on Jerusalem in the Provisional State Council on 24 June. Indeed there is no more illuminating expression of the Prime Minister's pragmatic image: the issue was not whether to include Jerusalem in the state, but how to achieve this goal in the light of military and economic obstacles and conditions.

We understand the need for our comrades from Jerusalem to pour out their hearts. Whether the discussion is worthwhile is another question. . . .

Comrades from Jerusalem: do not assume that the basic problem of Jerusalem is one of arrangements or politics: *it is*, in the first place, *a question of military capability*. Will we have the strength a) to capture the Old City, b) to capture as wide a corridor as is necessary from here [Tel Aviv] to Jerusalem so that we have . . . a sufficiently populated area to link Jerusalem to the rest of the State, and c) to rout the Jordan Legion from the Triangle? Without these three things we cannot say with confidence that Jerusalem is liberated. . . . These deeds must be done not only inside Jerusalem but, in the main, outside of it. . . .

[Moreover,] with military strength alone we cannot solve all the problems of Jerusalem. After the Jewish Army liberates the heart of Jerusalem, the Old City, conquers the territory between Tel Aviv and Jerusalem which is still not in our hands, and the strength of the Legion is destroyed, a problem of the first order will arise: how to secure *a healthy economic base*, large and wide, *not only for the present population of Jerusalem, but also for long-term immigration to this city*.

The third question is the most pressing . . . , the question of maintaining a large supply of water, gasoline, food, and materials to Jerusalem all the time that the shelling is going on. . . .

The Chosen City has not had luck. King David chose for his capital one of the most difficult places in the Land. The people who returned to Zion in our generation did not worry about communications or *territorial access to the capital*. A miracle happened, and the Jewish majority in the city was preserved. . . . But a Jewish majority in Jerusalem is not enough. We need surrounding Jewish agricultural areas and a road to Jerusalem clustered with Jewish settlements. We are being punished now for this sin of omission, and *we must accomplish now in war what evaded us in peace*. In our army's hands—and this time only in our army's hands—we will make amends. . . .

The basic question now for our existence and future is our military strength. On it depends the entire fate of Jerusalem. . . . The redemption of Jerusalem depends upon the redemption of the way to Jerusalem, and this is not only in conquering it, but in rebuilding it. . . .

It is not possible nor advantageous to say everything now. . . . In a war we must be silent about many things. . . .

[Finally, his image of the status of Jerusalem was unmistakable.] With regard to the question whether or not Jerusalem is within the country. . . . *Until peace is proclaimed* and boundaries are decided upon by international authority, with the agreement of all sides, *we speak of Jerusalem as within the boundaries of the Jewish State . . . (as of now, to my regret, without the Old City) exactly as Tel Aviv*. And there

---

[1] Interview, 1966.

is no difference between Jerusalem and Tel Aviv, Haifa, Hanita. *They are all part of the Jewish State.*[1]

All subsequent actions of Ben Gurion on the Jerusalem issue were derived from this unshakeable image of Jerusalem as an integral part of Israel: it was enunciated with his typical admixture of realism, logic, and vision. Among others, James McDonald, the first US Ambassador to Israel, caught its spirit and wider significance: '. . . there were some important Israeli leaders who considered the strategic vulnerability of Jerusalem and the economic advantages of its internationalization more important than its historical and religious appeal. These "realists" would, had they dared, have favored a compromise or at any rate a less unyielding attitude than that adopted by Ben Gurion and his Cabinet. . . .' Moreover, Ben Gurion was here expressing the unyielding view of the Israeli public—which had hardened even more as a result of the siege of the City in 1948.[2]

The Prime Minister's extraordinary emphasis on the military dimension was also recorded by one of his closest aides at the time: '"I find it difficult now to understand any other language than the language of war", he remarked during one discussion. ". . . I have heard it said that the wisdom of Israel is the wisdom of salvation, and these words too are inexplicable to me. I feel that the wisdom of Israel *now* is the wisdom to wage war, that and nothing else, that and only that".'[3]

Sharett participated in the June 1948 debate, but briefly. It was in reply to *Mizrahi*'s Warhaftig about demilitarization. 'First of all, we must demand that the Arab Legion leave Jerusalem and then it will be possible to talk of the demilitarization of Jerusalem also on the inside.'[4] The tone was very different from Ben Gurion's militant and military attitude, partly, no doubt, because of their roles (Defence Minister and Foreign Minister) but also because of Sharett's predominantly 'outer-directed' image of foreign policy problems.[5] In this regard, the Military Governor of Jerusalem at the time wrote: 'There was, in fact, a difference of opinion between our Foreign Minister . . . and myself in connection with the use of the side roads to bring food over and above the quantities specified by the Truce Commission. . . . It seemed to me that he was anxious to satisfy the demands of the UN authorities even when they were not juridically justified, in order to achieve an atmosphere of good will.'[6] And, judging from his later behaviour, both at the time of the strategic decision and with regard to the transfer of the Foreign Office (to be examined later), Sharett's image of Jerusalem fell into McDonald's category of 'less unyielding'.

[1] RPSC, pp. 18–21 (emphasis added). [2] McDonald, p. 207.
[3] Sharef, p. 191. [4] RPSC, p. 20.
[5] The contrasting images of Ben Gurion and Sharett were analysed in Brecher, ch. 12.
[6] Joseph, p. 236.

The prevalent Ben Gurion image and its policy implications were also noted at the time by a perceptive American journalist, Kenneth Bilby: they received further confirmation from another high-policy decision-maker and from the Director-General of the Foreign Ministry:

In the summer of 1948 . . . I wrote a speculative article . . . prophesying a fairly imminent declaration of Jerusalem's incorporation into Israel. Afterward, worried over possible denials, I showed a copy to Dr. Walter Eytan, and he was reassuring: 'You needn't be concerned. It may be a question of weeks or months, *but you can be certain it will happen.*'

[Further.] Israel's Immigration Minister, Moshe Shapira, admitted when I sought to explore this argument, that big plans were afoot for Jerusalem. He expected the Jewish population to jump another 100,000 within a few years. . . . The UN plan called for an immediate cessation of immigration; Shapira said most of the immigrants who docked at Haifa port expressed a desire to settle in Jerusalem—and *Israel would* funnel them there as fast as the state's resources permitted.[1]

Many years later Shapira remarked: 'For us, the State of Israel without Jerusalem is an amputated state. True, we agreed to a state without Jerusalem in 1947; but we merely waited until an opportunity arose to rectify the situation.'[2] And he, like many others, emphasized that Jerusalem had occupied a pivotal position as political and cultural centre of the *Yishuv* during the Mandate.

Ben Gurion's speech to the Provisional State Council in June 1948 was clearly the image of a war-time leader, responding to the reality of siege and the challenge to Israel's physical survival. The claim and commitment to Jerusalem were assumed; his focus was on the task of achieving a 'vital national interest'. What made Jerusalem vital to Ben Gurion (and to Israelis as a nation) was contained in his provocative statement to the *Knesset* eighteen months after the War of Independence, as quoted earlier. In short, the dominant strand in his attitudinal prism was the historic, national, and emotional links between Jewry and Jerusalem. And, just as military and economic capability were the dominant image-components in June 1948, so interest groups and competing élites (public opinion) were central to his outlook in December 1949, along with the global component of the external setting, as represented by the United Nations. He was also aware of Israel's more advantageous M and E capability. It was this psychological environment which shaped Israel's strategic decision on Jerusalem.

Sharett was in New York during the critical last phase of the decision process, representing Israel before the world body. Yet his image of the Jerusalem issue is evident in two speeches, especially his address to the General Assembly's *Ad Hoc* Political Committee on 25 November 1949:

[1] Bilby, pp. 195, 204–5 (emphasis added).   [2] Interview, 1968.

(1) Their attachment to Jerusalem led the Jews to form the majority of its inhabitants and to recreate their spiritual, cultural, and political centre in the Holy City.

(2) An immense sacrifice was entailed in the 1947 renunciation of the Jewish claim to the inclusion of Jewish Jerusalem in the Jewish State—an unparalleled sacrifice.

(3) Another source of the indissoluble link between Jerusalem and Israel was the 'dictates of self-preservation' which 'prevailed against the original willingness to accept an international verdict'.

(4) Israel's ordeals, sacrifices, and responsibilities, as the sole guardian of Jerusalem's historic values, along with economic and moral considerations, 'have impelled and continue to impel the transfer to it of central institutions such as always have been housed in Jerusalem'. And

(5) The Jewish inhabitants of the city have the elementary right of self-determination enjoyed by their compatriots elsewhere.[1]

Sharett's image did not encompass the passionate commitment to Jewish sovereignty over Jerusalem so conspicuous in Ben Gurion's pronouncements. Even in his lengthy survey to the *Knesset* after the hostile UN vote his reaction was restrained: the solitary exception was his remark that 'the Assembly Resolution amazed and shocked our public. It was as though an arrow had been shot into our heart from the very fortress to which we had looked for protection and support.'[2] That restraint was to be reflected in his subsequent behaviour—as were Joseph's and Maimon's vocal support for Ben Gurion's advocacy.

(c) DECISION PROCESS

Israel's decisions relating to Jerusalem extended over a period of more than seventeen years, from November 1949 to June 1967. They may be grouped into four clusters or stages:

(1) from 15 November 1949 (Ben Gurion's advice to the Cabinet to act quickly in the matter of Jerusalem as Israel's capital) to 11 December 1949 (the decision to make Jerusalem the seat of government);

(2) from 11 December 1949 to 23 January 1950 (the implementation of that strategic decision);

(3) from 4 May 1952 (a formal announcement that the Foreign Office would move to Jerusalem) to 12 July 1953 (the actual transfer of the ministry); and, after a lengthy lapse of time,

---

[1] 'Israel's Proposal', in *The Peace of Jerusalem*, pp. 5–17. His address to the plenary session of the General Assembly on 9 December 1949, just before the adverse vote reaffirming territorial internationalization, is entitled, 'For Jerusalem's Sake I Will Not Rest'. Ibid., pp. 56–68.

[2] It was the opening speech in the *Knesset*'s foreign affairs debate on 2 January 1950, *Divrei Ha-knesset*, iii, pp. 375–80.

(4) from 7 June to 28 June 1967 (the integration of West and East Jerusalem).

There was, too, an important stage of pre-decisional events, beginning with the UN Partition Resolution of 29 November 1947.[1]

Under the terms of Resolution 181 (II) the City of Jerusalem was to become a *corpus separatum*, administered by the Trusteeship Council, acting on behalf of the United Nations as the Administering Authority. An appointed Governor would serve as the chief administrative official, with the assistance of an administrative staff, principally of Palestinians, a police force composed of non-Palestinian nationals, and an elected Legislative Council. Jerusalem was to be demilitarized and neutralized. It was to form part of the Economic Union of Palestine, including the independent Jewish and Arab states, and was designated the Head-quarters of its Economic Board. Representatives of the two states were to be accredited to the Governor of Jerusalem and were to be responsible for the protection of the interests of their states and nationals in the City. There were also provisions concerning the administration of justice, citizenship, local autonomy, freedom of transit, the acceptance of two official languages, Arabic and Hebrew, though other 'working languages' could be adopted, and the special powers of the Governor for the protection of the Holy Places.

The Trusteeship Council (TC) was directed to prepare and approve a detailed Statute within five months. It was to take effect no later than 1 October 1948 and was to remain in force initially for ten years. Thereafter the Statute was to be subject to re-examination by the TC. Residents of Jerusalem were to be 'free to express by means of a referendum their wishes as to possible modifications of the regime of the City'.[2]

The *Yishuv* acquiesced in the proposal for territorial international-ization on purely pragmatic grounds: it was, as noted, the perceived *sine qua non* of independence. Among many, too, there was the convic-tion that the unfolding of events would prove a *corpus separatum* unwork-able. Joseph summed up the decision-makers' mood: 'We hoped that Jerusalem would be part of the state eventually. We thought that because we had a clear majority this would take place. But we didn't think about what would happen ten years later [referring to the referendum proviso]. We were then in the midst of a struggle over

---

[1] The Jerusalem issue, like the larger Arab-Jewish conflict, has deeper roots, of course: the Peel Commission Report of 1937 and the disturbances from which it arose; the earlier disturbances of 1920–1 and 1929; the League Mandate; the Balfour Declaration; the return of Jewry to its ancestral homeland from the 1870s; and the claims to Jerusalem inherent in Jewish nationalism and a decisive majority for a century on the one hand, and prolonged Arab presence on the other. Yet viewed as a decision of the State of Israel, the UN Partition Resolution is the most appropriate and relevant first pre-decisional event.

[2] The text of the Partition Resolution is in UN Doc. A/519, 29 Nov. 1947.

corpus separatum. The outcome was far from certain. It could have turned out better than it seemed.'[1] And, indeed, as the appointed day for the termination of the Mandate approached, the battle for, over, and in Jerusalem rendered the plan abortive—at least until the first Arab–Israel War came to an end.

The pre-decisional events of 1948–9 concerning Jerusalem may be summarized briefly. The Trusteeship Council completed the task of drafting the Statute on 21 April but postponed *formal approval* pending the receipt of further advice from the General Assembly.[2] By that time Jerusalem was the scene of fighting. Thus towards the end of April the Assembly set the Statute aside and instructed the TC 'to submit within the shortest possible time proposals [for] . . . suitable measures for the protection of the city and its inhabitants'.[3] The Council initiated negotiations with the Jewish Agency and the Arab Higher Committee and informed the Assembly of their agreement to a cease-fire effective on 2 May. This proved abortive because the Arabs insisted on the return of an Arab suburb, Katamon, captured by the *Hagana* on 30 April, and the Jewish Agency refused.

Pursuing an alternative path, the TC recommended that the Mandatory Government appoint a Special Commissioner for Jerusalem before 15 May. The General Assembly added its support by approving the proposal on the 6th. The designated Commissioner, Harold Evans, a Philadelphia lawyer, arrived on the 11th. A cease-fire was in force between the 8th and the 12th of May. By then, however, it was apparent to all that the protection of the City and its residents would devolve upon the two contending communities, their political organizations,

[1] Joseph interview, 1971. According to an official estimate the population of Jerusalem in 1946 was 164,440, comprising 99,320 Jews, 33,680 Muslims, 31,330 Christians, and 110 others. Government of Palestine, p. 13. A Jewish plurality of 50 per cent dates back to 1884. In the period 1898–1912 the Jewish majority in Jerusalem ranged from 64·3 to 67·4 per cent. The official census thereafter indicated the following figures:

TABLE I. JERUSALEM: DISTRIBUTION OF POPULATION 1922–46

	Jews	Per cent	Muslims	Per cent	Christians	Per cent	Others	Per cent	Total
1922	33,971	54·3	13,413	21·4	14,699	23·5	495	·8	62,578
1931	51,222	56·6	19,894	22·0	19,335	21·4	52	·0	90,503
1944	97,000	61·7	30,630	19·5	29,350	18·7	100	·1	157,080
1946	99,320	60·4	33,680	20·4	31,330	19·1	110	·1	164,440

Source: Government of Palestine, pp. 148, 151. Supplement, p. 13, as reproduced in Bovis, p. 128.

[2] For the text of the Draft Statute for the City of Jerusalem, which was faithful to the spirit of the Partition Resolution, see UN. TCOR, II, Annex, Doc. T/118 Rn. 2, 21 April 1948.

[3] UN Doc. A/543, 26 April 1948.

and their military capability, not on UN-designated officials without any effective sanction.[1]

When the *Minhalat Ha'am* (National Administration) met on 12 May, three separate truce proposals for Jerusalem were under consideration—one from the High Commissioner, another from the Consular Committee (US, French, and Belgian Consuls in Jerusalem), and a third from the Red Cross. Intertwined, was a proposal for a country-wide truce. It was rejected by 6 to 4. And that act 'meant *ipso facto* that in two days' time the State [of Israel] would come into formal being', immediately after the termination of the Mandate.[2]

The Proclamation of Independence on 14 May did not refer specifically to Jerusalem—nor to any other town or district in the Land of Israel. But within hours Arab armies invaded the new state, and Jewish Jerusalem came under siege. In the midst of that first assault, while Israel struggled for survival, Prime Minister Ben Gurion, as noted, assured a receptive provisional parliament: 'Until peace is proclaimed . . . we speak of Jerusalem as within the boundaries of the Jewish State . . . (as of now, to my regret, without the Old City), exactly as Tel Aviv. . . .' It was not a governmental *decision*. But as the first declaration on Jerusalem by Israel's Head of Government before an official forum, it symbolized the national will and the decision-makers' resolve. As Joseph recalled: 'From the first day of the state, we behaved as if Jerusalem were part of Israel—with one difference: many ministries were not yet established there.'[3]

The UN Mediator, Count Bernadotte, startled and angered Israel's leaders on 29 June by proposing the transfer of Jerusalem—as a whole—to Jordan.[4] It was dismissed out of hand, and formally rejected by the Provisional Council of State on 5 July. Yet a mistrustful Israeli High Policy Élite perceived it as symptomatic of a pro-Arab outlook in the UN establishment.[5]

In mid-July *Tzahal* (the successor to *Hagana*) made an ill-fated attempt to liberate the Old City: Operation *Kedem* failed, and East

---

[1] On the April–May events in the Trusteeship Council and the General Assembly see Bovis, pp. 53–7, and Schechtman, pp. 390–6.

[2] The relevant events from the UN Partition Resolution to the Declaration of Independence are chronicled from the inside by Sharef, pp. 108–23; the extract is from p. 123. See also Horowitz, Part IV; Hurewitz, ch. 23; and, with reference to the Holy Places, Zander, pp. 72–6.

[3] Joseph interview, 1971.

[4] S/863 in UN. GAOR III, Suppl. 11, pp. 25–6. The text read: 'Part III Annex to Suggestions: Territorial Matters 3. Inclusion of the City of Jerusalem in Arab territory, with municipal autonomy for the Jewish Community, and special arrangements for protection of the Holy Places.' All Arab states at that point supported the proposal and opposed internationalization.

[5] Eban's letter to the Secretary-General on 7 July 1948 is in S/870. For the Israel Prime Minister's memoir on the Bernadotte proposals see Ben Gurion 1971, pp. 197–202, 207–11. See also Bovis, pp. 59–64, 135.

Jerusalem remained under Jordan's control for the next nineteen years.[1] Nevertheless, the New City was under effective Israeli authority. To meet the needs of international law in a conflict situation and to regularize the *de facto* situation since the end of the Mandate, several formal steps were taken by the Israel Government on 2 August: the most important was the appointment of a Military Governor of Jerusalem. The person selected was Dov Joseph, a resourceful, decisive, Canadian-born lawyer with impressive administrative talent.

The New City held fast against the assault of Jordan's Arab Legion during the four-week war (14 May–11 June) and again, after the first truce, during the ten-day war (9–19 July). The prolonged second truce (19 July–22 October) witnessed limited hostilities on every front.[2] One of the victims was Bernadotte. But on 16 September, just a day before his assassination, the UN Mediator reverted to the idea of internationalization: he proposed to the General Assembly a 'special and separate treatment' for the City 'under effective United Nations control with maximum feasible local autonomy for its Arab and Jewish communities'. He also recommended two major territorial modifications of the 1947 Partition plan: to give the Negev to Egypt, and, as compensation, Western Galilee to Israel.[3]

The General Assembly, acting on the late Mediator's suggestion, instructed the newly-created Palestine Conciliation Commission (PCC)

[1] The second truce in the 1948 War was to take effect at dawn on 17 July. Ben Gurion issued an order to the commander of the Etzioni Brigade to inform the Consular Committee in Jerusalem that he would cease fire in accord with the Security Council decision on condition that he was informed by midnight on the 16th that the Arabs, too, had accepted the decision and would cease fire at the same time. Yadin, the *Tzahal* Chief of Operations, then sent the following order to the brigade commander: 'Following the telegram of the Minister of Defence . . . concerning the truce, you are to decide what you will be able to carry out during this night. The evident possibilities: Sheikh Jarrah or a bridgehead in the Old City. In case only one possibility is feasible before the truce, you are to carry out Sheikh Jarrah.' The brigade commander in Jerusalem decided to carry out Operation *Kedem*—the capture of the Old City, in a frontal attack, without prior encirclement. It failed, and at dawn all *Tzahal* forces returned to their bases. The Old City remained in Arab Legion hands. The truce went into effect on the evening of 18 July. Soon after, Shaltiel was replaced by Dayan as commander of the Jerusalem front. Lorch, pp. 295–6. The controversy simmered and exploded periodically, with Ben Gurion blaming Shaltiel and Yadin, and the latter charging Ben Gurion with responsibility both as Defence Minister and for failing to order an assault on the Old City earlier. In this context the key point of controversy was Dayan, whom Ben Gurion praised to the extent of arguing that, had he been in command of *Tzahal*, 'the map of Israel would have been different'. *Ha'aretz*, 10 March 1964. See also Narkiss.

[2] For an informative and moving account of Jerusalem under siege see Joseph, *passim*. Graphic journalists' reconstructions are to be found in Kurzman, Parts II and III, and Collins and Lapierre, *passim*.

[3] A/648, 20 Sept. 1948, in UN. GAOR III, Suppl. 11, esp. 7ff., 17–19. On the Mediator's views concerning the Jerusalem issue see Bernadotte, *passim;* Bovis pp. 65–8, 135.

on 11 December 1948 to 'present detailed proposals for a permanent international regime for the Jerusalem area. . . .'[1] There was no immediate official Israeli reaction, unlike a year later, 'because we weren't sufficiently strong and we wished to enlarge our presence in Jerusalem. We knew that the population division was clearly in our favour. And we wanted, if possible, to avoid an open conflict with the UN', especially when Israel was about to seek admission to the world organization.[2]

The first step towards a State of Israel presence in the New City had already been taken, namely, the appointment of a Military Governor. In mid-September 1948 Israel's Supreme Court was established in Jerusalem. In late September Ben Gurion suffered a setback when three *Mapai* ministers (Sharett, Kaplan, and Remez) aligned themselves with lesser Coalition party members to reject his proposal for a military operation against Latrun—in order to ensure a Jewish Jerusalem. The Prime Minister, in anguish, warned his colleagues that their inaction would cause a tragedy for generations ('*Behi'a Ledorot*').[3] Nevertheless, soon after the General Assembly's reaffirmation of intent to establish a 'permanent international regime', the Israel Cabinet decided, on 20 December, to transfer 'government institutions' to Jerusalem. As if in anticipation of that UN resolution, the Cabinet decided on 6 October, by a vote of 7 to 4 with 2 abstentions, to revoke an earlier Government decision, which had stated that internationalization was preferable to giving part of the City to the Arabs. The new decision stated that 'if Israeli control over all of Jerusalem is not achieved, and partition becomes necessary, the Israeli UN Delegation would agree to it'.[4]

The most conspicuous acts to create an irrevocable state presence occurred in mid-February 1949: the First *Knesset* convened in Jerusalem on the 14th, and three days later Dr. Chaim Weizmann took the oath of office as Israel's first President. The new state's prestige was now

---

[1] UN. GAOR III, Part 1, Doc. A/810, 11 Dec. 1948. This resolution also contained the highly controversial clause, odious to Israel, which was (incorrectly) interpreted by many as granting the Arab refugees the unqualified right to return to their abandoned homes.

[2] Joseph interview, 1971.

[3] Ben Gurion and Rosen interviews, 1971. The vote was 7 to 5 against the proposal, with 1 apparent abstention. In favour were: Ben Gurion (*Mapai*); Bentov and Zisling (*Mapam*); Rabbi Maimon (*Mizrahi*); and Gruenbaum (General Zionists). Opposed were Kaplan, Remez, and Sharett (*Mapai*); Bernstein (General Zionists); Rabbi Levin (*Agudat Yisrael*); Rosenblueth, later Rosen (Progressives); and Shapira (*Ha-po'el Ha-mizrahi*). Shitreet (*Sepharadim*) apparently abstained. Ben Gurion's rationale was stated by him thus: 'It is necessary that Jerusalem will be Jewish, and it will not be Jewish unless Latrun is conquered.' For detailed extracts from the minutes of the Government meeting on 26 September 1948, when the decision was taken, see Nakdimon. BG made a similar proposal in 1952 with the same result—'because I didn't want to engage in internal party consultations . . . , because I did not prepare my colleagues'. Interview with Eli Eyal, *Ma'ariv*, 28 April 1971.

[4] As quoted in Nakdimon.

committed to Israel's claim of sovereignty over (West) Jerusalem. Early in 1949, too, the Prime Minister informed the PCC that Israel rejected 'an international regime' for the City, though he reportedly accepted 'without reservation, an international regime for, or international control of, the Holy Places' in Jerusalem.[1] But even that concession was modified during the debate on Israel's admission to the United Nations, in May 1949. Eban then spoke instead of 'full security for religious institutions . . . , supervision of the Holy Places by those who hold them sacred . . . , and the fullest international safeguards . . . for their immunity and protection'.[2]

By that time the Military Government in Jerusalem had been disbanded (in early March), another signal of Israel's intended permanent presence. On 3 April Israel and Jordan signed a General Armistice Agreement, which set the demarcation line in Jerusalem as that defined by their Cease-Fire Agreement of 30 November 1948. The City, moreover, was to be virtually demilitarized, with both parties in (undisputed) authority over their respective zones.[3] In mid-September 1949 the PCC proposed a modified form of internationalization: a permanently demilitarized Jerusalem would be divided into autonomous Arab and Jewish zones, with the authority of a UN Commissioner being limited to international matters, notably jurisdiction over the Holy Places.[4] In the developing conflict over control of the City the PCC plan was ignored.

As the General Assembly convened for its annual autumn session, pressures for internationalization mounted once more. There were several sources. One was the Vatican-launched massive press campaign which urged Catholic states around the world, notably the influential Latin American group, then constituting 40 per cent of the UN membership, to support *corpus separatum*. A special envoy to Jerusalem, recalled Ben Gurion, 'came to see me and told me [in August 1949] that if they [the Vatican] had been aware of the fact that we were going to proclaim Jerusalem as our Capital, the State of Israel would not have been established at all'. He was emphatically rebuffed by the Prime Minister with the theme: '"I don't understand you"; Jerusalem was Israel's capital a thousand years before the birth of Christianity.'

---

[1] Second Progress Report of the PCC, UN. GAOR IV, *Ad Hoc* Pol. Cttee., Annexes, II, p. 5.

[2] UN. GAOR III, Pt. 2, *Ad Hoc* Pol. Cttee., 5 May 1949, pp. 233ff.

[3] For the text of the Armistice Agreement see UN Treaty Series, vol. xlii (1949), no. 655, p. 251. Apart from Rosenne, op. cit., a brief analysis may be found in *Israel and the United Nations*, pp. 109–13.

[4] The text of a *Draft Instrument Establishing a Permanent International Regime for the Jerusalem Area* is in A/973, 12 Sept. 1949, UN. GAOR IV, *Ad Hoc* Pol. Cttee., Annex I. There were four Progress Reports of the PCC in that year relating to Jerusalem: A/819, 15 March 1949; A/838, 5 April 1949; A/927, 21 June 1949; and A/992, 22 Sept. 1949.

Monsignor McMahon was not easily moved.[1] Nor did the efforts at persuasion by Ya'acov Herzog, the Foreign Office Adviser on Jerusalem, have any effect on the hierarchy in Rome or New York; the spearhead for territorial internationalization came from Cardinal Spellman's domain.

A second source of pressure, largely influenced by the first, was Latin America. It had supported the Partition plan of 1947 on the understanding that Jerusalem would be internationalized—under *de facto* Catholic control. That expectation—and demand—remained undiminished in 1949. Another substantial pressure group at the UN was the Arab states, all of whom, except Jordan, reverted to a pro-internationalization stand in the autumn of 1948, when Bernadotte's proposal to give Jerusalem to Abdullah proved abortive. And finally, the Soviet Union and her clients were still committed to an internationalized Jerusalem. It was a formidable alliance—Catholics, Muslims, and Communists—with Australia's External Affairs Secretary, Herbert Evatt, playing the role of saviour-advocate, largely, it seems in retrospect, because of his dependence upon the Catholic vote to buttress his domestic political position.[2]

As late as November 1949 the Prime Minister was cautious in asserting Israel's resolve. The Government, he told the *Knesset*, 'has in the past and will in the future stand on the *full right* of Jewish Jerusalem to be an inseparable part of the State of Israel'. Begin, as frequently in the past, was not satisfied to affirm Israel's right; he advocated its assertion, in the form of a proposal to enact a law making Jerusalem the capital at once. The area was to comprise the City in its entirety; and the President, Government, and *Knesset* were to move there immediately. Surprisingly, none of the speakers who followed him, including BG in his reply, made any comment on the *Herut* leader's concrete suggestion.[3]

On 22 November he persuaded Begin not to press his motion to a vote but, rather, to transfer it to the Legislative Committee of the *Knesset*. 'Formally, it is impossible to vote on this now', he told the House; 'but I do not wish to stand on formality. There are other reasons why we should not have a discussion about Jerusalem right now.' The principal reason was secret negotiations with Jordan then in motion for

---

[1] For a discussion of the position of the Roman Catholic Church on *corpus separatum*, see Zander, pp. 76–8, Ben Gurion interviews, 1966 and 1971, and Herzog interview, 1966. The first US Ambassador to Israel recorded his view that McMahon caused the Vatican to exercise its influence on Catholic states in favour of internationalization. 'That influence was sufficient to carry the day' in December 1949. 'The greatest single factor in Israel's failure was the Vatican . . . .' McDonald, pp. 205–6.

[2] This, too, provides an illustration of the interplay between internal environmental stimuli upon decision-makers' images and their foreign policy decisions.

[3] Among those who participated were Lavon, Lowenstein, Naftali, and Herzfeld (*Mapai*), Bernstein (General Zionists), Warhaftig and Nurock (Religious Front), Granat (Progressives), Elizur (*Sepharadim*), Yelin-Mor (*Lehi*), Hazan (*Mapam*), and Mikunis (*Maki*). *Divrei Ha-knesset*, iii, pp. 15ff.

an overall settlement which would have included a division of Jerusalem between the two states.[1] By that time, however, his acute concern and his determination to act were known within the high policy élite.

The first and most decisive stage in the decision process began in mid-November 1949. On the 15th, following Sharett's report to the Cabinet on the imminent Assembly discussion of Jerusalem, the Prime Minister urged his colleagues to act quickly and transfer the seat of government to Israel's historic capital. There was no decision. A week later, as noted, Ben Gurion followed the path of prudence in the *Knesset*. On the 25th Sharett tried to dissuade the Assembly's *Ad Hoc* Political Committee from the surge to territorial internationalization.[2] Eban used his powers of advocacy before the Committee four days later—without effect.

On 5 December the Director-General of the Foreign Office informed the Cabinet that the hard-line Australian draft resolution had been approved in sub-committee and had been returned to the *Ad Hoc* Political Committee.[3] The same day Sharett telephoned to convey the alarming news that the Australian proposal was assured of a large majority. Ben Gurion urged an immediate session of the *Knesset* to hear a Government Statement. He also advised the Cabinet to transfer the Government to Jerusalem immediately after the Assembly session.[4]

The Prime Minister's statement to the *Knesset* on 5 December was a conscious, unequivocal act of defiance. His words were blunt and firm:
. . . we will not consider any attempt made by the United Nations to forcibly remove Jerusalem from the State of Israel, or to interfere with Israel's authority in the eternal capital . . .
. . . we declare that Israel will never willingly give up Jerusalem, as she has never surrendered her faith in the thousands of years of peoplehood, her national

---

[1] The Ben Gurion statement of 22 Nov. is ibid., pp. 135–6. How advanced those negotiations were was revealed by Eytan: 'Conversations with him [King Abdullah] . . . were carried on intensively, especially between November 1949 and March 1950. A draft treaty was prepared and initialled, but the King . . . was unable in the end to carry it through.' Eytan, pp. 42–3. See also McDonald, pp. 192–6.

[2] See p. 19 above for the essence of his case.

[3] The procedure followed in the Assembly and its committees during the November–December 1949 debate on Jerusalem was as follows: after a general debate, the *Ad Hoc* Political Committee referred all proposals to a special sub-committee. These included the Australian draft, amended by Lebanon and the USSR, which called for a reaffirmation of the *corpus separatum* formerly approved by the Assembly as part of the Partition plan of 29 November 1947; an Israeli proposal, advocating international supervision of the Holy Places, along with international measures to assure freedom of access; and a compromise pro-Israeli, Swedish–Netherlands draft—to appoint a UN Commissioner to supervise the Holy Places on behalf of the UN. (Sharett accepted it as a possible 'starting point'.) UN. GAOR IV, 275th Pl. Mtg., 9 December 1949, p. 600.

[4] Ben Gurion's memoir on the Jerusalem issue is in Ben Gurion 1971, pp. 378–82, and Ben Gurion 1973.

unity, or her right to Jerusalem, to Zion—in spite of the persecution of which there has been no likeness in history. . . .
And we cannot look upon the decision of November 29 [1947] as binding, since the UN did not succeed in carrying out its decision. In our opinion, the decision of 29 November on Jerusalem is null and void.[1]

Ben Gurion's objective was to persuade the *Ad Hoc* Political Committee to reverse course on the Australian draft resolution. In fact, his speech was dysfunctional and was perceived by many UN members as provocative. The next day the Committee voted overwhelmingly in favour of complete territorial internationalization. And three days later, on 9 December 1949, the General Assembly reaffirmed the plan for *corpus separatum* by a vote of 38 to 14, with 7 abstentions. It was even more decisive than the vote for the Partition plan itself.[2] The Trusteeship Council was directed to revive and revise its Statute for Jerusalem, suspended in April 1948, and, further, to implement it immediately. It was also specifically instructed not to 'allow any actions taken by any interested Government or Governments to divert it from adopting and implementing the Statute. . . .' No coercive sanctions were provided.[3]

It was that UN act which served as the decisive input into Israel's Foreign Policy System, generating a strategic decision on Jerusalem. News of the Assembly vote reached the Government of Israel in the early hours of Saturday morning, 10 December. The next day, the Cabinet decided to make Jerusalem the seat of government, that is, the capital of Israel. It was an historic decision, nineteen months after the proclamation of independence. Ironically, it was in response to a perceived threat from the world organization which, at the outset, had provided international sanction to the new Jewish state.

There is no doubt as to the date of the strategic decision—11 Decem-

---

[1] *Divrei Ha-knesset*, iii, p. 221. Almost all speakers who followed took a similar hard line: they represented *Herut*, the Religious Front, General Zionists, *Sepharadim*, Progressives, *Mapam*, and *Lehi*. The only dissent came from *Maki*'s Wilner who praised the Soviet plan as one which would enable Israel and Jordan to decide the future of Jerusalem! Ibid., pp. 222–6.

[2] UN. GAOR IV, Rev. 303, approved at the 275th Plenary Meeting. For the Assembly's deliberations see Bovis, pp. 74–80, 137. The General Assembly's voting record on proposals recommending territorial internationalization was as follows:

TABLE 2. UN GENERAL ASSEMBLY VOTING RECORD ON JERUSALEM: 1947–52

	For	Against	Abstentions	Results
1947 (29 Nov.)	33	13	10	Res. 181 (II)
1948 (11 Dec.)	35	15	8	Res. 194 (III)
1949 (9 Dec.)	38	14	7	Res. 303 (IV)
1950	30	18	9	(no resolution; less than 2/3 majority)
1951		(no discussion)		
1952	28	20	12	(no resolution; less than 2/3 majority)
1953–67		(no discussion)		

[3] UN. GAOR IV, Supp. 14, Doc. A/1306, 7 Dec. 1949.

ber. Nor is there any dissent on the basic question: what induced the Israel Government to make the decision on Jerusalem at that time? All persons responded without hesitation to the Assembly resolution of 9 December. Ben Gurion confirmed this on several occasions: '*My* decision stemmed from the fact that the UN passed a resolution once more concerning Jerusalem.'[1] Joseph termed Israel's decision 'a deliberate defiance of the United Nations; there was a direct connection between the two'. Indeed, 'without the Assembly resolution on December 9th we would not have made the decision to move to Jerusalem at that time. But of course we would have done it later.' It was 'a deliberate attempt to prevent the implementation of the UN decision—to confront them with a *fait accompli*'.

Eban reflected that, in one of those quirks of history, Jerusalem became Israel's capital in 1949 primarily because of errors and massive pressures from the UN. 'Had the United Nations recognized our deep emotional attachment to Jerusalem, that might well have been sufficient, for many of our leaders thought of Jerusalem as an educational and cultural centre, but not necessarily, not even ideally, as the political capital. It was the violation of that intangible bond by the UN, its insensitivity that pushed us to action, by asserting Jerusalem as an integral part of the state, as its capital.' Herzog referred to the Cabinet decision of 11 December as 'a reflex assertion of Israel's rights'. And, while Sharef emphasized that Israeli leaders perceived Jerusalem as part of Israel from the very outset, 'the role of the General Assembly resolution was to catalyse the timing of our decision'.

Perhaps the most impressive evidence of a direct input–output relationship is the fact that the idea of Jerusalem *as the capital* was not discussed by the Cabinet *until a few weeks before the strategic decision was made*. Sharef, who as Secretary to the Government attended almost all Cabinet meetings, recalled: 'I did not meet people who thought Jerusalem would be the capital—all through 1948 and until the last months of 1949. The question was not put to a serious discussion, as far as I know.' Ben Gurion acknowledged that 'the question of Jerusalem didn't reach the Government table until after the Armistice Agreements, because the main problem was to win the war. After the United Nations resolution in December 1949 I called a Government meeting and we decided to transfer it to Jerusalem.'

There were, indeed, various proposals about a seat of government during the months preceding independence. Ben Gurion suggested Kurnub, a Negev settlement (later called Memsheet), near Dimona; but he quickly realized it was impracticable. Golda Meir proposed Mount Carmel (Haifa), for several reasons: 'because Herzl, when he visited Israel [Palestine], had said something about the Carmel as a

---

[1] The following seven extracts are taken from interviews with Ben Gurion, Joseph, Eban, Herzog, and Sharef, 1960–71.

place for the capital and because I disliked the idea of a capital being located in German houses, in Sarona'—a suburb of Tel Aviv and the ultimate choice. There was, she added, another factor: the Carmel was situated near a complex of *kibbutzim, moshavim*, and industrial enterprises, as well as having the deepest hinterland in the settled part of the country.[1] The elders of Zikhron Ya'acov, the oldest settlement in the north (1882), invited the *Yishuv* to establish the seat of government there. So too did the town fathers of Herzliya, further south along the coastal plain. The National Administration finally decided, on 13 May, in favour of Sarona, because of its proximity to Tel Aviv and, relatively, to Jerusalem, and because of the availability of housing space for a government in the making. They called it *Ha-kirya*, the Government Quarter.[2]

As for the strategic decision, Ben Gurion took the final initiative. He was actively encouraged, and on earlier occasions prodded, by two other ministers—Rabbi Maimon (Religious Affairs) and Dov Joseph (Supply and Rationing): the former was deeply committed to Jerusalem on spiritual grounds; the latter viewed it as Israel's eternal link with the past. Ben Gurion was no less attached, but he waited for a favourable moment to act; it came the day after the Assembly's reaffirmation of *corpus separatum*. Most of the other ministers supported the decision. A few were hesitant (Kaplan, Remez). And one dissented —Sharett.[3] The Foreign Minister cabled his resignation from New York immediately after the Cabinet decision: he felt responsible for Israel's setback at the Assembly which, he acknowledged, he did not anticipate; and his view that Israel should not act directly against an Assembly resolution had been rejected. 'I never showed the cable to my colleagues', recalled Ben Gurion. Instead he wrote to Sharett that the Assembly vote was not his responsibility and that the Cabinet of ten voted against him, too![4]

It remained to operationalize Israel's high-policy decision on Jerusalem. This was done simultaneously by the Cabinet in four steps. The Government's position as expressed by the Prime Minister in the *Knesset* on the 5th was reaffirmed. Secondly, the Assembly's resolution was termed unworkable, and Israel's policy would be non-cooperation.

[1] Meir interview, 1966.

[2] Sharef, pp. 158–62. Joseph, among others, opposed the name, on the grounds that there could be only one *Kirya*—in Jerusalem. Sarona was, he added, merely a choice of convenience—and not as the capital but as a seat of government. As for the various proposals about a seat of government, they were the result of necessity and were not seriously discussed. Interview, 1971.

[3] Based upon discussions with participants in the 11 December meeting. Nine of the twelve ministers were present: Rabbi Levin and Sharett were abroad; and Shazar was ill. Two civil servants were present—Eytan and Sharef.

[4] Ben Gurion interview, 1966. Several Foreign Ministry sources opined that, if anyone was responsible for the setback, it was the Permanent Representation to the UN, not Israel's Foreign Minister; but Sharett assumed the responsibility.

Further, the transfer of the Government and its ministries would be hastened; and to that end a special ministerial committee was established, with Joseph as chairman, Maimon, Shitreet, and Shapira as the other members. Finally, the *Knesset* would be urged to move permanently to Jerusalem. All this was to be announced to the *Knesset* by the Prime Minister in a statement approved that day (11 December) by the Government.

Rarely has there been a more illuminating example of a strategic decision in foreign policy as the direct output of pressure from the external, global setting, in the form of the world organization, and from interest groups and competing élites within Israel. Those inputs, as perceived by Israel's decision-makers, were the decisive image-components in the decision process.

(D) IMPLEMENTATION

The Prime Minister served notice of Israel's defiance immediately after the Cabinet meeting on the 11th. To journalists he remarked: 'Jerusalem is an inseparable part of Israel and her eternal capital. No United Nations vote can alter that historic fact.'[1] In his statement to the *Knesset* two days later Ben Gurion elaborated on this theme, conveyed the Government's decisions, and left no doubt as to Israel's resolve:[2]

My statement [on the 5th] stands as is, and there was not, nor will there ever be, any change in our stand. . . .

This [UN] decision is incapable of implementation if only because of the determined, unalterable opposition of her inhabitants. We can hope that, in time, the UN will correct the mistake made by its majority. . . .

. . . the State of Israel has always had, and it will always have, one capital—Eternal Jerusalem. This was how it was 3,000 years ago . . .

The *Knesset* responded to the Prime Minister's urging by approving a motion on 15 December favouring a return to Jerusalem as quickly as possible. On the 17th it was announced that certain ministries would be transferred shortly. The first to go, almost at once and without waiting for further Government prodding, were Supply and Rationing (Joseph) and Religious Affairs (Maimon); others, recalled Joseph, 'had excuses to delay their move'.[3] The Trusteeship Council severely criticized Israel's actions and called upon her 'to revoke those measures', as well as 'to abstain from any action liable to hinder the implementation' of the Assembly's resolution.[4] Israel replied on 30 December, denying any authority to the Trusteeship Council to demand that UN members revoke administrative acts in territories under their responsibility. She

---

[1] *Jerusalem Post*, 12 Dec. 1949.   [2] *Divrei Ha-knesset*, iii, p. 281.
[3] Interview, 1971.   [4] UN. GAOR V, Suppl. 9, Doc. A/1286, p. 1.

noted, further, that her highest state organs were already in Jerusalem.[1]

There was a major *Knesset* debate on the Jerusalem issue on 2–4 January 1950. It was opened by Sharett with a lengthy, somewhat apologetic survey of the Assembly's decision. By contrast, Ben Gurion's closing remarks were in the assertive tone of his December statements, along with a strategic perspective of the City, as expressed in his June 1948 address to the Provisional State Council. An assault from the Right, notably by Begin and the General Zionists' Saphir, failed: a *Herut* motion of no-confidence, on the grounds that the government had systematically prevented the proclamation of Jerusalem as the capital, was defeated (11 to 63). So too was a *Mapam* motion, criticizing the legitimization of the *de facto* partition of Jerusalem (23 to 63). A pro-Government motion was approved by 62 to 28.[2] The way was now clear for further implementing steps.

The Cabinet approved on 17 January a one-sentence draft of a motion to be presented by the Prime Minister to the Legislative and Foreign Affairs and Security Committees of Parliament. It was passed by them on the 19th: 'With the creation of a Jewish State, Jerusalem again became its capital.' Always conscious of continuity and Israel's history-rooted claim, Ben Gurion observed that no legislative act was required because Jerusalem had been made Israel's capital by King David.[3] The issue of law versus statement was debated once more and was settled (by 48 to 5) in favour of the latter. It took the form of Parliament's declaration on 23 January: 'The *Knesset* expresses its wish that the construction of the seat of the Government and the *Knesset* (*Kirya*) in Jerusalem be proceeded with speedily. . . .'[4]

That wish was not completely fulfilled for many years: the permanent home of the *Knesset* was inaugurated in August 1968—in the New City.[5] But more important, Parliament has met continuously in Jerusalem since December 1949; and all ministries but two had moved to the capital by 1951. One stayed by choice—Defence: it was universally

---

[1] Eban, as often, presented an elegant defence of Israel's case against internationalization, before the Trusteeship Council on 20 February 1950. His final cutting remark was that it would be incongruous for the UN to promote freedom everywhere but to deny self-government in the City where democracy was born. 'If I Forget Thee, O Jerusalem', Eban 1962, pp. 45–61.

[2] The principal speakers, apart from Ben Gurion, Sharett, Begin, and Saphir, were Riftin (*Mapam*), Aranne (*Mapai*), Burg (Religious Front), Harari (Progressives), Mikunis (*Maki*). *Divrei Ha-knesset*, iii, pp. 375–448.

[3] *Jerusalem Post*, 20 Jan. 1950.

[4] *Divrei Ha-knesset*, iv, pp. 602–18; the Declaration is on pp. 602–3.

[5] Many Israelis would have preferred to have their parliament in the Old City—as an expression of their deep commitment to a united Jerusalem. Thus, Ya'acov Shimshon Shapiro, former Minister of Justice (1966–73), revealed that, as early as 1954, he had recommended deferral of construction of the new *Knesset* building until it could be located in the Old City. *Jerusalem Post*, 7 Aug. 1972.

agreed in Israel that the conditions of prolonged war and Jerusalem's isolation required that *Tzahal* be directed from a relatively secure headquarters in the Tel Aviv area. The other was the Foreign Office, which remained there until July 1953.

The Prime Minister and others were annoyed by what they perceived as procrastination. As Navon recalled, every other day he would telephone the Foreign Minister's Political Secretary and say: 'Ben Gurion wants to know from Sharett, "when are you coming to Jerusalem?" '[1] Sharett remained unmoved because of his acute sensitivity to international repercussions; it was another illustration of his 'outer-directed' image. His first Director-General suggested 'practical' reasons as well: the diplomatic corps was already settled in Tel Aviv and would be inconvenienced; and congestion in Jerusalem made housing very difficult. But the principal concern, he acknowledged, was not to sever links with the diplomatic community.[2] In Mrs. Meir's view, 'no doubt that was a consideration. We wanted to do it with as little pain as possible. What would the embassies in Tel Aviv do if we moved to Jerusalem?' Joseph remarked succinctly about the reason for delay: 'not to irritate the Great Powers'. And further, 'Sharett was afraid they [the diplomats] wouldn't come to his ministry.' Herzog's comment was more colourful: 'We were under the lash of the UN. A transfer was possible after the trauma had weakened.'

There is a high direct correlation between declining UN pressure and declining hesitation to transfer the Foreign Ministry. On 17 April 1950 the Secretary-General was informed that the Soviet Union withdrew her support of territorial internationalization.[3] At the Fifth Session of the General Assembly in the autumn the debate on Jerusalem was inconclusive. Neither a Belgian draft, which in essence reaffirmed the Catholic preference for *corpus separatum*, nor a Swedish draft, incorporating Eban's ingenious formula of 'functional internationalization', commanded the necessary majority.[4] Thus the high tide of

---

[1] Interview, 1966.

[2] Eytan, pp. 74ff. The next three extracts are taken from interviews with Meir, Joseph, and Herzog, 1966, 1960, and 1966.

[3] UN. GAOR V, Suppl. 1, p. 5.

[4] For the Belgian and Swedish drafts see UN *Ad Hoc* Pol. Cttee., Doc. A/AC 38/ SR73, 7 Dec. 1950, and A/AC 38/L 63, 13 Dec. 1950, respectively. Israel's success in defeating the Belgian draft resolution was greatly assisted by a massive public relations campaign around the world, the riposte to the Vatican's press campaign during the months preceding the Assembly's reaffirmation of *corpus separatum* a year earlier. Crucial roles were also played by the April 1950 Soviet volte-face on Jerusalem and by a cable from the Greek Orthodox Patriarch in Jerusalem to the General Assembly urging that the *status quo* be maintained. Herzog interview, 1966.

The term 'functional internationalization' was elaborated in Eban's Memorandum to the Trusteeship Council on 26 May 1950. The object, he explained later, was to retain the idea and the substance of internationalization, about which many states felt strongly, but applied to the focus of concern, the Holy Places. In that connection

external pressure from the UN, the Vatican, and the Powers, had begun to recede.[1]

Jerusalem was not discussed at the Sixth General Assembly session in 1951. Thus the Government of Israel took its first cautious step—by announcing on 4 May 1952 that the Foreign Office would move as soon as the 'necessary technical arrangements' had been completed. This was a signal to the world body that Israel had decided to wait another year. The US and the UK protested. However, once more the UN failed to act: Jerusalem was not on the agenda of the Seventh General Assembly session in 1952. The issue was raised, indirectly, in the form of a Vatican-inspired Philippine amendment to a draft resolution recommending direct Arab–Israel negotiations; but the attempt to reaffirm territorial internationalization was defeated.[2] 'The Assembly's silence and inaction', Eytan wrote later, '*were taken* to indicate acquiescence.'[3] Finally, on 13 July 1953 the Foreign Office was transferred to Israel's capital. It was the last implementing act concerning the strategic decision of 11 December 1949 on Jerusalem.

The domestic response was enthusiasm, but reaction abroad was undisguised anger. A boycott of the Foreign Ministry was declared by the US and the UK. Other states followed their lead: diplomats from many missions were not permitted to conduct business or to attend official functions in Jerusalem; and all communications continued to be sent to the Ministry's Liaison Office in Tel Aviv. Washington even scolded Israel for the transfer, claiming that it had a solution for the Jerusalem issue, about to be unfolded.[4] The boycott was gradually relaxed, with the turning point in 1955, when US Ambassador Lawson conveyed the State Department's willingness to deal with the Ministry in Jerusalem. From 1956 onward all new diplomatic missions—with the notable exception of West Germany in 1965—were established in

---

he noted his constant communication with Jordan's UN Representative in 1950–1— and the latter's complaint that Israel was letting Jordan down, because virtually all the Holy Places to which the proposal of 'functional internationalization' would apply were located in the Jordan-controlled Old City. Eban interview, 1965.

[1] The defeat of the Belgian draft resolution in 1950 appears, in perspective, to have persuaded the Vatican that *territorial* internationalization could no longer be pushed through the Assembly. For informative surveys of the UN role in the Jerusalem issue see Bovis, ch. 3–5, *Israel and the United Nations*, ch. 5, and Pfaff, ch. 3. A succinct summary is in Wilson, Appendix F.

[2] The eight-power draft resolution on direct negotiations is in UN. GAOR VII, 1 A/AC. 61/L23/Rev. 4, 11 Dec. 1952. The Philippine amendment is ibid., Annexes, Agenda Item 67, p. 19 and ibid., 406th Pl. Mtg., 18 December 1952.

[3] Eytan, p. 79 (emphasis added).

[4] The Rusk plan provided for *de jure* territorial internationalization. Israel and Jordan were to be designated by the Trusteeship Council as Administering Authorities of their respective zones with complete *de facto* control. Their only obligation would be to send an annual report to the TC. It was discussed with Eban in 1950 but never formally proposed. Eban interview, 1965.

Jerusalem. Certain anomalies remained, especially with regard to the Consular Corps in Jerusalem.[1] By 1972, 23 of the 47 diplomatic missions in Israel were located in Jerusalem, most of them from Latin America and Africa.[2] But the high-policy decision to establish Israel's seat of government in (West) Jerusalem had been successfully implemented.

The Jerusalem issue lay dormant for fifteen years: there was no discussion in the General Assembly after 1952;[3] and *de facto* partition of the City remained unchallenged from within. It erupted once more in global and subordinate system politics in the context of the 1967 War. The result, in terms of Israel's policy towards Jerusalem, may be designated a tactical decision.

The crucial input for that decision is readily known. On the morning of 5 June Jordan launched a full-scale military assault along the entire demarcation line separating West from East Jerusalem—despite an explicit Israel pledge conveyed to King Hussein via UNTSO Chief General Odd Bull that Jordan would not be attacked if she stayed out of the Egyptian–Israeli hostilities. It was a foolhardy Jordanian act, for all of East Jerusalem came under Israeli military control on the 7th.[4] That day, too, Defence Minister Dayan declared before the Western (Wailing) Wall: 'The Israel Defence Forces have liberated Jerusalem. We have reunited the torn city, the capital of Israel. We have returned to this most sacred shrine, never to part from it again.'[5]

[1] Most governments did not recognize Israeli or Jordanian sovereignty over Jerusalem and did not permit their consuls to present their commissions to either government. Since Israel can issue an exequatur only at a consul's request and upon presentation of his commission of appointment, all but a few are 'unofficial', i.e., they may not perform functions which require recognition from the Government of Israel. They are accredited to the District Commissioner of Jerusalem.
A similar though short-lived problem relates to the presentation of credentials. President Weizmann received new heads of missions at his home in Rehovoth or at his Tel Aviv Office. The Dutch Minister, Boissevain, was the first to present credentials in Jerusalem, to President Ben-Zvi on 4 May 1953. The Chilean representative followed later in the year. The first Great Power envoy to present credentials in Jerusalem was the Soviet Minister, Abramov, on 4 Dec. 1953. There was an amusing 'crisis' over the new Italian Minister, who became accredited in Tiberias on 16 Dec. 1953, the last occasion outside Jerusalem. Thereafter Israel was firm; US and UK envoys presented their credentials in the (unrecognized) capital on 10 and 12 Nov. 1954, despite Arab pressure. The anomaly had ended. These details are drawn from Eytan's instructive discussion (ch. 4) of the Jerusalem issue, as well as from Bovis, p. 93.
[2] See Note to Table 3 following p. 55 below.
[3] There were, however, occasional protests against the transfer of Israeli ministries to Jerusalem. For the early years see UN. GAOR VII, 405th Plenary Meeting, 18 Dec. 1952, p. 400, and ibid., *Ad Hoc* Pol. Cttee., 26 Nov. 1954, p. 159.
[4] For an exhaustive account of the 1967 military campaign in Jerusalem see Harel and Gur, *passim*; Rabinovich, *passim*; Churchills, ch. 7; and Wilson, pp. 98–107. For an Arab view of the 1967 battle for Jerusalem see Schleifer.
[5] *Jerusalem Post*, 8 June 1967. The *New York Times* reported on the 15th that severa

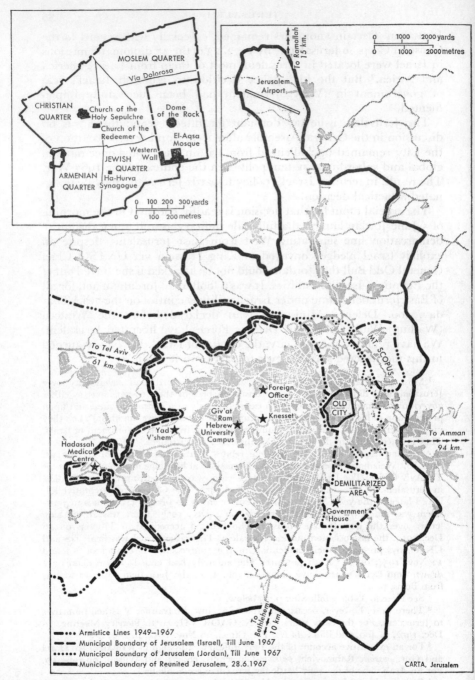

MOSLEM QUARTER

Via Dolorosa

CHRISTIAN
QUARTER

Church of the
Holy Sepulchre

Church of the
Redeemer

Dome
of the Rock

El-Aqsa
Mosque

Western
Wall

JEWISH
QUARTER

Ha-Hurva
Synagogue

ARMENIAN
QUARTER

0   100 200 300 yards
0   100   200 metres

0   1000 2000 yards
0   1000 2000 metres

To Ramallah
15 km.

Jerusalem
Airport

To Tel Aviv
61 km.

MT. SCOPUS

Foreign
Office

Giv'at
Ram
Hebrew
University
Campus

Knesset

OLD
CITY

Yad
V'shem

To Amman
94 km.

Hadassah
Medical
Centre

DEMILITARIZED
AREA

Government
House

To Bethlehem
10 km.

••••• Armistice Lines 1949–1967
– – – Municipal Boundary of Jerusalem (Israel), Till June 1967
••••• Municipal Boundary of Jerusalem (Jordan), Till June 1967
▬▬▬ Municipal Boundary of Reunited Jerusalem, 28.6.1967

CARTA, Jerusalem

JERUSALEM: BOUNDARIES 1949–1973

During the next three weeks Israeli authorities acted swiftly to integrate the two zones of Jerusalem. The Master Plan was expanded to include East Jerusalem. The water, sanitation, telephone, and electrical systems were united. The municipal bus service extended its routes. New trilingual street signs were installed. And, most important, the physical barriers which had separated East and West Jerusalem for nineteen years were removed, permitting free movement between Jews and Arabs throughout the City.

The political process was no less swift. The following discussion of process and images, not normally done for a derivative tactical decision, is offered here because of the eighteen-year gap between the S and T decisions, and because of the continuing post-1967 international political significance of that decision. Administrative unification was first discussed formally by the Government on 16 June. The next day the Cabinet decided to annex East Jerusalem and surrounding areas. It was a significant decision, no less so than the 1949 Israeli decision to make Jerusalem the seat of government. Indeed its importance may appear to justify the designation strategic, rather than tactical. However, the unification of West and East Jerusalem was a logical extension, after a lengthy lapse of time, of the initial high-policy decision to assert Israel's overall claim to the City, both as an integral part of the state and as its capital: unification was both possible and meaningful only in that context. Everything that followed was in the nature of operationalization and implementation of that core decision. Indeed, if King Hussein had responded positively to Eshkol's message on 5 June, Israel would not have acquired control over East Jerusalem. But the strategic decision making Jerusalem the capital would have remained intact. Thus the June 1967 decision to unify Jerusalem is termed a tactical decision, the consummation—fourth stage—of the decision process relating to the Jerusalem issue.

That decision was made by the second largest Coalition in Israel's history, the National Unity Government of 21 persons, representing 5 parliamentary parties or blocs:

The Alignment (Mapai/Ahdut Ha'avoda)

Levi Eshkol	Prime Minister
Yigal Allon	Minister of Labour
Zalman Aranne	Minister of Education and Culture
Moshe Carmel	Minister of Communications and Transport

---

hundred Arabs living close to the Wall had been given 24 hours to leave before bulldozers cleared the area. See also the *Guardian*, 26, 27 April and 9, 11, 13 and 16 May 1972 for articles and letters to the Editor on the Jerusalem controversy, notably D. Hirst, 'Bulldozing through Arab History', 27 April, and W. Schwartz, 'The Worst— the Best—of Both Worlds', 9 May 1972.

Moshe Dayan[1]	Minister of Defence
Abba Eban	Minister for Foreign Affairs
Yisrael Galili	Minister without Portfolio
Haim Gvati	Minister of Agriculture
Pinhas Sapir	Minister of Finance
Eliyahu Sasson	Minister of Police
Ya'acov Shimshon Shapiro	Minister of Justice
Ze'ev Sharef	Minister of Commerce and Industry
Yisrael Yeshaiahu	Minister of Posts

Gahal (General Zionists and *Herut*)

Menahem Begin	Minister without Portfolio
Yosef Saphir	Minister without Portfolio

Independent Liberals

Moshe Kol	Minister of Development and of Tourism

Mapam

Yisrael Barzilai	Minister of Health
Mordekhai Bentov	Minister of Housing

National Religious Party (*Mafdal*)

Yosef Burg	Minister of Social Welfare
Moshe Shapira	Minister of Interior
Zerah Warhaftig	Minister of Religious Affairs

Within that 'wall-to-wall' Coalition there was no open dissent from the decision 'to fuse' East and West Jerusalem. Yet there was a wide spectrum of attitudes, derived from diverse images of 'the Arabs', Israel's just claims, Israel's standing at the UN, the conditions of peace, and probable US reaction. The decision-makers may be classified into five groups:

Nationalist Hawks	*Gahal*'s Begin and Saphir, and Allon, Carmel, and Galili from the *Ahdut Ha'avoda* wing of the Alignment; (5)
Religious Hawks	*Mafdal*'s Shapira and Warhaftig; (2)
Pragmatic Hawks	*Mapai*'s Eshkol, Dayan, Gvati, Sasson, Y.S. Shapiro, Sharef, and Yeshaiahu, and *Mafdal*'s Burg; (8)
Pragmatic Doves	*Mapai*'s Aranne, Eban, and Sapir, and Independent Liberal Kol; (4)
Ideological Doves	*Mapam*'s Barzilai and Bentov. (2)

[1] A member of *Rafi*, which was to merge with the Alignment parties seven months later to form the Israel Labour Party.

Yet all favoured the permanent end to a tortured, physical partition of Jerusalem; none favoured a return to the *status quo ante* or to any variant of territorial internationalization.

The implementation of that tactical decision was delayed slightly. Enabling laws to integrate East and West Jerusalem were to be introduced into the *Knesset* on 18 June, but pressures intervened. An important policy speech on the Arab–Israel conflict by President Johnson was awaited on the 19th. At the same time Foreign Minister Eban was sending urgent cables from the UN, strongly advising caution—as Sharett did in December 1949; he was, ironically, supported in this advocacy of prudence by Arye Ben Eliezer, one of *Herut*'s respected leaders. They, among others, feared widespread UN censure.

That pressure notwithstanding, three enabling laws were placed before the *Knesset* on 27 June and were approved the same day. The basic enactment was the *Law and Administration Ordinance (Amendment No. 11) Law 1967*. The others were the *Municipal Corporations Ordinance (Amendment) Law 1967* which empowered the Minister of Interior to enlarge the area of any municipality by the inclusion of an area designated under the first Ordinance; and the *Protection of the Holy Places Law 1967*.[1] Acting under the authority of the first two ordinances, the Interior Minister, on 28 June, extended Israel law and administration to an enlarged Jerusalem, including the Old City, Kalandia Airport, Sheikh Jarrah, Sur Bahir, etc. The strategic decision had now been fully consummated.

External reaction to Israel's integration of Jerusalem was unconcealed anger. Non-Arab Muslim states took the lead before a highly-receptive Emergency Session of the General Assembly, convened in late June 1967 to consider the consequences of the Six Day War. The outburst of condemnation acquired Assembly sanction in the form of two Pakistani-sponsored resolutions. The first declared Israel's action invalid, called upon her 'to rescind all measures already taken and to desist forthwith from taking any action which would alter the status of Jerusalem', and instructed the Secretary-General to report back within a week on the implementation of this resolution. It was approved on 4 July by the extraordinary vote of 99 to 0, with 20 abstentions; Israel did not participate.[2]

Eban attempted to blunt the assault by replying to U Thant: 'That term "annexation" used by supporters of the resolution is out of place. The measures adopted relate to the integration of Jerusalem in the

---

[1] The texts are in *Sefer Ha-hukkim*, no. 499, 28 June 1967, pp. 74–5. They are summarized and discussed in *Israel Digest*, X, 14, 14 July 1967, p. 1; Lauterpacht, pp. 50–1; and Zander, pp. 102–5.
[2] The final draft is in UN Doc. A/L 527, Rev. 1, 3 July 1967. Guinea, Iran, Mali, Niger, and Turkey became co-sponsors. The text as approved is in UN. GAOR, ES-V, Res. 2253, 4 July 1967.

administrative and municipal spheres. . . .'¹ Israel's critics were not persuaded. On 14 July the Assembly passed another resolution, which 'deplores the failure of Israel to implement' its earlier admonition, reiterated the call 'to rescind' and 'to desist', and again asked the Secretary-General to report back; no time was specified. The vote was 99 to 0, with 18 abstentions; once more Israel remained aloof.²

The Jerusalem issue had been activated in the universal organization once more. It remained in a state of high verbal activity. In 1968 the Security Council approved three resolutions on Jerusalem in stronger language. One 'deeply deplores the holding by Israel of the military parade in Jerusalem'. Another, referring back to the 1967 resolution, 'urgently calls upon Israel to rescind . . . and to desist forthwith. . . .'³ The scenario was repeated in 1969 with even stronger language: 'censures in the strongest terms all measures taken. . . .' It was adopted unanimously by the Security Council.⁴ And in 1971 the Council once more called upon Israel 'to rescind . . . and to take no further steps in the occupied section of Jerusalem. . . .'⁵ Israel's Cabinet responded within hours by deciding unanimously on 26 September not to enter into discussion with any 'political factor' on the basis of the Council's resolutions. US approval of the resolution caused dismay in Jerusalem, but the storm passed quickly. Two months later Eban conveyed Israel's formal rejection to the Secretary-General, who acknowledged to the Security Council his inability to fulfil its mandate to dispatch a mission of inquiry to the City.⁶ Jerusalem had been united as an integral part – and as the capital – of Israel.

Israel held a military parade in 1968 through the heart of East Jerusalem, as a symbol of the political transformation wrought by the Six Day War. There was no military presence in the capital during the next four Independence Day celebrations. In April 1973 the President

¹ UN Docs. S/8052 and A/6753, 10 July 1967.

² Afghanistan, Guinea, Iran, Mali, Somalia, and Turkey joined Pakistan as sponsors of that resolution. See UN Doc. A/L 528, Rev. 2 and UN. GAOR, S-V, Rev. 2254, 14 July 1967. The events of 1967 relating to Jerusalem are noted briefly in Bovis, pp. 103–8.

³ The texts and debate are contained in UN. S/PV 1417, S/RES/250, 27 April 1968; S/PV 1420, S/RES/251, 2 May 1968; and S/PV 1426, S/RES/252, 21 May 1968.

⁴ S/RES/267, 3 July 1969.

⁵ S/RES/298, 25 Sept. 1971.

⁶ The Cabinet decision is discussed in *Jerusalem Post*, 27 Sept. 1971. The text of Eban's firm reply of non-compliance in a letter to U Thant, and the latter's reaction, are ibid., 23 and 26 Nov. 1971. A month earlier Israel rejected a resolution by the Executive Board of UNESCO calling for a UNESCO 'presence' in East Jerusalem to protect the City's cultural and historical sites. Ibid., 24 Oct. 1971. A selection of documents relating to the Jerusalem issue after the 1967 War, especially to the UN involvement, is to be found in *Journal of Palestine Studies*, 1, 1, Autumn 1971, pp. 178–94. For a controversial Israeli view on developments in Jerusalem since the Six Day War, see Benvenisti, *passim*.

of the Security Council, acting on Jordan's protest, conveyed to Israel's
UN delegate the displeasure of Council members over Israel's decision
to hold a military parade in Jerusalem on 7 May to mark the state's
twenty-fifth anniversary of independence. And when the parade was
revived it skirted the Arab quarters of the city, at the insistence of
municipal officials, *Tzahal* recommendations notwithstanding.[1]

(E) DECISION FLOW

Pre-Decisional Events

1. 29 November 1947	The UN General Assembly approved the Partition Resolution which, *inter alia*, provided for the territorial internationalization of Jerusalem as a *corpus separatum*. The Trusteeship Council was directed 'to elaborate and approve a detailed statute' for the City within five months.
2. 21 April 1948	After two months of deliberations, the Trusteeship Council completed, but did not formally approve, the Statute for Jerusalem.
3. 8 May 1948	After almost six months of *de facto* civil war, a cease-fire came into effect and continued to 12 May.
4. 12 May 1948	The National Administration decided to proclaim the State of Israel immediately after the termination of the Mandate two days later. It also rejected three separate truce proposals for Jerusalem put forward since the 8th.
5. 15 May 1948	The armies of the Near East Core Arab states invaded Israel, within hours of the proclamation of independence; the siege of Jewish Jerusalem isolated the City from the rest of the state.
6. 24 June 1948	Prime Minister Ben Gurion declared before the Provisional State Council: 'There is no difference between Jerusalem and Tel Aviv, Haifa, Hanita. They are all part of the Jewish State.'

[1] *Jerusalem Post*, 29 April 1973. The decision in favour of a military parade in
Jerusalem on the 25th anniversary was taken by the Israeli Cabinet in September
1972, with two dissenting votes, Defence Minister Dayan and *Mafdal*'s Welfare
Minister, Hazani. The former reportedly urged that the parade was 'not essential
in view of the cease-fire and the current security lull. Hence it is inadvisable.' *Jerusalem
post*, 26 Jan. 1973.

7. 29 June 1948   The UN Mediator, Count Bernadotte, proposed in a secret letter to Foreign Minister Sharett, that Jerusalem be placed under Jordan's sovereignty. It was rejected formally.

8. 16 July 1948   Operation *Kedem*—the attempt to capture the Old City of Jerusalem—failed; it remained under Jordan's control for the next nineteen years.

9. 2 August 1948   Dr. Dov Joseph was appointed Military Governor of Jerusalem.

10. 14 September 1948   Israel's Supreme Court was established in Jerusalem.

11. 16 September 1948   The UN Mediator proposed 'special and separate treatment' for Jerusalem 'under effective United Nations control, with maximum feasible local autonomy for its Arab and Jewish communities'.

12. 30 November 1948   A Cease-Fire Agreement was signed between Israel and Jordan.

13. 11 December 1948   The UN General Assembly, following the Mediator's suggestion, instructed the Palestine Conciliation Commission (PCC) to present 'detailed proposals for a permanent international regime for the Jerusalem area', with maximum municipal autonomy for the two communities.

14. 20 December 1948   The Israel Cabinet decided to transfer 'government institutions' to Jerusalem.

15. 14 February 1949   Israel's First *Knesset* was convened in Jerusalem; and, on the 17th, Dr. Chaim Weizmann took the oath of office as first President of Israel.

16. 3 April 1949   Israel and Jordan signed a General Armistice Agreement, which set the demarcation line in Jerusalem as that defined by the Cease-Fire Agreement of 30 November 1948. Moreover, the City was virtually demilitarized.

17. August 1949   Vatican pressure for internationalization was conveyed personally to Ben Gurion and Sharett by Monsignor McMahon.

18. 1 September 1949   The PCC proposed a *de facto* partition of a demilitarized Jerusalem into autonomous

Arab and Jewish zones, with the authority of the UN Commissioner being confined to international matters, especially jurisdiction over the Holy Places.

19. 8 November 1949   Ben Gurion reaffirmed to the *Knesset* the full right of 'Jewish Jerusalem' to remain 'an inseparable part of the State of Israel'.

20. 15 November 1949   In the course of a Cabinet discussion on the impending General Assembly session, Ben Gurion advised his colleagues to transfer the seat of government to Jerusalem—quickly.

Decisive Inputs into Strategic Decision

21. 5 December 1949   The probability of majority support in the General Assembly's *Ad Hoc* Political Committee for an extreme Australian draft resolution reaffirming *corpus separatum* was conveyed by Sharett to the Israel Cabinet by telephone. In response Ben Gurion urged an immediate session of the *Knesset* to hear a statement by the Prime Minister.

22. 5 December 1949   Ben Gurion informed the world, especially the UN, through the *Knesset*: 'We will not consider any attempt made by the United Nations to forcibly remove Jerusalem from the State of Israel. ... In our opinion, the decision of 29 November [1947] on Jerusalem is null and void.'

23. 9 December 1949   The General Assembly passed Resolution 303 (IV) reaffirming the territorial internationalization of Jerusalem.

Strategic Decision

24. 11 December 1949   The Government of Israel decided to make Jerusalem the seat of government (the official capital).

Implementation of Strategic Decision

25. 11 December 1949   The Cabinet empowered the Prime Minister to make a fresh statement to the *Knesset* confirming Israel's basic position on Jerusalem.

A four-man ministerial committee was formed to organize the transfer of government ministries to Jerusalem.

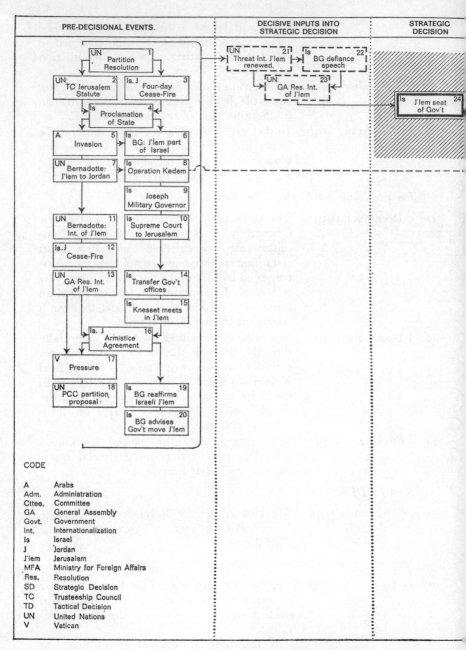

| PRE-DECISIONAL EVENTS. | DECISIVE INPUTS INTO STRATEGIC DECISION | STRATEGIC DECISION |

UN — 1 Partition Resolution

UN — 2 TC Jerusalem Statute

Is.J — 3 Four-day Cease-Fire

Is — 4 Proclamation of State

A — 5 Invasion

Is — 6 BG: J'lem part of Israel

UN — 7 Bernadotte: J'lem to Jordan

Is — 8 Operation Kedem

Is — 9 Joseph Military Governor

UN — 11 Bernadotte: Int. of J'lem

Is — 10 Supreme Court to Jerusalem

Is.J — 12 Cease-Fire

UN — 13 GA Res. Int. of J'lem

Is — 14 Transfer Gov't offices

Is — 15 Knesset meets in J'lem

Is. J — 16 Armistice Agreement

V — 17 Pressure

UN — 18 PCC partition proposal·

Is — 19 BG reaffirms Israeli J'lem

Is — 20 BG advises Gov't move J'lem

UN — 21 Threat Int. J'lem renewed.

Is — 22 BG defiance speech

UN — 23 GA Res. Int. of J'lem

Is — 24 J'lem seat of Gov't

CODE

A	Arabs
Adm.	Administration
Cttee.	Committee
GA	General Assembly
Govt.	Government
Int.	Internationalization
Is	Israel
J	Jordan
J'lem	Jerusalem
MFA	Ministry for Foreign Affairs
Res.	Resolution
SD	Strategic Decision
TC	Trusteeship Council
TD	Tactical Decision
UN	United Nations
V	Vatican

FIGURE 2. DECISION FLOW: JERUSALEM

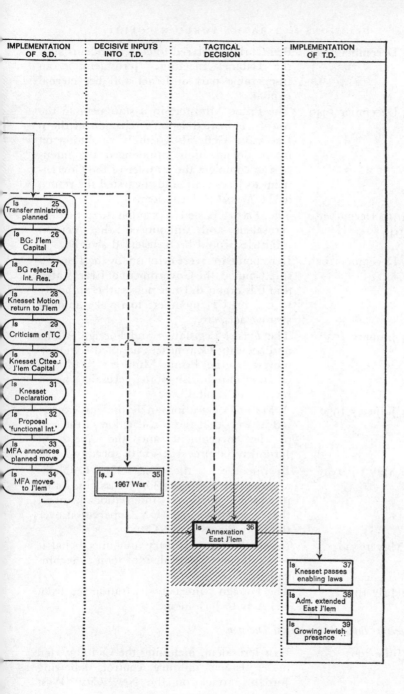

IMPLEMENTATION OF S.D.	DECISIVE INPUTS INTO T.D.	TACTICAL DECISION	IMPLEMENTATION OF T.D.

Is 25 Transfer ministries planned

Is 26 BG: J'lem Capital

Is 27 BG rejects Int. Res.

Is 28 Knesset Motion return to J'lem

Is 29 Criticism of TC

Is 30 Knesset Cttee.: J'lem Capital

Is 31 Knesset Declaration

Is 32 Proposal 'functional Int.'

Is 33 MFA announces planned move

Is 34 MFA moves to J'lem

Is. J 35 1967 War

Is 36 Annexation East J'lem

Is 37 Knesset passes enabling laws

Is 38 Adm. extended East J'lem

Is 39 Growing Jewish presence

26. 11 December 1949   Ben Gurion declared to correspondents after the Cabinet meeting: 'Jerusalem is an inseparable part of Israel and her eternal capital.'

27. 13 December 1949   The Prime Minister, in a statement to the *Knesset*, indicated Israel's rejection of the 9 December General Assembly resolution on internationalization, announced the intention to complete the transfer of the Government to Jerusalem, and suggested the return of the *Knesset* to Jerusalem.

28. 15, 17 December 1949   The *Knesset* passed a motion to return to Jerusalem and announced that certain ministries would be transferred shortly.

29. 30 December 1949   In response to severe criticism by the Trusteeship Council, the Government of Israel stated that this organ did not possess the authority to call on UN members to revoke administrative acts, etc.

30. 19 January 1950   The *Knesset* Legislative and Foreign Affairs and Security Committees adopted a motion moved by the Prime Minister: 'With the creation of a Jewish State, Jerusalem again became its capital.'

31. 23 January 1950   A *Knesset* Declaration on Jerusalem 'expressed its wish that the construction of the seat of the government and the *Knesset* in Jerusalem be proceeded with speedily . . .'.

32. 26 May 1950   In response to the Trusteeship Council's approval of a Statute for Jerusalem, Israel proposed 'functional internationalization', that is, international (UN) supervision over the Holy Places in the City.

33. 4 May 1952   Israel's Foreign Ministry announced that it would move to Jerusalem as soon as technically feasible.

34. 12 July 1953   The Foreign Ministry was transferred from Tel Aviv to Jerusalem.

Decisive Input into Tactical Decision

35. 7 June 1967   East Jerusalem, including the Old City, fell under Israeli military control, following Jordan's attack on the New City (West Jerusalem) on the morning of 5 June.

Tactical Decision

36. 18 June 1967   The Government of Israel decided to annex
                          East Jerusalem and surrounding areas.

Implementation of Tactical Decision

37. 27 June 1967   The *Knesset* approved three enabling laws
                          for the 'fusion' of East and West Jerusalem,
                          the basic enactment being the Law and
                          Administration Ordinance (Amendment No.
                          11) Law.

38. 28 June 1967   Israeli law and administration were extended
                          to an enlarged Jerusalem, including the Old
                          City, Kalandia Airport, Sheikh Jarrah, etc.

39. 1968ff.   Majority Jewish presence in Jerusalem area
                          became evident in East Jerusalem through
                          large-scale reconstruction and population
                          settlement.

(f) FEEDBACK

Israel's strategic and tactical decisions on Jerusalem (1949, 1967)
were found to be primarily due to *external* stimuli: the strategic decision
—to make Jerusalem the seat of government—was in response to global
pressure, real and perceived, manifested through the UN General
Assembly Resolution of 9 December 1949 reaffirming *corpus separatum*
for the City as a whole; and the tactical decision to unify West and East
Jerusalem was in response to the actual and discerned change in the
immediate-neighbour setting created by Jordan's attack of 5 June and
the consequent conquest of East Jerusalem by *Tzahal* within the next
two days. In both cases domestic pressures, that is, public opinion
acting through interest groups and competing élites, performed a supportive function in the decision process. Thus the feedback effects on
Israel's Foreign Policy System were experienced mainly by the *external*
components of her operational and psychological environments.

The most direct and continuous flow of (negative) influence is
evident in the *global* setting of Israel's foreign policy. The Jewish state
had been admitted to the UN with the active support of the super
powers in May 1949. Yet within seven months a formidable coalition—
of Catholic, Muslim, Soviet, and Arab states—with diverse interests in
Jerusalem, competing with, and hostile to, those of Israel, had succeeded
in securing Assembly approval for a harsh internationalization
resolution. The reactive Israeli decision alienated the UN and large
blocs within the organization and the global system as a whole, then
and later. For, while later attempts (1950, 1952) to reaffirm *corpus*

separatum failed, the UN remained seized of the Jerusalem Question: it was dormant for many years (1952–67) but tensely active thereafter.

Israel's tactical decision (June 1967) reactivated the hostile coalition of forces at the United Nations: recurring votes of massive condemnation of her unification of Jerusalem (99 to 0, in 1967, 1968, 1969) aligned Israel, objectively, with such pariah member-states as Portugal and South Africa. Moreover, they fed the propaganda machine of her Arab adversaries, which used Israel's posture on Jerusalem to portray her as an expansionist, recalcitrant, and inflexible state. And Israel's insistence on sovereignty over all Jerusalem, though muted occasionally by statements that 'every issue is negotiable', spilled over to the general global system image of the parties' behaviour after the Six Day War. In short, the perception of Israel's 'rigidity' on terms for a political settlement was accentuated by the 1967 decision to annex East Jerusalem and by her frozen negotiating posture on that sensitive issue. For two decades Israel had successfully resisted global system pressures on her claim to Jerusalem; but the price was increasing isolation within the world organization and the international system as a whole.

That strand of feedback was accompanied and fortified by the unconcealed displeasure of the super powers (DB) and their non-acceptance of Israel's decisions. Neither the US nor the USSR has recognized Jerusalem as Israel's capital; their diplomatic missions have always been located in the Tel Aviv area. For two years (1953–5) Washington boycotted the Foreign Office in Jerusalem. And, while the Soviets in 1950 withdrew their support for internationalization, their increasingly hostile policy towards Israel from 1955 onwards found in the Jerusalem issue another focus for anti-Israel coalition-building at the UN and elsewhere.

That DB facet was merely an extension of a general deterioration in Israel–Soviet relations, culminating in a prolonged diplomatic break (1967–). But the effect of Israel's Jerusalem decisions on her relations with the United States was adverse to a perceived vital Israeli interest, namely, continued assistance by the other super power in the protracted conflict. US support of the principle of internationalization from 1949 onward, her diplomatic boycott of Jerusalem, however brief, her adherence to the harsh General Assembly resolutions on Jerusalem since the Six Day War—all this weakened the Israel–US alignment which, by 1967, had become *the* pillar of Israel's foreign policy. Objectively, her stand on Jerusalem was exploited by hostile American pressure groups in a persistent attempt to secure sanctions or 'even-handedness' or a conspicuous pro-Arab policy by the US Government.

Feedback to the *Middle East subordinate system* (S) is too obvious to require elaboration. Suffice it to note that, from 1949 to 1967, Jerusalem was, for all Arab states engaged in the conflict except Jordan, another 'front' in the 'struggle for Palestine'. For non-Arab Muslim states (Turkey, Iran) Israel's 1949 decision was repugnant but tolerable, for the Old City, which contained virtually all Muslim—and Christian —Holy Places in the Jerusalem area, remained under control of a Muslim state. (That attitude was shared by Christian nations in the Middle East and elsewhere: they had long acquiesced in Muslim control (protection) of the Holy Places of Christendom but found intolerable, control (protection) of their shrines by a Jewish state.) What had been tolerable for fifteen years became odious to all in June 1967, following Israel's decision to unify Jerusalem under her authority.[1] And since the Six Day War the Jerusalem issue has appeared to be among the most intractable in the Arab–Israel conflict.

Another *subordinate system* (SO) in Israel's foreign policy setting has also been the recipient of adverse feedback from her Jerusalem decisions. Latin America, it was noted, had played a crucial role in securing the required two-thirds majority for the UN Assembly's Partition Resolution in November 1947; yet it did so in the expectation of a Catholic-dominated, internationalized City of Jerusalem. Thus the 1949 Israeli decision to make Jerusalem the seat of government was offensive to most of Latin America's decision-making élites. The consequence was a persistent thorn in an otherwise friendly alignment, indeed a vital friendship, for the Latin American group frequently used its voting strength to deny a two-thirds majority in the Assembly to anti-Israel draft resolutions moved by the Arab–Soviet–Muslim– 'radical' Third World coalition.

Latin America, like most other actors in the global system, adapted to the new *status quo* of 1949—a *de facto* partition of Jerusalem, with UN retention of the issue as a continuing symbol of the international community's legitimate interest in the Holy City. Israel's 1967 decision revived Latin America's antipathy to Israeli control over Christian Holy Places and its (long-dormant) expectation of an international city under predominant Catholic influence. Thus, while using its influence to defeat a harsh anti-Israel Assembly resolution on the conditions for a general Arab–Israel political settlement, the Latin American group joined the vociferous anti-Israel coalition and others to criticize, and later to deplore and condemn, her 1967 annexation of East Jerusalem. Israel's friendly relations with Latin America have withstood the disagreement over Jerusalem, but the adverse consequences are incontrovertible.

For the same reasons Israel's *bilateral* relations with several Catholic

---

[1] For a discussion of the Holy Places under Jordanian and Israeli rule see Zander, pp. 87–9 and 98–110 respectively, and Wilson, ch. vii. A Palestinian critique of Israeli policy in Jerusalem since the Six Day War is in Muhammad Abu Shilbaya, 'Jerusalem Before and After June 1967: An Arab View', *New Middle East*, nos. 42 and 43, March/ April 1972, pp. 43–5.

states, notably France, Belgium, and the Philippines, have periodically experienced negative effects from her decisions on Jerusalem. France has, for centuries, assumed the role of Protector of Christian interests in the Near East Core. Jewish control of Christian Holy Places was not only offensive; it provided Paris with an opportunity to reassert that role. French influence was also exerted to boycott Israel's diplomatic presence in Jerusalem and to rally Catholic support for internationalization. During the decade of *de facto* alliance with Israel (1955–66), French hostility to a Jewish (and Israeli) Jerusalem was muted. It re-emerged in 1967 and was expressed frequently thereafter. Belgium and the Philippines were in the forefront of UN campaigns for internationalization (1947–52). They have, in other respects, maintained friendly relations with Israel, but her insistence on sovereignty over Jerusalem alienated interest groups and decision-makers in those states. Adverse feedback has also been evident in Israel's relations with Italy and, more conspicuously, in her non-relations with the Vatican. While its massive campaign to internationalize Jerusalem did not succeed beyond the December 1949 Assembly resolution, the Holy See has not abandoned that goal. Israel's 1967 decision provided a pretext to reactivate the Vatican's aim; and the Pope continued to advocate territorial internationalization of the City.[1]

He did not do so directly, however, at the 'historic meeting' with Israel's Prime Minister Meir held in the Vatican on 15 January 1973. According to the jointly approved communiqué, 'His Holiness . . . presented the view of the Holy See . . . on the problems especially pertaining to its religious mission and relating to the Holy Places and to the sacred and universal character of the city of Jerusalem.'[2] And, despite the statement by the Vatican press spokesman, Professor Federico Alessandrini, that the meeting left Vatican–Israel relations unchanged, Mrs. Meir related: '. . . the Pope said, "thank you", three times, for our conduct in respect to the Holy Places in Jerusalem, and to the Christians. And he emphasized in the clearest fashion, at his initiative, that he was not speaking of internationalizing Jerusalem, and was not asking for an international treaty.'[3] Nevertheless, Vatican recognition of Israel, let alone her claim to Jerusalem, was not forthcoming.

In summary, all the external components of Israel's operational environment received negative feedback from her decisions on Jerusalem. Yet in none was the impact decisive. Israel's increasingly isolated position in the UN was the result of two developments: the massive influx of Third World states in the 1960s and the skill of the

---

[1] See, for example, his reported speech in Rome on 25 June 1971, *Jerusalem Post*, 26 June 1971. See also Zander, pp. 111–18.

[2] *Jerusalem Post*, 17 Jan. 1973.

[3] *Ma'ariv*, 19 Jan. 1973.

Arab–Soviet coalition in mobilizing their support on the Near East conflict; and secondly, the transformed global images of Israel and her Arab adversaries in the light of the outcome of the Six Day War. Her 1967 decision on Jerusalem was a contributing—but not a pivotal —cause of these structural and image changes in the world organization.

Similarly, Israel's relations with the super powers were only marginally affected by the Jerusalem issue. Soviet patronage of the Arab cause (from 1954 on) and the abrupt diplomatic breaks of 1953 and 1967 were due to more fundamental factors. This formulation is no less valid for Israel–US relations: Washington's reluctance to provide a formal guarantee of Israel's independence was not caused—or even influenced—by Israel's Jerusalem decisions. Nor was US refusal to provide arms until the 1960s. And her military, economic, and political support since the 1967 War has not been diminished by Israel's annexation of East Jerusalem or her rejection of the Rogers Plan for a territorial settlement (1969–70), with its special attention to the future of Jerusalem.

Israel's relations with Latin America and other Catholic actors have not been determined by the Jerusalem issue either. It has been, rather, in the nature of a pinprick to friendly alignments or, for some, notably France, a pretext to adopt an anti-Israel posture at a specific time and context, convenient to their interests. And while Israel's Jerusalem decisions have offended the Vatican, they did not result in the latter's denial of legitimacy to Israel as an independent state. Nor did they serve as an obstacle to the liberalizing thrust of Vatican II in redefining traditional relations between Catholics and Jews.

The dual character of the Jerusalem feedback to Israel's external environment—negative but marginal—had its counterpart in the psychological environment of her decision-makers. For one thing it was accurately perceived. For another, their image has been undifferentiated as to component; that is, they have recognized a near-universal opposition to Israel's decisions at all levels of the external setting. At the same time criticism has been correctly discerned:

(a) as vocal but not operational, i.e. not accompanied by sanctions of any kind;
(b) as spasmodic, not persistent (1949–50, 1952, 1967ff.);
(c) as not vital to Israel's relations with most international actors.

That perception, too, was accompanied throughout by an Israeli image of Jerusalem as an indispensable part of a revived Jewish state, a view rooted in the pervasive Jewishness of Israel's political culture, the historical legacy, and, more generally, the attitudinal prism.

Those contrasting perceptions—of marginal negative consequences for Israel's foreign policy and security interests, and of Jerusalem's centrality for Israel as a political society—created clear policy pre-dispositions:

(1) to withstand all external pressures, at first for internationalization (1947–52), and later for the revocation of measures to unify Jerusalem (1967ff.); and

(2) to assert an unshakeable claim to sovereignty over all of Jerusalem, using every opportunity in the changing operational environment to transform that claim into reality, such as a common interest with Jordan in *de facto* partition (1948–67) and a military windfall due to Jordan's strategic blunder in 1967.

That dual policy predisposition found expression in several courses of action:

(a) in prudent silence regarding the General Assembly's 1948 resolution on internationalization on the eve of the debate over Israel's admission to the UN;

(b) in the defiant riposte to the 1949 Assembly reaffirmation of internationalization, through the decision to make Jerusalem the seat of government;

(c) in the successful special effort to turn back the Vatican-led campaign for *corpus separatum* at the UN Assembly in 1950;

(d) in the display of patience over the transfer of the Foreign Ministry to Jerusalem in 1953, by which time the issue had become moribund;

(e) in surmounting the diplomatic boycott of Israel's capital (1953–5);

(f) in persuading all states but one (West Germany) which established diplomatic relations with Israel since 1956 to locate their missions in Jerusalem;

(g) in unifying West and East Jerusalem immediately after the June 1967 War, when unique circumstances of liberation obtained; and

(h) in withstanding the annual condemnation of that act by a near-unanimous UN Assembly vote.

Those policy acts, and especially the decisions of 1949 and 1967, flowed directly from the dual perception of Jerusalem's *external marginality* and *internal centrality*.

The latter image was immensely strengthened by a visible and articulate national consensus on Jerusalem. Only *Maki* openly dissented from the claim that it was an essential part of Israel. There were some persons more willing to compromise on control over the Old City; but even they insisted upon the retention of West Jerusalem and Israel's right to establish her capital there. The *political structure* was, indeed, the only internal component of the operational environment to experience feedback from the Jerusalem decisions. The effect was, essentially, to strengthen Israel's unity. Both within the coalition government and between government and opposition parties the decisions on Jerusalem created cohesion and commitment. Thus, while Israel's decisions caused hostility and adversity abroad, they led to support and unity at home.

Her decision-makers perceived this national consensus, especially in 1949 and 1967 but on other occasions as well, such as the transfer of the Foreign Office to Jerusalem in 1953. That image and its underlying reality both permitted and stimulated Israel's assertive policy, detailed above, which led to the *de facto* incorporation of the entire City into the Jewish state by June 1967 and the refusal to yield to external pressures. Finally, the act of unification (tactical decision), which was implemented in the subsequent years by controversial measures such as large-scale Jewish settlement in East Jerusalem, intensified the universal deep attachment of Israelis to their historic capital.

It remains to note that Israel's decisions on Jerusalem affected subsequent behaviour and outcomes in two issue-areas of her foreign policy—political-diplomatic and cultural-status. The core decisions (1949, 1967) had multiple spillovers in the P-D issue area—on Israel's position at the United Nations, on her relations with the US, UK, Latin American states, France, Belgium, the Philippines, the Vatican, etc. Indeed those decisions, along with the transfer of the Foreign Ministry to Jerusalem, sparked short-term diplomatic crises for Israel, involving her in acrimony and open disagreement with friendly as well as hostile international actors. The C-S issue-area encompassed the same decisions, for they all impinged on an outstanding illustration of a status issue in foreign policy—the right to establish the seat of government in a portion of territory claimed by the state concerned and challenged by (a broad spectrum of) actors in the global and subordinate systems of which it is a member. In the case of Jerusalem the status dimension rests on a deep cultural-historical commitment of decision-makers and their nation as a whole.

FIGURE 3

FEEDBACK: JERUSALEM

Operational Environment	Psychological Environment and Policy Derivatives
External	External

G Weakened Israel's position at the UN by providing focus for mobilization of diverse groups—Catholic, Muslim, Communist, and Arab—with anti-Israel interests in Jerusalem. (S)

The 1967 decision catalysed massive anti-Israel policy on Jerusalem at UN and in global system as a whole. (T)

S The 1967 decision, in particular, added further dimension to protracted Arab-Israel conflict and antagonized other Middle East system actors. (S, T)

SO Latin America's traditionally friendly policy towards Israel was adversely affected because of expectation that Jerusalem would be internationalized under Roman Catholic control. (S, T)

Integration of East with West Jerusalem accentuated Latin America's alienation on this issue. (T)

DB Both 1949 and 1967 decisions complicated Israel's friendly relationship with the US, including diplomatic boycott of Foreign Ministry in Jerusalem (1953–5). (S, T)

B Israel's relations with several Catholic states, notably France, Belgium, and the Philippines, as well as the Vatican, have been irritated by her insistence on sovereignty over Jerusalem. (S, T)

Israel's decision-makers correctly perceived negative consequences flowing from all external components of the environment. However, they discerned all as marginal for Israel's vital foreign policy predisposition:

(a) to withstand all external pressures, at first for territorial internationalization (1947–52), and, later, for the revocation of measures to unify Jerusalem (1967ff.); and

(b) to assert an unshakeable claim to sovereignty over all Jerusalem, using every opportunity in the changing operational environment to transform that claim into reality. (P–D, C–S)

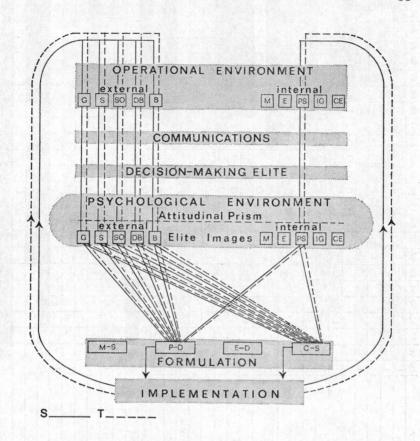

S————   T— — — — —

Internal	*Internal*
PS The overwhelming national consensus on Jerusalem removed one area of competition and friction from the political system and provided mass support for Government policy. (S, T)	The decision-makers' perception of total national support strengthened their resolve to establish capital in Jerusalem (1949) and to unify the City when the opportunity arose (1967). (P–D, C–S)

TABLE 3
DIPLOMATIC REPRESENTATION TO ISRAEL: 1949–1972

COUNTRY	49	50	51	52	53	54	55	56	57	58	59	60	61	62	63	64	65	66	67	68	69	70	71	72
Argentina	L	L																						
Australia	L							E																
Austria								L				E												
Belgium	L									O						E								
Bolivia										O														
Brazil				L					E															
Bulgaria		E																						
Burma								L		E														
Cambodia																		O	O	O	O	O	O	O
Canada														E										
Central African Republic							E																	
Ceylon												O	O											
Chile				O	O	L	E				E				O	E								
Colombia									O	O	O	O	O	O	O	E								
Costa Rica									O	O	O	O	O	O	E			O	O	O	O			
Cuba								L																
Cyprus															O	O	O	O						
Czechoslovakia	L						L										E							
Dahomey														E										
Denmark			O	O	O	O	O	O	O	O	O	O	O	E										
Dominican Republic								O	O	O	L	O	O			E								
El Salvador		C												E				O	O	O	O	O	O	
Finland				L										E										
France	L																							
Gabon																		E						
Germany (West)																		E						
Ghana											O	E												
Great Britain	L				E																			
Greece	DR		DR																					
Guatemala							E																	E
Haiti												O	O	O			O	O						
Holland	E																						E	
Honduras																	O	O	E					

Source: Ministry for Foreign Affairs, *List of Members of the Diplomatic Corps in Israel*, The Jerusalem Post Press, Jerusalem, 1948–72 (annual).

L Legation

E Embassy

O Representation abroad

C Consulate

DR Diplomatic Representation

[shaded] in Tel Aviv

[dark] in Jerusalem

Note. Eight African states severed diplomatic relations with Israel during the eighteen months preceding the Yom Kippur War, beginning with Uganda in March 1972. Another 20 African states did so during that war. Of those 28 countries, 14 had had missions in Israel, 11 of them in Jerusalem. By mid-November 1973 Israel's diplomatic ties with Africa were confined to Lesotho, Malawi, Mauritius and Swaziland, none of which has its diplomatic representation in Jerusalem.

Iran
Italy
Ivory Coast
Jamaica
Japan
Kenya
Korea
Laos
Liberia
Malagasy Republic
Malawi
Malta
Mexico
Nepal
Nicaragua
Niger
Norway
Panama
Peru
Philippines
Poland
Republic of Congo
Rumania
Sierra Leone
Sweden
Switzerland
Thailand
Turkey
Union of Soviet Socialist Republics
United States of America
Upper Volta
Uruguay
Venezuela
Yugoslavia
Zaire

CHAPTER 3

German Reparations

The Holocaust was an unparalleled human and national tragedy: six million persons, one third of the Jewish People, perished in a conscious plan of collective destruction by Nazi Germany. The 'Final Solution' was not attained, but most of the great centres of Jewish culture in central and eastern Europe were expunged between 1939 and 1945. The trauma experienced by Jews everywhere created a vast and seemingly unbridgeable gulf between Jewry and the Germans. Yet within a few years Israel made the first of several strategic decisions concerning Germany, which were to create, however painfully, a setting for conciliation and co-operation:

on 3 January 1951	the Government of Israel made a high-policy (strategic) decision to seek German reparations for plundered Jewish property in Europe. Simultaneously it decided to pursue that objective *indirectly*, through the Four Occupying Powers; (S)
on 30 December 1951,	after this approach had failed, a tactical decision was made—to accept an invitation to enter into *direct* negotiations with the West German Government. (T)

There was also an array of implementing decisions, culminating in the Luxembourg Agreement of 10 September 1952.[1] That decision flow will be analysed in depth after exploring the operational environment, the decision-making group, and the images which shaped their decisions.

(A) OPERATIONAL ENVIRONMENT

The setting for Israel's strategic and tactical decisions was inauspicious in almost all respects.

The *global system* (G) was in the grip of increasingly tight bipolarity towards the end of 1950, as war enveloped Korea. Indeed, the danger of

---

[1] All these events will be analysed in sections (c) and (d) below. A summary of the decision flow is provided in section (e). The dates and substance of the two basic Government decisions (3 January and 30 December 1951) were made known to the author by participants.

direct confrontation between the two super powers was intensified by a dramatic two-step escalation of that conflict: first, the UN-sanctioned crossing of the 38th Parallel by US-led United Nations forces in October; and the massive response of Chinese 'volunteers' in December. And while the Soviet Union was not formally involved in the war, her sympathy and material support for North Korea and the People's Republic of China were unconcealed.

For Israel the consequence of a sharpening global bifurcation was the abandonment of Non-Identification. With it came the certainty of a hostile response—or none at all—from one of the two German regimes which would, it was hoped, provide reparations. Moreover, Israel's alignment with the United States on the Korea issue during the autumn of 1950 was not likely to induce Soviet pressure on East Germany in the matter of reparations.[1] Thus the unique constellation of global forces which had led to American and Soviet support for Israel's independence no longer existed to her advantage. As partial compensation she had received a verbal security commitment from the US, UK, and France, in the form of the Tripartite Declaration of May 1950.

The *subordinate system* (S) was more tranquil than the global environment. This was partly because of the attitude of the Western Powers—the Soviets had not yet established a Middle East presence—and partly because of the reality and the image of Israel's victory in the 1948 War. Arab hostility was a constant, as was the perceived threat of annihilation. But the danger to Israel was less urgent in the autumn of 1950 than at many other periods in the protracted conflict.

As for the most significant *bilateral* (B) variable in the reparations equation, there were no objective grounds for Israeli optimism. Partitioned and occupied since 1945, West Germany had not revealed evidence of a capacity to pay large-scale reparations; the 'economic miracle' lay in the future. Further, there were competing claims upon that truncated economic capability from the victor–creditors in the Second World War. And no German leader had yet publicly admitted his nation's guilt for the heinous crimes of the Nazi regime—or had offered to make amends by massive reparations to the Jewish People and to Israel. In short, the external environment for a decision on reparations late in 1950 was partly *negative* (Soviet and East German attitudes to Israel's claim) and partly *uncertain* (West German and Western attitudes, as well as Bonn's capacity to pay). The regional setting was irrelevant.

The internal dimension of the operational environment was much more significant in the decision, serving as both obstacle and inducement. The Holocaust and the very name, 'Germany', evoked the most powerful feelings of revulsion among Israelis, crossing ideological lines.

[1] An analysis of Israel's response to the Korean War is contained in the following chapter.

In fact, no other issue in Israel's foreign policy throughout the period of independence was as explosive as relations with Germany—economic, military, cultural, and diplomatic.

There was no sustained outcry when Israel made known her claims in the Notes of 16 January and 12 March 1951 to the Four Powers— because that strategy avoided the substance and even the appearance of direct contact with a German government.[1] The Western Powers, however, declined to serve as intermediaries with Bonn. And Chancellor Adenauer's Declaration before the *Bundestag* on 27 September 1951 posed the issue of direct talks starkly. It was only then that opposition parties and pressure groups mounted a campaign, which was to reach its peak in the violent demonstrations outside the *Knesset* during the debate of 7–9 January 1952.

The amount of attention devoted to the reparations issue by Israel's *competing élites* (CE) exceeds all foreign policy advocacy on a single issue except that relating to the Rogers Proposals and the Jarring Talks in 1969–72. And furthermore, Israeli images of Germany and the policies they advocated reveal a highly consistent pattern during a period of two years. *Herut*, representing the nationalist Right, and *Maki*, then Stalinist, manifested a simple, direct, and unqualified perception of the Adenauer regime as dominated by neo-Nazis: the related advocacy was total rejection of any offer of reparations; indeed, of any contact with West Germany. The Left-socialist *Mapam* (which included at the time the Left-nationalist *Ahdut Ha'avoda*) shared their harsh perception and firm advocacy but emphasized a global strand as well—Bonn as a danger to international peace. The religious party, *Ha-po'el Ha-mizrahi*, also perceived Nazism in West Germany but did not attack the Adenauer Government directly; it urged permanent remembrance of the German nation's iniquity to the Jews—but in policy terms it followed the lead of *Mapai*, the repository of institutionalized political power in Israel. So did the Progressives. The General Zionists did not, and they expressed distrust of West Germany's *bona fides*.

Among *interest groups* (IG), many of the highly vocal and militant

---

[1] Ishar Harari of the Progressive Party was articulately opposed from the outset to seeking reparations in any form. Indeed, he correctly predicted that such a claim would inevitably involve Israel in direct negotiations with Germany. The great majority of speakers following Sharett's presentation of the 12 March Note to the *Knesset* supported the Government's approach to the Four Powers, though some doubted its practicality. The main criticism, by Rabbi Mordekhai Nurock and others, was that Israel had waited too long in asserting her claim. *Divrei Ha-knesset*, viii, 1951, pp. 953–6.

Begin, the *Herut* leader, charged in the *Knesset* on 2 April 1951 that some passages in the 12 March Note implied that Israel would not object to recognition of Germany if her demand for reparations were met. The allegation was stoutly denied by *Mapai* members Pinhas Lavon and Meir Argov. *Divrei Ha-knesset*, viii, 1951, pp. 1545–6, 1549, 1560.

associations of partisans and ghetto fighters merged their demands, their activism, and their tactics with the *Mapam* campaign against the Government. Nationalist groups within the wartime Jewish underground found a no less congenial framework within the ideologically akin *Herut*. A large number of persons who would benefit materially from any reparations agreement performed as a supportive interest group, pressing their views through party and other affiliations—though many were absolutely opposed to any deal with Germany and have refused to submit claims, to this day. Institutional interest groups, such as the higher army officers corps or the senior cadres of the bureaucracy, did not participate as such in the tempestuous struggle over reparations, but few, if any, were immune from the controversy. Among the formally non-party newspapers, *Ha'aretz* and the *Jerusalem Post* supported the decisions; *Ma'ariv* and *Yedi'ot Aharonot* were opposed.[1]

As for the *political structure* (PS), the characteristics most relevant to the decision process were the multi-party system of Israel and the centrality of coalition politics. *Mapai* alone did not command a *Knesset* majority for its reparations policy: it held only 45 seats—and even with its Arab allies, only 50—in a House of 120. Furthermore, its coalition partners (the Progressives and the Religious Front, comprising *Mizrahi*, *Ha-po'el Ha-mizrahi*, and *Agudat Yisrael*) were in turmoil over the first great foreign policy issue of conscience. Yet their support, even if only in part, was the *sine qua non* to parliamentary approval. Thus the internal fragmentation of parties imposed severe strains on the Coalition and on each member.

Israel's *military capability* (M) at the end of 1950 was relatively reassuring in the short run. *Tzahal* (Israel Defence Forces) was still heavily dependent on external sources for weapons; and none of the Powers was then prepared to perform the patron function. Yet Egypt was in the same position. And other Arab states in the Near East Core were too weak, alone or even in concert, to pose an immediate threat. Rather, the balance of forces created by Israel's triumph in 1948 remained essentially unchanged. Thus the military component of the environment was not a compelling source of pressure, though any improvement in Israel's economy was bound to have spillover effects on her defensive capability.

The *economic* (E) situation of Israel was harsh in the last months of 1950; graver, perhaps, than at any other period in the state's independent existence. All the indicators were negative as a result of the mass

---

[1] *Ha'aretz* was at that time closely associated with the Progressives; its editor was to become a member of the Third *Knesset* on that party's list. The *Post* has always reflected *Mapai* views. And the two evening newspapers were staffed overwhelmingly by *Herut* members; in fact, the editor of *Yedi'ot Aharonot* signed the Declaration of Independence for the Revisionists.

immigration that predominantly characterized that austerity period: from May 1948 to the end of 1951 Israel's Jewish population more than doubled, from 650,000 to 1,324,000. The major tasks were to provide food, clothing and shelter to the impoverished survivors of the Displaced Persons camps in Europe and Cyprus, and to the underprivileged immigrants from Iraq and Yemen, as well as employment for immigrants and demobilized soldiers. Yet that economic challenge had to be met by an underdeveloped economy without reserves of capital or foreign exchange.

The austerity programme, through stringent price controls and rationing of food, raw materials, and other basic necessities, ensured minimum standards of consumption for the entire population. The Israeli economy, however, was precarious and insecure. And external sources of aid were grossly inadequate—a total of $118 million in unilateral transfers in 1949, and $90 million in 1950, all of it from world Jewry.[1] This was hardly sufficient to cover a rising import surplus: exports barely increased from a minuscule $43 million in 1949 to $45·8 million in 1950, while imports rose from $263 million to $327·6 million. Although Israel was to be faced twenty years later with a massive deficit of more than $1 billion in her balance of payments, her economy was much less capable of coping with the deficit of $220 million in 1949 and $281·8 million in 1950.[2]

Other indicators were also disturbing. The Gross National Product in 1950 was less than half a billion Israeli pounds (£I458 million) for a population of 1·4 million: the annual *per capita* output of £I340 was tiny, compared to the rapid growth of ensuing years. Moreover, unemployment in 1950 was at its peak—an official estimate of 11·5 per cent, representing 52,000 persons; and even this 'seems low', remarked Professor Patinkin, in the light of the 50,000 added to the labour force that year through immigration and the 80,000 the preceding year, along with thousands more demobilized soldiers.[3] The living conditions of the 420,000 persons who poured into Israel in 1949 and 1950 were grim—overcrowding in immigrant centres and transit camps, scarcity of employment, inadequate educational facilities. And finally there was a drought in 1950–51, which imposed even more stringent austerity measures. Not all of these components were directly relevant to the reparations decisions. And those that formed part of the decision-makers' psychological environment, to which we now turn, were not perceived with equal intensity.

---

[1] Halevi and Klinov-Malul, Appendix Table 9, 'Unilateral Transfers: 1949–65', pp. 294–5.

[2] Ibid., Table 50, 'Balance of Payments on Current Account: 1949–65', p. 141. 'Billion' is used throughout in the US sense of 'a thousand millions'.

[3] Patinkin, p. 31. Israel's economic plight during the gestation period of her strategic and tactical decisions on reparations is described in detail in Balabkins, ch. 5.

(B) DECISION-MAKERS AND THEIR IMAGES

The decision to seek German reparations, by an approach to the Four Occupying Powers, was taken by Israel's Government at a meeting on 3 January 1951, after a debate extending over three Cabinet sessions. At that time the Coalition comprised the following parties and persons:[1]

Mapai

David Ben Gurion	Prime Minister and Defence
Dov Joseph	Transport
Eliezer Kaplan	Finance
Pinhas Lubianiker (Lavon)	Agriculture
Golda Meyerson (Meir)	Labour and National Insurance
David Remez	Education and Culture
Moshe Sharett	Foreign Affairs
Behor-Shalom Shitreet (*Sepharadim*)	Police

Religious Front
  Agudat Yisrael

Rabbi Yitzhak Meir Levin	Welfare

  Ha-po'el Ha-mizrahi

Moshe Shapira	Immigration and Health, and Interior

  Mizrahi

Rabbi Yehuda Leib Fishman (Maimon)	Religious Affairs and War Victims

Progressives

Pinhas Rosen	Justice

Non-Party

Jack Myer Geri	Commerce and Industry

Mapai held a decisive majority (8 of 13 ministers).[2] And, given internal party cohesion, it could secure Government approval for any foreign policy proposal—except when Prime Minister Ben Gurion and Foreign Minister Sharett disagreed. Thus, while all 13 ministers were formally equal as high-policy decision-makers, preponderant *influence* lay with the Big Three of *Mapai*—Ben Gurion, Sharett, and Kaplan. The views of three minor-party ministers—Rosen, Shapira,

[1] This, the 2nd Government of Israel, was a short-lived one—from 1 November 1950 to 14 February 1951, when it resigned; it continued until 7 October 1951 as a caretaker Government. Not all ministers were present at the Cabinet meetings when discussions took place and decisions were taken on the issue of reparations. The participants in crucial meetings will be specified later.

[2] As noted, it did so in all Governments from May 1948 to the end of 1965 and, thereafter, as the pre-eminent group in the Labour Alignment. For the details see n. 1, p. 13 above.

and Maimon—commanded respect on this as on many other issues. And Joseph, by the forcefulness of his advocacy, was a central figure in the debate.

Among the principal decision-makers Sharett was more responsive to the idea at the outset. Ben Gurion became central to the drama when it developed into an issue of national controversy, and *Herut* mobilized the opposition forces. That clash between parties (*Mapai* and *Herut*) was accentuated by the bitter personal rivalry between Ben Gurion and Begin. A negative vote in the *Knesset* in January 1952 would have been construed as a victory for Begin—which Ben Gurion was unwilling to tolerate—even if the decision on reparations had had less significance for Israel's 'national interests'. The result was BG's total commitment.

The pre-eminent role of the Prime Minister and Foreign Minister was acknowledged by several persons who participated in some stage of the decision process on German reparations.[1] Avner observed: 'Ben Gurion swung it in the Party and the *Knesset*—but Sharett never wavered.' Shinnar concurred: 'Ben Gurion was the only Israeli leader who could have pushed the decision through. Sharett favoured it but he needed the initiative.' Sharett's role, said Horowitz, was 'very important, because he gave full support at the beginning and guided us through the negotiations'. Kaplan did not speak in the *Knesset* debate. He could have vetoed the idea at an early stage but 'he was enough of a realist to know that it had to be done'. As Mrs. Meir put it succinctly, in reply to a question about who were the key actors: 'Sharett in Israel; Ben Gurion supported it, as did Kaplan.'

None was enthusiastic about reparations; all clearly preferred *indirect* arrangements. Thus it was decided to approach the US, UK, France, and the USSR, in the hope that Israel's claim could be met without the need for any contact whatsoever with Germany or Germans. When that hope proved illusory, the ministers remained publicly united, that is, in the *Knesset* vote to accept Adenauer's invitation to enter into *direct* negotiations. It was Goldmann who secured Adenauer's agreement to negotiate on the basis of Israel's claim and thereby made possible the tactical decision to enter into direct talks. He had little to do with the initial high-policy decision.[2]

How did the decision-makers perceive the setting for decision on a controversial and emotion-filled issue in Israel's foreign policy? Stated schematically, what components of the operational environment did they regard as relevant, and in what order of importance? There was no substantive *Knesset* discussion of reparations preceding the first

---

[1] The following five extracts are from Avner, Shinnar, Horowitz, Eytan, and Meir interviews.

[2] In his memoirs Goldmann wrote: 'In all the campaigns I have participated in ... I never had a chance *to plan and lead one so definitely from its very start....*' Goldmann 1969, p. 277 (emphasis added).

basic decision and the dispatch of the first Notes to the Powers, on 16 January, dealing with personal restitution, and on 12 March 1951, concerning reparations to the Jewish People.[1] Nor are Cabinet minutes of that period available for research. Thus the evidence concerning images of decision-makers at that time is drawn from contemporary speeches, memoirs of participants, written and oral, and eye-witness accounts.

Ben Gurion, in one of his published memoirs, recalled:[2]

If you want the overall reason in a single sentence, it was the final injunction of the inarticulate six million, the victims of Nazism whose very murder was a ringing cry for Israel to rise, to be *strong* and *prosperous*, to safeguard her peace and *security*, and so prevent such a disaster from ever again overwhelming the *Jewish people.* . . . I was proposing neither forgiveness nor wiping the slate clean when I presented the demand for reparations from West Germany at the *Knesset* session in January 1952.

This refers to the tactical decision. There is no evidence to suggest that Ben Gurion's view of the world and, specifically, of Germany, of Israel's need, and of her historic obligations, changed during the twelve months between the decision to seek reparations indirectly, and the decision to seek them directly. Nor does the long-term consistency of Ben Gurion's images suggest the probability of a change. And ministerial colleagues at the time confirm his consistent view. For example, Rosen remarked: '*Right from the beginning* he put forward the view of "the other Germany", first, that Germany had ceased to be a real danger, and secondly, that Germany had learned her lesson.'[3]

The pre-eminence of the Jewish prism is striking in Ben Gurion's

[1] There were, however, numerous earlier and concurrent discussions in the *Knesset* pertaining to Germany, especially the debate on the rearming of Germany, in October 1950, and again, by way of approving a resolution of the Committee on Foreign Affairs and Security, on 10 January 1951, a week before the dispatch of the first Note. Nothing was then said on the Note, and no Cabinet member participated. Other discussions were held on:
trade relations, budget debate, 29 June 1949
the Nazis and Nazi Collaborators (Punishment) Bill, 27 March 1950
the Four Powers' attitudes to Germany, 8 May 1950
a report of an approach by *Agudat Yisrael* to the West German Government, 17 May 1950
a German Property Bill, Aug. 1950
restitution, 5 Dec. 1949, 23 Jan., 22, 27 March, and July–Aug. 1950
Nazi crimes against Jews, 26 Dec. 1949, 27 March, 2 May, 26 July, Aug. 1950
the termination of the state of war with Germany by the Western Powers, 25 December 1950.
All these are contained in *Divrei Ha-knesset*, 1st *Knesset*, i–vii. In addition, there were occasional proposals by *individual* MKs that the Government of Israel claim and accept the reparations which Israel deserved.
[2] Ben Gurion 1965, p. 162 (emphasis added).
[3] Rosen interview, 1971 (emphasis added). Ben Gurion's closest aides, like Navon and Peres, confirmed this consistent perception. Interviews, 1965–6.

memoir—his sense of historical continuity, the obligation to the Six Million, the concept of Israel as the territorial base and political bastion of the Jewish People. Within that prism the focus was on 'strong' and 'security' (M), and on 'prosperous' (E): these were the two most relevant environmental variables, as well, of course, as Germany (B), the last as the source of Jewry's tragedy and of Israel's demand. The M component, in the form of a preoccupation with security, is central to his general view of the world and is ubiquitous in his words and deeds. The E and B components, as stimuli to the reparations decisions, were expressed by Ben Gurion with convincing simplicity after his retirement: 'The economic factor was important, but it was not the only thing. There was also the moral obligation of Germany to pay for the crimes it had committed.'[1]

These image-components are also evident in the most important articulation of Ben Gurion's image at the time—his Statement to the *Knesset* on 7 January 1952, introducing the Government's Motion on the issue of direct negotiations. Other perceptual elements are also apparent, namely, DB—the attitudes of Washington and Moscow, other B relationships—the reaction of London and Paris, and the dual view of Germany, with the emphasis on her never-to-be-forgotten or forgiven crimes against Jewry. And all this demonstrates what I have called the Jewish prism. Thus, in surveying the developments of the preceding year, from the Notes of 16 January 1951 to the Powers onward, the Prime Minister declared:[2]

The State of Israel took upon itself the great effort, and there is no precedent for this . . . , to absorb and to settle quickly hundreds of thousands of immigrants. . . . This enormous burden was accepted by a State without capital and is greater than her capacity . . . [E]

[The Soviet Union did not bother to answer Israel's Notes.] The Three [Western Powers] do not feel they can demand any more from Germany at this time, neither for themselves nor for others . . . [but they influenced Bonn to offer reparations to Israel.] [DB and B]

There is no precedent for this action because the State of Israel did not exist in the days of the Holocaust. . . . But . . . neither has there been a precedent for the massacre and slaughter in such enormous proportions like that which the German people committed under Hitler's leadership against the Jews of Europe. More than six million Jews were murdered, by torture, starvation, asphyxiation. Many were buried alive; no mercy was given to the aged, to women and children; babies were torn from their mothers' arms and thrown into the ovens. Before, during, and after this planned murder of millions, despoliation took place, and this too in immense proportions without precedent. . . . Crimes of these enormous proportions cannot be absolved in material terms. . . .

[1] Ben Gurion interview, 1966.
[2] The original Hebrew text is in *Divrei Ha-knesset*, x (2), 1951–2, 38th Sitting, 2nd *Knesset*, 7 Jan. 1952, pp. 895–6, and in *Documents* . . . , pp. 57–60 (emphasis added).

But the *German people, all of whom are responsible for the destruction wrought by their government under Hitler,* continue to benefit, both in the East and the West, from this slaughter and the shame of the robbery of the murdered Jews. . . . These atrocities will never be forgotten. . . . *Let not the murderers of our people be their inheritors as well!* [B]

The Jewish *Weltanschauung* was certainly pervasive in Ben Gurion's view of Germany. But which of the specific image-components dominated his thought—and decisions—on reparations remains a topic of controversy. Like all other persons in the decision-making group, he was aware of Israel's grave economic condition in 1950–1. And he was persuaded that massive foreign aid was imperative to cover the mounting import surplus. Thus he perceived the immediate economic value of reparations. He himself acknowledged this, as noted. Yet, like many charismatic figures, especially those cast in the role of 'Father of the Nation', he revealed a certain disdain for the economic dimension of public policy. He never attended meetings of the Cabinet's Economic Affairs Committee, he proudly recalled. 'I left this to Kaplan and, later, to Eshkol.'[1] According to his long-time Political Secretary, 'it is incorrect to see Ben Gurion's motive in the reparations issue as purely or even primarily economic. Whatever Ben Gurion has done at any time is dominated by concern with security and the survival of the state.'[2] And Rosen recalled: 'Ben Gurion was not indifferent to the Holocaust—but he was able to forget. Other things were more important to him, especially the building of Israel. The Holocaust was like a lost war for him.' Moreover, 'Ben Gurion was fond of prophecies. The whole trend of his thinking would indicate his awareness of political implications from the beginning.'[3] Stated differently, Ben Gurion felt that Germany was one of the few areas where Israel could pursue an independent policy—because of the uniqueness of the issue.

That concern with Israel's future is evident in his reported remarks to Haim Yahil the day the Luxembourg Agreements were signed: 'This is an historic day, though I do not think the Germans will pay.' Its significance, he explained, was twofold—the first formal international recognition of Israel as the address of the Jewish People, and the involvement of Germany on Israel's side in her struggle for survival.[4] Yet there is contrary testimony of other participants: that Ben Gurion

---

[1] Ben Gurion interview, 1966.   [2] Navon interview, 1965.
[3] Rosen interview, 1971.

[4] Yahil interviews, 1966, 1971. Ben Gurion denied part of this report: 'I had no reason to think they would not pay, though I couldn't give an assurance that they would.' But he did not contest his reported emphasis on the *political* significance of reparations. Ben Gurion interview, 1966.

Yahil reaffirmed to the author in 1971 this reported conversation with BG, adding about Ben Gurion's partial denial: 'You cannot expect Ben Gurion to remember everything *he* said to people—but *I*, like others, would remember what Ben Gurion told *me*!' Later, he wrote: 'I have no doubt about BG's political awareness of

was not ardently responsive to the idea of reparations at the outset; that he did not assert his leadership in the Cabinet meetings, when the issue was debated and decided; and that he did not intimate his political-security calculus *at that time*. This was to come later, from about 1957 on, they concluded.[1] Perhaps the simplest explanation was that offered by a non-*Mapai* Cabinet colleague whom Ben Gurion respected: 'He was primarily interested in the future of the state and he knew we needed financial aid.'[2]

From these diverse strands there emerges a Ben Gurion image, with constant and variable elements:

the fixed *attitudinal prism* was Jewishness in its broadest meaning—historic past, continuity, responsibility for the future;

the short-term environmental factor most directly perceived by Ben Gurion (and all other decision-makers) was the compelling need of Israel's economy (E);

while E was the catalyst to the decisions, it was perceived as an instrumental goal to achieve a higher value, the survival and security of Israel (M);

when the reparations decisions were consummated (the Luxembourg Agreements), regional and global components (S and G) replaced the economic stimulus in the hierarchy of Ben Gurion's images, partly because of scepticism about West Germany's fulfilment of her obligations, but mainly because of his recognition of Germany's revival as a Power and the symbolic international sanction which he perceived for the legitimate unity of Israel and world Jewry.

Stated in schematic and simple quantitative terms—ordinal ranking of image-components—Ben Gurion's articulated image may be designated for the three crucial dates in the decision flow, within a constant attitudinal prism of Jewishness. (See Table 4 on the following page.)

Other components of the environment were marginal in Ben Gurion's image: the attitudes of the Four Powers (DB and B_2, B_3—i.e. France, UK) were of possible instrumental relevance only; and the vocal opposition of parties and pressure groups in Israeli society (CE and IG) were perceived as legitimate and deserving of a hearing but they were rejected by him as *the* basis for making a high-policy decision.

Germany's importance already in 1952. I have ample proof of that.' Yahil letter, 1972. And Rosen recalled: 'He was certainly sceptical of the Germans, saying "I always believed there would be a Jewish State but I never thought the Germans would pay." ' Rosen interview, 1971.

The belief that Bonn would not fulfil its obligations was deep-rooted in Israel's high-policy and technical élites: it stemmed from experience with German default on debts in the inter-war period—another striking illustration of the effect of historical legacy on the psychological environment of decision-makers.

[1] Avner, Eytan, Horowitz, Shinnar interviews, 1966–71.
[2] Rosen interview, 1971.

TABLE 4

RANKING OF BEN GURION'S IMAGE-COMPONENTS RELATING TO
GERMAN REPARATIONS: 1951–1952

S(*trategic*)	T(*actical*)	De Facto I(*mplementation*)
(3 January 1951)	(30 December 1951)	(10 September 1952)
M (Israel's security) 10	M (Israel's security) 10	S M (German support for Israel's security in regional conflict) 10
E (Israel's economy) 9	E (Israel's economy) 9	G (International recognition of Israel–Jewry link) 9
B (Germany's crimes against Jewry) 8	B (Germany's crimes against Jewry) 8	E (Israel's economy) 8
		B (Germany's crimes against Jewry) 7

The Jewish prism was no less pronounced in Foreign Minister Sharett's image of German reparations. In September 1950 he advocated one exception to the principle of universal membership in the United Nations. 'The people of Israel and Jews throughout the world', he told the General Assembly, 'view with consternation and distress the progressive readmission of Germany to the family of nations, with her revolting record intact, her guilt unexpiated, and her heart unchanged.'[1] Moreover, after reading Israel's second Note to the Powers, he declared before the *Knesset*: '... The Government of Israel cannot imagine that the gates of the cultured and peace-loving world will be opened to the German people, not only because their hands are still smeared with blood, but also when their plunder is still under their cloak. There is a day of reckoning—and this day has arrived.'[2] The same theme is evident in his defence of Government policy during the January 1952 *Knesset* debate.[3] Any successor to Nazi Germany, he noted, would be considered by Israel 'the heir to the reign of blood, violence and destruction which preceded it'. Yet there was a fundamental *moral duty* of Jewry: 'Is it not our sacred duty to rescue whatever is still obtainable, to bring it here and turn it to creative uses? ... And if there is no other way of recovering this property except by negotiation with the heirs of the robbers, or even with the robbers

---

[1] GAOR, 5th Session, 286th Plenary Mtg., 27 Sept. 1950, p. 136. The same theme was reiterated in GAOR, 6th Session, 341st Plenary Mtg., 13 Nov. 1951, p. 87, and in the *Ad Hoc* Political Committee, 15th–16th Meetings, 4 Dec. 1951, pp. 77, 86.

[2] Statement on 13 March 1951, in *Documents* . . . , 6, p. 28.

[3] *Divrei Ha-knesset*, x (2), 1951–2, 40th Sitting, 2nd *Knesset*, 9 Jan. 1952, pp. 953–6. The following four extracts are taken from Sharett, pp. 7, 20–1, 12, 30.

themselves, then it is not merely permissible but our bounden duty to enter into such negotiations.'

Sharett's attitudinal prism thus reflected Jewishness and Jewry as a nation—its past tragedy and its inherent rights. An important image-component was clearly Germany's iniquity (B). The attitude of the Four Powers (DB and B_2, B_3) was marginal for him, as for Ben Gurion. 'You cannot demand of other people to do the dirty work for you', he chided the critics, 'while you keep your hands lily-white and retire into the rarefied atmosphere of an exalted morality.' Like Ben Gurion, too, he was aware of Israel's long-term security obligation as an independent actor in international politics (M), for which reparations were essential: 'A scattered and defenceless people can and, perhaps, must live only in the memories of the past. . . . But a people which exercises political sovereignty over a territory of its own is in a very different category. It knows that its land is part of a larger world and that it cannot escape contact with other nations. . . . It must follow every shift in the balance of forces around it and in the world at large; it dare not neglect any opportunity of increasing its strength.' And even more than Ben Gurion he was conscious of the economic dimension. Sharett acknowledged this with candour on the eve of the Wassenaar negotiations with West Germany: 'The crux of our problem is production. Our balance of trade is staggeringly adverse. . . . The inordinately wide gap between imports and exports creates a state of high economic tension characterized by acute shortage and strict rationing.'[1] In short, the same three components are evident in the perceptions held by Ben Gurion and Sharett—E, B, and M. Indeed, this confirms the consensus among participants that, on the reparations issue, the two men thought and acted alike.

Kaplan, the Finance Minister, perceived reparations in utilitarian (E) terms, as necessary to Israel's economic growth in a period of peril. That was natural for, as a Cabinet colleague remarked, 'He was Treasurer—he needed the money.'[2] Yet he was sceptical, as in most things, that anything would emerge from an indirect approach to the Powers. To Horowitz, his Director-General, he said late in 1950: 'You think you can do this through the Powers alone. You are wrong. The only way will be direct talks with Germany—and for that the country is not ready.'[3]

Mrs. Meir, who was Minister of Labour at the time, strongly opposed negotiations with Germany during the preliminary discussions; and she hesitated long whether to approve. But when she was won over, mainly by Ben Gurion's arguments, she became a forceful advocate.

[1] Y.L., no. 473, 14 March 1952, p. 1. Horowitz, Shinnar and others also recalled to the writer how important was the economic component in Sharett's image.

[2] Rosen interview, 1971.

[3] Horowitz interview, 1971.

During the January 1952 debate she used symbols of Jewish survival
and national pride in defending the Government's proposal of direct
negotiations:[1]

Why was it placed upon us, a small people, to bear such a large part of the
terrible cruelties that have befallen the world? There is only one answer. We
were weak, we had no independence, we had no state. . . . We must make
ourselves stronger in every way in order to save quickly . . . Jews from all over
the world. . . .

We are going to demand what is coming to us; and the responsible people of
the Government of Israel . . . know how to speak to the enemy with pride,
Jewish pride . . . in a manner which will add to the strength and honour of
Am Yisrael.

In retrospect, fifteen years later, she perceived three other environmental components—economic need (E), security (M), and international recognition of Israel's organic links with the Jewish People (G),
all within a Jewish prism:[2]

The economic factor was clearly pre-eminent but not in the narrow sense of
wanting aid for the immediate problem of Israel's shortages in 1951. We wanted
reparations because we needed enormous funds for development. We had to
develop the country, to absorb large numbers of refugees.

There was another reason. This would be the first time the Jews received
reparations for atrocities committed against them. And it would be the first
time that a Power would deal with Jews as a nation—and with a Jewish state.

[And thirdly] why should we have attached a higher value to the million
children killed by the Nazis than to the million who had to be rehabilitated in
Israel? The only thing to do was to establish Israel on such firm foundations
that this could never happen again.

The most forceful critic within the Government was *Mapai*'s Dov
Joseph, who held a number of economic portfolios in the early years.[3]
A decade later, he expressed the mood of 1950 thus: 'We were consumed
by anger and grief at the Holocaust.' Within that Jewish prism he

---

[1] *Divrei Ha-knesset*, . . . 8 Jan. 1952, p. 941. Although not one of the key foreign
policy decision-makers at the time, Mrs. Meir's subsequent influence on decisions
relating to Germany—during her tenure as Foreign Minister, 1956–66, and later as
Prime Minister—gives special interest to her image of Germany and her advocacy
concerning Israel's policy in 1950–2.

[2] Meir interview, 1966.

[3] After serving as the highly respected Military Governor of Jerusalem during the
1948 siege, Canadian-born and educated Bernard Joseph held 7 portfolios succes-
sively:

Supply and Rationing, and Agriculture March 1949–Nov. 1950
Transport Nov. 1950–Oct. 1951
Commerce and Industry, and Justice Oct. 1951–Dec. 1952
Without Portfolio Dec. 1952–June 1953
Development June 1953–Nov. 1955
(Also Health June–Nov. 1955).

After a period outside the Government, he returned to the Justice portfolio from
November 1961 to January 1966.

referred to two components: E—'we needed foreign currency' and 'we felt entitled to get restitution for German Jewish property—to absorb refugees'; and B—'the Germans could not be left with vast stolen property; we had a moral duty to recover part of the enormous plunder'.[1] Twenty years after the events, with the aid of notes to recall specific dates, he added fresh light to his advocacy at the outset:

I don't need these notes to remember exactly what I said. 'No one will object to the Jewish People claiming compensation from the German People', I said at the time. My objection was to the method of dealing with the matter. I said two things basically. First, I objected to direct contact with the Germans. I thought we should use the good offices of friendly powers. Secondly, I objected to German goods being brought into Israel. My idea was to take them elsewhere and sell them, even if at a loss. We should take compensation, I said, but not through direct talks.[2]

Among the lesser Coalition partners, *Ha-po'el Ha-mizrahi*'s leader, Moshe Shapira, recalled: 'The economic situation was grave, but that was not the only reason; on principle, the Germans stole billions from the Jews, and whatever we could reclaim, we simply had to do.'[3] The Progressive Party leader, Pinhas Rosen, spoke in a similar vein during the *Knesset* debate of January 1952:

We cannot be content with the expression of our feelings of hate and revenge. . . . Who gave you, [*Herut* leader] Begin, the right to give up the debts that we all agree are coming to us. . . . I would say to [*Mapam* leader] Hazan—*davka* [just because] they are Nazis we must claim from them. . . . Gentlemen! A state must take a rational course. . . . As a people we could be an exception but not as a state. . . . We must build the country and gather all the funds we are entitled to. We must not give them up.[4]

Among those involved in the negotiations with Bonn and other implementing decisions, E was designated as the dominant image-

---

[1] Joseph interview, 1960.

[2] Joseph interview, 1971. Joseph's advocacy of an *indirect* channel for the payment (and guarantee) of reparations reflected, in an acute form, the psychological effect of the reparations issue following the First World War on the generation which came into political prominence in the 1930s. In particular, the Dawes Plan (1924) and Young Plan (1929) to solve the problem of German reparations to the victorious Allies seemed to provide a model for the problem of German reparations to Israel and world Jewry; that is, indirect payment.

[3] Shapira interview, 1968. He added in retrospect: 'I don't know whether Ben Gurion thought that Germany would be an important Power with consequences for Israel in the future. He did so later.'

[4] *Divrei Ha-knesset* . . . 8 Jan. 1952, p. 913. Rosen recalled to the writer in 1971: 'I was always in favour of receiving Germans here, especially youth groups. But I, myself, couldn't return to Germany. I never went to visit there after 1932. My attitude always was—"I don't accept the *Herut* party argument, that to forgive the Germans means a lapse from moral stature. I respected anyone who could forgive them, though I personally couldn't do it after." ' Rosen interview, 1971.

component of Israel's decision-makers *at the time*.[1] Goldmann observed: 'The main consideration was economic—the need to absorb half a million refugees.' Shinnar, Co-Head of Israel's delegation to the Wassenaar Conference, remarked: 'The main stimulus was definitely economic, and rightly so, in view of the difficult situation of the state in its initial period and in view of general public opinion, which refused to think of any other aspect in Israel–German relations.' Eytan, then Director-General of the Foreign Office, recalled: 'The motive for demanding reparations was financial—Israel needed the money; we were taking in hundreds of thousands of displaced persons.' Avner, who was Head of the West European Department in the Foreign Ministry and a member of the negotiating team, referred to 'economic distress as one factor; the other was a feeling that "we must get something from the Germans—it is something the Jews should do"'. Bartur, Assistant Head of the Foreign Ministry's Economic Department, noted 'the overriding economic consideration; there was a desperate need of funds for immigration absorption and economic development'. But the most graphic portrait of the pervasive E image came from Horowitz: 'We were in desperate economic straits. We looked into the face of possible collapse. Foreign exchange reserves were practically exhausted. Every ship was important, for the reserve of bread in the country [1950–1] was sufficient for one week only.'

The view that E was the pre-eminent image-component was shared by many others—academics, journalist-commentators, and civil servants.[2] Even those who perceived a 'political motive' acknowledged the immediacy of the economic peril facing Israel in 1950 and 1951, stimulating a foreign policy initiative. Indeed, like the high-policy decision of 11 December 1949 to make Jerusalem the seat of government, the strategic and tactical decisions concerning reparations were precipitated by one component in the psychological environment. In the former it was external pressure from the international system through the United Nations (G). In the latter it was internal pressure, in the form of the demands of immigrant absorption and economic growth (E). For both the attitudinal prism was pervaded with Jewishness.

(c) DECISION PROCESS

The cluster of decisions relating to reparations extended over a period of 29 months, from October 1950 to March 1953. Four distinct stages are evident:

(1) from 30 October 1950 (the first substantive reference to reparations

---

[1] The following half dozen extracts are taken from Goldmann, Shinnar, Eytan, Avner, Bartur, and Horowitz interviews, 1965–71.

[2] Interviews in Israel in 1960, 1965–6, 1968, 1969–71.

in the Cabinet) to 18 February 1952 (Israel's formal decision to
enter *direct* negotiations with West Germany);
(2) from 21 March 1952 (the opening of the Wassenaar Conference)
to 10 June 1952 (the agreement on substance);
(3) from 28 June 1952 (the resumption of formal negotiations) to 10
September 1952 (the signing of the Luxembourg Agreements);
(4) from 10 September 1952 to 22 March 1953 (the ratification
process).[1]

There was, too, a pre-decision stage of thought and deeds lasting almost
a decade.

Nahum Goldmann raised the issue in public as early as 1941: 'If
reparations are to be paid [by Germany], we are the first to have a
claim to them', he told a meeting of the World Jewish Congress (WJC)
in Baltimore. That claim was given concrete form two years later by
the WJC Legal Adviser, Dr. Nehemia Robinson, and was approved at
an international Jewish conference in Atlantic City: the resolution
demanded restitution for losses suffered by Jewish communities and
individuals, along with recognition of the principle that the Jewish
People has a right to collective compensation.[2] In 1944 the value of
Jewish property seized or destroyed by the Nazi regime was estimated
at more than $6 billion.[3] That same year Dr. Siegfried Moses, who was
later to be Israel's State Comptroller, published a booklet setting out
the moral nature of future claims to restitution. His proposals, based
upon a memorandum prepared in 1943 by Dr. Georg Landauer of the
Jewish Agency for Palestine, dealt mainly with community and heirless property; they were, to a large extent, embodied in the final
agreement.[4]

Soon after the end of the Second World War the Jewish claim was
formally presented on behalf of the Jewish Agency by Dr. Weizmann.
The principles laid down in his letter to the four victorious allies were
to form the basis and to set the tone of all subsequent claims by the
State of Israel in her Notes and during the negotiations with West
Germany:

[1] Ratification by Israel was a formality. The six-month struggle for German ratification, which culminated in that act by the *Bundestag* on 18 March 1953, was a *German*
foreign policy decision—though not without the pressure of Israeli inputs. On this
point see note 3, p. 97 below.
[2] Goldmann 1969, p. 250. There was an indirect reference to this issue as early as
the spring of 1940, when the AJC set up a Committee on Peace Studies under Professor
Morris R. Cohen. American Jewish Committee, Research Institute on Peace and
Post-War Problems, *Preliminary Announcement*, New York, 1941, p. 9.
[3] N. Robinson, *Indemnification and Reparations*, Institute of Jewish Affairs, New York,
1944, p. 83, as cited in *Documents* . . . , 5, p. 20.
[4] Moses and Landauer. Among others who suggested a claim to compensation for
German material destruction and plunder was Shalom Adler-Rudell, also of the Jewish
Agency in Jerusalem. Shinnar 1966.

(a) That with regard to the problem of Jewish property . . . , so far as the individual or communal owners of such property cannot be traced, the title should pass to the representatives of the Jewish people, the realizable assets to be employed for the rehabilitation of Jewish men, women and children.

(b) That . . . such assets . . . should be entrusted to the Jewish Agency for this purpose. [And]

(c) That the Jewish people should be allotted a proper percentage of reparations . . .[1]

Within Germany the idea of reparations received its earliest expression at the highest governmental level on 11 November 1949. Just two months after his election as Chancellor of the Federal German Republic, Konrad Adenauer told the editor of a German-Jewish weekly: 'The German people are resolved to make good the wrong done to the Jews in their name by a criminal regime, so far as this is still possible now that millions of human beings have been destroyed beyond recall. This reparation we regard as our duty. Far too little has been done . . . since 1945. The Federal Government is determined to take the appropriate steps.' He acknowledged that 'the State of Israel is the outwardly visible concentration of the Jews of all nationalities'. And then, in a premature and insensitive gesture of intended goodwill, he offered, 'as a first direct sign' of that intent to make amends, a gift to Israel of goods to the value of DM 10 million (less than $3 *million*). Apart from the fact that this offer was premature, the amount suggested was perceived as ridiculously inadequate: the value of Jewish property plundered or destroyed by the Nazi regime was, as noted, estimated as at least $6 *billion*.[2] There was an indirect response from the World Jewish Congress, in the form of a five-point declaration issued in December 1949: It called for (a) acceptance by the German parliament of moral and political responsibility for Nazi deeds towards Jews; (b) material indemnification; (c) legislation against anti-Semitism; (d) re-education of German youth; and (e) a check upon nationalistic tendencies in the West German Government.[3]

A major personal influence in the German quest for conciliation was Herbert Blankenhorn, a foreign policy confidant of Adenauer from the outset and later West German Ambassador to London and Paris.[4] At

[1] *Documents* . . . , I, pp. 9–12. Goldmann's memoir (1969) conspicuously omits reference to this landmark statement of the Jewish claim or to the proposals of other Jewish officials during the Second World War. The Government of Israel restated Weizmann's 1945 claims in an *aide-mémoire* to the Four Occupying Powers on 18 January 1950.

[2] Adenauer's interview with Karl Marx first appeared in the *Allgemeine Wochenzeitung der Juden in Deutschland*, Issue 33, 25 Nov. 1949. An English version, from which the above extracts are taken, is in Vogel, pp. 17–18. See also Deutschkron, pp. 33–4.

[3] Noted by Balabkins, p. 86, from an unpublished account by Noah Barou.

[4] Recalling his talks with the Chancellor 'in the very first weeks of the existence of

the Chancellor's request, he began informal talks in London early in 1950 with the European representative of the World Jewish Congress, Noah Barou. Like others to follow, Barou emphasized two pre-conditions of Jewish contact with the Bonn regime: a solemn public declaration by the Chancellor acknowledging Germany's national responsibility for the horrible deeds committed against the Jews of Europe during the Second World War; and an expressed willingness to compensate Jewry for material losses.[1] Adenauer, too, recalled in his memoirs: 'The first feelers . . . began already in early 1950; but they did not lead to practical results.'[2]

Among those contacts were conversations between Jakob Altmaier, a Jewish Social Democratic member of the *Bundestag*, and Dr. Eliyahu Livneh, Israel's Consul in Munich from 1949 to 1953.[3] Livneh came to Israel in the spring of 1950 to consult Sharett and Kaplan as to how to proceed: he was told that it was not yet appropriate to enter into direct contact with the German authorities concerning *reparations*.[4] An elaborate memorandum on 'The Problems of Reparations and Restitution for Israel' was submitted to Israel's Finance Ministry on 1 July 1950 by Hendrik van Dam, Secretary-General of the Central Council

---

the Federal Government, around October and November of 1949 . . .', he shed much light on the motivations of the German offer: 'In these talks it was constantly maintained by me—and the Chancellor fully accepted this reasoning—that the new German state could regain confidence, reputation, and credibility in the world only if the Federal Government and the Diet, in a freely decided act of will, disavowed the past and contributed through impressive reparation payments to the relief of the incredible extent of distress suffered. . . . Such an act of true reparation *was intended to help surmount the unimaginable bitterness that National Socialist crimes had inspired* in the Jews the world over and in all right-thinking people. *Its purpose was further to make the German people realize the dreadfulness of the past and the necessity of a radical conversion.*' Tape-recorded Blankenhorn memoir in 1965. Vogel, p. 21 (emphasis added).

[1] Blankenhorn interview with Deutschkron, 8 March 1968. Deutschkron, pp. 36–7. Goldmann also noted Barou's role in bringing him into contact with German officials in 1950. Goldmann interview, 1966 and Goldmann 1969, p. 254.

[2] Adenauer, p. 133. In that connection, there occurred a near-meeting between Adenauer and Weizmann, both of whom were vacationing at a Swiss resort in 1950. The Chancellor sent word to Israel's first President that he would welcome an opportunity to exchange greetings. The reply was courteous but negative, on the grounds that such a meeting was premature. The two leaders passed each other in the garden, but no interchange took place. Related to the author by a member of Weizmann's entourage. Adenauer mentioned this incident to David Horowitz the following year in Paris. Horowitz interview, 1966.

[3] Livneh, like his predecessor Haim Hoffmann (Yahil), was accredited to the United States Military Government in Munich, not to a German governmental authority. Altmaier was one of Adenauer's key links to the opposition Social Democratic Party, to world Jewry, and to Israeli officials.

[4] Yahil interview, 1971. On funds due to *individual* Jews in *Germany* the Government of Israel had, on 15 February 1950, authorized the Finance and Foreign ministries to deal directly with officials of the Federal German Republic. Related by a participant in the Cabinet decision.

of German Jews. Its essential proposal was that Israel 'dispatch a "Reparation and Indemnification Mission" with authority to negotiate with German government agencies [regarding individual compensation] . . . and . . . also make preparations for the general reparation claim'.[1] Still another person who attempted to persuade Israeli leaders to enter into *direct* talks with Bonn was Robert M. W. Kempner, the Deputy United States Prosecutor at the Nuremberg Trials, during his visit to Israel late in 1950. But the idea of negotiating directly with the successor to Nazi Germany was still anathema, as the deliberations and initial decisions of Israel's Government were to demonstrate. By that time, too, the idea of seeking substantial German reparations *indirectly* offered a viable solution to the dilemma of Israel's decision-makers.

The idea of making an indirect claim to German reparations, as a concrete, operational policy act by the Government of Israel, was mooted by David Horowitz in September 1950. Then in London on one of his frequent foreign-currency search missions as Director-General of the Finance Ministry, he 'phoned Sharett, who was attending the UN General Assembly in New York, and warned him of a potential economic collapse. 'I have ideas for a radical departure', he said: 'they involve Germany.' A sceptical Sharett met Horowitz at the Hotel Rafael in Paris and was persuaded of the merits of the proposal—to approach the Four Occupying Powers on the basis of a precise claim: half a million Jewish refugees were being absorbed by Israel, at a cost of $3,000 per person, justifying a claim to $1·5 billion from the successor governments to Nazi Germany. Horowitz, upon his return to Israel some weeks later, convinced Ben Gurion of its necessity and feasibility. Kaplan's approval had already been given though, as noted, with doubts about its practicability.[2]

The reparations issue came before the Cabinet on 30 October 1950, in the context of a general discussion about Germany prompted by information that the three Western Powers intended to end the state of war with the Federal German Republic. Sharett opened 'a very brief debate'. As Joseph recalled, 'it was said that the time has come— and we will have to take a decision; although stated in general terms, the obvious intent was direct contact with the Germans. I was alone in my dissent.'[3] No substantive decision was taken.[4]

---

[1] As cited in Vogel, pp. 21–6. The extract is from pp. 25–6. Another major document on collective Jewish claims was submitted by A. L. Easterman, Political Secretary of the World Jewish Congress, to Lord Henderson, Permanent Under-Secretary at the British Foreign Office, on 25 July 1950. The text is in Balabkins, Appendix A. Other persons who were active in those early contacts were Karl Marx, as noted, Kurt G. Grossmann, and Yossele Rosenzaft, a leader of the survivors of the Bergen–Belsen extermination camp. For a succinct survey of pre-decisional events see Balabkins, pp. 81–7.   [2] Horowitz interviews, 1966 and 1971.
[3] Joseph interview, 1971.
[4] Nine of the 12 ministers were present: Kaplan and Meir were abroad; Rosen

The issue was debated at greater length on 27 December. Eytan spoke about the desirability of taking the matter up with Germany—and Joseph proclaimed his emphatic opposition to direct contact. Eytan recalled the scene vividly. '"If a German official walked in here today and placed $10 million on the table", said Joseph, "I would reject it as dirty money".'[1] Joseph added that, at this meeting, he was joined in dissent by others, notably Rabbi Maimon.[2] The forcefulness of his plea led to a further postponement of a decision—and to rejection of the premature proposal for direct talks.[3] A week later, *on 3 January 1951, a high-policy decision was taken: to seek and to accept reparations for Jewish property plundered by Nazi Germany.* This would be done through an approach to the Four Powers occupying Germany.[4]

That decision took the form of two Notes to the Powers, dated 16 January and 12 March 1951.[5] Both were drafted by Dr. Leo Kohn, Political Adviser to the Foreign Minister (from 1948 until his death in 1961), and Horowitz. Kohn contributed the rationale of the historical continuity of Jewry and the legitimacy of the claim to reparations. Horowitz provided the economic formula for the claim to $1·5 billion.[6]

There were two types of claim set forth in the January Note. The first pertained to dispossessed *individuals* and urged upon the Powers

(a) The retention of control over restitution and indemnification among the powers reserved to the Allied Occupation Authorities. . . .

(b) The improvement of the existing indemnification laws—in particular, the adoption of a General Claim Law for the whole of the Federal Republic of Germany.

(c) The immediate assumption by the Government of the German Federal Republic of financial liability under the indemnification laws, jointly and severally with the Länder.

(d) The speeding up of actual restitution and payment of compensation claims.

(e) The urgent solution of the transfer problem between the parties concerned.

---

was absent. Secretary to the Government, Ze'ev Sharef, and Horowitz also attended the meeting.

[1] Interview, 1971.   [2] Interview, 1971.

[3] In the interim (November), Shazar left the Cabinet, while Lavon and Geri became ministers, forming a Cabinet of 13, noted on p. 61 above, which made the first basic decision. Of the 13 ministers, 3 were absent—Kaplan, Rosen and Sharett. Sharef and the Head of the Foreign Ministry's Economic Department, Gershon Meron, were also present.

[4] Present at that formally decisive meeting were 12 of the 13 ministers (Sharett was abroad), Sharef, Attorney-General Haim Cohen, and Foreign Office legal specialist Eli Nathan.

[5] Identical Notes were sent to the US, UK, and France, and a similar one to the Soviet Union, on 16 January, those to France and the USSR in French. Identical Notes were later sent to the Four Powers, to France on 11 March, to the others the following day. *Documents* . . . , 3–5, pp. 13–24.

[6] Many persons confirmed Kohn's primary drafting role—Ben Gurion, Eytan, Horowitz, Meir, Shinnar, etc.

The second was a general claim in respect of the wholesale destruction of European Jewry: 'The Government of Israel cannot reconcile itself to the enjoyment by Germany of the fruit of its rapine and murder, while the victims of an unholy regime are denied all comfort and redress.'

That specific claim was to form the subject of the March 1951 Note. The value 'of the Jewish property confiscated and plundered by the Germans . . . is authoritatively estimated to aggregate over six billion dollars'. But the basis of the claim was the cost of absorbing 500,000 refugees from Nazi-decimated Europe, 'which would involve an overall expenditure of one and a half billion dollars. This figure corresponds approximately to the value of exports from Western Germany alone in 1950. . . .'[1] Israel sought acceptance of 'the justice of its claim' and 'an early expression of views . . . concerning the practical steps . . . towards implementing the proposals. . . .' The following day, 13 March 1951, Sharett read the second Note to the *Knesset* and concluded with the pungent words noted earlier—'German . . . hands . . . still smeared with blood . . . , their plunder . . . still under their cloak'.

The formal response of the Powers was disappointing. Moscow acknowledged Israel's Notes but never answered them. The Western Powers were sympathetic but declined to intervene. The British, for example, wrote on 5 July: 'His Majesty's Government regret that they cannot see their way to impose upon the Federal Government the task of making reparation to the Government of Israel as a condition' to the normalization of relations. Washington and Paris echoed this sentiment.[2] Later Sharett referred to these replies 'as an attempt to force us into the Procrustean frame of a request for war reparations', which would have 'obliterated the unique nature of our cause . . . [But, unlike the Soviets, they] were at least frank in telling us what they thought of our claim.'[3]

The issue which had been avoided now began to emerge—whether or not to accept the idea of direct negotiations with West Germany. There were as yet no formal bids from Bonn, though several signals had been transmitted. One came on 8 April 1951, when 'Adenauer sent someone to our people to say that he had considered our Note and had come to the conclusion that Germany should pay substantial compensation'.[4] Another took the form of a remark by West German

---

[1] *Documents* . . . , 5, p. 24. Although persuasive at first glance, the Horowitz formula of $3,000 per immigrant absorbed proved to be a bargaining liability for Israel. The German delegation was able to argue, from Bonn's considerable experience in rehabilitating refugees from Poland and East Germany, that the cost of absorption was less; and this enabled it to press for a substantial reduction of the total reparations figure.

[2] The Western Powers' replies to Israel's Notes of 16 January and 12 March 1951 are in *Documents* . . . , 7–12, pp. 28–41. The extract is from p. 37.

[3] Sharett, pp. 8–9.

[4] Joseph interview, 1971.

President Heuss in mid-July that Germany was ready for talks with Israel on all outstanding problems.[1] The most important, however, was the first high-level contact between Israeli and West German officials.

The meeting was held at the Hotel Bristol in Paris on 6 May 1951, 'a cloak and dagger affair', recalled Horowitz, one of the four persons present: the others were Adenauer, Blankenhorn, and Maurice Fischer, Israel's Minister (later, Ambassador) to France. Horowitz began by describing Nazi persecution of the Jews as the greatest crime in human history, which could neither be forgiven nor forgotten: 'you owe it to yourselves to make amends'. At Sharett's behest he emphasized two points: (a) Germany must issue a 'guilt declaration' before financial negotiations began: Adenauer remarked, 'I always condemned those crimes and was a friend of the Jews'; Horowitz insisted that the declaration be a solemn act of state; Adenauer was reluctant but he agreed; (b) 'if reparations are to be paid, they must be of the order of our claim', though there could be minor changes: 'Adenauer tried to avoid a commitment but he finally yielded on this too.' They agreed to deny the meeting had taken place and to inform, respectively, the US State Department and the US High Commissioner in Germany.[2] How significant that confrontation was in the decision flow is difficult to measure. Shinnar sheds some light on this point: 'David Horowitz expressed his views forcefully and with great emotion. In July 1958 I visited Chancellor Adenauer with Maurice Fischer— and he remembered the meeting that took place seven years ago, and the persuasive content of Horowitz's words. He even remembered

---

[1] He added, in an interview with the New York Jewish magazine *Aufbau*, that 'it will take a long time', but he was confident that 'love between one human being and another will form a bridge between the two groups . . .' Reported in *Jerusalem Post*, 20 July 1951.

[2] Horowitz interview, 1966. His written account, in unpublished memoirs of the period 1948–70, which was shown to the author in 1971, is substantially the same but more detailed. Apparently it was United States pressure, quietly exerted, which led to the German initiative. Horowitz's recollections on the background made the United States' role clear. Early in April he went to Washington, London, and Paris to enlist support for the Israeli claim to reparations. Secretary of State Acheson was sympathetic but noncommittal. Assistant Secretary Byroade remarked, 'you have an irresistible moral case', and sent him to the US Representative to the Tripartite Commission on Germany, who received him warmly, as did Lord Henderson of the British Foreign Office. Parodi of the Quai d'Orsay was 'receptive but negative', saying, 'Israel had no legal case'. Soon after, a cable from Jerusalem informed Horowitz in New York: 'Contact established with Germans; you will shortly meet Adenauer.' A few weeks thereafter Fischer telephoned him in London to say that a cable from Sharett indicated a meeting had been arranged the next day at 3 p.m. Only behind-the-scenes 'advice' by American officials could have led to the meeting. Many of the facts recalled by Horowitz 15 years later, but not the meeting with Adenauer itself, were reported in the press at the time. See *Jerusalem Post*, 28 June and 1 July 1951. The Horowitz–Adenauer meeting, a vital input into the decision process for the tactical decision, was first recorded in Shinnar 1967, p. 18.

with what passion and stormy feelings these words resounded in his ears. . . .'[1]

There were other encounters, notably one between Israeli and West German delegates to the Congress of the Inter-Parliamentary Union at Istanbul at the beginning of September 1951. Carlo Schmid, who later served as Vice-President of the Diet, recalled the protest of Yitzhak Ben Zvi against the German presence at the Congress as 'a terrible and dreadful philippic . . . , a fearful speech. I have seldom heard anyone speak with such passion.' Yet the two delegations met, and an 'agreement' reportedly emerged that the Israelis would inquire whether a Bonn offer to negotiate reparations would be acceptable.[2]

All of these contacts, along with continued prodding by the United States, led to Adenauer's solemn Declaration of 27 September before the *Bundestag*. Guilt was acknowledged by the Chancellor, but he made a precise distinction between the German nation and the Nazi regime: 'The great majority of the *German people* abhorred the crimes committed against the Jews and had no part in them. . . . Many Germans . . . were prepared to help their Jewish compatriots. . . .' And he cited 'the immense destruction of Jewish valuables by *National Socialism*'. Even the operative passage absolved Germany from collective guilt, while assuming responsibility for restitution: 'But unspeakable crimes were perpetrated *in the name of the German people*, which impose upon them the obligation to make moral and material amends . . . first steps have already been taken, but much remains to be done.' Thus the Federal Government 'is prepared, jointly with representatives of Jewry and the State of Israel, which has admitted so many homeless Jewish refugees, to bring about a solution of the material reparation problem. . . .'[3]

---

[1] Shinnar 1967, p. 18. Goldmann, in his account of the reparations issue (for example, interview 1966; 1969) makes no mention of this meeting or, indeed, of Horowitz's role. Yet he was aware of that role, as is evident in the text of a cable sent jointly by Sharett and him to Horowitz on 10 September 1952: 'On the day of the signing of the Agreement on Reparations we remember with gratitude the exemplary role that you played in initiating the claim and the first thrust of the effort.' English translation from a photostat copy of the Hebrew cable.

[2] The other Israeli delegates were *Mapai*'s David Hacohen, who served later as Minister to Burma and as Chairman of the *Knesset* Committee on Foreign Affairs and Security, and Ya'acov Klebanoff, a prominent General Zionist. The other German representatives were Heinrich von Brentano, later Foreign Minister of West Germany, and Robert Tillmann of the Christian Democratic Union, a Minister without Portfolio at the time. Schmid's tape-recorded account is in Vogel, pp. 19–20.

[3] For the German text and Hebrew translation see *Documents* . . . , 13, pp. 41–3. An English version, from which the above extracts are taken, is in Grossmann, Appendix IV, pp. 59–60 (emphasis added). A somewhat different English translation, along with statements by representatives of all German parties, is contained in Vogel, pp. 32–5. Adenauer, in his memoirs, devoted a paragraph to this development (p. 136). The influence of external pressure on Bonn's formal acknowledgement of crimes against Jewry (issued six years after the end of the Second World War) is evident in the opening passage: 'Recently the world has on various occasions occupied itself

The Government of Israel's initial reaction was cautiously positive:
'The Chancellor's declaration appears to represent an attempt on the
part of the Government of the German Federal Republic at last to
face this great issue and to initiate some measure of moral and material
reparation to the Jewish people.' It added, pointedly: 'No such
acknowledgement of "unspeakable crimes" has come from the East
German Republic, which is under an equal obligation.'[1]

Adenauer's Declaration 'did not come as a surprise to us'; in fact, the
draft was scrutinized by Jewish and Israeli representatives, including
Barou, Goldmann, and Shinnar. The first draft was prepared by the
West Germans in July 1951. It took almost three months of negotiations
to agree upon a text which satisfied 'justified Jewish demands'. And it
was Barou, generally credited with a vital role in the pre-decision phase,
who convinced Adenauer that Israel must be the principal beneficiary
of collective compensation.[2] Adenauer himself referred to these consultations: 'I had previously enquired whether my offer would not be
declined in Israel and by the Jewish world organizations. I received
favourable answers.'[3] Yet he had not acknowledged German national
guilt.[4] Nor had he accepted the amount of the Israeli claim as the basis
for a settlement. And he had intruded a bargaining element into a
solemn act: 'With regard to the extent of reparations . . . the limits
must be considered which are set by the German ability to pay. . . .'
Thus it was accepted only as a first step.

It was one of Goldmann's major achievements to ease Israel's path
to the highly controversial tactical decision. This he accomplished
during his first meeting with Adenauer, at Claridge's Hotel in London
on 6 December 1951. After a 25-minute peroration (Barou and
Blankenhorn were the only others present), Goldmann indicated that
Ben Gurion would not take the issue of direct talks to the *Knesset*
unless he could be assured that Adenauer accepted the $1 billion claim
as the basis for negotiations. 'You do not know me,' replied the
Chancellor, 'but people who do, know that I am a man of few words.
While you spoke, I felt the winds of world history about me.' Then and
there he offered a commitment and asked Goldmann to prepare a

---

with the attitude adopted by the Federal Republic toward the Jews. Now and then
doubts have been expressed as to whether the new state of West Germany is guided
by principles in respect of these important questions which take into consideration
the terrible crimes of the past epoch. . . .'

[1] Government of Israel Statement, 27 Sept. 1951. *Documents* . . . , 14, p. 45.

[2] Shinnar interview, 1965; Barou, pp. 6, 7; Goldmann 1969, p. 256. On Barou's
role see Fraenkel and Goldmann in Infield, pp. 7, 11. Goldmann also recalled (interview, 1966) that Jacob Altmaier brought the Adenauer draft to him for approval and
that some of his proposed changes were accepted.

[3] Adenauer, p. 136.

[4] Goldmann sought only an acknowledgement of the German People's 'responsibility for Nazi crimes', not of 'guilt'. Goldmann interview, 1966.

draft. The letter was brought to Adenauer the same day at Chatham House, where he was to deliver a lecture, and was signed at once. The operative clause read: 'The Federal Government is ready to accept the claims which the Government of the State of Israel has formulated in its note of 12 March 1951 as the basis for these negotiations.'[1]

That letter was written to Goldmann as Chairman of a newly established Conference of Jewish Material Claims Against Germany, an umbrella organization of twenty-two Jewish groups to speak for

[1] The Chancellor mistakenly identified Barou as Israel's Ambassador to the UK, present under an assumed name. For his account of the meeting and the German text of his letter see Adenauer, pp. 137–9. An English translation of Adenauer's letter, from which the above extract is taken, is in Grossmann, Appendix V, p. 61. The English version in Vogel is slightly different. More significant and unsubstantiated is Vogel's remark that 'Konrad Adenauer's generous offer ... was made against the will of the Allied powers' (p. 36). In perspective, Israel had committed a major error in directing her original claim to both German states—in a 2:1 ratio, $1 billion from West Germany and $0·5 billion from East Germany, for Bonn claimed to represent all of Germany on all foreign policy issues. It was the only time that Bonn acquiesced in representing a part of Germany! And East Germany never formally replied to the Israeli appeal, though she made known her refusal in principle to pay reparations to Israel or Jews. Before the meeting, Goldmann demanded full authority from Ben Gurion to speak in the name of Israel, as well as of world Jewry. Goldmann believed he had received such authority. This point and the above account of their meeting is based upon Goldmann interview, 1966.

Adenauer, too, perceived Goldmann's dual representative role. In his letter to Finance Minister Schäffer on 29 February 1952, urging that 'negotiations be prepared and conducted in a spirit appropriate to the moral and political weight and the uniqueness of our obligations', the Chancellor referred to Goldmann as 'chairman of the Conference on Jewish Claims against Germany and delegate of the government of the State of Israel ...' Vogel, pp. 37–8. Adenauer had conferred with his financial adviser, the prominent banker Hermann Abs, in London on 3 December, just before his scheduled meeting with Goldmann. Abs urged the Chancellor not to incur any new obligations. Abs later declared that he did not know of Adenauer's 6 December commitment to Goldmann until 29 February 1952, when an Israeli diplomat mentioned it to him. Only on 8 March was he informed, in Bonn, of the forthcoming Wassenaar talks. He wished to resign but was dissuaded by Adenauer. Abs interview with Balabkins, 21 July 1966; Balabkins, p. 126.

More than twenty years after her original Notes to the Four Powers, Israel's Foreign Ministry urged friendly governments, including the US, Canada, Belgium, and Holland, who were about to recognize the German Democratic Republic, to press the Pankow regime to pay restitution to Israel for Nazi war crimes. On 31 December 1972 the Israeli Cabinet decided to further this diplomatic campaign. A full-dress *Knesset* debate on Israel's demand for reparations from East Germany was to be held early in 1973. *Jerusalem Post*, 4 Jan. 1973. The most active public role in the quest for East German reparations was taken by Goldmann, who sought the intervention of West German Chancellor Brandt and other Bonn officials. *Jerusalem Post*, 7 Feb. 1973.

The official newspaper of the East German Communist Youth Organization, *Junge Welt* (Young World), repeated on 8 March 1973 that the German Democratic Republic would not recognize Israel or pay reparations to her. *Jerusalem Post*, 9 March 1973.

world Jewry in negotiations with Germany. It was convened by Goldmann at Sharett's suggestion and held its inaugural meeting in New
York on 25–26 October 1951. The Conference extended 'its whole-
hearted support of the [Israeli] claim . . .', demanded 'satisfaction of all
other Jewish claims against Germany . . .', and called for 'immediate
steps to improve existing restitution and indemnification legislation and
procedures', to enact further laws, and 'to speed up the settlement of
claims'. The Conference also established an Executive Committee of
thirteen, headed by Goldmann, and 'authorized [it] to take such practical steps as developments may necessitate'.[1]

Just before that conclave 'a stormy discussion' took place at Kaplan's
home in Jerusalem over the issue of co-ordination between Israel and
the Claims Conference; the protagonists were Goldmann and Georg
Landauer, a highly respected figure in the Zionist Movement. A
formula prepared by Shinnar 'in good faith . . .' was accepted by
Kaplan and Sharett but was forcefully 'opposed by . . . Goldmann: in
his opinion I emphasized too much—out of naiveté and lack of knowledge ("what a nest of wasps I was getting into")—the special right of
the State of Israel as representative of the Jewish People. . . .' The
disagreement was quickly resolved.[2]

With Bonn's acceptance of the Israeli claim as the basis of negotiations, Israel's decision about direct talks could no longer be delayed.
Thus the period 6 December 1951 to 9 January 1952 was to see an
increasingly tense political battle, which split the nation and caused
agony across the land. Ranged on one side were diverse parties,
interest groups, and individuals who were repelled by the idea of direct
contact with the successor to Nazi Germany. On the other were the
'realists', mostly in *Mapai*.

The issue was debated by *Mapai*'s leadership at a tense evening session
on 28 November. Ben Gurion led off with a résumé of informal contacts
and proposed approval of direct negotiations. He emphasized Israel's
'right' to reparations, the unwillingness of the Western Powers to act as
intermediaries, the necessity of direct talks, and the economic importance of restitution funds. Sharett followed with a similar line of argument. Sprinzak, the first Speaker of the *Knesset*, was strongly opposed,

---

[1] The text of the main Claims Conference resolution is in Grossmann, p. 17. The
membership of the Executive Committee was as follows:
President: Nahum Goldmann
Senior Vice-President: Jacob Blaustein
Vice-Presidents: Jules Braunschvig, Samuel Bronfman, Rudolph Callman, Adolph
Held, Barnett Janner, Noah Barou, Henry d'Avigdor Goldsmid, Bt., Frank Gold-
man, Israel Goldstein, Isaac Lewin, Shad Polier.
Treasurer: Moses A. Leavitt
Secretary: Saul Kagan.

[2] Shinnar 1967, pp. 19–20. Shinnar had served in several economic posts in the
Israeli bureaucracy from 1948 to 1951. On 1 July 1951 he became Adviser to the
Foreign Ministry on the reparations issue.

emphasizing the moral standing of Jewry: this dictated, he said, that Israel not meet with the present generation of Germans. Dvorjhetsky, a partisan leader in Nazi-occupied Europe, spoke in the same vein, provoking the Prime Minister to term this a *'Galut'* view, that is, a view of Jewry in exile; further, 'a free people has a right to decide'.

There were other clashes, notably one between Mrs. Meyerson (Meir) and Peretz Naftali, then Minister without Portfolio. The future Prime Minister recalled: 'My own view was, by all means, yes, but this did not imply forgiveness. At a party meeting I said, "it must be clear that we are demanding what is ours by right and that we are not making up with the Germans".'[1] Naftali dissented, and he urged that Israel not go to the talks with this 'racist' attitude. Despite these and other critical voices, there was a clear majority in favour of direct negotiations.[2] That decision was to determine the voting behaviour of *Mapai* ministers in the Cabinet session which followed two other discussions: (1) by the Directorate of the Jewish Agency, on 10 December; and (2) by the *Knesset* Committee on Foreign Affairs and Security, on 17 December.

By that time there were changes in the composition of Israel's Government, both parties and persons. After the Second *Knesset* elections on 30 July 1951 the Progressives had refused to join a narrow Coalition, leaving a four-party Government of thirteen ministers with even greater *Mapai* domination: *Mapai* (9); *Ha-po'el Ha-mizrahi* (2); *Mizrahi* (1); and *Agudat Yisrael* (1). There was also a turnover of five ministers: Geri, Lavon, Maimon, Remez, and Rosen were replaced by Dinaburg (Dinur), Eshkol, and Naftali of *Mapai*, Burg of *Ha-po'el Ha-mizrahi*, and Pinkas of *Mizrahi*.

The issue of direct negotiations was discussed and decided by the Cabinet on 30 December 1951. As Mrs. Meir recalled: 'Within the Cabinet many sat on the fence, but we [*Mapai*] took a stand.'[3] Joseph

[1] Meir interview, 1966.

[2] This account is based upon a participant's recollection: Yahil interview, 1971. Zalman Aranne, then a member of the *Knesset* Committee on Foreign Affairs and Security, was also reportedly opposed to direct talks (Shinnar 1966). Three days earlier the issue was discussed before the Young *Mapai* Circle. The party newspaper reported that emotional objections were strongly voiced, but that 'correct information ... [provided by speakers Yahil and Shinnar] will do much to cancel the unbased suspicions'. *Ha-dor*, 26 Nov. 1951. A reading of the *Mapai* press, which reported all party meetings of any consequence, indicates that the reparations issue was not a topic of frequent discussion and debate in party organs. During the entire period of the decision process the daily *Ha-dor* carried three editorials (17 Jan., 28 Sept., and 9 Dec. 1951) and three articles (13 July and 5, 16 Oct. 1951). The party weekly, *Ha-po'el Ha-tza'ir*, carried only one editorial on reparations (30 Oct. 1951) and two advocacy articles (18 Dec. 1951 and 15 Jan. 1952).

[3] Meir interview, 1966. All thirteen ministers except Pinkas were present at the 30 December 1951 meeting, along with Sharef and Abba Eban, then Ambassador to the US and Permanent Representative to the UN.

himself had become reconciled to the inevitable: 'No one in the Government doubted the desirability of making the Germans pay; but it became clear after a while that it had to be negotiated directly.'[1] The decision, one of the most controversial in Israel's foreign policy, provided for a *Government Statement to the Knesset on 2 January 1952, requesting authority to act in the best interests of Israel.*[2] Sharett was initially designated to present the Statement; but under the impact of events that task was assumed by Ben Gurion. The appointed date was postponed to the 7th, and ten hours were allocated to parliamentary debate.

The first nine days of January 1952 were among the most tempestuous in Israel's history. The contending political coalitions marshalled their forces, and the rising crescendo of bitterness and hate was felt all across the land. In political terms the choice was simple—an Israeli initiative or allowing the matter to fade away through inaction.

On 1 January Members of the *Knesset* (MKs) from Coalition parties met in Jerusalem to debate the Government proposal. *Open* dissent was limited to the religious parties, and after a three-hour discussion the Cabinet stand was approved. Three days later the Executive of *Ha-po'el Ha-mizrahi* decided to support direct negotiations but to allow its dissenting MKs to abstain in the *Knesset* vote (it was known that six would support the Government and two would abstain). Another religious faction within the Coalition, *Mizrahi*, decided to treat the issue as a matter of conscience (Communications Minister Pinkas was committed to vote for direct talks, while Rabbi Nurock would oppose).

The two extremes of the legitimate political spectrum—*Herut* and *Mapam*—held protest meetings at Mograbi Hall in Tel Aviv on the 4th and 5th.[3] Begin, an advocate of nationalist purity down through

---

[1] Joseph interview, 1971.

[2] It can be argued that the *de facto* decision to enter into direct talks with Bonn was taken before Adenauer's Declaration of 27 September 1951, on the grounds that he would not have made it without an advance, though informal, positive response from Israel. Adenauer and others, as noted, confirmed these consultations. Yet in terms of a decision flow this was a pre-decisional act. The decision itself was not taken by the Government until 30 December (the date was explicitly foreshadowed by the *Mapai* newspaper *Ha-dor*, 26 Dec. 1951); and it was not confirmed until after the *Knesset* and its Foreign Affairs and Security Committee authorized the Government to act, in mid-January 1952. Moreover, as late as 30 November 1951 Israel had approached the three Western Powers once more, seeking their intervention to 'impress on the . . . Federal Republic of Germany the urgent and compelling necessity to give effective satisfaction to its claims. . . .' Note to the United Kingdom. The text of the three similar Notes is in *Documents* . . . , 16–18, pp. 47–56. Only *after* Adenauer's letter to Goldmann on 6 December and *after* the Western Powers reaffirmed their policy in favour of direct negotiations (their replies were sent in mid- and late January, after the Israeli decision was made (*Documents* . . . , 23–24, pp. 62–3), but their view was communicated informally in December 1951) were all of the external inputs present in Israel's Foreign Policy System. It then proceeded to generate the tactical decision.

[3] *Maki*, the Communist Party of Israel, was a legal organization, but being outspokenly anti-Zionist it was beyond *political legitimacy* in Israel. That pariah status

the years, called for active dissent, in the form of an open letter to all Israelis to volunteer in this 'hour of emergency' to save Israel's honour.[1] This was echoed the following day by the editor of *Ma'ariv*, E. Karlebach, who attacked the Government stand on material and moral grounds. *Yedi'ot Aharonot*, too, was strongly opposed to direct talks, in its editorials on the 6th.

Constitutionally, the Government of Israel is not bound by *Knesset* directives unless they are embodied in a legislative act. On the issue of direct talks with West Germany, however, the Cabinet sought *Knesset* approval because of the gravity of the act. This had been pledged at the previous parliamentary debate on Foreign Affairs. Thus the matter was brought to the House as a Statement, not a proposal.

The three-day debate (7, 8, and 9 January) took place in an atmosphere of violence unprecedented in Israeli parliamentary life. The Opposition—*Herut*, General Zionists, *Mapam*, and *Maki*—were known to control 51 certain votes in a House of 120. When Prime Minister Ben Gurion rose to present his Government's Statement on the evening of the 7th, the scene outside the *Knesset* building on King George Street in Jerusalem was one of mounting tension, with angry demonstrators in the thousands, the sirens of police cars and ambulances, and sporadic explosions of grenades. Window panes were splintered by rocks, while the fumes of tear gas bombs entered from the streets. In the two-hour mêlée 92 policemen and 36 civilians were reported injured. At 7 p.m. an army detachment arrived, and by 7.30 order was restored. A few blocks away, in Zion Square, Begin, with the venerable Professor Joseph Klausner by his side, had roused passions even further by charging that the police were using gas grenades made in Germany!

The debate began with Ben Gurion's moving Statement. His concluding remarks, already cited, were not easily stilled: 'Let not the murderers of our people be their inheritors as well!' This was followed by three passionately critical speeches by Elimeleh Rimalt (General Zionists), Ya'acov Hazan, the second-ranking leader of *Mapam*, and Begin. 'We are torn between the rational and logical, and the emotional, in this debate', Rimalt began. 'Compensation will ease the conscience of the Germans, but this is something we should not do. How will we educate our youth that materialism cannot substitute for moral qualities? What will happen to our moral uniqueness . . .?'

Hazan attacked Adenauer's Germany as unrepentant and he ridiculed the *Mapai* illusion of confining relations to reparations: '. . . this is impossible. Negotiations mean recognition of a neo-Nazi Government, managed mostly by ex-Nazis, whose Military [Establishment] is already Nazi today.' Furthermore, 'we cannot be on the same side as

---

changed in 1965 when *Maki* split into two, and Dr. Moshe Sneh led the Jewish remnant to a nationalist stance. See Brecher, pp. 166–8.

[1] *Herut* (Tel Aviv), 5 Jan. 1952.

the Nazis in the Cold War'. In the midst of Hazan's speech *Herut*'s Yohanan Bader entered the *Knesset* yelling, 'gas against the Jews; with that you will win!' *Maki* leaders Meir Wilner and Esther Wilenska entered and cried out: 'People are being murdered outside, they are shooting.' Stones came crashing through the window, and then gas fumes where *Mapam* members were sitting. Some sought safety, others remained in their seats.

The stoning continued when Begin rose to address the House. A gifted orator, with a demagogic capacity to sway a crowd, he carried his rage from Zion Square to the floor of the *Knesset*. He attacked the Bonn regime as Nazi and asked rhetorically about Adenauer: 'In which concentration camp did he sit during the Nazi era . . . [And] who are his aides . . .?' Charging that Israel would receive at most $300 million (of $6 billion in plundered property), he demanded: 'Who gave you the right to take only 5 per cent and leave 95 per cent to the murderer?' Further, 'you will be sellers of German goods produced by Nazi factories'. Turning to the Prime Minister, he implored: 'I ask Mr. Ben Gurion as a son of an orphaned nation to a son of an orphaned nation— don't! Go to the nation. Hold a referendum. Actually, I think this referendum was already rejected by those killed at Auschwitz, Treblinka, etc. . . . I ask the members of the House to take no part in the vote.' He even appealed to Arab MKs to abstain, on moral grounds, this being something for Jews to decide. (Had they heeded his call, the Government's majority would have been reduced to 3 or 4 votes.) Then, taunted by the Prime Minister who, from his seat, referred to a petition against reparations signed by distinguished men, who 'are not identified with your hooligans in the street', Begin accused Ben Gurion of being a 'murderer'. Deputy Speaker Yosef Serlin called on Begin to retract, but he refused until BG did so. Ordered to leave the rostrum, Begin raged: 'If I don't speak, nobody will speak.' And finally, in a typical Begin flourish, he waived his parliamentary immunity, said it would be his last *Knesset* appearance, and exclaimed: 'I know we will be dragged to the concentration camps. . . . We will die together.'

The meeting was adjourned at 6.45 p.m. amidst disorder and was reconvened three hours later—after Begin had retracted his epithet. Lavon concluded the debate on the 7th with an attack on Begin's threat of rebellion: 'The *Herut* leader speaks in the name of the Six Million. Who gave you a monopoly on their ideas? Those who are alive must decide, according to their responsibility to the future of this nation.'

The debate continued the next day in a tense but quieter atmosphere. Rosen led off and supported direct talks. 'We cannot hate and seek revenge now', he said; 'we are responsible for the building up of our country.' He was followed by *Mapai*'s Zalman Shazar, later President of Israel, who proclaimed, 'The restitution money is ours, it belongs to us, it's Jewish money'; *Maki*'s Mikunis, who emphasized US pressure and accused the Government of treason; and *Mizrahi*'s Nurock, who referred to talks with Germany as 'a spiritual and moral catastrophe'. Then, with varying degrees of intensity and with different arguments, came supporting speeches by *Mapai*'s Aranne and Meyerson (Meir), *Ha-po'el Ha-mizrahi*'s Michael Hazani, and *Mizrahi*'s Pinkas, interspersed with opposing speeches by General Zionist Yosef Saphir, *Mapam*'s Yisrael Bar-Yehuda (from the *Ahdut Ha'avoda* wing), and the Progressives' Ishar Harari, among others.[1]

The debate was closed by Sharett on the 9th with a speech revealing much about his own image, as noted. He dismissed Begin's words and *Herut*'s deeds as 'throes of death . . . the pangs accompanying the death of a political party and the decline of one who aspired to leadership . . . [by] a return to the technique of blood-letting. . . .' He chided Nurock for his descent to the level of expediency and he showed respect for Harari's principled opposition and prescience. The main thrust of his remarks, however, was directed to the criticisms levelled by *Mapam* and General Zionist speakers. Patiently, in the manner of a school teacher, he explained why Israel ought to enter into direct talks with Bonn. And he reminded his listeners that direct contact with the Germans by private Jewish organizations had been the norm for some years. Yet to forestall any misunderstanding among his friends and foes in Israel, among the Germans, and among people elsewhere, the Foreign Minister read out a three-point statement as the Israel Government's formal reply to Adenauer's Declaration before the *Bundestag*:

First, the Government adheres steadfastly to the view that the *entire German people* bears responsibility for the mass murder of European Jewry.

Secondly, the Government sees no convincing signs that, since the conclusion of the War, anti-Semitism has been eliminated from the German people either in Eastern or Western Germany.

Thirdly, we do not consider that the mere payment of reparations constitutes a complete settlement of this grave account. . . . [It] cannot wipe out the fearful crimes committed by the Nazis and the stain they left on the German people.[2]

Two proposals were before the House. The Government Motion read:

The *Knesset*, after hearing the Government's Statement on the demand for reparations from Germany, for plundered Jewish property, empowers the Committee on Foreign Affairs and Security to determine finally the action in accordance with the circumstances and conditions.[3]

---

[1] Other speakers opposed to direct negotiations were General Zionists H. Boger, C. Beba, and Yisrael Rokah; *Mapam*'s M. Erem and Y. Riftin; *Maki*'s Wilenska, and the Yemenites' S. Garida. Others supporting the Government were *Mapai*'s Meir Argov, Herzl Berger, Y. Han, Yona Kessah, and M. Namir; and just before Begin spoke, Yitzhak Rafael of *Ha-po'el Ha-mizrahi*.

[2] Sharett, pp. 3, 4, 12, 22–4, 25, 31 (emphasis added).

[3] That Motion was unique in the annals of Israel's parliamentary history: the

The Opposition Motion, proposed by Yosef Saphir and four other MKs, read:

The *Knesset* does not agree to negotiations between the Government of Israel and Germany concerning reparations.

The Government proposal was approved by 60 to 51, with 5 abstentions and 4 members absent: the narrow majority comprised *Mapai*'s 45 MKs, 5 Arabs belonging to affiliated parties, 6 from *Ha-po'el Ha-mizrahi*, 3 Progressives, and 1 from *Agudat Yisrael*; the opposition parties voted *en bloc*; and 5 MKs from religious parties abstained.[1]

It remained for the *Knesset* Committee on Foreign Affairs and Security to authorize direct negotiations. This was done on 15 January 1952 by a vote of 8 to 6, with a *Mapam* member absent. The operative clause read:

... the Committee on Foreign Affairs and Security decides to authorize the Government to act in the matter of reparations from Germany including the possibility of direct negotiations, according to the needs of the issue and the hour. ...[2]

Thus ended the decision-making process on the tactical decision, the most agonizing and controversial act in the drama of German reparations.[3]

The transfer of authority from the Government to the *Knesset*

Plenary was not to decide anything on substance, but to leave everything in the hands of its Foreign Affairs and Security Committee. This was designed to evade another expected storm in the House. Of course, the party composition of that Committee assured the Government Motion a majority.

[1] It was the third and last time in 23 years that the personal vote of each MK was taken and recorded; usually the vote is by a show of hands, generally uncounted, sometimes with a count. The abstentions were M. Genihouski of *Ha-po'el Ha-mizrahi*, Z. Warhaftig of *Mizrahi*, K. Kahana and B. Minz of *Po'alei Agudat Yisrael*, and Rabbi Levin of *Agudat Yisrael*. Rabbi Nurock, the Progressives' Harari, and *Sepharadi* MK B. S. Sasson, voted for the Opposition Motion. The climax was heightened by the scene of *Herut* MK Arye Ben-Eliezer, then suffering from a heart ailment, being brought into the House on a stretcher to cast his vote. *Mapai* member David Hacohen, who was attending the General Assembly in Paris, was flown back for the same purpose. This account was based upon *Divrei Ha-knesset*, x (2), 38th, 39th, and 40th Meetings of the 2nd *Knesset*, pp. 895–964, supplemented by the detailed reports in *Ha'aretz* and *Jerusalem Post*, 8–10 Jan. 1952.

[2] The Hebrew text is in *Documents* . . . , 22, p. 61.

[3] Ben Gurion later wrote that 'the request for and acceptance of [direct negotiations] created a tremendous storm in the *Knesset* and the newspapers, the like of which had never before been seen in Israel'. Further, 'this stormy debate [7–9 Jan. 1952] . . . had no precedent in the annals of the *Knesset*. . . .' Ben Gurion 1969, pp. 421–3. A slightly different English translation is in Ben Gurion 1971, pp. 399–400. Despite its emotion-charged character and its links to the Holocaust, and despite the US Government's involvement, the *Knesset* debate and decision was virtually ignored in the American press, except by Yiddish newspapers, all of which, except the Communist daily, supported the decision.

Foreign Affairs and Security Committee was one noteworthy feature of the decision. Another was that, although a foreign policy issue in the strict sense, the Government Statement was, at the last moment, presented to the *Knesset* by the Prime Minister, not by the Foreign Minister. As Ben Gurion remarked many years later, 'we knew it would be a stormy debate'.[1] Moreover, as Mrs. Meir recalled, 'it was a matter of national importance, not just a foreign policy issue';[2] and, as many added, they wanted to provide the sanction of full support by the highest governmental authority.

(D) IMPLEMENTATION

To classify all Israeli (and world Jewry) acts in the decision flow after 15 January 1952 as of the implementing type is not to denigrate their importance. Yet the first Note (16 January 1951) may be regarded as irrevocable; that is, 'from then on our energy was geared to making it a success; the decisions thereafter were self-propelled'.[3] Adenauer had accepted the Israeli claim for $1 billion from West Germany as 'the basis for negotiations', but the path to agreement was strewn with obstacles. In overcoming them, those who negotiated with the Bonn regime performed an invaluable function, especially the 'crisis intervener' for both delegations, Goldmann, and the Joint Heads of the Israeli team, Giora Josephthal (political) and Shinnar (economic).[4]

The pre-negotiation preparations began at once. On 20 January

[1] Ben Gurion interview, 1966. The tension did not abate quickly. On 19 January 1952, after the decision was authorized, Begin threatened to advocate non-payment of taxes if German money were accepted. The following day he was suspended by the *Knesset* (56 to 47) for the rest of the session for 'threatening the *Knesset* with acts of violence'. *Jerusalem Post*, 22 Jan. 1952.

[2] Meir interview, 1966.

[3] Bartur interview, 1966. Many other observers and participants agreed.

[4] Other members of the Israeli negotiating team were:
Gershon Avner (Political Adviser)
Eli Nathan (Legal Adviser)
Georg Landauer (Expert)
Zvi Shariv (Economic Adviser)
Jacob Robinson (Legal Adviser)
S. Adler-Rudell (Expert).

The first choice for Head of the Israeli delegation was Horowitz. However, at a meeting in Kaplan's home in mid-January 1952, attended by Ben Gurion, Sharett, Kaplan, Naftali, and Pinkas, Horowitz was emphatic in refusing. Naftali and Kaplan agreed: 'in view of the state of Kaplan's health and the state of things in the Treasury', he was needed at home. Horowitz proposed Zvi Dar, then in charge of military industry, but Ben Gurion refused. Sharett then suggested Josephthal, and this was approved. Horowitz interview, 1966, and his unpublished memoirs. Shinnar related that he had expected to be selected Head after Horowitz declined, that Sharett had informed him Josephthal would lead the Israeli team, that he had refused to serve as second-ranking member, and that the compromise formula of two Joint Heads was devised. Shinnar 1967, pp. 26–7.

1952 the Claims Conference assembled in New York and endorsed the Israel Government's policy. Goldmann met Adenauer in London on 4 February to arrange the form and place of the talks. From the 11th to the 13th a joint meeting of the Israel negotiating team and the Executive Committee of the Claims Conference was held in Paris to co-ordinate plans: Sharett, Goldmann, Josephthal, and Shinnar were present.[1] On the 18th the Government of Israel, acting upon the mandate of the *Knesset* Committee, formally decided to accept Bonn's offer of negotiations and asked Goldmann so to inform the West German Government. A parallel conference on Germany's external debts, which almost wrecked the talks on reparations, opened in London on the 28th.[2]

The tripartite conference on reparations began on 21 March 1952 at Wassenaar, a quiet resort between The Hague and Leiden. Israel's opening statement reiterated the basis and purpose of her claim to $1·5 billion from Germany as a whole as set out in the Note of 12 March 1951 to the Powers; in fact, most of the statement took the form of reading into the record large extracts from that Note.[3] The Claims Conference recapitulated the grim tale of German atrocities and concentrated its demand on restitution to individuals, as well as on the problem of heirless and unclaimed Jewish property.[4] The German delegation countered that Bonn's willingness to meet their claims was restricted by Allied legislation and that the Israel/world Jewry claims would have to be co-ordinated with those of Germany's creditors then being discussed at the London Conference.[5]

It was clear from the outset that hard bargaining lay ahead. The issue was complicated by the constricted terms of reference of the German delegation, led by two persons sympathetic to Israel's claim: the former Rector of the University of Frankfurt, Professor Franz Böhm, and his deputy, Otto Küster. As Avner recalled: 'We felt that

[1] A further joint meeting at the highest level was held in London on 16–18 March to complete plans for co-ordination. The Claims Conference negotiating team was not appointed until 18 March, a few days before the first round of talks with the Germans was to begin. With Goldmann as super-Head, its role and influence were distinctly less important than that of the Israeli team. From all accounts co-operation was excellent.

[2] Adenauer's perception of the link between these two events offers a glimpse into one strand of his image of Jewry (another, his abhorrence for anti-Semitism, was well-known): 'It was clear to me that, if the negotiations with the Jews fail, the negotiations at the London Debt Conference will also take a negative turn, as the Jewish banking circles would then exercise a not-to-be-underestimated influence on its course.' Adenauer, p. 141.

[3] *Documents* . . . , 27, pp. 69–74.

[4] Ibid., 28, pp. 75–9.

[5] Ibid., 29, pp. 79–81. Josephthal described the 'first encounter' as 'a dramatic one. Everyone got up when we came in. . . . Nobody shook hands with anybody but just bowed mutely when introduced. . . . The Germans left the room with deep bows, leaving us behind.' Letter of 27 March 1952, Josephthal, p. 146.

the sum was fixed and that the only issue was the types and forms of allocations.' In truth, the German delegation had no authority to settle the issue. For Germany it was a preliminary clarification of Israel's claim—why, how much, what criteria were being used by Israel in formulating its demands, etc.[1]

The first stage of negotiations lasted two weeks and ended in total deadlock.[2] The Israeli team rejected the German attempt to link the Wassenaar and London Conferences, a strategy pressed most vigorously by Abs;[3] it asserted, rather, the uniqueness and primacy of the Jewish claim. The German team went to Bonn for consultations on 30 March. Two days later Adenauer accepted—in principle—Böhm's proposal of a severely qualified 'offer' of DM 3 billion ($715 million).[4] On the 5th of April the German delegation made this 'offer' known through a statement which challenged the basis of Israel's financial (though not her moral) claim: the *per capita* cost of immigrant absorption, it asserted, was about one third less than Israeli estimates, thereby reducing the maximal basis of the claim to DM 3 billion. Moreover, the satisfaction of even that reduced claim was linked to the outcome of the London Conference, thereby undermining the *bona fides* of the 'offer'. The Israelis reacted sharply, rejecting both points in the German statement and requesting 'the date upon which a binding [unqualified German] proposal . . . will be available' on the amount, the period over which payment would be spread, and the principles of implementation. The Germans promised a reply in a month. It was to take a little longer.[5]

[1] Interview, 1968.

[2] The Germans met daily with the Israeli team in the morning and with the Claims Conference delegation in the afternoon. Israeli/world Jewry statements were delivered in English, with a German translation given to the other side; the language of the German delegation's communications was the reverse. After a few days German became the working language at Wassenaar. The gruelling pace of work was described by Josephthal, letter of 27 March 1952, pp. 147–8.

[3] Abs' 1967 memoir on this controversial issue is in Vogel, pp. 39–41.

[4] Also present at the meeting were Finance Minister Schäffer, Abs, and Küster. US High Commissioner McCloy was informed of the 'offer' the same afternoon and was reportedly concerned lest Germany's precarious financial situation at the time impose part of the burden on the Western Powers. Deutschkron, pp. 64–5.

In his quest for a settlement Böhm had sought the advice of two economists, Professor Wilhelm Röpke of the University of Geneva and Professor Fritz W. Meyer of Bonn University. Both prepared memoranda arguing that payments in kind by Germany were not identical with payments in foreign exchange: that is, they would not cause a 'transfer problem'. Meyer interview with Balabkins, 27 July 1966, Balabkins, pp. 132–3.

[5] The German statement of 5 April 1952, the Israeli reply on the 8th, and the German response on the 9th are in *Documents* . . . , 30, 31, 32, pp. 82, 82–4, and 85, respectively. Goldmann's memoirs (1969) gloss over the extreme tension created by German bargaining tactics. Earlier, however (interview, 1966), he noted that there was 'very tough bargaining'. From the outset Josephthal adopted a tough and realistic posture. At the second session, 'I made a sharp reply, hinting strongly at breaking off

The period of quiet diplomacy lasted two months, from the suspension of the talks on 9 April to 10 June 1952. It was then that Goldmann made his significant contribution to the consummation of Israel's reparations decisions. As he wrote later, he had stayed out of the Wassenaar talks 'so that I could more effectively intervene in a crisis'.[1] He met Adenauer frequently and successfully pressed the claims of Israel and world Jewry. Shinnar was present at several of these discussions (Josephthal as well, though less often), and he conducted most of the economic negotiations separately. The flow of events during that behind-the-scenes implementing phase may now be sketched.

Pressure was exerted by American Jewry, through talks with US Government officials and Congressmen. In particular, Jacob Blaustein, then Chairman of the AJC and Senior Vice-President of the Claims Conference, pleaded with President Truman to help break the impasse —during a conversation in early April and through an exchange of letters on the 11th and the 15th. Josephthal, too, was busy lobbying for British support, through conversations with Selwyn Lloyd, Hugh Dalton, influential economic correspondents of the London press, etc.[2] These efforts were to bear fruit, though not for another two months of adamant advocacy by Josephthal, Goldmann, and Shinnar.

On 19 April Goldmann and Shinnar met with Abs in Bonn for further discussion on the mutual impact of the Wassenaar and London talks. The next day Adenauer promised Goldmann an early indication of a precise German offer. On the 6th of May the *Knesset* 'noted' by 50 to 34 a resolution by the Foreign Affairs and Security Committee recommending the Government not to renew the negotiations until a 'clear and binding offer' was received concerning the amount of reparations and the schedule of payments.[3]

A crucial bargaining session took place in London on 19 May. Abs tried to persuade Shinnar (and Moshe Keren, Economic Minister at the Israel Embassy) to be more 'realistic' and 'flexible'. A vague offer of $100 million, to be paid as an advance in four annual instalments, was rejected as 'totally unacceptable'. Shinnar rightly called this a turning

---

the negotiations'. On 3 April he warned of an impending crisis. And on the 8th he threatened once more to terminate the negotiations, because 'they constantly play us off against the other creditors . . .'. Letters of 27 March, 3, 8 April 1952, Josephthal, pp. 147, 149, 150. Shinnar described the German 'offer' of 5 April as 'extremely disappointing; it led to a breakdown'. Interview, 1965.

[1] Goldmann 1969, p. 263.
[2] Blaustein, pp. 7, 12; Josephthal, letters of 19, 23 April 1952, pp. 154, 155.
[3] The Hebrew text is in *Documents* . . . , 37, p. 90. That day, *Herut* introduced a motion of no-confidence in the Government; it was defeated by 3 against 57 with 33 abstentions. Then three Motions for the Agenda were introduced, as well as the Committee's resolution, reported by its chairman for 'notification'. After a lengthy debate the three motions were defeated and the Committee's resolution was 'noted' with approval. *Divrei Ha-knesset*, xi, 6 May 1952, pp. 1928–44.

point, for Abs reported to Adenauer immediately that Israel would stand firm. Josephthal's hard line had the desired effect even though, as he acknowledged, 'We are colossal bankrupts: $20 million in debts every month and an income of $10 million at most, and all this without additional expenses for defense.'[1] This was confirmed by Böhm, who recalled the content of a telephone call from Blankenhorn to him late at night on the 19th: 'He [Adenauer] was great. He carried all of them [the West German Cabinet] with him. Besides, we have just heard that Abs did not succeed in persuading the Jewish party that his $100 million offer is worth discussing.'[2]

The decision of the Bonn Cabinet that day was to make an offer of DM 3 billion to Israel, entirely independent of the outcome of the London Conference: the catalysts were pressure from the *Bundestag* Foreign Affairs Committee, Küster's resignation as Deputy Head of the German delegation to the Wassenaar talks, and Böhm's widely-reported dissent from Bonn's niggardliness.[3] Goldmann, too, pressed the Israeli claim by following up the Shinnar–Abs deadlock in London with a letter to Adenauer the same day (the 19th), emphasizing the negative impact on Germany's image in the West if the talks broke down. On that occasion, however, his *démarche* arrived too late to affect Adenauer's decision.[4] Böhm was persuaded by the Chancellor to

---

[1] Josephthal also reported at the time: 'They [the Germans] got *ibergeshrekt* [scared]. Nahum [Goldmann] thought I was too aggressive and rigid and should have been more patient; for otherwise they would have treated us like a commercial creditor.' Letter of 19 April 1952, pp. 154–5. On the eve of the 19 May meeting Josephthal expected a 'scandalous . . . first proposal'. See letters of 18, 21 May 1952, pp. 157–8.

[2] Böhm interview with Deutschkron, 17 Feb. 1969, Deutschkron, p. 70.

[3] The *Bundestag* Foreign Affairs Committee issued a unanimous statement on 12 May declaring that Jewish/Israeli claims were of a *moral* character and should be given precedence over *commercial* claims at the London Conference. Finance Minister Schäffer, whom Goldmann included among Israel's friends during the negotiations, reportedly attacked Küster for his resignation and for his statement upholding Israel's cause against his own country. He also pleaded West Germany's 'great' poverty. *Jerusalem Post*, 26 May 1952.

Böhm arrived in Bonn for consultations on the 19th. The Chancellor sought his advice and was urged to order the resumption of negotiations without reference to the London Conference. Böhm recalled that Adenauer said: 'I shall see what I can achieve tonight in the Cabinet meeting.' He was successful, as the extract from Blankenhorn testifies. Deutschkron, p. 70. Abs pressed for a figure considerably lower than Böhm's proposed DM 3 billion. And Finance Minister Schäffer thought in terms of DM 2 billion. Reported in Balabkins, p. 132, based upon information provided by Schäffer on 5 August 1966.

Perhaps apocryphal, perhaps not, is the report (widely-believed among Israeli decision-makers) that Adenauer finally convinced his Cabinet with an adage that future German history books would contain 20 lines on German cruelty to the Jews— and that there was need for one line on German reparations to the Jews!

[4] The text of Goldmann's letter is in Grossmann, Appendix VI, pp. 61–3. A copy was pointedly sent to McCloy. Adenauer, in his memoirs, conspicuously dates the German Cabinet decision (19 May) before the arrival of Goldmann's letter: 'On the

withdraw his planned resignation and to proceed to Paris to convey the new offer. McCloy telephoned Goldmann on the 21st and informed him that important news would be forthcoming shortly. A few hours later the Böhm–Goldmann meeting was arranged. The Western High Commissioners conferred with Adenauer on the 22nd.[1]

The Böhm offer on 23 May was very similar to the final terms of agreement. In essence, it provided: (1) a total sum of DM 3 billion ($715 million), to be paid over a period of eight to twelve years, exclusively in goods (for West Germany lacked foreign exchange); (2) the amount and type of goods per year would be jointly determined; (3) after the conclusion of the London Conference, Bonn would apply for a foreign loan to be placed at the disposal of Israel; and (4) reparations were to be fixed for the first two years at 200 million marks annually. The Israeli and world Jewry delegation leaders agreed that it was a fair offer.[2] Ben Gurion, Sharett, and Kaplan also responded favourably.[3] Abs continued to resist from London, saying that, while Israel's claim to immediate payment was just, it was 'neither legally correct nor economically possible for Israel to get full payment before anyone else received a penny'.[4] But once Adenauer had decided, the outcome was assured. He met with Goldmann again on 28 May in Paris: a communiqué indicated their agreement that early resumption of negotiations was desirable and that another informal discussion was planned.[5] It took place in Bonn on 10 June.

De facto agreement on all major points was reached at two meetings that day. At the morning session the German team comprised Secretary

---

21st of May 1952 a letter from Dr. Goldmann was submitted to me in which he expressed his great concern about the situation that had been created, in the meantime. The letter carried the date of 19 May 1952.' Adenauer added that Abs' offer to Shinnar on the 19th was made without his knowledge, pp. 145–7.

[1] Böhm told Deutschkron that Adenauer had convinced his Cabinet (on the 19th) that they should go along with *US views* on the terms of a reparations agreement. Deutschkron, p. 70. American-Jewish and Israeli pressure was confirmed to the author by several knowledgeable Israelis.

[2] Böhm met first with Goldmann alone for an hour on the morning of the 23rd. Then Josephthal, Shinnar, Avner, and Barou joined them for a further three-hour discussion. Böhm noted that Adenauer wanted Israeli and Jewish reactions before seeking *formal* German Cabinet approval. Goldmann, on his own, suggested that all Bonn commitments be made to Israel, which would then satisfy the Jewish organizations on a previously agreed-upon basis. Adenauer, pp. 148–51. Böhm's lengthy report to Adenauer on the 23 May discussions in Paris is in Vogel, pp. 49–53.

[3] Goldmann claimed that Ben Gurion had urged him, at an earlier stage, to accept $300 million—but he had refused. Interview, 1966. Ben Gurion did not deny or affirm it: 'I can't recall having said it.' Interview, 1966. Kaplan was reportedly ready to settle for $500 million if more could not be attained. Yahil letter, 1972. Josephthal wrote to his wife on 9 April 1952: '. . . I believe that we shall get $300–400 million within ten years.' Josephthal, p. 151.

[4] United Press, reported in *Jerusalem Post*, 1 June 1952.

[5] The text is in Adenauer, p. 151, and (in English) in Vogel, p. 53.

of State Hallstein, Assistant Secretary Blankenhorn, Abs, Böhm, and a Foreign Ministry official, Frowein; Goldmann, Shinnar, and Barou spoke for Israel and world Jewry. The total payment was fixed at DM 3 billion to Israel and DM 500 million to the Claims Conference (of which DM 50 million was to be assigned to Jews converted to Christianity). Abs insisted that all reparations be paid in goods. This was agreeable, provided part would take the form of crude oil purchased by Germany for Israel.[1] The final decision was left to the afternoon session, as was the disagreement over the schedule of payments. Israel pressed for a maximum of ten years, the Germans, fourteen.

Adenauer played the decisive role in the afternoon session. The Israeli reluctance to waste reparations funds on consumer goods evoked his respectful comment (only 3 per cent was allocated for that purpose). The crude oil proposal was accepted in principle. And the Germans agreed to make 30 per cent of the annual payments in foreign exchange, largely for oil. Finally, they agreed to make advance payment in later years, if financially feasible. The Chancellor, who had been called away during the discussion, prevailed upon a reluctant Abs to remain until agreement was reached. At Adenauer's suggestion, a memorandum was prepared—by Shinnar, Hallstein, and Abs—and was initialled by the parties.[2] A week later the German Cabinet approved those terms.[3]

[1] According to this proposal Germany would pay the Shell Oil Company in marks via the European Payments Union (EPU), in order to ensure a steady flow of oil to Israel. The agreement was finally concluded by Shinnar on 10 September 1952, 'the last possible date, for Israel's oil funds were exhausted'. Shinnar interview, 1965. Goldmann (1969) takes credit for this ingenious plan. Every other knowledgeable source on the Israeli side ascribed it to Shinnar, with Josephthal negotiating the political aspects. Josephthal, letters of 14, 18 July 1952, pp. 164, 165.

[2] The text of the 10 June Memorandum is in Grossmann, pp. 24–5. The accounts of that decisive meeting are almost identical: see Adenauer, pp. 152–3; Goldmann interview, 1966, and Goldmann 1969, pp. 269–76; Josephthal, pp. 160–1; Shinnar interview, 1965, and Shinnar 1967, pp. 37–41. The Wassenaar talks are summarized in Balabkins, pp. 123–36.

[3] Adenauer's motives in paying reparations to Israel were undoubtedly complex. One strand—German national interest—was illuminated by Blankenhorn (see pp. 73–74, n. 4 above). The moral stimulus is evident in the following passage from the Chancellor's memoirs:

'The Agreement with Israel was something different from the usual contracts between two states. It was based upon a pressing moral obligation. The Federal Republic was determined, within the framework of its capacity, to restitute what Hitler had done to the Jews. It would have been shameful if we would have wavered in our decision only because adverse economic consequences were threatening. *There are higher things than good business. We wanted another Germany than Hitler's Germany. We had to pass the test and not only with nice words but also with material sacrifices.* I was convinced that the German people and the German economy stood behind me.' Adenauer, p. 155 (emphasis added).

In reflecting upon Adenauer's 'generous' offer in 1952 (DM 3 billion), compared with his initial offer of DM 10 million in 1949, Yahil emphasized the critical role of

Formal negotiations were resumed at Wassenaar on 28 June and continued through the summer. There were many contentious points.[1] Just as Goldmann's role was primary in the 'crisis negotiations', Josephthal was the dominant negotiator at the Wassenaar talks, and Shinnar was the principal figure in securing optimal economic and technical conditions, with a display of ingenuity in the last phase.[2]

There were four separate but related agreements. In the first, the Reparations Agreement proper, the Federal Republic of Germany undertook to pay DM 3 billion ($715 million) to the Government of Israel over a period of twelve to fourteen years. In Protocol Number One, Bonn pledged itself to enact new legislation for individual compensation. Protocol Number Two provided for the payment of DM 450 million ($107 million) to the Jewish Claims Conference to cover Jewish property without known heirs. Israel was to receive the full amount of DM 3·45 billion ($822 million) and to transfer to the Claims Conference its share in goods. And in Protocol Number Three Israel undertook to refund the value of the property of the German Templars in Israel, which had been nationalized.[3]

The agreements between West Germany and Israel were signed by Adenauer and Sharett, and those relating to the Claims Conference by Adenauer and Goldmann at a solemn, sombre, simple ceremony in Luxembourg's City Hall on 10 September 1952. There were no speeches, not even a perfunctory handshake among the principals.[4] However else Israel reacted, it was a distortion of reality to say, as Goldmann

---

West Germany's 'economic miracle' in the interim, in contrast to the slow process of Bonn's international political rehabilitation. And that gap, in turn, explains much about the success of Israel's reparations policy: 'Germany, in 1952, was financially strong but still politically insecure and anxious to improve her image. Two years *earlier* we would have had to settle for a much smaller sum [see Israeli expectations, p. 94, n. 3 above]. Two years *later* we would have encountered a much more arrogant and self-confident Germany.' Yahil letter, 1972.

[1] They included: a suitable preamble; a clause to ensure the real value of reparations against possible devaluation of the mark; the technical aspects of the fuel oil arrangement; the preparation of lists of merchandise for payments during the first year; compensation for the property of German Templars in Israel taken over by the Israel Government, etc. Much light is shed on the second phase of negotiations by Josephthal, letters of 27 June–31 August 1952, pp. 162–72. It is clear that they were not smooth: 'The discussions are endless and quite tense'; 'We are nervous and can only hope everything will turn out all right' (pp. 167, 172).

[2] The task of legal drafting was performed largely by Dr. Jacob Robinson, then Legal Adviser to the Israel Delegation to the UN. Josephthal paid frequent tribute to him as 'doing a magnificent job' (pp. 162, 163, 165, 166).

[3] The official name of the Agreement was 'Agreement Between the State of Israel and the Federal Republic of Germany. Signed on 10 September 1952, at Luxembourg'. *Documents* . . . , pp. 125–72. The basic text is also in Grossman, Appendix II, pp. 37–57 and in Vogel, pp. 56–68. See also Balabkins, pp. 143–7. On the legal aspects see Honig. For a cursory general analysis see also Giniewski, and Prittie, pp. 203–8.

[4] On the signing ceremony see Adenauer, pp. 155–6; Goldmann 1969, pp. 273–4; Shinnar 1967, pp. 43–6; and Balabkins, pp. 137–8.

did, that 'the signing of the agreement was greeted with . . joy . . .'.[1]
The more sober judgement of Shinnar was closer to the truth: 'I
believe one may say that public opinion and the prevailing opinion in
parliament welcomed this treaty . . . as a serious contribution to reparations for the material wrong done and the resulting damage; at
least a clear difference was apparent as against the reception by public
opinion at the beginning of the negotiations.'[2]

It remained to ratify the Agreements. The process took six months,
largely because massive Arab pressure was directed toward the Bonn
regime, political parties and MPs, and toward German firms with an
interest in the Middle East. Egypt went so far as to demand equal
compensation. But Arab pressure was rebuffed, and the *Bundestag*
approved the Agreements on 18 March 1953.[3] Four days later the
Government of Israel ratified the Agreements. Thus ended a two-year
process of foreign policy decision-making by Israel on the issue of
reparations.

(E) DECISION FLOW

Pre-Decisional Events

1.	1941	Goldmann asserted a Jewish claim to German reparations after the Second World War.
2.	1943	An international Jewish conference in Atlantic City demanded restitution to individuals and invoked the principle of Jewry's right to collective compensation.
3.	1943–4	Landauer-Moses memorandum and book set forth the Jewish claim.
4.	20 September 1945	A Weizmann letter to the Occupying Powers

[1] Goldmann 1969, p. 274. Goldmann also claimed that Ben Gurion spoke of the
Reparations Agreement as one of two miracles he had witnessed, the other being
the creation of the State of Israel; further, that he, Ben Gurion, had presided over the
second, and Goldmann over the first. To place these two events on the same level of
historical significance, whether secular-inspired or other, requires an extraordinary display of personal vanity. To assert that Ben Gurion would do so is fanciful. To this
writer Ben Gurion cited Josephthal as having played the *key* role in negotiating the Luxembourg Agreement (interview, 1966), while not denying Goldmann's important role.

[2] A comment in 1962. Vogel, p. 87.

[3] The vote was 239 to 35, with 86 abstaining. There was marked dissent in Adenauer's
own party, the Christian Democrats (for example, Finance Minister Schäffer voted
against), in contrast to overwhelming support by the Social Democrats. Ratification
by the *Bundesrat* (Upper House) on 20 March came just before the end of the parliamentary session. Any further delay would have meant the loss of a year (1953–4) in
the beginning of the flow of reparations payments—at a time of grave economic
distress for Israel. The struggle for ratification in West Germany is discussed at length
in Balabkins, pp. 147–50; Goldmann 1969, pp. 275–6; Grossmann, pp. 27–9, 31–5;
Shinnar 1967, pp. 49–56; and Vogel, pp. 69–87.

formally presented the claim of the Jewish
People to reparations and restitution.

5. 11 November 1949   Adenauer, in an interview with Karl Marx,
indicated the determination of West Germany
to pay reparations to Israel.

6. 1950   Secret conversations took place, notably
between Blankenhorn and Barou in London,
and between Altmaier and Livneh in West
Germany.

7. 1 July 1950   The van Dam Memorandum was submitted
to Israel's Finance Ministry.

Decisive Inputs into Strategic Decision

8. all 1950   Israel's economic situation was grave.

9. September 1950   Horowitz suggested an indirect approach to
the Four Occupying Powers of Germany.

10. 30 October—   The reparations issue was discussed by
27 December 1950   Israel's Cabinet; opposition to direct talks
with Germany was expressed.

Strategic Decision

11. 3 January 1951   The Government of Israel decided to seek and
to accept reparations for Jewish property
plundered by the Nazi regime.

Implementation of Strategic Decision

12. [A.D.* 3 January   The Government of Israel decided upon an
1951   indirect approach, through the Four Occupying Powers.]

13. 16 January 1951   Israeli Notes were sent to the United States,
United Kingdom, France, and the Soviet
Union asserting, in general terms, Jewish
claims for '(a) Restitution of identifiable
property, including communal and heirless
property; (b) Indemnification for injuries to
life, liberty and health . . .', etc.[1]

14. 12 March 1951   Identical Israeli Notes were submitted to the
Four Powers setting forth the claim to $1·5
billion worth of reparations, $1 billion from
West Germany, $500 million from East
Germany.

* Abortive Decision.
[1] *Documents* . . . , 3, p. 14.

Decisive Inputs into Tactical Decision

15. all 1951   Israel's economic situation remained grave.

16. 6 May 1951   At the Horowitz–Adenauer meeting in Paris, Israel's two conditions for direct negotiations were conveyed.

17. 27 September 1951   A Declaration was made by Chancellor Adenauer before the *Bundestag* affirming West Germany's readiness to enter into negotiations on material reparations to the State of Israel and to world Jewry.

18. 6 December 1951   Adenauer, in writing, informed Goldmann, President of the Conference on Jewish Material Claims Against Germany: 'The Federal Government considers that the time has come when . . . negotiations should begin [and] . . . is ready to accept the claims which the Government of the State of Israel has formulated in its note of March 12, 1951 as the basis for these negotiations.'[1]

19. December 1951   Further to their Notes of 20–21 March and 5 July 1951, the United States, the United Kingdom, and France informally conveyed a negative reply to Israel's Notes of 30 November requesting them to put pressure on Bonn, reaffirming their support for direct negotiations between Israel and West Germany.

Tactical Decision

20. 30 December 1951   The Government decided to recommend to the *Knesset* that Israel enter into direct negotiations with West Germany for reparations.

Implementation of Tactical Decision

21. 7–9 January 1952   At the conclusion of the stormiest debate in its history, the *Knesset*, by a vote of 60 to 51, empowered its Committee on Foreign Affairs and Security 'to determine finally the action in accordance with the circumstances and conditions'.[2]

22. 15 January 1952   The *Knesset* Committee on Foreign Affairs and Security, by a vote of 8 to 6, with an

[1] Grossmann, Appendix V, p. 61.
[2] *Documents* . . . , 21, p. 61.

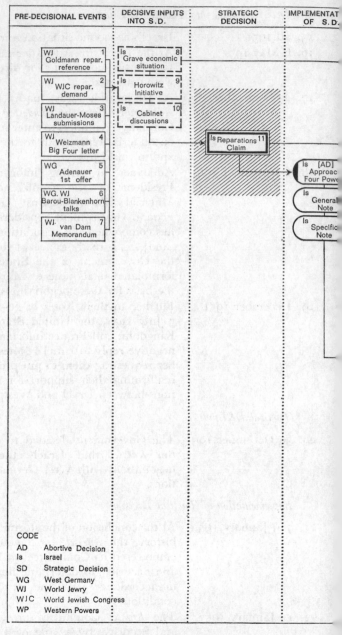

PRE-DECISIONAL EVENTS	DECISIVE INPUTS INTO S.D.	STRATEGIC DECISION	IMPLEMENTAT OF S.D.

WJ 1
Goldmann repar. reference

WJC 2
WJC repar. demand

WJ 3
Landauer-Moses submissions

WJ 4
Weizmann Big Four letter

WG 5
Adenauer 1st offer

WG. WJ 6
Barou-Blankenhorn talks

WJ. 7
van Dam Memorandum

Is 8
Grave economic situation

Is 9
Horowitz Initiative

Is 10
Cabinet discussions

Is Reparations 11
Claim

Is [AD]
Approac Four Powe

Is General Note

Is Specific Note

CODE
AD   Abortive Decision
Is   Israel
SD   Strategic Decision
WG   West Germany
WJ   World Jewry
WJC   World Jewish Congress
WP   Western Powers

FIGURE 4. DECISION FLOW: GERMAN REPARATIONS

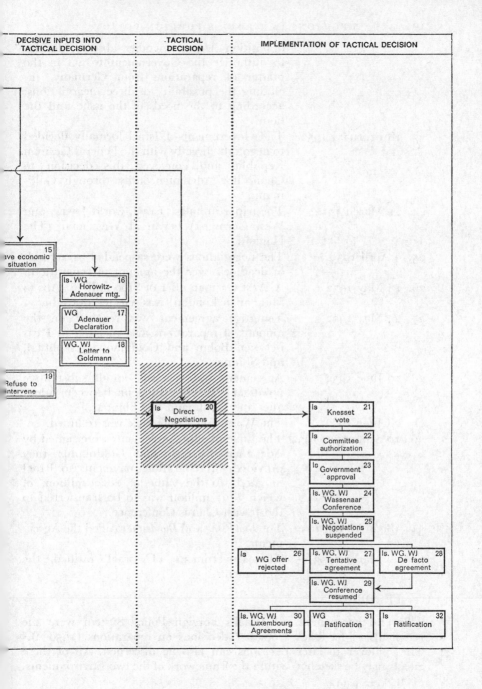

DECISIVE INPUTS INTO
TACTICAL DECISION

TACTICAL
DECISION

IMPLEMENTATION OF TACTICAL DECISION

15
...ave economic
situation

Is. WG   16
Horowitz-
Adenauer mtg.

WG   17
Adenauer
Declaration

WG. WJ   18
Letter to
Goldmann

19
Refuse to
intervene

Is   Direct   20
Negotiations

Is   Knesset   21
vote

Is   Committee   22
authorization

Is   Government   23
approval

Is. WG. WJ   24
Wassenaar
Conference

Is. WG. WJ   25
Negotiations
suspended

Is   26
WG offer
rejected

Is. WG. WJ   27
Tentative
agreement

Is. WG. WJ   28
De facto
agreement

Is. WG. WJ   29
Conference
resumed

Is. WG. WJ   30
Luxembourg
Agreements

WG   31
Ratification

Is   32
Ratification

		opposition *Mapam* member absent, 'decides to authorize the Government to act in the matter of reparations from Germany, including the possibility of direct negotiations, according to the needs of the issue and the hour'.[1]
23.	18 February 1952	The Government of Israel formally decided to negotiate directly with the Federal German Republic and conveyed this decision to Chancellor Adenauer orally through Goldmann.
24.	21 March 1952	The tripartite talks (Israel, world Jewry, and West Germany) began at Wassenaar (The Hague).
25.	9 April 1952	The negotiations were suspended as a result of deadlock over the amount of reparations.
26.	19 May 1952	A West German offer of $100 million (Abs to Shinnar in London) was rejected outright.
27.	23 May 1952	Tentative agreement was reached on the amount of reparations at a meeting in Paris between Böhm and Goldmann, Josephthal, and Shinnar.
28.	10 June 1952	Agreement was reached on all substantive points at a meeting in Bonn between Adenauer and Goldmann and Shinnar.
29.	28 June 1952	The Wassenaar Conference was resumed.
30.	10 September 1952	The Luxembourg Agreements were signed by Adenauer, Sharett, and Goldmann: they provided for reparations payments to Israel in goods to the value of $822 million, of which $107 million was to be transferred to the Jewish Claims Conference.
31.	18, 20 March 1953	The *Bundestag* and *Bundesrat* ratified the Agreements.
32.	22 March 1953	The Government of Israel ratified the Agreements.

(F) FEEDBACK

Several components of Israel's Foreign Policy System were the recipients of feedback from her decisions on reparations (1950–2).[2] The spillover to later decisions can also be discerned. All of these effects may be sketched within the framework of the two Environments.

[1] Ibid., 22, p. 61.

[2] These are portrayed graphically and are summarized on pp. 108–9 below.

It should be emphasized that the concept of feedback applied here does not imply a one-one mechanical relationship between the initial high-policy decision (concerning reparations) and all subsequent decisions within a designated issue (relating to Germany). Rather, the contention is that the strategic decision of 1951 was the *necessary*, *but not sufficient*, condition for later Israeli strategic decisions on Germany.

In the *external* sphere, a cumulative impact is evident in two components: relations with Germany (B); and, partly as a consequence of that relationship, Israel's growing association with a regional system other than the Middle East, that is, Western Europe (SO). As a former Director-General of the Foreign Ministry observed: 'The reparations decision made it easier for us to take later decisions about Germany—to reconcile to the reality of a "new Germany".'[1] The evidence bears this out. For one thing the tension during the decision crises of 1957–8 (arms purchased from Germany), 1959 (arms sales to Germany), and 1965 (diplomatic relations), while greater than for most other foreign policy decisions, was less in duration and intensity than the initial explosion of 1951–2. Further, each successive act, including the Ben Gurion–Adenauer meeting of 1960 and the (secret) arms aid agreement of that year, eased the way to *rapprochement*, forged closer links and broadened support for Israel from a re-emerging Great Power in the conflict with her Arab adversaries. Stated briefly, the reparations decisions were the first step not only on 'West Germany's path to Israel' but, in terms of her foreign policy capability, on 'Israel's path to West Germany'.

Although the relationship never attained the status of a formal alliance or even, as with France, a *de facto* alliance, Germany was to become an increasingly valuable bilateral component in Israel's Foreign Policy System. It was to contribute economic aid (to the value of $35–40 million per annum) after the conclusion of reparations payments in 1965; military assistance (approximately $50 million a year from 1960–5); and political support in Israel's prolonged efforts to secure a viable association with 'Europe'.

From 1960 Israel was engaged in a massive campaign to obtain entry into the European Common Market. Her principal supporter within the Community was the Benelux group, especially Holland. France was not unfriendly. But Italy used her influence to prevent any relationship beyond a preferential trade agreement. Even that minimal form of association was achieved (in 1964) only after an intense struggle. West Germany's role was vital, not only as one of the most powerful members of the Market, but also through her pressure on the other important state in the EEC, France. Thus, reparations, by reopening the door to West Germany, eased the (limited) entry of Israel to

[1] Eytan interview, 1971.

'Europe', with the economic and, indirectly, the political and diplomatic benefits that ensued.

These objective changes, which can be traced partly to the reparations decisions, were accompanied by a fundamental shift in the perceptions of Germany held by Ben Gurion and his closest aides. Undoubtedly a mutual interaction was operating in the two environments.

From 1957 onward Ben Gurion was to give continuous public expression to his image of: (*a*) a basic difference between Nazi Germany and Adenauer's Germany; (*b*) the importance of Bonn to Israel, both as a direct source of economic and military assistance, and as a friend within Europe, particularly *vis-à-vis* France; and (*c*) of Israel as part of Europe. All of these images were also articulated by Shimon Peres, then at the height of his influence as Director-General of the Defence Ministry and, from 1959, as Deputy Minister of Defence.[1]

How important Adenauer's Germany had become, in Ben Gurion's psychological environment, is evident in his speeches and writings during the late 1950s and early 1960s. None is more revealing than the following remarks to the *Knesset* in 1959:

When I say that the Germany of today, the Germany of Adenauer and the Social Democrats, is not the Germany of Hitler, I am referring not only to the new regime . . . but also to the geo-political transformation that has taken place in Western Europe and in the world. . . . Germany as a force hostile to Israel . . . also endangers the friendship of the other countries of Western Europe and might even have an undesirable influence on the United States and the other countries of America. She is a rising force . . .—and her attitude to us will have no small influence on the attitude of other countries that are allied with her.

In my profound conviction, the injunction bequeathed to us by the martyrs of the Holocaust is the rebuilding, the strengthening, the progress and the security of Israel. For that purpose we need friends . . . especially friends who are able and willing to equip the Israel Defence Forces in order to ensure our survival. . . . But if we regard Germany, or any other country—as Satan, we shall not receive arms.[2]

Whether Ben Gurion perceived Germany's re-emergence as a Power in 1951–2 as lucidly as he did in 1959 is subject to controversy. There can be no doubt, however, that his iron-willed insistence on forging ever-stronger links with Bonn via the arms decisions of 1957, 1959, and 1960, was the logical policy consequence of the image so starkly portrayed by him before the *Knesset* and elsewhere at the time. And that image, in turn, derived from a judgement which appeared to be confirmed by the Israeli decisions on reparations in 1950–2 and West Germany's subsequent behaviour.

---

[1] Interview, 1960.
[2] 'Address by the Prime Minister, Mr. David Ben Gurion, in the *Knesset*, July 1, 1959.' State of Israel, Government Press Office, Jerusalem, p. 14.

The establishment of *diplomatic* relations between Bonn and Jerusalem was consummated by Ben Gurion's successor, in 1965. Yet that formal act of 'normalization' must be viewed as the logical end-product of Israeli decisions in 1950–2 to seek and accept reparations from the successor to Nazi Germany. The process began with economic ties (1952); then came the purchase and sale of arms (1957, 1959, and 1960); cultural links (1962); and finally, as the climax to an intercontinental political crisis, diplomatic relations. In fact, there is some evidence that 'Adenauer tentatively offered Israel diplomatic relations . . . at the time of the Luxembourg Agreement'.[1]

There was a significant effect of the time lag and the disharmony in Israeli and German attitudes. At the time of the Luxembourg Agreement West Germany was eager for diplomatic relations; but Israel was not ready, for internal reasons. More than a decade later the roles were reversed: Bonn hesitated because of formidable Arab pressure, which led to the severance of ties with many Arab states from 1965 until 1972. Thus 'a mortgage' on Israel–German and German–Arab relations was taken out in the early 1950s because of Israel's reluctance then to establish full diplomatic relations with the Federal Republic.

An incidental (and incomplete) feedback from the reparations decisions to the perceptions of Israel's decision-makers concerned Spain: 'If we could deal with Germany, which had killed six million Jews, how could we refuse to deal with Franco Spain, which though Fascist, saved many Jews. The anti-Franco feeling [which was responsible for Israel's rejection of Madrid's overtures in 1949 for diplomatic relations] would have faded anyway. But our decision on German reparations made it easier to accept the idea of relations with Franco Spain. Then it was too late—Spain was no longer interested.'[2]

The feedback from reparations to the *internal* environment was more dramatic and had, perhaps, more durable effects on the political structure and economic capability. The demonstrations before the *Knesset* in January 1952 and the atmosphere of invective, hostility, and hate illuminated the conflict that enveloped both Israel's political élite and her mass public. The mutual disdain of Ben Gurion and Begin was fortified. And the more basic institutional hostility between *Mapai* and *Herut*, with its roots in the *Yishuv*, was given a sharp infusion of rancour not to be forgotten by either party. Indeed, the violence of the January street riots revived the spectre of *Herut* as a *'putschist'* party which had not outgrown its origins in the *Irgun Tzva'i Le'umi*, or

---

[1] Prittie, p. 207, based upon a conversation with Hans Globke, then one of the Chancellor's closest political confidants. Prittie also reported that Adenauer asked US Ambassador David Bruce to sound out Washington's attitude. 'American advice was allegedly against this proposal.' A knowledgeable Israeli source, too, related to this writer the German offer of diplomatic relations in 1953. Yahil interview, 1966.

[2] Eytan interview, 1971.

Etzel. And it was that image of *Herut* as an anti-democratic threat to Israel's parliamentary system which sustained the *Mapai*-inspired animosity towards the party of the nationalist Right. In terms of Israel's *political structure*, the consequence was more rigid exclusion of *Herut* from a role of possible Coalition partner. Certainly its inclusion in the Cabinet was unthinkable for Ben Gurion: deep-rooted hostility and distrust of Revisionists became immovable. That fissure was widened by other controversies relating to Germany in 1957–8, 1959, and 1965. Indeed, it required the enormity of the May 1967 crisis to heal the wounds sufficiently to enable *Herut* to enter a *Mapai*-dominated 'National Unity Government'. To the leaders of both parties Germany was an insuperable obstacle to political co-operation; and the conflict over reparations heightened the hostility.

Inter-party (*competing élite*) conflict was more extensive. *Mapam* and *Ahdut Ha'avoda*, then united, had opposed direct talks with Bonn just as vigorously as *Herut* had, though less violently. And in 1957–8 and 1959, as Coalition partners of *Mapai*, they contributed to the dissolution of the Government over decisions about arms relations with West Germany.[1] On those occasions, too, Israel's political structure was destabilized by the fallout from her decisions on reparations. There were also serious consequences for the psychological environment. Mistrust escalated, especially among leaders: Ben Gurion, in particular, perceived the two smaller Labour parties as unreliable and opportunistic; they reciprocated this image. Those personal and party animosities were periodically rekindled by the German question, which thereby contributed to the delay in the reunification of *Mapai*, *Ahdut Ha'avoda*, and *Rafi*. That event (1968), which was to signal a basic shift in Israel's political structure, was unthinkable as long as Ben Gurion remained at the helm.

The impact of reparations on Israel's *economic capability* is the most susceptible to precise measurement. The flow of goods and services began in 1953, a critical time in Israel's struggle for economic viability. Other sources of foreign exchange were inadequate and insecure. For a period of twelve years the infusion of unilateral transfers in German goods to the value of $715 million helped to propel the Israeli economy on the path to rapid growth. Imported goods consisted of ships and equipment (38 per cent), fuel (30 per cent), and raw materials (24 per cent); the balance was for services abroad. Israel's largest bank summed up the effects on Israel's economy—and on the multi-faceted Israel–German relationship—as follows:

There can be no doubt that the past nine years (1953–62) have seen a revolution in the Israel economy, brought about in large part by reparation goods. Over 1,300 Israel firms received new equipment under the Agreement. Reparation

---

[1] These decisions were analysed in Brecher, ch. 16.

goods were largely instrumental in the development of such basic plants as the Timna Copper Works . . . and several electric power stations.

The larger part of Israel's new merchant marine of some 50 ships of 450,000 tons deadweight was purchased under the Agreement.

. . . implementation of the Reparation Agreement has brought about close commercial ties between the two countries which will no doubt continue after the terms of the Agreement have been fulfilled. Israel industry now relies to some extent on German-made spare parts and semi-processed goods. Such commercial ties naturally bring in their wake a demand for diplomatic and cultural exchanges.

Personal restitution payments to Israelis have further strengthened commercial intercourse between the two countries. Many recipients of such payments used a part of them for purchasing West German products. . . . And the receipt of German Reparation goods was one of the factors which led to the steep rise in the living standards of the Israel man-in-the-street.[1]

Shinnar, who supervised the implementation of the Reparations Agreement as Head of the Israel Purchasing Mission in Cologne, proudly remarked: 'Some 80 per cent of the Agreement was accepted in shipments of capital goods of all kinds, and accordingly . . . were a visible, lasting constituent of the building-up of industry in Israel in those first years, so decisive for the economic consolidation of Israel.'[2]

Whether Israel's economy could have achieved one of the most impressive performances in the contemporary era without such an infusion of foreign aid is a matter of conjecture. And whether the moral standard of Israel would have been purer without German reparations is a matter of individual conscience. There can be no doubt, however, that the inflow of almost $5 billion to the end of 1965 markedly strengthened Israel's economic capacity to support her foreign policy decisions throughout the period 1953–65.[3]

The spillover benefits to Israel's *military capability*—as the underpinning to her security—are also unmistakable. The stimulus to economic growth also affected that large and important segment of the

---

[1] 'Review of Economic Conditions', *Bank Leumi Le-Israel*, no. 36–7, May 1962.

[2] Taped comments in 1962. Vogel, p. 88.

[3] According to the Federal German Finance Ministry, reparations payments to the end of 1966 comprised the following:

Federal Indemnity Law	DM 21,400 million
Federal Restitution Law	DM 2,750 million
Reparations Agreement	DM 3,450 million
General treaties with 12 German States	DM 1,000 million
Other payments (public service, etc.)	DM 2,700 million
Total	DM 31,300 million.

Of this approximately DM 19,500 million was allocated through the Federal Budget. Not all of these payments went to Israel or Israelis. The sum of $5 billion is an estimate. As cited in Vogel, p. 99. On the implementation of the Luxembourg Agreements see Balabkins, pp. 169–88, 256–69, and ch. 10, 11. See also Report on the delivery of goods under the Agreement by the Federal Minister of Economic Affairs, Bonn, March 1966, in Vogel, pp. 89–99.

Figure 5

FEEDBACK: GERMAN REPARATIONS*

Operational Environment	*Psychological Environment and Policy Derivatives*
External	*External*
SO Strengthened Israel's ties with West Germany and thereby facilitated Israel's later (1960 ff.) quest for association with 'Europe'	Perception of 'Israel as part of Europe' from late 1950s, with Germany as complementary (to France) path to 'Europe': policy derivative was goal of link with European Common Market, realized in part with Preferential Trade Agreement, 1964 (E–D)
B Created precedent for multiple ties to West Germany by easing psycho-political barriers to normal bilateral relations	Image of 'new' Germany as economic, political, and military support for Israel, both on Common Market issue and in conflict with Arab adversaries: notable policy derivatives were (secret) arms agreements (1959, 1960) and diplomatic relations (1965), as well as economic aid (post-1965) (M–S, P–D, E–D)
Internal	*Internal*
M Broadened and deepened material underpinning of military capability; also stimulated expansion of arms production industry	Sense of greater security arising from massive infusion of foreign aid—its contribution to Israel's self-reliance and to a firmer base for defence capability: policy derivatives were arms sales agreement of 1959 with Bonn to sustain and expand 'Rafael'— the Israel armament authority—and the arms agreement (1960) (M–S)
E Contributed critical input to economic growth in period 1953–65	Awareness of economic dependence upon annual infusion of unilateral transfers from Germany: policy derivative was attempt to perpetuate West German economic aid (Ben Gurion–Adenauer meeting 1960) and annual foreign aid agreements since 1965 (E–D)

* All feedback flowed from the combination of the strategic and tactical decisions on reparations; the tactical decision represents an integral second-level policy decision, a direct extension from the fundamental decision to accept reparations at all.

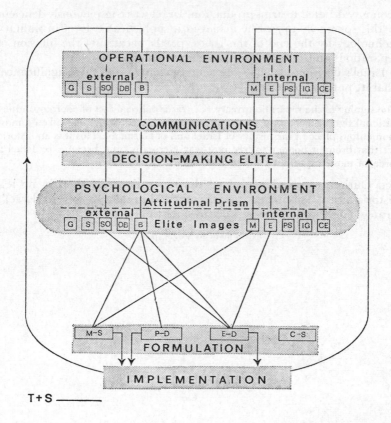

PS	Destabilized political structure	Intensification of personal and party
CE	(1957, 1959 crises over arms	resentments in leaders' images: policy
	relations); also made more	derivatives were internal only: (*a*) to
	rigid the exclusion of *Herut*	delay unification of *Mapai* with *Rafi*
	from role as Coalition partner	and *Ahdut Ha'avoda*: and (*b*) con-
		tinued treatment of *Herut* as perma-
		nent opposition party (to 1967)

economy devoted to arms production. Israel was conspicuously deficient in this sphere in 1953. She achieved a sophisticated level in military technology by the end of the 1960s, partly because of the infusion of reparations and related West German payments.

Israel's decision-makers were acutely conscious of their significance. Sharett put it succinctly:

The signing of the reparation treaty . . . was a political fact of enormous international significance, something quite unprecedented, which has taken a most momentous place in the history of Israel and of Germany. This was an historic act that brought honour to free post-war Germany, and became for Israel a force of most important constructive aid.[1]

Ben Gurion, as noted, perceived the reparations decisions in no less historic terms. This image was instrumental in shaping some of Israel's strategic decisions in the two decades that followed.

[1] Comment to Vogel, p. 55.

CHAPTER 4

Korean War and China

Several important decisions relating to East Asia and the inter-bloc struggle were made by Israel during the first half of the 1950s. Two were of the tactical type, in terms of a foreign policy system, and two were at the strategic level:

on 9 January 1950   Israel's Cabinet decided to accord *de jure* recognition to the People's Republic of China (PRC), which had been proclaimed in Peking the preceding October; (T_1)

on 2 July 1950   Israel's Cabinet decided to convey official support for UN resolutions and actions taken in response to the outbreak of the Korean War—and thereby abandoned the fundamental policy of non-identification; (S_1)

on 25 May 1954   the Ministerial Committee on Foreign Affairs and Defence decided against active pursuit of diplomatic relations with Peking until after the Geneva Conference on Indo-China; (T_{2a})

on 14 November 1954   the Government of Israel approved the dispatch of an official *trade* delegation to China; (T_{2b}) and

on 28 March 1955   Israel's Prime Minister–Foreign Minister decided to decline Peking's overtures for diplomatic relations at that time. (S_2)

There was also a plethora of related implementing decisions on the Korea/China issue.

The pattern of Israel's decisions on the Korean War and China differed from that on other foreign policy issues. The strategic decision on China (1955) was, firstly, *negative* in character. That, in turn, accounts for another atypical trait of a high-policy decision. Implementing decisions were stillborn. Moreover, the tactical decision on China (1950) preceded the strategic decision. And thirdly, the strategic decision on China was the outcome of a 'conflict' between the thrust of the preceding (1950) tactical and strategic decisions, both with intense Cold War overtones. Despite these differences and the substantial gap in time between them, they may be analysed as a *decision cluster*, both because they are objectively interrelated and because the principal decision-makers thus perceived them. Their importance lies not only in the issue itself. In symbol and substance the Korean War/China decisions mark the great divide in the policy orientation of the Jewish state: from July 1950 onwards non-alignment gradually gave way to the conscious quest for US patronage in the form of an American guarantee of Israel.

(A) OPERATIONAL ENVIRONMENT

Only three components of the environment were relevant to Israel's decisions on the Korea/China issue. One was the dynamics of the global system (G), notably the pressures flowing from the world organization and the inter-bloc struggle. Another was Israel's pre-eminent bilateral relationship, universally recognized by her decision-makers—'the American factor' (DB). The third was a domestic input, in the form of demands from the Left parties, *Mapam* and *Maki*, to establish normal relations with the People's Republic of China (CE). All three are evident in the setting for Israel's decisions on Korea, 1950–1. The internal component was marginally present in the decision to recognize the Peking regime, in 1950. And the US factor was striking in the environment for the 1954–5 negative decisions on diplomatic relations with the PRC. These may now be explored.

World politics became increasingly bipolarized during the months preceding Israel's tactical decision on China. The formation of NATO in April 1949 completed the process of bifurcation in Europe and symbolized the growing confrontation between the blocs. In the perspective of history, however, the decisive development of that year was the triumph of Communism in China after a protracted civil war. The proclamation of the People's Republic of China on 1 October 1949 not only caused a sense of irreparable 'loss' in the American psyche: it also meant a qualitative change in the global balance of power. And with that cataclysmic event came an intensification of the inter-bloc struggle, though not in the immediate, direct, and dramatic form produced by the outbreak of the Korean War.

During the autumn and, especially, in the first few days of 1950, the Left urged Israel's Government to recognize the Peking regime: the thrust of their case was Israel's need to maintain access to both camps, whose leaders, the USSR and the US, had contributed greatly to Israel's independence and her survival against powerful adversaries; and this could be achieved only by adherence to the policy of non-identification. The Government of Israel did not yield to internal pressure. As late as 4 January the Foreign Ministry spokesman responded thus to a *Mapam* journalist's pointed inquiry: 'This is not a burning issue'; and 'mutuality remains a basic principle in our policy'.[1] Yet a few days later the Cabinet decided in favour of recognition: domestic pressure from the Left, which held 23 of 120 parliamentary seats, was thereby satisfied. And there was no discernible opposition from other parties, except *Herut*. Finally, the *Mapam–Maki* advocacy coincided with the *Mapai*-dominated Government's commitment to non-identification, as embodied in its March 1949 'Basic Principles...'.[2] As Sharett stated it bluntly in the *Knesset*, Israel will 'in no case ... become identified with one of the great blocs in the world against the other'.[3]

The outbreak of war in Korea on 25 June 1950 was one of several crises between the two blocs from the onset of the Cold War. But it was unique in the extensive involvement of the United Nations and of the super powers, supporting their respective clients. Israel could remain aloof, non-identified, during the Berlin confrontation of 1948–9 and earlier inter-bloc conflicts. But the Korean War caused a major infusion of tension. The inter-bloc struggle became sharply focused on East Asia. And, for the first time since Israel's independence, the United States demanded that the Jewish state 'stand up and be counted'.[4] In short, the two salient external components, G and DB,

---

[1] *Al Ha-mishmar*, 5 Jan. 1950.

[2] The first foreign policy point read: 'Loyalty to the principles of the United Nations Charter and friendship with all freedom-loving states, and in particular with the United States and the Soviet Union.' *Divrei Ha-knesset*, i, 8 March 1949, p. 55.

[3] Ibid., i, 15 June 1949, pp. 718–19. The policy of *ee-hizdahut* had crystallized as early as a half-year *preceding* Israel's independence. This is evident in some of Ben Gurion's pronouncements:

(a) 'We have no basis for joining one of the sides; they are not fighting yet and they will make peace tomorrow. ...'

(b) 'The Jewish State will not come into being—I doubt if it will be created—if it identifies *a priori* with one of the sides.'
(To the *Mapai* Central Committee on 3 December 1947. Israel Labour Party Archives.)

(c) 'I don't know why the Jewish Nation should not have the ambition to create an organization with other small nations, which should not be involved in the conflict between the large bears, *a bloc for peace*.'
(To the Zionist Executive in Jerusalem on 7 April 1948. Israel Labour Party Archives. Emphasis added.)

Yet Ben Gurion was not oblivious of the possibility of pressures which would lead to Israel's alignment:

(d) 'In a year or two we may take our place in the world, and if necessary we will change it [the policy of *ee-hizdahut*]. ...' It is evident from the context that he meant a pro-US orientation.
(To the *Mapai* Central Committee on 3 December 1947.)

[4] Evidence of US pressure will be indicated in sections (c) and (D) below.

contributed powerful inputs into Israel's Foreign Policy System, to which her decision-makers could not remain indifferent. Any response was fraught with grave consequences for Israel's basic global orientation, with probable spillover effects on the conflict with her neighbours, on her military and economic capability, and on the nation's morale.

Within Israel the significance of the Korean War was recognized at once. Decision-makers sensed that this was the great divide in Israel's foreign policy, a point which will be elaborated later. And competing élites marshalled their forces to advocate a 'correct' line for the Government to pursue. On the Left, *Mapam* and *Maki* adopted a virtually identical position. The Korean War began as a civil war, they argued, a revolt of an oppressed people against a corrupt and reactionary regime. The Government was urged to reject the Security Council's interpretation of events which charged North Korea with a 'breach of the peace'. Israel must understand—and aid—other peoples' struggles for freedom. The *Mapam* organ went further, calling upon Israel not to forget Soviet assistance in the past. Moreover, the Security Council's decisions were termed not binding because Communist China was absent from the proceedings. Support for the UN would also cause turmoil and animosity for Jewish communities in the two camps. In any event, the Security Council had not helped Israel in her hour of need. And finally, Israel must not show herself as less independent than Egypt, which had not approved the Council's resolutions. It was a formidable set of 'theses', thrust into the debate on the origins of the war and on the proper policy response for Israel.[1]

All other parties but one advocated precisely the contrary. The General Zionists accepted the Security Council findings that North Korea had started the war; and they insisted upon Israel's approval of its resolutions—because she wanted aggression anywhere to be crushed, because the enhancement of UN prestige was in her interests, and because world Jewry was allegedly in favour of the United Nations stand.[2] *Mizrahi*, too, termed North Korea an aggressor because she tried to solve the dispute by force rather than by mediation. Morally, it asserted, Israel could not refrain from raising her voice against aggression. And, while she may be neutral between the blocs, Israel's duty is to support and strengthen the United Nations, especially because Egypt refused to do so. In short, Israel's vital interests required this.[3] The Progressives concurred in the UN analysis of the origins of the war

---

[1] *Al Ha-mishmar*, 2, 3, 5, and 6 July 1950. The *Maki* reaction was expressed in *Kol Ha'am*, 2, 3, 12, 14, and 17 July 1950.

[2] *Ha-boker*, 2 and 3 July 1950.

[3] *Ha-tzofeh*, 30 June, 3, 7, and 8 July 1950. Parenthetically, that religious party advocated Israel's use of an unusual opportunity to fortify her position, by stimulating mass immigration of Jews from all over the world, regardless of cost, and by stockpiling foodstuffs and raw materials. Ibid., 13 July 1950.

and urged Israel's 'moral support' of the world organization, for the Council was defending the rights of all peoples to freedom and independence, 'humanity's supreme possession'.[1] Only *Herut* dissented. While it accepted the repudiation of North Korea's actions, the nationalist Right disparaged the UN as a dubious guardian of peace and the rights of small states; and it urged an Israeli policy of caution towards international intervention in the Korean conflict.[2]

All of these competing élite attitudes and advocacies were elaborated in a major *Knesset* debate on 4 July 1950, soon after the Government announced its support for initial UN resolutions and actions in response to the outbreak of war. *Mapam* formalized its opposition with a motion of no-confidence; it was defeated by 70 to 19; *Herut* moved another motion, critical of the 'unconditional UN-orientation of the Government's policy'; it, too, was defeated, by 68 to 20, with 8 abstentions.[3]

As to the meaning of Israel's decision, *Mapam* and *Maki* had no doubts: the Government had abandoned non-identification and had aligned Israel completely with the Western bloc, the 'Imperialists', the 'warmongers'. The General Zionists, *Mizrahi*, and the Progressives saw no contradiction between support for the UN resolutions and aloofness from the inter-bloc struggle. And *Herut* had always opposed non-identification as a pillar of Israel's foreign policy. The Establishment-*Mapai* view, as expressed by the *Histadrut* daily, was in terms of the formula: 'Israel decided in favour of non-identification with either bloc but not for non-identification with the UN.'[4]

Competing élite advocacies followed a consistent pattern on subsequent implementing decisions. The Left parties opposed the offer of medical aid to South Korea in August 1950; the Government's support of the General Assembly resolution authorizing UN forces to cross the 38th parallel in October 1950 (*Mapam* called for abstention); the branding of the People's Republic of China as an aggressor, in February 1951; and the imposition of an embargo on trade in strategic goods with China, in May 1951. The Centre and Right parties supported the Government's pro-UN/US acts, some actively, others by silent acquiescence.

One further example will suffice. During the *Knesset* foreign policy debate in late January 1951, a *Maki* motion, harshly critical of Government policy, received 2 votes. A *Mapam* motion advocating a peaceful settlement via negotiations, including Moscow and Peking, was defeated 74 to 17. *Herut* called for an alliance with the United States. And the General Zionists acknowledged, approvingly, Israel's policy

---

[1] *Ha'aretz*, 3 and 5 July 1950.

[2] *Herut*, 3, 5, and 6 July 1950.

[3] For the debate and the motions of no-confidence, including Sharett's statement explaining the Government's decision, see *Divrei Ha-knesset*, vi, 1950, pp. 2057–87.

[4] *Davar*, 3 July 1950.

on Korea as a departure from non-identification.[1] In short, the articulation of CE views was vocal and, in the case of the Left, persistently strident. However, it was the least important environmental element impinging upon Israel's Korea decisions: the external variables, G and DB, were considered far more compelling by the decision-makers, as will be indicated.

When Chinese feelers about diplomatic relations were put out at the end of 1953 the global system (G) was somewhat more tranquil. The long and bloody Korean War had ended in stalemate. The first Indo-China War was still raging but it too had been terminated by the time Peking invited Israel to send a Goodwill Mission to China, in September 1954. Stalin was dead, and his successors had embarked upon a policy of international and domestic relaxation. The United States, with Foster Dulles at the helm of foreign policy, was engaged in feverish 'pactomania'. Yet the Cold War had become stabilized, and the inter-bloc struggle was beginning to move from rigid or tight bipolarity to a lesser form of bipolar system. China was still a pariah state—in the United Nations and elsewhere—but several non-Communist states which had recognized the PRC in 1950 now moved to the stage of diplomatic relations (the UK, Norway, the Netherlands, in June, October, and November 1954, respectively, and Afghanistan in January 1955). Thus the global system in 1954-5 was decidedly less hostile to ties with Peking.

Israel's relations with the United States (DB), always complex, were enmeshed in multiple negotiations and concerns. The Jordan Waters controversy was, throughout that period, under active mediation by President Eisenhower's personal representative, Eric Johnston. As always, there were discussions about additional economic aid. The possibility of military assistance was being seriously probed, especially in the early months of 1955, when the strategic decision on China was approaching a climax. Washington had revealed a tough, demanding posture in the voting of friends and allies in the UN over China's representation in September 1954. American public opinion, including middle-class American Jewry, was sharply antagonistic to Communist China in the aftermath of the Korean War. And Israel's high-policy élite, prodded by the General Zionists, then an active constituent of the Sharett-led Coalition Government, and some *Mapai* ministers, were actively seeking a defence alliance with the United States.

---

[1] *Divrei Ha-knesset*, viii, 23-4, 30 Jan. 1951, pp. 848-69, 875-85, 914-38. No less than 34 MKs participated in the three-day debate, including *Maki*'s Mikunis and Wilner, *Mapam*'s Ben Aharon, Ya'ari, Riftin, and Sneh, the General Zionists' Bernstein and Serlin, and *Herut*'s Bader and Landau. For the Left advocacy during the crucial summer and autumn of 1950 see, in addition to pp. 112-15 above, *Al Ha-mishmar*, 3, 4, and 6 Aug., and 8 Oct. 1950; and *Kol Ha'am*, 13 Aug. and 6 Oct. 1950; for the Right and Centre views see *Ha-tzofeh*, 6 and 24 Oct. 1950; and *Ha'aretz*, 24 October 1950.

The significance of that relationship was accentuated by the deterioration in Israel's relations with the other super power. Diplomatic ties had been severed by Moscow in February 1953—following a bomb blast in the compound of its Tel Aviv embassy. And, while they were resumed five months later, the Soviet Union had begun to court the Near East Arab states, notably Egypt and Syria. Non-alienation of the US, in that context, became a high Israeli foreign policy value. Indeed, the 'American factor' was a constant in the decision-process, ultimately creating the psychological environment for the negative strategic decision.

Within Israel there was spasmodic advocacy of relations with the People's Republic of China. After the initial flurry of January 1950, at the time of recognition, the issue was raised again, in the form of *Knesset* questions, in July and August 1954. But it was not until the eve of departure of Israel's Mission to China and, especially, after its return, that demands from the Left mounted. *Maki*, supported by *Mapam*, moved a motion on 12 January 1955 urging that a discussion of relations with China be placed on the *Knesset* agenda. Sharett chided them, noting that Israel's desire for 'friendly relations' was clearly indicated: 'Our aim is friendship with People's China.' But he insisted that any further steps would have to await the report of the Israeli delegation. The proposal was defeated.[1] At the end of February *Mapam*'s Ya'acov Riftin attacked Israel's UN policy: 'This line can rightly be viewed by the Asian peoples as pro-Imperialistic; it would be an error not to see this as the disturbing factor in the opening of relations with other Asian countries . . .'; the context was his demand for an Israeli legation in Peking.[2] *Maki* leader Shmuel Mikunis was even more scathing:

Israel's vote against China's admission to the UN (September 1954), the non-establishment of diplomatic relations with that country, despite the stand of the head of Israel's delegation to China . . . , pointing out the many possibilities of trade with her—and against this the haste of the Government to recognize Laos and Cambodia, which are ruled by American agents, but not the Democratic Republic of [North] Vietnam—add all this together and you get a foreign policy picture of complete dependence on Washington.[3]

Another attack which cut close to the bone was delivered by Hanan Rubin of *Mapam* on 28 March 1955, when the strategic decision was about to be made:

Let the Director of Information explain why diplomatic relations have not been opened with China. Let him explain to the Cabinet members that every fifth person in the world is a Chinese. I ask myself—what's happening here? . . . Occasionally we are told, 'Hold on; there was a delegation; in the course of

[1] *Divrei Ha-knesset*, xvii, 12 Jan. 1955, p. 563.
[2] Ibid., 28 Feb. 1955, p. 947.   [3] Ibid., 1 March 1955, p. 966.

time we shall advance.' But how long will you wait? Even England has diplomatic relations with China, as do other countries. What is the reason that we have not? Of course there is an answer to that question—you have been forbidden to do so. Our Ambassador in Washington, or someone else, was told, 'Don't do it' . . .[1]

From the other extreme of the political spectrum, Arye Altman or *Herut* warned of the dangers along the road to Peking: 'Why did we hurry to recognize China before many other free countries? If we want good relations with the United States we should know that in America 79 per cent object to recognition of China. Does this contribute to an improvement of our relations? . . .'[2]

In their contrasting advocacies both Left and Right shared an awareness of the pre-eminent component in the setting for Israel's strategic decision on China—'the American factor'. They differed only in their attitude: the Left wished to ignore—or reject—that constraint; the Right urged that Israel yield to it. The Government, more correctly Sharett, yielded to his perception of 'the American factor'. But while he was aware of these advocacies from Left and Right, they were, at most, marginal in the shaping of the decision. To the determining images of the key decision-makers on the Korea/China issue we may now turn.

(B) DECISION-MAKERS AND THEIR IMAGES

The composition of Israel's Government was identical for the two basic East Asia decisions of 1950—the recognition of Communist China (9 January) and support for initial UN reaction to the Korean War (2 July). *Mapai* dominated the Coalition, as always, with 8 of the 12 Ministers:

Mapai

Ben Gurion	Prime Minister and Defence
Joseph	Supply and Rationing, and Agriculture
Kaplan	Finance, and Commerce and Industry
Meir	Labour
Remez	Communications and Transport, and Posts
Sharett	Foreign Affairs
Shazar	Education and Culture
Shitreet (*Sepharadim*)	Police

Progressives

Rosen	Justice

Religious Front
  Agudat Yisrael

Levin	Social Welfare

---
[1] Ibid., xviii, 28 March 1955, p. 1326.   [2] Ibid., 28 March 1955, p. 1324.

Ha-po'el Ha-mizrahi
Shapira   Immigration, Interior, and Health
Mizrahi
Maimon   Religious Affairs

It was the same Cabinet which had decided to establish the seat of government in Israel's 'Eternal Capital'. But whereas all ministers were involved in the Jerusalem issue, through emotional, religious, historic, and/or national associations, China was remote and esoteric. It fell within the exclusive realm of foreign affairs and, as such, was entrusted to the duumvirate in foreign policy during the early years, Prime Minister Ben Gurion and Foreign Minister Sharett. The Korean War evoked more interest because of its global implications and potential spillover to the Arab–Israel conflict. But in that decision, too, Cabinet members looked to the PM–DM and the FM for guidance.

Insight into the relevant images of these pre-eminent decision-makers is limited by the paucity of hard data. There are no recorded statements, speeches, or interviews, before the *Knesset*, a party group, or the press at the time Israel decided to recognize the People's Republic of China. As for the Korean War, Sharett delivered an important address to Parliament soon after the decision. For the rest, perceptions must be reconstructed from secondary sources, especially Foreign Ministry officials, and Ben Gurion's oral memoirs.

No less than eight components may be discerned. The reality of Communist control over the Chinese mainland was central to their image. The principle that recognition did not connote approval of a political system or its prevailing ideology was another vital component. The absence of any sense of obligation to Taiwan for past behaviour was a third element. The 'national interest' calculus that recognition of the actual governing authority in China would strengthen Israel's claim to universal acceptance was not lost on some. The legitimacy acquired by UK and Scandinavian recognition of Peking made it easier to take that decision.

The problem of recognition was also perceived in terms of Israel's prevailing global policy of non-alignment: to recognize the People's Republic of China, especially in the face of US displeasure, would conform with, and strengthen, Israel's posture of *ee-hizdahut* or non-identification with the competing blocs. It would also satisfy the vocal demands of the second largest organized political force in Israel at the time, the Left-socialist *Mapam*. And finally, there was a sense of obligation to the Jewish community of China, refugees from the Bolshevik Revolution and, later, from Nazi terror in Europe.[1] All but the last

[1] At the end of the Second World War there were approximately 22,000 'Western' Jews in China, and by September 1948 about 10,000, mostly in Shanghai, Harbin and Tientsin. About 8,000 migrated to Israel from the autumn of 1948 to early 1950. Yuval interview, 1972.

two image-components are evident in the reflections, many years later, of decision-makers in the Korea/China issue.

Ben Gurion replied to the question, 'Why did Israel recognize the People's Republic of China in 1950?': 'For the simple reason, "why not". Also, you could not consider Formosa as China. There are 600 million people in China. It would be an insult.'[1] On another occasion he added: 'The Government in Peking was in control. We had to recognize it as a fact, as an important fact. China deserved her rightful place in the world.'[2]

Walter Eytan, who knew Sharett's mind well as the first Director-General of the Foreign Ministry, referred in his published account to three image-components: 'Quite apart from the fact that she had no special cause for gratitude to the Formosa regime, Israel, in her own recognition policy, made a practice of acknowledging established fact. . . . There could be no doubt that the Government of the People's Republic was the effective government of continental China. [Moreover,] the domestic political system of China was none of Israel's concern, any more than it was that of Switzerland or Sweden.'[3]

Abba Eban, who was then Permanent Representative to the UN, with exceptional influence on Israeli foreign policy decisions, dismissed the 'no obligation to Formosa' theme: 'Formosa had performed a valuable service in the debate on Israel's application for UN membership, in both March and May 1949; there was nothing in her behaviour to warrant our displeasure or dissatisfaction.' (He might have added that, on 2 March 1949, the Nationalist Government accorded recognition to the State of Israel.)[4] At the same time, Eban concurred with the 'recognition of reality' element and cited two other components of Sharett's image: 'First, we were more attracted to the pragmatic, liberal view of the Scandinavians and the British than to the rigid animosity of the Americans at the onset of the McCarthy era; secondly, we were conscious of the impression of our constantly being with the United States—and this was an opportunity to establish the sense of our voting as our interests dictated; and thirdly, the Peking regime was a fact which could not be ignored by the United Nations or the world.'[5]

There is, too, the recollection of Ya'acov Shimoni, who was most directly concerned with China at the time, as Head of the newly-established Asian Division in the Foreign Office. He emphasized the issue of principle in Sharett's image—along with 'national interest' as a secondary component:

---

[1] Ben Gurion interview, 1966.   [2] Ben Gurion interview, 1971.

[3] Eytan, pp. 188–9.

[4] Cable from Wu Te-shen, Nationalist China's Minister of Foreign Affairs, in Canton, to Shertok (Sharett). Made available to the author. It was in reply to a cable from Sharett dated 27 February 1949.

[5] Eban interview, 1965. These remarks were directed to the issues of Israel's recognition *and* China's representation in the UN.

As far as I can remember—and this was a decision which I initiated and laid before Sharett—the reasons of principle given *were* the real reasons: the Communist Government of China was undoubtedly in full control, and we acted on the assumption of principle that recognition had nothing to do with approving political or ideological systems of government, but had to be given when a government proved to be in control of a state. The fact that we were still struggling at that time for the recognition of Israel by many countries, and were using the same arguments of principle, probably made it appear doubly necessary that we ourselves should implement a principle that we so constantly held up to others for our own sake.[1]

Shimoni wrote on another occasion: 'Beyond the application of this principle ... Israel was obviously hoping for the development, in a not too distant future, of close and friendly relations with the great Chinese people. Certainly China's potential as a major power was fully appreciated by some at least of Israel's leaders, including David Ben Gurion.'[2] Another knowledgeable civil servant, Ze'ev Sharef, Secretary to the Government during the early years, remarked: 'Ben Gurion always looked at China as one of the super powers. Privately, from time to time, in the early days, he made reference to it.'[3] Yet there is no evidence to indicate that BG or Sharett was moved to act in 1950 by a carefully considered image of China's long-term significance for global and/or Middle East international politics.

Stated in terms of the psychological environment for the recognition issue, Israel's principal decision-makers perceived the following components in order of importance:

B   the reality of political power in Mainland China and the absence of obligation to Taiwan;

G_1 the principle of recognition and its implications for Israel's acceptance by states which had not yet recognized her;

G_2 the Israeli policy of non-alignment and the internal pressure to
CE   maintain its credibility; and

IG   the need to safeguard the interests of China's Jewish community.

The decision to recognize the Peking regime was a Government of Israel initiative.[4] There was, therefore, ample time, in fact more than three months, for images of China to gestate. By contrast, perceptions of the Korea crisis had to crystallize within days, in order to shape the *wholly reactive* decision to support the initial UN response to the outbreak of war. That time factor, in turn, led to a narrowing of the perceptual focus among Israel's decision-makers.

Two components dominated the psychological environment of Ben Gurion, Sharett, and members of the Foreign Service Technical

[1] Shimoni letter, 1966.   [2] Shimoni 1972.   [3] Sharef interview, 1971.
[4] It need not have responded to the PRC's request for recognition; most states did not do so at that time.

Élite involved in the strategic decision of 2 July 1950. These were succinctly summarized by Shimoni:[1]

'(a) the wish to support the UN, especially when it was acting to defend a small country against aggression from the outside; [G]

'(b) the need to go along with vital policies of the USA.' [DB]

All concurred with this assessment.

Ben Gurion emphasized the second element, in a direct—and unhesitating—reply to the question, 'What were the considerations leading to Israel's decision on 2 July 1950 to support the UN action in Korea?': 'Sympathy for America; it was merely for the sake of America. I knew that Truman wanted peace.'[2] Yet the UN dimension was also present in his thinking, as is evident from his unusual proposal to dispatch a *Tzahal* contingent to Korea as part of the UN Command.[3]

Sharett cited two reasons, in his explanatory *Knesset* speech soon after the Cabinet decision:

The Government of Israel . . . as a member of the United Nations which has undertaken faithfully to abide by the Charter, and which has based its foreign policy, in the first place, on support of the UN, is unable to agree that the United Nations' right to exist and capacity to act can be stultified by the failure of any one nation actively to participate in its work. . . .
Moreover, as a small nation, and more especially as a nation which in the past was itself a victim of aggression, and which is likely any day again to be attacked . . . Israel cannot under any circumstances willingly reconcile itself to the paralysis of the UN and to the surrender by the UN of its right to intervene for the restoration of international security and the defence of peace. . . . Just as Israel will not waive its rights and claims *vis-à-vis* the international organization, so it cannot escape its obligations towards it. . . .[4]

There is also evidence of Sharett's (and others') perception of US pressure: it was forcefully reported to the Foreign Office by Israeli diplomats in New York and in Washington. 'Once it began,' recalled R. Kidron, then with Israel's UN Mission, 'American pressure was intense, with us as with everybody. They approached me with unmistakable expectation that Israel would toe the line.'[5] Moreover, Sharett appreciated the political implications of Israel's decision. He reiterated, in the same *Knesset* speech, the 'principle of non-identification', but he juxtaposed a higher obligation: 'this principle . . . cannot be perverted into repudiation of world peace, nor can it serve as a pretext for running away from responsibility towards the UN. . . .' The shift from non-identification was subtly hinted at: 'Israel is aligned

---

[1] Shimoni letter, 1966.   [2] Ben Gurion interview, 1966.
[3] To be elaborated in sections (c) and (D) below.
[4] Foreign Minister's Statement to the *Knesset* on 4 July 1950. *Divrei Ha-knesset*, vi, pp. 2057–8. An English translation, from which the following extracts are taken. was issued the same day by the Government Press Office, Tel Aviv.
[5] Kidron interview, 1966.

with those nations who see in the UN a first line of defence against a world catastrophe. . . .'

Eban confirmed 'the American factor' in Israeli decision-makers' thinking: 'it [US lobbying for Israeli support] was not easy to ignore or resist'. They were also conscious, he remarked, of the strong backing of the world community, as expressed in the overwhelming approval of UN action in the Security Council and, later, in the General Assembly. Thirdly, there was an Israeli predisposition to favour intervention by the Great Powers and, even more, by the UN to protect weak states at the mercy of aggressors. Israel, it was perceived, might again be in that position: 'We saw everything at that time in terms of 1948: North Korea's invasion of the South was equated with Arab aggression against Israel.' In short, there was concern lest UN inaction in Korea be a precedent for future inaction in the Middle East.[1]

According to Eytan, Sharett (and senior officials in the Foreign Ministry) perceived *at that time*, accurately but with regret, the strategic significance of Israel's initial decision on the Korean War: 'He knew it was the end of his policy of non-identification—but he knew it was the world in which he lived.' Furthermore, 'we had lived with the illusion that Israel could retain non-identification, but then came the Korean War. The issue was clear. People said, "it is a pity", but we had no alternative.'[2]

The composition of Israel's Government had changed drastically by 1954. Ben Gurion had 'retired'—temporarily—to his Negev *kibbutz*, Sde Boker. Sharett became Prime Minister in January of that year, as well as retaining the Foreign Ministry. And Pinhas Lavon succeeded to the crucial Defence portfolio. In structural terms the basic change was the presence of the conservative General Zionists in the Coalition. (They had joined the Fourth Government in December 1952 and continued in the Sharett Cabinet.) In September 1954, when China's interest in diplomatic relations with Israel was publicly announced by Chou En-lai, the Israeli Government comprised four parties; *Mapai* retained its majority with 9 of the 16 ministers:

Mapai

Moshe Sharett	Prime Minister and Foreign Affairs
Zalman Aranne	Without Portfolio
Ben-Zion Dinur	Education and Culture
Levi Eshkol	Finance
Dov Joseph	Development
Pinhas Lavon	Defence
Golda Meir	Labour
Peretz Naftali	Agriculture
Behor Shalom Shitreet	Police

[1] Eban interview, 1965.   [2] Eytan interview, 1971.

General Zionists

Peretz Bernstein	Commerce and Industry
Yisrael Rokah	Interior
Yoseph Saphir	Communications and Transport
Yoseph Serlin	Health

National Religious Party

Yoseph Burg	Posts
Moshe Shapira	Religious Affairs, and Social Welfare

Progressives

Pinhas Rosen	Justice

The duumvirate in foreign affairs (Ben Gurion and Sharett) was no longer in force. Sharett's primacy in this field was recognized, but his lesser stature as Prime Minister permitted a more active role in discussion and decision by *interested* colleagues. Notable among them were Joseph, Lavon, and Aranne for *Mapai*, Bernstein and Saphir for the General Zionists, and the Progressives' Rosen. In an issue with Cold War implications, the pronounced pro-American outlook of Israel's most conservative Cabinet in her entire history would—and did— assert itself.

Sharett was undoubtedly the principal decision-maker on the issue of relations with Peking. Yet there is little hard evidence about his image of China in 1954–5. His occasional remarks to the *Knesset* were either laconic or diplomatically evasive. 'We have not forgotten that Peking exists', he said on 8 March 1954, in the course of a Foreign Ministry budget debate.[1] Replying to a leftist Motion for the Agenda in mid-July 1954, he chided his critics: 'The fact of the existence of People's China, her importance in Asia, even the possibility of trading with her, has not escaped the Israeli Foreign Office.'[2] 'The Government of Israel assumes that there will be progress in this direction at the appropriate time', he declared the following month, in reply to a question by *Maki*'s Meir Wilner, whether Israel was prepared to take active steps towards diplomatic relations. 'I can elaborate no further...: [it will be discussed] at the appropriate time.'[3]

Many who worked closely with Sharett during that period affirmed that he favoured formal ties with Communist China—among them Eytan, David Hacohen (one of the principal figures in tactical and strategic decisions 2, as Israel's Minister to Burma), Daniel Lewin (Head of the Foreign Ministry's Asian Department), and Ze'ev Shek (his Political Secretary).[4]

Yet Sharett's image of China was one of insensitivity to her global importance. He was neither hostile nor sympathetic—but remote. It

---

[1] *Divrei Ha-knesset*, xv, 8 March 1954, p. 1083. This was in reply to comments by *Mapam* MK Ya'acov Riftin.   [2] Ibid., xvi, 14 July 1954, p. 2164.
[3] Ibid., xvi, 10 Aug. 1954, p. 2361.   [4] Interviews in Israel, 1966 and 1971.

was not that he was oblivious of *Asia*. Indeed, more than a year before independence Sharett had declared:

The next item and the principal one is Asia. . . . We are facing a wall there; they see us as a sword the West is thrusting into the East. There is a natural emotional tendency to identify with the Arab Movement. There will be need of a great effort which may not succeed, but which may blaze a path to the hearts of many people. . . . Our starting point is that we exist in Asia, we are part of it, part of the renewed Asia and part of ancient Asia, whether we like it or not.[1]

His focus, however, was on India and her National Movement, not on China. This is illuminated by Hacohen's vivid recollection of a lengthy discussion with Sharett in Jerusalem late into the night in September 1954. He had emphasized the far greater importance to Israel of China than India in political, economic, and diplomatic terms. Sharett, like many Israeli leaders, long mesmerized by the Gandhi–Nehru–Indian National Movement symbols, turned to his lifelong friend: 'David, you have revolutionized my thinking about Asia; I never saw China in this light before.'[2]

More generally, for Sharett as for the entire Israeli high policy élite, China was peripheral to a Euro-America-centred world view. By contrast, he was acutely conscious of the DB variable in the equation; that is, of the possible impact on Israel's relations with the United States, the vital source of economic assistance, diplomatic support—and, it was to be hoped, arms. In his perception no foreign policy step that could undermine America's patron role should be undertaken by Israel.

That bifocal image is evident in Sharett's speeches—to the *Knesset* on 4 July 1950, announcing Israel's initial decision on the Korean War, as noted, and in his increasingly pro-Western (US) statements to the UN General Assembly during the autumn and winter of 1950–1. It is no less apparent in his behaviour. He never displayed a sense of urgency about relations with Peking. And he explicitly sought Washington's approval or, at least, acquiescence, in his proposed Israel–China ties by an approach through Israel's Ambassador to the US.[3]

The only other strand in Sharett's perception of China is the persistent pressure from *Mapam* and *Maki* to establish relations with the second Communist Great Power (CE). But apart from a pinprick role, through frequent questions in the *Knesset*, that domestic environmental

[1] To the Jewish Agency Executive, 18 March 1947. Zionist Archives, File S25 1621.

[2] Hacohen interview, 1971. Ben Gurion, who attached great importance to China in the 1960s, was indifferent to both East and South Asia on the eve of Israel's independence. '. . . When we say the whole world it is an exaggeration', he told the Zionist Executive on 6 April 1948; 'we never think of India or China or similar countries, but rather about the countries in which Jews have lived or are living.' Zionist Archives, File S5 322.

[3] These points will be elaborated in the following section.

variable did not influence Sharett's thought or action, unlike its role in the decision to recognize Peking, when the Left was a much stronger force in Israeli politics. In short, his behaviour in 1954–5 was dominated by one image-component, relations with the United States (DB). That concern with 'the American factor' was not unnatural, for Washington's capacity to vent anger and to retaliate was known: it had been felt in October 1953, when US economic aid was cut off for ten days to compel Israel's suspension of the Huleh reclamation project in the Demilitarized Zone bordering on Syria.

Sharett's US orientation was strengthened by his most striking personality trait—caution, especially in the face of a venture into the unknown.[1] This was emphasized in the form of a nuance revelation about another aspect of Israel's East Asia policy. 'Sharett was personally rather hesitant [about China]', wrote a knowledgeable Foreign Ministry official. 'I recall, for example, that I had a difficult time persuading him that we should establish relations with Japan, as he still regarded [the Japanese] as Fascist war criminals on the same line as Germany: if memory serves me right, we got BG's approval for relations with Japan while Sharett was on vacation.'[2]

Among Sharett's colleagues the perceptual imbalance between the United States and China was even more glaring. The four General Zionist ministers were programmatically committed to a policy of alignment with 'the free world' and, especially, with the United States. China was not only geographically and psychologically remote; it was also Communist. The religious party ministers normally followed *Mapai*'s lead and, in any event, felt no less an ideological affinity with America. And the normally active Rosen and Joseph seem to have been uninvolved, judging by their indifferent recollection of the China issue in Cabinet discussions.[3]

Among the *Mapai* ministers the two most vigorous participants were Lavon and Aranne. Their general view, shared passively or actively by many colleagues, was, in effect: the US was vital to Israel's survival and progress; and it would be irresponsible to yield to Hacohen's pressure on something so remote as China. More specifically, their image was shaped by developments at the turn of 1954–5: Washington's courting of Nasser; the coming to fruition of the Baghdad Pact; delicate negotiations on US arms aid; and the Eric Johnston Jordan Water Plan. With that perception, Lavon and Aranne strenuously urged Sharett *not* to proceed along the path to diplomatic relations with Peking.

The only person who could have effectively countered the 'American lobby' in the Government was Ben Gurion. He was in the Negev from December 1953 until February 1955; and, on several occasions, he

---

[1] For an analysis of Sharett's personality see Brecher, pp. 247–9, 253–7.
[2] A private communication to the author.
[3] Rosen and Joseph interviews, 1971.

asserted that he had *not* been consulted by *anyone* on the China issue during his 'retirement'. BG returned to the Cabinet on 21 February 1955 as Defence Minister—the only change in the high policy élite for the strategic decision on China. Yet, ironically, he claimed that, as a member of the Government, he remained oblivious of the issue of diplomatic relations with Peking.[1] Given the extraordinarily narrow—single-component (DB)—image of that issue, the decision was not surprising.

(c) DECISION PROCESS

(d) IMPLEMENTATION[2]

The initial stimulus to Israel's first major decision on China was the proclamation of the PRC on 1 October 1949 and its request for recognition from all states. The Soviet bloc responded at once. Others, well-disposed or committed to the principle of recognizing reality, waited for the dust to settle. Burma recognized the new regime on 16 December. India followed two weeks later. And several other non-Communist countries, notably the United Kingdom and Norway, did so in the first days of 1950. It was the behaviour of London and Oslo which served as the second decisive input for Israel's tactical decision to recognize Communist China. In a larger framework this flowed from the strategic decision at the very birth of Israel to pursue a policy of *ee-hizdahut*, non-identification, with the two power blocs.[3]

The tactical decision was formalized at a Cabinet meeting on 9 January 1950. Preceding discussion followed a normal step-by-step ascent along the ladder of authority. Recognition of Peking was recommended by the Head of the Foreign Office's newly-formed Asian Department, Ya'acov Shimoni. The Director-General, Eytan, approved the step. And Sharett concurred. The Foreign Minister presented the proposal to Cabinet after consultation with Prime Minister Ben Gurion. There was no open dissent—despite criticism by the US Government. 'They were angry with us and made their displeasure known', recalled BG; it was done through normal diplomatic channels.[4]

Israel's decision was implemented by a cable from Sharett to Chou En-lai the same day:[5]

I have the honour to inform Your Excellency that the Government of Israel

[1] Ben Gurion interviews, 1966, 1971.

[2] The character of the Korea/China decision cluster, as noted in the introduction, justifies the fusion of these two facets of foreign policy analysis for this issue.

[3] On Israel's non-identification policy see Brecher, pp. 39–41, 270 ff., 561–2.

[4] Ben Gurion interview, 1971. See also Shimoni 1972.

[5] That day, too, Sharett conveyed to the Prime Minister of Indonesia, Dr. Mohammed Hatta, Israel's *de jure* recognition of the new state in South-East Asia. The English text was issued on 9 January by the Foreign Press Division of the State of Israel Information Services, Tel Aviv.

has decided to recognize your Government as the *de jure* Government of China. I gladly avail myself of this opportunity to express to Your Excellency my Government's sincere hopes for the prosperity of the Chinese nation, as well as my own best wishes for Your Excellency's personal well-being.

China's Prime Minister–Foreign Minister responded warmly, concluding with friendly greetings and wishes for the prosperity of Israel.[1] 'The wording of the Chinese reply', as Eytan observed, 'was appropriate in every sense to the recognition statement. In our telegram we did not mention diplomatic relations and therefore they did not mention them in their reply.'[2]

Israel was among the earliest, in fact, the seventh, of all non-Communist states to recognize the PRC. But she was hesitant about normalizing relations. Eytan's explanation was twofold: '. . . Israel always thought of establishing an embassy at Peking as soon as budgetary provision could be made for it'; and 'there were other places of greater interest to us—states with large Jewish communities, etc.'[3]

The Foreign Ministry official in direct charge of Asian affairs ascribed 'weighty political reasons' to Israel's reluctance to establish full diplomatic relations with Peking: 'The mere recognition of Communist China had, as foreseen, displeased the US; the establishment of full relations might well be considered as an unfriendly act, and thus have dire consequences. Moreover, in mid-1950 China became involved in the Korean War. . . . It was inconceivable that Israel should provoke most of the world by establishing relations with China at that juncture.'[4]

The first cautious step towards some form of relations was taken three weeks after recognition. On 31 January 1950 the Foreign Ministry instructed Israel's Minister in Moscow, Mordekhai Namir, to suggest to the PRC Embassy that Israel's Embassy there be the link between Israel and China, 'as we do not intend to open a legation in Peking'. Namir urged that he wait a little longer—for the Chinese Ambassador to the USSR to inform him of his appointment, in accordance with protocol—but to take the initiative if no such notification reached him. Eytan, the Director-General, agreed: 'There is no reason to be hasty . . . you will be able to wait . . . with your approach to the Ambassador.' There was still no contact in April, reported Namir; and the Chinese Military Attaché, who had been invited to an Israeli reception, did not attend.

Suddenly on 20 June 1950, the Chinese Chargé d'Affaires in Moscow visited Arye Levavi, Israel's Chargé, in Namir's absence. Levavi re-

---

[1] A communication from a Foreign Ministry official long involved with Israel's Asia policy.
[2] To Israel's Minister to Moscow, in early February 1950. Namir, p. 148.
[3] Eytan, p. 189 and Eytan interview, 1971, respectively.
[4] Shimoni 1972.

ported to the Foreign Office the same day as follows: 'He asked me, on instructions of his government, whether Israel was planning to send them a diplomatic mission. I replied . . . that the problem was only financial, and that we are highly desirous of maintaining close contacts with People's China. He said that this was understandable.'[1] At the end of June the Foreign Office informed Levavi: 'The Government has decided in principle to establish diplomatic relations with People's China. However, nothing will be done in this direction until the situation in the Far East clears up. This is for you only, and you are to do nothing until you hear further from here.'[2]

The Government of Israel's decision was taken at a meeting on 28 June, following a recommendation by the Foreign Ministry Directorate three days earlier that Israel's Minister to the Soviet Union be appointed, concurrently, as non-resident Minister to the PRC. That belated decision was stillborn: like the basic principle of non-identification, of which it was a part, it became a casualty of the Korean War. It was also Israel's first 'missed opportunity' to normalize relations with Peking.[3]

Israel's strategic decision on Korea was in response to a global crisis; but it was not, in terms of *Israel's foreign policy*, a crisis decision. The outbreak of war at that time came as a surprise; and there was little time to react. However, the Korean War was not perceived as a threat to basic Israeli values.

A number of interrelated decisive inputs flowed into Israel's Foreign Policy System during the last week of June 1950:

the war began at dawn on 25 June;
within hours President Truman ordered US forces in the Far East
    to provide massive air and sea support for South Korea, as well as
    protection for Taiwan (Formosa) against any thrust from Main-
    land China;[4]
the same day, 25 June, the Security Council criticized North Korea
    for attacking the South, termed it a breach of the peace, ordered
    the immediate cessation of hostilities and the withdrawal of

[1] The text is in Shimoni 1972.

[2] Namir, pp. 147–9. Levavi related the June 1950 approach to him by China's Chargé in Moscow five years before that episode was published by Namir. Interview, 1966.

[3] It is noteworthy that all other (13) non-Communist states which recognized the PRC during the first wave (1949–50) established diplomatic relations with Peking, though some of the European countries did not do so until 1954–5, when Israeli diplomacy recorded another, more significant, 'missed opportunity'. Indeed Israel is one of the few among 52 states which recognized the Peking regime until 1 March 1965 without diplomatic ties with the PRC. For details of the PRC's bilateral diplomatic relationships until that date see Halpern, Appendix A, pp. 495–9.

[4] An illuminating and systematic analysis of the US Government's response to the Korean crisis is in Paige, *passim*.

forces to the 38th Parallel, and invited assistance from UN members;[1]

on the 27th the Council reported the failure of North Korea to comply with its instructions, termed military action urgent, noted the Republic of (South) Korea's appeal for help, and recommended that all UN members extend assistance to the Republic of Korea;[2]

on 29 June Secretary-General Trygve Lie requested the governments of all member-states to inform the UN Secretariat of the nature of their proposed aid.

Most important for Israel's decision was the flow of US pressure 'to stand up and be counted'; apart from the UN channel already cited, the word was passed to Ambassador Elath in Washington via Truman's personal adviser and friend of Israel, Niles, that the President wanted Israel's support; more pointedly, that he was seeking and expecting the first reciprocal act of friendship, considering all that America had done for the new state; that pressure, real and intense, was conveyed to *Ha-Kirya*—by Elath and Eban.[3]

The demand for identification, which does not appear to have been matched by counter-pressure from Moscow, was considered irresistible by Israeli decision-makers: in Eytan's words, 'it was clear what had to be done'.[4] Indeed, with that recognition Israel's non-alignment phase was over. The issue was the extent and form(s) of support for UN–US policy in Korea. This, in essence, was the focus of discussion at the extraordinary Cabinet session held on 2 July at Weizmann's residence in Rehovoth, with the President in attendance.

Sharett dominated the discussion and recommended—as did Eban and others—diplomatic and political support, but no more. Ben Gurion startled his colleagues with a proposal to contribute a contingent of Israeli soldiers to the UN Command—on the (logical) grounds that, 'if we are really serious in saying this is aggression, we should send troops'. The Prime Minister stood alone in the Cabinet; *Tzahal* leaders, too, were opposed.[5]

There was no vote: the decision was made by consensus and took the form of a Government statement on the Korean War: 'The Government of Israel opposes and condemns aggression wherever it

---

[1] UN.SCOR, 5th year, 473rd Mtg., 25 June 1950, pp. 4–5.

[2] UN.S/1511, and UN.SCOR, 5th year, 474th Mtg., 27 June 1950, p. 5.

[3] The essence of Elath's cable was summarized by Eban. Interview, 1965.

[4] Eytan interview, 1971. Other members of the FSTE expressed the same view to the author. Interviews, 1960ff.

[5] Ben Gurion acknowledged that he had made this recommendation. Interview, 1971. Other participants, too, recalled the proposal and the outcome to the author. There was no immediate pressure on Israel to send troops. Eban recalled, however, that he was approached by US diplomats in 1951 and 1952 in this matter: 'they were keen to broaden the international character of the UN Force'. Eban interview, 1965.

may occur and from whatever quarter it may emanate. In fulfilment of its clear obligations under the Charter, Israel supports the Security Council in its efforts to put an end to the breach of the peace in Korea and to restore peace to that area. . . .'[1] That position was conveyed to the UN the next day.

The Cabinet decision of 2 July 1950 marked the first step away from non-identification towards alignment with the West. Indeed, it is that dimension which merits the designation *strategic* decision. It was operationalized by the tactical decision to support UN (and US) actions on Korea during the early days of the War.

Awareness of the foreign policy significance of the first Korea decision is already evident in the *Knesset* debate on 4 July and in press editorials at the time, as noted. The Left condemned the Government line as a violation of *ee-hizdahut*, while the Centre and the Right approved, except for *Herut*, which criticized its 'unconditional UN-orientation'. Nonetheless, two no-confidence motions were easily defeated, *Mapam*'s by 70 to 19, *Herut*'s by 68 to 20 with 8 abstentions.[2]

The implementation of Israel's strategic and tactical decisions on Korea took the form of an increasingly open alignment with US policy towards the war. The pattern is evident in both Israel's behaviour and in the tone of Sharett's and Eban's speeches before the General Assembly. The first act was an effort to maintain the image of non-involvement: on 3 August 1950 Israel offered medical aid to South Korea, and later, food supplies for civilian relief; both contributions totalled $100,000.

The effort failed, according to an Israeli report to the Foreign Office:

. . . while until recently we were regarded as a more or less neutral nation, we are now [March 1951] well on the way to becoming 'a running dog of American imperialism'. The single act which did most to procure this unsatisfactory state of affairs was the sending of medical supplies to Korea. Korea is a very touchy subject with the Chinese, who are also a practical people. If we had satisfied ourselves with following the Indian lead and merely voting that there had been aggression when the North attacked the South, the repercussions would not have been great. But the actual sending of medical supplies to Korea damned us in Chinese eyes. It received a very great amount of publicity in the Chinese press, which is interested in Asiatic reactions, and did us enormous harm.[3]

During the autumn Assembly pretence at lingering non-identification vanished. As one Foreign Ministry official observed, 'we were

[1] UN.S/1553 and UN.SCOR, 5th year, Suppl. for June–August 1950, pp. 52–3.
[2] *Divrei Ha-knesset*, vi, pp. 2057–87, 4 July 1950.
[3] This report by an Israeli who had spent some weeks in the Far East was considered sufficiently interesting to be distributed in the internal Foreign Service Information flow (Y.L. no. 239, 14 March 1951). It is a well-researched report, accurate on matters which can be empirically tested.

merely applying, or continuing, a basic policy decision, with support for the US the decisive factor.'[1] Eytan was more blunt and colloquial: 'Sharett was just dotting the i's and crossing the t's; he knew that Israel had moved into the Western camp.'[2] The record confirms this assessment.

In his address to the Assembly on 27 September, Sharett rejected as fallacious the tight ideological division of the world into two camps. He termed the 'point at issue' whether any system should be imposed by force. And he emphasized Israel's value affinity to the West: 'Freedom is the very breath of Israel's existence and development. Its democracy is based upon full political and cultural liberty in its internal life and on unrestricted contact of its citizens with the world outside.' It was in that speech, not surprisingly, that he indicated Israel's support for the novel 'Uniting for Peace' idea then being mooted by the US as a way of overcoming the paralysing Soviet veto in the Security Council.[3]

A week later Sharett's perception of the struggle over Korea became indistinguishable from that of the United States: on 4 October he replied to the Soviet delegate that, 'at worst', the evidence on the origins of the Korean War 'indicated the South Korean Government as having, at a certain stage, nurtured aggressive designs but there was a great difference ... between intention and physical action'.[4] With that shift in his articulated image came a change in his views about Israel's proper policy in the bloc struggle—from *non-identification* to an *independent* foreign policy. In practice this meant growing alignment with the West, to the extent that it permitted Israel's attachment.

Three days later, on 7 October, Israel voted for the (Western) Eight-Power draft resolution which authorized UN forces to cross the 38th Parallel, a momentous escalation of the war.[5] Sharett had prepared the ground for this vote by declaring that, because of North Korea's attitude, the 38th Parallel had 'lost whatever temporary validity it had had'; further, that he now believed [4 October] the 'occupation of all Korea by the United Nations forces might be the only method to achieve effective unity and peace in Korea'; and that the Israeli delegation favoured a call for an immediate cease-fire, 'provided that call was addressed to North Korea alone'.[6]

That unqualified approval for crossing the 38th Parallel by UN forces was restated even more forcefully by Sharett on 13 December 1950. He cited three reasons: (1) military—UN forces would be exposed to 'grave peril' if they halted their progress at an arbitrary straight

[1] Lewin interview, 1965.   [2] Eytan interview, 1971.
[3] UN.GAOR, 5th Session, 286th Plenary Mtg., 27 Sept. 1950, p. 135.
[4] Ibid., 1st Comm., 352nd Mtg., 4 Oct. 1950, pp. 45–6.
[5] UN.GA Res. 376 (V), 7 Oct. 1950, pp. 9–10.
[6] UN.GAOR, 5th Session, 1st Comm., 4 Oct. 1950, p. 46.

line; (2) political—it was 'politically essential' to provide them with 'the indispensable latitude to consolidate their position, to ensure their substantial control of Korea . . .'; and (3) moral—'on the purely moral side, the concept of the 38th Parallel seemed already to have lost its validity. . . .'[1]

Many years later Eban provided further insight into the rationale for Israel's strong backing of the decision to cross the Parallel:

(a) It provided an opportunity—and a challenge—to construct an effective system of international law;
(b) UN action conformed to Israeli vital interests—the defence of the doctrine of territorial conservatism, or opposition to all efforts to alter the *status quo* by force; any action elsewhere which strengthened the doctrine was valuable for Israel; [and]
(c) the US delegation were absolutely convinced that the Chinese Communists would not become directly involved, that there was no risk of escalation, that UN action would bring North Korea to the bargaining table, and that the UN would have something to concede.[2]

On 13 December 1950 Sharett opposed a Soviet draft resolution calling for the *immediate* withdrawal of all foreign troops from Korea: 'A progressive withdrawal, over a period of, say, six months . . . could be envisaged as desirable.' Rather, Israel voted for a 13-Power Western resolution calling for the appointment of a three-man committee of Good Offices to seek a basis for a cease-fire.[3]

In late January 1951 Eban echoed the US line on the massive intervention of Chinese 'People's Volunteers' in the Korean conflict: 'Such action was undoubtedly illegitimate. It was no doubt possible to explain the origins of that aggression or even to find extenuating circumstances, but it was impossible to deny its existence.'[4] With that rationale Israel voted for the draft resolution of 1 February 1951, which termed the People's Republic of China an aggressor in Korea.[5]

In the same spirit, Israel supported a Western draft resolution on 18 May 1951 recommending an arms embargo by all UN members against China.[6]

The last two implementing acts represented Israel's 'public' shift from non-identification to alignment with the West on the Korean issue. Yet at the turn of the year, 1950–1, there was an important Israeli

---

[1] Ibid., 416th Mtg., 13 Dec. 1950, p. 443.
[2] Eban interview, 1965.
[3] UN.GAOR, 5th Session, 1st Comm., 416th Mtg., 13 Dec. 1950, pp. 443-4.
[4] Ibid., 432nd Mtg., 26 Jan. 1951, p. 559.
[5] UN.GA Res. 498 (V), 1 February 1951, and UN.GAOR, 5th Session, 327th Pl. Mtg., 1 Feb. 1951, p. 696. Israel abstained on some individual paragraphs but supported the resolution as a whole. She also abstained on a competing neutralist Asian resolution on that issue.
[6] UN.A/1799, 14 May 1951, in Annex: Item 76, pp. 20-1, and UN.GAOR, 5th Session, 330th Pl. Mtg., 18 May 1951, p. 742.

initiative to mediate the conflict. It began on 4 December at a dinner which the Secretary-General gave for a special PRC delegation to the UN. The 'chief delegates from a number of key countries which had recognized the Peking government' were present, including those from the UK, India, Pakistan, Sweden, and Israel. 'At this dinner Mr. Sharett broached the principles of the cease-fire resolution which the General Assembly later adopted.'[1] The three-point plan called for a cease-fire, the withdrawal of all non-Korean forces from Korea, and the settlement of all Korean issues by the UN, with China's participation.

The Foreign Minister outlined the plan in his 13 December speech to the Assembly; the informal reaction was positive. The PRC dampened enthusiasm by rejecting a demand for a prior cease-fire. Israel persisted with the initiative. On 13 January 1951 Eban elaborated the proposal before the Assembly in the form of seven principles for a settlement. These were: an immediate and unconditional cease-fire; the affirmation by all governments concerned of the goal of a unified, independent Korea, to be achieved by nation-wide elections under UN supervision; the participation of Korea's neighbours, i.e. China, in the work of the UN agencies; an agreement for the progressive withdrawal of non-Korean forces during a specified period; the initiation of rehabilitation and reconstruction projects; a UN guarantee of an independent Korea—with China concurring; and a declaration that urgent consideration be given to all outstanding questions between the PRC and the UN. It was a neat compromise—pro-West in its call for an independent, united Korea, UN-supervised elections, and the withdrawal of forces, and sympathetic to China in calling for her participation in a Korean settlement and, later, in the UN.[2] Those principles were later embodied in an Israeli draft resolution which Ross, a member of the US delegation, requested Eban to propose.

The proposal was welcomed by many—the Commonwealth Prime Ministers, then meeting in London, the UN representatives of the US, UK, other Western states, neutralist India—and even the Arab states. But, as Canadian External Affairs Secretary Pearson informed Eban, the Arabs would withhold support if the resolution were moved by Israel—and that would seriously reduce the majority. The pitfall awaiting any Israeli initiative at the UN had been revealed. Eban yielded—reluctantly—to the Norwegian delegation, which was prepared to put forward a virtually identical draft—and did so. The resolution was approved, but Peking rejected the plan. In recalling that episode, the only sustained Israeli attempt to mediate an international conflict, Eban termed the attitude of *Ha-Kirya* as polite indifference: 'No one really attached any importance to it. Ben Gurion

---

[1] Lie, p. 352.
[2] UN.GAOR, 5th Session, 1st Comm., 425th Mtg., 13 Jan. 1951, p. 496 and Annex: Agenda Item 76, p. 13.

took no interest. It did not come before the Cabinet.'[1] There was an abortive sequel to this mediation effort in mid-March 1951.[2]

During the next two and a half years, until the August 1953 cease-fire agreement, Israel was inactive on the Korean issue—apart from an important abstention on a US-opposed, narrowly defeated proposal of 27 August 1953 in the General Assembly to include India in a Political Conference on Korea, then being mooted. By then alignment with the United States within the global system had become the pillar of Israel's foreign policy.[3]

After a lapse of almost four years another opportunity arose to establish diplomatic relations with the People's Republic of China. The principal setting was Burma, where Israel had opened her first Asian diplomatic mission towards the end of 1953. The initial approach was surprising, as David Hacohen, Israel's first Minister to Rangoon, reported in his diary. Late in December, during his first courtesy call on China's Ambassador, then Dean of the Diplomatic Corps, Yao Chung-ming 'was interested to learn why we had chosen to send a Minister to Burma and whether we had considered forming closer ties with Peking'. Although not a professional diplomat—he had long been a prominent figure in *Solel Boneh*, the industrial empire of the *Histadrut*—Hacohen fielded the inquiry with skill: 'I made a point of stressing that I had been instructed by my Government to cultivate good relations with representatives of China and to send greetings

---

[1] Eban interview, 1965. Ben Gurion confirmed that the mediation effort was not discussed, let alone approved, by the Cabinet. 'In foreign policy I mixed in only on the big problems, not the day-to-day questions. The Ministry of Defence was enough for me.' Ben Gurion interview, 1966. (See also Brecher, pp. 379–84, for BG's view of his role in foreign policy decision-making.)

Eban was less than generous in claiming the entire initiative as his own. Sharett, by contrast, paid 'special tribute to the brilliant ability and creative political thought' of Eban 'throughout all the stages of our participation in this complex and decisive discussion'. Address to the *Knesset* on the activities of Israel's Delegation to the Fifth General Assembly, 23 Jan. 1951. *Divrei Ha-knesset*, viii, pp. 848–54. An English translation, from which the above extract is taken, was issued the same day by the Foreign Press Division of the Israel Information Services.

[2] On 15 March 1951 Eban sent to Sharett a Memorandum containing further proposals aimed at finding a solution to the Korean War. He noted that a military stalemate existed, that this might induce China to accept proposals which she had rejected when she thought military victory was possible, and that the gap between UN and Chinese views was not irremediably wide. Thus he proposed a two-stage solution: a preliminary meeting to achieve the two objectives of a cease-fire agreement and a conference agenda; and secondly, a full-dress conference to discuss all the political issues relating to Korea and the Far East, the conference to be convened the day the cease-fire became effective. The full text of the Memo and Eban's letter to Sharett are reproduced in Y.L. no. 243, 28 March 1951. Nothing came of this second initiative.

[3] A useful summary of Israel's behaviour at the UN on the Korea question is to be found in *Israel and the United Nations*, pp. 227–39.

through the courtesy of the Ambassador to his Government.' Further, he expressed the hope 'that in the wake of the relaxation of international tension [the end of the Korean War] . . . our contacts would certainly become closer and deeper'.[1]

A few weeks later, on 16 January 1954, Yao conveyed orally to Hacohen an official message from Peking: 'The Government of China has ordered me to inform you that it welcomes the fact that the State of Israel has opened a legation in Burma and regards this as a suitable opportunity to notify you that it wishes to form trade ties with the State of Israel. The intention is to seek imports . . . and we would ask you to inform us what goods and what quantities and prices you would be prepared to sell us.'[2] A similar signal was communicated at the beginning of 1954 by the Chinese Ambassador in Helsinki to the Israeli Chargé d'Affaires, Eliahu Ben-Zvi.[3]

The Soviet Ambassador to Burma urged Hacohen (Israel) to respond quickly to Peking's initiative, adding that 'those to arrive first would be the beneficiaries'. He even suggested that, to evade the US–UN embargoes on trade with China, Israel could transfer shipments to Odessa and from there overland via Siberia to China. Hacohen replied that he did not think his country would circumvent the existing UN embargo.[4]

There was a further Rangoon exchange in mid-February, when Hacohen explained to his Chinese colleague the problems involved in Israel-China trade, notably the 1951 UN embargo and Egypt's denial of passage to Israeli shipping and Israeli goods through the Suez Canal and Tiran Straits. At the same time he conveyed Israel's positive interest and her wish to send a trade delegation to China. Hacohen added that this 'was in itself indicative of the thaw in Israel's attitude to China'.[5]

Behind the scenes Israeli decision-makers were engaged in a deadly serious discussion. The process led to an important but *not irrevocable* negative decision on China: it was therefore tactical, rather than strategic, in the typology used here.

Two views competed for authoritative sanction within Israel's Foreign Policy System. The most forceful advocate of a positive response to Peking was the pragmatic and unconventional Hacohen. From Rangoon, China seemed not only massive in size and population; it was also another, and even more important, window to the

---

[1] Hacohen, p. 34, entry 26 Dec. 1953.   [2] Ibid., pp. 61–2, entry 18 Jan. 1954.

[3] Ben-Zvi recalled that there were many friendly personal contacts, largely at the Chinese envoy's initiative. There were several hints about China's interest in 'relations'; diplomatic ties, as such, were not specified. Communicated to the author in September 1971. Eban, in recalling the Helsinki feeler, dismissed the Chinese approach as 'perhaps merely to get rid of an embarrassing situation'. He did not elaborate. Eban interview, 1965.

[4] Hacohen, p. 63, entry 19 Jan. 1954.   [5] Ibid., p. 91, entry 17 Feb. 1954.

non-Western world. Moreover, unlike India, Pakistan, Indonesia, etc., she had neither a Muslim majority nor a pro-Arab tradition or vital interest. This assessment was strongly supported within the Foreign Ministry by Eytan, the Director-General, and Lewin, Head of the Asian Department. Lewin's reasoning focused on short-term opportunities and long-term prospects: (1) China was a major power and would attempt to extend her influence in the Middle East as soon as her resources permitted; (2) for China's leadership the victory of Communism was certain, and all of Asia fell naturally within Peking's sphere of influence; they would therefore want a diplomatic base in the Middle East; (3) since all Arab states recognized the Taiwan (Nationalist) regime at the time, Israel had a unique advantage; (4) Israel had a brief period, perhaps a few years, to exploit this advantage by establishing diplomatic relations before China turned to the Arabs; and (5) the Chinese were loyal; if diplomatic ties were forged with Israel, they would not abandon her.[1]

At the other extreme stood Israel's Minister (No. 2) to the United States, Reuven Shiloah. His contention was simple and direct: relations with Peking would bring no tangible benefits to Israel and would almost certainly offend the US Government, at a time when vital negotiations were taking place for arms and economic assistance. The resurgence of border violence and heightened tension in the Near East Core made it even more imperative to retain Washington's friendship. That advocacy was staunchly supported—at first—by Ambassador Eban and by Teddy Kollek, then Director-General of the Prime Minister's Office, and was sympathetically transmitted by Ya'acov Herzog, Head of the United States Department in the Foreign Ministry.

Among the high-policy decision-makers, Sharett was favourably disposed but, as always, hesitant. To Hacohen's persistent urging that he be authorized to conclude diplomatic relations, he reportedly said: 'I am prepared to go along but I am not prepared to rush and, certainly, not to gallop.'[2]

At the time Prime Minister and Foreign Minister, Sharett was acutely conscious of 'the American factor' as a permanent component of Israel's Foreign Policy System. Thus he sought the reaction of Israel's Washington Embassy throughout and, at the outset, the US Government's attitude as well.[3] His exchange of cables

---

[1] Lewin interview, 1965.　　　　　[2] Hacohen interview, 1966.

[3] His sensitivity to 'the American factor' was so great that, in late 1947–early 1948, Sharett went so far as to propose postponing immigration from the Soviet bloc, owing to concern about the loss of United States support arising from her fear of Communist penetration of the Jewish state, in the guise of *aliya*. Cables to Ben Gurion on 23 Oct. 1947 and 11 Feb. 1948. Zionist Archives, Files S25 1698 and S25 1702.

Even more striking was Sharett's attitude to the proclamation of independence with the approaching departure of the British. On several occasions he advised against

with Eban and Shiloah during the early 1954 phase is illuminating.[1]

On 9 January, in response to Sharett's initial inquiry, Eban expressed emphatic opposition to any move in the direction of diplomatic relations with Peking. On the 29th, shortly after the Chinese Ambassador's official approach to Hacohen in Rangoon, Sharett asked Eban to inform the State Department that Israel was considering a positive response and to elicit the US attitude. Sharett cabled the Ambassador again on 11 February and elaborated on his thinking at the time. He noted that, at the end of 1950, Washington's reaction to the idea of Israel establishing relations with the PRC was absolutely negative, because China had been regarded as an aggressor and the aggression had continued. It is true, he observed, that the deadlock continued even after the Korean Armistice Agreement of August 1953—and, therefore, the complaint that Israel missed an opportunity to establish relations with China was erroneous. Israel could not do with China what had been done with Japan (diplomatic relations). But that act, along with her appearance in Rangoon, represented a stage towards the establishment of relations with Peking.

'In the meantime', Sharett noted, 'we decided to propose to the Chinese, as an answer to their approaches in Helsinki and Rangoon, to send a delegation headed by our Minister in Rangoon, with two economists, to ascertain the possibilities of commercial relations and to clarify also the consequences of relations, especially in the economic sphere; that is to say, what is being considered at present is a one-time visit.' He did not know what Peking's reaction would be; and certainly months would pass before something concrete was done by Israel. Eban was requested to note this possibility in his discussions with the State Department and to clarify Israel's position in the matter of

---

a *formal* proclamation—lest the US reaction, both governmental and public opinion, be adverse. Typical was his cable to Ben Gurion on 14 April 1948: 'In my opinion an armistice should not be refused, and any demonstrative step of proclamation on 15 May should be avoided.' Zionist Archives, File S25 1704. And, after his meeting with Secretary of State Marshall on 8 May, Sharett left for Tel Aviv with the aim of persuading Ben Gurion and other colleagues to avoid a *formal* proclamation of independence when the Mandate came to an end a week later. He denied the charge of 'softness' and explained that he was motivated by an intense wish to reach an agreement with the US. Ibid., File 15, package Z.6.6. See also Files Z5 2386; S25 1710; Z5 2388; and E. Wartman, Interviews with the Signatories to the Declaration of Independence, 1961. State Archives.

Parenthetically, Hacohen, with all his interest in Israel–Chinese relations, urged, as early as February 1954: 'We must be careful to do nothing which would upset relations between us and America . . . [and] we must involve our Embassy in Washington in consultations on such issues and coordinate every move together.' Hacohen, p. 92, entry 17 Feb. 1954.

[1] The contents of all Foreign Ministry cables and letters noted hereafter, without specific source, were made available to the author.

future relations with China. 'We shall, of course, take into account the US reaction', concluded Sharett.

Shiloah replied to the PM–FM on 15 February—before informing the State Department. The Embassy was giving much consideration to the issue of relations with China, he began, and from day to day their doubts increased. The intensification of the (first) Indo-China War, he went on, had created an almost hysterical atmosphere in the United States towards China, and therefore 'it is necessary to behave with maximum caution'. Shiloah also transmitted the reaction of Teddy Kollek, Director-General of the Prime Minister's Office, then in the US on an important financial mission. He did not wish to comment on the political aspects of the issue, said Kollek, but he felt obliged to note that the consolidating operation, which had been assigned to him, would be demolished by any action towards a diplomatic *rapprochement* with China. The knowledge, in the United States, that an Israeli Minister, accompanied by economists, visited China, even once, would raise a wave of attacks upon Israel, and the heads of this consolidating operation would encounter grave difficulties. And it was probable that a number of communities would cease their negotiations with the banks to get loans for Israel. Kollek's reaction was intense indeed. 'You cannot imagine', he cautioned Sharett, 'how great a sensitivity there is among Americans, Jews and non-Jews, in the matter of China and, especially, towards governments that increase their commercial relations with China.' He therefore recommended that any action, including the dispatch of a delegation, be postponed.

Sharett was unconvinced and conveyed his dissent on 21 February. Further, he introduced an economic argument: 'We need to strengthen our economy and must search for new markets.' More pointedly, he asked, rhetorically, why it was 'permissible' for Israel to establish relations with the Soviet Union but not with the ideologically-akin People's Republic of China. In any event, he added, it would take some months for the Israeli delegation to leave; by that time the effective period of fund-raising for that year will have passed.

Shiloah was adamant in his 'absolutely personal' reply to Sharett on 24 February, just after he and Eban had discussed the issue with the Under-Secretary of State—without any US aides present. Bedell-Smith replied to their inquiry that, as a friend of Israel, he advised postponing the matter for the time being. Who better than they, he continued, knew that he personally—for important reasons—would like to see an Israel mission in Peking. But in view of the situation prevailing in public opinion and in Congress, he was prepared to sacrifice certain interests and to recommend to them to refrain from any step that could be interpreted as encouraging the process of (People's) China's joining the UN family. Israel must understand that this was not a question of political logic. The crux of the matter lay in the emotional complex which deflects people from their powers of clear thinking. Israel could not have chosen a less appropriate timing. His advice to them was to postpone the matter for a more propitious moment. As they bade him farewell at the end of their talk, Shiloah concluded in his report to Sharett, Bedell-Smith again emphasized that, as a friend of Israel, he advised them to abstain for the time being from any act of drawing close to China.

These dire forebodings from Washington had a profound continuing effect upon Sharett's thinking and behaviour. Soon after the Chinese *démarche* in December 1953, he had decided to recommend to his Cabinet colleagues that the Government actively pursue the objective of diplomatic relations with Peking. 'You can certainly say that we are at the brink of this decision', said Sharett to a Foreign Ministry aide. Then 'something happened'; and the official was called to Sharett's home on Saturday evening, 27 February 1954: the recommendation was to be considered at the Government meeting the next day. 'I cannot swear on it under oath; but my recollection is that it was an incoming cable from Shiloah in Washington marked "Top Top Secret". It arrived Saturday night, just before the Cabinet meeting where the proposal was to be discussed.'[1] 'This item must be deleted from the agenda', said the Prime Minister–Foreign Minister, pointing to 'Diplomatic Relations with China'. The 'something' was the pressure from Israel's embassy in the US. Eban, too, confirmed that Sharett's decision not to seek Cabinet approval at that stage to proceed towards *diplomatic* relations was taken on the basis of his advice.[2]

The opposition of Israel's Washington Embassy was also influential in the deliberations of the Ministerial Committee on Foreign Affairs and Defence, to which Sharett brought the China issue in late May 1954. Their emphasis on the 'American factor'—the need not to alienate Israel's principal benefactor—was shared by most and articulated especially by two *Mapai* members, Defence Minister Pinhas Lavon and Minister without Portfolio Zalman Aranne. The decision—T_{2a}—was taken on 25 May: not to go ahead right now with the active pursuit of diplomatic relations; the specified intent was to wait until after the Geneva Conference on Indo-China, then in progress.[3]

To the most senior Foreign Ministry official at the time, the role of Israel's US Embassy was decisive. Eytan, who was involved at every stage of the process, recalled vividly the cables from Washington and their impact upon the China decisions: 'Sharett and I wanted to instruct the proposed delegation [to China] to negotiate diplomatic relations; I pressed extremely strongly, and Sharett was one hundred per

---

[1] Private communication to the author.
[2] Eban interview, 1965. Others concurred.
[3] Private communication to the author.

cent in support. Then came the powerful, repeated, and persistent opposition from Eban. He pressed his opposition ferociously. His argument was that diplomatic relations with Peking would cause incalculable harm to Israel's relations with the United States. Sharett was not persuaded; he had not changed his opinion. However, his Cabinet colleagues decided against him.' And, he added, 'We (Sharett and I) felt the time was ripe. Here was a golden opportunity.'[1]

In the perspective of a decade Eban termed it 'a constructive and considered decision' and explained his reasoning thus: if the opportunity for diplomatic relations existed then, it would obtain six months or a year later as well, since there was a probability of a rapid extension in the number of states recognizing Peking; therefore, why should Israel be out of step and risk near-certain American displeasure, possibly worse, for a doubtful benefit in the future—especially when relations with the PRC would still be available later.[2] The Under-Secretary's conclusion had been that 'Israel's relations with Peking would mean sacrificing something tangible for some possible remote gain'. Bedell-Smith's reaction, he recalled, had been mild and not unfriendly. His considered view had been that the State Department would not be openly hostile or upset—'but your problem is the Congress', and some important economic negotiations were then going on. US public opinion, too, would be annoyed.

Eban remarked that Sharett's method of soliciting American reaction indicated uncertainty about the right course of action. 'We should either have taken a decision to establish relations and then explained our action to Washington or not raised it at all with the State Department; to do it as Sharett suggested could only lead to a negative reply.' And he was convinced, in 1954 as in 1965, that, 'had we proceeded we could have explained it to Washington and avoided adverse effects'.[3]

Seventeen years after the events Eban summed up his role in the 1954–5 decision process on China: 'I never recommended not to establish relations with China. I was asked to clarify the position of the United States Government and we [Eban and Shiloah] passed on the results of this clarification.'[4] It is apparent that, during most of 1954, he shared Shiloah's opposition to a proposal to seek *diplomatic* relations. However, subsequent cables demonstrate that Eban did not oppose this step *in principle* or *indefinitely*. Thus on 24 November 1954 he informed Eytan that Dutch diplomats told him their decision to establish

---

[1] Interview, 1971.
[2] An unpersuasive thesis that Peking was 'really' not interested in diplomatic relations with Israel in 1954–5, which misinterprets the glaring evidence to the contrary, is to be found in Medzini.
[3] Eban interview, 1965.
[4] A communication from Eban to the author, August 1971.

diplomatic relations with Peking was taken after a lengthy resistance because of possible US reactions. Moreover, they now found American opinion more moderate than a few months earlier. This, Eban continued, confirmed his own impression that now was a good time to go forward with some stages, especially economic, but he would not exclude diplomatic ties, if available. He also referred to a talk between Hacohen and Robert Murphy of the State Department, with Shiloah and himself present, which showed moderation.[1]

In reply to an inquiry from the Foreign Office, he expressed the view on 3 January 1955 that, in the light of the Dutch and Norwegian experience, it would be desirable to discuss with China the establishment of diplomatic relations. The US, he added, needs the assistance of non-Communist states represented in Peking until she solves the problem of her relations with China.

Eban's most elaborate and positive statement on this issue was contained in a cable to the Ministry on 14 January 1955, two weeks before the Hacohen Mission set out for China. His stand, he began, was as follows: relations with China would strengthen Israel's international position and therefore should not be postponed. Moreover, the US Government would reconcile itself to this act and even try to benefit from it. Israel has arguments to soften the negative American reaction, and these should be exploited. Nor are the Americans fanatical in their stand. In fact, Eban continued, they too were seeking a path to relations with Peking, though Israel should not expect plaudits for her initiative. He again referred to the Dutch experience—they thought that their act in establishing diplomatic relations did not cause them any harm in the US; and further, that it is easier for Washington to acquiesce in bilateral relations with Peking than in Peking's entry into the UN. 'In the light of the Dutch precedent,' he concluded, 'I tend to regret that we approached along the line of commercial relations and not diplomatic relations', though he cautioned against the risk of trading in goods that other non-Communist states were not selling to China. Finally, on 15 April 1955 he reaffirmed the view that Israel should establish normal diplomatic ties with Communist China. Nevertheless, his opposition *in early 1954* must be considered a major input into the May tactical decision on China.

Another source of pressure, then and later, as noted, was the stern opposition of senior *Mapai* Cabinet colleagues Lavon and Aranne. Indeed, it was they, far more than the ideologically pro-American General Zionist Ministers, who turned the tide against a positive response to Peking's overtures, in May and again in the post-September 1954 phase. As such they were constituents of 'the American lobby'.

---

[1] Hacohen recalled that Murphy had reacted favourably to the planned Israeli mission—and that he, Hacohen, had said to Eban and Shiloah after the discussion: 'Now I have my American visa to China.' Hacohen interview, 1966.

Peking does not seem to have been aware of the complex Israeli decision-making process in January–February 1954—which, in any event, was concealed by Hacohen's indication of Israel's wish to send a *trade* mission to China. This is evident from Ambassador Yao's apology to Hacohen for the six-week delay in a reply, when they met again on 26 March 1954. Further, he said 'he wished to tell me that the Chinese Government felt friendship for Israel and was convinced that this feeling was reciprocated by Israel'. Moreover, 'there were no grounds for giving the impression that China had ceased to be vitally interested in forming commercial and diplomatic (he used the word deliberately) ties with Israel'.[1]

Three months later, on 29 June 1954, Hacohen met Chou En-lai who was passing through Rangoon en route to Geneva for the Conference on Indo-China. The Chinese Prime Minister 'said he hoped I would pay a visit [to Peking] and that, following his return home, he would find time to deal with the visit of the Israeli delegation. He hoped to meet me there.'[2] The formal invitation was conveyed by Yao to Hacohen on 13 September, just as Israel's Minister was about to depart for the UN General Assembly: the delegation, he hoped, 'would be authorized to conduct negotiations on questions of commerce and *all issues* affecting "two friendly states". He emphasized that we would be welcome as guests. We could stay in the country and visit as long and wherever we pleased.'[3]

One week *after* this invitation Israel inadvertently took a sharp turn to the Right in her public posture towards the PRC: on 21 September Eban voted in favour of the US 'moratorium' resolution, that is, not to consider the question of China's representation at the current (ninth) session of the General Assembly. The reason for the abrupt change was simply 'the American factor'. 'Eban was instructed not to oppose; but he took it upon himself to vote against Peking', asserted the Head of the Asian Department at the time.[4] And a member of the UN delegation in 1954 was emphatic in stating that Eban knew precisely the Jerusalem intent but came under massive American pressure at the UN to shift Israel's stand.[5]

Eban himself acknowledged a decade later that *he* had taken the decision. In the context of the 1954 UN vote he also recalled the wide discretion he enjoyed throughout his tenure as UN Representative—1949–59. And, as already noted, he emphasized the persistent US pressure on the Korea/China issue in Israel's foreign policy.[6] Finally,

---

[1] Hacohen, p. 158, entry 28 March 1954.
[2] Ibid., pp. 244–5, entry 30 June 1954.
[3] Ibid., pp. 304–5, entry 14 Sept. 1954 (emphasis added).
[4] Lewin interview, 1965.
[5] A private communication to the author.
[6] Eban interview, 1965. All persons interviewed confirmed Eban's exceptional discretion.

in a rare display of open disagreement, Sharett and the Foreign Office disassociated Israel from the vote—for it was a qualitative, conspicuous, and unauthorized shift in policy.[1]

Hacohen, then in Israel en route to New York, was appalled by the vote. His concern was assuaged by the explanation of Foreign Ministry officials that there had not been a desire to offend Peking. More scathing was the extraordinary public dissent:

Commenting last night on the Israel vote in favour of deferring consideration of the admission of the Chinese People's Republic to the UN, the Foreign Ministry spokesman said that the Israel delegation had been given a directive in this connection, the *essence of which was that it should not vote against the admission of the People's Republic of China.*

The motion tabled at the Assembly did not, in fact, fully correspond with the position that had been anticipated, and for which the original instructions had been framed. Under these changed circumstances the Delegation decided that it must vote as it did although *this was not in accordance with the principal*

---

[1] In 1950 Israel had voted for Indian and Soviet draft resolutions to seat Peking's delegation as the representative of China in the General Assembly; the Soviets added a provision for the expulsion of Taiwan's delegation. Sharett explained Israel's position thus: 'My delegation feels that it would be unwise for the United Nations, in disregard of compelling realities, artificially to bolster up a regime of the past, which has lost its hold on the territory and people it claims to represent.' On the Indian draft resolution the vote was 16 to 33, with 10 abstentions. On the Soviet draft resolution to seat Peking the vote was 10 to 38, with 8 abstentions; on its resolution to expel Taiwan the vote was 4 to 37, Israel among those in favour, with 8 abstentions. All 3 resolutions were voted on 19 September. UN.GAOR, 5th Session, 286th Pl. Mtg., 27 Sept. 1950, p. 136. The following year a Byelorussian draft resolution 'to regard as invalid the credentials of the representatives of the so-called Kuomintang Government . . .' was defeated by 39 to 7, with 4 abstentions, Israel among them. Ibid., 6th Session, 351st Pl. Mtg., 25 Oct. 1951, p. 167.

The change to a non-aligned stance came in 1952, when Israel abstained on a draft resolution to postpone consideration of the China representation issue until the next Assembly; she was in 'respectable' company—with such neutralists as India, Indonesia, and Yugoslavia, and, ironically, three Arab states! The vote was 42 to 7, with 11 abstentions. 'Israel', explained her delegate, 'is in agreement with the view that the time is not propitious to discuss the question of Chinese representation as long as hostilities against the United Nations in Korea continue.' On the other hand, he urged that the possibility for consideration should be left open. Ibid., 7th Session, 389th Mtg., 25 Oct. 1952, p. 167. Israel abstained on an identical resolution in 1953. The vote was 44 to 10, with 2 abstentions. Ibid., 8th Session, 432nd Pl. Mtg., 15 Sept. 1953, p. 10. Then in 1954 came the sudden shift—in contravention of instructions from Jerusalem, as noted. The vote on the US 'moratorium' resolution was 43 to 11, with 6 abstentions. Ibid., 9th Session, 473rd Pl. Mtg., 21 Sept. 1954, p. 142. Eban's explanation was: 'My Government could not oppose the [US] view that little useful purpose could have been served in discussing this question in circumstances which were bound to lead only to bitterness and to failure. The question of untimeliness, however, does not affect the ultimate issue of principle. The interests of the United Nations would be best served by the participation of the Central People's Government of China in its membership and its work.' Ibid., 491st Pl. Mtg., 6 Oct. 1954, p. 211.

intention as originally laid down. There was no time for the Delegation to seek fresh instructions before the vote. . . .[1]

The Chinese were piqued but they seemed determined not to be diverted from their path. *Two days after* the UN vote Chou En-lai informed the first session of the first National People's Congress during a major foreign policy address: 'Contacts are being made with a view to establishing normal relations between China and Afghanistan, as well as between China and Israel.'[2] Moreover their criticism of the Eban vote was muted, as well as being delayed: *a month and a half* after Jerusalem's apologetic cable, Ambassador Yao wrote that the PRC 'assumes that the Government of Israel, desiring to establish and maintain mutual relations with China, will in future adopt a correct stand concerning China's status at the United Nations'.[3]

Peking's invitation to send a mission to China to discuss 'all issues affecting "two friendly states"' and Chou En-lai's statement about 'normal relations' posed a fresh challenge and created an opportunity—for Israel's decision-makers. Indeed these were two decisive inputs into the strategic decision on China: there could no longer be any reasonable doubt about the PRC's intention or about the genuineness of the Rangoon (and other) feelers during the preceding nine months.

The real issue at that time (September–November 1954) was whether the Mission should actively pursue the aim of *diplomatic* relations or confine its discussions to *commercial* matters. The upshot was a compromise Government decision on 14 November—T_{2b}—the appointment of a middle-ranking Trade Delegation, without broad *negotiating* authority, but with diplomats in the group to *sound out* Peking's 'real' intentions. The process leading to that tactical decision was illuminated by two Foreign Ministry officials and by Sharett himself.

Lewin remarked:

In the course of consultations within the *Misrad* (Ministry) the 'American lobby' argued strenuously against acceptance of diplomatic relations. The reason given was that it would offend the US Government and American Jewry; both would cut off economic aid. The effect of the pressure was a compromise, that is, Israel would send a trade delegation. This proposal went to the Cabinet, along with Hacohen's plea for authority to negotiate diplomatic ties. The Government agreed to a trade mission, without dissent, but did not give it authority to initiate talks or to negotiate on diplomatic relations.

After the Cabinet decision, new pressures arose within *Mapai*; Lavon and Aranne wanted to cancel the delegation altogether. Sharett refused, but all freedom of action on diplomatic ties was removed from the mission's terms of reference. Just before we left Rangoon for China, Hacohen and I sought—

---

[1] As reported in *Jerusalem Post*, 23 Sept. 1954, with the caption, 'Israel's Vote on China Explained'. For Hacohen's account of this episode see pp. 318–19, entry 25 Sept. 1954.

[2] Chou En-lai Report, p. 43.

[3] Hacohen, p. 435, entry 1 April 1955.

without success—Sharett's permission to *react favourably, with a commitment*, i.
Peking spokesmen indicated an interest in diplomatic relations.[1]

Herzog recalled 'a crucial meeting' at Sharett's home in December
1954, a few weeks before the Mission was to depart: Eytan, Levavi,
Meir de Shalit, and Herzog were present. He transmitted the strong
opposition from Israel's Embassy in Washington. And it was decided
that the delegation should *probe* the issue of diplomatic ties *informally,
without any commitment*.[2]

Sharett confirmed the essence of that decision—in some illuminating
remarks reported after his death by Moshe Rivlin, Director-General
of the Jewish Agency: 'He [Sharett] went on to relate that when he
received Mr. Hacohen's report on his talk with the Chinese Ambassador
in Burma, he referred the matter to the proper authority. He reported
on Mr. Hacohen's stand on the issue and *demanded* that *the proposal to
establish ties with China be approved*. But the majority voted against it, and
obviously he yielded to the majority opinion, and replied in the
negative to Hacohen's proposal.' Furthermore, to Rivlin's comment:
'Look here, today [1963] you are being attacked for this negative
reply . . . why don't you tell the nation the truth?' Sharett 'retorted in
anger': 'Do you realize what you are suggesting? . . . I was then
Foreign Minister, and as such I assumed responsibility for all decisions
taken authoritatively and here you ask me to disown such responsibility.
No, I am not the sort of man to do that.'[3]

Parenthetically, Sharett gave his stamp of authoritative accuracy to
Hacohen's account of the China issue in Israel's foreign policy, 1954–5,
in reply to Rivlin's criticism of the latter's *Burma Diary*: 'David [Haco-
hen] showed me the manuscript and told me that he was prepared to
delete the chapter [on China] from his book. [Hacohen and Sharett
were lifelong friends.] I begged him not to do so. *The facts are correct*;
one must not cover them up; one must not delete them, even though it
may prove uncomfortable to someone, even to myself.' Many years
after the decision, in reply to a question about diplomatic relations,
Sharett observed: 'There were doubts whether to *embark* upon such a
decision, and the Cabinet finally decided against it.'[4] And when
Hacohen asked Sharett in 1962 what was the stumbling block to
giving him a clear signal on diplomatic relations, surmising that it must
have been his General Zionist coalition partners, Sharett replied:
'What, General Zionists! It was those —, Aranne and Lavon.'[5]

---

[1] Lewin interview, 1965 (emphasis added). Nineteen years after the events, Hacohen
revealed that, in October 1954, just after Israel's negative vote on the admission of
Peking to the UN, Sharett told him that '. . . he came up against fierce opposition
from Zalman Aranne and Pinhas Lavon [on relations with China] arising from
fears of a negative reaction from the United States . . .' Hacohen (4).

[2] Herzog interview, 1966.   [3] Rivlin (emphasis added).
[4] Interview in *Ha'aretz*, 28 July 1963.   [5] Hacohen interview, 1966.

Many persons, as noted, confirmed Sharett's *basic predisposition* in favour of diplomatic relations with the PRC. Yet because of powerful constraints within the Cabinet and the Foreign Service he acknowledged Peking's offer of hospitality with coolness. 'After contact with the Government of China,' he informed the *Knesset* on 15 November 1954, 'we are about to explore the possibilities of direct *commercial* relations ... by sending to Peking a special *trade* delegation. . . . It was agreed between the two sides that Israel will dispatch a mission to China, and then the Chinese Government announced that during their stay in Peking, the members of the delegation will be their guests.'[1]

The Government of Israel's acceptance of Peking's invitation in November 1954 was another decisive input into the strategic decision— despite the emasculation of the Mission's terms of reference. So too was the tour of the five-man delegation and its resultant pressure. Led by the irrepressible Hacohen, it comprised Lewin and de Shalit of the Foreign Ministry, Joseph Zarchin, Head of the Export Department of the Ministry of Commerce and Industry, and Moshe Bejarano, an industrialist who had served as Commercial Attaché in Moscow. The Mission spent three days in Canton and arrived in Peking on 31 January 1955.

There it was received by the Deputy Minister of Commerce, in charge of Foreign Trade, Li Jen-min, and lesser officials from the Foreign Office. Li emphasized that the PRC was interested in developing commercial relations with all states. He recalled that Israel was among the first to recognize the new regime. He emphasized the equal status of all countries, small and large. He noted that both China and Israel had an ancient tradition. And the Chinese, he observed, respected the Jews for standing firm through all their trials.[2]

During the next two weeks the Israeli delegation toured factories, agricultural settlements, schools, and social institutions in Peking, Tientsin, Chenyang (Mukden), and surrounding areas. Discussions were resumed in mid-February and centred on the goods which China wished to purchase, notably chemicals and fertilizers, spare parts, trucks, and industrial diamonds. The formal outcome was a five-point Protocol signed on 18 February:

1. Both sides desire trade relations on the basis of equality and mutual benefit;
2. Both sides presented the foreign trade problems of their countries, studied the lists of commodities available for foreign trade, and examined other questions relating to commerce;
3. Both sides agreed that the mutual talks and exchange of information had laid the foundation for the development of closer commercial ties between the two countries;
4. Both sides agreed to present reports to their Governments on the atmosphere

---

[1] *Divrei Ha-knesset*, xvii, p. 104, 15 Nov. 1954 (emphasis added).
[2] Hacohen, pp. 385–8, entry 1 Feb. 1955.

prevailing during the Peking talks, and to continue, through existing channels and others to be formed in the future, to develop the commercial ties between the two countries;

5. On behalf of the Government of Israel, the Israeli delegation expressed the hope that the Government of the People's Republic of China would send a trade delegation to visit Israel as the official guests of the Israeli Government.[1]

The Chinese parried an Israeli request to commit themselves to send a reciprocal mission to Israel. However, during informal talks they did not conceal their interest in diplomatic relations. Hacohen and Lewin sought and were granted meetings, respectively, with the Deputy Foreign Minister and the Head of the Asia Department in the Chinese Foreign Office. Both left without any doubt that the Chinese officials desired to establish relations—and believed the presence of Israel's delegation symbolized her interest in normal ties as well.

Illuminating in this context is the 'offer' made by their Chinese hosts. In the course of his discussion with Chang Han-fu, who was Chou En-lai's deputy, with a reputation for great influence, Hacohen raised the issue of Jewish property which had been donated to the State of Israel by Shanghai Jews before leaving China and had been confiscated by the PRC. Chang replied: 'You will need a compound in Peking for your activities. Other countries represented here before 1949 had them. We will exchange your [Jewish] property in Shanghai for a compound here. I will give you a protocol officer—go around the city and look for a suitable building. Why take a dollar as compensation?'[2] Lewin recalled an identical offer and, conscious of his instructions, replied that he had to report back to Jerusalem, for his Government had not yet made a decision about diplomatic relations. This elicited a reciprocal response. 'I was absolutely certain that his remarks were *pro forma*, to save face, a matter of dignity, and that, at that time, Peking was keen about diplomatic relations.'[3]

Meir de Shalit gave a different version of the Shanghai property episode, many years later: 'The Israelis said they would like to exchange this property for a house in Peking in which to set up an Embassy. Again, there were polite smiles, but no reaction.' (If so, they were different—and lower-ranking—Chinese officials.) He also dissented sharply from the Hacohen–Lewin interpretation of Peking's intent at that time: '. . . it was seen as a unique opportunity that was lost . . . I disagree heartily.' Further, he believed that there never had been a chance to establish formal relations with Communist China.[4]

---

[1] The text is in Hacohen, p. 416, entry 19 Feb. 1955. The Mission's visit to China is discussed ibid., pp. 378–420. An English translation of some salient Hacohen diary entries concerning Israel–China relations, 1953–5, is to be found in Hacohen (2). See also Hacohen (3) and Hacohen (4).

[2] Hacohen interview, 1971.   [3] Lewin interview, 1966.

[4] 'No Chance for Ties with China', interview with Sraya Shapiro, *Jerusalem Post*, 22 Aug. 1971.

The Mission's inability to do more than 'report back' was the price of the dilution of its terms of reference. The severe constraints are evident in Sharett's letter of instructions to Hacohen, dated 19 January 1955:

The delicate point on the Mission's agenda is the problem of diplomatic ties. It would be best not to raise this question in the first stages of the visit but to restrict yourself at first to general talks about our desire to tighten the ties of friendship, of this delegation being an explicit sign of our desire and hope that China will quickly dispatch a reciprocal mission to us. One must give as much opportunity as possible for the Chinese to take the initiative and raise the issue of formal ties as a subject for discussion and then you should respond to this positively: To say that the Government is thinking in this direction, and that *the Mission received instructions to clarify the possibilities and conditions* and that the *Government will certainly decide on the question in the light of the Mission's report*—if not immediately, then within a not too lengthy period of time. But should several days pass without a word from the Chinese side, then the question should be touched upon, at first *with caution*, and then carry on according to the reaction. If the Chinese latch on to the matter, you can delve into it in depth as said above, but if there is a retreat from their side—you must drop this subject immediately and not return to it. Under no circumstances should a situation be created wherein we are clinging to them and persuading them of our rights to diplomatic ties, while they are imposing reservations and are retreating. These are the lines that I have seen fit to lay down and I rely on your common sense and good taste to guide you on the correct path.[1]

The tone was one of extreme caution, with emphasis on *Chinese* initiative, a non-committal, though positive, Israeli response, and the preservation of Israel's *amour propre* at all costs. As so often with Sharett's diplomacy, form seemed to take precedence over substance. To the *Knesset* Sharett reported in the same vein:

The step we are about to take will be executed, as befits the nature of things, on the basis of a completed agreement between us and the Government of China. As well, we shall rely upon the clarification . . . , as a result of this visit, concerning the possibility of further tightening relations. *When the Mission returns and submits its report, the Government will have to decide* if a further step will be necessary, *which* step will be required, and *when* it should be taken. In any event our aim is friendship with People's China. . . .[2]

Hacohen conducted himself accordingly. But he was absolutely convinced of genuine Chinese interest. Thus, upon his return to Rangoon, he urged an immediate decision. 'We must remember to ensure that this mission does not remain an isolated episode', he wrote at the end of February, 'which will be forgotten in the course of time and which will lose all value because of procrastination on our part—and

[1] Photostat copy of the letter made available to the author by Hacohen in 1971 (emphasis added).
[2] *Divrei Ha-knesset*, xvii, p. 563, 12 Jan. 1955.

perhaps also under external influence. The Government must act without delay. . . . [Finally], in my opinion we shall not make any progress in political, commercial, and cultural relations with China if we do not take the decisive step of exchanging Ambassadors.'[1] Hacohen sent a stream of letters and cables to Jerusalem during the next month requesting 'immediate telegraphic instructions to contact China in order to clarify whether they wished to establish diplomatic relations with us . . . including, if necessary, another visit to Peking for this purpose'. 'All my letters and telegrams', he wrote in despair in his diary, 'have been of no avail.'[2] Lewin, too, upon his return from China, tried on several occasions to secure Sharett's permission to write to his opposite number in Peking, indicating the Government of Israel's approval. 'I could not get him to say "yes".'[3]

Sharett's response during that crucial month was typical. He refused to be stampeded. Furthermore, he invoked the sacred principle of mutuality. On 28 March 1955 Lewin informed Hacohen of Sharett's decision: 'The Foreign Minister, before bringing the matter of diplomatic relations to a decision, emphasizes that the Chinese delegation which was invited by us must first come to Israel.' This was to be the 'test' of China's *real* interest—'only if, and only after, it takes place' would Israel decide upon the issue of diplomatic relations.[4] As one Foreign Ministry official remarked, correctly: 'Sharett was a stickler for small formal details.'[5]

The tone and essence of the decision were also evident in the letter of 3 April, which Lewin sent to his opposite number in the Chinese Foreign Office, Chen Chia-kang. The Israel delegation was preparing a detailed report, he wrote, *more than five weeks* after it left China, and the Government of Israel would be able to decide on what steps to take 'only on the basis of their report'. The invitation to China to send a mission was renewed—with the aim of realizing 'close friendly trade relations'. Reference to diplomatic ties was studiously avoided. It was, in short, a negative, masked decision, in the form of a stalling operation.

Hacohen was appalled by Sharett's decision on 'reciprocity as a precondition to any further Israeli action'. He had already, in his letter of 28 March, warned of the adverse consequences at the approaching Bandung Conference and had stressed the need for speedy action. He did so again on 4 April and asked, 'why link the two issues, and why "only after" the Chinese delegation visits Israel?' It was in vain: the game was lost, for the decision on an immediate Israeli initiative for diplomatic relations remained negative, until it was too late. The

[1] Hacohen, p. 424, entry 12 March 1955.
[2] Ibid., pp. 435–6, entry 1 April 1955, and p. 425, entry 12 March 1955.
[3] Lewin interview, 1965.   [4] Hacohen, p. 436.
[5] Shimoni letter, 1966.

acceptance of Peking's overtures, when it did come, was belated and grudging.

As in 1950, there was an abortive implementing sequel to the strategic decision on China. Hacohen was asked to tell China's Ambassador to Burma that Israel was 'considering' the establishment of diplomatic relations. He replied to the Foreign Office on 13 April that this 'was not meaty enough'. Then, as reports filtered in about the probability of Arab success in securing an anti-Israel resolution at the Bandung Conference, which began on 17 April, Sharett sought Lewin's advice on how this could be offset. Lewin again emphasized the cardinal importance of diplomatic relations with the PRC for Israel's relations with the Third World.[1]

Eban, too, was consulted by Sharett. It seemed to him, began the PM–FM, that the delegation to China did not cause Israel any damage in the US. What would happen, he asked, if she moved now towards diplomatic relations with China. There is the view, he continued, referring to Hacohen and Lewin, that a favourable decision is urgent because of China's contacts with the Arabs at Bandung. 'Please answer me immediately', he concluded.

Eban replied the next day that his stand had not changed, that is to say, diplomatic relations with China would strengthen Israel's position —and therefore one should act immediately. He could not guarantee that there would not be a negative echo, but it would not cause basic damage. Israel's step, he advised, should be described as a natural outgrowth of her recognition of Peking and as part of her widening network of representation in Asia. Then it would be well received. At the same time, Israel's act should not appear as support for the PRC's claim to a right to conquer Formosa.

Sharett continued to procrastinate. On the 19th Hacohen wrote a postmortem to Lewin, the essence of which was that 'we have lost the moment' and 'if we would have approached the Chinese they would have responded positively'. The same themes were elaborated by Hacohen in a letter to Sharett on the 20th—in a desperate effort to secure a reversal of the 28 March decision.[2] He also reported to Lewin on 22 April that Chou En-lai had identified China with the pro-Arab resolution at Bandung. Nevertheless, he still thought that Israel should act.[3] At that point—and *only in the 'defeat at Bandung' context*—

---

[1] Lewin interview, 1965.

[2] Hacohen, pp. 449–58. Over the years he persisted with this theme of Israel's diplomatic blunder. See, for example, Hacohen (3) and Hacohen (4).

[3] The resolution, more moderate than the initial extreme pro-Arab draft, read as follows: 'In view of the existing tension in the Middle East caused by the situation in Palestine and of the danger of that tension to world peace, the Asian-African conference declared its support of the rights of the Arab people of Palestine and called for the implementation of the United Nations resolutions on Palestine and of the peaceful settlement of the Palestine question.' *New York Times*, 24 April 1955. The Arabs were

Sharett finally authorized Lewin to inform Chen that the Government of Israel 'desires to establish full diplomatic relations with the Government of the People's Republic of China at the earliest convenient moment'. The letter was dated 29 April. The reply was polite but non-committal: on 21 May 1955 Chen wrote that he had already reported the proposal to his government. There was no further word from Peking.

Sharett's act was belated. By then the Sino-Arab link had been forged at Bandung: there, Chou En-lai had invited all Arab states to send missions to Peking. They were soon to comply.[1]

Sharett's central decision-making role is evident despite the fact that, when he finally took the path to diplomatic relations, he did so with Cabinet approval. But caution had triumphed—and Israeli diplomacy had blundered.[2]

---

elated; Israel was dismayed. But the resolution was very mild, compared with many to follow. And the Chinese Ambassador conveyed his regrets to his Israeli colleague in Rangoon, stating that Chou did not wish to oppose the strong desire at Bandung for unanimity. Hacohen interview, 1965.

[1] Informative surveys of the origins and evolution of China's relations with the Arab states are to be found in: W. A. C. Adie, 'The Middle East: Sino-Soviet Discord', *Survey* (London), no. 42, June 1962, pp. 132–47, and 'China's Middle East Strategy', *The World Today* (London), 23, 8 Aug. 1967, pp. 317–26; Malcolm H. Kerr, 'The Middle East and China: The Scope and Limits of Convergent Interests', in Halpern, ch. 15; Joseph E. Khalili, 'Sino-Arab Relations', *Asian Survey* (Berkeley), viii, 8 Aug. 1968, pp. 678–90; G. A. Masannat, 'Sino-Arab Relations', *Asian Survey*, vi, 5 April 1966, pp. 216–26. For Israeli assessments see Joseph Ben-Dak, 'China in the Arab World', *Current History*, lix, 349, Sept. 1970, pp. 147–52; Z. Katz, 'Sino-Soviet Conflict and the Arabs', *New Outlook*, 7, 4 (62), 1964, pp. 35–7, and 'China's Role in the Middle East, *Asian Analyst*, July 1967, pp. 10–12; Meron Medzini, 'Chinese Penetration in the Middle East', *New Outlook*, 6, 9 (58), Nov.–Dec. 1963, pp. 16–28; M. Nahumi, 'China and Israel', *New Outlook*, 9, 6 (81), 1966, pp. 40–8; Shimoni 1972; and Rafi Yisraeli, 'China's Struggle in the Middle East', *Hamizrah Hehadash* (The New East), 18, 1–2, 1968/5728, pp. 79–105 (in Hebrew).

[2] This writer has derived much benefit from a lively and continuous dialogue during the past twenty years with the leading Asia expert in Israel's Foreign Service, Ya'acov Shimoni. He served as Head of the Asian Department, 1949–52 and 1960–4, Minister to Burma 1955–7, and has been Assistant Director-General of the Foreign Ministry in charge of Asia (as well as Africa and Latin America) since 1969. There is no disagreement about the empirical data presented in this chapter. There is, however, basic disagreement about the appropriate terminology applied to the several decisions and, even more important, about the significance, actual and speculative, of Israel's decisions relating to China in 1954–5. His considered view was conveyed to the author and is presented here in full—as the most knowledgeable Israeli Establishment interpretation of this issue in Israel's foreign policy.

Israel's decision, in January 1950, to recognize Communist China—in the face of well-known US opposition and in expectation of US displeasure—was a strategic decision, concerning both relations with China and Israel's non-aligned posture.

That decision implied a tactical follow-up: the establishment of full diplomatic relations. This implication was formally spelled out in the summer of 1950, with the proviso that the follow-up should be postponed to a time tactically propitious.

Contact between Israeli and Chinese officials continued spasmodically:
1. On 23 May 1955 China's Ambassador to Burma explained—in a friendly and apologetic spirit—Chou's behaviour at Bandung. In Hacohen's words, he said that 'China wanted true friendship and relations of mutual respect with Israel. Relations between China and Israel had not been harmed in any way. Chou En-lai wanted to avoid saying anything on the [Arab-Israeli] problem but the prevailing sentiment at Bandung was in favour of issuing a joint declaration on all issues on the agenda . . . etc.' Hacohen, pp. 479–80, entry 23 May 1955.
2. In July 1955 Israel's Ambassador to Moscow, Avidar, visited Peking. The

---

This tactical decision was overridden and frozen by the strategic decision concerning the Korea conflict, i.e. it became inoperative as long as China was considered an aggressor and ostracized from the family of nations.

The tactical decision—to implement full relations with China at a propitious moment —became operative again after the Korean cease-fire of 1953.

The decisive mistake was made during 1954 when the time should have been judged propitious for the establishment of relations, especially after Chou En-lai's surprising statement of September 1954 (which is still inexplicable, coming out of the blue, unpreceded by any contacts or negotiations). This mistake of 1954 was largely determined by objections voiced by the USA and/or Israel's representatives in the USA. But it remains a *tactical* mistake, deriving from an excess of hesitation and not from a negative strategic decision concerning relations with China.

Despite that mistaken tactical decision of 1954 not to go ahead with diplomatic relations, Israel decided to send a mission to China. The fact that some Israeli politicians and/or diplomats opposed even that mission, is interesting in terms of Israeli politics and public opinion; but it had no relevance to or influence on relations with China, since it remained unknown to China: once China was informed, in November 1954, of Israel's desire to send the mission, the delay until late February 1955 was entirely China's and not Israel's.

Early in 1955 it was decided to go ahead with the establishment of diplomatic relations. The fact that Israel's representatives in the USA had removed their objection late in 1954 and were now actively advocating relations with China, may well have been an important element. The Prime Minister–Foreign Minister did not need a formal Cabinet endorsement of his decision, since it remained within the previously determined tactical follow-up to the strategic decision of 1950. (The fact that the matter was not brought formally before the Cabinet reconfirms its tactical nature.)

The question now became sub-tactical, i.e. what was the best procedure and who should take the initiative. Sharett's instructions to Hacohen have to be understood in that sub-tactical sense only. During the Mission's visit to China, China's preparedness for diplomatic relations was several times implied but never spelled out (despite Chou En-lai's September 1954 statement). Sub-tactically, therefore, the question remained should Israel take a formal initiative—with no complete certainty that China would respond favourably.

Sharett's decision not to take the formal initiative for diplomatic relations at that juncture was a mistake deriving from an excess of hesitation and an over-insistence on diplomatic procedure. But it remained a purely tactical or even sub-tactical mistake and did not imply by any means a strategic decision not to establish diplomatic relations with China.

This tactical mistake had no real influence on China's decision, after the Bandung Conference, to prefer relations with the Arabs and freeze those with Israel. The hesitation of 1954 may have had such influence, but not the tactical delay of March 1955 (which may even have been unknown to China). China's evaluation that a

Chinese Deputy Foreign Minister told him that the present situation was unfavourable for diplomatic relations but he hoped that mutual interest and friendship between the two countries would continue to develop. He avoided reacting to a hinted inquiry about the invited Chinese delegation to Israel. (A communication to the author from a Foreign Ministry source.)

3. Between July and October 1955 Mordekhai Gazit, Israel's Chargé d'Affaires *ad interim*—from Hacohen's departure to Shimoni's arrival as Minister—spoke with China's Ambassador to Burma several times. At his first meeting, in July, he transmitted Lewin's reminder to his opposite number in Peking, who had not written after his acknowledgement of Lewin's early letters—on 21 May 1955 he had asked whether the PRC was prepared to enter diplomatic relations. The reply was: 'The People's Republic of China wishes to have relations with all countries which follow a policy of peace.' Gazit persisted: 'Does that include Israel?' The Ambassador repeated, 'The People's Republic of China wishes . . .'. This was reported to Jerusalem without any formal recommendation as to what Israel should do next. Gazit saw the Ambassador again in August and, once more, in October 1955. He inquired afresh if Peking was ready for diplomatic ties. The reply was evasive—that China's leadership was preoccupied with an impending session of the National People's Congress and could not take a decision at this time. He also reiterated, 'the People's Republic of China . . .'. Gazit surmised then and later that Israel could have 'shot its way into Peking' even at that date; that is, she could have taken the initiative, interpreting the formula, 'all countries which follow a policy of peace' as including Israel—he noted that Israel was not explicitly excluded—and sent an envoy to Peking with the goal of establishing a mission. 'I could have got a visa to China right then', he added; and 'Israel would have succeeded in forming normal diplomatic ties'. (Gazit interview, 1966.)

4. On 26 August 1956 the Chinese Ambassador to Budapest said to an Israeli diplomat: 'It is a pity there are no regular diplomatic relations between our

---

breakthrough to the Arabs was possible and its resulting decision that relations with the Arabs were preferable to those with Israel and that the latter had to be sacrificed for the sake of the former, was a strategic, basic policy decision on the part of China and did not result from Israel's hesitation, at least not from that of 1955. The Mission had clearly indicated that Israel was interested in fostering relations, even if at present it had not yet formally proposed diplomatic relations.

This leads to speculation as to what would have happened had Israel proposed in March 1955 the immediate establishment of diplomatic relations instead of proposing a Chinese mission to Israel. It took China two months to agree to the Israeli mission. I cannot suppose that China would have responded to an Israeli proposal to establish diplomatic relations, in March 1955, with an immediate positive reply. The Bandung Conference would have intervened before such a positive reply or, at any rate, before its consummation. The overriding basic policy considerations that led China in April to its pro-Arab decision would in any case have been the determining element. Even had diplomatic relations been established—which it seems quite unrealistic to suppose—China's pro-Arab policy would have led it to break them off—soon, or in 1956, or at the latest in 1967.

The tactical decision of March 1955 was a mistake. But it had little, if any, causal influence on China's Middle East policy. That policy was determined by a basic, global decision—taken despite China's knowledge that Israel was interested in full and friendly relations. Shimoni communication, 1972.

two countries, but your region boasts such unrest that, firstly, you must settle your differences with the Arabs.' (A communication to the author from a Foreign Ministry source.)

5. In December 1961 Israel's Ambassador to the USSR, Arye Harel, made a semi-private visit to China; nothing came of his discussions.

6. There were other contacts. As a Foreign Office summary-memo observed: 'Israeli diplomats in various capitals persevered on instructions from their government, in their attempts to cultivate relations with their Chinese colleagues, but no results of substance emerged.'

A notable instance of inter-governmental contact occurred in 1963, when Chou En-lai addressed a letter to all Heads of Government concerning the nuclear test ban treaty, about to be signed, and urging a total ban on nuclear weapons. The letter arrived in Israel by 'Ordinary Mail'. Prime Minister Eshkol replied in a friendly tone and again conveyed Israel's interest in relations. The letter was personally transmitted by a senior Israeli official to the Chinese Embassy in Stockholm. The Chinese Ambassador listened politely to his suggestion for the resumption of contacts. Peking did not respond. (A communication to the author from a Foreign Ministry source.)

7. Israeli inquiries about trade have all been rebuffed. In one case a private request for a PRC visa received the following response: 'When you can show us your Egyptian, Syrian or Iraqi visa, you can come back for your Chinese one.' (A private communication to the author.)

8. In July 1971 it was divulged that *Mapam*'s representative in Paris, Eli Ben-Gal, had held conversations with members of China's Embassy in Paris during the preceding three years. The Chinese desired the contact, but. . . . This episode was widely reported, at first in *Ma'ariv* on 26 July 1971, then in *Jerusalem Post*, *Ha'aretz*, and *Al Ha-mishmar* on 27 July ff.

There were also several press reports at the same time about alleged Chinese interest in diplomatic relations with Israel, communicated by Roumania's Deputy Foreign Minister to Prime Minister Meir, during his first visit to Israel, and via Israeli diplomats in Africa. *Jerusalem Post* and *Ha'aretz*, 27 July 1971 ff. Early in November 1971 China's Prime Minister, Chou En-lai, declared that Peking was not planning to establish normal relations with Israel. 'But it is not impossible', he reportedly stated, 'to develop friendly relations with the people of Israel.' Interview reported in Tokyo, as carried in *Ma'ariv*, 7 Nov. 1971. This question arose following Israel's voting behaviour on the issue of China's admission to the UN. There were four resolutions:

(a) to postpone all voting from 25 to 26 October 1971 (53 for, 56 against, 19 abstentions): Israel abstained;

(b) to vote first on a US proposal to require a 2/3 majority to expel the (Nationalist) Republic of China (61 for, 53 against, 15 abstentions): Israel was for;

(c) to require a 2/3 vote to expel the Nationalist regime, i.e. the first substantive resolution (55 for, 59 against, 15 abstentions): Israel was for; and

(d) to expel Nationalist China and to seat the PRC (76 for, 35 against, 17 abstentions): Israel was for. *Jerusalem Post*, 27 Oct. 1971.

In an opening speech to the UN General Assembly, China's Deputy Foreign Minister, Chiao Kuan-hue, strongly supported the Arab cause: 'The essence of the Middle East question is aggression against the Palestinian and other

Arab peoples by Israel and Zionism, with the support and connivance of the super powers. The Chinese Government and people resolutely support the Palestinian and other Arab peoples. . . .' *Jerusalem Post*, 17 Nov. 1971. Later that month the Italian Socialist leader, Pietro Nenni, brought a personal despatch from Mrs. Meir to Chou but was rebuffed in his effort to build a bridge between Jerusalem and Peking. *Ma'ariv*, 26 Nov. 1971.[1] One incontrovertible fact remains. The strategic decision of March 1955 to decline the PRC's overtures for diplomatic relations resulted in a prolonged absence of normal, in fact any, Israeli ties with the third super power and a pivotal state in the non-Western world.

(E) DECISION FLOW[2]

Decisive Inputs to Tactical Decision 1

1. 1 October 1949	People's Republic of China (PRC) was proclaimed in Peking, following total Communist victory in Chinese Civil War; the new regime requested recognition from all states.
2. 2 October 1949– 7 January 1950	More than a dozen states, including several non-Communist countries (Burma, India, Pakistan, Ceylon, Norway, and, especially, the UK), recognized Peking.

Tactical Decision 1 (China)

3. 9 January 1950	Government of Israel decided to accord *de jure* recognition to People's Republic of China.

Implementation of Tactical Decision 1

4. 9 January 1950	Foreign Minister Sharett cabled Israel's recognition to Chou En-lai, Prime Minister and Foreign Minister of PRC.
5. [A.D. 31 January 1950	Israel's Minister to Soviet Union was instructed to suggest to PRC Ambassador that Israeli delegation in Moscow be liaison between Israel and China; 'suitable occasion for contact did not arise'.]

[1] For further data on China's attitudes to Israel from 1955 to 1973 see Brecher 1974, Appendix III.

[2] Items within round brackets have been included in an earlier phase of the Decision Flow and, therefore, are not given a separate step-number. Items within square brackets are stillborn or unfulfilled steps. A.D. refers to abortive decision.

6. [A.D. 28 June 1950   Government of Israel decided, in principle, to establish diplomatic relations with PRC but to delay announcement and implementation because of Korean Crisis; decision was stillborn.]

Decisive Inputs into Strategic Decision 1

7. 25 June 1950   Korean War broke out.

8. 25 June 1950   President Truman ordered air–sea support for Republic of Korea (South Korea) by US forces in Far East.

9. 25–27 June 1950   Security Council passed two resolutions:
(1) calling for cease-fire (25th) and
(2) requesting member-states to assist Republic of Korea (27th).

10. 29 June 1950   UN Secretary-General requested all member-states to inform Secretariat of their proposed aid.

11. 26 June 1950ff.   United States diplomats at UN and in Washington conveyed Truman's expectation of Israel's support for UN–US actions.

Strategic Decision 1

12. 2 July 1950   Government of Israel abandoned its basic policy of non-identification by aligning with the West (US) in critical inter-bloc crisis through decision to support UN resolutions and actions in response to outbreak of Korean War.

Implementation of Strategic Decision 1

13. 3 July 1950   Government of Israel's decision was conveyed to UN Secretary-General.

14. 3 August 1950   Israel offered medical aid, via UN, to Republic of Korea.

15. 7 October 1950   In line with Sharett's pro-Western speeches to General Assembly on 27 September and 4 October, Israel voted for Eight-Power draft resolution enabling UN forces to cross 38th Parallel, but at same time attempted to find compromise formula.

16. 13 December 1950   Israel opposed Soviet draft resolution

	calling for immediate withdrawal of all foreign troops from Korea.
17. 1 February 1951	Israel voted for a US-sponsored General Assembly resolution which branded Government of PRC aggressor in Korea.
18. 18 May 1951	Israel supported a Western-sponsored General Assembly resolution recommending arms embargo against China.

Pre-Decisional Events to Strategic Decision 2

(9 January 1950	As noted, Israel recognized People's Republic of China.)
(28 June 1950	As noted, in response to direct inquiry by China's Chargé d'Affaires in Moscow of his Israeli counterpart on 20 June, about Israel's intent re diplomatic relations, Government of Israel made decision in principle to establish diplomatic relations with PRC—but not to announce or to implement decision until Far East crisis cleared up; it remained abortive decision.)
(... 1950	As noted, Israel supported UN acts on Korean War on 2 July, 3 August, 7 October, etc.)
19. 19 September 1950	Israel voted for Indian and Soviet draft resolutions to seat Peking's delegation as sole representative of China in General Assembly.
(... 1951	As noted, Israel supported Assembly resolution terming China an aggressor, on 1 February, and Assembly resolution calling for arms embargo against China, on 18 May.)
20. 25 October 1952, 15 September 1953	Israel abstained on Western 'moratorium' resolution to postpone for a year consideration of all proposals to exclude Nationalist representatives and to seat PRC delegation.
21. 23 December 1953	China's overtures to Israeli envoys in Rangoon and Helsinki expressing wish to form ties. (Hacohen told China's Ambassador to Burma on 16 February

that Israel wished to send trade delegation to China.)

Decisive Inputs into Tactical Decision 2(a)

22. 9 January 1954

Eban conveyed opposition to any move in direction of diplomatic relations with Peking.

23. 15 February 1954

In response to Sharett's inquiry, Shiloah conveyed from Israel's Washington Embassy strong opposition to relations with Peking, on grounds that it would alienate US Government and American Jewry. He reiterated opposition on 24 February, buttressed by his (and Eban's) discussion with Under-Secretary of State Bedell-Smith. This persuaded Sharett to cancel planned Cabinet discussion of that issue.

Tactical Decision 2(a)

24. 25 May 1954

Ministerial Committee on Foreign Affairs and Defence decided not to proceed with active pursuit of diplomatic relations until after Geneva Conference on Indo-China, then in process.

Decisive Inputs into Tactical Decision 2(b)

25. 13 September 1954

Following Chou En-lai's informal invitation to Hacohen on 29 June to visit China, China's Ambassador in Rangoon informed him of official Peking approval for visit of Israeli delegation to negotiate on all issues, affecting the 'two friendly states'.

26. 23 September 1954

Notwithstanding apparent shift in Israel's policy on China representation issue at UN—from abstention to vote for US 'moratorium' resolution, on 21 September—Chou En-lai informed National People's Congress of intention to establish 'normal relations' with (Afghanistan and) Israel.

27. October–November 1954 Continued opposition to diplomatic

relations with Peking regime flowed
from *Mapai* ministers Lavon and Aranne
and others in 'the American lobby'.

Tactical Decision 2(b) (China)

28. 14 November 1954   Government of Israel approved dispatch of official *trade* delegation to
China—without authority to negotiate
on diplomatic relations; Sharett informed *Knesset* of invitation and decision
on 15th.

Implementation of Tactical Decision 2(b)

29. 28 January–   Five-man trade delegation, headed by
    24 February 1955   Hacohen, toured China, negotiated
principles of commercial ties, and held
informal talks on diplomatic relations.

Decisive Inputs to Strategic Decision 2

(13 September 1954   As noted, Peking invited Israeli delegation to visit China and to negotiate
on all issues.)

(23 September 1954   As noted, Chou En-lai informed
National People's Congress of intention
to establish 'normal relations' with
Israel.)

(October–November   As noted, powerful opposition to diplo-
1954   matic relations with Peking regime
flowed from *Mapai* ministers Lavon and
Aranne and others in 'the American
lobby'.)

30. 27 February–   Following return of trade delegation,
    28 March 1955   Hacohen dispatched stream of cables
and letters from Rangoon to Jerusalem
advocating immediate decision and
action to establish diplomatic relations
with PRC and warning of adverse
consequences of inaction at approaching Bandung Conference.

Strategic Decision 2 (China)

31. 28 March 1955   Prime Minister–Foreign Minister Sharett decided *not* to pursue *actively*
diplomatic relations with Peking—by

imposing as precondition a visit to Israel of reciprocal Chinese delegation.

Implementation of Strategic Decision 2

32. 3 April 1955

Head of Israel Foreign Ministry's Asian Department wrote letter to counterpart in Peking renewing invitation to send Chinese delegation to improve *trade* relations.

(Post-Strategic Decision 2) Events

33. 4 April 1955

In reply to Sharett's 'reciprocity' decision, Hacohen asked Foreign Office why Israel should link indissolubly issues of diplomatic relations and prior reciprocal PRC delegation to Israel.

34. 13 April 1955

Hacohen decried as inadequate Jerusalem directive to him to inform Chinese Ambassador in Rangoon *orally* that Israel was considering establishment of diplomatic relations.

35. 15 April 1955

In response to Sharett's further inquiry, on 14 April, Eban renewed his advocacy of diplomatic ties with PRC.

36. 22 April 1955

Hacohen informed Foreign Ministry that Chou En-lai supported pro-Arab resolution at Bandung Conference; and Hacohen renewed plea for immediate Israeli action on issue of diplomatic relations.

Belated Reversal

37. [A.D. 24 April 1955

In 'defeat-at-Bandung' context, Government of Israel authorized Sharett's decision to convey Israel's wish for diplomatic relations with PRC. Head of Foreign Ministry's Asian Department informed Head of Chinese Foreign Office's Asian Division on 29 April that Government of Israel 'desires to establish full diplomatic relations'. Noncommittal reply from Peking on 21 May 1955 was last formal communication on issue of relations.]

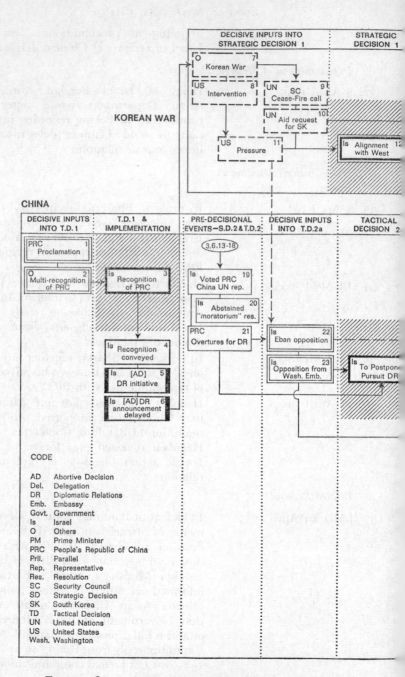

FIGURE 6. DECISION FLOW: KOREAN WAR AND CHINA

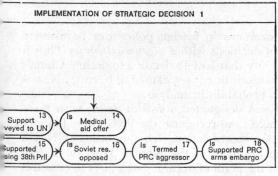

IMPLEMENTATION OF STRATEGIC DECISION 1

Support 13 veyed to UN	Is Medical 14 aid offer		
Supported 15 sing 38th Prll	Is Soviet res. 16 opposed	Is Termed 17 PRC aggressor	Is Supported PRC 18 arms embargo

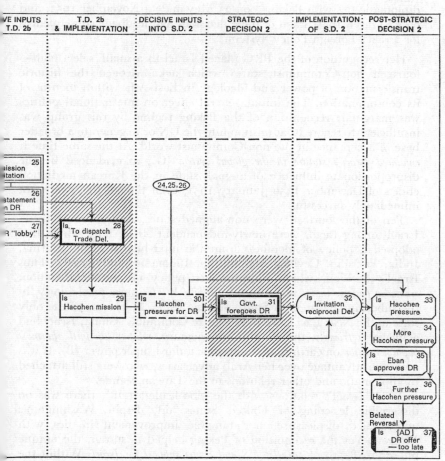

VE INPUTS T.D. 2b	T.D. 2b & IMPLEMENTATION	DECISIVE INPUTS INTO S.D. 2	STRATEGIC DECISION 2	IMPLEMENTATION OF S.D. 2	POST-STRATEGIC DECISION 2

ission 25 tation

statement 26 n DR

R "lobby" 27

Is To dispatch 28 Trade Del.

24,25,26

Is Hacohen mission 29

Is Hacohen 30 pressure for DR

Is Govt. 31 foregoes DR

Is Invitation 32 reciprocal Del.

Is Hacohen 33 pressure

Is More 34 Hacohen pressure

Is Eban 35 approves DR

Is Further 36 Hacohen pressure

Belated Reversal

Is [AD] 37 DR offer — too late

(F) FEEDBACK

The impact of *positive* decisions in foreign policy can be assessed more precisely than that of decisions with a *negative* outcome. Thus it cannot be stated with certainty that Israel's decision to decline China's overtures for diplomatic relations in 1954–5 caused a, b, c, . . . Nevertheless, one may engage in probabilistic analysis.

The Korea/China issue was designated a *decision cluster*, with three basic, interrelated decisions: (1) to recognize the PRC, on 9 January 1950; (2) to abandon non-identification, by supporting UN–US actions in response to the outbreak of the Korean War, on 2 July 1950; and (3) to hesitate to the point of declining overtures to establish diplomatic ties with Peking—on 25 May and 14 November 1954, and on 28 March 1955. Each of these decisions had feedback consequences for Israel's Foreign Policy System.

Her recognition of the PRC placed Israel in a small, select club— fourteen non-Communist states which acknowledged the historic transformation of power and ideology in East Asia within months of its consummation. The initial general effect on international politics was marginal: recognition of the Peking regime by this group was insufficient to secure its admission into the UN or to generate a broader base of acceptance in the non-Communist world. At the same time it *enhanced Israel's stature in the global system* (G), as evidenced by the disproportionate influence of a small state in the Korean mediation efforts of December 1950–January 1951, even though they were not immediately successful.

Ten of the fourteen were non-aligned states. And seven of these, Israel among them, were newly-independent *Asian* states which had adopted a policy of aloofness from the inter-bloc struggle (Burma, India, Pakistan, Ceylon, Afghanistan, Indonesia, and Israel). Thus Israel's decision, which reflected her policy of non-identification, *created a positive image in the emerging Third World*, more particularly, in the subordinate system of Southern Asia (SO). Moreover, as the only state in the Near East Core to recognize Communist China, Israel had achieved *a friendly*, though still rudimentary, *relationship with the most populous nation* on earth, soon to become a third super power (B). It was a unique advantage over her Arab adversaries, who were still attached by diplomatic and other relations to the Taiwan regime.

As for Israel's relations with the bloc leaders (DB), there was no discernible lessening of United States aid, despite Washington's unconcealed displeasure, nor tangible improvement in ties with Moscow. Yet the recognition of Peking helped to sustain the unique phase (1948–50) of *parallel US and Soviet support for Israel*. Within the internal environment only one component was the modest recipient of feedback: the act of recognition, strongly urged by the Left and carried out by a Centre Coalition, *removed one source of friction within the political structure* (PS). It was a minor contribution to the accommodation process in an emergent parliamentary democracy.

All of those feedback strands were limited in scope and time. They were, firstly, *confined to the operational environment*; that is, they did not penetrate further into Israel's Foreign Policy System—through the communication network to the high policy élite and its psychological environment. Stated differently, *the flow was aborted*. It was, secondly, short-lived. The outbreak of the Korean War less than six months later—and Israel's response—stimulated a new set of feedback effects, which *overflowed the earlier unfulfilled impact* on several environmental components.

The Korean War greatly intensified the inter-bloc struggle. As bipolarity became tighter, the policy of non-alignment came under severe attack from both camps. Some states which had chosen to remain uninvolved or non-attached experienced powerful pressures to 'stand up and be counted'—and yielded. Israel was one of them. Indeed the Korean War marks the great divide in Israel's foreign policy, the shift from non-identification to alignment with the US. Her entry into the Western camp did not affect the balance of global power; it merely added one more vote to the already large—and unreal—Western majority in the UN General Assembly. Rather, it initiated *Israel's declining stature in the global system* (G), a by-product of the end of the early phase of autonomous behaviour on issues outside the Near East Core.

Similarly, the *image of Israel* in the Third World was rapidly transformed into that of a *Western 'camp follower'*. Ironically, Israel's move away from non-alignment occurred at a time when it was a thriving international pressure group, making important contributions to the solution—or at least easing—of international conflicts, notably the Korean and first Indo-China Wars. Israel's 'membership' in the non-aligned group, always challenged by her Arab enemies and their Muslim friends, had been affirmed by the policy of *ee-hizdahut*. By 1953–4, all the epithets of 'Zionism as a puppet of Imperialism', 'Western beachhead in the Near East', etc., found a more receptive audience in the Third World, especially in Asia. Thus the positive feedback to SO of Israel's decision to recognize Peking, along with other non-aligned (and some aligned) states, was erased by a negative image, assiduously cultivated by her adversaries.

The flow effect of Israel's Korea decisions on her relations with China (B) was faint. Certainly they did not deter Peking from making recognizable overtures to Israel after the Korean War had ended. Thus *the earlier positive effect was muted—but not transformed* into hostility or even indifference.

Israel's relationship with one super power, the US, undoubtedly benefited by a pattern of consistent pro-American speeches and voting at the United Nations, but it was not enough to achieve a defence alliance or even the direct supply of arms from the United States. The impact on relations with the other super power was further deterioration, caused primarily by several pressures, some within the Soviet political system and power élite, others due to Moscow-perceived vital interests. The abandonment of non-identification contributed an added stimulus to, or rationalization for, Soviet anti-Israel behaviour, or both. In short, *the dual friendship with the super powers* (DB), a product of special circumstances in 1947–8 but sustained by the policy of non-identification, *was undermined* by Israel's responsive decisions to the Korean War. Whether those decisions were necessary cannot be verified. More important, that question is irrelevant to the incontrovertible fact that Israel's strategic, tactical, and implementing decisions on the Korean War terminated the phase of non-identification and ushered in the enduring period of aspiring alignment with, and increasing dependence upon, the West.

In the long run the effect of Israel's Korea decisions was even greater on the psychological environment of her decision-makers. The swing to the West was accompanied by, and accentuated, an image of Israel's vital interests as linked indissolubly with those of the West. Sharett's image of the global system now became identical to that of Washington; that is, a tight bipolar system dominated by the conflict between 'the free world' and the Communists. Moreover, his perception of the United States as patron became increasingly crystallized, as did his image of a hostile Soviet Union.

The Government's Korea decisions did not penetrate deeply into Israeli public opinion. Yet they caused sharp and persistent criticism from the Left, which (correctly) perceived them as a fundamental departure from Israel's foreign policy since independence. The turn to the West *aggravated the relations between Mapai and Mapam*, which then included the Left-nationalist *Ahdut Ha'avoda*. But it did not prevent those parties joining the Government in the mid-1950s and remaining within successive coalitions under Ben Gurion, Eshkol, and Meir.

The decision not to pursue actively the path of diplomatic relations with Peking in *March 1955* has been deplored by some Israeli decision-makers and dismissed by others as inconsequential. Ben Gurion remarked: 'It was wrong—and a terrible mistake.'[1] Yigal Allon, later Deputy Prime Minister, stated in 1959: 'It seems to me there then existed more opportune and easier circumstances than today to establish such ties, and to my sorrow they were missed by us and not missed by other states which had strong ties as well with the other part of the

---

[1] Ben Gurion interview, 1966.

world.'[1] Mordekhai Namir, Israel's Minister to Moscow when the first PRC approach was made in 1950, wrote in sorrow: '. . . to this day [1971] a feeling is nestled in my heart that we probably missed a once-in-a-lifetime opportunity that, despite our being one of the first states which accorded formal recognition to the new regime, we made do with pseudo-contacts by means of People's China's Embassy in Moscow only.'[2]

Eytan declared: 'Looking back historically, it was a serious mistake. It would have been a first-class move. It might have transformed Israel's position in Asia and the Third World generally.'[3] Herzog concurred: 'It was a great, great mistake—retrospectively, but one must bear in mind the background of 1954–5.'[4] R. Kidron, then with Israel's UN delegation, said: 'Looking back, it was an error'; but he hastened to add, 'we had little freedom of manoeuvre, given the intense American feeling and pressure'.[5] Lewin, naturally, was distressed by the decision, terming it a blunder of the first magnitude.[6]

Eban, as noted, defended the February 1954 decision as 'a constructive and considered decision'. He added: even if there had been relations, 'what would our wretched Chargé have accomplished?'[7] One former Director-General of the Foreign Office, Levavi, doubted that the decision was 'very meaningful' or that the relationship would have been any different (in 1966) if there had been an Israeli diplomatic mission in Peking.[8] Ya'acov Shimoni, who has alternated with Lewin in responsibility for Asian affairs in the Foreign Office most of the time since independence, was almost certain about the opportunity: 'I have little doubt that, had we made any move for diplomatic relations up to 1954, it would have been accepted [by Peking].'[9] On the insignificance of the negative Israeli decision he appears to be certain. 'I have no doubt', he was reported to have said in 1971, 'that, if we had established diplomatic relations with the Chinese then, they would have closed our embassy and expelled us like dogs, at one of the later stages: either in 1957 after the Sinai Campaign, or in the 'sixties, or at the latest, after the 1967 War. They put all their eggs in the Arab basket.'[10]

Hacohen was unconvinced: 'There is no basis for this assumption.

[1] *Divrei Ha-knesset*, xxvi, p. 1724, 30 March 1959.

[2] Namir, p. 146. Eban, then Permanent Representative to the UN, concurred with the last part of Namir's comment. He expressed the view at that time that the PRC Embassy in London would be a more appropriate place for diplomatic contact between Israel and China, *inter alia*, to avoid an impression of Israel's total identification of China with Russia. Reported by Eytan to Namir in February 1950. Namir, p. 148.

[3] Eytan interview, 1971.   [4] Herzog interview, 1966.
[5] Kidron interview, 1966.   [6] Lewin interview, 1965.
[7] Eban interview, 1965.   [8] Levavi interview, 1966.
[9] Shimoni letter, 1966.   [10] Eyal.

Why would they throw us out, any more than the Turks or the Iranians or the Roumanians? Turkey and Iran are Muslim, and Roumania a Communist state. On the contrary, just as for Roumania relations with Israel are a sign of independence, so too perhaps the Chinese would have proved they are not wagging the Soviet tail. And bear in mind we would have been sitting there for ten years in contact with the governmental leaders, explaining daily complex and difficult matters. Our ambassador would be travelling there; and the Chinese ambassador here, and reporting to Peking. Who knows how things would have developed? It is all in truth speculation. . . . But we must remember that Mao Tse-tung is no Stalin. He is Lenin. He is not irrational . . . I am not at all certain, therefore, that they would have severed diplomatic relations. . . .'[1]

The debate over what the Chinese would or would not have done in the 1960s is indeed speculation—and of the most intellectually spurious kind. So too is the *ex post facto* rationalization that the decision was right—or inconsequential—because 'it would not have made any difference anyway'. More systematic speculation is possible and necessary.

One strand of feedback is incontrovertible: the negative Israeli decision in 1955 led to a *deterioriation in relations with China* (B). The failure to seize an opportunity for diplomatic relations sundered even the embryonic commercial ties initiated by the Hacohen Mission. The non-relationship has continued—almost twenty-five years since Israel recognized the PRC and nineteen years since Israel's too-hesitant pursuit of Peking's overtures. Whether other factors, either international or domestic Chinese, helped *to perpetuate* the delay in normal relations is *irrelevant* to the *catalytic role* of the 1955 decision.

There was, too, an adverse effect of Israel's decision on China's role in the Middle East Subordinate System (S). From 1950 to the early 1960s Peking was preoccupied with domestic and regional issues. But with the development of the Palestine guerrilla organizations, Peking began to funnel arms into the Near East Core. Compared with US and Soviet involvement, China's Middle East 'presence' has been rudimentary. However, to the extent that it exists, including diplomatic recognition of *Al-Fath*, the largest of the Palestinian militant organizations, *China's role in the conflict is hostile to Israel and her interests*.[2] And that role is an indirect consequence of a triangular China–Israel–Arab states relationship in the mid-1950s: Sino-Arab friendship was made easier by Isael's failure to exploit a five-year advantage over her Arab adversaries *vis-à-vis* the PRC. From her recognition of Communist China in January 1950 to her hesitant response of March

---

[1] Ibid. The Eyal article is a useful and, in general, accurate report of the 1954–5 China Diplomatic Relations affair.
[2] See the bibliography cited in n. 1, p. 152 and n. 1, p. 156.

1955 the road to Peking was open to Israel alone among all Middle East states.

A more speculative strand of feedback from the 1955 decision may be discerned in Israel's relations with the Third World (SO). From 1948 to 1950 Israel was non-aligned. And, though the Arab states prevented her inclusion in the embryonic Asian Group at the UN, Israel's image in the world body and elsewhere was that of a new state desirous of remaining uninvolved in inter-bloc conflict. Her alignment with the US during the Korean War marred that image but not irrevocably.

China's overtures to Israel occurred at a seminal phase in the emergence of the Third World. Non-aligned India had led the way to a Korean settlement and had played a worthy role in the first Indo-China accommodation. The Colombo Powers had formed a loose association. And preparations were under way for Afro-Asia's dramatic arrival on the stage of world politics. Sino-Indian friendship was at its height. India was staunchly pro-Arab, but Communist China had been ignored, worse, rejected by *all* the Arab states.

A decisive positive response to Peking's overtures in March 1955 or, even better, in January, May or November 1954, would almost certainly have created a friendly Chinese *predisposition* towards Israel's claim to participate in the Bandung Conference. China could have—and, it is reasonable to surmise, would have—used her influence to persuade Nehru not to yield to Arab pressure on the Colombo Powers to exclude Israel. Chou En-lai's advocacy of Israel's rightful place at Bandung as an Asian state—it is illogical to assert he would not have done so immediately after diplomatic relations were established with Israel—might have been the decisive input into the wrangle over Israel's invitation. Burma's U Nu sponsored her—but Burma alone was not strong enough to turn the tide.

Once at Bandung the task of breaking down the remaining barriers to Israel's acceptance in Asia would have been eased. And the steady erosion of her image, effectively exploited by the Arab states, would have been halted. Israel's membership in the Third World would also have provided both balance and alternative paths to her *general foreign policy orientation*—preventing the increasingly narrow dependence upon Western Europe and/or the United States.

The 1954–5 decisions on diplomatic relations with China *had an adverse feedback on Israel's subsequent relations with the Third World* (SO), both in reality and in her image. That, in turn, caused her decision-makers to perceive Israel's alignment in the future *exclusively in Western terms*. They became disenchanted with the Third World of non-alignment—and were rejected by it, a mutual interaction of operational and psychological environments. It was a lengthy process, not initiated nor wholly caused by the negative decision on diplomatic relations with China. But that process was given a thrust at a crucial moment in

FIGURE 7

FEEDBACK: KOREAN WAR AND CHINA[1]

Operational Environment	*Psychological Environment and Policy Derivatives*
External	*External*

G   Enhanced Israel's stature in global system, especially in UN, as small, non-aligned state (T_1)

Reduced Israel's stature in global system (S_1)

Perception of Israel as part of 'free world' and of North Korea-cum-China as aggressors; policy derivative was alignment with West (P–D)

S   Eased Arab path to Peking and facilitated Chinese penetration of Near East Core as propaganda and arms supporter of Arab states and Palestinian guerrilla movement (S_2)

SO Created positive image of Israel in emerging Third World (T_1)

Created image of Israel as Western 'camp follower' (S_1)

Dealt severe blow to Israel's aspiration for acceptance as part of non-aligned, anti-colonial Third World (S_2)

Perception of hostility among non-aligned states, especially in Asia; policy derivative was increasingly open alignment with West (P–D)

DB Helped to sustain non-identification and, thereby, USSR support for Israel (T_1)

Shattered dual friendship with super-powers and undermined support from USSR (S_1)

Perception of US as guardian of small states, victims of aggression; policy derivative was abandonment of non-identification, and increasing dependence on US for political and economic support (P–D, E–D)

B   Initiated rudimentary friendly relationship with People's Republic of China (T_1)

Erased friendly relationship with PRC—but did not transform it into hostility (S_1)

[1] Tactical decision 2—to dispatch an official trade delegation to China (14 November 1954)—did not yield autonomous feedback; its consequences for Israel's Foreign Policy System are subsumed in the feedback from Strategic Decision 2.

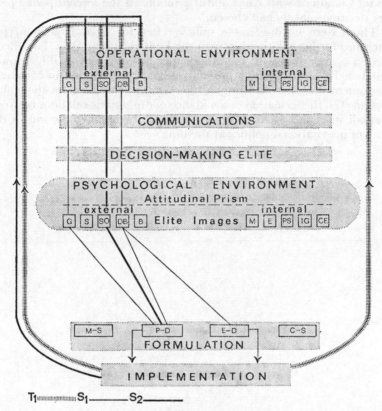

T_1—————S_1————S_2————

S_1 erased all feedback of T_1 in Operational Environment except for B (China), which was erased by the S_2 decision

Led to prolonged period of non-relations and, from mid-1960s, increasingly hostile Chinese behaviour towards Israel (S_2)

Internal

PS Removed one source of friction between Left opposition and Coalition Government (T_1)
Aggravated relations between Centre Coalition and Left Opposition (S_1)

Israel's relations with Asia; and it symbolized the foreign policy path her decision-makers had chosen.

There were no discernible spillover benefits from Israel's 1954–5 decisions for her relationship with the United States (DB). The effect, if any, on relations with the other super power is not readily known, but Israel's China decision probably added confirmation to Moscow's assessment that she was firmly in the Western camp. As for the global system (G), the formation or avoidance of diplomatic relations between a small state and a pariah great power was a minuscule event in the flow of international politics at the time.

CHAPTER 5

Jordan Waters

The quest for water has been a persistent theme in *Yishuv*-Israeli activity during the past half century. It was, indeed, another front in the struggle for increasing immigration into the Jewish National Home; that is, the battle over Palestine's absorptive capacity. And, after independence, the expansion of irrigation and electric power resources was sought relentlessly, to enhance the new state's economic and survival capability.

Israel made several decisions concerning the Jordan River and its tributaries during the decade of the fifties. Two of them may be designated tactical, in terms of their scale and duration of importance, one preceding, the other following the basic, strategic decision on this issue:

in late July 1953 — Israel's Prime Minister–Defence Minister and her Foreign Minister approved a recommendation by a Government-designated, *ad hoc*, Committee, which included the Agriculture and Finance Ministers, to activate an engineering proposal to divert the Upper Jordan at Gesher B'not Ya'acov[1] and to transport that water to the arid Negev; (T_1)

on 22 February 1955 — Israeli leaders decided to accept the Revised (Johnston) Unified Water Plan. (S)

The strategic decision of 1955, so designated because it remained the foundation of all subsequent Israeli behaviour regarding the Jordan Waters issue, was put into operation during the following nine years.

Shortly after 18 November 1958 — the derivative tactical decision was finally taken by Israeli leaders: to shift the diversion point to Eshed Kinrot, at the north-western corner of Lake Tiberias (Kinneret, Sea of

[1] The 'Bridge of Jacob's Daughter', the Arab rendition of which is Jisr Banat Ya'qub.

Galilee) and to activate the
National Water Carrier Project,
part of Israel's Ten Year Plan,
which had been approved in
February 1956. (T₂)

The diversion scheme was so designed as to ensure that Israel would
draw from the Jordan River (no more than) the quantity of water
allocated to her in the Unified Plan. From 1958 onwards her actions
were co-ordinated with the United States Government and, informally,
through Washington, with the Jordanian Kingdom's irrigation-cum-
hydroelectric projects. Israel's National Water Carrier Project was
completed in June 1964, despite Arab threats and attempts to divert
the Hasbani and Banyas headwaters of the Jordan River.

(A) OPERATIONAL ENVIRONMENT

The setting for Israel's strategic decision was complex, with both
external and internal inputs into her Foreign Policy System. There were
six relevant components of the environment, of varying intensity and
persistence.

The United Nations (G) was active and influential at an early stage
of the decision flow. In October 1953 the Chief of Staff of the UN
Truce Supervisory Organization (UNTSO), General Bennike, ruled
that Israel must suspend work on her canal project at Gesher B'not
Ya'acov which had begun the preceding month. That, in turn,
catalysed an important United States act—to withhold economic aid
to Israel until the UN ruling was obeyed. Thus the world body was
instrumental in preventing the implementation of Israel's decision to
divert the Jordan within the Demilitarized Zone. The legacy of UN
intervention in 1953 is also evident in Israel's later decision to shift the
diversion point to Lake Tiberias, which is entirely within Israeli territory.
That decision, the *sine qua non* for the construction of the National Water
Carrier, was made in a setting in which UN disfavour was a known,
though passive, restraint on Israel's perceived freedom of choice.

The Near East Core of the Middle East subordinate system (S) was
the pervasive geo-economic component of the setting for the entire
decision flow, from the pre-decisional events beginning in 1920 to the
completion of the project in 1964. In fact, the Jordan Waters issue
focused on the system's capacity to mobilize meagre water resources
for the benefit of all riparian states—Israel, Jordan, Syria, and
Lebanon—and thereby to create a precedent for regional co-operation
among those conflicting states.

The headwaters of the Jordan River rise in the foothills of Mt.
Hermon, the second highest peak—after Mt. Lebanon—in the Near
East Core (2,840 metres). Its spring-fed sources flow in three separate

rivers—the Hasbani, in Lebanon, the Banyas, in (pre-1967) Syria, and the Dan, in Israel. These converge in Israeli territory about 8 kilometres south of the Lebanese frontier at the northern edge of the Huleh Valley, to form the Jordan River Fork. The Dan descends 185 metres and the Banyas more than 300 metres before reaching that valley. Just beyond the Gesher B'not Ya'acov, south of the drained Lake Huleh area, the Jordan makes a drop of 270 metres on its short (15 km.) course towards Lake Tiberias. The Lower Jordan is joined by its main tributary, the Yarmuk, soon after emerging from the southern end of the Lake near Israel's oldest *kibbutz*, Degania. Eleven smaller streams and rivulets flow into the Jordan between the Lake and the Dead Sea, into whose salty wastes the river empties after a tortuous course of 110 km.; during that journey it drops another 200 metres—to the lowest point on earth.

The path of the Jordan River and its tributaries creates a complex geopolitical pattern of rivers and borders among the riparians. Syria and Lebanon have the status of upstream states *vis-à-vis* Israel and the Kingdom of Jordan, as far as the Hasbani and Banyas are concerned. Israel, on the Jordan River, is a downstream state in relation to Syria and Lebanon but an upstream state relative to the Kingdom of Jordan. The Yarmuk is a frontier river between Jordan and Syria (32 km.) and then becomes the border between Israel and Jordan (14 km.) until it joins the Jordan River. And the Jordan River forms the boundary between Israel and Jordan for about 30 km. before continuing its flow through the Jordanian Kingdom to the Dead Sea.[1]

Thus the near-success of the Johnston Mission (1953–5), incorporating formal co-operative sharing of the region's water and *de facto* recognition of Israel by her Arab neighbours, makes the Jordan Waters issue unique in the pattern of Arab–Israel relations.

Another persistent environmental input was the United States (DB). Her roles ranged from effective restraint (the imposition of economic sanctions in October 1953) to quiet approval for Israel's behaviour (especially, the unilateral withdrawal of Jordan water). Indeed the DB component (Israel's relationship with a super power, in this issue the United States) was dominant throughout the decision flow.

Israel's first tactical decision was aborted by US action. The strategic decision, too, revealed the presence of 'the American factor'. The implementation of that decision took the form of a *Draft Memorandum of Understanding* in mid-July 1955, the result of three months of bilateral negotiations in Washington. The decision to shift the diversion point to

---

[1] Since the 1967 War, the Jordan River became the *de facto* frontier between Israel and the Kingdom of Jordan for its entire length between its junction with the Yarmuk south of Lake Tiberias and the Dead Sea. For relevant geo-economic and demographic data see AFME, pp. 1–3; Doherty, pp. 3–7; Garbell, pp. 25–8; Rosenne, pp. 3–6; Stevens 1956, pp. 234–5.

Lake Tiberias was made in a setting of continued opposition by both the United Nations and Washington to the Gesher B'not Ya'acov project. Finally, Israel's construction of her National Water Carrier (1959–64) was made possible by US approval and financial aid.

The internal setting was less conspicuous, but three domestic components are readily discerned—economic capability (E), and the advocacy of interest groups (IG) and competing élites (CE). Israel's economic growth is, in large measure, dependent upon accessible water from the Jordan–Yarmuk River System for irrigation. One constraint is the need to share that water with the three other riparian states, none of which acknowledges Israel's legitimacy. Another (more severe) limitation is the paucity of water in the region of the Jordan–Yarmuk River System.

The amount of water available to Israel from all sources has long been subject to controversy, but there is a consensus about its inadequacy. Israeli officials, following the optimistic estimate of 'large, unused water resources' by Lowdermilk and others in the 1940s, perceived Israel's water potential, in 1952, to be 3,200 million cubic metres (henceforth referred to as mcm) per annum. This was gradually reduced to 2,400 mcm and, a decade later, according to an informed publicist, to no more than 1,500 mcm.[1] And an authoritative Israeli source, in 1964, cited 1,700 mcm as 'the average annual amount of water that can ultimately be brought into use by employing present-day methods': that referred to all resources—groundwater, rivers, springs, diversion of the Jordan, etc.[2]

The total annual flow of the Jordan–Yarmuk River System, the allocation of which was central to the Johnston Mission, was about 1,000 mcm, almost equally divided between the two rivers.[3] Even the maximum figure (1,880 mcm) is tiny, in comparison with other rivers in the Middle East: about 1 per cent of the Nile, less than 3 per cent of the Tigris, and less than 8 per cent of the Euphrates, the principal rivers of Egypt, Iraq, and Syria–Iraq, respectively.[4] This does not diminish its significance, for 'History has magnified the Jordan in the thinking of reverent or merely interested millions out of all proportion to its actual size. To be sure, its basic importance cannot be magnified, because its role in history has been great beyond all rational measure-

---

[1] Schiff, p. 27.   [2] Prushansky, p. 14.

[3] The Hasbani supplies about 150 mcm, the Banyas 120 mcm, and the Dan 240 mcm; that is, about 510 mcm in all to the Upper Jordan or Jordan Fork. The Yarmuk contributes a little less to the Lower Jordan. The average annual discharge at the Allenby Bridge near Jericho is 1,250 mcm.

[4] AJC, p. 2, note. In terms of eastern US rivers: '. . . this would be comparable to the flow of only a relatively small river such as the Genesee River of Portageville, New York or the Passaic River at Paterson, New Jersey'. M.V.C. Hare, 'The Jordan Valley of the Future: Desert or Garden', *The Near East*, 7, 6, June 1954, p. 12, as cited in AFME, p. 2.

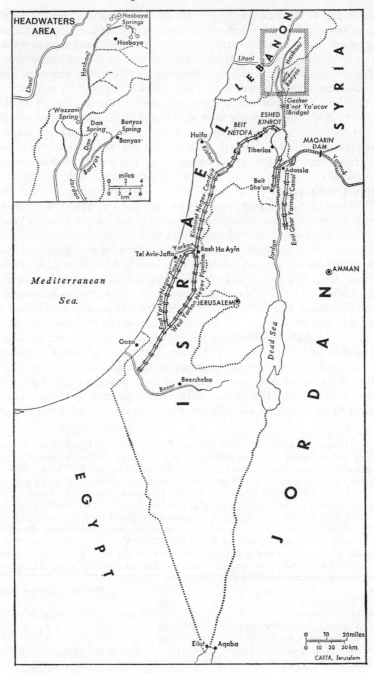

HEADWATERS AREA

Hasbaya Springs
Hasbaya

Litani

Hasbani

Wazzani Spring
Dan Spring
Banyas Spring
Dan
Banyas
Banyas

Upper Jor...

miles
0 2 4
0 2 4 6
km

LEBANON

Litani

Hasbani
Banyas

SYRIA

Gesher B'not Ya'acov (Bridge)

ESHED KINROT

BEIT NETOFA

Haifa

Tiberias

MAQARIN DAM

Yarmuk

Adassia

Beit She'an

East Ghor Yarmuk Canal

Kishon

Kinneret Negev Conduit

Mediterranean Sea.

Yarkon
Tel Aviv-Jaffa
Rosh Ha Ayin

East Yarkon Negev Pipeline

West Yarkon Negev Pipeline

JERUSALEM

Gaza

Besor Beersheba

I S R A E L

Jordan

Dead Sea

AMMAN

J O R D A N

E G Y P T

Eilat Aqaba

0 10 20miles
0 10 20 30km
CARTA, Jerusalem

THE NATIONAL WATER CARRIER OF ISRAEL

ments. . . . It is in connection with the revelation of the divine that the importance of the Jordan becomes paramount, exceeding that of any other river in the world.'[1] Moreover, the dispute involves four states in protracted conflict, with Jordan Waters one of many 'fronts'.

Even without the conflict, economic development imposes heavy demands for water. About 60 per cent of Israel's pre-1967 territory was desert. Her principal water resources are in the north, while large tracts of cultivable, though then arid, land lie in the northern Negev. By 1970, with a population of three million (excluding territory occupied in the Six Day War), almost all available water was in regular use (1,500 mcm). Yet maximal immigration continues to be encouraged, to achieve the core national goal of *kibbutz galuyot* ('ingathering of the exiles'), with its multiple implications—ideological, economic, and military–security enhancement. Thus the acute shortage of water (E) was a major environmental input for decisions on the Jordan Waters issue—in the 1953–5 period and again in 1963–5.

Compared with other major foreign policy issues, Jordan Waters did not arouse strong and continuous criticism from Israel's opposition parties (CE). For one thing the dispute, the data, and the decisions were highly technical in nature. Secondly, other objects of attention, more dramatic and more receptive to rhetoric, were present at the time, notably the Lavon Affair[2] and escalating border tension. Moreover, the Jordan Waters issue lacked a crisis atmosphere; in fact, it dragged on for many years. When, as in the case of Israel, a political system is accustomed to an environment of crisis, a non-crisis foreign policy issue does not stimulate sustained advocacy by competing élites. This is evident from the infrequent reference to Jordan Waters during *Knesset* foreign policy debates in 1953 and 1954.[3] Even in 1955,

---

[1] Glueck, p. 62.

[2] The *cause célèbre* of Israeli politics since independence, the Lavon Affair began in 1954 as a result of an Israeli intelligence fiasco in Egypt. At first it caused political rumbling and important personnel changes, with Lavon leaving the Defence Ministry and Ben Gurion returning to that post in February 1955. Revived in 1959, it created havoc within Israel's political system, notably by causing the split in *Mapai* in 1965 which gave birth to the *Rafi* party (*Reshimat Po'alei Yisrael*—Israel Workers' List).

[3] Thus, only 8 of 21 participants (4 of them from parties in the Coalition Government) referred to the water controversy during a two-day debate shortly after Israel was compelled to suspend work on the Gesher B'not Ya'acov project—and that indifferent advocacy followed a lengthy statement on the issue by Foreign Minister Sharett. *Divrei Ha-knesset*, xv, pp. 270–314, 30 Nov. and 1 Dec. 1953. The pattern was repeated in more acute form on subsequent occasions:

Date	Speakers	Speakers on Jordan Waters
1. 2–3 March 1954	16	5
2. 10–11 May 1954	21	4
3. 30 August–2 September 1954	25	1
4. 15–16 November 1954	31	1

1. *Divrei Ha-knesset*, xv, pp. 1045–9, 1056–71. 2. Ibid., xvi, pp. 1596–1638. 3. Ibid., pp. 2547–70, 2575–87, 2602–10. 4. Ibid., xvii, pp. 64–109.

when the strategic decision was made, Jordan Waters was a peripheral *Knesset* issue: there was a brief discussion in January, Motions for the Agenda in February and May, a Question in March, and a foreign affairs debate in October, with two of seventeen participants referring to the controversy.[1]

The most vocal critics were *Mapam* and *Herut*, with rare interventions from members of Coalition parties, *Ha-po'el Ha-mizrahi* and the Progressives. The nationalist Right asserted Israel's sovereignty over the Demilitarized Zone and attacked the Government for yielding to external pressures. *Herut* leader Begin spoke thus in March 1954:

You began very important development work in the channel of *our* Jordan. Along came General Bennike, the water governor in Israel and ordered you to stop work. . . . The American Foreign Minister, who gives Naguib pistols of steel, pulled his 'silver' gun from his pocket and pointed it at your forehead. . . You stopped work—you received the US money. . . . Why do you not resume work? Do you at all suspect another implementing order? . . . There have suddenly appeared in the northern Demilitarized Zone new citizens, 'citizens of the United Nations, the first world citizens on the globe', and they are found within the State.[2]

The initial Left-socialist view was stated by *Mapam*'s Ya'acov Riftin—in the context of an attack on Dulles and the US as the principal source of international tension: 'Since his visit [to Egypt] the Washington Government's pressure on Israel has greatly increased; a grant was delayed. And after this delay the Government of Israel gave in. . . .'[3] Yitzhak Ben Aharon voiced the hard line of the nationalist Left, the *Ahdut Ha'avoda* splinter from *Mapai*, which had, for some years (1948–54), been part of *Mapam*:

We are speaking here of the question of our sovereignty on sources of living and on our rights to develop the great wastes, the Negev, with water the source of which is in our State. . . . It is an attempt to interfere in the physical and national future of this Land and State . . . because the Negev is required by them for strategic anti-Israel purposes opposing peace. . . .[4]

We demand that the Israeli Government veto on resumption of work in the Jordan Channel be removed. This would be a sort of demonstration of our independence, more so than talk.[5]

Harari of the (liberal) Progressives urged caution on the resumption

---

[1] *Divrei Ha-knesset*, xvii, pp. 493–5, 508, 3–4 Jan.; ibid., pp. 913–14, 23 Feb.; ibid., pp. 1666–8, 18 May; ibid., p. 1109, 16 March; and ibid., xviii, pp. 85–106, 18 Oct. The principal engineering expert on that issue referred to discussion in the *Knesset* on Jordan Waters as 'simply chatter'. 'The critical stand of *Herut* was not the result of a demand for water in the Negev, but just a desire to change the Government.' Blass letter.

[2] Ibid., xv, p. 1065, 3 March 1954. See also Haim Landau's blunt attack, 'Our sovereignty is what counts'. Ibid, p. 281, 30 Nov. 1953.

[3] Ibid., p. 271, 30 Nov. 1953.   [4] Ibid., p. 305, 1 Dec. 1953.

[5] Ibid., p. 1601, 10 May 1954.

of the diversion project.[1] And a spokesman for the religious-workers party, *Ha-po'el Ha-mizrahi*, termed the Jordan Waters essential for development and immigration, with independent control of the water indispensable to Israel.[2]

Criticism was resumed in February 1955. *Maki*'s Moshe Sneh placed the Jordan Waters issue in the broad context of the Cold War, Western alliances in the Middle East, and Israel's global policy: 'Development schemes are impossible without the joint usage of water, and the joint usage of water is impossible without peace. Development requires peace, and peace requires opposition to joining war alliances. This requires a basic change in Israel's foreign policy.'[3] At the very end of the Johnston Mission, Begin taunted the Government: 'I sometimes wonder: What has happened to you "men of action", that you have been warning so much. If you have decided to act—do so! . . . Don't announce and warn again and again, but start the work, and the world will know we are a sovereign state, that Mr. Dulles as well cannot threaten us. . . .'[4]

The advocacy by *Mapam* reflected not only the ideological and programmatic alternative of an opposition political party (CE): the two main components of that party were agrarian movements, whose *kibbutzim*, scattered across the country, were heavily dependent upon water for irrigation—*Ha-kibbutz Ha-artzi* of the Marxist-Zionist *Ha-shomer Ha-tza'ir* and *Ha-kibbutz Ha-me'uhad* of the Left-nationalist *Ahdut Ha'avoda*. These powerful interest groups transmitted pressure through their *Mapam* spokesmen in parliament. A third *kibbutz* movement, the *Ihud Ha-kvutzot*, was linked with the mainstream governing party, *Mapai*. Its access to high-policy decision-makers was assured by the *kibbutz* membership of several *Mapai* ministers and their receptivity to the vital need of agricultural settlements, whose continued élite status belies their steadily-declining proportion of the population. The most important avenues of IG advocacy were Finance Minister Eshkol and the Director-General of his ministry, Pinhas Sapir, the latter conveying the shared interests of smallholder co-operative settlements, *moshavim*, in a larger water supply.

The *kibbutz-moshav* complex was the principal interest group in the setting for decision on Jordan Waters. Less cohesive was private and public industry, which perceived benefits in the form of larger electric power resources. Their pressure, too, was made known quietly through contacts in the bureaucracy and the Cabinet. Indeed this was the

---

[1] Ibid., p. 1618, 10 May 1954.

[2] Yitzhak Rafael, ibid., xv, p. 276, 30 Nov. 1953.

[3] Ibid., xvii, p. 914, 23 Feb. 1955. Similar statements were made by *Mapam*'s Riftin, ibid., and *Ahdut Ha'avoda*'s Zisling, on 18 May 1955, ibid., pp. 1666–7.

[4] Ibid., xviii, p. 90, 18 Oct. 1955. *Mapai*'s Herzl Berger replied that 'The stoppage of work in the Demilitarized Zone has not . . . seriously delayed the implementation of our irrigation plan . . .', ibid., p. 110, 19 Oct. 1955.

fundamental difference between advocacy by parties and interest groups: the first was more vocal (and can therefore be readily documented). The second used quiet—and no less influential—channels for communicating demands.

The presence, pressure, and power of the United States (DB)—to harm or to benefit Israel—was the most actively influential of the six relevant components. Demands by Israeli agricultural settlements (IG) were the pre-eminent internal input, a counterweight to American pressure for compromise, especially on water quotas. The pervasive hostility of Israel's neighbours (S) was a geopolitical given in the decision process, just as Israel's aspiration for more rapid growth (E) was a geo-economic constant. Party advocacy (CE) was essentially a visible supplement to interest group demands. And United Nations restraint (G) was important only in the early stage.

(B) DECISION-MAKERS AND THEIR IMAGES

When the decision was taken to divert the Jordan at Gesher B'not Ya'acov, in July 1953, Israel's Government was a four-party Coalition of 14 members—*Mapai* (8), General Zionists (3), *Ha-po'el Ha-mizrahi* (2), and Progressives (1). By then, Eshkol held the Finance portfolio as well as the key Agriculture post in the Jewish Agency; as such, he joined Ben Gurion and Sharett as the principal decision-makers on Jordan Waters. In February 1955, when the strategic decision was taken to accept the Revised Unified Plan, the four-party Coalition was still in office, but *Mapai* and the General Zionists were relatively stronger, with 9 and 4 members respectively; the other two constituents remained unchanged. The most striking change, however, was the formal absence of Ben Gurion from the Government and the division of his two ministerial posts between Sharett and Lavon. Israel's fourth Cabinet, formed on 26 January 1954, was as follows:

Mapai

Moshe Sharett	Prime Minister and Foreign Affairs
Zalman Aranne	Without Portfolio
Ben-Zion Dinur	Education and Culture
Levi Eshkol	Finance
Dov Joseph	Development
Pinhas Lavon	Defence
Golda Meyerson (Meir)	Labour
Peretz Naftali	Agriculture
Behor-Shalom Shitreet	Police

General Zionists

Peretz Bernstein	Commerce and Industry
Yisrael Rokah	Interior

Yoseph Saphir   Communications and Transport
Yoseph Serlin   Health

Ha-po'el Ha-mizrahi and *Mizrahi*
(National Religious Party)
Yoseph Burg   Posts
Moshe Shapira   Religious Affairs and Welfare

Progressives
Pinhas Rosen   Justice

The Government which authorized acceptance of the *Draft Memorandum of Understanding* with the United States was smaller—3 parties and 12 ministers: abstention on a vote of no-confidence by the General Zionists led Sharett to resign on 29 June 1955 and to re-form his Cabinet without them. Yet that change made no difference to the decision process, for, as the Government Secretary at that time remarked: 'Very little was said about Jordan Waters in meetings of the Government; certainly it was not discussed in detail.'[1]

There is a consensus that Ben Gurion, Sharett, and Eshkol were the decision-makers at the policy level.[2] BG was in 'retirement' at Sde Boker during the second and third Johnston tours but 'he was kept informed and participated in all major decisions, even when he was out of the Government'.[3] Sharett carried the issue through the Cabinet and the *Knesset*. And Eshkol was the central figure in the negotiations, especially as Head of Israel's delegation during the crucial third round. Both engineering experts on the delegation termed Eshkol's influence decisive. One of them, Simha Blass, explained it thus: 'The founder of *Mekorot* and a man of the settlements, he was considered knowledgeable in the matter.'[4] The other, Aharon Wiener, noted the interaction among the decision-makers and the intangible negative veto: 'Had Eshkol taken a negative stand, Sharett would have accepted it, for Eshkol was respected as having a special feel and knowledge about the water problem. At the same time, Eshkol was close to Ben Gurion then. If *he* had taken a hard line, it might have been decisive. They sought Ben Gurion's confirming support for a course of action already selected.'[5] Apart from Sharett and Eshkol, Blass and Wiener, the negotiating team included three civil servants—Pinhas Sapir, Teddy Kollek, then Director-General of the Prime Minister's Office, and Ya'acov Herzog, then Head of the Foreign Ministry's United States Department.

Ben Gurion rarely spoke about Jordan Waters. His frequent reference to 'making the desert bloom' indicates a perception of more water as vital to economic growth (E). Yet that aim was always defined in

---

[1] Sharef interview, 1971.   [2] Herzog interview, 1966.
[3] Wiener interview, 1971.   [4] Blass, p. 20.
[5] Interview, 1971.

instrumental terms, related to the constant core of his world-view—
security.[1] Indeed he acknowledged this candidly: 'The things I
thought about most concerned security. I didn't take a special interest
in economic matters. I left these to Eshkol and Kaplan.'[2] This is also
illuminated by several passages in his authoritative *gestalt* definition
of security:

... the scope of our defence ... does not depend on our army alone. ... Israel
can have no security without immigration. ... Security means the settlement
and peopling of the empty areas in north and south; ... the establishment of
industries throughout the country; the development of agriculture in all suitable areas; and the building of an expanding (self-sufficient) economy. ...
Security means economic independence. ...[3]

The link between water, growth, and economic independence—a
constituent of security—is also evident in BG's remarks to Blass at the
peak of the decision process, in July 1955: 'From whom will we get the
water', he asked; 'from the Americans or from the Good Lord?'
Blass replied: 'from God'. 'The main thing', responded Ben Gurion,
'is the possibility to start work and for us not to be dependent on other
developments.'[4]

There was one other strand in Ben Gurion's perception: 'We shouldn't
forget we are discussing a possible breakthrough with the Arabs.' Such
was the essence of BG's soft line on the proposed water quota for
Israel in February 1955. More precisely: '... the quantity was close
enough to what Israel would accept; a dialogue with the Arabs was
important in itself; and it was preferable to work on the basis of an
agreed distribution of water because the Jordan is an international
river.'[5] As another participant recalled, the BG view was: 'sacrifice a
certain amount of water, if that is necessary to get an agreement—but
keep the UN out of any central function'.[6] In short, the two pivotal
components of Ben Gurion's image for decision were security and peace
—in our terms, the enhancement of Israel's military (or survival)
capability (M) and an accommodation with Israel's neighbours (S);
economic growth was subordinate to the former objective.

Eshkol approached the Jordan Waters issue in more down-to-earth
economic terms. He had always been close to the land, by experience
and conviction: he was a *kibbutz* member for almost fifty years and an
active rural labourer for fifteen; he admired A. D. Gordon's call for
national redemption through a return to the soil, and by predisposition
he was an '*eesh meshek*', that is, a practical man concerned with the day-
to-day problems of increasing productivity. As he recalled to his biographer in 1968: 'No one had been keener than I was on getting back

---

[1] For a general analysis of his psychological environment see Brecher, pp. 261–9,
381–2.   [2] Ben Gurion interview, 1966.
[3] Ben Gurion, pp. 22–4.   [4] Blass, p. 35.
[5] Wiener interview, 1971.   [6] Herzog interview, 1966.

to the land. I loved the land, and it was central to my philosophy of life.'[1] Moreover, Eshkol was the pre-eminent Israeli public figure in the related fields of immigration absorption, land settlement, and economic development, through his dual posts at the Jewish Agency and in the Government. And from 1952 onwards, as Finance Minister, he held primary responsibility for national economic growth.

In his only remark to the *Knesset* on Jordan Waters he declared, simply: 'Certainly when Johnston was here, we argued for our rights and for the quantity of water. In general we are arguing over water. The water is required by someone. We are arguing over the area and the quantity per dunam.'[2]

Eshkol's image thus focused primarily on economic capability (E), with the demand by *kibbutzim* and *moshavim* for more water (IG) providing an additional stimulus to his behaviour. He was not oblivious of its security implication: all Israeli decision-makers are aware of the link. But unlike Ben Gurion he did not approach Jordan Waters (or any other economic issue) primarily from a security (M) perspective.

Nor did Sharett, the most active Cabinet participant in public discussion over Jordan Waters. Always articulate, Israel's first Foreign Minister (he was Prime Minister for most of that period as well) illuminated his image of the setting in several statements to the *Knesset*. The most revealing was made in November 1953, soon after the first round of talks with Johnston.

He was not indifferent to the United Nations' role (G): 'Of course, it is desirable for us to resume work on the basis of a final agreement with the United Nations.' (That external component was soon to be replaced by 'the American factor' (DB).) He affirmed support for the principle of regional water planning (S). He placed special emphasis, however, on the economic dimension: the term 'development project' was used four times. More important was the following passage:

All who are interested to receive our co-operation in this area must be aware of one thing. Water for Israel is not a luxury; it is not just a desirable and help-ful addition to our system of natural resources. *Water to us is life itself.* It is bread for the nation—and not only bread. Without large irrigation works we will not reach high production levels, to balance the economy and to achieve economic independence. And without irrigation we will not create an agricul-ture worthy of the name . . . and without agriculture—and especially a deve-loped, progressive agriculture—we will not be a nation rooted in its land, sure of its survival, stable in its character, controlling all opportunities of production with material and spiritual resources. . . .[3]

---

[1] Prittie 1969, p. 181. Eshkol's daughter, Dvorah, conveyed to Prittie 'his excite-ment over the building of a new pumping station near Haifa', adding that 'being in charge of Israel's agriculture gave him a supreme sense of purpose and achievement'; pp. 147–8.

[2] *Divrei Ha-knesset*, xvii, p. 495, 3 Jan. 1955. A dunam is a quarter of an acre.

[3] Ibid., xv, pp. 270–1, 30 Nov. 1953.

In the spring of 1955, replying to a question about Israel's 'national interest' in continuing the negotiations with Johnston, Sharett stated: 'Israel's national interest is to get . . . an efficient and undisturbed use of the sources of her water for purposes of irrigation and production of power.'[1] Thus, while alluding to the larger purposes of survival (security), which was central to Ben Gurion's image, Sharett's perception was much more akin to that of Eshkol: for them E was the most salient component of the environment. For both, too, the advocacy by agricultural settlements (IG), though not publicly acknowledged, was a closely related input to decision. Yet with Sharett another strand is apparent. Throughout, he related an agreement on water to the larger task of accommodation with Israel's Arab enemies (S). As the 'Weizmannist' *par excellence*, any decision that strengthened the path to peace through diplomacy, compromise, and co-operation was welcome.[2] Even more than Ben Gurion, his behaviour during the negotiations revealed the dominant role of that regional component in his image of the Jordan Waters issue.

(c) DECISION PROCESS

The roots of the Jordan Waters issue lie in the convergence of geo-economic and historical phenomena. The first is the paucity of natural resources in Palestine—water, coal, oil, and other—and the consequent dependence of a viable economy on the development of hydro-electric power; this was perceived as best provided by the falls of the Litani and the Yarmuk rivers. The second strand is Zionism's aspiring claim to a restored national home in the Land of Israel.[3] Throughout 1917 and 1918 Jewish nationalists and pro-Zionist Englishmen advocated the continued integration of 'Eastern' and 'Western' Palestine. More pointedly, the Advisory Committee on Palestine proposed, 'on historical, economic and geographical grounds', that its boundaries should include, 'in the North, the Litani River, the Banyas, close to and north of the sources of the River Jordan . . .'.[4]

Great Power considerations dictated a less generous territorial settlement. British Government promises to Weizmann notwithstanding, the UK yielded to France's insistence that the waters of the Upper Jordan—the Hasbani and Banyas—and the Yarmuk, as well as the Litani, remain in French-controlled Lebanon and Syria. An Anglo-French agreement on the boundary issue was signed on 23 December 1920; the report of the Boundary Commission was approved on 3

---

[1] Ibid., xvii, p. 1109, 16 March 1955.

[2] 'Weizmannism', as compared with 'Ben Gurionism' and 'Buberism', is discussed in Brecher, pp. 280–90.

[3] The founder of political Zionism was conscious of this dimension, as is evident in his diary entry for 23 Aug. 1896. See Herzl, p. 195.

[4] *London Bureau*, 1586, 6 Nov. 1918, as quoted in Ra'anan, p. 101.

February 1922 and took effect from 10 March 1923. Formal international sanction was provided by the Council of the League of Nations
in 1924.[1] Thus ended the first attempt by the Jewish national movement
to secure control over the headwaters of the Jordan–Yarmuk River
System and the hydro-electric potential of the Litani. The blow was
softened by the final demarcated frontier which placed all of Lake
Tiberias in Palestine, along with a tiny strip of territory to the east and
a fertile, triangular area bounded by the Jordan, the Yarmuk, and the
Lake.[2] Those by-products of negotiations by colonial Powers were to
remain regional realities in the environment for Israel's decisions on
Jordan Waters.

The Anglo-French agreements of 1920 and 1922 were the first two
pre-decisional events. The third occurred in 1926, when the Mandatory
Government granted to the (Zionist) Palestine Electric Corporation
exclusive rights—for seventy years—to use Jordan and Yarmuk waters
in order to generate hydro-electric power. The 'Rutenberg Concession'
was approved by the Transjordan Government two years later and
did not arouse objections from the French Mandatory authorities in
Lebanon and Syria. During the next two decades the Concession
became a pillar of industrial development in the *Yishuv*'s economy. It
was, too, a valued precedent for further exploitation of the Jordan–
Yarmuk River System.[3]

The first hydrographic survey of the Jordan Valley was conducted—
by the Transjordan Government—as an outgrowth of the Peel Commission's recommendations (1937). The ensuing Ionides Report impinged upon the subsequent Arab–Israel dispute because of three
pivotal features: a proposed diversion of Yarmuk water—through an
East Ghor canal, with a feeder canal from the south end of Lake
Tiberias—to irrigate 75,000 acres of Transjordanian land; an insistence on the primary use of the Jordan River water within the Jordan

---

[1] The texts of the Anglo-French border agreements are in Cmd. 1195, London
1920 (*Franco-British Boundary Convention of December 23, 1920*), and Cmd. 1910, London
1923 (*Agreement between H.M. Government and the French Government respecting the boundary
line between Syria and Palestine from the Mediterranean to El-Hammé*). For a careful discussion of the frontier problem in Mandatory Palestine, 1918–25, see Ra'anan, ch. v.

[2] There were two other 'compensations': (1) the 1920 Franco-British convention
permitted the use of Upper Jordan and Yarmuk water in Palestine *after* the self-
defined requirements of French-mandated Lebanon and Syria had been met; (2)
the Boundary Protocol of 1922 authorized the Palestine Government to construct
dams on Lakes Huleh and Tiberias, with adequate compensation to owners and
tenants of flooded lands.

[3] Israel's most prominent water engineer wrote many years later that Rutenberg
probably constructed the hydro-electric works at Naharayim, in Transjordan, in
order to control in one plant the three topographical components of the Concession—
the Jordan, the Yarmuk, and the Kinneret; further, that it affirmed—in an unconventional manner—a Jewish presence, a fact, where Jews were a small minority.
Blass, p. 1.

Valley's drainage basin (both of these were to be integral parts of all later Arab plans); and the suggestion that Lake Tiberias be used as a reservoir for Yarmuk flood waters. The scheme was not implemented for almost twenty years because the Woodhead Technical Commission (1938) reversed the thrust of the Peel Report's Partition Plan.[1]

The *Yishuv's* hopes concerning the Litani received support from an unexpected source in 1943: a joint study by Jewish engineers of the Palestine Water Company and a Lebanese engineering firm headed by Albert Nakkache concluded that only one-seventh of that river's flow could be effectively harnessed in Lebanon and that the rest might beneficially be diverted to the Jordan Valley. The following year Jewry's optimism about Palestine's absorptive capacity was given its most imaginative expression by a distinguished US conservationist.

Drawing upon the TVA's experience, W. C. Lowdermilk recommended a large-scale Jordan Valley Authority (JVA) which would irrigate the arid land of the Jordan Valley on both sides of the river; create a power programme in the deep incline of the river; introduce sea water from the Mediterranean to develop power and to compensate the Dead Sea for the loss of diverted Jordan sweet water; and transmit surplus water thus derived to the Negev desert. The crucial proposal was to divert the sweet water of the Upper Jordan, Yarmuk, and Zarqa Rivers into open canals or closed conduits running around the slopes of the Jordan Valley. Lowdermilk estimated the total irrigation potential as 1·2 million dunams (300,000 acres), almost double the area of irrigable land in the Valley, thus leaving a substantial surplus for irrigation elsewhere, including the Negev. The power potential of his scheme was estimated at a billion kw. hours per year. As the Ionides Report did for all Arab plans, so the Lowdermilk proposals permeated all Israeli plans, especially the 'out-basin' use of surplus water 'to make the desert bloom'.[2]

The Lowdermilk vision was given operational content in engineering studies prepared by other Jewish Agency consultants, notably J. B. Hays and J. L. Savage. The ensuing Hays Plan, which was published on the eve of Israel's independence, set out eight stages for the realization of a Jordan Valley Authority, designed to permit irrigation of two-thirds of the proposed total land area without the co-operation of neighbouring Arab states. Lowdermilk had estimated Palestine's absorption capacity at 4 million Jewish refugees—beyond the existing population of 1·8 million. Hays and Savage were more cautious but optimistic nonetheless: a viable economic basis for 1·75 million—in

[1] See Ionides (1) and (2); AFME, p. 12; Doherty, p. 13; and Stevens 1965, p. 238.
[2] See Lowdermilk, ch. xi; AFME, pp. 13–15; and Doherty, pp. 13–14.

agricultural settlements and towns—as a result of 2·4 million dunams of newly irrigated land.[1]

Planning for irrigation and power continued after the 1948 War, but no decision relating to the diversion of Jordan Waters was taken for five years.[2] In the interim Israel became embroiled in acute international tension as a result of her attempt, early in 1951, to implement one of the projects in the Hays Plan—the drainage of the Huleh marshes, then located in the Israel–Syria Demilitarized Zone.[3] Syria protested to the Security Council on 14 February 1951, asserting that Israel's action violated the Armistice Agreement of 1949 because it would increase her military capability. Israel countered that the Demilitarized Zone fell within her sovereign jurisdiction. Nevertheless, she accepted a Security Council resolution of 18 May, calling upon the Palestine Land Development Company to 'cease all operations in the Demilitarized Zone until such time as an agreement is arranged'

---

[1] The eight stages were as follows:

'1. development of underground water resources, principally along the coast but also in Emek Esdraelon and Jordan Valley;
'2. utilization of the Upper Jordan summer flow including Hasbani storage water for irrigation of . . . Lower Galilee, Emek Esdraelon and Afula-Beit Alfa;
'3. diversion and storage of Yarmuk River, with a 50-50 division of water between Palestine and Transjordan;
'4. the implementation of the Mediterranean seawater–Dead Sea Hydroelectric project;
'5. recovery of winter surplus waters of Upper Jordan with storage at Sahl al Battauf, to irrigate Afula area and Coastal Plain down to Rehovot;
'6. reclamation of Huleh Lake and Swamps;
'7. utilization of remaining Jordan Waters . . . for irrigation in Jericho area; [and]
'8. storage of flood water in *wadis* along the Coastal Plain, for irrigation in the Negev.'

Hays, p. 16, as quoted in AFME, pp. 16–17. See AFME, pp. 16–26, for a detailed technical summary of the Hays Plan; also Doherty, pp. 15–17.

[2] The effect of the war and a reason for the delay were explained thus: 'According to the boundaries of the British Mandate it was possible to begin the diversion of the Jordan tributaries (the Dan, Banyas and Hasbani) starting from the height of the Dan (+182) and to bring them to Beit Netofa by gravitation. Because the Banyas enters our legitimate border at a height of +300 and the Hasbani at +145, the engineer G. B. Hays suggested building (in Lebanon) a higher dam and flow the water by gravitation to the same height as the Dan. But after the War of Independence a section of the Banyas flow canal remained in the demilitarized zone and we could not reach the required height. Also, no one believed we would reach an agreement with Lebanon about the Hasbani. In spite of this, it took a long time for us to give up the nice idea of gravitation. We thought that a miracle might occur and we would reach an agreement with the Arabs.' Blass letter.

[3] *Yishuv* planners had long aimed to reclaim this highly-fertile land, especially after the 44 square miles of the Huleh Valley were sold, in 1934, to the (Jewish) Palestine Land Development Company. The Peel Commission had endorsed the project. (Cmd. 5479, London 1937, p. 258, as quoted in Stevens 1956, p. 237.) And both Lowdermilk and Hays had emphasized its role in increasing Palestine's absorptive capacity.

on compensation to Arab landowners and tenants in the Huleh region.[1]

The 1951 Huleh incident did not, *per se*, affect Israel's decision to proceed with her Jordan diversion project. Yet they were related in several foreign policy dimensions: both were located in the Demilitarized Zone and aroused international tension; Israel suspended activities in both cases under UN pressure; and Israel used the 1951 ruling which authorized civilian projects in the Zone as a precedent for her diversion project in 1953.[2] The stimulus to the first tactical decision lay elsewhere, however.

In 1952 an American engineer, M. E. Bunger, proposed the construction of a high dam at Maqarin on the Jordan–Syria border, to create an artificial lake of 500 mcm. A canal would lead to Adassiya, where a diversion dam would carry that impounded Yarmuk water along to East Ghor—to the exclusive benefit of land in the Kingdom of Jordan. A related electric power project, to generate 40,000 kw. per year, was also suggested, for Syria's use. Most important, no reference was made to Israel, a riparian state with the legal right to use Yarmuk water. An agreement to execute the Bunger Plan was signed between Jordan and UNRWA in March 1953, and work started in July, a month after an agreement between Jordan and Syria to exploit Yarmuk water.[3] It was those Arab activities which catalysed an Israel Foreign Ministry interest in the Jordan Waters issue.

In a memorandum to policy-makers prepared in October 1952, Blass noted that large-scale Israeli water projects had been prepared and he advised that the time had come to implement these, in part. 'In the meantime', he remarked, 'several real questions have appeared: drying the Huleh [marshes] and irrigating it, commencing construction of the Gesher B'not Ya'acov–Beit Netufa Canal', etc. Nothing was done. Then, in the spring of 1953, Prime Minister Ben Gurion mooted

---

[1] UN.SCOR, 546th Mtg., 16 May 1951, pp. 2–5. The UNTSO Chief of Staff, General Riley, ruled in June 1951 that civilian land conservation was permitted in the Demilitarized Zone by the terms of the Armistice Agreement and authorized Israel to implement the project—subject to the proviso regarding compensation. This incident and the UN role is examined in Bar-Ya'acov, ch. 4, esp. pp. 66–93. The Huleh Project was completed in 1956, restoring 45,000 acres of fertile land.

[2] On the link between the two projects in Israel's case before the UN see Eban, pp. 7–15, especially the sections 'Huleh Scheme Similar', 'The Moral of 1951', and 'Continuity in Principles'.

[3] Miles E. Bunger was attached to the Point 4 Technical Co-operation Agency in Amman. His report was prepared jointly with the Jordan Government's Department for Water Resources Development. On the Bunger Plan see Bunger (1) and (2); AFME, pp. 32–4; Doherty, pp. 20–1; and Nimrod (1), p. 39.

Another plan, commissioned by Jordan's Government in 1949, was prepared by a British engineering firm, Sir Murdock MacDonald & Partners; it was published in 1951 but never implemented. See MacDonald, *passim*; AFME, pp. 27–31; and Doherty, p. 20.

the idea of dividing the Demilitarized Zone with Syria. In conversation with Blass he revealed the 'peace with Israel's neighbours' component of his image of the Jordan Waters issue: 'We are in a quarrel with all the Arab States. There is much political significance, if at least one Arab State would sign any agreement with us. Possibly from here there is hope for a peace pact. Your contentions [Blass opposed the idea of partition on technical, water, grounds] are very important, but a hopeful outlet to peace is more important.' Blass persuaded Dayan, *Tzahal* Commander of the Northern Front. And Ben Gurion's proposal failed to secure a Cabinet majority.

Israel's decision to divert the Upper Jordan at Gesher B'not Ya'acov (tactical decision 1) was made in late July 1953. Concern about the Bunger Plan, which had just been activated, is evident in a Blass memorandum to a Cabinet *ad hoc* committee, urging that work be started on the diversion project: 'a Government decision is necessary'. 'I was asked', he wrote many years later, 'whether there was no choice but to begin at Gesher B'not Ya'acov, which was in the Demilitarized Zone. I replied that the actual diversion and the portion of the Canal in the Zone were but a small part of the project and it was possible to delay this work for a number of years, when political conditions would be appropriate. It was possible to draw the water from the Kinneret: it would cost about a million dollars [then, 3 million Israeli pounds] more per annum.'[1] Finance Minister Eshkol and his DG, Sapir, were sceptical, especially because funds were not available—and the Yarkon–Negev Project, then under way, demanded large sums. The Foreign Office representative was opposed, because of political complications. In favour were Agriculture Minister Naftali and Aluf Dayan, whose rationale was that Syria's ruler, Colonel Shishakly, was then preoccupied with internal political problems and would not interfere.

The Dayan–Naftali view prevailed in the Committee: Blass referred to the former as 'the decisive force'. The decision was not taken by the Government as a whole, for this issue—a water project—lay, formally, within the jurisdiction of the Agriculture Minister. As noted, Naftali actively supported the proposal. Eshkol acquiesced. And, shortly after, the recommendation was approved by the two other senior ministers directly involved—Prime Minister–Defence Minister Ben Gurion and Foreign Minister Sharett.[2]

---

[1] Blass letter. Blass explained his own rationale thus: 'I had two reasons: The Jordanians would build a water project from the Yarmuk, and if they finished before us, they would claim that they needed more of our water. Therefore we must not lag behind. And secondly, I knew that implementation of the Jordan–Negev Project was a complicated and expensive operation and required a lot of time: if it were needed in 10 to 12 years, we had to start immediately.'

[2] The analysis of the decision process from October 1952 to July 1953 is based primarily on Blass's detailed memoir, pp. 2–6, supplemented by the Blass letter. The

In a larger sense the politically hazardous decision was made primarily on technical grounds: Blass had advised diversion at Gesher B'not Ya'acov because there was no salinity in the Jordan at that point, in contrast to Lake Tiberias. Ben Gurion confirmed this basis of the decision: 'We knew that the water in the Kinneret was salty—and there it is pure.' Equally important, 'the Lake is 200 metres below sea level; Gesher B'not Ya'acov is higher. These were the two important reasons.'[1] Eshkol remarked: 'It was taken on technical grounds,' adding, 'in fact, the advice of the engineers was less than ideal.'[2] And a senior Foreign Ministry official recalled that, when Eban asked Blass in New York in October 1953 if the diversion could be done outside the Demilitarized Zone, he acknowledged: 'Yes, but it would cost Israel an extra 3 million [Israeli] pounds.'[3] The cost of ignoring the political dimension proved to be much higher: the decision was not implemented, and the diversion point was later changed.

The intent to proceed with the project was communicated to the UN Chief of Staff orally on 31 July 1953, and in writing on 2 September. On 2 September 1953 Israel began work on the canal at Gesher B'not Ya'acov: it extended from the River to the Lake and was designed to use the 270-metre drop in the Jordan flow between the diversion point and the Kinneret—and to use that power to pump water into the diversion canal southwards. As might have been anticipated, Syria protested once more to the Security Council. On 16 October she charged that: (a) diversion of the Jordan infringed upon the right of (Arab) inhabitants of the Demilitarized Zone to exercise their normal activities; (b) Israel's acts would prevent Syrians from irrigating their lands with Jordan water; and (c) Israel had conducted military operations in the Zone. General Bennike had called upon Israel on 23 September to cease work on the canal and now ruled in favour of Syria. The ruling was ignored—until Secretary of State Dulles announced, on 20 October, that the US Government was withholding funds earmarked for Israel by the Foreign Operations Administration.[4] Economic sanctions, the

---

idea of diverting the Jordan at Gesher B'not Ya'acov was conceived earlier. Blass himself referred to it in his October 1952 memorandum. One writer ascribed it to an 'All-Israel' Plan of November 1950, as part of a four-stage programme (Doherty, p. 17); but she acknowledged that the 'Plan' was never published and relied upon a single secondary source (Bowman). Another analyst mentions the 'All-Israel Plans' but without data or content (Peretz 1955, p. 404). Neither Blass nor Wiener recalled it in connection with Gesher B'not Ya'acov (interviews, 1971). In any event, the decision on Gesher B'not Ya'acov was not made until July 1953. The 'All-Israel' Plan of 1950 may, at best, be regarded as a pre-decisional event.

[1] Ben Gurion interview, 1966.

[2] Interview, 1966. The first technical plan to divert Jordan water to the Negev was submitted by Blass as early as 12 February 1941. The idea reappeared in *Yishuv* and Israeli planning for the next dozen years and beyond.

[3] Gazit interview, 1966.

[4] USSD, pp. 589–90. President Eisenhower made it known the following day that

only *publicly announced* instance of direct US pressure of this kind, were heeded within two weeks.[1] On the 27th Israel accepted a temporary discontinuance of the Gesher B'not Ya'acov project but 'without prejudice to [her] rights, claims, or position in the matter'. President Eisenhower responded by announcing the resumption of economic aid to Israel.[2]

The dénouement of tactical decision 1 coincided with the initial phase of decisive inputs into the strategic decision on Jordan Waters. On 16 October 1953, two days after Israel's major reprisal at Kibya, President Eisenhower announced the appointment of Eric Johnston as his personal envoy to seek, with Near East states, a comprehensive programme to develop the Jordan River's water resources 'on a regional basis'. Underlying the initiative were three postulates: the successful Marshall Plan experience could be transposed to the Middle East; the optional path to solution of political problems was economic aid and co-operation; and the Arab–Israel conflict required a piecemeal, constructive approach, not a 'package deal'. In this perspective Johnston's stated objectives were a viable solution to the Arab refugee problem and, more generally, economic progress and stability of the area.[3]

Direct US Government intervention was one decisive input. Another, intimately related, was a comprehensive report to UNRWA, prepared by Charles T. Main, under the direction of the TVA and with the backing of the State Department. The Main Plan, announced on 19 October, provided the technical basis for Johnston's initial negotiations with Israel and the neighbouring Arab states.[4]

The essence of the report is this:

As a problem of engineering the most economic and the quickest way to get the most use from the waters of the Jordan River System requires better organization of the headwaters on the Hasbani and in the Huleh area to serve the lands by gravity flow within that part of the Jordan watershed and use of Lake

---

he had been consulted by Dulles and that he approved the sanctions decision. *MEA Chronology*, iv, 12, December 1953, p. 429.

[1] At the height of the Sinai–Suez conflict, on 7 November 1956, the US Government conveyed through diplomatic channels (Acting Secretary of State Hoover to Israel's Minister to the United States, Shiloah) a threat to apply economic sanctions. It was not publicized and proved to be unnecessary, as will be elaborated in ch. 6 below.

[2] For Israel's case before the Security Council see Eban, *passim*; see also Shimoni. A detailed analysis of the 1953 UN episode is to be found in Bar-Ya'acov, pp. 117–30, and pp. 151–65.

[3] The text of Johnston's terms of reference is in *MEA*, iv, 12, Dec. 1953, p. 413. See also *New York Times*, 17 Oct. 1953, and Bar-Ya'acov, pp. 130–5.

[4] The Main Plan resulted from an UNRWA request to the TVA in 1952 to prepare a plan for the unified development of the Jordan–Yarmuk River System. It was submitted to the Governments concerned in August 1953, after approval by UN authorities, and was published in October following press leaks.

Tiberias as a storage reservoir for the flood flows of the Jordan and Yarmuk Rivers. From Lake Tiberias these waters would be made available by gravity flow to irrigate lands on the east and west sides of the Jordan Valley to the south. Gravity flow eliminates expensive pumping facilities. Storage reservoirs save flood waters for use in the dry months. Use of the natural reservoir afforded by Lake Tiberias takes advantage of an asset already at hand; there is no known alternative site, at any cost, for a reservoir that would effectively regulate and store the flood flows of the Jordan and its main tributary, the Yarmuk.[1]

The pivotal idea of the Main Plan was *integrated regional planning* for irrigation and power projects, this despite Clapp's conclusion in 1949 as Chairman of the UN Economic Survey Mission for the Middle East:

The region is not ready, the projects are not ready, the people and Governments are not ready, for large-scale development of the region's basic river systems or major underdeveloped land areas. To press forward on such a course is to pursue folly and frustration and thereby delay sound economic growth. . . . Engineering, technical and financial assistance must assume peace and co-operation before men and money can be applied to the development of the Jordan River System as a whole.[2]

The pre-conditions were as remote from reality four years later. Yet folly was pursued, frustration was endured—and the Johnston effort, based upon the Main Plan, came closer to success in breaking the Arab–Israel impasse than any other act of mediation since the onset of the conflict. The Plan intentionally disregarded political boundaries and aimed at the resettlement of about 200,000 Palestinian Arab refugees in Jordan and the West Bank. There was some affinity with Israeli plans; for example, diversion of the Yarmuk into Lake Tiberias and of part of the Upper Jordan before it reached the Lake, as well as support for the Tel Hai power project. Main emphasized, as did the Arabs, in-basin use of the Jordan Waters. He rejected the Bunger proposal to use the Maqarin Dam for irrigation, though endorsing it for power generation. And no reference was made to power development in Lebanon or to Israel's hoped-for use of Litani water. On the crucial question of water allocations the Plan was cautious, but it did specify the additional land to be irrigated if carried out in its entirety and the quantum of water 'within present political boundaries':

	Dunams	mcm water
Israel	416,000	394
Jordan	490,000	774
Syria	30,000	45

[1] TVA Director Gordon Clapp's letter to L. Carver, Director of UNRWA, as cited in AFME, p. 35.

[2] UN.CCP, Final Report of UNESMME, Part I, 28 Dec. 1949, p. 13. See also Stevens 1956, pp. 251–4.

The cost was estimated at $121 million, most of which was to be borne by the US (apart from the $14 million Jordanian Yarmuk Dam and $76 million Israeli Mediterranean–Dead Sea project). Finally, the Plan recognized that the states concerned might have different ideas on several aspects of regional economic development, including the specific areas within their boundaries to which these waters might be directed.[1]

The Johnston mediation effort was enacted in four rounds of negotiations between October 1953 and October 1955. Of his extraordinary persistence his closest aide throughout wrote later:

No man ever worked harder at a job than Johnston worked at this one. On the four separate visits to the Middle East over a span of three years on which I accompanied him as an adviser, I watched him argue and cajole his way through hundreds of weary hours of the most detailed and harassing negotiations it is possible to imagine. He burned the midnight oil in every US Embassy in the area preparing argumentation and counterproposals for the next meeting with one side or the other. American ambassadors winced at his tough talk to Presidents, Prime Ministers, and Kings, watched him shatter all the rules of diplomatic exchange, and ended up with a considerable amount of admiration for what several of them now call the 'Johnston technique'.[2]

The day he arrived to consult with Israeli Government leaders about the Main Plan (27 October 1953), Israel published her own Seven Year Plan, prepared for an international Jewish Economic Conference then assembled in Jerusalem. While based on the Lowdermilk and Hays principles, it aimed specifically at doubling the water supply (from 810 mcm in 1952–3 to 1,730 mcm in 1960–1) in order to treble the area of irrigated land: the goal was to meet three-fourths of the total production required by Israel for an estimated population of two million by the end of 1960.[3]

The first, three-day, discussion defined the parameters of negotiation. Sharett, Head of Israel's delegation, agreed that regional co-operation was desirable, both for the optimal use of limited water and as a possible breakthrough to a peace settlement, eased by the long-term US presence that would ensue. At the same time the Israeli team rejected the basic principles of the Main Plan advocated by Johnston: the primacy, if not exclusivity, of 'in-basin' use of the Jordan Waters— that is, within the Jordan Valley—and unqualified prior claim of the downstream state (Kingdom of Jordan) before satisfying the needs of upstream states (Israel, Lebanon, and Syria). Israel countered that the international law of rivers contained several principles, none of which exclusively supported the 'in-basin' concept. Thus she was prepared to

[1] See Main, *passim*; AFME, pp. 35–40; Doherty, pp. 22–4; *New York Times*, 20 Oct. 1953; Nimrod (1), pp. 40–1; Nimrod (4), pp. 37–9; Peretz 1955, pp. 398–401; and Schmidt, pp. 5–6.   [2] Barnes, pp. 25–6.
[3] National Water Plan 1953; UNRWA, pp. 95–7, as cited in AFME, pp. 56, 59.

discuss water quotas 'on the pragmatic basis of what is acceptable to all sides. Moreover, we made it clear to Johnston that his [water] figures were not acceptable. Johnston said he didn't expect our agreement immediately.'[1]

Israel was invited, as were the Arabs, to submit an assessment of the Main Plan, and did so. *Tahal* (Water Planning for Israel Ltd.) cited precedents, even in the United States, for use of river water outside of its basin and termed the Plan openly discriminatory on this point. The Kingdom of Jordan's water quota and estimated irrigable land were designated 'exaggerated'. Moreover, 150 mcm of water were to be permitted to flow, wastefully, into the Dead Sea, despite Israel's demonstrable needs in the Negev. And the full electric power potential of the River System, argued Israel's brief, was not exploited, notably her proposed Kinneret power station.[2] Although not included in the critique, Israel was also concerned about the authority of the 'Supervisor' who, according to the Main Plan, would be responsible for the actual division of water, a perceived threat to Israel's sovereignty and, in particular, to control over her development plans.[3]

Sharett's reaction to the US envoy's initial proposals was, as always, the most moderate. Not without reason did an early account of the Johnston Mission observe:

In [his] view . . . the advantages to Israel of improved relations and possibly direct dealings with the Arabs which might result from joint acceptance of the water plan were worth weighing. Furthermore, international financing of the joint plan would aid Israel greatly. Finally . . . [there was] the possibility of renewing negotiations eventually with Lebanon for exchange of power for water from the Litani. The long view, required of the diplomat, was at war nevertheless with the spirit of direct action prevailing in many other official [Israeli] departments. . . .[4]

Thus Development Minister Dov Joseph declared a few days after Johnston's departure: 'Since the Arabs have already announced that they do not agree to any co-operation with Israel in such a plan, there is nothing left for us to decide, but we have told Johnston that without the waters of the Litani of Lebanon there can be no regional water plan.'[5] And Defence Minister Lavon denounced plans to deprive Israel of water rightfully hers.[6] In short, Israel's attitude during the

---

[1] Wiener interview, 1971. All subsequent quotations attributed to Wiener are taken from that interview.   [2] The critique is summarized in Blass, pp. 17–18.

[3] This concern was expressed by *Mapai*'s semi-official organ, *Davar*, on 22 Oct. 1953, a few days before Johnston's arrival: '. . . the Clapp [Main] Plan is designed to sabotage the Israeli Plan for the exploitation of all water resources in Israel. Its transparent purpose is to hamstring Israel and transfer the control over its water to foreigners.' Blass, pp. 8–9, alludes to a similar expression of disquiet in the discussions of Israel's UN delegation at the time.

[4] Stevens 1956, pp. 264–5.   [5] *Davar*, 8 Nov. 1953.

[6] In a speech to the *Ihud Ha-kibbutzim Veha-kvutzot*, as reported in *Davar*, 1 Nov. 1953.

first round reflected the enduring cleavage in the images and advocacy of her high policy élite—'Ben Gurionism' *v.* 'Weizmannism'.[1]

Johnston himself reportedly termed Israel's (and Lebanon's) response 'far from enthusiastic, but slightly interested'. As for Jordan, 'the door is closed but not locked'; Syria—'the door is ajar'; and Egypt 'hinted at readiness to influence the Arab League and encourage it to take an interest in the project'.[2] Some months after the first round he remarked: 'Neither Israel nor the Arab States liked the proposals. . . . This was to be expected. But it made it clear to all of them that . . . it is not a hard-and-fast proposal, a take-it-or-leave-it proposal. On the contrary, it is open to modification.'[3] The two sides responded—with what became the bargaining postures for the second phase of indirect negotiations under the auspices of the US President's envoy (June 1954).

The Arab Plan is an unique document in the protracted Arab–Israel conflict. For one thing, it is explicitly based upon the principle of *regional* water development, though, following Ionides, MacDonald, and Bunger, exclusive 'in-basin' (Jordan Valley) use was stipulated. More important, it implied *de facto recognition* of Israel by acknowledging her status as a riparian 'state' with a right to share the Jordan Waters. The major difference from the Main Plan was the quantity of water granted to Israel—17·4 per cent instead of 32·5 per cent. But the *qualitative* change in Arab policy was, potentially, far more significant.[4]

Israel's reaction was less than enthusiastic. As Wiener recalled: 'We

---

[1] These are examined in Brecher, ch. 12, esp. pp. 280–90.

[2] *Davar*, 20 Nov. 1953.

[3] *This Week*, 14 Feb. 1954. The first round is examined carefully in Nimrod (4), pp. 41–6.

[4] *The Arab Plan for Development of Water Resources in the Jordan Valley* was produced by a Committee of Arab experts, headed by a US-trained Egyptian irrigation engineer, Dr. Mohammed Salim, and established by the Arab League Council in January 1954. Approved by the League Council on 5 April, the Plan's contents were first reported by Kenneth Love in the *New York Times* on 21 May 1954. The details are less significant and may be noted briefly:

use of the Upper Jordan and the Hasbani for irrigation and power, including the provision of water to Israel's Huleh region;

the construction of two storage dams on the Yarmuk (at Maqarin and Adassiya) to generate power and irrigate Jordan Valley lands in Jordan territory;

rejection of Lake Tiberias as the principal storage site for surplus Yarmuk waters— because it lies wholly within Israel and because the Lake's higher salinity would cause deterioration in the irrigation waters to be stored there;

utilization of the Lower Jordan, south of Lake Tiberias, and its tributaries, for irrigation of the Jordan Valley;

allocation of modest water supply to Lebanon (which the Main Plan had excluded); and

UN supervision over the distribution of water.

The text is in EEPSR, 2 Oct. 1955, pp. 42–4. For analyses see AFME, pp. 64–9; Doherty, p. 25; Nimrod (1), pp. 46–8; Peretz 1955; pp. 402–3; Rizk, p. 8; Stevens 1956, pp. 266–7; and UNRWA, p. 95.

saw it in a negative light, as a counter-bargain; what we found unacceptable in the Main Plan [the water quota] was cut almost in half.
By that time, too, we started ventilating the idea that the Jordan was
Israel's river and the Yarmuk Jordan's river, with a certain allocation
to the other state from each river.' That principle of predetermined
fixed allocation to the lesser riparian state was eventually incorporated
in the Revised Unified Plan. In the spring of 1954, however, Israel
responded with a *gestalt* conception of *regional* development in which
no water would be wasted.

The guiding principle of her Cotton Plan was to provide 'for the
full irrigation of all irrigable lands in the Kingdom of Jordan, . . . [and]
all irrigable areas in Southern Lebanon as well as Syrian lands in the
Upper Yarmuk basin, leaving Israel *all* the surplus water from the
Jordan–Yarmuk System *and the Litani flow*'.[1] The Cotton Plan envisaged
twice as much water as the Main Plan (2,345 mcm to 1,213 mcm);
almost three times the irrigated land, including a quadrupling of
Israel's area and a tenfold increase in Lebanon's share—compared
with the Arab Plan—as compensation for inclusion of the Litani in the
scheme; seven times the amount of electricity; and a fourfold increase
in cost (from $121 million to $470 million), the bulk of which would be
provided by the US Government. As with all *Yishuv* and Israeli plans
in the past (Lowdermilk, Hays, Seven-Year), the Cotton Plan also
insisted on Israel's sovereign right to use her share of water *anywhere*
within her territory; the intent was reiterated—'to make the [Negev]
Desert bloom'. Another major feature was the physical separation of
Israeli and Jordanian irrigation networks. The diversion canal at
Gesher B'not Ya'acov was incorporated once more, as was the Mediterranean–Dead Sea project. The entire plan was to be implemented in
stages within twenty-five years (compared to ten years for the Main
Plan). There was, conspicuously, no reference to a UN (or other international) supervisory role.[2]

---

[1] The inclusion of the Litani River was patently a bargaining counter; for, while
a strong case could be made on technical and geo-economic grounds, Israel's legal
claim was non-existent; the Litani was a wholly *national* river—of an *enemy* state.
The reason for her decision to press that 'claim' was illuminated by Blass: 'It is clear
that without the mutual consent of the interested countries, the Cotton Plan cannot
be implemented, and even though for the time being no such consent appears imminent, the Plan will fulfill several important functions . . .'. *Jerusalem Post*, 25 June
1954. As Wiener noted: 'Israel did not make inclusion of the Litani a *condition*; we
couldn't reject outright a plan by the President's Representative.'

[2] The Consulting Board associated with J. S. Cotton comprised H. W. Bashore,
former US Commissioner of Reclamation, Dr. J. L. Savage, former Chief Designing
Engineer of the US Bureau of Reclamation, and Dr. A. Wolman, former Chairman of
the US National Water Resources Commission. The Cotton Plan was submitted to
Israel's Government on 1 February 1954 and presented to Johnston at the beginning
of June. See Cotton, *passim*; Blass, pp. 18–19; Doherty, p. 24; Nimrod (2), pp. 19–23;
Nimrod (4), pp. 47–9; Peretz 1955, p. 404; and Schmidt, pp. 6–9.

No decisions were made during Johnston's second visit, in June 1954. The bargaining was brisk; there were some concessions by the US envoy; but several points remained in dispute. Israel's delegation was again headed by Sharett, then PM as well as FM, and included Eshkol, Sapir, Kollek, Y. Herzog, Blass, and Wiener. The Johnston team comprised two State Department specialists, Arthur Gardiner and Oliver Troxell, a personal assistant, George Barnes, and two engineers.

Sharett led off with the Cotton Plan and urged use of the Litani surplus and Lake Tiberias in a genuine *regional* scheme. Johnston replied that Lebanon's Litani could not be included. Sharett countered that the Lake, too, was an exclusive national resource; further, that Israel would not accept any plan which did not recognize her right to divert water to the Negev. This resulted in Johnston's first concession: while noting the Arab objections to 'out-basin' use, he expressed support for that fundamental Israeli demand.

Negotiations then moved to political and technical 'working groups'. Israel was urged to accept three themes: (*a*) the Kingdom of Jordan's prior claim to water, to permit the resettlement of 200,000 Arab refugees, half in the Jordan Valley, half in nearby urban centres; (*b*) joint use of Lake Tiberias as a regional reservoir; and (*c*) the necessity of a neutral supervisory agency. The Israeli reply was negative on the first two and a qualified affirmative on the third, i.e. agreement to *limited* supervision.

On the all-important issue—the quantity of water—Johnston pressed Israel to accept 400 mcm, claiming that an agreement with the Arabs would clear the *political* air. Blass, the maximalist throughout, demurred. Sapir, an outspoken minimalist, 'got excited. . . . At an internal [delegation] meeting after midnight in the Prime Minister's home, [he] shouted at me . . .: "Do you give the Prime Minister the power-of-attorney to close at 460 mcm?"' Blass explained that this figure included 60 mcm in the form of 'returning water' from irrigation of fish ponds, which belonged to Israel, and concluded: 'In reality Johnston was not so generous.'

So matters stood at the end of the second round of talks. Disagreement had not been reduced on the water quotas for each riparian state, which Israel and Jordan in particular termed insufficient; the degree and type of international supervision; the use of Lake Tiberias as a reservoir, which both Israel and the Arabs opposed—for different reasons; and the Litani River, which the Arabs and Johnston refused to incorporate into a regional plan.[1] Sharett confirmed the impasse on

---

[1] This account is based on Blass, pp. 17–22, and on Blass and Wiener interviews, 1971. See also Nimrod (4), pp. 51–4. The extent of Israeli distrust was expressed many years later by Blass: 'Johnston wanted to hold the keys to the water in the hands of the "neutral authority", who would operate according to American instructions.' Blass letter.

28 June, especially over the last two issues.[1] Thus the joint Johnston–Israel communiqué noted 'a common desire to arrive at a coordinated development of the area. As yet', however, 'they have not reached the stage of definite agreement.' By contrast, the US envoy and the four Arab states declared that they had 'reached agreement on general lines of an overall plan for the development of the Jordan Basin, and on the need for its immediate implementation'.[2] Closer examination showed that the difference was semantic. As so often in the conflict, an impression of greater Arab flexibility was created—and communicated: for example, a State Department official remarked: 'Johnston came very close to agreement with the Arabs, but the negotiations with Israel are liable to prove extremely difficult.'[3] At the same time an Israeli official noted a 'Tentative Agreement' in the working groups on 28 July 1954.[4]

'By the close of the second round', recalled Wiener, 'we decided to abandon the debate on "principles" and to concentrate on figures. From then on the main point was bargaining over the quantity of water.' That task, for Israel and the Arabs, was eased by the findings of a soil-cum-hydrological field study of the Jordan Kingdom in 1954. The Baker–Harza Report proved that the available water could irrigate more land than previously estimated, i.e. that less water was required per acre. Moreover, it demonstrated the existence of more irrigable land in Jordan's sector of the Valley. 'The Master Plan envisaged major storage of water within Arab territory, at Maqarin . . . with storage in Lake Tiberias . . . only of surplus Yarmuk flood waters. . . . Lake Tiberias storage', it asserted, 'is an absolutely essential element. . . .'[5]

Israel rejected once more the Baker–Harza assumption of an *a priori* claim to 'in-basin' use of the water within the Jordan Valley. More important, she was able to demonstrate that the Baker–Harza figures of water required per acre were too high. And the amount of available ground water, argued her engineers, showed that the Kingdom of Jordan needed less water from the Jordan River.

The technical conditions for an agreement now seemed at hand. Thus, when Johnston arrived in Israel at the beginning of his third visit (26 January–23 February 1955) he was able to offer her a substantially higher water quota—from 400 mcm to 492 mcm (62 mcm from the drainage of the Huleh marshes, not to be included in Israel's share of the Jordan Waters, and 30 mcm from her 'historic usage', also

---

[1] To a conference of editors in Tel Aviv. *MEJ, Chronology*, viii, 4, Autumn 1954, p. 456. [2] *New York Times*, 27 June 1954.

[3] Reported in *Davar*, 27 Aug. 1954, as cited in Nimrod (2), p. 26.

[4] Shimoni interview, 1971.

[5] See Baker–Harza, *passim*; AFME, pp. 75–82; Doherty, pp. 25–6; Peretz 1955, pp. 408–9; Stevens 1956, p. 269; and UNRWA, pp. 101–9.

not to be counted). Moreover, while on tour of the Arab States he sent Barnes back to inform Israel that Jordan would give her 40 mcm from the Yarmuk; this was reduced to 25 mcm by the time Johnston returned to Jerusalem for a crucial negotiating session (21–23 February).

The US envoy insisted that no agreement could be reached without the use of Lake Tiberias to store Yarmuk flood water (for the benefit of Jordan). To ease Israel's concern about possible Arab demands for territorial changes to ensure their flow of water from the Lake, Johnston promised a letter of explanation and, as a further guarantee, a letter from President Eisenhower. Sharett seemed well-disposed and re-marked: 'If this is the case we will consider the matter.' After further internal consultation the Israeli delegation agreed to recommend to their Government joint use of the Lake—if Israel received letters from Johnston and the President, as well as an explicit provision in the final agreement, and if the engineering problems were solved.

It was during this session, too, that Johnston finally accepted the Israeli proposal for an unencumbered division of water, that is, the Jordan River to Israel and the Yarmuk River to the Kingdom of Jordan, with fixed assignments to the lesser riparian party. This took the form of a revision of the Unified Plan water quotas, the so-called 'Gardiner Formula':

Syria: 20 mcm from the Banyas, 22 mcm from the Jordan, and
            90 mcm from the Yarmuk (132 mcm)
Lebanon: 35 mcm from the Hasbani (35 mcm)
Jordan: 100 mcm from the Jordan and the residue—the bulk—
            from the Yarmuk[1]
Israel: 25 mcm from the Yarmuk and the residue—the bulk—
            from the Jordan.

Of the 100 mcm to Jordan, Israel was to be permitted to provide 30 mcm from the salty springs which would be diverted around Lake Tiberias. As a further inducement Johnston pledged an effort to secure for Israel another 15 mcm from the Yarmuk. Eshkol countered that Israel's share of Yarmuk water should be at least 40 mcm, the amount first indicated by Johnston; further, that part of the 100 mcm to be supplied to the Kingdom of Jordan should be drawn from under-ground wells in her territory. The US envoy (correctly) noted that the distance between the parties was very small—it appeared to be a matter of 15 mcm!

That night, 22 February 1955, Sharett and Johnston had a stormy exchange at a farewell reception for the US delegation. Johnston hinted at a threat to terminate his mission and to charge Israel with intran-

---

[1] A month earlier, in January 1955, Johnston had offered Amman 260 mcm from Lake Tiberias, 160 mcm to be derived from the Jordan River, 100 from the Yarmuk. The 'Gardiner Formula' gave her a little more, an estimated 280 mcm.

sigence. Gardiner tried to persuade Blass to relent and throw his support behind the 'Formula'. The issue was Israeli dissatisfaction over the exchange of 100 mcm (of which 70 mcm was sweet water) from the Jordan–Kinneret to the Kingdom of Jordan, in return for 25 mcm from the Yarmuk. Eshkol, who was Head of Israel's delegation during the third round, then intervened and assured Johnston: 'If you bring the Arabs' agreement to the Revised Plan [i.e. the 'Gardiner Formula'], we will go along with it.'[1] When Blass objected to this 'improvisation', without consulting the delegation, the Finance Minister replied brusquely: 'This is how I understand it and we must finish it.'

Eshkol's attitude was undoubtedly strengthened by the concurrence of the other two persons in Israel's decision-making triumvirate. Sharett had, from the outset, emphasized the larger political dimensions of a Jordan Waters agreement. Ben Gurion was much more 'water-minded' but he was no less aware of the political implication. Then in the final days of his 'retirement' at Sde Boker, his advice was sought by a Government delegation—Eshkol, Sapir, and Wiener. BG decided on 17 February to return to the Government as Minister of Defence; he took the oath of office in Jerusalem on the 21st, the day of the crucial last negotiating session with Johnston during the third round. 'Ben Gurion's point was that we were discussing a difference of a few per cent [the 15 mcm]; was this enough to torpedo an agreement? He felt we should make the sacrifice and advised acceptance of the Revised Plan.' Wiener added: 'Johnston returned to Israel with a set of figures and related conditions close to what we considered acceptable. All of us except Blass felt that we should see this in the larger terms of an accommodation with the Arabs.'

The conditional acceptance of Johnston's Revised Plan in February 1955 was Israel's strategic decision on Jordan Waters: it shaped all subsequent Israeli behaviour on that issue, i.e. it was strategic in terms of significance and duration. Yet like T_1 the S decision was not made by the Government as a whole. Wide discretion on authority had been granted to the negotiating team headed by Sharett, later by Eshkol, with the other one actively involved. On the basis of Johnston's assurances in February 1955 the Israeli delegation recommended acceptance. The confirming support of Ben Gurion was sought—and received.

In the interplay of forces Eshkol played the *crucial role*. The final *decision*, however, must be ascribed to the Sde Boker meeting with Ben Gurion. The delegation's decision was tentative. Further, Eshkol by temperament never regarded decisions as final. And he held BG at that time in awesome respect. Thus, as noted, if 'the Old Man' had opposed the Revised Plan Eshkol would almost certainly have changed his stance; so too would Sharett. At the same time, Eshkol was known as a 'water man', strongly drawn to the arguments of the engineers,

[1] Herzog interview, 1966.

though he too recognized the larger political aspects of the decision; the fact that he—and Sharett—favoured acceptance of the Plan were important environmental stimuli to BG's attitude. In the event Israel's three most influential decision-makers concurred: the delegation's decision (Eshkol, Sharett, *et al.*) was necessary but not sufficient; the Sde Boker meeting sealed the decision.[1] And Eshkol conveyed it to Johnston on 22 February.

Eshkol remarked about the decision: 'We *did* accept but did not say so in writing, officially, because we were afraid that, if we did so, the Arabs would bargain for more, as is the Oriental mentality in these matters. Later [July 1955] we put our acceptance of the Johnston Plan in writing.'[2] And Ben Gurion replied to the question, why did Israel not officially accept the Johnston Plan—unconditionally: 'The fact is that *we* accepted.'[3]

Israel's *de facto* strategic decision became formalized during intensive negotiations over the ensuing five months.[4] Eshkol was told early in March, at a Washington meeting with Johnston, that the 'Gardiner Formula' was the last word on Israel's quantity of water. All his colleagues, except Blass, concurred that this should now be formally accepted: 'Eshkol suggested that I go to Washington to try my luck.' Sharett expressed concern lest Blass act without consulting Jerusalem. The result was a delegation comprising Blass and Wiener, with Shiloah and Shimoni, Minister and Counsellor at Israel's Embassy to the US, and Kollek, then in America, providing political expertise.

That the core decision had already been made was acknowledged by the two influential Israeli engineers. 'At the beginning of April 1955', wrote Blass, 'we left for Washington, with a secret decision to accept the conditions if there is no other way out.' And Wiener observed: 'All the main points had been agreed to earlier.'[5] The talks lasted from 12 April to 17 July and resulted in a *Draft Memorandum of Understanding*, an agreement signed by authorized Israeli and US representatives but never published: it incorporated the precise terms of the Revised Unified Plan.[6] '. . . preliminary understanding on all major points has

---

[1] This account of the January–February 1955 negotiations, including direct quotations not specifically attributed, is based upon Blass, pp. 23–9, and on Herzog and Wiener interviews. The analysis of the informal decision process and mutual interaction among the triumvirate also benefited from Arnon and Yahil interviews. Nimrod (2), pp. 27–8, discusses Arab concessions on water quotas and on 'out-basin' use of Israel's water.

[2] Eshkol interview, 1966.   [3] Ben Gurion interview, 1966.

[4] A detailed account of these negotiations is in Blass, pp. 30–4. See also Nimrod (4), pp. 55–8.

[5] Blass, p. 30, and Wiener interview, 1971. The latter added that every phase was carefully dissected and referred to the Israel Embassy for advice and approval.

[6] The following extracts and summary are taken from a draft of the *Draft Memorandum of Understanding*, made available to the author. There were no substantial changes in the signed Memorandum two months later. Eban, Sapir, and Wiener concluded

been achieved', it began, referring to storage, supervision, sovereignty, and water allocation. 'The purpose of this memorandum is to set forth the elements of the understanding . . . subject to final approval by the Governments of Israel and the United States.'

1. *Storage* facilities were to be constructed on the Yarmuk—the Maqarin Dam. As for the contentious issue of Lake Tiberias, Blass scored a major victory—owing to disarray in the ranks of American negotiators: '. . . final decision as to the use of the Lake . . . will be made by the Neutral Engineering Board by 1960', a five-year delay.

2. *Supervision* was to be exercised by a three-man Neutral Engineering Board, the chairman to be selected by the two members whom Israel and 'the other Jordan Valley states' were to designate.

3. *Sovereignty* by Israel over all existing Israeli territory was carefully assured.

4. *Water Allocations* were set forth in accordance with the 'Gardiner Formula'.

Blass summed up the results pithily: 'With regard to the quantity of water we argued and failed . . . the American stand was like a fortress. . . . With regard to the [Lake Tiberias] reservoir we stalled, the thing was left in the hands of experts [for five years], and we succeeded.'[1]

In essence, Johnston was concerned with the allocation of about 1,000 mcm, almost equally divided between the two rivers. Stripped of all technical details, the core of his Revised Plan was the following: the Kingdom of Jordan would receive most of the Yarmuk water and a little from the Jordan, while Israel would get the bulk of water from the Jordan River and a small amount from the Yarmuk; Syria and Lebanon were treated as lesser riparians. The range of bargaining and the differences in water quotas, from the initial Main Plan figures to those of the Revised Unified Plan, are evident in the gross figures (see Table 5).

The overall increase in estimated available water, from the Main Plan to the Revised Unified Plan (124 mcm), was due to the Baker–Harza and ground water findings. These also permitted the reduction of Jordan's quota, an allocation to Lebanon, and the increase to Syria and Israel. The quotas for Lebanon and Syria were identical in the Arab Plan and the Revised Unified Plan. The Cotton Plan figures were never seriously discussed because they depended on the inclusion of the

---

the negotiations; Blass, dejected, withdrew from active participation when the outcome became certain.

[1] Blass credits Wiener and an engineer of the US team, Kelvin Davis, with this achievement. Upon reflection he added: 'Probably it was a tactical error on our part in the negotiations with Eric Johnston that we did not begin to claim half of the Yarmuk waters, for the Arabs were interested in more water from the Yarmuk in exchange for Jordan Waters. In my opinion we could have reached an agreement according to my principles—for us, the Jordan, and to the Arabs, the Yarmuk. But for the weakness of our leaders we would have convinced Johnston.' Blass letter.

Litani River. The final figure for Israel was 15 per cent higher than that in the Main Plan, more than 25 per cent higher if the 60 mcm of the Huleh Valley is added to the quota of 450 mcm. In essence the Jordan-cum-Yarmuk Waters were divided on a 60–40 basis between the two Arab riparians and Israel. That substantial gain for Israel was the product of prolonged and tenacious bargaining.

TABLE 5

COMPARISON OF JORDAN VALLEY REGIONAL WATER PLANS:
1953–55

| | Main Plan | | Arab Plan | | Cotton Plan* | | Revised Unified Plan | |
	Water	Area	Water	Area	Water	Area	Water	Area
Jordan	774	490	861	490	575	430	720†	
Lebanon	—	—	35	35	450·7	350	35	35
Syria	45	30	132	119	30	30	132	119
Total for Arab States	819	520	1,028	644	1,055·7	810	887	
Israel	394	420	200	234	1,290	1,790	450‡	
Total	1,213	940	1,228	878	2,345·7	2,600	1,337	

Water—million mcm.   Area—thousands of dunams.

* Cotton Plan includes water of Litani River, as well as Jordan and Yarmuk Rivers.

† An estimate, not specified in the Revised Plan, because it includes the residual (bulk) amount from the Yarmuk, which varies annually.

‡ An estimate, not specified in the Revised Plan, because all but 25 mcm is the residual (bulk) amount from the Jordan River which varies annually. Moreover, it does not include 60 mcm accruing to Israel from the Huleh area. The estimate for Israel—water from the Upper Jordan along with other Revised Plan water quotas—was first cited by Peretz, 1964, p. 297, note.

This gain, along with the potential political benefits, was emphasized by Sharett in his exposition before *Mapai*'s Political Committee after the *Draft Memorandum of Understanding* had been signed. Ben Gurion spoke briefly in the same vein. The leadership was given a free hand. That pattern was re-enacted at meetings of the Government. No formal vote was taken on the *Memorandum*. Rather, Sharett (and Eban) reported to the Cabinet on the outcome of the Washington negotiations and recommended acceptance. Blass, who was present and who dissented throughout, wrote, in defeat, that 'there was no point in opposing the agreement'; and he assured the Cabinet that it was a great advance on the Main Plan—'if we have to accept it, it would not be a tragedy'.[1] As a close observer remarked: 'The real struggle [within Israel] over the Johnston Plan was between politicians, who saw the

[1] Blass, p. 36.

water problem as part of a larger political issue, and the engineers, for whom all that mattered was more water for Israel.'[1] In that form Israel's Government 'decided' to confirm the *Memorandum* embodying the Revised Unified Plan.[2]

Armed with Israel's agreement, Johnston set out on his fourth visit to the Near East (25 August–15 October 1955), 'in an effort', according to Secretary of State Dulles, 'to eliminate the small margins of difference which still exist'.[3] The Arab Experts Committee approved the *Draft Memorandum of Understanding* and in late September 1955 recommended it to the League Council. In the interim, however, inter-Arab conflicts and political instability, especially in Lebanon and Syria, made the Revised Unified Plan much less attractive than at the beginning of that year. All the traditional arguments against acceptance now gathered fresh force: the acknowledged purpose of the Plan—to resettle the refugees permanently in their place of residence—was an abandonment of Palestinian rights; agreement meant recognition of Israel; and Israel's (the enemy's) economic capability would benefit greatly from the Plan.

The League Council debated the issue for four days. The outcome, on 11 October 1955, was a diplomatically phrased rejection, through the time-honoured technique of 'further study':

> Representatives of the Arab countries concerned . . . have studied the Arab Plan [!] for the exploitation of the waters of the River Jordan and its tributaries. . . . They have found that despite the efforts exerted there remain certain important points which need further study. It has, therefore, been decided to instruct the Experts' Committee to continue their task until a decision is reached which would safeguard Arab interests.[4]

Johnston remained optimistic, in his public posture:

> When I left the Near East only two days ago, there was not the slightest doubt that Israel and her Arab neighbors . . . recognize the Jordan Valley Plan as the only logical and equitable approach to the problem of developing a river system which belongs, in some part, to all of them.
>
> They have made it clear to me that, in the main, the technical and engineering aspects of the Plan—including the proposed division of the water—are now satisfactory to them. They believe the remaining minor differences can readily be reconciled. I am sure that they can be.[5]

The reason, perhaps, was a warm letter from the Arab League's

---

[1] Arnon interview, 1971.

[2] There is no evidence in Government Minutes of a positive *decision* on the Jordan Waters issue in July–October 1955.

[3] Statement on Arab–Israel Affairs, 26 Aug. 1955. The text is in *MEA*, vi, 8–9, Aug.–Sept. 1955, p. 270.

[4] Statement issued by the Arab News Agency, Cairo, 11 Oct. 1955, as quoted in *MEA, Chronology*, vi, 11 Nov. 1955, p. 372.

[5] *New York Herald Tribune*, Forum Press Release, 17 Oct. 1955.

Secretary-General dated 11 October: he expressed 'deep gratitude' to Johnston 'for the cooperation you have shown to the Arab Technical Committee. The Political Committee also expresses the hope that continued discussions and efforts by both sides [the Arabs and Johnston] will lead to satisfactory results.'[1]

President Eisenhower confirmed the US Government's perception of virtual agreement: 'By their end [the Johnston negotiations], all the major technical problems of an overall plan appeared to have been resolved satisfactorily. . . . At the end of Ambassador Johnston's last visit to the area in [August–October] 1955, only formal political concurrence on the plan remained to be obtained.'[2] But Arab concurrence remained elusive—and unattainable.

One Israeli analyst interpreted the League's 11 October statement as 'a retreat from the negative decision [outright rejection of the Unified Plan] previously reached in Damascus [at the beginning of October]'. He criticized Israeli 'impatience' and ascribed it primarily to the return of Ben Gurion as PM, 'pressing for resumption of work in the Jordan Valley, thereby turning all further talks on the water problem into a series of threats and counter-threats'.[3] Johnston and his assistant knew better. Barnes wrote with candour:

This was diplomatic double talk: rejection of the plan had nothing to do with technical matters. The League's action was motivated wholly by political considerations. It was a clear reflection of the obsessive hatred of Israel that pervades the Arab world. The effect of the League's action was to kill any immediate possibility of going ahead with a major undertaking that offered indisputable benefit to the Arab states themselves.[4]

Three years after the impasse Johnston wrote:

A comprehensive plan for the Jordan Valley is already in being. Its technical aspects have been approved by the Arab States and Israel. All that it lacks is the political go-ahead signal.

. . . in October 1955, it was rejected for political reasons at a meeting of the Arab League. Syria objected to the project because it would benefit Israel as well as the Arab countries. . . . [Thus] every year a billion cubic metres [1,000 mcm] of precious water still roll down the ancient stream, wasted, to the Dead Sea.[5]

[1] Private communication to the author. Wiener remarked that 'he probably had the agreement of all—except Syria' and recalled that, a few days before his visit to Israel in September 1955, Johnston sent Barnes to work out the timing and wording of the statement on an agreement. Wiener interview, 1971.

[2] *Report by the President for 1955*, pp. 70–1.

[3] Nimrod (2), pp. 32, 33. The reason was phrased in the form of a question, but the author's intent was unmistakable.

[4] Barnes, p. 26.

[5] Johnston (2), p. 47 and Johnston (3), p. 80. The most generous phrasing of the Arab League's decision is that by Georgiana Stevens: '. . . the Arab Governments could not bring themselves to give formal acceptance to an arrangement that would also help Israel's development . . . [and] accept a plan that was tantamount to tacit

(D) IMPLEMENTATION

The Arab League's decision of 11 October was one decisive input into Israel's post-1955 behaviour on Jordan Waters. There were others. Formally, the League had postponed a decision; further discussions in late March 1956 had the same outcome. Then, as Lebanon's Prime Minister acknowledged, 'in 1956, the water question was shelved because of the successive political and military events in the area'.[1] In short, continued refusal to co-operate with Israel on a *regional* plan was a related input. As Wiener recalled: 'We did not take the League's October 1955 decision as a final rejection. We hoped the Plan might have a chance at a more opportune time. But as 1956 went on we realized that war was coming.' Thirdly, the (correct) Israeli perception that the US Government and the UN were still opposed to diversion at Gesher B'not Ya'acov was the persistent catalyst to Israel's implementing acts after the Johnston Mission.

On 9 February 1956 the National Planning Board of Israel adopted a Ten Year Plan, based upon the Seven Year Plan of 1953. It included all the earlier projects but placed special emphasis on the National Water Carrier, designed to divert 500 mcm annually from the Upper Jordan (compared with 340 mcm in the Seven Year Plan) and to convey this by a canal to the Beit Netofa Reservoir and then, by a new 108-inch main conduit, to the northern Negev. The point of diversion at that time remained Gesher B'not Ya'acov. The goal was to double Israel's water supply within ten years in order to triple the irrigated area of the country, so as to support an estimated population of 3 million by 1966.[2]

---

acceptance of Israel's existence. . . . Thus the momentum achieved during the Johnston negotiations died out.' Stevens 1965, pp. 32, 33, and Stevens 1956, p. 278. Doherty denies that the League 'vetoed' the Johnston Plan, preferring the formulation, 'the Arab League's decision not to accept the Unified Plan', and apportions equal responsibility for the collapse of the Johnston Mission (pp. 54–5). Nimrod (4) (pp. 65–7) takes a similar line. In truth, Israel accepted the Plan, as demonstrated.

An authoritative explanation of Arab behaviour was provided by Johnston's closest aide: 'The negative vote that killed the project under the Arab League's unanimity rule was cast by Said el-Ghazi, then Premier of Syria, who feared the possible political consequences of acceptance. . . . On the following morning . . . [I was told] that el-Ghazi had acted under instructions from Nasser of Egypt, who had repeatedly assured Johnston that he would support the plan.' Barnes, p. 26. A different interpretation was that Cairo cautiously urged the other Arab States to accept but that Nasser told Johnston he was unable 'to take an unpopular action'. Copeland, p. 92. The League's decision was, at all events, clear Arab rejection of the Johnston Plan and the principle of any co-operation with Israel for regional economic development.

[1] Premier Uwayni's Statement in the Chamber of Deputies, Beirut, 21 Jan. 1965, on the Cairo Summit Conference. The English text was made available to the author.

[2] For details and analysis see AFME, pp. 54, 56–61; Doherty, p. 31; *Israel Digest*; JOMER, p. 13; MFA 1959, pp. 5–7; and UNRWA, pp. 95–9.

Apart from the formal adoption of the Ten Year Plan, the Jordan Waters issue was relegated to the background of Israeli policy during the late 1950s. From the Czech (Soviet) arms deal with Egypt and Syria (September 1955) to the spring of 1957 Israel was preoccupied with escalating border strife, the Sinai Campaign, and the ensuing political struggle.[1] Another year of 'low posture' policy towards Jordan Waters followed, in the wake of recovering from the trauma of the Sinai Campaign and its aftermath. The year 1958 was dominated by Middle East upheavals in Lebanon and Iraq. Thus it was not until the autumn of that year that Jordan Waters came to the fore as a policy issue. Ben Gurion recalled that period of inactivity and the reason: 'There were many acts of Government in which I did not take part—technical and economic matters without political significance. There may have been many reasons—money; we were trying to desalt the Kinneret . . .'.[2]

The focus of discussion was where to divert the Upper Jordan. Gesher B'not Ya'acov was still preferred on economic and technical grounds. One expert, the Jewish Agency's Kublanov, advocated the Dan Springs, north of the Demilitarized Zone. And Lake Tiberias, though more costly, had the merit of being entirely within Israeli territory. The decision—to shift the diversion point to Eshed Kinrot at the north-western corner of Lake Tiberias—was taken by Israeli leaders shortly after 18 November 1958, upon the recommendation of a committee, headed by Agriculture Minister Peretz Naftali and comprising representatives of the Finance, Agriculture, Foreign Affairs, and Labour Ministries, as well as *Tzahal*, with the professional advice of *Tahal*.[3] Eshkol gave the reason without hesitation: 'It was simply due to our concern about international repercussions; both Gesher B'not Ya'acov and Dan Springs sites might have provoked Syria and antagonized the US and the UN.'[4] A senior Foreign Ministry official remarked: 'It was obvious that the political danger of going back to Gesher B'not Ya'acov outweighed the economic costs.' In essence, the

[1] To be analysed in the decision study of the Sinai Campaign (the following chapter).

[2] Ben Gurion interview, 1966.

[3] The *ad hoc* Naftali Committee, appointed by Finance Minister Eshkol to examine the Kublanov proposal, recommended that work start at Eshed Kinrot, in its report dated 18 November 1958. There is no evidence in the archives of the Prime Minister's Office of a statutory decision—by the Cabinet, or its Ministerial Committee on Economic Affairs, or, indeed, any other body. The pattern of decision-making at that time and BG's known interest in the major policy aspects of Jordan Waters suggests that the Naftali Committee's recommendation was conveyed to the Prime Minister, as well as to Eshkol, probably by Naftali himself; that Ben Gurion approved the Eshed Kinrot operation, either himself or through an informal meeting with key persons—Eshkol, Naftali, probably Foreign Minister Meir, and the Chief of Staff or *Tzahal* Commander of the Northern Front. That approval may have been granted a week or two or a month or two after the Naftali Committee recommendation, but no more.

[4] Eshkol interview, 1966.

decision was to have as little to do with the UN as possible, especially after the experience with the Security Council in the autumn of 1953, a view strengthened by the UN role in the Sinai Campaign. Ben Gurion was the strongest in his abhorrence of UN involvement in the water issue—or any other issue.[1] That decision (tactical decision 2) was never announced as such: it was mentioned, parenthetically, in an Israeli Foreign Office Background Note at the end of 1959.[2]

The National Water Carrier, or the Lake Kinneret–Negev Project, is succinctly summarized in the following passage:

The project consists of a conduit 105 km. long, with intermediate reservoirs and pumping and booster stations. The intake is at Eshed Kinrot, in the north-west corner of Lake Tiberias. The water will be lifted by pumping from the Lake level to that of the conduit 40 m. above sea level (a total lift of about 250 metres). From the point of intake to the operational reservoir at Beit Netufa in Lower Galilee, a distance of more than 65 km., the water will flow in a canal. After that, it will pass through concrete-lined tunnels in the Galilee and Menashe Hills for eight km. and then for about 80 km. through a 275 cm. diameter pipeline, mostly along the coast, to the headworks of the Yarkon–Negev Project, at Rosh Ha'ayin, east of Tel Aviv. From there, the water will be carried further south in the two existing Yarkon–Negev pipelines.[3]

The main constituent parts of the National Water Plan are the Huleh Marshes Drainage Project, completed in 1956; the Western Galilee–Kishon Project, which, 'when completed and integrated into the National Water Plan . . . will deliver 180 million cubic metres'; the Yarkon–Negev Project, designed to supply the northern Negev with 100 mcm by diverting the Yarkon from its source north of Tel Aviv to the Negev; and the National Water Carrier itself.

[1] Yahil interview, 1966. Others concurred. Gazit, Herzog interviews, 1966. The decision was made easier by the fact that technical difficulties associated with the Beit Netufa Reservoir dictated that work be started at Eshed Kinrot. 'Everyone agreed that Eshed Kinrot should be the first phase.' Moreover, 'we always decided to keep the B'not Ya'acov option open—down to 1967—but every time we agreed that the political costs were greater than the economic benefits.' Wiener interview, 1971.

[2] MFA 1959, p. 6. T_2 was the outcome of lengthy gestation. The Ten Year Plan, made known towards the end of 1955 and adopted in February 1956, already acknowledged that the Gesher B'not Ya'acov project could not readily be resumed. 'As long as there exist difficulties in operating the diversion from Gesher B'not Ya'acov,' it declared, 'the plan will be based in its first stages on drawing water from the Kinneret.' A few months later, in April 1956, *Tahal* published a pamphlet on 'A Comparison of Various Options for the Implementation of the Jordan–Beit Netofa Project': it was prompted by continuing obstacles in the Demilitarized Zone to the Gesher B'not Ya'acov project. And then, after a lengthy hiatus, the Naftali Committee recommended diversion at Eshed Kinrot. As one Foreign Ministry official observed, 'we knew as early as the beginning of 1956 that we would have to divert the Jordan elsewhere. It took a few years to formalize the decision.' Shimoni interview, 1971.

[3] Rosenne, p. 6; see also MFA 1959, pp. 5–7. The Central Israel Water Conduit was to form the central section of the Jordan project. Its main purpose was to convey water surpluses from the Galilee to the Negev.

The Water Carrier Project was facilitated by a $15 million US *loan* in early 1959, to develop the central conduit—'compensation' for the $4 million US *grant* to Jordan to complete her East Ghor project, to irrigate 120,000 dunams in the Jordan Valley.[1] There were also assurances from Washington that Amman had pledged itself to abide by the Revised Unified Plan water allocations. Thus, ironically, while the Arab League decision of 11 October 1955 'killed the Johnston proposal as a regional development scheme . . . it did not kill the Johnston formula'.[2] By mutual self-restraint Israel and Jordan achieved the intent of the Johnston Mission—use of the 1,000 mcm of the Jordan–Yarmuk River System for irrigation and power in the Near East Core.

Israel's decisions on Jordan Waters (S and T_2) were implemented over a period of five years by two interrelated processes:

(1) negotiations with Washington for political and economic support of her (restrained) unilateral actions; and

(2) the construction of her National Water Carrier in a setting of Arab threats—and attempts—to divert the headwaters of the Jordan.

The attainment of the first eased but did not, *ipso facto*, assure successful completion of the Carrier by target date—1964.

The catalyst to reaffirmation of US backing was Jordan's approach to the World Bank for a loan, in September 1961. Israel cautioned that the Bank might undermine the *de facto* agreement to abide by Johnston Plan allocations.[3] In May 1962 the State Department offered to put into writing the oral assurance of support—by Dulles in 1955 and again in 1958—for Israel's right to divert Jordan Water, within the Revised Unified Plan quotas. This was accepted, but Israel also sought a letter from the President to this effect. Written by Kennedy to Ben Gurion in November 1962, its importance lies in the level of commitment, especially in the context of renewed Arab threats. Israel also received a State Department assurance that Washington would strongly oppose submission of the issue to the World Court and any action by the Security Council to stop the flow of water.[4]

All decisions relating to the completion of the National Water Carrier were made by an *ad hoc* Cabinet Committee comprising Agriculture, including *Tahal*, Defence, Finance, and the Foreign Ministry. For the most part it was a committee of senior officials: DG Finance (Arnon); DG Foreign Office (Yahil); Chief of *Tzahal*'s General Staff Branch

---

[1] When the East Ghor project was announced in February 1958, the Government of Israel conveyed its dissatisfaction. The result, more than a year later, was the $15 million US loan. Herzog interview, 1966. On Jordan's East Ghor and other projects see Dees, *passim*; AJC, p. 11; Ghobashy, p. 21; and Stevens 1965, pp. 49–54.

[2] Geyelin.

[3] The real Israeli concern stemmed from a fundamental distrust of a World Bank role comparable to its initiative in the India–Pakistan Indus Water Agreement of 1960.   [4] Interviews with Gazit, Herzog, Yahil, 1965–6.

(Rabin); and, for Agriculture, the Minister himself, Dayan. Important political decisions were made with the ministers present, including Ben Gurion, in his capacity as Defence Minister; technical-implementing decisions were taken by the committee of officials.

Late in 1959 the Arab League began to consider methods of obstructing Israel's Water Carrier Project. Three paths were debated: (1) military action, advocated by the Nasserite wing of Syria's Ba'ath Party and the ex-Mufti of Jerusalem; (2) diversion of the Jordan's headwaters; and (3) political action through the UN, with Syria taking the lead. The second alternative was chosen as the most viable and the least likely to harm Arab, especially Jordanian, interests.[1] The League's Experts Committee, revived on 28 August 1960, prepared a plan in November: to build a dam on the Hasbani and to carry its water to the Litani River via a tunnel; to divert the Banyas southwards so as to irrigate lands up to the Yarmuk; and to dam the Yarmuk in Jordan, along with the completion of the East Ghor Canal.[2]

The League's Political Committee adopted these proposals on 30 January 1961. However, no decisions were taken until the first Arab Summit Conference of January 1964. There it was decided to implement the diversion plan during the next eighteen months, and an initial budget of $17·5 million was allotted for this variously estimated ($168–$235 million) project.[3] The second Arab Summit Conference, at Alexandria in September 1964, decided to construct a $28·7 million dam on the Yarmuk at Makheiba, with a storage capacity of 200 mcm to be diverted from the Banyas and the Hasbani. The timetable for completion of the Arab diversion project was the end of 1966, but the plan remained unfulfilled.[4]

Israel was not alarmed by these Arab threats and plans, for vital support from the United States had been obtained. In the words of a State Department interpretation of the Revised Plan:

The waters accruing to Israel represented its share after equitable Arab claims had been deducted. There was in 1955 clear understanding that this Israel share could be used legitimately either in or out of the basin. . . .

Technical representatives of the riparian states . . . unanimously endorsed it . . . no feasible alternative has been suggested. . . . The U.S. therefore

[1] The Jordan Kingdom followed a two-track policy: the US-supported unilateral withdrawal of Jordan Water through the East Ghor canal; and acquiescent participation in the Arab League diversion decisions—which would have given her even more water had they been implemented.

[2] Rizk, p. 13.

[3] The Cairo Summit Conference also established a Unified Military Command with an annual budget of $42 million—but rejected Syria's demand for immediate war, if necessary, to prevent the completion of Israel's National Water Carrier. See Mahdi, pp. 25–8.

[4] Excerpts from the Report to the Alexandria Summit Conference on the diversion of the Jordan tributaries appeared in an article by Mahmoud Riad. In *Al Gumhuriya* (Cairo), 14 Oct. 1964.

considers that the Unified Plan represents the tacit but effective consensus of the international community.[1]

This view was publicly expressed on 9 May 1964 by a senior State Department official, who affirmed Washington's policy to 'support and endorse any project of any of the riparian states which remains within the limits of the Unified Water Plan'.[2] And while Israel was ready to begin her diversion project at once, the Arab project was still at the planning stage.

Eshkol, who had succeeded Ben Gurion as Prime Minister in June 1963, replied to the Cairo Summit resolution with a firm declaration before the *Knesset*, on 20 January 1964. He noted that the Revised Plan had 'assured Syria and Lebanon all the quantities of water demanded by them in the Arab plan, without any cuts whatsoever'. Their diversion scheme, therefore, was designed only 'to injure Israel' and 'to deny Israel's right to exist'. He announced that Israel would soon begin to divert Upper Jordan water from Lake Tiberias, and emphasized: 'We have undertaken to remain within the quantities specified in the Unified Plan—and we shall honour this undertaking.' Finally, he warned the Arabs: 'Israel will oppose unilateral and illegal measures by the Arab States and will act to protect her vital rights.'[3] That statement was reiterated by Israel's Government on 13 September 1964, in a plea to the UN, 'peace-loving states', and international public opinion to oppose the Alexandria Summit Conference's 'public announcement of aggressive intent'.[4]

---

[1] 'Summary of 1955 Unified Plan', March 1964 (unpublished).

[2] As cited in AJC, p. 6.

[3] *Divrei Ha-knesset*, xxxviii, 20 Jan. 1964, pp. 8–13; the text of Eshkol's speech was issued as a *Press Bulletin* on the same day by the Government Press Office, Jerusalem. For a succinct presentation of Israel's case see MFA 1959, MFA 1964 (1), MFA 1964 (2); and for the legal bases, Rosenne, *passim*. See also Doherty, pp. 47–48. Typical of the obfuscation surrounding the inherently complex Jordan Waters issue is the following comment by Charles Douglas-Home:

'Israel actually gave an assurance that her independent plans would never involve drawing more than that amount to which she was entitled under the *original* American scheme. . . . However, this ignored the fact that the total amount of water available all around was less than it would have been if the littoral states had jointly developed the water resources. Israel would have been more correct to say that she would not draw more than the *percentage* awarded to her under the Johnston entitlement, which would have brought her less water but possibly more tolerance from the Arabs' (p. 58).

There are three errors here. First, the Israel share of water referred to was that contained in the *final* American plan, known as the Revised Unified Plan, and was agreed to by both the US Government in the *Draft Memorandum of Understanding* and the Experts Committee of the Arab League. Second, it is obscurantist reasoning to criticize party X for utilizing its resources allocation formally agreed to by the sponsoring party because the third party has decided, for its own reasons, not to utilize its share. Most important, Israel's behaviour could not—and did not—affect the *total quantity* of available water.

[4] *Press Bulletin*, 13 Sept. 1964. This was followed up with a note to the President

By that time the first section of the National Water Carrier had begun to operate. Following test pumping through the main conduit in May 1964, Agriculture Minister Dayan announced on 11 June the successful link of the southern end of the Carrier to the Yarkon–Negev pipeline. And in September the reservoir at Beit Netofa was completed. Thus began the flow of water from the Jordan Valley to other parts of Israel, at first to replenish the depleted water table on the coastal plain and, eventually, to the Negev.[1] That Egypt had heeded Eshkol's warning was evident in Nasser's declaration to a Palestine Congress in Cairo, in May 1965: 'There are some [Syria] who say that we should start a war immediately, but those who say this are joking or lying. . . . We shall act only in accordance with our strength and if we will not be able to defend the [Arab] plan to divert the Jordan's tributaries we shall not carry the plan out.'[2] The Arab diversion plan was abortive. And the Israeli Carrier, starting with an annual flow of 150–180 mcm, reached its designed maximum of 320 mcm in 1970.

(E) DECISION FLOW

Pre-Decisional Events

1. 23 December 1920   Jordan River System was sundered by Anglo-French settlement over Near East Mandates: two of three principal headwaters (Banyas and Hasbani) were excluded from territory of Palestine. So too was Litani River.

2. 3 February 1922   Anglo-French Protocol fixed boundary line, incorporating all of Lake Tiberias in Palestine, and authorized High Commissioner of Palestine to raise levels of Lakes Huleh and Tiberias by construction of dams, with adequate compensation to owners and tenants of flooded lands.

3. 5 March 1926   Rutenberg Concession, with exclusive rights to utilize Jordan and Yarmuk Rivers for generation of hydro-electric power—for 70 years— was granted by Mandatory Power to Palestine Electric Corporation; it was ratified by Transjordan Government in 1928.

4. 1937–9   First hydrographic survey of Jordan Valley was

---

of the Security Council on 18 September 1964—as part of a major diplomatic and public relations campaign to frustrate Arab designs.

[1] The implementation of the National Water Carrier Project is surveyed in Bar-Ya'acov, pp. 138–51. Its legal aspects are explained on pp. 165–81.

[2] *Al Ha-mishmar*, 1 June 1965. For a discussion of the post-Johnston phase, especially 1959–65, see Nimrod (3) and Nimrod (4), pp. 87–109.

conducted by Ionides, whose Report and proposed diversion of lower Yarmuk to irrigate land on east bank of Jordan River became authoritative source for all subsequent Arab plans concerning Jordan System.

5. 1943   Joint study by *Yishuv* and Lebanese engineers concluded that only one-seventh of Litani's water could be effectively used in Lebanon and that remainder might be beneficially diverted to Jordan Valley.

6. 1944   Lowdermilk proposed Jordan Valley Authority (JVA); called for diversion of Upper Jordan, Yarmuk, and Zarqa Rivers, to irrigate all Jordan Valley irrigable land, with surplus water to reclaim Negev; and estimated Palestine's absorptive capacity as additional 4 million persons. It served as technical and philosophical guide for all subsequent Israeli water plans.

7. 1948   Hays Plan operationalized Lowdermilk ideas in eight-stage programme, designed, *inter alia*, to permit irrigation of two-thirds of proposed total land area without Arab states' co-operation.

8. 1948   Israel's War of Independence and *de facto* partition of Palestine necessitated modifications of Hays Plan.

9. November 1950   Four-stage 'All-Israel' Plan proposed, *inter alia*, diversion of Upper Jordan water and storage at Beit Netofa; construction of pipelines from north to south; and building of Mediterranean–Lake Tiberias tunnel to generate electric power and to replace diverted water.

Decisive Input into Tactical Decision 1

10. July 1953   Work began to implement 1952 US-supported Bunger Plan for Maqarin Dam on Jordan–Syria border; purpose was to impound 500 mcm of Yarmuk water and to divert bulk to Jordan Kingdom.

Tactical Decision 1

11. July 1953   Government-appointed *ad hoc* Committee (Eshkol, Naftali, Sapir, Dayan, Blass, FO representative) recommended that Israel begin

> work on diversion canal at Gesher B'not
> Ya'acov in Demilitarized Zone. Recommen-
> dation was approved by Prime Minister Ben
> Gurion and Foreign Minister Sharett.

(uncompleted) *Implementation of Tactical Decision 1*

12. 2 September 1953 Israel began work on Gesher B'not Ya'acov
    Canal.

13. 20 October 1953 Following Syria's protest to Security Council,
    on 16 October, and General Bennike's ruling
    to cease work on Canal, Secretary of State
    Dulles announced that US was withholding
    foreign aid funds earmarked for Israel until
    she accepted UN Chief of Staff's decision.

14. 27 October 1953 After two weeks of US economic sanctions
    Israel announced temporary discontinuance of
    work on Gesher B'not Ya'acov project, but
    'without prejudice to [her] rights, claims, or
    position in the matter'. (The same day Presi-
    dent Eisenhower announced resumption of
    economic aid to Israel.)

Decisive Inputs into Strategic Decision

15. 16 October 1953 President Eisenhower announced appointment
    of Eric Johnston as his personal envoy to con-
    duct discussions with Near East states regarding
    mutual development of Jordan River water
    resources 'on a regional basis', primarily to
    contribute to solution of Arab refugee problem
    and, more generally, to economic progress and
    stability.

16. 19 October 1953 Main Plan, technical basis of Johnston Mis-
    sion, was published. It disregarded political
    boundaries and sought most efficient use of
    Jordan River System as a whole—to provide
    irrigation and electric power for three riparian
    states: Jordan would receive 774 mcm, Israel
    394 mcm, and Syria 45 mcm, at cost of $121
    million, to be financed mainly by United
    States.

17. 5 April 1954 Arab League approved Arab Plan, in response
    to Main Plan: accorded 17·4 per cent of
    Jordan–Yarmuk water to Israel, implying *de*

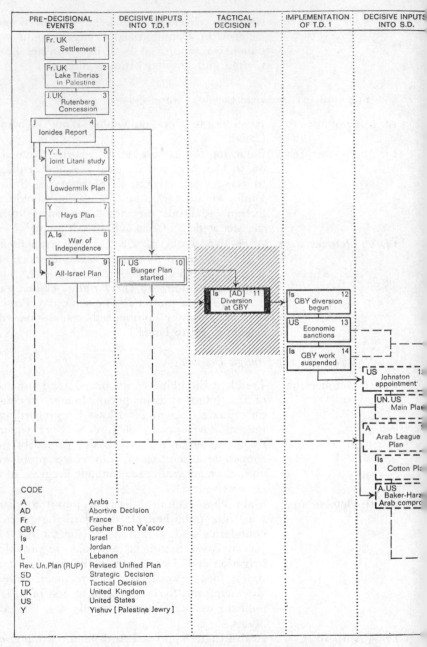

| PRE-DECISIONAL EVENTS | DECISIVE INPUTS INTO T.D. 1 | TACTICAL DECISION 1 | IMPLEMENTATION OF T.D. 1 | DECISIVE INPUTS INTO S.D. |

Fr. UK   1
Settlement

Fr. UK   2
Lake Tiberias
in Palestine

J. UK   3
Rutenberg
Concession

J   4
Ionides Report

Y. L   5
Joint Litani study

Y   6
Lowdermilk Plan

Y   7
Hays Plan

A. Is   8
War of
Independence

Is   9
All-Israel Plan

J. US   10
Bunger Plan
started

Is   [AD]   11
Diversion
at GBY

Is   12
GBY diversion
begun

US   13
Economic
sanctions

Is   14
GBY work
suspended

US   1
Johnston
appointment

UN. US
Main Pla

A
Arab League
Plan

Is
Cotton Pla

A. US
Baker-Harz
Arab compro

CODE

A	Arabs
AD	Abortive Decision
Fr	France
GBY	Gesher B'not Ya'acov
Is	Israel
J	Jordan
L	Lebanon
Rev. Un. Plan (RUP)	Revised Unified Plan
SD	Strategic Decision
TD	Tactical Decision
UK	United Kingdom
US	United States
Y	Yishuv [Palestine Jewry]

FIGURE 8. DECISION FLOW: JORDAN WATERS

STRATEGIC DECISION	IMPLEMENTATION OF S.D.	DECISIVE INPUTS INTO T.D.2	TACTICAL DECISION 2	IMPLEMENTATION OF T.D.2

	facto recognition; but forbade use of water outside Jordan Valley.
18. 1 June 1954	Israel's counter-proposal (made known in February 1954), Cotton Plan, included surplus Litani water and insisted on right to utilize her share of Jordan water to irrigate Negev. Envisaged twice as much water as Main Plan, trebling of region's irrigated land, including large share for Lebanon, seven times the amount of electricity, and fourfold increase in cost ($121 million to $470 million).
19. mid-February 1955	Johnston informed Israel that, on basis of Baker–Harza survey in Jordan, conducted throughout 1954, revealing greater irrigation potential, Arab water experts agreed to larger Israel share of water and withdrew objection to use of her water outside of Jordan Valley.

Strategic Decision

20. 22 February 1955	At Sde Boker meeting with Eshkol and Sapir, Ben Gurion approved conditional acceptance of Revised Unified Plan, including 'Gardiner Formula' for water allocation, as recommended by Israel's delegation to Johnston Talks— Eshkol, Sharett, *et al.* (Decision was conveyed to Johnston by Eshkol on 22 February.)

Implementation of Strategic Decision

21. 12 April–17 July 1955	Negotiations in Washington by Israeli delegation, following Eshkol–Johnston meeting in US in March, led to signed but unpublished *Draft Memorandum of Understanding* containing Revised Unified Plan. (Arab League Technical Committee representatives also approved it.)

Decisive Inputs to Tactical Decision 2

22. Post-20 October 1953	Reality of continuing US and UN opposition to Israel's diversion project at Gesher B'not Ya'acov was correctly perceived by Israel.
23. 11 October 1955	Towards end of Johnston's fourth and last visit, Arab League Council returned to its Experts Committee for 'further study' his Revised Unified Plan, 'until a decision is reached which would safeguard Arab interests'.

24. Post-11 October 1955   The four interested Arab states refused to accept Unified Plan, i.e. continued their policy of non-co-operation with Israel in any regional water plan.

Tactical Decision 2

25. Post-18 November 1958   To shift diversion point from Gesher B'not Ya'acov to Eshed Kinrot, at north-west corner of Lake Tiberias, and to activate National Water Carrier Project, as part of Ten Year Plan of 1956, a revision of Seven Year Plan of 1953. Goal was to double Israel's water supply within ten years in order to support estimated population of 3 million. Diversion project was carefully designed to accord with Israel's water allocation in Unified Plan and to refrain from invalidating its general principles.

Implementation of Strategic Decision and Tactical Decision 2

26. 11 June 1964   Israel's National Water Carrier was completed after five years of uninterrupted work, despite persistent Arab threats and periodic attempts to divert the Hasbani and Banyas headwaters of Jordan River. From 1958 onwards Israel's actions were co-ordinated with US and, through her, informally, with irrigation-cum-power projects of Kingdom of Jordan. (Subsequent Arab diversion *threats*, at Alexandria Summit Conference in September 1964 and Casablanca Summit Conference in September 1965, remained ineffective: diversion *work* began, slowly, in January 1965, and *acts* ceased in July 1965.)

(f) FEEDBACK

Israel's major decisions on Jordan Waters (1953, 1955, 1959) were seen to be the product of both external and internal stimuli. The United States presence (DB), whether in the form of restraint or mediation or support, was a pervasive component of the setting. So too was the Near East Core (S), whose Arab members bitterly opposed the two Israeli decisions concerning diversion, and whose apparent readiness to co-operate in a regional plan eased Israel's strategic decision. The United Nations role (G) was negative for both diversion decisions: along with United States pressure, it prevented the fulfilment of T_1 and induced T_2—the shift from Gesher B'not Ya'acov. Among internal components the perennial shortage of water (E) and the articulated needs of agricultural settlements (IG) operated as parameters for decision. Advocacy by Right and Left parties (CE) fused with interest-group demands.

Feedback may be analysed in two streams—the flow from the 1953 tactical decision and the effects of the strategic decision as implemented in 1964, that is, the completion of Israel's National Water Carrier. The decision to divert the Upper Jordan at Gesher B'not Ya'acov created a harsher environment for Israeli foreign policy among the three relevant external components. The United Nations openly criticized a development project in the Demilitarized Zone and called for its cessation (G). The United States Government took the extraordinary step of imposing economic sanctions against Israel to prevent the implementation of the diversion decision (DB). And the Near East Arab states, notably Syria, denounced the project, thereby heightening the level of conflict in the region (S). Yet the first two flows of alienation were short-lived: they were erased by Israel's 'temporary' suspension of work at Gesher B'not Ya'acov on 27 October 1953—indefinitely as time was to demonstrate. And even the third focus of antagonism, her Arab neighbours, was changed, briefly, into a forum of incipient accommodation during the Johnston mediation phase (October 1953–October 1955).

The effects of T_1 on the internal environment were marginal or nil. The decision was welcomed by *kibbutzim* and *moshavim*, who perceived it as symbolic of the Government's determination to enlarge Israel's water supply. The opposition parties favoured the decision for the same reason and for the related assertion of sovereignty. Suspension of the project met with criticism, especially vocal among *Herut* and *Mapam* spokesmen in the *Knesset*.

Domestic pressure was reflected in the efforts of Israeli negotiators to secure a massive increase in water: the Cotton Plan was its formal expression. Yet the decision to accept the 'Gardiner Formula' did not have significant feedback effects internally. Two reasons may be adduced. The (strategic) decision of February 1955 to accept the Revised Unified Plan was conditional upon Arab acceptance and was not announced as such, in the *Knesset* or the press; nor was the *Draft Memorandum of Understanding*, which formalized Israel's acceptance. Secondly, the strategic decision was not implemented *in its intended form*—as part of a regional co-operative water scheme. When the Arab League, in effect, rejected the Johnston Plan, it aborted Israel's conciliatory decision and thus defused the hostile reaction that might have been generated among interest groups and competing élites.

The strategic decision did have a profound continuing effect on one aspect of the environment. Israel's abandonment of a claim to the Litani surplus, her acceptance of the 'Gardiner Formula' on water quotas, as well as a neutral supervisory board, and, in principle, the use of Lake Tiberias to store Yarmuk flood waters for the benefit of Jordan—in general, her conciliatory, co-operative approach, with marked concessions—created a predisposition in Washington to support Israel's efforts to expand vital water resources. This positive feedback flow became evident in the post-Johnston phase, especially from 1959 onward.

An incipient but unrealized consequence of Israel's strategic decision is also discernible in the Near East Core (S). Arab engineers had evinced a willingness to co-operate with Israel in a regional water scheme and recognized her legitimate riparian rights. Arab political leaders approved the Arab Plan, which included the allocation of 17·4 per cent of the total Jordan–Yarmuk flow to Israel. Moreover, the Arab League's Experts Committee accepted the final terms of the Revised Unified Plan including an Israeli share of 40 per cent of Jordan–Yarmuk water and the right to use it outside the Jordan Valley. There can be little doubt that had the League decision on the Revised Unified Plan been positive, the first breakthrough in the Arab–Israel conflict would have occurred: co-operation on water and *de facto* recognition of Israel would have signalled an Arab willingness to live at peace with the Jewish State and would have created the indispensable condition for *rapprochement*. That it did not occur meant, in this context, an abortive feedback from Israel's strategic decision to the Near East Core.

The construction of Israel's National Water Carrier may be regarded as the consummation of a decision process that began in 1953: it was given strategic policy content in the acceptance of the Revised Unified Plan and was operationalized by the decision (T_2) to shift the diversion to Eshed Kinrot. What were the feedback effects on Israel's operational environment? Four consequences may be discerned:

(1) The relationship with the United States (DB) was further strengthened by Washington's active aid and official support for Israel's unilateral withdrawal of water via the Carrier.

(2) The conflict with Near East Core Arab States as a whole (S) was sharpened by their efforts, from 1960 to 1965, to nullify Israel's water plan by diversion of the Jordan headwaters to Arab lands.

(3) A quiet pattern of informal co-operation between Israel and Jordan (B) developed from 1958 onward: both displayed moderation in adhering to the Unified Plan quotas of water withdrawal from the Jordan–Yarmuk River System.

(4) Israel's economic capability (E) was enhanced by the increase in her overall secure supply of water; both agriculture and industry benefited from the completion of the National Water Carrier and related projects.

FIGURE 9

FEEDBACK: JORDAN WATERS

Operational Environment	*Psychological Environment and Policy Derivatives*
External	*External*
G Alienated all three relevant ex- **S** ternal components—the UN, **DB** Near East Core Arab states, especially Syria, and the US. The first and third were short-lived and the second changed to incipient co-operation during Johnston negotiations (T_1)	Israel correctly perceived threefold negative effect of T_1. Policy consequence was to shift diversion point, first to suspend the diversion at Gesher B'not Ya'acov and five years later to shift operations to Eshed Kinrot, i.e. T_2, because of known continued opposition by UN, US, Syria to GBY
	DB component (Johnston Mission aftermath to uncompleted T_1) also created perception of strong US interest in regional plan and consequent **S** decision—concessions and co-operation *vis-à-vis* Revised Unified Plan (P–D)
G Shift of diversion point, as noted, erased earlier friction with UN (T_2)	Israel correctly perceived elimination of UN antagonism; but there was no policy derivative
S Incipient but unfulfilled effect was strengthening in Arab world of forces for accommodation and co-operation with Israel, reflected in behaviour of Arab League Experts Committee (S)	Awareness of non-rejection, formally, by Arab League, left open option of regional co-operation in future (P–D, E–D)
Conflict with Arab states was intensified by threats and attempts to divert Jordan headwaters from Israel flow (T_2)	Image of unmitigated Arab hostility strengthened policy of unilateral actions on water (P–D, E–D)
DB Acceptance of Revised Plan 1955 and shift in diversion point in 1959 erased earlier friction, generated US financial aid and diplomatic support for Israel's unilateral withdrawal of Jordan water (S, T_2)	Awareness of US backing and of tangible benefits that would—and did—follow acceptance of Plan provided security for subsequent implementing behaviour—notably unilateral withdrawal of water 1964ff. (P–D, E–D)
Israel's credibility in Washington and, therefore, potential for further US support on water plan-	

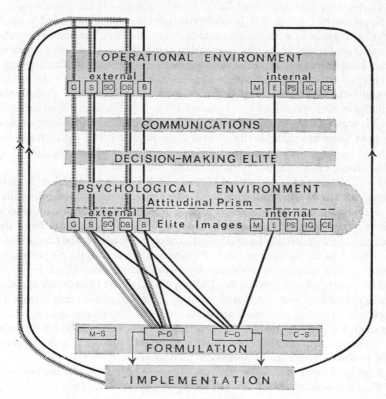

——— S+T₂ Erasure of feedback of T₁ in Operational and Psychological Environment
——— S+T₂ Independent effects

ning was enhanced by meticulous
adherence to Unified Plan allocations (S, T₂)

B	Non-official, parallel, uni-lateral withdrawal by two main riparians strengthened pre-conditions for Israel–Jordan accommodation (S, T₂)	Awareness of *de facto* Israel–Jordan co-operation strengthened policy of seeking separate political and economic settlement with Jordan (P–D, E–D)

Internal   *Internal*

E	Israel's capacity for economic growth was enhanced, including first stage in irrigation of Negev (S, T₂)	Benefit to national economy was correctly perceived and added in-centive to search for more water (E–D)

There were parallel—and interrelated—effects on the psychological environment. During the Johnston talks, especially the third round, Israel's high-policy decision-makers were acutely conscious of the 'American factor' (DB), in particular the benefits that would accrue from concessions. And these concessions—the essence of the strategic decision—created an awareness of probable US support in subsequent Israeli behaviour on Jordan Waters, as long as it did not violate the principles and quotas of the Unified Plan. That positive feedback, as noted, was further strengthened by US financial aid and assurances of support—the State Department and Kennedy letters of 1961 and 1962. Those, in turn, fortified Israel's resolve to 'go it alone' in this as in other areas of overlapping Israeli–Arab interests.

The primary effect of the League's October 1955 decision was to reconfirm the predispositional Israeli image of constant Arab hostility (S). The corollary was the need to pursue water planning in unilateral terms, a prospect made easier by US approval. At the same time the absence of formal Arab League rejection of the Unified Plan meant the continued presence of a possible framework for regional co-operation; and this was viewed as desirable by Israel's decision-makers (S).

The willingness of Jordan to abide by the Unified Plan water quotas, demonstrated during the implementation of Israel's strategic and T_2 decisions (1959ff.), created an image of parallel water development between the two major riparians of the Jordan–Yarmuk River System, to their mutual benefit. That in turn induced hopes of a quicker pace to a political accommodation with Jordan (B).

Finally, Israeli decision-makers accurately perceived the importance of the National Water Carrier's completion for a rapidly developing economy desperately short of water to meet its multiple demands (E). All of these feedback effects are presented graphically in Figure 9 and its accompanying summary.

CHAPTER 6

Sinai Campaign[1]

The first phase of Israel's foreign policy reached its climax with the Sinai Campaign. A myriad of decisions preceded and followed that second Arab–Israel War. Almost all, however, were either preparatory or implementing in character, functionally related to a cluster of three decisions with long-term significance:

on 20 September 1956	Prime Minister Ben Gurion decided to co-ordinate Israel's military and political actions with France in order, at some unspecified date in the near future, to wage war against Egypt; (T)
on 25 October 1956	following the 'Treaty of Sèvres', a secret alliance with France and the UK, Ben Gurion decided to launch the Sinai Campaign, to begin on 29 October; (S_1) and
on 8 November 1956	the Government of Israel agreed, in principle, to withdraw from occupied territory —after 'satisfactory arrangements' were made with the UN International Force. (S_2)

The autonomous tactical decision was implemented immediately and merged into a decisive input for Israel's first strategic decision—to wage war against Egypt. That strategic decision, too, was carried out at once, with total military triumph in Sinai and Gaza within eight days. The withdrawal decision, by contrast, was implemented in stages

[1] Despite the extensive literature on the Suez crisis (see introductory note to Sources, pp. 602–3), the Sinai Campaign remains virtually unexplored as a decision study in *Israel*'s foreign policy. There are valuable insights and (partial) descriptions but not a systemic analysis: of the setting in which perceived challenges had to be met; of the psychological environment perceived by Israel's Sinai decision-makers; of the processes leading to the strategic and tactical decisions and their implementation; and of the feedback (consequences) of their decisions for subsequent Israeli foreign policy. This will be the analytic focus for the Sinai decision cluster. The well-known details concerning the *Suez* conflict will be noted only to the extent necessary to dissect the dynamics of *Israel*'s behaviour, that is, the *Sinai* issue in her foreign policy. Both qualitative and quantitative methods of analysis are used. The principal sources are the diaries, memoirs, and speeches of decision-makers; interviews with them and their advisers in the Foreign and Defence Ministries, and Prime Minister's Office; and *Knesset* debates. These and the voluminous secondary sources are indicated in the Bibliography.

during a tenacious four-month political struggle at the United Nations and in the United States. The consequences of those decisions were evident especially during the decade 1957–67 but after the Six Day War as well.

(A) OPERATIONAL ENVIRONMENT

The setting for Israel's decisions on the Sinai Campaign was complex: no less than seven components impinged upon her behaviour or the outcome of her actions; several reinforced each other over time. In the external arena only other subordinate systems (SO) were irrelevant. Among the internal variables, economic capability (E) and political structure (PS) did not affect Israel's decisions; and interest groups (IG), with one notable exception, *Tzahal*, fused with, that is, articulated their views through, the larger aggregative competing élites (CE), or political parties.

The universal actor in the *global* system (G) was omnipresent. UN Secretary-General Hammarskjöld visited the area of conflict in January and April 1956, in a futile effort to curb the spiral of *feda'iyun* raids and Israeli reprisals. After three international conferences (August–September) had failed to ease the crisis over Nasser's nationalization of the Canal, the Security Council laid down six guideline principles, in mid-October. The Council once more, and the Emergency Session of the General Assembly, were deeply involved in the search for a cease-fire as a result of Israel's massive raids into Sinai on 29 October and the Anglo-French assault in the days that followed. The Assembly created a UN Emergency Force early in November. Its relentless pressure contributed to Anglo-French withdrawal from the Canal Zone in November–December. And Hammarskjöld's defence of Egypt's legal rights, as well as his insistent demand for unconditional Israeli withdrawal, strengthened US and General Assembly resolve. The result was Israel's final withdrawal from Gaza and Sharm-e-Sheikh in March 1957, on the basis of 'assumptions' proclaimed by her Foreign Minister in the Assembly.[1]

The dominant systemic trait, bipolarity, had already undergone change—from the rigidity of Stalin's last years (1948–53) and its aftermath to the inter-bloc dialogue beginning with the 'spirit of Geneva', the summit conference of May 1955. That did not prevent a deep Soviet penetration of the Near East Core, through the arms agreements with Egypt and Syria. Yet the Cold War, *per se*, did not impinge on the developing crisis between Israel and her Arab adversaries. Rather, the contestants for global hegemony pursued *parallel* policies during the Suez–Sinai conflict, exerting complementary pressures on the UK,

---

[1] The UN role, as an externally-based institutional interest group, will be explored in section (D) below.

France, and Israel—Moscow with unremitting harshness, Washington with embarrassment. In short, global bipolarity was in abeyance during the period of Israel's tactical and strategic decisions.[1]

The DB component, by contrast, had profound significance for those decisions. The Soviet arms deal was a decisive input into the processes leading to both Israel's alignment with France (T) and the launching of the Sinai Campaign (S_1). Moreover, the grave warning of imminent intervention by Bulganin on 5 November 1956, along with symbolic acts during the next forty-eight hours, was a crucial catalyst to the withdrawal decision (S_2). Thus, that strand of Israel's *dominant bilateral* relationships was persistently relevant. They had moved from tangible super-power support (1947–9) to correctness (1950–3), to rupture (1953), to minimal contact, and then, steadily, to Moscow's patronage of Israel's declared enemies (1955ff.) and direct threat to Israel's existence (November 1956). Only during the dogged Israeli resistance to unconditional withdrawal after the Sinai Campaign did the Soviet factor in Israel's Foreign Policy System become marginal: it merged with UN and Asian–African pressure and was secondary to Israel's other DB relationship.[2]

United States behaviour, too, was a vital part of the setting for Israel's decisions. There were no drastic shifts along the friendship–hostility spectrum, as with Soviet attitudes and actions. The US supported Israel's independence and accorded her immediate recognition. Economic aid was granted. Large-scale private financial assistance was permitted under favourable conditions. Free contact between American Jewry and Israel was unhindered. And Washington was a party to the Tripartite Declaration of 1950, a form of guarantee of the *status quo* enshrined in the Armistice Agreements. Yet military assistance was denied to Israel during the first half of the 1950s and beyond. Indeed that was a key environmental influence on Israel's Sinai decisions: the US Government's negative response to Jerusalem's overtures for a security guarantee quickened the pace of her French orientation, culminating in the *de facto* alliance of September 1956—the T decision.

[1] On the characteristics of global politics in 1955–6 see G. Barraclough and R. F. Wall, *Survey of International Affairs 1955–1956*, Oxford University Press, London, 1960, ch. x, xii, xiv, and G. Barraclough, *Survey of International Affairs 1956–1958*, Oxford University Press, London, 1962, ch. vi; P. Calvocoressi, *International Politics Since 1945*, Praeger, New York, 1968, ch. 1 (3); D. F. Fleming, *The Cold War and its Origins 1917–1960*, Allen and Unwin, London, 1961, Vol. 1, Part IV, ch. xxv; L. J. Halle, *The Cold War as History*, Harper and Row, New York, 1967, ch. xxxii; W. LaFeber, *America, Russia and the Cold War, 1945–1966*, John Wiley, New York, 1967, ch. viii; J. Lukacs, *A New History of the Cold War*, Doubleday & Co., New York, 1966 (Anchor Books), pp. 123–54; and W. A. Williams, *The Tragedy of American Diplomacy*, World Publishing Co., New York, 1959, ch. 7.

[2] For a general survey of Soviet–Israel relations in the mid-1950s see Dagan, ch. x–xii. Substantial work is at present being done on Soviet–Israel relations, 1947–55, by Ya'acov Roy, as a Ph.D. dissertation at the Hebrew University of Jerusalem.

President Eisenhower tried, unsuccessfully, to dissuade Ben Gurion from implementing the decision to launch the Sinai Campaign (S_1). Massive pressure from the White House and the State Department was a decisive input into the 8 November withdrawal decision (S_2). And the US factor was overwhelmingly decisive in affecting its implementation during the political struggle from November 1956 to March 1957.[1] Thus both super powers loomed large in the operational environment.

So too did one *bilateral* relationship (B), that with France. From its origins in 1952–3, the alignment was forged in 1955 and 1956 to become the *sine qua non* of Israel's first strategic decision on Sinai and, in fact, the pillar of her foreign and security policy for a decade. More specifically, it was French initiative, soon after the nationalization of the Suez Canal, which led a cautious but not unwilling Ben Gurion to respond favourably to military co-operation against Egypt. The flow of French arms, beginning in earnest in April 1956 and reaching a climax during the forty-eight hours before the Campaign, was its indispensable prerequisite. The French initiative to hold tripartite talks (with the UK), leading to the 'Treaty of Sèvres', was the last of the decisive inputs into Israel's S_1 decision. Thereafter, too, the French factor was vital—in the setting for Israel's S_2 decision and its implementation: the use of her veto twice in the Security Council, on 29 and 30 October 1956, thereby delaying UN intervention in the crucial first thrust of Israel's advance into Sinai and Gaza; the advice on 6 November to agree to withdraw because of an insufficient Franco-Israeli deterrent to Soviet threats; and the 'assumption' formula—by Mollet and Pineau in Washington in late February 1957—which broke the deadlock over the conditions of Israel's final withdrawal, in what seemed at the time Israel's optimal interests.[2]

The only other state to impinge on Israel's behaviour was Britain. For the most part her role was a constraining element. Her pro-Arab stance was evident in a military alliance with Jordan and in her periodic warnings to Israel about reprisal raids, as late as 14 October 1956. Prime Minister Eden's proposals for a territorial settlement more than a year earlier had only deepened distrust of the former Mandatory Power. Indeed it was primarily responsible for the delay in Ben Gurion's first strategic decision: only after the written British commitment at Sèvres did that anxiety lessen. Like France, the UK vetoed the preliminary Security Council resolutions calling for a cease-fire and Israeli withdrawal. However, London became increasingly indifferent to the interests of an embarrassing ally. Thus while relevant to

[1] US–Israel relations during the first phase are examined in Safran 1963, ch. xiv.

[2] The French component in Israel's Sinai decision process, like the role of the UN, US, USSR, and UK, will be discussed at length in sections (c) and (d) below.

Israel's S_1 decision, the UK did not influence the T or S_2 decisions—or their implementation.

Escalating border violence in the Near East Core was the *a priori* environmental condition for Israel's Sinai decisions. The pattern of *feda'iyun* attacks and Israel's retaliation, beginning with Gaza (February 1955) and continuing with increasing frequency, intensity, and loss of life, defined the territorial setting of active conflict: the result was intolerable disruption of civilian life, with grave effects on national morale, and a rising barometer of perceived threat to Israel's existence.[1] There were, in fact, several inputs from the *subordinate system* (S) into the decision process: the transformation of the military balance caused by Soviet–Arab arms agreements in September 1955; the enlarged scope of Egypt's blockade of the Tiran Straits, to include air traffic; the rising curve of Israeli casualties from Arab hit-and-run raids (1951—137; 1952—147; 1953—162; 1954—180; 1955—238);[2] the growing influence of Nasser's leadership, more and more widely accepted in the Arab world; and the demonstrable encirclement of an Israel already feeling the pangs of siege, which reached their peak with the formation of a unified command over the armies of Egypt, Jordan, and Syria (23 October 1956). It was that Near East setting of inflationary violence which served as the first decisive input into Israel's search for security in the mid-fifties: first, with an approach to Washington; simultaneously, through Paris; then, after the American option proved unproductive, the forging of an alliance with France, as the perceived Arab threat became ominous; and finally, the strategic decision to invade Sinai. By that time all of the four external components (G, DB, B, and S) were interacting to induce, through the images of Israel's decision-makers, the predisposition to make the T and S_1 decisions. The regional environment, however, did not influence Israel's withdrawal decision and its implication: Egypt was militarily prostrate from November 1956 to March 1957; and Jordan and Syria had remained aloof when Israel had been relatively weaker. They could be—and were—ignored.

Near East violence acquired political significance with the transformation of the *military* balance (M). A tolerable situation had been maintained by the three Western Powers through careful rationing

[1] The rising tension level in 1955 and 1956 is discussed in virtually the entire Suez–Sinai literature. See, for example, Azar; Ben Gurion 1971, pp. 451–60, 470–6; Berger, ch. 2; Blechman 1971, ch. III; Blechman 1972; Burns, ch. 1, 5–12; Campbell, ch. 7; Dayan 1966, pp. 4–57; Eden, Book 3, ch. 1, 6, pp. 329–30, 341–7; Macmillan, ch. 4; Peres, 1970, ch. 9; Robertson, ch. 1; Stock, pp. 67–75; and H. Thomas, pp. 20–30.

[2] Cited by Yisrael Galili, *Ahdut Ha'avoda* leader and MK, in the parliamentary debate on foreign and security policy, 15 Oct. 1956, *Divrei Ha-knesset*, xxi, Part 1, p. 83. Burns cites as Israeli figures 1,237 Israelis killed or wounded by infiltrators between the 1949 Armistice and October 1956, p. 60. Blechman 1972 indicates 561 Israeli 'casualties' for the same period, p. 165.

during the first half of the 1950s. As a result neither of the adversaries was then a grave military threat to the other.[1] Into that relatively stable equilibrium came a massive input of planes, tanks, guns, and naval vessels. Estimates of the value of the Soviet arms deal vary—up to $450 million, to be paid for in Egyptian cotton. A precise account was provided by a professional military student of the Sinai Campaign:

Egypt was to receive 50 Stalin III (heavy) tanks, 150 T.34 (medium) tanks, 200 armoured troop carriers, 100 self-propelled guns (S.U. tank destroyers), 120 Mig-15 fighters, 50 Ilyushin-28 twin-engined jet bombers, 20 Ilyushin-14 transport planes, 2 destroyers, 15 minesweepers, 2 submarines, 200 anti-tank guns, 50 guns of 122 mm., 100 5-ton vehicles, 50 10-ton vehicles, radar, recoilless rifles, and thousands of semi-automatic weapons; Syria was to receive 100 T.34 (medium) tanks, 100 Mig-15 fighters, troop carriers, anti-aircraft guns, howitzers, and lesser arms.[2]

Moshe Dayan, who has always been free of self-deception in military matters, designated the contents of the arms deal in essentially the same terms.[3]

There were few, if any, then and later, who doubted that 'the entire military and political structure of the Middle East changed drastically,

---

[1] By the late summer of 1955 Egypt possessed about 200 tanks, most of them Sherman Mark IIIs but including 40 of the advanced Centurions, and 100 planes, 80 of them jet fighters—Meteors, Vampires, and Furies. She had also received two British destroyers, a consignment of French 150 mm. guns and 120 mm. mortars, four frigates, and 600,000 tons of supplies and equipment left by the departing British in the Canal Zone. Israel at that time possessed 200 tanks, but no Centurions, about 50 jet fighters, including a single squadron of Ouragans, and two destroyers. Nor did the further flow of Western weapons early in 1956 alter the balance appreciably: to Egypt, 20 additional French 150 mm. guns, 40 French Amx-13 tanks, and 200 Valentine (Archer) tank destroyers from Britain; to Israel, eight Mystère IVs, a small number of French Amx-13 tanks, radar equipment, etc. Ra'anan, pp. 49–51. The data are drawn from Henriques, pp. 26–7; Jules Menken, 'Problems of Middle Eastern Strategy', *Brassey's Annual: The Armed Forces Year Book*, 1956 ed., Praeger, New York, 1956, ch. XIII; Dayan 1966, pp. 4–5; Barker, pp. 59–61; Bar-Zohar 1964, pp. 72–120; Monroe, p. 185.

[2] Henriques, pp. 42–3. A similar set of data on the Israel–Egypt arms balance from 1948 to 1955 and the post-Soviet arms deal is provided by Safran 1969, pp. 209, 217, 223.

[3] Dayan 1966 (pp. 4–5) wrote: 'The Czech arms received by Egypt included 530 armoured vehicles—230 tanks, 200 armoured troop-carriers and 100 self-propelled guns; some 500 artillery pieces of various types; almost 200 fighters, aircraft, bombers and transport planes; and a number of warships—destroyers, motor-torpedo-boats and submarines. By the standards of arms acquisition in the Middle East at that time, the scale of this deal was very much larger than anything known before. . . . Before, Egypt had eighty jet warplanes as against Israel's fifty. Now, the number of Egyptian jet fighters and bombers shot up to 200—four to one. In artillery, naval vessels and infantry weapons, the Israel picture was no better. It was not only the disparity in quantity but also the superiority in quality which decisively upset the arms scales. The Migs and Ilyushins which the Egyptians received were at least two stages ahead of the Meteors and Ouragans then in our possession; and their modern T-34 Soviet tanks were infinitely better than our old Sherman Mark 3s.'

ominously'.[1] The Soviet-bloc arsenal reached its destination by July 1956 and triggered a chain of events that was to culminate in the Sinai Campaign three months later. In the interim Israel had pressed her search for French arms successfully, and the imbalance was corrected in September–October 1956, especially after the 'Treaty of Sèvres'.[2]

Only one of Israel's *competing élites* (CE), the Left-nationalist *Ahdut Ha'avoda*, was partly aware of the intense negotiations which led to the French alignment and the Sinai Campaign: the other leaders were informed by Prime Minister Ben Gurion between 25 and 28 October 1956.[3] This is evident from the party press and periodic parliamentary debates on foreign policy and security. The most dramatic of these was held on 15–17 October, barely a fortnight before the Campaign and a week before Israel's first strategic decision. All of the competing élites participated with certain common themes in the speeches of their leaders: an assault upon UN behaviour, including the alleged pro-Arab partisanship of the Secretary-General; preoccupation with the threat of Iraqi troop entry into a crumbling Jordan; and the intolerable burden of casualties and terror created by *feda'iyun* raids. Beyond that they articulated the general foreign policy programme of their parties.[4]

Herut called for drastic measures to seize the opportunity; in short, war. *Ahdut Ha'avoda* was no less militant in its demand for action. At the other extreme of the spectrum, *Maki* pressed for a fundamental revision of Israel's foreign policy, with an emphasis on peace, negotiation, and compromise. *Mapam* spoke in essentially the same vein. The Progressives were closest to the Government's stand on the enveloping Middle East crisis, though the religious parties and General Zionists were not in basic disagreement. They criticized specific points in Israel's behaviour: the quality of her propaganda abroad; the degree of publicity given to receipt of weapons, and the designations 'offensive' and 'defensive'; the lack of sufficient religious spirit in Israeli society, etc. But all of these pragmatic parties (in foreign policy) followed *Mapai*'s lead. Only Harari of the Progressives drew attention, marginally, to the impending confrontation with Egypt. The lacuna

---

[1] Robertson, p. 17.

[2] Yet even then the operational strength of Israel's Air Force on 29 October was barely 136, of which only 82 were reliable fighters (16 Mystères, 22 Ouragans, 15 Meteors, and 29 Mustangs). Egypt's first-line strength was 245—but only half were operational. Cited by Jackson, pp. 82–3.

[3] Even *Ahdut Ha'avoda* first learned of the French alignment only at the end of September, when Moshe Carmel, one of its leaders and then Transport Minister, was added to a high-level mission to Paris. To be discussed in (c) below.

[4] The foreign policy debate on 15–17 October 1956 is recorded verbatim in *Divrei Ha-knesset*, xxi, pp. 66–114. Speeches by the main participants were: Begin (*Herut*), 66–71; Bernstein (General Zionists), 78–81; Rafael (*Mizrahi*), 81–3; Galili (*Ahdut Ha'avoda*), 83–5; Hazan (*Mapam*), 85–8; Levin (*Agudat Yisrael*), 92–4; Wilenska (*Maki*), 94–6; Harari (Progressives), 97–9.

was not due to diffidence; rather it was due to lack of knowledge of what was afoot. Thus this component of the environment did not affect the tactical and strategic 1 decisions, though the decision-makers knew of their concern about Israel's increasingly insecure position and valued their near-consensus support for a riposte.

These decisions were profoundly affected by one of the most powerful *interest groups* (IG) in Israel's Foreign Policy System. The Defence Establishment—*Tzahal* and the Defence Ministry—has functioned as a permanent arms lobby and has made known its views on foreign policy issues, especially those perceived as likely to affect Israel's security. In the context of the Sinai Campaign it was the Defence Ministry, acting through Director-General Shimon Peres, which took the initiative in the arms discussions in Paris in 1954–5 and which shaped the decision to align Israel, militarily and politically, with France. Moreover, *Tzahal*'s advocacy of the policy of retaliation contributed to the growing tension in the Near East Core. Through both strands it was an important internal environmental input into the tactical and strategic 1 decisions.

Senior army officers also attempted to abort the final implementation of the decision to withdraw—by making known their dissent to Ben Gurion through Chief of Staff Dayan. The Prime Minister called about twenty officers to his residence in mid-March 1957, listened to their views, and explained the compelling reasons for that decision: the dissenters, led by Deputy Chief of Staff Haim Laskov, yielded to his persuasion. As related by Ben Gurion in his memoirs, 'The Defence Minister saw a need to explain to the army commanders the essence of the political struggle after the Sinai Campaign. . . . While the UN's pressure was increasing [he] invited the General Staff to a meeting to convey the Government policy. He explained that "we need now most of all a delay so that the world would be able to think again and see that we are right".'[1] Thus both external and internal components of the operational environment impinged on one or more of the basic Sinai decisions, as well as their outcomes.

(B) DECISION-MAKERS AND THEIR IMAGES

The formal decision-making unit for Israel's strategic decisions on the Sinai issue was her seventh Government: formed in November 1955, its internal political–ideological balance was drastically changed by the resignation of Foreign Minister Sharett in June 1956 and his replacement by a devoted Ben Gurionist, Mrs. Meir.[2] At the time of

---

[1] Ben Gurion 1966, *Davar*, no. 71, 5 Aug. 1966. Ben Gurion also narrated this incident to the author (interview, 1966). See also his reflections in Moncrieff, p. 72.

[2] On Sharett's resignation and its significance see Brecher, pp. 387–91 and Ben Gurion 1971, pp. 493–4.

the decisions the Cabinet comprised the following persons, with the usual *Mapai* majority (9 of 16 ministers, in that period):

Mapai

D. Ben Gurion	Prime Minister and Defence
Z. Aranne	Education and Culture
L. Eshkol	Finance
K. Luz	Agriculture
G. Meir	Foreign Affairs
P. Naftali	Without Portfolio
M. Namir	Labour
P. Sapir	Commerce and Industry
B. Shitreet	Police

Ahdut Ha'avoda

Y. Bar-Yehuda	Interior
M. Carmel	Communications and Transport

Mapam

Y. Barzilai	Health
M. Bentov	Development

National Religious Party

Y. Burg	Posts
M. Shapira	Religious Affairs and Social Welfare

Progressives

P. Rosen	Justice

The Cabinet participated in the *crisis* strategic decision on 8 November (S_2), but Ben Gurion possessed paramount influence—to approve or reject the demand for Israel's agreement to withdraw. As for the decision to launch the Sinai Campaign (S_1), Israel's commanding figure revealed that a major military operation against Egypt was not discussed in Government meetings at any time from the negative December 1955 Cabinet decision on his proposal to open the Tiran Straits by force until 28 October 1956, when the Government authorized Operation *Kadesh*, to begin the next day.[1] A month earlier the Cabinet had approved the dispatch of a four-man team to a high-level conference in Paris concerning French arms deliveries (30 September–1 October); but that was to implement the tactical decision of alignment which Ben Gurion had already made and communicated to the French

[1] Ben Gurion interview, 1971. Meir, Rosen, and Sharef concurred. Interviews, 1966, 1971, and 1971 respectively. This does not mean, *ipso facto*, that it was not discussed among Cabinet colleagues informally. Yet that too was very limited, for only ten persons apart from General Staff Officers knew of the Sinai Campaign before 25 October, among them only three ministers—Meir, Eshkol, and Carmel.

Government some days earlier (20 September). In short, the decision-making group was much smaller, with the Government's role confined essentially to authorization. Ben Gurion made all three decisions. However, Peres and Dayan were so influential as initiators, advisers, and negotiators of the 'French orientation' that they, too, must be designated *de facto* decision-makers for T and S_1. And Meir, as Foreign Minister, was a member of the Inner Circle throughout the Sinai issue.

Important technical roles were played by several senior members of the Foreign Service: Abba Eban, Israel's supreme advocate as Permanent Representative to the UN and her principal negotiator over the conditions of withdrawal—from November 1956 to March 1957; Ya'acov Herzog, then Head of the United States Department in the Foreign Ministry, who was seconded to the Prime Minister's Office on 28 October and served as Ben Gurion's diplomatic counsellor throughout the implementation of both strategic decisions; Reuven Shiloah, Minister (No. 2) in the Washington Embassy of Israel; and Gideon Rafael and M. Kidron of Israel's UN Mission, who were Eban's principal aides in the political struggle to safeguard Israel's interests during the withdrawal process.[1] To this group must be added Ben Gurion's Political Secretary, Yitzhak Navon, and his Military Secretary, Nehemia Argov.[2]

The images of the four persons who were crucial in shaping Israel's Sinai decisions—Ben Gurion, Dayan, Peres, and Meir—will now be explored, in the following sequence: their perceptions of the global and dominant-bilateral setting; of the regional environment and Israel's near-neighbours; of Israel's relative military and economic capability; and their goal-advocacy. Both qualitative and quantitative data will be used in the analysis of their psychological environment.[3]

Ben Gurion's enduring interest in the global system was rooted in three fundamental perceptions: the dispersion of world Jewry, Israel's only truly reliable ally; *Tzahal*'s dependence upon external sources for vital arms; and the potentiality of forging inter-state relations to counter and, possibly, to reduce Arab hostility. These were expressed in many speeches and writings during his lengthy tenure as Prime

---

[1] Herzog later served in Washington (Minister) and Ottawa (Ambassador) and was Director-General of the Prime Minister's Office from 1965 until his death in 1972; Shiloah died in 1959; Rafael later became Director-General of the Foreign Ministry (1967–71); and Kidron served as Permanent Representative to the UN (Geneva). For further biographical and career data see Brecher, ch. 17.

[2] Navon was Ben Gurion's Political Secretary from 1952 to 1963, except during the latter's 'retirement' to the Negev in 1954. He entered the *Knesset* in 1965 and later served as Deputy Speaker. Argov died in 1958.

[3] Ben Gurion's perceptions will be given the most attention because of his pre-eminent role as decision-maker throughout the Sinai issue. Extracts from the articulated images of others will be cited as supplementary evidence or when the passage communicates the overall élite view.

Minister–Defence Minister, nowhere more cogently than in his illuminating assessment of the Sinai Campaign:[1]

. . . there were two reasons why Israel could not ignore the wider [global] sphere: (1) it contains the great majority of the Jewish people, from which we draw manpower, material and cultural resources, and moral and political support; (2) the forces at work in the wider sphere will not lightly accept all the decisions secured by the Israeli forces. . . . And there is another reason, no less decisive: the Israel Defence Forces depend, in regards to the prospects of obtaining equipment . . . on the goodwill of those who manufacture the arms, which only a few of them are prepared to place at our disposal. . . .
This friendship . . . with as many nations and states as possible . . . is important and necessary in itself . . . but it can also bring about the weakening and the collapse of the Arab wall of hatred, and finally pave the way for a pact of peace and co-operation between Israel and the Arabs.

Ben Gurion's image of the 'wider sphere' embraced the United Nations and the Great Powers, including the United States, the Soviet Union, France, and Britain; that is, he grouped together the G, DB, and the two most relevant B components. For the universal actor he had always manifested a mixture of disdain, regarding its role in the Arab–Israel conflict, and hope, concerning its potential contribution to world order. Throughout the decision flow on Sinai, however, it was the denigrating 'oum shmoum' image which prevailed. This is starkly evident from several passages in his most important public *tour d'horizon* before the strategic decision to launch the Sinai Campaign, his review of the security situation before the *Knesset* on 15 October 1956:[2]

The U.N. authorities have demonstrated their incapacity . . . to put an end to repeated and systematic murders of Israeli citizens.
The U.N. authorities ignore breaches of the Agreements by Egypt, Jordan and Syria.
. . . what have the institutions of the U.N. done, or attempted to do, to safeguard our elementary rights according to the Charter . . . ?
The latest Security Council meeting did not even condemn the violation of Israel's freedom of navigation.

Ben Gurion's unpublished remarks were much harsher: their tone and substance revealed deep mistrust of the UN, especially of the Secretary-General, because of perceived pro-Arab bias.[3] Among the various pressures leading to the withdrawal decision on 8 November 1956, the UN demand was the least heeded by Ben Gurion. His concern about Hammarskjöld's behaviour during the political struggle over the terms of withdrawal was reflected in an instruction to Eban on 24

---

[1] Ben Gurion 1960, pp. 58, 79–80.
[2] Ben Gurion 1956 (3), pp. 21, 23, 26, 34. The bulk of that important speech was reproduced in Ben Gurion 1971, pp. 495–502.
[3] Interviews with members of Ben Gurion's Secretariat, Cabinet colleagues, and civil servants, including Navon and Kollek, Sharett, Meir, Joseph and Rosen, Peres and many Foreign Service officers, 1960–70.

December to approach the Secretary-General as little as possible and to use the General Assembly platform instead.[1] The six Assembly withdrawal resolutions were ignored by BG as being inconsequential. And throughout the implementation of Strategic Decision 2 UN assurances were regarded as much less valuable than US guarantees.

Ben Gurion's image of the United Nations was shared by Dayan and Peres, as well as by Meir. Indeed the two young men of the Defence Establishment (Dayan was 41 in 1956, Peres 33) displayed near-total indifference to the universal actor: the Chief of Staff made only four references to the UN, out of 212 global-system references, in his content-analysed speeches; the Director-General of the Defence Ministry mentioned the UN twice among 354 references to the global system. This was partly a function of their role. By contrast, Ben Gurion devoted much more public attention to the world body, 120 of 224 references, most of them critical. And the Foreign Minister, Meir, accorded it pre-eminent attention—75 per cent of her references to G, as is evident in Table 6.[2]

An elaborate content analysis of Israeli élite perceptions of the UN revealed a sharp change, from disdain for the United Nations in July 1956 (85·8 per cent *negative* evaluation) to high respect immediately after the outbreak of war (83·6 per cent *positive* evaluation).[3] This

---

[1] Eban 1957, p. 113.

[2] Approximately 12,000 words were analysed for each decision-maker. Where less than 11,500 words or more than 12,500 were available, raw totals of frequency were weighted. It is these weighted totals which appear in Tables 6–11. All speeches analysed antedated or immediately followed the Sinai Campaign. Where possible, a variety of audiences was selected. The usual rules of content analysis were followed. Each sentence was analysed in the active tense and all compound sentences were broken down. Each reference was counted only once. Intercoder reliability was verified at 81 per cent. The coded speeches for this content analysis were as follows:

Ben Gurion: Address to the *Knesset*, 15 Oct. 1956.
　　　　　　　Address to the *Knesset*, 7 Nov. 1956.
Dayan:　　　 Selections from *Diary of the Sinai Campaign*, 1956, ch. 2, pp. 28–43, and ch. 4, pp. 58–76.
Meir:　　　　Address to Jerusalem Press Club, 2 July 1956.
　　　　　　　United Nations Day Address to Jerusalem Rotary Club, 24 Oct. 1956.
　　　　　　　Address to the Emergency Session of the General Assembly, 5 Dec. 1956.
　　　　　　　Address to the 11th Session of the General Assembly, 11 Dec. 1956.
Peres:　　　　Lecture to Representatives of American Jewry, May 1956.
　　　　　　　Address to *Mapai* Party Workers, Tel Aviv, 21 Aug. 1956.

[3] Siverson 1969, p. 19. This study was based upon 47 Israeli documents (speeches, statements, etc.) by Ben Gurion, Meir, Peres, Dayan—and Eban—during five specified periods: I(2); II(27); III(7); IV(7); V(4). (Siverson also analysed Egyptian élite perceptions.) The results are not exactly comparable to those cited earlier (Table 6); because of his role Eban was the most sensitive of all Israeli public figures to the 'UN factor'. See Eban 1957, p. 53. And throughout the political struggle which followed, Eban perceived the UN's (and its Secretary-General's) attitudes as deserving of major Israeli consideration. This reflected, perhaps, Eban's perception and implied advocacy in July 1955: 'The very exercise of seeking the support of world opinion imposes restraints of reason in development of national policies, and operates against

TABLE 6

DECISION-MAKERS' IMAGES OF THE GLOBAL SYSTEM:
MARCH–OCTOBER 1956

Variable	Peres	Meir	Ben Gurion	Dayan	Total
United Nations	2	203	120	4	329
Britain	107	3	24	86	220
United States	89	25	27	39	180
France	98	0	7	72	177
Soviet Union	44	13	22	11	90
Jewish People	14	21	22	0	57
Cold War	0	0	2	0	2
Total	354	265	224	212	1055

was probably because of surprise at the UN's swift reaction to the Suez–Sinai conflict. Herzog recalled, 'We didn't realize how quickly and how far the Assembly would move in ordering Israel to withdraw.'[1] Surprise, in turn, was due to several misperceptions or miscalculations:

(1) of UN members' bewilderment resulting from the information gap—Eban's first defence of Israel's strike into Sinai, with its powerful theme, 'embattled, blockaded, besieged', was only delivered to the Assembly 72 hours after the Campaign began;[2]

(2) of the negative spillover effect on Israel's image in the UN caused by the violent attack on the Anglo-French assault on Egypt—by the US, the USSR, and the Asian Group;[3]

(3) of the haunting fear of global war, the gloom and near-panic in the Assembly, created by Soviet threats—the notes to the British, French, and Israeli Governments on 5 November;

(4) of the cumulative effect on UN members of the Hammarskjöld–Burns pressure for a cease-fire and, later, for Israeli withdrawal;[4] and finally,

(5) of the catalytic role of the Hungarian uprising in speeding UN

the formulation of national policies on the sole basis of egocentric emotion.' Eban 1969, p. 211. Thus the proportionate positive evaluation of the UN by the four decision-makers would be much lower.

[1] Interview, 1966.

[2] The full text is in Eban 1969, pp. 276–92. That state of shock also affected the North American Jewish community, which rallied to Israel's defence only *after* Eban's 1 November speech. Eban and Meir interviews, 1965 and 1966 respectively.

[3] Herzog interview, 1966.

[4] As one writer correctly noted: 'Critically aggravating the withdrawal issue ... was the Israeli belief that Hammarskjöld was negotiating with a pro-Arab bias, that he delineated his responsibilities too legalistically and narrowly. There seems little doubt that the aloof, austere Secretary-General probably preferred dealing with Egypt's UN Representative Fawzi whom he found more flexible than the obdurate Mrs. Meir.' Robertson, p. 324. The alienation of Israel caused by this friction with Hammarskjöld was confirmed by Kidron. Interview, 1966.

cease-fire and withdrawal resolutions; as Ben Gurion's Political
Secretary at the time remarked, 'The Western world was furious
that, by our action, we made it easier for the Russians to do what
they wanted to do in Hungary.'[1]

For the most part, Ben Gurion and his followers—Dayan, Peres,
Meir—retained their contempt for the international organization.
Suspicion of the Secretary-General was expressed with characteristic
bluntness by Meir: 'He was consistently anti-Israel; his attitude during
the Sinai period followed this pattern.'[2] And the categorical refusal to
accept UNEF units on Israeli territory illuminated that mistrust. Peres
expressed the general decision-makers' perception on this point: UN
behaviour was rarely to Israel's benefit; UNEF's presence would delay
a direct Arab–Israeli diplomatic confrontation; and Israel's sovereignty
would be jeopardized by the UN's desire to impose a super-govern-
ment upon her.[3] Ben Gurion's view was the same: 'We didn't want them
to be bosses in our country. Behind the UN force in Israel would be
the United Nations and the Powers. A foreign military force in our
country—never.'[4] Indeed, there was a sharp drop in their short-lived
positive perception—to 59 per cent in March 1957, providing further
evidence of the decision-makers' combined images: of disdain for the
United Nations; and of Israeli insecurity—even at the point of final
compromise.[5]

The Cold War dimension of global politics is virtually absent from
the content-analysed speeches delivered before Strategic Decision 1:
it accounts for only 2 of 1,055 references to G components, both by

[1] Navon interview, 1965.   [2] Interview, 1966.   [3] Interview, 1966.

[4] In that context Israel's Prime Minister added his perception of Nasser's view of
Sinai and the UN: 'And I am sure that Nasser did not regard Sinai as part of Egypt.
He would not have, and did not, allow UN troops on *Egyptian* territory.' Interview,
1966.

[5] So too does a revised Index of Injury, applied to Israeli perceptions throughout
the Sinai issue. Siverson defined the Index of Injury as

$$\frac{\text{Negative Units as Target} + \text{Positive Units as Agent}}{\text{Negative Units as Agent} + \text{Positive Units as Target}}$$

Index results in excess of 1·00 indicate perceptions of injury, while those below 1·00
indicate a perception of friendship for the target by the relevant actors in the international system at the time. Siverson's research revealed Israel's perception of injury
by target and time period, as follows:

Perceived Target	Time Period				
	I	II	III	IV	V
Israel	2·25	2·82	2·19	3·40	1·09
United Nations	1·30	·85	1·25	·73	1·46
Egypt	—	·49	·35	·36	·86
Arab States	·24	·29	·35	·23	·39

Although the UN was viewed as a more injured actor than Egypt or the Arab States,
Israel was perceived as a subject of qualitatively greater injury than the UN during
the Sinai–Suez Crisis as a whole. Siverson 1970, pp. 161–3.

Ben Gurion. Thus, Soviet–American competition for Middle East or world hegemony did not find expression in Israeli élite images relevant to the Sinai issue. Nor did three of the four DB relationships—Israel–USSR, Arabs–US, or Arabs–USSR. Only the Israel–US relationship was articulated: Peres (15), Dayan (10), Meir (8), and Ben Gurion (4), making a total of 37 references.

In qualitative terms there was a consensus, asymmetrical, image of the super-powers—a fundamental kinship for, and assumed friendliness by, the United States; a rooted mistrust of, and expected hostility from, the Soviet Union. Ben Gurion expressed this clearly in two important speeches of 1956:[1]

the 'Czechoslovakian Deal' is only a new and pointed expression of a process which began with the Bolshevist Revolution and sharpened after Lenin's death . . . [indicating] the Soviet Union's constant opposition on principle to Zionism, which is the lifeblood of the State of Israel . . .;
The United States, to whom we owe our thanks for much political and financial assistance from the day the State was founded. . . . Hence we insist on our demand for arms—first of all from the United States, which does not desire war in the Middle East and wishes well both to Israel and the Arab peoples.

About their probable roles in the developing crisis Ben Gurion spoke with candour on several occasions during the month preceding the Sinai Campaign. On 1 October he remarked to some visiting French generals:[2]

. . . we must not forget that [the Soviet Union] is a nation of 200 millions, which constitutes a gigantic global factor, and which defeated Napoleon in his time. . . .
We must not ignore the possibility of 'volunteers' being sent from Russia, and also the encouraging of the tyrant Nasser—*and this encouragement might complicate matters.* . . .

The Prime Minister reaffirmed his image of possible Soviet intervention, at the beginning of the Sèvres Conference, on 22 October. 'The position of the United States, too, is not clear', he added; 'now, Eisenhower is bound to his slogan "peace at any price"; however, it is possible that, after the elections, he will feel himself freer to act. . . .'[3]

Ben Gurion's cautious optimism about American support quickly vanished, undoubtedly because of the US President's mounting pressure. Thus to Israel's Cabinet he 'confessed' on 28 October, the day before the Campaign began:

I imagine that if we occupied the Sinai Peninsula a certain number of Powers would force us to evacuate it. France and Britain are with us, but they are not

[1] The extracts are from Ben Gurion 1956 (1), p. 1, and 1956 (3), pp. 7, 14.
[2] Peres Diary (Evron), pp. 86–7. The authenticity of this and subsequent extracts from Peres' Diary, as quoted in Evron, was confirmed to the author by Peres himself in 1972.
[3] Ibid., p. 126.

everyone. There's America and Russia, there's also the United Nations and Nehru, Asia and Africa; and I'm thinking more of the Americans than the others, because they would force us to withdraw. The United States wouldn't need to send troops; it would be enough for them to announce that diplomatic relations were being broken off, that collections for the Jewish funds were forbidden and loans to Israel blocked.[1]

Ben Gurion consistently ascribed greater importance to the United States than to the Soviet Union as decisive inputs into Israeli behaviour. A decade and more after the events, he observed about the crucial withdrawal decision of 8 November: 'The only way Bulganin could act was to send an army—or attack by air. And I knew he would not do so. But the Americans—I knew they didn't have to send an army. Therefore I was more concerned about the Americans.'[2] That concern did not lessen during the ensuing political struggle. On several occasions the Israeli Prime Minister instructed Ambassador Eban to concentrate on US guarantees, not on UN assurances; the Soviets were ignored throughout the four-month diplomatic campaign. Moreover, the combined inducements and implied threats by Eisenhower and Dulles in February 1957 moulded Ben Gurion's perception of global constraints at the time. And it was US pledges, absorbed into a pre-dispositional image of friendliness, which shaped his final decision to withdraw from Gaza and Sharm-e-Sheikh.

All the high-policy decision-makers were more aware of the United States than of the Soviet Union during the Sinai issue, according to the frequency of reference data in Table 6: Peres (89–44), Meir (25–13), Dayan (39–11), and Ben Gurion, with the smallest margin, 27 to 22. That difference in attention is accentuated by the DB data already noted—37 references to the Israel–US relationship, none to Israel's ties with the USSR.[3] In substance three lesser decision-makers shared

---

[1] Ben Gurion Documents (Bar-Zohar 1968), p. 224. A slightly different wording appears in Ben Gurion 1971, p. 505.

[2] Ben Gurion interviews, 1966 and 1971. But many others, who participated in, or observed, the decision process of 7–8 November, termed 'the Russian factor' more compelling for Ben Gurion (to be elaborated in section (D) below). The Prime Minister himself did not minimize *joint* super-power influence on the Arab–Israel conflict: 'Ten years ago, I was absolutely certain that, if Russia and America wished it, there would have been peace. . . . Even now', he added, 'if the two Great Powers want it, they could bring it about—by pressing Nasser.' Interview, 1966.

[3] The perception of a pivotal US role, as often, was cogently elaborated by Eban, Israel's principal negotiator in the post-Sinai battle for guarantees, in reply to the question, 'Was the Sinai Campaign necessary?' 'If the Americans had given us 40 planes at the right moment, in January 1956, the kind of psychological and military build-up that occurred after the Czech arms deal need not have occurred. The Arabs and Israel, and the world at large, would have known and accepted the fact that Washington would always act to rectify an arms imbalance in the Middle East. Sharett's position and policies would have been greatly enhanced; the concern in Israel would have been less; and the psychological and military build-up would have been less compelling. But the Americans did not respond—because they did not cor-

Ben Gurion's image. Peres wrote at the time of the Soviet arms deal: 'The Russians penetrated—and Nasser's glory rocketed sky-high. . . . To the word "Mig", there was then a magic ring. . . . To the technical entanglement there was added, as well, the Soviet mystique. . . .'[1] And in May 1956, as often, he referred, decisively, to 'the totalitarian regime which made the deal with Egypt and not only supplied them with an abundance of air, land and sea weapons, but also sold equipment directly from their military stockpile at prices which seem to be a token payment'.[2] Dayan manifested the greatest concern about 'the Russian factor', especially during the tense days of 5–8 November 1956: it was characteristic of his image of global politics over the years, during the May–June 1967 crisis and the post-Six Day War period as well. The consensus among colleagues, subordinates, and observers is persuasive.

Among the global system components Britain and France attracted the most attention in the content-analysed images of Peres and Dayan: the former, 107 and 98 respectively, almost 60 per cent of his total G references; the latter, 86 and 72, together almost 75 per cent of his references to the global system. This reflected in large part their primary roles: Peres, architect of the 'French orientation' from 1954 onwards; Dayan, an activist Chief of Staff drawn steadily to France as indispensable arms supplier, especially after the Soviet–Egyptian deal and the US refusal to rectify the balance; and both as principal advocates of alliance with France, a goal consummated with the tactical decision of September 1956. The two men also perceived the value, later the necessity, of a joint military campaign with France and Britain against an assertive and well-armed Egypt.

Peres wrote in his diary in July 1954, after a discussion with Selwyn Lloyd: 'In general, I have had the impression that the English have still not recognized the State of Israel and certainly have not yet made peace with her independent existence.' The French, by contrast, perceived her with marked affection, as the following passages in September 1955 reveal:

I discovered there a sympathy for the Jewish People, its fate, the tragedy which afflicted it. We received from France many negative replies but never did we have the feeling that any reply carried any sense of finality. The French are a people with an open heart and a never-ending dialogue. . . . In France there exists a double aesthetic: both of rationality and sentimentality.
A Frenchman of high status will always, always be found . . . who will be bound with Latin enthusiasm and courage to fight for a 'lost cause'.[3]

---

rectly understand the depth of Israeli insecurity. They saw the Middle East solely in terms of their Cold War with the Soviets; thus they denied us arms in January. They did move towards a rectification of the arms imbalance, haltingly and inadequately, indirectly through Canada and others, in April; but it was too late.' Interview, 1965. The same perception was articulated by Herzog: interview, 1966.

[1] Peres Diary (Evron), pp. 20–1.   [2] Reported in *Jerusalem Post*, 14 May 1956.
[3] These two extracts are from Peres Diary (Evron), pp. 17, 19. A decade after Sinai,

Dayan perceived France as a pragmatic ally, with England's role necessary for Ben Gurion's peace of mind: 'If it were not for the Anglo-French operation,' he wrote in his diary, 'it is doubtful whether Israel would have launched her campaign.'[1] And the French inability to counter Soviet threats, communicated to Peres and Meir in Paris on 6 November, influenced the withdrawal decision two days later. Their image of all G components thereafter was irrelevant, for the implementation of that strategic decision lay essentially in other hands.

Ben Gurion's contrasting images of Britain and France are evident in his *Knesset* speech of 15 October 1956:

The British Government, which sold the Egyptian dictator heavy tanks, knowing that they were intended to strike at Israel, obstinately refused to sell them to Israel. And this England is . . . a party to the Tripartite Declaration of 1950. . . .

We owe profound appreciation and sincere thanks to France, which was the first to supply us with 24 modern Mystère IV jet planes. . . .[2]

A few weeks earlier Dayan recorded in his diary: 'He [BG] is . . . suspicious of Britain. He feels that Britain may wish to demonstrate her friendship for the Arabs by employing her forces against us in going to the help of Jordan.'[3]

Ben Gurion's mistrust of 'perfidious Albion' is also conveyed in a letter to the Chief of Staff in mid-October, explaining his decision to stop reprisal raids against Jordan: 'I think that Eden will eventually join in "the Cyprus action". In my opinion, France will not act without Britain, so we must not give the British any pretext just now to slip out of the affair.'[4] Peres' diary entry for 16 October provides further insight into Ben Gurion's image of Britain nine days before Strategic Decision 1:

Another problem . . . was the deep mistrust which Ben Gurion harboured towards the British Government—and to Eden in particular. He saw in him not only the progenitor of antagonism to Israel, but also a weak leader whose deeds do not match his declarations. . . . Ben Gurion took into account the possibility of . . . the British . . . even joining the Arab camp at the last moment.

A crisis of confidence towards England came from long years of bitter ex-

---

Peres reflected upon his impressions of the four key French actors in the drama: 'Mollet felt that Nasser was a dictator à la Hitler. To him there was no contradiction among three strands—socialist ideology, French interests (Algeria), and a gesture to Israel, a social democracy.

'Bourgès-Manoury saw Israel as a Middle East extension of France *libre*. He and Thomas viewed Suez as another potential Munich, hence the need for action.

'Pineau was the least political of the four; brilliant in analysis, a man of dignity, he became disillusioned with Nasser and threw his support whole-heartedly to Israel.

'It was a happy collaboration.' Peres interview, 1966.

[1] Dayan 1966, p. 3. This theme is striking in Peres' 1970 account, ch. 10, esp. pp. 188–205.

[2] Ben Gurion 1956 (3), pp. 7, 30.   [3] Dayan 1966, p. 28, entry 27 Sept. 1956.

[4] Ben Gurion Documents (Bar-Zohar 1968), p. 208.

perience and from acquaintance with the pro-Arab tradition of the 'Foreign Office' . . . .[1]

Of the events of 22–24 October he has written: '. . . again there was the attempt to allay Israel's mistrust of Britain. Pineau [the French Foreign Minister], with a sardonic touch, said: "We've brought the British round from complete misunderstanding to partial misunderstanding." When Ben Gurion heard this, he exclaimed: "Why didn't you get them to banish all misunderstanding?"'[2] Eden's behaviour the day after that conference sustained Ben Gurion's mistrust: 'I owe nothing to Eden; he did not behave well.'[3] So too did the delay in the Anglo-French landing, which Israeli decision-makers blamed entirely on London; the tone of British statements in the General Assembly from 1 November onwards; and the premature British insistence upon a cease-fire—before the entire Canal Zone was secure under Anglo-French control. Thereafter Ben Gurion simply ignored the UK in weighing Israel's course of action, at the UN and elsewhere: to the image of mistrust was now added a perception of weakness and irrelevance to the outcome of Israeli political goals.

One theme dominates the content-analysis data on Israel's near-neighbours, as is evident in Table 7: the decision-makers were preoccupied with Egypt and Nasser in the Near East Core.

Almost two-thirds of all country references were directed to Egypt. In terms of individual images the emphasis ranged from Meir (73 per cent) to Dayan (57 per cent). The focus on Egypt's President is even more striking—90 per cent of all references to Near East Arab leaders. Only Dayan distributed his attention widely, mentions of Nasser being just over half of the total. Among all other units in the Core, Jordan alone attracted more than marginal verbal interest from Israel's decision-makers during the six months preceding the Sinai Campaign—21 per cent of the total country references. Dayan's quantitative image of Jordan is the most striking—94 references, 26 per cent of his total and almost half of his references to Egypt. The gap in attention to Arab *leaders*, however, is much greater: King Hussein was mentioned 10 times, only 4 per cent of the total, equally divided between Ben Gurion and Dayan.

The concentration on Egypt and Nasser from March to October 1956 was blurred at the time, partly by Israel's successful diversionary tactic of reprisal raids against *Jordan* and partly because of the *failure to analyse Israeli decision-makers' perceptions*. The last speech explored by content analysis was Ben Gurion's review before the *Knesset* a fortnight

---

[1] Peres Diary (Evron), pp. 100–1.

[2] Peres 1970, p. 200. There is no explicit reference to the Sèvres Conference in Peres' 1970 account but it is clear from internal—and other—evidence that the episode occurred at that historic Franco-Israeli-British secret meeting.

[3] Ben Gurion interview, 1966. This point will be elaborated in the following section.

before the Campaign. By that time the *direction* of Israel's approaching strategic decision was unmistakable.

TABLE 7

DECISION-MAKERS' IMAGES OF NEAR-NEIGHBOURS:
MARCH–OCTOBER 1956

(a) Actors

Variable	Dayan	Ben Gurion	Meir	Peres	Total	Per cent
Egypt	214	140	100	94	548	63·4
Jordan	94	48	14	25	181	21·0
Iraq	30	15	8	10	63	7·2
Syria	14	20	12	8	54	6·3
Palestine (community)	0	8	3	0	11	1·3
Lebanon	3	3	1	0	7	·8
Total	355	234	138	137	864	100

(b) Leaders

Variable	Peres	Ben Gurion	Meir	Dayan	Total
Nasser	102	62	33	14	211
King Hussein	0	5	0	5	10
King Abdullah	0	0	3	4	7
King Farouk	4	1	0	1	6
King Feisal	0	0	0	2	2
King Saud	1	0	0	0	1
Total	107	68	36	26	237

Throughout the pre-decision phase, 1954–6, Israeli decision-makers perceived 'the Arabs' as hostile, threatening, unwilling to recognize Israel's right to exist, and certain to exploit every sign of weakness to destroy the Jewish state. In short, the core perception was the identity of security and survival. And that 'trauma' image was strengthened by a series of events in the operational environment: the rise to power of a young, assertive, charismatic leader in Egypt, openly aspiring to hegemony in the 'Arab Circle'; Britain's withdrawal from the Canal Zone; escalating *feda'iyun* raids in 1955–6; the Soviet–Egyptian arms deal; and the broadening of the blockade of the Tiran Straits. By the time the Suez Canal was nationalized, Israeli decision-makers' distrust had registered a negative perception rating for Nasser of 90·2 per cent. On the eve of the Sinai Campaign that negative rating had declined to 68·2 per cent, reflecting greater Israeli security as a result of the rectification of the arms imbalance and the alignment with France.[1]

[1] Siverson 1969, p. 18.

Ben Gurion, as always, enunciated with candour his image of the Arab threat. On 15 April 1956, Independence Day, he warned the nation:

It may be that in the ninth year of our renewed independence we shall have to face a supreme test, graver and more difficult than that which we faced successfully eight years ago. For our enemies are concerting their designs against us. . . . We see with open eyes the dangers that threaten us from the constantly increasing pace at which *our enemies, especially Egypt,* are rearming.[1]

And on 15 October he informed the world from the *Knesset* podium:

The Egyptian dictator and his supporters openly declare that he is preparing to liquidate Israel. . . .
[And, at the end of a long review,] We are faced with the need for a supreme effort in the field of security, for *it is forced on us by external factors and hostile forces*; we may be facing *fateful decisions and events*. Let us stand ready and united. . . .[2]

Perception of threat was combined with a respectful image of Nasser's survival capacity. On 1 October Ben Gurion remarked: 'It is not at all certain, even if the airfields, installations, ports of the enemy, and his army be destroyed, that the tyrant would be deposed. . . . Possibly a military débâcle would bring his annihilation—but this is not certain.'[3]

The Sinai Campaign was the culmination of a period of Arab raid and Israeli retaliation. It was Dayan who provided the clearest rationale for that policy consequence of a long-term Israeli image of insecurity in an environment of Arab hostility:

We must regard the events which came up under the heading of 'current security' not as transient episodes but as a basic condition over a long period. Is it 10 years? Or 20? Who can say how long we shall have to live under current security conditions? . . .
We must set up fixed rules of what is permissible and what is forbidden in the relations to us of the Arab countries and their populations, and take care not to tolerate or accede to any assaults against us, even if minor, when we are in a position to prevent them. . . .
The motive that could bring the Arab government and armies to follow such a course [imposing severe punishments and opening fire on Arabs by their own forces . . . fighting extremist bands]—and make the people understand why— must be something hard and real and certain; reprisal actions by the Israel Army, and the fear of such actions.

---

[1] Ben Gurion 1956 (2), pp. 1, 4 (emphasis added). Long before that, indeed a year before the Sinai Campaign, Eban perceived a grave threat and urged a military riposte. 'I recommend', he cabled Sharett, early in November 1955, 'that, in the light of the possibility of an increase of aggressive pressure on Egypt's part, a plan of action be prepared aimed at using force against Egypt, either by our strength alone or in co-operation with other states.' As quoted in an interview by Eli Nissan, 'An Hour with Abba Eban', *Davar*, 29 Oct. 1965.
[2] Ben Gurion 1956 (3), pp. 13, 43 (emphasis added).
[3] To visiting French generals. Peres Diary (Evron), p. 86.

. . . it is in our power to set a high price on our blood, a price too high for the Arab community, the Arab army, or the Arab governments to think it worth paying.[1]

During the summer preceding the Campaign Dayan conveyed with typical directness his image of Nasser, the Middle East—and, *en passant*, of France, the West, and the Soviets:

There are two dangers threatening the Middle East—the annihilation of European influence and Soviet penetration. Egypt is gradually turning into a Soviet base [June 1956, not 1968 ff.], and the West is losing its influence in this part of the world. To Israel and France there is a common enemy in the region—Gamal Abd-el Nasser. *For the purpose of the struggle against him Israel is prepared to co-operate with the French.*[2]

Neither Peres nor Meir dissented from the image of threat and insecurity, or from the general policy of retaliation and the specific policy of alignment with France: the consensus among Israel's decision-makers was complete.

Two images of M were manifested by Israel's decision-makers during the period March–October 1956: concern about the military balance; and confidence about the outcome of another war. The first strand is evident from content-analysis data, the second from qualitative indicators. Taking the period as a whole, the frequency count, coded along a three-point scale (increasing, same, decreasing), reveals cautious optimism about Israel's *military capability*. At the same time, all except Dayan perceived a rise in their enemies' M as well. When the frequency data for Israel and her adversaries are combined into a rough indicator of military balance, the *image of concern* is strengthened.

TABLE 8

DECISION-MAKERS' IMAGES OF ISRAEL'S RELATIVE MILITARY
CAPABILITY: MARCH–OCTOBER 1956

Image of	Peres	Ben Gurion	Dayan	Meir	Total
Increasing*	10	14	11	4	39
Same†	32	13	38	3	86
Decreasing‡	15	29	0	15	59
Total	57	56	49	22	184

* Increasing = 'increasing' for Israel's M, 'decreasing' for enemies' M
† Same   = 'same' for both Israel's and enemies' M
‡ Decreasing = 'decreasing' for Israel's M, 'increasing' for enemies' M

[1] From a lecture to *Tzahal* officers in November 1955. Dayan 1955 (1). For a more formal articulation of Israel's security complex during the pre-decisional phase see Dayan 1955 (2), pp. 250–67.
[2] To a group of French military officers near Paris, on 23 June 1956. Peres Diary (Evron), p. 42.

The image balance is heavily weighted to concern: for all but Dayan the references to 'decreasing' relative Israeli military capability exceed those to 'increasing' M, in the case of BG by 2 to 1, and for Meir almost 4 to 1. If concern is defined as non-increasing M, a valid criterion in the light of the permanent Arab–Israel arms race, the image balance is sharply accentuated: Peres 47 to 10; Ben Gurion 42 to 14; Dayan 38 to 11; and Meir 18 to 4; for none is the negative image of Israel's M less than 1 to 3; and for the group as a whole the image of concern is 145 to 39, almost 4 to 1. Only Dayan referred to Israel's mobilization potential: while he made no references to 'low', the frequency count for 'medium' outweighed 'high' by 13 to 5, a further indication of concern.

That concern was a direct result of the Soviet (Czech)–Egyptian arms deal. Dayan perceived it thus: '. . . it wiped out in a flash the shaky arms balance which existed between the Arab States and Israel. . . . Now, Egypt's armoured force alone . . . had an ascendancy over Israel of nearly four to one. This was true also for the air force.'[1] Ben Gurion expressed an identical view: 'The Czech–Egyptian arms deal transformed Israel's security situation for the worse at one stroke. The quantitative inferiority of our military equipment, which had existed ever since the War of Independence, became a dangerous position of qualitative inferiority as well.'[2] And for the decision-making élite as a whole, 'it really threw us into a deep anxiety'.[3] Indeed, that perception triggered Ben Gurion's instruction to the Chief of Staff in October 1955 to prepare plans for a strike against Sharm-e-Sheikh—and Dayan's response: 'As to *time*, it does not seem to me that the moment for action . . . will be more favourable a few months hence. With the strengthening of the Egyptian forces, particularly in the air, our military prospects of succeeding in such an operation will be weakened.'[4]

A favourable change in the operational environment—the flow of French arms—produced a discernible change in articulated image. Thus in May 1956 Peres expressed confidence: 'If the Egyptians attack us, we have no doubts of our ability to come out victorious, even though the price of victory will necessarily be high because of the threat of bombers to non-combatants . . . in our cities.'[5] Four months later Dayan told Peres that arms from France should not be regarded as a *sine qua non* to Israel's action—because *Tzahal* could conquer Sinai even without further military aid.[6]

The most dramatic shift in élite perception of military capability

---

[1] Dayan 1966, p. 4.   [2] Ben Gurion 1960, p. 25.

[3] Herzog interview, 1966.

[4] Letter to Ben Gurion, 5 December 1955, as quoted in Dayan 1966, p. 14. That important event will be elaborated in the following section.

[5] *Jerusalem Post*, 14 May 1956.

[6] On 26 Sept. 1956. Peres Diary (Evron), p. 78.

was expressed by Ben Gurion in the *Knesset* on 15 October 1956. The arms flow from France was at its peak. The Prime Minister chose to reveal this by quoting from a poem celebrating Israel's greater security. He also cited with approval Dayan's words a few weeks earlier about the strength of Israel's army, and added: 'I am as confident as every one of our commanders that any conflict with the Egyptians or the rest of the Arab armies will end in our victory. . . .'[1]

He was not without worry, however. In rejecting a UK plan for Israel to attack—without any British or French military involvement until later—BG told his colleagues at Sèvres on 22 October: '. . . the Egyptians have the capability of bombing Tel Aviv within minutes of flight . . . and we must assume they have about 50 bombers. Even if they were to send but 10 planes at one time, they have the power to attack five times a day. . . .'[2] Indeed, it was that concern which led to Ben Gurion's insistence upon French air cover for Israel's cities from the very outset of the Sinai Campaign.

None of Israel's Sinai decision-makers articulated a perception of economic capability (E) or political structure (PS) as *relevant* to their decisions. The attitudes of other parties were known and absorbed but they were not significant, perhaps because of the near-total support of competing political élites (CE), as well as of the press and the mass public, for strategic decision 1—to launch the Campaign. More dissent was perceived regarding S_2 and the actual withdrawal, as is evident in *Knesset* debates and press comments; but that dissent did not affect either the decision or its implementation. As for interest groups (IG), only Dayan made (marginal) explicit reference to them in his speeches —Defence (8), Finance (1), and the Prime Minister's Office (5). In short, the psychological environment was dominated by external components—G (United Nations); DB (United States and Soviet Union); S (Near East Core); and B (France and Britain), with one internal

---

[1] The most poignant passages of Natan Alterman's poem are as follows:

'Perhaps it is a night that has been. Or the night of a dream. In its dream—
    iron, much iron, new iron,
With long muzzles, thundering on steel chains,
Arriving from afar, climbing onto the shore, and while it is all vision it is all
    substance,
And when it first touches the soil it is transformed into Jewish power.

Perhaps this is a night of dreams, but waking
    and in fact it saw melting away the terror of the gap
Between ourselves and the forces of destruction . . . Iron
    steadily comes,
    and the bowels of the earth tremble . . .

Good that Israel's day should know that from the night it draws the power of
    life, the power of fire . . .'

Ben Gurion 1956 (3), pp. 10, 12, 13.
[2] Peres Diary (Evron), p. 126.

component, M, as the logical extension of the perception of threat from Israel's neighbours.

The external focus is also illuminated by the data on *symbols*, *advocacy*, and *objectives* of the Campaign, as enunciated by Israel's decision-makers. The wealth of symbolic imagery is evident in the raw facts. There were 1,228 references to 17 symbols. Meir contributed 44 per cent of the total (548), Ben Gurion 29 per cent (363), and Dayan and Peres the rest, 180 and 137 references respectively. Three of these symbols account for more than half of the total; and the four most frequently noted, almost two-thirds of all references, reveal the stimuli to strategic decision 1 and its goals—Conflict (308), Peace (236), Terrorism (154), and Freedom of Navigation (66).[1]

Advocacy statements are those which propose, urge, or recommend a policy position; they usually contain the verbs 'must', 'should', or 'has to'. All such statements were ranked on a special nine-point scale, with 9 representing the most militant posture and 1 the most conciliatory point. The *advocacy statement scale* which guided the coding was as follows:

9. We cannot tolerate any further increase of *feda'iyun* raids into Israel.
8. We cannot tolerate the continuing blockade of Israeli shipping.
7. We must act before the Arab forces on our borders unite.
6. We must not permit Egypt (Nasser) to acquire superiority in weapons.
5. We must strengthen our military capability to defeat an Arab attack.
4. We must seek allies to ensure our defence.
3. We must persuade the Arabs that we are not expansionist.
2. Co-existence with our neighbours should be our highest policy objective.
1. We should seek peace through mutual compromise.[2]

[1] There were only three internal symbols, comprising barely 8 per cent of the total references—Economic Development (47), Freedom (27), and Justice (24). Their most frequently cited symbol was Conflict, with Peace second and Terrorism third. Moreover, the attention curve is much broader: the first symbol accounts for only 25 per cent of Meir references, and 24 per cent for BG; and the three leading symbols constitute 52 per cent and 57 per cent of their total references respectively. That difference was partly a function of role—and audience—and partly of predisposition.

There was much greater symbolic concentration in the images of Dayan and Peres than of Meir or Ben Gurion. No less than 55 per cent of all Dayan references were to Conflict (99 of 180); along with Terrorism (17) and Defence (15), there emerges a homogeneous Dayan cluster of *security* symbols, accounting for 73 per cent. Conflict accounted for 45 per cent of Peres' symbol articulation; if Freedom of Navigation and Security are added, they make a security cluster embracing 63 per cent of his references. The distribution for Meir and Ben Gurion is conspicuously different.

The other 10 coded symbols were: Aggression, Danger, Defence, Destruction of Israel, Enmity, Friendship, Independence, Inequality, Nationalism, and Security.

[2] Several alternative scaling procedures were considered. The Q-Sort method was

The results are evident in Tables 9 and 10 and Figure 10.

TABLE 9

DISTRIBUTION OF ADVOCACY OF DECISION-MAKERS, FREQUENCY
AND INTENSITY: MARCH–OCTOBER 1956[1]

INTENSITY			FREQUENCY		
	Scale Point	Meir	Ben Gurion	Peres	Dayan	Total
Maximum						
Militancy	9.	5	7	1	2	15
	8.	2	6	0	0	8
	7.	0	2	0	2	4
	6.	0	3	1	0	4
	5.	12	9	9	1	31
	4.	1	2	0	2	5
	3.	3	2	0	0	5
	2.	16	6	1	0	23
Minimum	1.	1	0	0	0	1
Militancy						
Total		40	37	12	7	96

TABLE 10

MEDIAN VALUE OF ADVOCACY STATEMENTS BY DECISION-MAKERS:
MARCH–OCTOBER 1956

Dayan	6·8
Ben Gurion	5·8
Peres	5·4
Meir	3·5
Decision-Makers' Median	4·9

The salient points emerging from the advocacy data are as follows:

(a) one-third of the total statements cluster around the mid-point of
the scale (5), which emphasizes military superiority to defeat an
Arab attack, not the more militant 'not permit', 'act', or 'cannot
tolerate';

---

rejected because of its forced distribution, which did not allow for optimal treatment
of the data, given the interest in policy positions as well as intensity of advocacy. The
pair-comparison method did not permit comparison *across* decision-makers. Thus we
superimposed on the data an external scale, which neither forces distribution nor
eliminates comparison. The 9-point scale was developed from the writer's general
knowledge of competing advocacies and was pre-tested for sensitivity. The results
should not be considered interval data.

[1] All advocacy statements were extracted from the texts by two coders; inter-coder
agreement was 83 per cent. All statements were placed on separate cards; and the
names of all countries, places, and leaders were masked. Inter-coder agreement on
the scaling was 85 per cent.

FIGURE 10
ADVOCACY POSITION OF ISRAELI DECISION-MAKERS:
MARCH—OCTOBER 1956

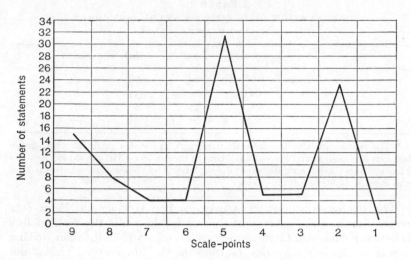

(b) the only two other focal points are the upper extreme of militancy and the conciliatory call for co-existence;[1]

(c) Meir was the most moderate advocate—21 of her statements fell below the mid-point, 16 of them at very conciliatory point 2, and only 7 statements were above the median;

(d) Peres was the epitome of the median advocate—three-fourths of his statements fell around point 5;

(e) Ben Gurion was more 'hawkish', with 18 statements above the median and only 10 below;

(f) Meir and Ben Gurion contributed 80 per cent of all advocacy statements, with Peres and especially Dayan playing a marginal role in this decision-making function; and

(g) Dayan was the most militant advocate of the four decision-makers, with a median value of advocacy at 6·8.[2]

---

[1] It seems plausible to discern in these points of high frequency a complementary relationship, for, in the image of Israeli decision-makers, ample Israeli military capability is a precondition to viable coexistence.

[2] According to Dayan's biographer, '. . . after the Czech Arms Deal in September 1955, Dayan aspired more than Ben Gurion to intensify border disputes—by means of more and more crushing reprisal actions—which would lead to an undoubted Israeli victory in war. . . .' Tevet, p. 430.

The average intensity of *Eban*'s advocacy statements during that period was also computed; it fell at the 7·14 level on the scale; that is, he was the most militant among Israeli leaders. Other content analysis data on Eban and his peers support this finding.

In this context it remains to note the proximity—or distance—
among the decision-makers as advocates of policy in 1956.

TABLE 11
CORRELATION OF DECISION-MAKERS' ADVOCACY:
MARCH–OCTOBER 1956*

	Ben Gurion	Peres	Meir	Dayan
Ben Gurion	—	·82	·66	·24
Peres	·82	—	·57	·23
Meir	·66	·57	—	·01
Dayan	·24	·23	·01	—

* The Spearman Rho (ρ) correlation of rank order was used. The correlation
between Ben Gurion and Peres is significant at the ·01 level. The correlation between
Meir and Ben Gurion is significant at the ·05 level. And the correlation between Meir
and Peres is significant at the ·10 level.

The strongest association is between Ben Gurion and Peres (·82
correlation and significance at the ·01 level), while the weakest link
is between Meir and Dayan (·01 correlation). Indeed, the most striking
aspect is Dayan's maverick position on the Sinai issue. This is not
surprising: rather, it conforms to the reality of Dayan's 'loner' role
within Israel's political élite. Similarly, the very high correlation between
Ben Gurion and Peres found continuing expression in the political
battles of the next decade, with Peres as the most devoted Ben Gurionist
and the managerial director of the BG-inspired splinter party, Rafi. And
the distance between Foreign Minister Meir and Chief of Staff Dayan
corresponded to the consensus view of Israel's attentive public at the
time. Ben Gurion, as the central figure and as mediator between
Foreign Office and Defence Ministry, was strongly associated with both
Meir and Peres. Only the relatively high correlation (·57) between the
latter is surprising, in the light of other evidence of friction. However,
as Meir remarked, their disagreement was on tactics, not strategy or
goals at that time; it centred on institutional roles—of the two ministries—in forging the French alliance, not the wisdom of the alignment
per se.[1]

There was a near-total consensus on the goals of the Sinai Campaign.
Dayan's objectives are stated in the epilogue to his Diary: '. . . its three
major purposes were . . . freedom of shipping for Israeli vessels in the
Gulf of Aqaba; an end to the feda'iyun terrorism; and a neutralization

See Brecher, Appendix D. Eban himself perceived his attitudes thus: 'There are hawks
dressed in the feathers of doves', he remarked in 1970, 'and vice-versa.' Interview on
Galei Tzahal (Army) radio station, reprinted in Bemahane, 3 February 1970.
[1] Interview, 1966.

of the threat of attack . . . by the joint Egypt–Syria–Jordan military command'.[1] Peres defined the objectives thus: 'End the *feda'iyun* raids; break the unity of the Arab camp; [and] secure free passage through Eilat.'[2] Meir's view of the goals was no different. 'There were two: to get rid of the *feda'iyun*, who had become a real nuisance; and to clear the Straits; and both were achieved.'[3]

While reflecting upon the Sinai Campaign many years later, Ben Gurion cited two goals only—*to free the Straits* for Israeli shipping and *to eliminate the feda'iyun bases*.[4] Members of his staff concur. Yet there is evidence that the Prime Minister contemplated other objectives as well. One was the *fall of Nasser*, a goal which he conveyed to French generals on 1 October 1956: '. . . without the speedy annihilation of the tyrant there is no security that the struggle would be ended *quickly*— even if there would be military successes in the first stage'. Another was *peace*. '*After every war*', he told *Tzahal* officers a few weeks before the Campaign,

and after every war from which we will emerge victors we will again face the same problem . . . the threat of a third round, fourth, fifth—and so on with no end. . . . We must remember that the vision of peace *is a Jewish vision*; however, even without the moral motive . . . this actual situation compels us always, to-gether with increasing military preparedness, never to forget, that our his-torical goal for the long run *is peace* . . . [War must be viewed] never as a goal in itself.[5]

Still other objectives were indicated by Ben Gurion at the Sèvres Conference (22–24 October): 'the *Suez Canal* must be turned into an international waterway;[6] Israeli control must be permitted over the approaches to Eilat; and the *Sinai Peninsula* is to be *demilitarized* . . .'.[7]

---

[1] Dayan 1966, p. 203 and p. 22 (entry 17 September 1956). Dayan, a decade after the Campaign, also referred to the goals of overthrowing Nasser and the concluding of a peace settlement. 'Ten Years After Sinai Campaign', reprinted from *Jewish Chronicle* (London) in *Jerusalem Post*, 28 Oct. 1966.

[2] Interview, 1966.   [3] Interview, 1966.   [4] Interview, 1971.

[5] The last two extracts are from Peres Diary (Evron), pp. 87, 114–15.

[6] Noteworthy in this context are the divergent views of Dayan and Peres. Six weeks before the Campaign the former told his General Staff: 'We have no aspirations to reach Suez and become an involved party in this dispute.' Dayan 1966, p. 22 (entry 17 Sept. 1956). Peres was even more distant from his mentor's goal: 'Deep in our hearts we thought of Suez as an Egyptian canal, built through Egyptian territory and belonging to Egypt—unfortunate as it might seem. But Tiran was a genuine international waterway, where we had the same rights as anyone else. *We never saw Suez as a casus belli, whereas we saw the Gulf of Aqaba as an extension of Israel's territorial rights.*' Interview, 1966 (emphasis added).

[7] Peres Diary (Evron), p. 123 (emphasis added). As for Eilat, two other indications of its pivotal role in Ben Gurion's image are noteworthy. As early as 4 June 1935 he sent a memorandum on Eilat to US Zionist leader Justice Brandeis. He referred to its importance in Biblical days and predicted that 'in the near future Eilat will play a more important part, politically and economically . . .'. Furthermore, 'there is no other route to India except through the Red Sea, from Haifa by way of Eilat'. Quoted

Moreover, Peres noted in mid-October BG's preoccupation with *keeping casualties to a minimum*: 'No one will understand David Ben Gurion correctly if he does not take into account that . . . a report on the death of a soldier shrouded him in depression. . . . How many boys would fall as a result of his fateful decision?'[1] As for Gaza, he wanted— and tried to achieve—the non-return of Egypt in any form. But he was not sanguine about its value. 'I fear that it will be embarrassing for us', he told the Cabinet the day before the Campaign. 'If I believed in miracles I would pray for it to be swallowed up in the sea. . . .'[2]

Among these eight goals there can be no doubt that freedom of navigation through the Straits was the highest priority for Israel's Prime Minister. Mounting terror from across the borders was the short-term catalyst. And peace, as always, was the long-term goal. To the extent possible, casualties should be minimal. All other objectives were qualitatively less important. Such was the hierarchy of Ben Gurion's advocacy and specific aims in launching the Sinai Campaign.

(c) DECISION PROCESS AND IMPLEMENTATION: T AND S$_1$

There are several plausible starting points in the Sinai decision process, for its roots lie deep in the Arab–Israel conflict: the military assault on 15 May 1948, immediately after the proclamation of Israel's independence; Egypt's blockade of the Gulf of Aqaba (1 July 1951); the seizure of power in Cairo by Free Officers (26 July 1952); and the formal dismissal of Neguib by Nasser, on 14 November 1954. There may be others. Certainly the emergence of a youthful, vigorous, and ambitious regime in the largest Arab state was viewed by Israel's decision-makers as creating a more formidable enemy in the protracted conflict. But the regime was not a *threat*, real or perceived, as long as Britain exercised direct control over the Suez Canal Zone.

The end of that military presence was heralded by the Anglo-Egyptian Agreement of 1954, initialled on 27 July and formally signed on 19 October: its central provision was the evacuation of all 70,000 British troops from their Suez base within twenty months.[3] As such it

---

in Ben Gurion 1957 (1), p. 828. During the third week of October 1956 Ben Gurion discovered from a Greek text the existence of a Jewish community on Yotvat (Tiran) in the 6th and 5th centuries B.C. He informed Dayan, Eshkol, and Meir, and ordered a search for more historical evidence. Several interviews, 1966.

[1] Peres Diary (Evron), 16 Oct. 1956, pp. 100–1.
[2] Ben Gurion 1971, p. 505. More than four months later, at the very end of the political struggle, he reiterated this view about Gaza before Israel's parliament. Ben Gurion 1957 (2), p. 1240.
[3] The UK retained for seven years the right to reactivate and return to the Base in case of an attack by an 'Outside Power' against an Arab League state or Turkey;

signalled a fundamental shift in the geo-strategic character of the Near East Core, unfreezing a frontier which had been tranquil since the Armistice Agreement of 1949—by virtue of the British buffer. That change in the operational environment was correctly perceived by Israel's decision-makers.[1] Indeed, it is the congruence of the two environments which merit selection of the 1954 Suez evacuation as the first pre-decisional event in Israel's Sinai decision process: with the departure of the last British soldier on 13 June 1956 the path was open to direct physical confrontation in the desert. And the transfer of vast stores and equipment to the Egyptian Army, valued at £200–£300 million, added a new element of instability to the arms balance. But other pre-decisional events were yet to unfold.

After months of prodding by the US, a mutual defence treaty was concluded between Turkey and Iraq on 24 February 1955: it was the first link in Dulles's cherished 'Northern Tier' to encircle the Soviet Union. Britain joined the Baghdad Pact in April, Pakistan in September, and Iran in October. The United States, despite her sponsorship, remained formally aloof, though she participated in the Pact's committees. Nasser, who perceived it as a form of neocolonialism, splitting the (illusory) unity of the Arab East, bitterly opposed the Pact before and after its formation. Its effect on the Arab–Israel conflict was to raise the general level of tension in the Near East Core.[2]

More dramatic in the flow of events was Israel's Gaza Raid on 28 February: it was the most serious clash since the Armistice Agreement, with 38 Egyptians killed and 31 wounded. The psychological effect on Nasser was profound, especially because he perceived a link with Israel's explicit demands that he abstain from condemning to death and executing suspects in the Israeli (Marzouk) spy ring in Egypt.[3] The consensus is widespread that the raid was a shock and a catalyst to the search for arms—from UNTSO Chief Burns to pro-Arab publicists like Childers and Love, and to an Israeli biographer of Ben

---

at Egypt's insistence Israel was excluded from the designation 'Outside Power'. Moreover, select Base installations were to be maintained by British commercial firms. The text is in Cmd 9298, HMSO London, 1954. For a discussion of the Agreement see Campbell, p. 65 and Love, pp. 184–8. On the US role see Copeland, pp. 113–23.

[1] Many emphasized it in their analysis of the background to the Sinai Campaign: Ben Gurion, Meir, Peres, Eban, Herzog, Navon interviews. Most accounts of the Suez conflict, by contrast, barely mention the Agreement. Love, an exception, does not indicate its far-reaching implications.

[2] See Campbell, ch. 5; Love, pp. 17–18, 193–211, 273–5; and Seale, ch. 16, 17. Tsur, in a *tour d'horizon* on Franco-Israeli relations, termed the Baghdad Pact a turning point in *France*'s Middle East policy; more specifically, 'a catalyst to change in French policy towards Israel'. The US and UK, he observed, created the Pact without, even against, France—with their emphasis upon the build-up of Hashemite power relative to Syria, Lebanon, and Egypt. Interview, 1960.

[3] Private communication to the author.

Gurion, Bar-Zohar.[1] But if the Gaza Raid was significant for Nasser's decisions, it was for Israel merely another act of retaliation and therefore an event, not a decisive input into her Sinai decision process. It was preceded by Kibya (18 October 1953) and was followed by ten other such acts from September 1955 to October 1956.[2] Further evidence is the lack of any reference to the Gaza Raid in the memoirs of Ben Gurion, Dayan, and Peres on the Sinai Campaign.[3] It was not part of their psychological environment and therefore not central to the decision.

They were conscious of another event soon after the Gaza Raid—the Egyptian General Staff's decision in April 1955 to launch *feda'iyun* raids into Israel from camps in the Gaza Strip. In August these hit-and-run sorties, unorganized since the Armistice, began in a systematic manner. At first they were a nuisance, but within a year they had caused death, destruction, and demoralization to the point of intolerability. What began as a pre-decisional event was to become a decisive input. As with the Gaza Raid, Israeli reprisals in the autumn of 1955

[1] Burns referred to 'the blow at Gaza which has destroyed any possibility of negotiating an early peace'. He also cited Nasser's remark to him about his abrupt change in attitude to Israel 'after the shock of February 28 1955'. Yet Burns was not entirely convinced: 'It is difficult to determine exactly what weight to give to Nasser's words.' And he acknowledged that Nasser's nationalization of the Canal 17 months later 'shook the foundations of peace in the Middle East'. pp. 21, 18–19, 18, and 163.

Childers wrote: 'The Gaza raid was a shock of quite historic dimensions. Nasser's reference to it [as 'the turning point', 'the alarm bell'] reflected universal [Egyptian] feeling.' pp. 132, 125.

Love devoted an entire chapter of his massive work on Suez to the Gaza Raid: it 'gave history a rowdy shove that sent it reeling across the intervening months into the Suez Crisis. ... The Gaza Raid started a chain of reactions ... which developed a drift towards war that neither human will nor political impunity was able to deflect.' p. 1.

Stephens considered its main effect was 'sharply to accelerate the arms race between Israel and Egypt, and to inaugurate a new and far more bloody cycle of terrorism, guerrilla raids and reprisals.' p. 156.

Bar-Zohar (1968) referred to the Gaza Raid as 'the turning point in Nasser's relations with Israel. It was also an opening shot in the Suez affair.' p. 185. Others echoed this view. For example, Robertson wrote: 'Reeling from the shock of the Gaza raid, Nasser announced ...' p. 12. And Stock observed: 'the determination to obtain arms, it is clear, was present before the Gaza raid, but the raid strengthened it ...' p. 110. See also Copeland, p. 9. Notable exceptions are Finer, Nutting, and H. Thomas.

[2]

Khan Yunis	1 Sept. 1955	Dir-al-Balah	17 Aug. 1956
Kuntilla	29 Oct. 1955	Rahawa	12 Sept. 1956
Nitzana	3 Nov. 1955	Garandal	13 Sept. 1956
Kinneret	11 Dec. 1955	Husan	25 Sept. 1956
Gaza	4 April 1956	Kalkilya	10 Oct. 1956

The last four were against Jordan, the others against Egypt. The most thorough treatment of Israel's reprisal policy is in Blechman 1971.

[3] Nor is it mentioned in Eban 1969 or in Eytan. The latter was then DG of the Foreign Ministry.

(Khan Yunis—1 September, Kuntilla—29 October, and Kinneret—11 December) were part of a new routinized pattern of Arab raid and Israeli retaliation, signposts on the road to Sinai.

During that period there occurred three other events which became catalysts or decisive inputs into both T and S$_1$ decisions. The first was Egypt's sudden announcement on 12 September broadening and tightening the Gulf of Aqaba blockade. All shipping and air transport were henceforth required to give seventy-two hours' advance notice and to receive Egyptian permission before passing through or over the Tiran Straits. And the passage by Israeli planes and ships was totally banned, which meant cutting the only direct air link with Africa. Dayan referred to it as 'the last straw'; it was not quite.

The second decisive input was the Soviet (Czech) arms deal with Egypt and Syria. Although news of the impending agreement was known to Israeli intelligence towards the end of August, it was first disclosed by the British Foreign Office on 28 September 1955 and by Nasser the next day. The near-consensus view is that the Gaza Raid triggered Egypt's panic search for arms; that Nasser approached Chou En-lai at Bandung (April 1955); that China alerted Moscow; that Nasser approached the Soviet Ambassador in May; that the Soviets sent Foreign Minister Shapilov to Cairo in July; that negotiations continued through the summer; and that they were successfully concluded by the end of August. At that time—but not before then—the unfolding reality of massive Soviet-bloc arms shipments to Israel's Arab enemies entered the psychological environment of Ben Gurion, Dayan, Peres, et al.[1]

[1] There is evidence of Egyptian–Soviet contacts on the arms issue in 1954 and at the beginning of 1955, leading one analyst to term this a 'dubious version of history' and, mistakenly, to sever the arms deal from its Gaza Raid roots. Ra'anan, in an elaborate reconstruction of the 'Genesis of an Arms Deal', notes with approval the view that the Gaza Raid was 'tactically useful afterward in justifying [Nasser's] moves . . .' (p. 47). He notes discussions between 1951 and 1954 (p. 69). He discovers 'a decisive development in the genesis of the Arms Deal' between 14 and 21 February 1955 (p. 76) and declares that an arms *agreement* was reached at that time. However, he destroys his own tortuously-reasoned and Talmudically-researched thesis by acknowledging: 'If it is asked whether the Egyptian–Czech *talks* in February resulted in a *final* and *irrevocable commitment* . . . then the answer* would appear to be *negative*. . . . [It was] an essential *preliminary stage* rather than the culminating point in the long process to which historians refer as the "Arms Deal". . . . There is no indication whether the Czech delegation to Cairo even included military experts. . . . It seems probable that the initial . . . *discussions* [termed by him an "agreement" and a "decisive development"] produced only a very general arrangement of a primarily financial character . . .' (pp. 80–1, emphasis added).

The designation '*Czech* arms' was conscious distortion. The British Ambassador to Egypt at the time wrote: 'It was of course a deal with the Russians and the Czechs only came into it at the last moment as a front for political reasons. . . . It would sound better that way, since Israel had had considerable arms supplies from the Czechs.' Trevelyan, p. 30. And the manner of attributing the deal to Prague was reported by an eye-witness as follows: Trevelyan was about to arrive to see Nasser. 'What, under

The arms deal was undoubtedly 'a decisive event in the development of the Middle East crisis'.[1] So too was the enlarged blockade of the Gulf. There was a third, virtually unknown at the time. As early as the spring of 1955, with Sharett as Prime Minister and Foreign Minister, and Ben Gurion newly reinstalled as Defence Minister, Israel sent out feelers to Washington for a military alliance or treaty of guarantee. BG referred to it indirectly in his Independence Day speech on 27 April: 'We are a small people and a poor state but we have the same rights as all sovereign states. . . . To the extent that other peoples need alliances, we too need them. . . .' And the semi-official report of the Cabinet's proceedings the following day made this more explicit: 'One can assume that the central question was one of guarantees to the security of Israel. . . . Israel will continue to demand guarantees in a mutual treaty in which each side promises to come to the assistance of the other, if attacked.'[2]

The openly pro-Western posture of *Mapai* became an issue in the general elections that summer, with the General Zionists, Progressives, and religious parties in full support, and the Left harshly opposed.[3] Eban's efforts in Washington proved in vain. In September there were several reports that the 'Presidents Club' of American Jewry and the Israeli Ambassador were pressing Washington for a guarantee of Israel's existing borders. And on 12 October the authoritative *Davar* reported in headlines: 'Israel demands from the United States a security agreement and large arms supply quickly.'[4] But the US declined the overtures. The convergence of these three decisive inputs created a *sense of desperation*, and that, in turn, led to an important Ben Gurion initiative.

On 22 October he summoned the Chief of Staff from a vacation in France. 'At the end of the talk [the following day]', wrote Dayan, 'he, as Minister of Defence, instructed me, among other things, to be prepared to capture the Straits of Tiran . . . in order to ensure freedom

---

the circumstances, was Nasser to tell the British Ambassador? "Just to hold him until tomorrow night", said Roosevelt, "tell him the arms are coming from Czechoslovakia", the idea being this wouldn't sound so heretical . . .' Copeland, p. 135. See also Love, pp. 90–1, 98–102. Love cites 25 August 1955 as the date of Nasser's final decision.

[1] Monroe concurred: 'The whole elaborate structure of Anglo-American defence policy was altered by this coup.' p. 186. Burns blames Israel: 'the tough Ben Gurion–Dayan policy . . . had practically forced Nasser to accept the Russo-Czech arms proposals.' pp. 99, 101. So did Sharett, in a 1957 speech reflecting on the Sinai Campaign. *Jerusalem Post*, 18 Oct. 1966. Most Israelis disagree.

[2] *Davar*, 28 and 29 April 1955.

[3] For the foreign policy platforms in the 1955 election campaign see Brecher, pp. 165, 167–8, 171, 176, 178, 179.

[4] Campbell, p. 93 (emphasis added). The outcome was clarified in an exchange of letters between Ben Gurion and *Ahdut Ha'avoda* leader Galili, *then* vociferously opposed to any military tie with the United States. The excerpts are from *Davar*, 12, 20 Sept., 12 Oct. 1955.

of shipping through the Gulf of Aqaba and the Red Sea.'[1] Two other contingency plans were requested: to attack the Gaza Strip; and to advance into Sinai.[2] Egypt was publicly warned by Ben Gurion on 2 November, in a speech to the *Knesset* presenting his new Cabinet after the third (1955) general election:

It is Egypt that recently took the lead in this guerrilla warfare. Raids from the Gaza Strip alone in the first nine months of 1955 have caused 153 casualties. . . . Egypt now seeks to block the passage of Israeli ships through the Red Sea Gulf in contravention of the international principle of freedom of the seas. *This unilateral warfare must cease, for it cannot remain unilateral indefinitely.* . . . Our aim is peace—but not suicide.[3]

The Prime Minister sought Cabinet approval on 5 December for a strike at Sharm-e-Sheikh. It was denied—by a small majority consisting of *Mapai* moderates (Sharett, Aranne, Luz, Sapir), *Mapam* (Barzilai, Bentov), the National Religious Party's ministers (Shapira, Burg), and the Progressives' Rosen. Although abortive, this proposal indicated the dominant perception among the Sinai issue decision-makers, with a direct link to the first strategic decision a year later. Dayan, for example, urged Ben Gurion the same day: 'It is . . . my view that we should undertake as soon as possible (within one month) *the capture of the Straits of Tiran.*'[4] The issue remained dormant at Government level for almost a year: other decisive inputs were necessary to permit the triumph of the Ben Gurion–Dayan–Peres advocacy.

One was the collapse of the Anderson Mission, a secret high-level US attempt at peacemaking through personal diplomacy. It never reached the stage of direct talks. Robert Anderson, as President Eisenhower's personal envoy, did commute between Cairo and Jerusalem for two months—January–March 1956—but he could not break the impasse.[5]

---

[1] Dayan 1966, p. 12.   [2] Ben Gurion Documents (Bar-Zohar 1968), p. 192.

[3] *Divrei Ha-knesset*, xix, pp. 226–33. The extract is from p. 233. The section of this speech dealing with security is reproduced in Ben Gurion 1971, pp. 446–50.

[4] Dayan 1966, p. 15.

[5] An authoritative Israeli source (Isser Harel, then Head of the Secret Service) termed the Mission a result of Israel's pressure on Washington to do one of two things. Harel was sent to the US in the autumn of 1955, soon after the Soviet arms deal. He showed US officials a top-secret document of a Ben Gurion meeting with Defence Ministry officials in which the Prime Minister declared that, if Israel received weapons to counter the flow to Egypt there would be no war. The US did not comply but created the Anderson Mission as a sop. Bar-Zohar 1971, pp. 125–8.

The Gamma project has been credited to Kermit Roosevelt, the CIA chief in Cairo. His aide, Miles Copeland, described it thus: 'According to Gamma, Roosevelt and I would have talks with Nasser to arrive at a basic negotiating position with which to confront Ben Gurion, while two other Americans would have similar talks with Ben Gurion. Then Anderson would fly between Cairo and Tel Aviv to narrow differences to an irreducible minimum. After this would have been reached, Nasser and Ben Gurion would meet secretly on a yacht in the Mediterranean to try to close

Ben Gurion, in a detailed memoir based upon a diary account written at the time, was illuminating about that mediation effort. The first meeting was held in Jerusalem on 23 January 1956, with Sharett, Kollek,[1] and Herzog present. Anderson conveyed Nasser's two fundamental conditions of a settlement: a land bridge through the Negev, to link Egypt and Jordan; and return of the Palestine Arab refugees to their homes, along with compensation. Ben Gurion, as so often, termed the real issue the Arab desire for peace and asked how it could be achieved without a meeting between the parties. He also replied that the meaning of 'free choice' to the refugees was the creation of a fifth column inside Israel.

The next day BG proposed direct talks in Cairo, with Sharett representing Israel. Anderson conveyed this to Nasser and informed the Israelis on 31 January that Egypt's leader was prepared to consider this but was frightened of the possible consequences, for not even the intelligence and police chiefs in his regime were aware of the Anderson Mission: he feared a leak—and with it blackmail, loss of power and, possibly, assassination. Anderson returned for a final round of talks, which ended on 9 March. He showed understanding for Israel's stand that she could not undertake any commitments until she was free of concern over security. At the same time he asked Ben Gurion and Sharett to accept Dulles's view that 'Israel's security was not solely dependent on arms'.[2] They remained unconvinced—and emphasized the danger of war if the dramatic shift in the military balance (Soviet arms deal) was not corrected.

To Ben Gurion the cause of the deadlock was simple—Nasser's rigidity on the two conditions, his fear, and his unwillingness to take the risk of talks with Israeli representatives, official or unofficial.[3] Whichever version is correct, the relevance of the Anderson Mission was its effect on Israeli decision-makers' images: for Ben Gurion in particular it marked another vain effort to reach a peaceful settlement, further evidence that Egypt had no intention of accepting Israel as a legitimate state in the Middle East.[4]

---

the gap.' According to Copeland's view, Israel's Prime Minister was responsible for the deadlock, refusing to talk details and asserting: 'If I am going to make any concessions it will be [directly] to Nasser and to no one else.' *Sunday Times* (London), 24 June 1971.

[1] Director-General of the Prime Minister's Office from 1952 to 1965 and thereafter Mayor of Jerusalem.

[2] Eisenhower, in a letter to Ben Gurion on 27 February, promised only to give the request for arms careful attention 'in the light of the need to assure Israel's security and to create conditions that would help bring peace to the region'.

[3] Ben Gurion 1971 (2). Herzog reflected many years later: 'The discussions were doomed to failure from the beginning [for] . . . Nasser was pushing towards an Egypt-dominated Middle East.' Further, in reply to Copeland, 'we never heard that Israel was to blame for their failure'. Herzog 1971.

[4] Ben Gurion's memoir also revealed earlier indirect communications with Cairo—

That conviction seemed further confirmed by the UN Secretary-General's inability to effect a cease-fire for more than a few days, during his April visit to the Core. In fact, what made the failure of the Anderson Mission significant was its coincidence with another input. During the early months of 1956 the toll of Israel's civilian life and tranquillity grew steadily: *feda'iyun* raids were more frequent and more severe. No city or village seemed safe. Nerves became frayed, and the cry for reprisal grew louder—in parliament, press, party, and public. Once 'a nuisance', the *feda'iyun* were now a danger, especially to national morale. Navon summed up well the nightmare of insecurity: 'It couldn't go on for ever. This in itself provided the atmosphere, the mental preparation, the need to put an end to it. Government was being criticized. People were afraid to move at night [in] Nahal Oz, [due to] bombing [and] shooting. The *feda'iyun* danger was sufficient to lead to something drastic regarding Sinai and the Gaza Strip. Even without Soviet arms to Egypt we would have had to act.'[1]

By the spring of 1956 a qualitative change had occurred in the operational environment due to the convergence of several decisive inputs which have been noted. At that point Ben Gurion induced a further change—the resignation of Sharett. It was *not* a decisive input, rather, the removal of an obstacle to the policy of Ben Gurionism. As the Prime Minister remarked to the *Knesset* on 19 June, the day following Sharett's resignation: 'Recently the State's security situation became unusually grave. . . . I reached the conclusion that, in these circumstances, the interests of the State required, so far as humanly possible, full co-ordination between the Foreign Ministry and the Ministry of Defence. . . .'[2]

Of its significance for the Sinai issue a Ben Gurion biographer correctly noted: 'If Sharett had stayed, the Suez affair might never have happened. But with Sharett gone, the way was open for the war on Egypt which Ben Gurion had long envisaged.'[3] However, while

---

in April 1953 and again in December 1954, the latter through Maurice Auerbach, a British MP who went to Egypt on behalf of the World Jewish Congress and Sharett, to plead for the lives of those sentenced to death in the 'Lavon Affair'. For Auerbach's account see Finkelstone. Another, rather vague, account of the Anderson Mission, which 'failed because Ben Gurion deliberately set impossible conditions', is in Love, pp. 307–10. On the Menzies mission to Cairo see Menzies, pp. 153–72.

[1] Interview, 1965.

[2] Ben Gurion 1971, p. 492 (a slightly different translation). See also Love, p. 125, for a report on Sharett's account.

[3] Bar-Zohar 1968, p. 199. BG added insult to injury in a personal letter to Sharett: 'I fear I am going to cause you pain, and God is my witness that I don't want to hurt you, but I believe it my duty to give you my opinion on this painful subject—that I have come to the conclusion that your presence as Minister for Foreign Affairs is not beneficial to the good of the State. . . .' Ben Gurion Documents (Bar-Zohar 1968), ibid.

In that context the Kinneret Raid of 11 December 1955 is noteworthy. Carried out while Sharett was in Washington negotiating for US arms, it was perceived by the then-Foreign Minister as an attempt to embarrass him and to undermine his position.

Sharett's removal made the Sinai Campaign *possible*, that event did not make it *certain*. Nor did any of the decisive inputs discussed thus far: they were, at most, necessary but not sufficient conditions. The most decisive input was yet to come.

The 'French factor' was injected into the environment in two related acts. The first, on 27 June 1956, was a large-scale arms agreement, which included 72 Mystère IVs and 200 Amx-13 tanks, to counter the Soviet arms deal. French arms began to arrive a month later. Apart from vital material aid, the agreement was a tangible demonstration of France's military support role in a period of perceived peril. The second input was a French offer of political and military alignment. From early August to mid-September, in response to Egypt's military and propaganda assistance to Algerian nationalists and, especially, to Nasser's nationalization of the Canal on 26 July, French ministers inquired—of Peres—about Israel's willingness to co-operate with 'Operation Musketeer' against Egypt. To these decisive inputs, last in time but first in importance for Israel's tactical and first strategic decisions, we may now turn.

The flow of French aircraft to Israel was minimal *until July 1956*.[1] Early efforts to secure planes resulted in the purchase, in 1950, of surplus Mosquitoes, which had been acquired by France from the RAF. Late in 1953 Peres, newly appointed DG of the Defence Ministry, received Nord aircraft but no jets. Then in August 1954 a secret agreement between Peres and General Catroux, Secretary for Air, provided for the sale of 24 Ouragans: these, along with radar equipment and lesser weapons, began to arrive in February 1955.

The search for advanced aircraft (Mystères) and tanks was conducted by the indefatigable Peres, assisted by the Defence Ministry's Purchasing Mission in Paris, headed by Yosef Nahmias. Throughout 1954 they pressed French officials and the Dassault Company for Mystère IIs. In June the Quai d'Orsai told Ambassador Ya'acov Tsur it agreed to the sale of 6 planes! By then, on the basis of technical advice, Israel was reluctant, expressing a preference for Mystère IVs. In January

Sharett interview, 1960. Among the many who confirmed Sharett's bitterness over the Kinneret Raid were Navon, Peres (interview, 1966), and Dayan's biographer—Tevet, p. 426. More important, it led to a Cabinet decision that, thereafter, any reprisal action must first receive the approval of the Foreign Minister. This fall-out came after an angry cable from Sharett protesting against the Raid and the lack of consultation. All three contingency plans sought by Ben Gurion of Dayan, and even the Sinai Campaign, fell into the category of reprisal actions. And the display of Sharett's influence within the Government in 1955-6 was not lost on the Prime Minister: enforced resignation became imperative.

[1] The following account of Franco-Israeli arms discussions and agreements is based upon: Peres Diary (Evron), pp. 16–33, 41–3; Ben Gurion 1971, pp. 494–502; Tsur, Part 3, ch. 8, 10; Gee; Ben Gurion, Peres, Tsur interviews; Peres 1970, ch. 3; and Robertson, pp. 22–5, 132–3, 148–50. Typical of the distorted account of Franco-Israeli arms agreements, especially their number and scope, is Love, pp. 138–43.

1955 Catroux informed him of a willingness to sell Mystère IVs. In May Ben Gurion wrote to Defence Minister Koenig asking for a large quantum of military equipment—29 Mystère IVs, 30 Amx tanks, 200 guns, and 15 Vautour fighter-bombers. The French Defence Ministry approved the request in July, but the Foreign Office successfully opposed and delayed it.

Foreign Minister Sharett's widely publicized *démarche* at the Big Four Foreign Ministers Conference in Geneva during the last half of October 1955 met with polite attention but no pledge of arms. By contrast Peres' efforts at the French Defence Ministry appeared to be approaching success: on 26 October Peres was informed that the French agreed to supply 20 Amx tanks from the original (July) deal, an additional 60 tanks, some 75 mm. cannons, and 24 Mystère IV jets immediately, with another two squadrons (48) during the first four months of 1956; the agreement was to be signed on 4 November. However, US pressure, in the form of a revival of the Western, tripartite Near East Arms Commission (NEAC) on 7 November, foiled the deal once more. Only at the initiative of new Defence Minister Bourgès-Manoury did the French Cabinet Committee on Defence approve, on 11 December 1955, the sale of 12 Mystère IVs to Israel. This modest agreement was finally signed on the 23rd—three months *after* the massive Soviet arms deal with Egypt and Syria; the planes arrived in Israel on 12 April 1956.

Israel's search for arms was eased by two developments early in 1956: the assumption of power by the French Socialists at the end of January with Guy Mollet as Premier; and a US decision at the beginning of April to remove its veto on Western arms sales to Israel—in fact, to encourage France and Canada, in particular, to make weapons available to Israel.[1] Thus on 3 April Ben Gurion told Sharett, Dayan, and Peres: 'We must cease immediately all further efforts in the United States, and not even make use of her "good offices" to obtain arms from other countries, but approach them directly.'[2] A week later, the Prime Minister emphasized to them and Tsur the importance of obtaining more arms and aircraft before Egypt's superiority became alarming. And on the 12th the Ambassador to France delivered a personal letter from Ben Gurion to Mollet. He emphasized the threat posed by an aggressive Egypt, heavily armed by the Soviet bloc and using *feda'iyun* raids as a prelude to a general attack. And he concluded: 'At this dangerous time, the small and young Republic of Israel appeals to the older and great French Republic with the certainty of mutual

---

[1] As Herzog remarked: 'Dulles, fed up with Nasser, at long last permitted France to send the first 12 Mystères to Israel. They were then produced under US licence and needed American approval for sale. The US object was to get 24 Mystères and 24 F84s—via Canada—to Israel.' Interview, 1966.

[2] Peres Diary (Evron), p. 28.

understanding.'[1] The plea bore (modest) fruit almost at once: on 23 April Peres and Bourgès-Manoury signed an agreement for the sale of an additional 12 Mystère IVs, which arrived the following month. But it was not until the third arms agreement, on 23 June, and the beginning of the flow, on 24 July, that French arms became a decisive input into Israeli decisions. As Ben Gurion wrote in his memoirs: 'In the following three months—July, August and September—the [military] balance was to a large extent righted by the Socialist Government of Premier Mollet, which supplied Israel with tanks, guns, jet planes, machine-guns and ammunition. . . . Quantitatively the gap in arms was still considerable, but qualitatively it had been . . . reduced.'[2]

The origin of the final input into Israel's tactical decision can be traced to conversations between Bourgès-Manoury and Peres early in May and on 7 August 1956:

'How much time, do you reckon, it would take your army to cross the Sinai Peninsula and reach Suez?', asked the French Defence Minister. I replied that our army people estimated it would probably take from five to seven days. . . . He went on to ask whether Israel was thinking of taking action at some time along her southern borders, and if so where. I replied that our 'Suez' was Eilat . . . and any Israel operation would be aimed at freeing the straits. . . . We returned to this subject at greater length three months later.[3]

Israel was first informed about the date of the revised 'Operation Musketeer' on 1 September via her Military Attaché in Paris: the cable continued, 'it is in the mind of the French to invite Israel to take part in the campaign—one week after it begins. . . .'[4] On the 7th Admiral Barjot discussed practical matters with General Meir Amit, then Chief of the General Staff Branch of *Tzahal*, especially whether Israeli airfields would be available to the French; no decisions were reached. Two days later Dayan ordered his staff to check all operational plans relating to the Egyptian front, 'from the capture of the whole of

---

[1] A partial text is in Ben Gurion 1971, p. 475.

[2] Ibid., p. 495. Ben Gurion added later: 'The deal was made without the knowledge of the French Foreign Office. Pineau knew and approved, but not his officials. It was due mainly to Mollet and Bourgès-Manoury.' Interview, 1966. Bourgès-Manoury's account to Robertson (pp. 148–50) referred to 'the first meetings between myself and Mr. Peres . . . in the autumn of 1955. . . . They developed seriously in January 1956 when I became Defence Minister in M. Mollet's government. We reached complete understanding on Franco–Israeli co-operation, in the struggle against the Arabs during March and April.'

A. Thomas, Director-General of the French Defence Ministry, told Robertson (pp. 132–3) about the period July–October 1956: 'We could not supply everything ourselves, so we asked the Americans for material supplies. As a result . . . the unofficial list of arms supplied to Israel greatly exceeded the official list. . . .' Pineau offered further reflections on the tenth anniversary of the Sinai–Suez War, in Moncrieff 1966, nos. 2, 3, 4, in *Le Monde* (Paris), 4 Nov. 1966, and, along with Thomas, in an interview given to Yoel Marcus, *Ha'aretz*, 28 Oct. 1966.

[3] Peres 1970, pp. 185–6.

[4] Peres Diary (Evron), p. 62. See also Dayan 1966, p. 20.

the Sinai Peninsula to . . . control of the Straits of Tiran or of the Gaza Strip'.[1]

The precipitating event to the tactical decision occurred at a meeting between Peres and Bourgès-Manoury on 18 September. The latter referred to 'the French timing, which requires immediate action against Nasser, taking into consideration the situation in North Africa . . .', and 'the English timing, which prefers to act in a political framework in about two months . . .'. Peres was asked 'what we had in mind'. Once more he cabled Ben Gurion, who had ignored the several inquiries about alignment during recent months—because all pre-conditions of a decision had not yet crystallized. Finally on the 20th came Ben Gurion's *tactical decision* to co-operate politically and militarily with a view to war against Egypt: 'As for the three timings [Bourgès-Manoury had made a euphemistic reference to an American timing], the French timing is close to our hearts.'[2] It was not irrevocable and therefore *not* a strategic decision; further stimuli were necessary to make the high-policy decision to launch the Sinai Campaign.

Implementation of the tactical decision extended over a period of three weeks and then merged into the final inputs for the strategic decision. The French Cabinet decided on 22 September to enter into a tacit political and military alliance with Israel. Nahmias was notified at once by Bourgès-Manoury; and the following day Israel was requested to send representatives to a high-level conference in Paris. The discussion between Peres and France's Defence Minister was revealing:

Peres:	'Is it clear to you [the French Government] that we are talking about a partnership of full equality?'
Bourgès-Manoury:	'I did not think otherwise for a moment.'
Peres:	'But what about the British?'
Bourgès-Manoury:	'Their neutrality is assured. When Pineau left London disappointed the day before yesterday, he was able to throw this at Eden: "It seems that we have no choice but to work hand in hand with the Israelis. . . ." The British Prime Minister . . . reacted in a flaccid tone: "*On condition that they do not hurt the Jordanians . . .*". From this [it can be deduced that] the English will not attempt to interfere with the operation.'
Peres:	'And should one not be concerned about the interference of the United States?'

[1] Dayan 1966, p. 22.
[2] The following reconstruction, up to the 'St. Germain' Conference (30 Sept.–1 Oct.), is based upon Peres Diary (Evron), pp. 70–3, 74–5, 77, 84–5.

Bourgès-Manoury: 'It is in France's hands to prevent that. . . . On this subject [the Soviet stand] the information in our hands
is insufficient.'

Following Peres' report to Ben Gurion, the Israeli Cabinet was
convened on the 25th. The Prime Minister reportedly said: 'The
decision which faces us is perhaps the gravest since the founding of the
State but, in my opinion, we must accept the proposal [for alignment
with France] because who knows when such an opportunity will come
our way again.' The Cabinet concurred and decided upon the delegation: Dayan, Peres, Meir, and, at Ben Gurion's insistence, the *Ahdut
Ha'avoda*'s Moshe Carmel, Minister of Transport and commander of
the Northern Front in the 1948 War; the Prime Minister was trying
to broaden the basis of support for a *possible* preventive war. But the
Government was not then informed of further details, for the strategic
decision was yet to be made.

The 'St. Germain' Conference was held on 30 September and 1
October, with France represented by Pineau, General Challe, Thomas,
and Colonel Louis Mangin.[1] The political exchanges were frank and
friendly, the discussion on arms precise. Meir posed three questions:
how would the British react to a joint Franco–Israeli operation; what
would the Soviet stand be; and was there not worry about a total
American embargo against Israel? The French Foreign Minister
replied that Britain would 'no doubt . . . look with favour upon an
action against Nasser', that the US would do nothing before the
presidential election, and that the USSR would provide military aid
to Egypt but would not interfere directly. 'All of these things', he
continued, 'give decisive importance to the time factor. From the viewpoint of diplomacy there *is no doubt* that a short war would create many
fewer problems than a long one.' As for arms, Israel's *sine qua non* to
military alignment, her shopping list included 100 tanks, 50 tank
carriers, 300 four-wheel-drive trucks, 300 half-tracks, etc. Meir exchanged views with Mollet for the first time. And it was made clear
that Paris would act, with or without the British, the decision to be
taken after the approaching Security Council sessions. Peres later
summed up the results: 'The talks ended with agreement on two points:
further French military help to Israel [the fourth of the arms agree-
ments] and the maintenance of joint consultations on the development
of events.'[2]

On that basis Dayan issued an Early Warning Order to *Tzahal*'s
GHQ (2 October), indicating the likelihood of a campaign against
Egypt to begin on the 20th, with an estimated duration of three weeks;
and all officers on training overseas were summoned home. However,

---

[1] General Challe was Commander of the French Air Force. Mangin, a famed
Resistance fighter, was an aide to Bourgès-Manoury.   [2] Peres 1970, pp. 192–6.

the Chief of Staff was careful to note that a decision had not yet been made.[1] The following day, the 3rd, the alignment was given quasi-institutional form with a Ben Gurion–Mangin agreement to establish a joint Franco–Israeli planning staff in Paris. Communications—personal, cable, and telephonic—increased during the next thirteen days: in particular, Amit met with General Gazin on the 15th and again the next day with Gazin and Challe concerning the proposed Franco–Israeli operations plan; no conclusions were reached because new inputs at a high political level were about to be injected. In short, 2–16 October was a gestation period only: until mid-October Israel's decision process had sanctioned a tacit alignment with France—no more. As Peres remarked: 'There was practically nothing on paper. A word was a word, and formalities were put aside. It was informal collaboration at its best.'[2] By contrast, there was as yet no *direct official* contact between Israel and the UK on collaboration. However, London did convey informally to Ben Gurion about 20 September, via Colonel Robert Henriques, an English Jew, the British Government view. Further, while Britain would probably denounce Israel, she would support her claims at any peace conference to follow.[3]

Four of the decisive inputs into Israel's T decision performed the same function with respect to her S_1 decision: (1) Egypt's strengthening of the Gulf blockade (12 September 1955); (2) the Soviet Arms Deal (28 September 1955); (3) the escalation of *feda'iyun* raids throughout 1956; and (4) the demonstration of a French military support role (the arms agreement of 27 June 1956). However, two other inputs were necessary to generate the high-policy decision to launch the Sinai Campaign: one concerned the UK attitude; the other was the nature of the tripartite relationship. Both crystallized during the ten-day period 15–24 October. The flow of events was marked by suspicion and by illumination of different interests, as well as by the uncertain foundations of the alliance.

General Challe, Chief of the French Air Staff, met with Eden, Foreign Secretary Lloyd, and Antony Head, Secretary for War, at Chequers on the 15th: finally, he reported to Nahmias the same day, the British were prepared to *act*. This followed Challe's forthright presentation of a new plan, the essence of which he described on a map: 'The Israelis here, the Egyptians there. Where is our position? On the Canal.' An immediate reply was requested to a British 'plan' that Israel attack first, alone, along a broad front, right up to the Canal; Anglo-French forces would pose as saviours of the peace by intervening later. There were even reports (Paris to Jerusalem) that Lloyd had proposed

---

[1] Dayan 1966, pp. 31–4.   [2] Peres interview, 1966.

[3] Henriques referred to this episode in an article in *The Spectator*, 5 Dec. 1959. It was also noted in Eban's account (interview, 1965), in Love, p. 440, in H. Thomas, p. 95, etc.

bombing both Egyptian and Israeli forces to give credence to the façade of high *moral* content in Franco-British behaviour.[1] Ben Gurion summarily rejected the proposal and indicated two acceptable alternatives: indirect Israeli participation in an Anglo-French operation or a joint Franco-Israeli action, on condition the British did not interfere. The day his reply reached Paris (16 October), Eden and Lloyd were meeting Mollet and Pineau: their agreement to invade the Canal Zone after Israeli forces reached its eastern bank contemplated some form of co-operation with Israel and thus proved to be a decisive input. As one British scholar put it picturesquely: 'Although Eden doubtless did his best on this occasion to avoid direct commitment, there is today no doubt that he did indeed now nail Britain's colours to the unfamiliar mast of Franco-Israeli collaboration.'[2]

Ben Gurion, too, interpreted the 16 October meeting in this light, for when he learned of the Anglo-French summit he yielded to Peres' suggestion of *direct* talks. Paris was informed, and on the 17th an invitation arrived from Mollet to Ben Gurion to meet secretly in Paris. Only four of his colleagues were informed—Dayan, Eshkol, Meir, and Peres. BG was favourable but insisted that Mollet be informed of Israel's rejection of the British plan. The French Premier renewed the invitation, with this understanding, and the road to collusion lay open.

The 'Treaty of Sèvres' was the most decisive of all inputs into the process generating the Sinai Campaign. That function, however, derived from *Israeli* perceptions of what transpired, not the recall or memoirs of other participants or of commentators who, from the mid-1960s, shed increasing light on Sèvres and the *Suez* fiasco.[3] Thus the

---

[1] Bar-Zohar 1968, pp. 210–11; and Robertson, p. 147, based upon an interview with Bourgès-Manoury.

[2] H. Thomas, p. 114. In the first edition (1966) Thomas used the phrase, 'there now seems little doubt'. On the 15 October (Chequers) and 16 October (Paris) meetings see Robertson, pp. 147, 150–2; H. Thomas, pp. 110–11, 114–15; and Love, pp. 450–3. The Chequers meeting was first revealed by the Brombergers, p. 13. It is noted in Azeau, p. 240, and is discussed by Nutting, pp. 74–8. The Challe remark is quoted from H. Thomas, p. 111.

[3] Considering its fateful consequences for the Suez War, the decline of Britain and France as global powers, the Middle East conflict, Nasser's stature, and international politics generally, relatively little of value has been written about the Sèvres Conference and its 'Treaty'. The French contributed most to what was known until 1968: to accounts by the Brombergers and Tourneaux, based upon incomplete information from Defence Ministry sources in Paris; and to Robertson (ch. 8), who was aided by interviews with the four principal French actors—Mollet, Pineau, Bourgès-Manoury, and Thomas. Pineau also spoke of it in his tenth anniversary reflections, *Le Monde* (Paris), 4 Nov. 1966, Moncrieff 1966, no. 4, and in the *Daily Telegraph* (London), 6 June 1967. There are also discussions in Finer (ch. 13); Fontaine; H. Thomas (pp. 121–4); Moncrieff 1966, no. 4, based on discussions with, *inter alia*, Dayan as well as Pineau; and, marred by extreme bias, Love (pp. 460–6).

British participants (Lloyd, Patrick Dean) and high-policy decision-makers (Eden,

analysis which follows, focusing on Sèvres and Israel's *Sinai* decision, will be based on Israeli sources.[1]

Macmillan) have not spoken or written authoritatively about Sèvres. In their accounts the UK–Israel link appears as fortuitous or opportune. Lloyd is quoted by his deputy, Nutting, as having told him on 23 October, 'Oh! the cold! [with which Nutting had been put off by Lloyd's Private Secretary the previous day] Yes, well, I never had one. I went to see Ben Gurion outside Paris.' Nutting's brief report of Lloyd's account of Sèvres (pp. 101–2) tallies with those of other participants. At the time, 28 October 1956ff., Lloyd was less than honest to the US Ambassador:

'. . . on Sunday evening, 28 October . . . Lloyd replied that he had no evidence to show that the Israeli mobilization was directed against Egypt. . . . In the House of Commons he repeated the statement that he did not know what the Israeli mobilization signified at that moment.' Aldrich, p. 541.

Lloyd's words, in reply to Gaitskell's question, '. . . whether there has been collusion in regard to this matter', were simply: 'There was no prior agreement between us about it. . . .' As quoted in Moncrieff, p. 84. Eden's denial was no less at variance with the facts: 'I want to say this on the question of foreknowledge,' he told the Commons on 20 December 1956, 'and to say it quite bluntly to the House, that there was not foreknowledge that Israel would attack Egypt—there was not. But there was something else. There was—we knew it perfectly well—a risk of it. . . .' As quoted in H. Thomas, Appendix 7, p. 223. In his memoirs, too, Eden gave not the slightest hint of acknowledgement that the Sèvres Conference took place. Indeed, in a twenty-page chapter on the period 23–31 October (Book Three, ch. VII), there was no reference whatsoever to co-operation, even indirect, with Israel.

Macmillan's account was equally unflappable: there is no reference to Sèvres; in fact, there is a portrait of a UK–Israel non-relationship. Like Eden he was sympathetic: the tripartite Arab joint command meant that 'the stranglehold was complete. The Israel reaction . . . was not difficult to foresee.' He then referred to the Anglo-French ultimatum of 30 October to Egypt and Israel as if it were in good faith, impartial—and certainly without collusion. Macmillan, pp. 149–50.

Menzies, then Prime Minister of Australia, wrote blandly, in his memoirs, 'At the end of October, fighting having begun between Israel and Egypt, Britain and France sent their joint message to both countries. . . . Israel agreed. Egypt refused.' Menzies, pp. 176–7.

The precise date when British Cabinet Ministers learned of Franco-Israeli plans is subject to controversy. It ranges from 'late August', according to Beaufre, p. 94, through 23 September (Pineau–Eden talk) and 'early October', to 14 October (Nutting, p. 77). This point is discussed in H. Thomas, pp. 96–8. One thing is certain, however: Eden, Lloyd, Macmillan, *et al. did* know of the Franco–Israeli alignment at least a fortnight before the Sinai Campaign began.

[1] Ben Gurion's 93-page memoir on the Suez Crisis (1971, ch. 5) is silent on Sèvres. 'I will tell you everything about the Sinai Campaign but will not speak about Suez', he said to this writer in 1966. Five years later he acknowledged collusion and the Sèvres Conference—but did not indicate details. Interview, 1971. There is a conspicuous omission of entries for 22, 23, 24 October in Dayan's Diary (1966). In his Foreword (p. 1) he notes: 'In dealing with the political aspects, I have followed the direction of Mr. Ben Gurion . . . who felt that the time had not yet come for publication of the full record of the developments preceding the Sinai Campaign.' There is a brief reference to Sèvres in a semi-official biography of Dayan—Tevet, pp. 450–1. Using Ben Gurion documents, Bar-Zohar (1966, 1968) discussed Sèvres at some length, thought not without factual error. The most valuable source is Peres—excerpts from his diary, in Evron, extensive interviews (1966), and his own memoir (1970).

Ben Gurion decided upon the mission's members—Dayan, Peres, and his Military Secretary, Argov—on the morning of 18 October. That afternoon he reflected upon the approaching conference during consultations with Eshkol, Meir, Dayan, Peres, and Minister of Commerce and Industry Pinhas Sapir; only Sapir, an unabashed dove, then and later, reportedly expressed doubts.[1] Challe and Mangin arrived on the 21st—in de Gaulle's DC4, a gift from Truman—to escort the Israelis to their Paris rendezvous. They were received coldly at first because of their known 'softening-up' mission—to persuade Israel not to oppose the British-urged presence of Iraqi troops in Jordan, and, further, to yield to the original British 'neutral intervention' plan, now revived by London. 'If they do not understand', said Ben Gurion on his way to the airport, 'that our negative reply is final, there is no purpose to the whole trip.'[2] Moreover, he balked when told that Mollet was pleased to *receive* him—he had agreed to go to Paris if *invited* by the French Premier. His ruffled feathers were smoothed by Dayan and Peres.[3]

The Israeli visitors landed at Villacoublay airbase just outside Paris at 1.30 p.m. on 22 October. In the later afternoon they were joined by Pineau, Bourgès-Manoury and senior military officers—at a Sèvres villa midway between Paris and Versailles, made available by a Jewish friend of the French Defence Minister. The preliminary exchange was friendly, relaxed, and insubstantive—except for Ben Gurion's emphatic reassertion that Israel would not 'play' the British game. That night Challe flew to London to explain Ben Gurion's firm stand.

The conference began in earnest on the 23rd, with the arrival of Mollet. France's Premier sought the Israeli leader's views. The result was a long and comprehensive survey of the Middle East situation by Ben Gurion—Arab belligerency, *feda'iyun* raids, Soviet penetration, and the blockade of the Gulf:

[1] Sapir remarked that 'he got to know in Switzerland of oil discoveries in the Sinai Peninsula'. Ben Gurion responded with a touch of humour: 'Nevertheless I suspect that you are opposed to the whole business.' Sapir countered: 'It seems to me that you, too, are not completely at peace with it.' This time BG just gave a knowing smile. Peres Diary (Evron), p. 110.

[2] Ibid., p. 112. The British Chargé d'Affaires had informed Ben Gurion and Meir on 12 October of the plan to move an Iraqi Division into Jordan: the UK urged support; the US favoured it; and France acquiesced. The Prime Minister protested and reserved Israel's freedom of action; and the Foreign Minister wrote to US Ambassador Lawson, terming it a severe threat to Israel's security. This was followed by a day's notice from the British Consul in Jerusalem that Jordan had requested UK action under their mutual defence agreement. The Kalkilya raid (10/11 October), which sparked these moves, is discussed at length in Dayan 1966, pp. 43–57. Dulles reiterated US support for the Iraqi troop plan, in a talk with Eban on the 15th, and conveyed a message from Eisenhower to BG expressing the hope that Israel would do nothing to place herself in the wrong in the world's eyes. Ben Gurion replied on the 20th requesting US influence to frustrate the plan. Eban 1957, pp. 4–5.

[3] Peres interview, 1966. It was not mere pride, for BG felt that an invitation gave him much greater bargaining power.

The plan I will present before you, for the Middle East, may appear imaginary, perhaps . . . [Then came the goals noted earlier—the Canal as a *de facto* international waterway, Israeli control over the approaches to Eilat, and a demilitarized Sinai.]

In this way France will again regain for herself a foothold in the Middle East— by means of Israel and Lebanon. The entire West—including the United States—will gain. Soviet penetration of this part of the world will be stopped. The English would retrieve their influence in Iraq and assure their sources of oil. . . .

We must work out a political plan to which Eisenhower as well will agree—or at least to which he will not object. . . .

Personally I have great admiration for the British people, for its democratic regime. . . . But I doubt the strength and honesty of Eden.

Mollet reportedly replied: '. . . it [the plan] does not appear imaginary at all in our eyes. Moreover, it is a good plan.'[1]

The French premier offered his own assessment:

Nasser is growing stronger, and the Russians are strengthening their influence in the region. Perhaps, in the end we would convince the United States in favour of a common programme . . . but we would lose valuable time, and possibly even the chance to act. . . . As for British participation, any delay is likely to be fatal. I know Eden personally, and I am absolutely convinced that he is an enthusiastic supporter of common action—and he has no dual aims . . . but his domestic situation is deteriorating. . . .

Pineau added that the Russians were busy in Hungary; the US was preoccupied with her elections; winter conditions in the Mediterranean were approaching; and Britain would not agree to a separate Franco-Israeli operation.

Ben Gurion countered that there was nothing to prevent the Soviet Union from sending thousands of 'volunteers' to the Middle East. And he expressed one of his concerns: 'The suggested [military] plan does not come into account from the moral standpoint. If Israel would open the war, she would be branded an aggressor. The world does not like aggression, and we would not be able to face it.' It was in that context, too, that he referred to Egypt's air-strike capability, a major worry. 'We are suggesting co-operative action at a later date—after France persuades Britain of the general plan, and after US neutrality is assured.' Bourgès-Manoury emphasized that France would wait no more: the beginning of November was the last possible opportunity. Ben Gurion replied: 'If the war is conducted with full co-operation, we can start it even tomorrow. We would be ready to take upon ourselves the main land burden. . . . If the British send their bombers, you would be able

---

[1] Peres Diary (Evron), pp. 123–4. Peres termed Robertson's version of an impassioned speech (p. 159) 'sheer nonsense; Ben Gurion made no such plea; he spoke about philosophy and made general remarks about history and politics'. Interview, 1966.

to recall most of your conscripts. We will do the work on the ground. . . . Why give in to the British', he continued. 'Let us prepare a triple plan. We will try together to persuade the English, and we will proceed to implement it next week. It is possible to finish the action in a number of hours,' he promised, 'and you will be able to send your divisions home.'[1]

The discussion moved to technical matters, including how to legiti- mize Anglo-French intervention. One suggestion was that Israel attempt to send a ship through the Canal; Egypt would block passage, providing a signal for action. It was rejected, as was Pineau's proposal for a direct Anglo-French assault on the Canal Zone without waiting for an Israeli pretext. Finally, Dayan devised a formula—to satisfy French and Israeli needs. *Tzahal* would undertake a large-scale *reprisal*, not total war; this could be justified in terms of self-defence which, in turn, would reduce the danger of Egyptian bombing of Israel's cities and, at the same time, enable the British to invoke the intervention clause of the 1954 Anglo-Egyptian Agreement. The operative act would be a parachute drop at the Mitla Pass, to be followed by Anglo- French intervention to defend the Canal—no later than thirty-six hours after the Israeli raid.[2] Moreover, an understanding was reached on the French role: air cover for Israel's cities; a naval patrol of her coastline; the arrival of additional Mystère squadrons at Israeli air- fields on the 27th and 28th, with Israel's strike set for the 29th; and a parachute drop of arms and provisions to Israeli units moving across Sinai. An Israeli *decision*, however, had not yet been reached: Ben Gurion ordered Dayan to make no commitments when presenting the formula, for he was determined not to act without British approval.

Lloyd arrived from London at 7 p.m. on the 23rd, accompanied by Patrick Dean, then an Assistant Under-Secretary at the Foreign Office. He began by restating the discredited British plan, which Ben Gurion once more rejected—in an atmosphere of tension, hostility, and sus- picion. Indeed, he recalled, the Foreign Secretary tried to treat him as a subordinate.[3] After hours of discussion Lloyd accepted Dayan's formula—as well as the stationing of French Air Force planes in Israel to defend her cities during the first day of the Campaign—on condition London approved.[4] Pineau flew to London that night with Lloyd and returned on the 24th at 3 p.m. with news of British Cabinet authoriza- tion to proceed.

[1] The exchanges between Mollet, Ben Gurion, Pineau, and Bourgès-Manoury are taken from Peres Diary (Evron), pp. 124–7.

[2] Tevet, pp. 450–1 and Peres Diary (Evron), p. 133.

[3] Ben Gurion interview, 1971.

[4] Pineau's slightly different version is reported in Robertson, pp. 161–2. Of interest is his remark: 'I was struck by the fact that the English sought above all else a method of justifying their action in the eyes of the Arabs and before world opinion.' Thomas and Bourgès-Manoury concurred. Ibid., pp. 133, 148.

The final round of talks began at 4 p.m.: present were Ben Gurion, Peres, and Dayan; Pineau, Bourgès-Manoury, Mangin, and Challe; and Dean and Logan (Private Secretary to Lloyd). Devoted to technical details—dates, parachute operations, landings, etc.—it revealed the continued aloofness of the British, who refused to undertake support for Israel at the Security Council! A provisional protocol, drafted by a six-man committee, was initialled by Ben Gurion, Pineau, and Dean at 8 p.m. that evening. The 'treaty' was signed by them the following morning after Eden's final approval was given. As the signing was taking place, news arrived that Jordan had joined the Cairo–Damascus military pact, which placed all three armies under the Egyptian Commander-in-Chief. It was further confirming evidence of armed confrontation. Indeed, Ben Gurion reflected, his (strategic) decision 'became irrevocable with the tripartite Arab agreement' of 24 October.[1]

As Pineau reportedly observed about the 'treaty': 'it was incorporated into a formal document signed . . . by Patrick Dean for Britain, Ben Gurion for Israel, and myself for France . . . and we decided that the agreement should never be published.'[2] Eden sustained Israeli suspicion to the end: instead of sending his confirmation directly to Ben Gurion as arranged, he wrote to Mollet, on the 26th; a photocopy of his letter *to the French Premier* was dispatched to Jerusalem. No wonder Ben Gurion recalled, as noted: 'Eden didn't behave well; I owe him nothing.' Yet he had reason to be gratified, for all three basic Israeli aims had been achieved at Sèvres: (*a*) a shared burden, instead of Israel providing an aggressor's pretext for Anglo-French restoration of international order; (*b*) protection of Israel's cities by French air cover, a pledge which was sealed with a letter from Mollet; and (*c*) dissociation from Anglo-French war aims.

Neither Dayan nor Peres, let alone the French or British, *knew until 25 October* whether Ben Gurion would decide to go to war. That strategic decision was, in fact, not made until the last night at Sèvres, though Ben Gurion remarked that he had *thought* about a joint venture with France against Egypt as early as his letter to Mollet on 12 April 1956.[3] The making of the strategic decision was described by Peres thus:

I saw Ben Gurion when he faced momentous decisions, but I shall never forget that evening and the night which followed it—between October 24 and 25,

---

[1] Interview, 1966. Of this development Dayan wrote: 'The State of Israel thus found herself hemmed in on three sides, south, east and north. . . . , and her Government could be under no illusion as to the aggressive purpose of this united military organization . . .' 1966, p. 5.

[2] Robertson, p. 163. H. Thomas casts doubt on the importance of the 'document'—'the word "treaty" is a misnomer, for it was a "declaration of intent" . . .' p. 124. Certainly both the French and the Israelis regarded it as no less binding than a treaty. As for Ben Gurion's attitude at the climax of Sèvres, he 'folded "the Document" carefully and hid it in his breast pocket, his naughty wink as if saying "what is certain is certain".' Peres Diary (Evron), p. 141.   [3] Interview, 1971.

1956. . . . In a certain place, a certain man had to make the decision, despite the fact that some of the essential data, for and against, were yet unknown, unknowable. . . . We sat—Moshe Dayan, the late Nehemia Argov and this writer—with Ben Gurion: not one of us envied him the long night that lay before him. The next morning we saw him . . . the decision made. . . .[1]

On another occasion Peres added: 'He took all the necessary and permissive actions—so as not to stop it—but he *did not decide until the last minute.*' Apart from concern about the British role and fear of aerial bombardment of Israel's cities, 'the fate of the State was involved, and he was conscious of the way Israel would appear in history'.[2] Dayan confirmed this in his diary entry of 29 October: '. . . the decision taken to launch the campaign [by Ben Gurion] . . . occurred on the 25th, four days ago'.[3] And Ben Gurion himself was emphatic: 'The final decision was made by me by the time I returned from France.'[4]

As for the timing of the Campaign, the US presidential election was irrelevant, according to Peres. There was the problem of weather—it had to be before winter turbulence made transport by sea more difficult. Moreover, the French expected a nationalist offensive in Algeria before the end of 1956. And the Mollet Government was precarious. Hungary was 'important' but not 'decisive': the Revolt broke out while Israeli decision-makers were in Paris and *before* the final decision was taken.[5] Ben Gurion denied any link whatsoever with the US election or the Hungarian uprising.[6]

The decision was implemented swiftly, efficiently, and with total success. By the time Ben Gurion and his aides returned to Israel, late on Thursday 25 October, the mobilization of *Tzahal* reserves was under way. Within seventy-two hours the process was complete. And on Monday the 29th, at 4 p.m., a day after authorization was given by the Cabinet, a paratroop unit was flown to the Mitla Pass, deep in the Sinai desert. By the end of the first day Kuntilla, Ras-el-Nakeb, and Kuseima had fallen, along with three fortified points in the heart of Sinai on the way to the Canal—Bir El-Tamad, Tarat umm Basis, and El-Jofra. On 31 October Bir Hassneh, El-Nahal, and Abu Ageila were overrun. Rafiah and Bir Gafgafa were captured on the 1st of November. And on the 2nd both Gaza and the important coastal town of El-Arish were taken. The road to the Canal was open: within five days Israeli forces reached that principal objective in the west and stopped 10 km. east of the waterway. By the 5th all operations ceased, once Sharm-e-Sheikh and the islands in the Tiran Straits were cleared of Egyptian soldiers, long-range artillery, and aircraft.

---

[1] Peres 1965, p. 34. Only the location—Sèvres—was omitted, as it was from his later memoir on the conference. Peres 1970, pp. 200–5.

[2] Interview, 1966 (emphasis added).   [3] Dayan 1966, p. 75. See also p. 60.

[4] Interview, 1971.   [5] Interview, 1966.

[6] Interview, 1971.

It was a brilliant eight-day Campaign—at a cost of 171 killed and one prisoner, *Tzahal* had destroyed all *feda'iyun* bases in Gaza and Sinai, had occupied the Strip and the Peninsula, had terminated the blockade of the Gulf, had captured 6,000 Egyptian troops and vast quantities of Egyptian armour and other material, and had routed the army of its most formidable foe. As a result the Near East Core military balance had been abruptly transformed; Israel's insecurity gave way to security. Her citizen army had achieved a momentous victory, though not without substantial French aid. On 27 and 28 October, as promised at Sèvres, two additional squadrons of Mystère and Sabre jets arrived, to form an air umbrella over Israel's cities. Three French warships took up position along the coast. And, once the battle was joined, Nord Atlas transports flew supply drops from Cyprus to Israeli units in Sinai. On one occasion a French cruiser shelled Egyptian positions at Rafiah. But while they eased the cost of the Sinai Campaign, the triumph was wholly *Tzahal's*—under Dayan's masterful command.[1]

The political dimension of implementation was more complex. On Friday the 26th Ben Gurion informed all Coalition partners except *Mapam* of Operation *Kadesh*: first, the *Mapai* ministers other than Meir and Eshkol, and then, separately, Bar-Yehuda, Carmel, and Galili of *Ahdut Ha'avoda*, Shapira and Burg of the National Religious Party, and Rosen and Harari of the Progressives.[2] *Mapam* leaders were notified on Sunday morning, the 28th, just before the Cabinet met—as late as possible, 'because Ben Gurion knew they would be opposed'.[3] They were—but they agreed to share responsibility if all other Coalition members favoured the Campaign. All did so with the result that the

[1] The most authoritative account of Israel's military campaign is Dayan. Other informative studies are Henriques, Marshall, O'Ballance, and Fall. Barker and Beaufre provide excellent analyses of the *Suez* operations. See also Keightley, Schiff, Stockwell. Childers emphasizes French combat aid. Dayan acknowledged its value: the arrival of 200 trucks on 27 October, he wrote in his Diary, 'saved the situation . . . I do not know what we would have done if these French trucks had not arrived.' p. 68.

[2] Neither Galili nor Harari was in the Cabinet but both were respected members of the *Knesset* Committee on Foreign Affairs and Security. According to Sharef, then Secretary to the Government, it was he who advised Ben Gurion to do so, 'because, on an earlier occasion [December 1955] he had met defeat in the Government on a similar proposal, which had not been cleared in advance with key ministers'. Interview, 1971.

[3] Navon interview, 1965. That discriminatory treatment rankled deeply. Fifteen years later *Mapam*'s perennial leader, Ya'ari, spoke bitterly at a meeting of the Alignment's Executive about the lack of consultation on the part of its senior partner, the Israel Labour Party. In that connection he reportedly cried out: 'The same thing happened on the eve of the Sinai Campaign. Begin told me some time ago that Ben Gurion had informed him of the plans three weeks before he notified us. Even though we were members of the Coalition, we were told about it only a few hours before the Campaign was launched.' *Jerusalem Post*, 2 July 1971, and *Ma'ariv* (Tel Aviv), 4 July 1971.

Government meeting on 28 October formally authorized what ministers had approved informally.

The proposal could have been turned down—in theory. As Justice Minister Rosen recalled: 'It is quite true that Ben Gurion did not bring the issue to the Government until a day before the Campaign. But we could have reversed it. BG insisted at that meeting that we had a right to say "no"—and nothing would happen. "The French", he said, "had made the same reservation".'[1] In reality, however, the *decision* had been made. As Herzog observed: 'If Ben Gurion had seen that many of his Cabinet colleagues were opposed, he might have changed his mind; but in those days their dissent was unthinkable.'[2]

Bentov of *Mapam* asked: 'what is the ultimate objective of this invasion', and received Ben Gurion's reply already noted, including the 'prayer' that the Gaza Strip 'be swallowed up in the sea'. Bar-Yehuda raised some doubts but did not oppose the Campaign. Carmel, as always, was the most vocal hawk. And Shapira proposed the creation of an Inner Cabinet to conduct the war; it proved to be unnecessary. After the meeting, the Prime Minister informed President Ben Zvi. He then journeyed to GHQ in Tel Aviv, where he notified opposition General Zionist leaders—Bernstein, Rokah, and Serlin—and, on Monday morning, *Herut*'s Begin and Ben-Eliezer. All approved. Apart from *Mapam*, only *Knesset* Speaker Sprinzak was *vociferously* opposed.[3]

By that time pressure had mounted from a not unexpected quarter: it took the form of two urgent messages from Eisenhower to Ben Gurion. The first, which arrived on Sunday morning, the 28th, was a 'friendly' warning about mobilization: '. . . I renew the plea which was communicated to you through Secretary Dulles [on the 20th] that there be no *forcible initiative* on the part of your Government which would endanger the peace and the *growing friendship between our two countries*.' The second, communicated to Eban on the evening of the 28th by Dulles, was delivered to the Defence Ministry at 5 a.m. the following morning: 'Again', wrote the President, 'I feel compelled to emphasize the danger inherent in the present situation and to urge your Government to do nothing which would endanger the peace.'[4]

Both were processed by Herzog who on Sunday morning had been seconded by Meir to the Prime Minister as diplomatic adviser. The Foreign Minister made minor changes in his draft reply and then approved it, in the late morning of 29 October, as did Ben Gurion, who lay ill at home then and throughout the Campaign. At noon US Ambassador Lawson telephoned Herzog to read a cable from Dulles

---

[1] Interview, 1971. Sharef, who was present, concurred.

[2] Interview, 1966.

[3] The 28 October meeting is discussed briefly in Ben Gurion 1971, pp. 504–5.

[4] The texts are cited in part in Eban 1957, pp. 9, 10, and in Eisenhower, pp. 69, 70 (emphasis added). They are paraphrased in Finer, pp. 348–50.

ordering the evacuation of American nationals. The Ben Gurion reply to Eisenhower, delivered at 1.30 p.m., reiterated the view that Israel was in danger from Egypt, and provided a clear warning of what was to follow: '. . . the Government [of Israel] would not be fulfilling its elementary responsibilities if it did not take all possible measures to thwart the declared aim of the Arab rulers to destroy Israel.'[1]

At 4.30 that afternoon the technocrats met at Ben Gurion's bedside— Dayan, Peres, Isser Harel (Director of the Secret Service), Yehoshafat Harkabi (Director of Military Intelligence), Navon, Argov, and Herzog. The Prime Minister resolved a typical inter-ministerial dispute by authorizing two statements, one on the Mitla Pass operation, by the Defence Ministry, the other to the world, by the Foreign Office. The first was issued at 8.20 p.m., three hours after the parachutists had successfully occupied the Pass, the political statement two hours later because, as Herzog recalled, 'there was no time to prepare it earlier!' As for Ben Gurion, Navon remarked: 'I never saw him so calm as on that day, calm, calm, and quiet.'[2]

US pressure on Israel increased once the Campaign began. On the 30th the President's Special Assistant, Sherman Adams, conveyed a message from Eisenhower to Zionist leader Rabbi Abba Hillel Silver, by telephone:

The president would like you to contact Ben Gurion to give him the following message: 'The declared aim of the Israel Defence Forces that have invaded Egypt—liquidation of the *feda'iyun* bases—has been achieved. President Eisenhower porposes that you now voluntarily return immediately to your own borders. if you do, the President promises to publish immediately a declaration expressing his deep appreciation and firm friendship for Israel.

'The President emphasizes that, despite the temporary convergence of Israel's interests with those of France and Britain, you shall not forget that Israel's strength is principally dependent upon the United States. The President requests an immediate reply.'

Eban, learning of the approach to Silver, sent his advice at once: 'Please cable your reply immediately. Our relations with the United

---

[1] Ben Gurion 1971, p. 504. The cable reached Eisenhower at 4.30 a.m. on 30 October after Israel's official statements about the Mitla Pass Raid had been issued. Eisenhower, p. 73. Dayan noted (1966) that, at first, Ben Gurion was apprehensive about the President's pressure but then felt it could be 'swallowed'. Diary, entry 29 Oct., p. 71.

[2] Navon interview, 1965. Uncertainty to the end is evident in Dayan's diary entry on 29 October: when the announcement about the Mitla Pass was being drafted he was concerned that the Campaign would have to be cut short because of 'complex . . . political circumstances' (1966), p. 76. A detailed account of the Israeli decision process from 25 October to 8 March 1957 was given to the writer (Herzog interview, 1966) and was published later that year in virtually identical form (Herzog 1966). Among other insights there is the human aspect: the Ben Gurion reply to Eisenhower on the 29th was delayed because the typist had made an error, had refused to allow a 'dirty' copy to go out, and had sent out for an eraser!

States must be weighed carefully, especially in view of today's favourable [military] developments.'[1] When Ben Gurion did not reply at once, Eisenhower's 'carrot' pressure increased. First Adams and then the President spoke to Silver on the 31st:

I would like to know if Ben Gurion intends to withdraw his forces from Sinai? You can tell him, in my name, that I am interested in an immediate improvement of our relations with Israel. Please tell Mr. Ben Gurion that if I learn during the next few hours that Israel intends to withdraw her forces from Sinai and return them to her own borders, I am ready to broadcast a most friendly declaration toward Israel on a special television and radio programme tonight.

Eban added his own request: 'Please consider deeply and reply with highest priority.'[2] Ben Gurion did not respond, partly because he deemed it imperative not to blunt the thrust of *Tzahal*'s advance and partly because, with the Anglo-French air attack on Egyptian airfields on 1 November, the pressure on Israel declined momentarily.

That day also witnessed a dramatic shift of attention at the UN, from the Security Council to the General Assembly, and with it Eban's finest hour as the 'voice' of Israel. He did not know of Israel's decision to align with France. And he had been denied information on the Sèvres Conference, the decision to launch the Sinai Campaign—and the scheduled date.[3] Herzog wanted to cable Eban on the 29th, before

---

[1] That day, too, at 3.30 p.m. London time, the Counsellor of Israel's Embassy, Gershon Avner, was called to the Foreign Office to receive the (prearranged) Ultimatum. Neither he nor Ambassador Eliahu Elath knew of this; in fact, the latter was on leave. At 4 p.m. the Ultimatum was announced to the British Parliament, and then over the BBC. But the message did not reach Israel until 10.30 in the evening—because of a technical delay. It was of no consequence to Israel or the UK, merely a charade, in accordance with the Sèvres Agreement.

[2] The Adams–Silver and Eisenhower–Silver telephone conversations and the Eban cables are from Ben Gurion Documents (Bar-Zohar 1966), instalment 5. Eban's cables were also the result of perceived direct pressure: 'Our friends . . . advised and urged that we end the Campaign and the crisis quickly.' Eban 1957, p. 18.

[3] All four senior Israeli ambassadors—Avidar (Moscow), Eban (Washington), Elath (London), and Tsur (Paris)—had been demonstratively summoned home for consultations on 16 October but were not told of impending plans: it was a feint, one of many, to draw the world's attention to Jordan. Just before returning to New York on the 22nd Eban saw Ben Gurion and was given a hint: the Prime Minister told him something might happen soon, involving Egypt, which would cause him a great deal of difficulty; however, it might not happen at all. He did not know, Eban acknowledged later, the precise date of the operation, its scope, or the link with France and England. Interview, 1965. Another hint of a probable impending military operation, in co-operation with France, was conveyed to Eban by Harkabi in mid-October. The *Tzahal* Director of Intelligence had been sent to New York, at French request, to serve as liaison with the French Foreign Minister, then participating in the Security Council debate on the Suez crisis. It is doubtful if Eban accepted the signal as 'hard' information. Harkabi communication, 1972. All other envoys knew nothing. And within the Foreign Office Meir told senior officials—DG and Department Heads—on

the operation began, but Argov insisted that no military information be dispatched during a state of emergency.[1] The result was extreme embarrassment. At the very moment Israel's political statement was issued—late afternoon of the 29th, Washington time—Eban and Shiloah were in Dulles's office denying Israel's intent for war to Assistant Secretary of State for Near East Affairs William Rountree, and complaining at the US failure to protest as well against Arab mobilization. In the midst of the discussion Rountree was handed a note about the Mitla Pass operation. 'I think you will agree, Mr. Ambassador,' he said, turning to Eban, 'that the discussion has become academic.'[2]

At the second of three Security Council sessions on the 30th, the French delegate whispered to Eban: 'Don't worry—there will be a veto.' 'That was the first hint I had', Eban remarked, 'that we were not carrying on a lone campaign.'[3] US Representative Henry Cabot Lodge expressed the personal anger of Eisenhower, Dulles, and himself in presenting an American draft resolution at 11 a.m.: it urged the Council to order an immediate cease-fire and called for immediate withdrawal of Israeli forces behind the armistice lines. News of the Anglo-French ultimatum to Egypt and Israel, announced by the Soviet delegate moments later, caused shock and bitterness—and Lodge's insistence upon a vote without further delay, at the resumed Council session, starting at 4 p.m. The outcome heightened the tension even more: 7 to 2 (France and the UK), with 2 abstentions (Australia and Belgium). It was the first British veto ever, a stunning development at the UN. And again in the evening Israel's two allies vetoed a virtually identical Soviet draft resolution, with Belgium and the US abstaining. The following afternoon Yugoslavia moved that an Emergency Session of the Assembly be convened under the terms of the 'Uniting for Peace' Resolution, first used under the aegis of Washington to break the impasse over the Korean War towards the end of 1950. An attempt by the UK's Dixon to have it ruled out of order was defeated by 6 to 4,

---

Saturday evening, 27 October. According to Herzog, Ben Gurion did not know of this; and Navon added, 'if he had known he would have opposed'. Interviews, 1966.

[1] Herzog interview, 1966.

[2] Fraser Wilkins, who was in charge of Arab–Israel relations at the State Department, was also present. The incident is related in Beal, pp. 272–3, and Finer, pp. 353–4. Eban and Herzog also mentioned it. Interviews, 1965, 1966. Another embarrassed Israeli public figure was ex-Foreign Minister Sharett, who, the day the Campaign began, was assuring Nehru in New Delhi that there was no collusion with France and Britain. A few days later Sharett, while in Bangkok, received the shattering news of collusion, in a letter from Eytan, DG of the Foreign Office. Hacohen interview, 1966 (Hacohen was with Sharett on that Asian trip). Elath and Tsur were away from their posts, on leave, on 29 October.

[3] Eban 1957, p. 21.

with China abstaining. And the Yugoslav draft resolution was approved by 7 to 2 (France and the UK), with 2 abstaining (Australia and Belgium). Hammarskjöld's implied threat to resign, on the 31st, deepened the crisis.[1]

By the time the Emergency Session convened, in the evening of 1 November, Israeli forces had scored major successes on the battlefield. This news was telephoned to Eban by Meir and Peres, with the result that, when he and Shiloah saw Dulles that morning, 'we decided not to justify ourselves but to attack'. The tactic was not without effect, for the Secretary of State added a paragraph to the US resolution which he presented to the Assembly—urging that, upon the cease-fire becoming effective, steps be taken to reopen the Canal and restore freedom of navigation. And in his speech Dulles added a section on the non-return to the *status quo*.[2]

That evening Eban delivered perhaps the most brilliant speech of his decade at the United Nations. One paragraph reflects its spirit and essence:

Surrounded by hostile armies on all its land frontiers, subjected to savage and relentless hostility, exposed to penetration, raids and assaults by day and by night, suffering constant toll of life amongst its citizenry, bombarded by threats of neighbouring governments to accomplish its extinction by armed force, overshadowed by a new menace of irresponsible rearmament, embattled, blockaded, besieged, Israel alone amongst the nations faces a battle for its security anew with every approaching nightfall and every rising dawn. In a

---

[1] The surprise expressed by US leaders—especially by the President—at British and French behaviour, was either feigned or unjustified. Macmillan remarked: '. . . neither he [Dulles] nor Eisenhower could ever have been under any misapprehension . . . Britain and France in the long run would not shrink from force.' More specifically, (a) 'Eden's vital message to Eisenhower at the end of July left no room for uncertainty or equivocation'; (b) 'I made it quite clear [to Murphy on 30 July] that we and France must accept the challenge, or sink into the rank of second-class nations'; and (c) '. . . I told Foster [Dulles on 1 August] as plainly as I could, that we just could not afford to lose this game.' pp. 103, 104, 106. Murphy confirmed that conversation in his memoirs and added: 'I was not surprised at this reaction because it seemed not unjustified.' Moreover, 'The Anglo-French military operation was launched on 31 October strictly according to the staff plan which I had been told about in July.' pp. 380, 391.

French leaders, too, spoke of US foreknowledge. According to Bourgès-Manoury, 'the Americans knew just about everything that was going on in Paris'. And Thomas added: '. . . the Americans were constantly informed of all we were doing on the military side . . .'. Robertson, pp. 148, 132. More striking, CIA Director Allen Dulles (brother of the Secretary of State) knew of Franco–Israeli–British preparations for war, of their collusion, and of the French arms lift to Israel on 27–8 October. In fact, the US Air Force organized an air lift from Florida to France to provide, *inter alia*, additional reserve fuel tanks for the Sabre jets. The key source was Thero de Vijola, head of the French intelligence network in Washington. See Dan, and Ben Gurion Documents (Bar-Zohar 1966), 4th instalment.

[2] Eban 1957, pp. 27–31. The Eban–Dulles meeting on 1 November and the entire UN debate are narrated in detail in Finer, ch. 14.

country of small area and intricate configuration, the proximity of enemy guns is a constant and haunting theme.[1]

The speech, as Eban wrote, was 'heard and seen by millions, had a tremendous echo, and its impression . . . was considerable'.[2] Nevertheless, the Dulles draft resolution was approved by almost the entire Assembly—64 to 5 (Britain, France, Israel, Australia, and New Zealand), with 6 abstentions. The call for a cease-fire and withdrawal was not heeded—yet.

The idea of an international peace force was formally introduced by Canada's Pearson on 2 November. His basic motive was to find a face-saving device for Anglo-French withdrawal: the United Nations Emergency Force—UNEF, as it came to be known—would perform the same function that prompted Western intervention, namely to ensure an *international* waterway; it would be under Canadian command, without Soviet influence. After prolonged debate in the Assembly, it was approved in the early hours of 4 November by near-unanimity—57 to 0, with 13 abstentions (7 from the Soviet bloc, Australia, New Zealand, and the 4 belligerents, Egypt, France, Israel, and the UK). At the same time another cease-fire resolution was passed—by 59 to 5, with 12 abstentions.[3]

By that time Israel's military campaign was complete except for the destruction of Egypt's bastion at Sharm-e-Sheikh. Thus she accepted a cease-fire *conditionally*, in the form of a message from Meir to Hammarskjöld containing five questions for clarification. The French and British, too, stalled for time: finally, at dawn on 5 November, their airborne assault on the Canal Zone took place. But thirty-six hours later, at 11.59 p.m. on the 6th, they accepted a cease-fire: they had yielded to massive pressures from Washington and Moscow relentlessly pursued.[4] Israel had already the previous day conveyed to the Secretary-General her unconditional acceptance of the cease-fire.[5] The implementation of strategic decision 1 had been an unparalleled success: *Tzahal* now occupied the Gaza Strip and virtually all of Sinai; passage through the

---

[1] The full text is in Eban 1969, pp. 276–92; the extract is from pp. 279–80.

[2] Eban 1957, p. 32.

[3] On the origins of UNEF see Burns, ch. 14; Finer, pp. 402–6; Frye, ch. i, ii; Higgins, pp. 227–73; and Robertson, pp. 210–28, 270–6, 286–94, 327–32.

[4] The events of 5–6 November, from the Anglo-French invasion to their cessation of operations, and super-power pressures on London and Paris, are chronicled at length in Finer, ch. 15; Love, ch. 18; Robertson, pp. 247–82; and H. Thomas, pp. 157–168.

[5] It came none too soon, for on the 5th Britain had abandoned her: Lloyd announced in Parliament London's support for *Israel*'s withdrawal! Israeli delegates to the UN all noted British aloofness during that tense week of debate. By contrast, Franco–Israeli co-operation was very close, a diplomatic extension of the tacit alliance from September 1956 to March 1957, when the political battle at the UN ended. Eban, Kidron. and Rafael interviews, 1966.

Straits was freed; the *feda'iyun* bases had been obliterated; and Egypt's military power had been crushed.

(D) DECISION PROCESS AND IMPLEMENTATION: S₂

A mood of exhilaration permeated Ben Gurion's 'victory speech' to the *Knesset* on the evening of 7 November. 'This was the greatest and most glorious military operation in the annals of our people', he began, 'and one of the most remarkable operations in world history.' He challenged the near-universal view of Egypt's sovereignty over Sinai: '. . . . our forces were given strict orders not to cross the Suez Peninsula'. And he threw down the gauntlet to 'world public opinion' by proclaiming 'our stand . . . with full moral force and unflinching determination':

(1) The Armistice Agreement with Egypt is dead and buried, and cannot be restored to life. . . .

(2) In consequence, the Armistice Lines between Israel and Egypt have no more validity. . . .

(4) . . . we are ready to enter into negotiations for a stable peace, co-operation and good-neighbourly relations with Egypt, on condition that they are direct negotiations, without prior conditions on either side and not under duress from any quarter whatsoever. . . .

(5) . . . even if they are not prepared for permanent peace, so long as they observe the Armistice Agreements, Israel for her part will do so too.

(6) On no account will Israel agree to the stationing of a foreign force, no matter how called, in her territory or in any of the areas occupied by her. . . .

And as if to emphasize this disdain for her 'external factor' he concluded: 'These are the principles of our policy in these stormy times.'[1]

The 'victory speech' was a tactical error of the first magnitude, for it alienated not only '*oum shmoum*' and Israel's enemies—but her friends as well. Referring to 'whatever sympathy for Israel's grievances existed at the United Nations', one commentator wrote: 'Now, unaccountably and irascibly, he almost threw it away.' That view in turn was based upon Pearson's chagrin and his remark to Eban in the UN corridor 'that the speech must have been as offensive to the British, the French, and the Americans as it was to the Arabs. "If you people persist with this," he reportedly said, "you run the risk of losing all your friends." '[2] Eisenhower's rebuke—and threat—the same night (7 November, to be analysed shortly), adds credibility to this view.

According to Eban, 'The general reaction was confusion and consternation . . . and the demand for greater pressure to withdraw increased.' Further, 'Much of the sympathy that we had acquired

---

[1] There were seven points; two were marginal. The text is in Ben Gurion 1956 (4); the extracts are from pp. 1, 4, 8–9. Ten years later Ben Gurion reiterated: 'We did not regard Sinai as part of Egypt.' Moncrieff, p. 71.

[2] Robertson, pp. 277–8.

after October 29 was dissipated.'[1] One indicator was the *total* isolation of Israel in the General Assembly on the night of 7 November: the vote for an immediate cease-fire and *withdrawal* was 65 to 1 (Israel), with 10 abstentions (including Britain and France, their NATO allies, Australia and New Zealand, and South Africa). To the man who cast that sole negative vote Israel's aloneness was eerie and awesome.[2] Another indicator was intense pressure from Hammarskjöld the following morning: he blamed Israel for endangering world peace and raised doubts about her future existence; and he categorically refused to discuss any claims and grievances until she agreed to withdraw.

Ben Gurion's aides explained the 'victory speech' in somewhat different terms.[3] 'One must place it in the atmosphere of the time', said Herzog. 'Ben Gurion—and all Israelis—felt that we must terminate the nightmare once and for all—*feda'iyun* raids, threats of annihilation, etc. We were playing for big stakes—*peace*. We felt passionately that we must get peace before we withdraw.' In Peres' view, 'he created that impression [plans to annex Sinai] merely as a bargaining device to secure free passage through the Gulf. Later, Ben Gurion related this gambit to a group of junior officers who posed the same question.' And Mrs. Meir remarked: 'I think he believed that we could stay in Sinai and Gaza. He didn't take into consideration, nor did any of us, that the Soviets would respond as they did.' All three explanations are plausible. But the most convincing was Ben Gurion's candid and human admission: 'I made a few mistakes in that speech—saying that the Armistice Agreement was dead and buried, that Egypt would not be allowed to return to Sinai. I went too far; and it was against the views I had expressed in the Government [on 28 October], that they would not let us stay in Sinai—Russia, America, the UN, Africa and Asia.' And then, after a thoughtful pause, the essential truth was stated: 'But you see, Mr. Brecher, the victory was too quick. I was too drunk with victory.'

The 'fall-out' of that mood was a grave though very brief (16 hours) crisis in Israel's foreign policy and a second strategic decision related to Sinai. There were several decisive inputs, two of which have already been noted: the 'victory speech' itself, with its harsh, unremitting, and arrogant tone, causing anger and antipathy in the outside world; and, secondly, growing pressure from within the UN, which reached its zenith with the Secretary-General's unyielding stand and dire warning, on the morning of the 8th—along with 'advice' from Israel's friends, like Pearson. There were others, more important in the shaping of the *crisis* decision to withdraw—the 'Soviet factor', the 'French factor', the 'American factor', and the 'Jewish factor'.

---

[1] Eban 1957, pp. 46–7.   [2] Kidron interview, 1966.
[3] The following four extracts are from Herzog, Peres, Meir, and Ben Gurion interviews, 1966.

The first in time and, according to many, the most decisive input was the Soviet threat. It began on the evening of 5 November, with the arrival of a brutal, blunt, and belittling letter from Bulganin to Ben Gurion. Apart from the usual 'unqualified condemnation of . . . the criminal acts of the aggressors' and the accusation that Israel was 'acting as an instrument of external imperialistic forces', the Soviet Premier charged Israel with falsehood, 'while she prepared a treacherous attack on her neighbours'. Then came the unprecedented threat:

The Government of Israel is criminally and irresponsibly playing with the fate of the world, with *the fate of its own people*. It is sowing hatred of the State of Israel among the Eastern peoples, such as cannot but leave its mark on the *future of Israel* and *places in question the very existence of Israel as a State*. . . . The Soviet Government is at this moment taking steps to put an end to the war and to restrain the aggressors. . . . The Government of Israel should consider, before it is too late. . . . We hope that the Government of Israel will fully understand and appreciate this warning of ours.[1]

No decision-maker could be indifferent to such an official communication from a super power—and Ben Gurion was not. After immediate consultation with Meir, Dayan, and Peres, he decided to send the Foreign Minister and the DG, Defence Ministry, to Paris for advice. They left at 1 a.m. on the 6th and were received shortly after their arrival by the French Foreign and Defence Ministers. Peres' account is instructive:

We found them divided in their opinions about the significance of the Russian threat—but far from tranquil. Pineau defined the situation thus: 'France is ready to share with you whatever she has—but she cannot give you *more* than she has. . . . We have no means of defence against *missiles*. If you are attacked by the Russians, even if we rush to your aid with all our might—we are helpless against missiles.' . . .
The French Foreign Minister appeared very worried, and he took the Soviet threat very seriously. 'I suggest that you do not belittle Bulganin's warning', he said. . . .
The French Foreign Minister concluded with the following story: when Bulganin's letter arrived Adenauer was in Paris and at that hour was visiting Guy Mollet. When it was clear to him what was being said he remarked to his host seriously: 'It is best that you don't have any illusions. . . . Those Americans will not rush to your help, despite the Atlantic Alliance. . . .' The words of the German Chancellor worried the French Prime Minister, and Pineau immediately cabled his Ambassador to Washington to clarify the situation without delay. That same evening [the 5th, in the US capital], Ambassador Hervé Alphand met with the President. . . . Eisenhower was pale and nervous, and repeated again and again: 'You must stop this war. . . . You must withdraw from Egypt. . . . Our stand corresponds to the UN Charter. . . .' Suddenly the President looked at the Ambassador angrily and said: '*Permit me to say this to you,*

---

[1] As quoted in Ben Gurion 1956 (5), p. 2 (emphasis added). A slightly different translation of the text appears in Ben Gurion 1971, pp. 508–9.

Sir: Life is but a ladder, the top of which reaches the sky. I am very close to the upper end of the ladder. . . . I would like to present myself to my maker with clean hands. . . .'

An hour after meeting Pineau, Peres received a telephone call at his hotel from Bourgès-Manoury: 'In truth, I have no precise documentary evidence but in my view the Soviet threat is nothing but a bluff. . . . They will not create the danger of a third world war. . . . This is only a *personal* opinion, but it is well that you take this too into account. . . .'[1]

Ben Gurion's initial reaction to the Bulganin letter was noted by Dayan in his diary the following day:

[He] did not hide his deep concern over the Soviet stand, nor did he seek to ignore the full gravity of its significance; but his reaction was not a trembling in the knees. He was not seized with panic. . . . What particularly infuriated him was the difference between the letters sent to Britain and France and that sent to Israel. The one to us is couched in terms of contempt and scorn, and it threatens the very existence of Israel as a State.[2]

In fact, Ben Gurion followed the Bourgès-Manoury line—at first. The advice of Israel's steadfast ally reached him on the afternoon of the 6th, when he was drafting his 'victory speech'; but Pineau's words of caution did not deter him from adopting a tough stand in his address to the *Knesset* more than twenty-four hours *later*. It required the appearance of Soviet *acts* to make Bulganin's threat credible.

The CIA leaked a report to Paris on the 7th—ostensibly from US Ambassador Bohlen in Moscow—that the Soviets intended 'to flatten' Israel the next day. The French, in good faith, passed the grim 'news' on to Israel. It was believed by many, especially in the light of the shooting down of a British Canberra over Syria the previous afternoon, the consequent assumption of Soviet-controlled radar there, reports from Turkey of Soviet overflights, flashes of a Russian request to send five warships through the Turkish Straits to the Mediterranean, a report of an Anglo-French air alert against Soviet planes and submarines, etc.[3] There was also an urgent cable from Ambassador Eliahu Sasson that his Soviet counterpart in Rome had communicated the same threat. But what made Soviet words and reported acts so ominous was US behaviour, both negative and positive.

US Ambassador Dillon had assured Mollet in the early hours of the morning of 6 November that a Soviet missile attack on Britain or

---

[1] Peres Diary (Evron), pp. 152–5. See also Peres 1970, pp. 210–11.

[2] Dayan 1966, pp. 185–6. Dayan adds his own reflection: 'Who knows whether this Sinai Campaign would have been launched if the Russian messages had been sent . . . before the 29th of October.' On the Bulganin messages to Eden and Mollet and their reactions see Eden, pp. 554–6; Finer, pp. 427, 431–2; Love, pp. 610–13; Macmillan, pp. 165–6—'We never took them [Bulganin's threats] too seriously'; Nutting, pp. 143–4; Robertson, pp. 251–2; and H. Thomas, pp. 158–9.

[3] The Bohlen report about the probability of a massive one-day Soviet air assault on Israel was also noted by Eban, along with similar warnings by Communist-bloc diplomats in Israel. Eban 1957, p. 54.

France would lead to US retaliation: the conspicuous omission of Israel was not unknown to her decision-makers. Even more disturbing was a twin verbal assault from the President and the Secretary of State, the result of Ben Gurion's 'victory speech', reports of which reached Washington in the late afternoon of the 7th. Eisenhower wrote:

I must say frankly, Mr. Prime Minister, that the United States views these reports of Israel's refusal to withdraw, if true, with deep concern. Any such decision . . . could not but bring about the condemnation of Israel by . . . the United Nations. . . . It would be a matter of the greatest regret to all my country-men if Israeli policy on a matter of such grave concern to the world should in any way impair the friendly cooperation between our two countries.[1]

That 'concern' received blunt expression in the verbal threat of sanctions which Under-Secretary of State Herbert Hoover Jr. conveyed to Shiloah while transmitting the President's letter: 'I consider that this is the most important meeting ever held with Israel representatives. I am speaking on behalf of Dulles', who was then in hospital. There followed a picture of the dire consequences of non-withdrawal, notably Soviet penetration of the Middle East. 'Israel would be the first to be swallowed up.' And then came the direct threat: 'In these circum-stances Israel's attitude will inevitably lead to most serious measures, such as the termination of all [US] governmental and private aid, United Nations sanctions, and eventual expulsion from the UN. I speak with the utmost seriousness and gravity.' And Rountree, who was present, added: 'We have therefore been profoundly shocked at the report of the Prime Minister's latest stand.'[2]

The two messages were telephoned to Herzog at 8.30 a.m. on the 8th.[3] They were followed soon after by a cable from Eban, which proved to be crucial in devising a formula to permit a *volte-face* by Israel, yet retain for her bargaining power in the political struggle:

The world is waiting in a state of great tension for your reply to Eisenhower's letter. The appeals from Jews and others are increasing, all of them urging that you retreat from point 6 in your speech yesterday [refusing to allow an inter-national force in occupied areas]. There is a general feeling that fateful matters are in your hands. [Then came the recommendation about the *form* of accept-

[1] The full text is in Ben Gurion 1960, pp. 35–6.

[2] Eban 1957, p. 52. Shorter and less ominous paraphrases of that threat are to be found in Ben Gurion 1960, p. 35, and in Ben Gurion 1971, p. 514. Ben Gurion's Israeli biographer added that Hoover and Rountree also conveyed 'instructions from our Government to inform you that we will not be able to come to your aid in the event of your being attacked by Soviet "volunteers"'. Ben Gurion Documents (Bar-Zohar 1966), instalment 5.

[3] Ironically, owing to a mechanical difficulty at the US Embassy in Tel Aviv, the threat was conveyed to the victim through his own communication network, via the Israel Embassy in Washington!

ance.] '. . . the Government of Israel declares her willingness to withdraw her forces from Sinai *when satisfactory arrangements are made with the international force that is about to enter the Canal Zone.*'

Israel's envoy also emphasized the need for an announcement within twenty-four hours—because of growing 'evidence' of Soviet plans to intervene.[1]

The pressure from organized Jewry was conveyed with candour by Goldmann to Ben Gurion soon after the 'victory speech':

With regard to Israel's refusal to move from Sinai or even to transfer its positions to an international force . . . I must tell you that it will be impossible to mobilize an American–Jewish front to support this posture. If there will be an open dispute between Israel and the US Government on this point . . . [and] if this should lead to cessation of the UJA and Bonds, I foresee great difficulties in renewing these enterprises, even if the American authorities would again give their agreement. . . .

. . . what is needed is a step that will prevent an open split with Eisenhower. . . . I must add that I am certain that if the US takes steps against us, Germany will stop reparations.[2]

Despite the importance of American Jewry, there is virtually no evidence that the 'Jewish factor' was seriously considered by any of the decision-makers, though, like Eban's view, it did strengthen the position of the doves within Israel's Government.

By 9 a.m. on 8 November Israel's decision-makers faced a grave challenge. All three criteria of a foreign policy crisis were present—surprise, at the intensity of opposition by the two super powers, the UN, and friends; a perceived threat to basic values; and little time to respond.[3] How did they behave during the very brief crisis?

The Prime Minister's first reaction was to seek Eban's view as to whether an immediate summit meeting with the President could be arranged. It was impossible, the Ambassador replied. Ben Gurion then consulted Meir, and the first of two Cabinet sessions followed to consider the Soviet and American threats. President Ben Zvi, in a rare act, came to the Prime Minister's office that morning.

The Government met again, almost continuously from 5 p.m. until just before midnight. Multiple pressures upon the small, totally isolated Jewish state had reached their apex in the late afternoon, and the effect was visible. It was a tense, even stormy session, one of the most fateful in Israel's history. The doves, led by Aranne and Sapir, cried out that the state was in jeopardy, the danger of destruction real—they warned that History would never forgive Israel's leaders if another Holocaust ensued. They were supported more soberly by the two NRP ministers, Shapira and Burg, the Progressives' Rosen, and their *Mapai* colleague,

---

[1] Eban 1957, p. 53.
[2] Ben Gurion Documents (Bar-Zohar 1966), instalment 5.
[3] Hermann, pp. 29–36, 197–203.

Shitreet. The hard line was enunciated by *Ahdut Ha'avoda*'s two ministers, especially Carmel. *Mapam*'s members had executed a *volte-face*, from opposition to the Sinai Campaign to refusal to withdraw from Gaza! But the real power of decision lay with the 'Big Three' of *Mapai* at the time, Ben Gurion, Meir, and Eshkol, and in the last analysis with the Prime Minister himself—for the lines of division were vocal but not rigid. Rosen recalled: 'The Government decision was to leave the decision to Ben Gurion.'[1]

He decided to withdraw—*in principle*; for the combination of pressures on 8 November seemed insurmountable to BG as to most Israeli decision-makers. The decision was taken, after the leaders of all Opposition parties—except *Maki*—were consulted and informed by Ben Gurion formally, at about 9 p.m. However, the issue did not end thus. At the moment of decision Herzog urged an attempt to make withdrawal *conditional* and injected anew the Eban formula—'when satisfactory arrangements are made with the international force. . . .' 'Aranne and Sapir, more than others, feared world war and the danger of not withdrawing, and they felt haggling was wrong. Herzog persisted and got approval.'[2]

Ben Gurion favoured as much delay as possible, to allow Israel's propaganda to take effect. Yet a vital piece of information was lacking: would conditional withdrawal be acceptable to the Powers, especially to the United States? To fill that lacuna Herzog was instructed to secure Eban's judgement. He telephoned shortly after 9 p.m. Eban recalled speaking with Dulles, who raised no objection, and informing Herzog at 11.30 that 'the formula can stay in'. Rafael phrased Ben Gurion's parting remark as follows: 'If you [Eban] really take the responsibility that it is feasible, then I agree.' And Herzog confirmed the timing of the conversations, as well as the Cabinet debate.[3]

After the political struggle was over, Eban wrote of that episode: '. . . the Government decided to leave in my hands whether to undertake an immediate and unqualified withdrawal or to make the withdrawal conditional. . . . I decided in favour of the conditional sentence. Shiloah and Kidron participated in this fateful consultation.'[4] This summation reflects the important role of a diplomat in the decision-

---

[1] Interview, 1971.

[2] Navon interview, 1966. Herzog also referred to his own critical role at this juncture. Interview, 1966; but it was not mentioned in Herzog 1966.

[3] This reconstruction is based upon Eban, Herzog, Navon, Rafael interviews, 1965–6.

[4] Eban later offered three reasons for his recommendation: (1) the conditional sentence was important to gain time to continue the political struggle and to ensure the certainty that evacuated areas would not be handed over to the Egyptian Army; (2) a reply satisfactory to the UN was essential to remove the danger of Soviet intervention; and (3) if the Soviets hesitated because of possible UN reaction, then conditional withdrawal would be sufficient to win Western support; why concede everything? Eban 1957, p. 55.

making process but its spirit is not entirely accurate. The *strategic* decision to withdraw was taken by Ben Gurion, and formally by the Cabinet, *before* consulting Israel's envoy in America. The issue of *conditional* withdrawal was of a lesser order of significance. And Eban's recommendation to retain the formula followed approval by the US Secretary of State. At the same time his role was innovative. And the burden of responsibility placed upon him on 8 November was very heavy. He reacted decisively. Finally, the formula permitted *phased* withdrawal and therefore ample time to secure concessions, the *raison d'être* of the political struggle to follow.

A half hour after midnight on 8 November a weary and dejected Ben Gurion delivered a radio broadcast to his people. The mood of triumph just twenty-nine hours earlier (his 'victory speech') was now replaced by sober realism. He recounted the events of the day—the UN resolutions, the Bulganin and Eisenhower letters, the Cabinet meetings, and the decision. He also read his replies to Moscow and Washington. To the Soviet Premier he expressed 'surprise and sorrow at the threat against Israel's existence and well-being . . .'. He was also firm: 'Our foreign policy is dictated by our essential needs and by our yearning for peace. It is not and will not be decided by any foreign factor.' To the President he set out the conditional *withdrawal* formula, expressed satisfaction with his deep interest in Israel's welfare—and aligned Israel with the US: 'you will always find Israel ready to make its humble contribution at the side of the United States in its efforts to strengthen justice and peace in the world.' Finally, to the nation, he noted 'the political struggle with which we are confronted' and the three goals—destruction of Egyptian armed forces, 'liberation of the territory of the homeland . . .', and safeguarding of free navigation through the Gulf and the Canal. He expressed confidence that the second and third objectives would yet be achieved.[1] The next morning Meir sent a parallel reply (conditional withdrawal) to the UN Secretary-General. Eban informed Hammarskjöld before the Foreign Minister's message arrived, and noted: 'he expressed a tremendous relief . . .'. And Kidron telephoned the news to Sobolov of the Soviet delegation; but evaded the question, 'when?' The political struggle to implement Strategic Decision 2 was about to begin.

There remains the vital question: which input(s) shaped the decision to withdraw?[2] The prevailing mood among Israel's decision-makers on 8 November 1956 was acutely portrayed by Herzog: 'There was a genuine fear of world war that day. The conflict had escalated beyond the Middle East. The chasm of the unknown had opened for Israeli leaders—unlike any in the past. They shrank from the abyss.' He also

---

[1] Ben Gurion 1956 (5), pp. 1–6.
[2] The following eight extracts are taken from Herzog, Meir, Peres, Eban, Ben Gurion, Bar-Zohar, and Navon interviews and, for Eytan, Eban 1957, p. 56.

cited three specific factors—Soviet threats, US hints of sanctions, and UN pressure; but the general mood was termed decisive. This appreciation was correct for the Cabinet doves and other, uncertain, ministers. However, the near-consensus is that, for Ben Gurion, the pre-eminent decision-maker, the ranking input was the 'Soviet factor'.

Meir: 'I am convinced that this speech was definitely made in response to the Soviet threat';

Peres: What were the reasons for the decision? 'The Soviet threat';

Eban: 'the grave news—on the night of the 7th and all day on November 8th—of Soviet preparations to intervene in force';

Eytan: in a cable to Eban on the night of the 8th he noted that, in view of the well-founded fears of a Soviet air attack the next day, the Soviet UN Representative should be informed at once of Israel's decision to withdraw;

Ben Gurion was a conspicuous dissenter:

> 'I didn't care what Bulganin *said*. I knew that Bulganin would not *act*. But the Americans—I knew they had other means of pressure to compel us to withdraw. Therefore I was more concerned about the Americans';

Bar-Zohar: 'Ben Gurion was scared by the Russians but he preferred to surrender to the Americans.'

Navon was the most persuasive in relating the two principal inputs to each other:

After all we received two ultimata, from Russia and the United States. We didn't regard the US threat as serious—militarily—but the economic threat, yes. (Ben Gurion thought of standing fast and asked Eshkol for an assessment as to how long Israel could hold out economically.) The Russian threat we took as deadly—physically, militarily. We had information that it was real. American Jews, too, pressed for withdrawal.

If the US had been more sympathetic, we would have seen the Soviet threat as not too serious. Just as the US and Russian conjunction of policy led to the creation of the State, so on this occasion their conjunction led to our decision to withdraw.

We tried hard to create the impression that we withdrew in response to *US* pressure.

Khrushchev's reported view would thus appear to be in accord with Israeli perceptions:

... when we delivered our own stern warning to the three aggressors, they knew that we weren't playing games with public opinion. They took us very seriously. ... We only had to issue our warning once unlike the Chinese variety ... !

I think I can explain why Israel retreated from the territory it had captured. ... We put our conditions to Israel in very unambiguous terms: either the Israelis pull back their troops . . . or else . . . they might find themselves faced with our volunteers. . . .

It was a great victory for us when *we ended the crisis*.[1]

One of *Tzahal*'s most respected officers reflected a decade later: 'There was, unfortunately, an erroneous evaluation of the intervention of the United States and the Soviet Union. I don't think the Russians would have attacked.'[2] Most Israelis shared his view—later. But on the day of crisis the unknown dimension of Soviet intentions seemed awesome and shaped Israel's strategic decision to withdraw.

The decision to withdraw set in motion an intense political–diplomatic struggle lasting four months. Israel's goal was to retain the fruits of victory on the battlefield; in particular, guaranteed freedom of passage through the Straits, Egypt's non-return to Gaza, and the creation of an effective buffer by the demilitarization of Sinai. The struggle took place in New York and Washington (UN Headquarters and the State Department), with Israel's cause being advocated by her premier diplomat, Abba Eban, and by Foreign Minister Meir. The negotiations were protracted and often acrimonious: the Eban–Hammarskjöld dialogue went on for almost three months (21 November 1956–11 February 1957), with the Secretary-General insisting on unconditional withdrawal and Israel's Permanent UN Representative holding out for 'accompanying circumstances'; the Eban–Dulles dialogue was all-consuming from 11 to 28 February 1957.

Strategy remained under the control of Ben Gurion throughout. But the diplomatic Sinai Campaign which followed Operation *Kadesh* was conducted by a small group within the FSTE: Eban; his principal aides at the UN, Rafael and Kidron; Shiloah in Washington; and Herzog in Jerusalem. Indeed the implementation of S_2—the decision to withdraw—was an impressive display of talent by Israel's Foreign Service. The flow of events may be analysed in four stages.[3]

1. *Negotiations Culminating in the Withdrawal to El-Arish, 9 November–31 December 1956*

Soon after the cease-fire Eban and Herzog synchronized actions, the former to delay UN and US pressure for withdrawal, the latter to

---

[1] Khrushchev, pp. 436–7. On the Soviet role see also Hayter and Smolansky.

[2] Amit.

[3] The principal source for this analysis is a detailed, fascinating reconstruction prepared immediately after the struggle by Abba Eban. Unless otherwise cited, all quoted passages and data refer to this unpublished report, cited as Eban 1957, which was kindly made available to the author by Mr. Eban. The report was based upon a complete record of minutes of all meetings (October 1956–March 1957) between Israeli diplomats at the UN and UN officials—Secretary-General Hammarskjöld, Under-Secretary Ralph Bunche, and Special Assistant to the Secretary-General Andrew Cordier. Kidron interview, 1966. The only useful published work on this phase of Israel's Sinai decision process is Finer, ch. 17. It is not, however, always entirely accurate and it is insufficiently documented.

ensure a slow withdrawal of troops on the ground. The objective was to gain time in order to create a setting conducive to concessions.[1] Tenaciously pursued and skilfully executed, the tactic was not without success.

An urgent task at the outset was to mobilize support for Israel's claims—from American public opinion, the US Congress, and West European governments. The themes to be emphasized were set down by Ben Gurion in a briefing to Israeli envoys: Egypt's Army must not be allowed to return to Sinai; the International Force must remain in the Canal Zone—and ensure free passage for all; Egypt must be persuaded to negotiate a stable peace; and the western coast of the Tiran Straits, vital to Israel, should be retained by her. These 'maximum demands' were injected into the political game through a massive propaganda campaign, including speeches to key pressure groups and articles in the US press. As often in Israel's foreign policy, public relations were harnessed to the needs of diplomacy.

In mid-November Meir and Eban held talks with many Foreign Ministers at UN Headquarters. Pineau reported on the 15th that US Ambassador Lodge was optimistic about Israel remaining in Gaza. Canada's Pearson was sympathetic. Holland's Luns offered positive support. Norway's Lange was friendly but more reserved. Selwyn Lloyd, despite the 'Treaty of Sèvres', reiterated the UK Foreign Office view that the Partition Resolution of 1947 should be the basis of a settlement. Australia's Casey indicated that Washington expected Israel to be tough; and he recommended that she so act. And Spaak of Belgium supported a policy of no return to the *status quo*. All this Eban reported to Jerusalem on the 22nd, along with Hammarskjöld's remark the previous day: 'He begged me desperately that we do not hurry to withdraw from Gaza. We must not cause a void suddenly.' Eban noted that Deputy Under-Secretary of State Robert Murphy had expressed an interest in the demilitarization of Sinai and had assured him the US would oppose a return to conditions permitting closure of the Straits.

A Western-led bloc sympathetic to Israel crystallized at the General Assembly on 24 November, largely at Spaak's initiative; however, his proposal was defeated 37 to 23, with 18 abstentions, including the United States. An Asian–African resolution pressing Israel for immediate withdrawal was adopted by 63 to 5 (Australia, France, Israel, New Zealand, and the UK), with 10 abstentions.[2] At Eban's urging, Ben Gurion approved an announcement that by 1 December Israeli troops would withdraw to thirty miles east of the Canal; but 'he particularly insisted that I [Eban] omit mention of the armistice lines.

---

[1] Eban interview, 1965 and Herzog interview, 1966.
[2] Resolution 1120 (XI), GAOR, 24 Nov. 1956, 594th Pl. Mtg., pp. 295–307. See also *UN Yearbook 1956*, p. 56.

. . . We were not to mention the armistice lines with Egypt under any circumstances.'[1]

Negotiations with Hammarskjöld on withdrawal and guarantees began on 26 November. On 9 December Jerusalem instructed Eban to do everything possible to gain time, to avoid a clash with the Secretary-General, and to demand free passage through the Canal. If pressure for further withdrawal continued, Israel would halt at El-Arish in the first week of January and wait for real assurances. Indeed partial, stage-by-stage, withdrawal of Israeli troops was, throughout, the key bargaining device to extract guarantees. An agreement between Generals Burns and Dayan on 16 December provided for two further steps of withdrawal—thirty miles that week and fifteen miles the week after. Hammarskjöld, via Bunche, objected to the slow pace. After another meeting with the Secretary-General on the 20th Meir and Eban persuaded Jerusalem to agree to expedite the withdrawal—to the El-Arish line by the first week of January.

An important cable from Ben Gurion to Eban on 25 December set a new focus to Israel's political strategy, from UN assurances to US guarantees, with a clear scale of objectives:

(1) demilitarization of eastern Sinai;
(2) the retention of Israeli troops at Sharm-e-Sheikh until *real* guarantees were achieved; and
(3) the non-return of Egypt to Gaza.

Ben Gurion was prepared to recommend to Israel's Government concessions on Sinai but not on the Straits or Gaza. 'In relation to them,' he concluded, 'we are prepared to go to the bitter end.' Meir and Eban conveyed Ben Gurion's views to Dulles on 29 December; he was reported by them to be in agreement, to a large extent. The Prime Minister himself emphasized to US Ambassador Lawson and Bedell-Smith that Israel would not permit a blockade of the Straits under any circumstances. This was followed up by the Washington Embassy with an information drive via editors of key newspapers, Senate and labour leaders, and influential friends of Israel like Arthur Dean, Chester Bowles, and Paul Hoffmann.[2]

---

[1] Delayed at the request of Pineau and Lloyd, the Israeli announcement was made on the 1st—before them—and took effect on the 3rd. While re-emphasizing the principle of immediate withdrawal, the Belgian Amendment sought explicit reference in the Asian–African draft resolution to the fact that partial withdrawal of all three States' armed forces had begun, and called for a reference to UNEF, 'the most striking gesture of our action during the past few weeks . . .'.

[2] Dean had been a law partner of Dulles for many years (Sullivan and Cromwell, New York). Bowles was Governor of Connecticut, 1949–51, and had served as UN Ambassador to India from 1951–3. At the time of the Sinai Campaign he was a university lecturer. Hoffmann, a former President of the Studebaker Corporation, was then head of the influential Committee for Economic Development. There had been earlier

2. *Completion of the Withdrawal except for Gaza and Sharm-e-Sheikh and the coastal strip, Definition of the Demand for Guarantees, and the Crisis with Hammarskjöld, 2 January–11 February 1957*

On 2 January Eban presented a letter to the Secretary-General containing a demand for guarantees against a renewal of *feda'iyun* raids; for a delay in withdrawal from Sharm-e-Sheikh until permanent arrangements had been agreed upon; and for confirmation that he would implement free passage through the Canal, as well as, at a later stage, Israel's Gaza proposals. There were inconclusive meetings with Hammarskjöld on the 5th and with Bunche on the 8th and 12th. Simultaneously, on the 4th, there was a Burns–Dayan agreement for further withdrawal. And, under the pressure of an impending Asian–African resolution, Israel's Government decided on 13 January to complete her withdrawal from occupied territory except for Gaza and a strip from Eilat to Sharm-e-Sheikh. The Cabinet also accepted Ben Gurion's proposals: that *Tzahal* units remain in the western coastal strip until free passage was assured in the Straits *and the Canal*; that UN observers, but not UN forces, be assigned to Gaza, about whose affairs Israel would report to the General Assembly; and that the UN be asked to demilitarize all or at least the eastern half of Sinai. This policy line was approved by the *Knesset* on the 23rd.[1]

A major effort was made during the first half of January 1957 to convince friendly states of Israel's case on the Straits: Meir met with eleven UN delegates, Eban with seven others. Pineau, the UK's Sir Pierson Dixon, and Australia's Percy Spender spoke to Hammarskjöld in the spirit of Israel's demands. 'We did not neglect Dean, Clay,

---

meetings with State Department representatives: for example, Eban with Murphy on 3 December, the latter sympathetic, as he was to be throughout; Meir, Eban, and Shiloah with Hoover and Rountree on the 7th; and discussions with Dulles in Paris on the 11th. But these were secondary to the main focus of negotiations at the time—the UN, especially the Secretary-General.

[1] At one extreme *Herut*'s Begin termed any withdrawal 'a political defeat after military victory'. *Maki*'s Mikunis was harshly critical 'of national irresponsibility, of political blindness . . . of nihilistic adventurism . . .'. Representatives of the religious parties supported the Government, differentiating Gaza from the Straits: 'In the question of the Strip', said *Ha-po'el Ha-mizrahi*'s Raphael, 'there is no place for compromise. . . . [it] is again a part of our homeland. . . .' General Zionist leader Bernstein echoed Begin's admonition not to yield to sanctions or to withdraw any further. A softer line was expressed by the Progressives' I. Cohen who denied an Israeli interest in territorial annexation. The Left-socialists' Riftin reaffirmed the *Mapam* plan to retain Gaza and contribute to large-scale Arab refugee rehabilitation within an Israeli-controlled Strip. And *Ahdut Ha'avoda*'s Ben Aharon advocated the demilitarization of Sinai. A *Herut* motion against withdrawal received 11 votes. And a group of parties headed by *Mapam* received 54 votes for a motion supporting Government policy; as such, this motion carried; there was no count of negative votes. The verbatim record of the 25 January debate is in *Divrei Ha-knesset*, xxi, part 2, pp. 830–51. The motions are on p. 851.

McCloy, and Dewey.'[1] On 12 January Murphy promised to speak to Dulles about the guarantees. He also informed Eban and Shiloah that Hammarskjöld had told him two days earlier that Israel had an iron-clad case on the Straits. The lobbying penetrated many power centres in the US and the UN. Among the results was a moderated version of an Asian–African resolution, adopted on 19 January by 74 to 2 (France and Israel), with 2 abstentions. Latin American and other Western states had achieved the omission of condemnation, threats, and sanctions in exchange for support of the fifth Assembly call for withdrawal.[2]

Tension between Israel and the UN mounted in late January when Hammarskjöld began to retreat from his earlier stand that the Gulf of Aqaba was an international waterway. Moreover, he refused to separate the Gaza and Straits issues, preferring to use the latter to extract Israeli concessions on the former. 'We tried again to mobilize the State Department.' Shiloah reported differences, with Murphy heading a pro-Israel group, Rountree and Lodge opposed, and Dulles sympathetic, especially on the Straits.

On the 26th Murphy told Eban and Shiloah that sanctions were impossible and the Asians knew it, and that Israel was right to stress the question of the Straits, not Gaza. By contrast Pearson defended the Hammarskjöld report. So did Lodge in the Assembly on the 28th.

The Israel–UN crisis escalated following the Assembly's approval on 2 February of still another withdrawal resolution. Hammarskjöld told Eban on the 4th that withdrawal from Gaza meant civilian authority too. Nor did President Eisenhower's unmasked cable to Ben Gurion on the 3rd ease the political struggle for Israel: 'It is my earnest hope that this withdrawal will be completed without further delay. . . . Such continued ignoring of the judgement of the nations, as expressed in the United Nations Resolutions, would almost surely lead to the invoking of further United Nations procedures which could seriously disturb the relations between Israel and other member nations including the

---

[1] General Lucius Clay, a former US Military Governor of Occupied Germany, was then a prominent business executive, Chairman of the Board of the Continental Can Co. John J. McCloy was President of the World Bank, 1947–9, and served as US High Commissioner to Germany during the German reparations issue. At the time of the Sinai Campaign he was Chairman of the Board of the Chase Manhattan Bank. Thomas E. Dewey, a former Governor of New York (1942–54), had been the Republican candidate for the US presidency in 1944 and 1948.

[2] Resolution 1125 (XI), (A/3501/Rev. 1), 19 Jan. 1957, *UN Yearbook 1956*, p. 60. Altogether the General Assembly approved six resolutions calling for withdrawal of Israeli forces from Egyptian territory and from Gaza: three were during the Emergency Session—997 (ES–1), 2 Nov. 1956; 999 (ES–1), 4 Nov.; and 1002 (ES–1), 7 Nov.; and three were during the Eleventh Session—1120 (XI), 24 Jan. 1957; 1123 (XI), 19 Jan.; and 1124 (XI), 2 Feb. (UN.GAOR). The third resolution, on 7 November, was directed to British and French forces as well.

United States.'[1] Notwithstanding the signal, Israel's Government rejected the Assembly's latest withdrawal resolution on 6 February. And Ben Gurion, in his reply to the President on the 8th, rejected pressure—from all sources: 'It is unthinkable that, now that we have recovered our independence in our ancient homeland, we should submit to discrimination; our people will never accept this no matter what sacrifice it may entail.'

3. Negotiations with the United States on Guarantees, 11–28 February 1957

Israel's refusal to yield had the desired effect: on 11 February the threat of sanctions collapsed under pressure from the Senate, labour, American Jewry, and the press.[2] That day Dulles handed Eban and Shiloah a crucial aide-mémoire. On Gaza there was no change: '. . . we believe that Israeli withdrawal . . . should be prompt and unconditional, leaving the future of the Gaza Strip to be worked out through the efforts and good offices of the United Nations.' More important was the stance on the Straits: '. . . The United States believe that the Gulf [of Aqaba] comprehends international waters and that no nation has the right to prevent free and innocent passage in the Gulf and through the Straits giving access thereto. . . .' There was also a pledge that, 'in the absence of some overriding decision to the contrary, as by the International Court of Justice, the United States . . . is prepared to exercise the right of free and innocent passage and to join with others to secure general recognition of this right.' This, it was emphasized, depended upon prior withdrawal. In short, support on the Straits issue was the 'carrot' once the 'stick'—threat of sanctions—proved ineffective. Nonetheless, the aide-mémoire went a long way to meet Israel's basic demand.[3] Dulles was reported most friendly during the conversation, disclaiming pacifism, approving 'just' wars, and indicating that he still had an open mind on Gaza.

[1] Cited in Eisenhower, p. 184.

[2] By that time Israel's investment in public relations began to show results: 41 Republican Congressmen called on the US Government to oppose Israeli withdrawal until Egypt began to negotiate; and 75 Democrats demanded that the US insist on free passage through the Canal and the Straits before Israel's evacuation. There was also vocal pressure against any form of sanctions from Senator William Knowland (California), the Republican Senate Leader, Senator Paul Douglas (Illinois), and others. And an AFL–CIO manifesto urged the demilitarization of Sinai, as well as continued Israeli civil administration of Gaza. Goldmann claimed, in retrospect, that American Jewish pressure, through letters to Congressmen, protests, meetings, etc., played a key role in blunting the threat of US sanctions. Interview, 1966.

The bulk of the American press supported Israel's demand for assurances regarding free passage through the Straits and for security against the renewal of Egyptian hostility—but not for Israel's claims to Gaza. The Washington Post was the first (11 February) to call for a guarantee through the UN and, if necessary, a separate UN guarantee of free passage and secure borders.

[3] The text is in Eisenhower, Appendix J, pp. 684–5. See also Finer, pp. 473–5.

The next three weeks were devoted to the struggle for clarifications of US pledges. On the 12th Dulles regretted the inability to make them more formal and urged immediate Israeli withdrawal. Eban held his ground, 'and great tension prevailed in the room'. Eisenhower took an ominous initiative on the 16th, at a meeting with Dulles, Lodge, and Treasury Secretary Humphrey: '. . . I rejected, from the outset, any more United Nations resolutions designed merely to condemn Israel's conduct. . . . I preferred a resolution which would call on all United Nations members to suspend not just governmental but *private* assistance to Israel. Such a move', wrote the President later, 'would be no hollow gesture.'[1] It was a replay of the Hoover threat to Shiloah on 8 November 1956. Eban reported that the *aide-mémoire* was the outer limit of American concessions; but Ben Gurion was not persuaded.[2]

On 18 February, the day after the US published her *aide-mémoire*, the Prime Minister set down firm instructions for Eban, with two non-negotiable items: (1) no evacuation until *after effective* guarantees of free passage through the Straits; and (2) the non-return of Egypt to Gaza. Israel's people, he added, were prepared to suffer sanctions rather than yield; and, if faced with a choice, her security comes before public opinion abroad. The same day Ben Gurion requested Eisenhower's assistance to delay imminent UN discussion of the crisis: 'Withdrawal under present circumstances will spell disaster for us. . . . For the UN to take this course is to adopt a double standard of morality.'[3] There was a storm of protest in the Senate and the American press following Dulles's remark on the 19th that the United States did not rule out sanctions. The next day, at a special White House Conference with twenty-six Congressional leaders, Senators Lyndon Johnson and Knowland echoed the BG line about a double standard, pursuing one policy for the strong, the Soviet Union *vis-à-vis* Hungary, another for the weak, Israel.[4]

The President cabled an unmistakable warning to Ben Gurion immediately afterwards: 'I would greatly deplore the necessity of the

---

[1] Eisenhower, p. 185.

[2] Eban reportedly consulted Bedell-Smith on the 17th, before leaving for consultations in Israel. The latter recommended: 'Go ahead with what they have offered, and be a little more flexible than Ben Gurion has been till now!' Finer, p. 480. Almost identical language was used by empathetic American officials during the protracted Israel–US dialogue after the 1967 War.

[3] Eisenhower, p. 186.

[4] About the role of a future US President, an eye-witness reported: 'The Vice-President [Nixon] sat through the whole two and a half hours of serious, and sometimes heated debate without joining the argument. . . . [The reason was] his reluctance to become involved in a battle between Eisenhower and [his home state's Republican Senator] Knowland.' Adams, pp. 280–1. Knowland even threatened to resign from his position as a US delegate to the UN Assembly if sanctions were imposed on Israel. Adams, p. 225.

United States taking positions in the United Nations, and of the
United Nations itself having to adopt measures, which might have far-
reaching effects upon Israel's relations throughout the world.'[1] The
tone of Eisenhower's broadcast to the American people that evening
was even tougher: 'Should a nation which attacks and occupies foreign
territory in the face of United Nations disapproval be allowed to impose
conditions on its own withdrawal? . . . [And he concluded] The United
Nations must not fail.'[2] Ben Gurion replied to the President on the 21st
that Eban was en route to Washington with Israel's stand after an all-
day Israel Cabinet session; and he asked that the General Assembly
session, due that day, be postponed. It was—under US pressure—until
the 26th.[3]

A new crisis developed on 25 February, when the UN Secretary-
General reaffirmed to Eban his formal interpretation of Egypt's rights
under the Armistice Agreement. He refused to consider Egypt's non-
return to Gaza. He expressed doubt that the Gaza and Straits questions
could be settled separately. And he rejected as beyond his competence
the idea of a UN naval unit in the Gulf of Aqaba.[4] Dulles advised

---

[1] Eisenhower, p. 187.

[2] Ibid., p. 188. 'We are entitled to expect, and do expect, from such peoples of the
free world a contribution to world order which unhappily we cannot expect from a
nation controlled by atheistic despots.' As cited in Adams, p. 227. Another channel
of US pressure was used on the 21st: Bedell-Smith, a known friend of Israel, was called
to the White House and asked to contact Ben Gurion. He did so via Shiloah, stressing
that the formal and personal US–Israeli exchanges 'constitute in effect a strong moral
obligation on the part of this Administration'. He urged the Prime Minister to put
himself in the hands of the President. The State Department also reportedly tried—
and failed—to bring moderating pressure to bear upon Israel from a group of eight
prominent non-Zionist American Jews headed by motion-picture magnate Barney
Balaban. They met with Dulles on the 21st and conveyed their strong dissent from
Eisenhower's sanctions-threatening speech the previous night. They also declined
an invitation to meet the President that day. Finer, pp. 477, 484–5.

[3] The US aide-mémoire provoked another Knesset debate, on 22 and 25 February,
with no discernible change in the advocacy of competing élites. Noteworthy, however,
was the view of future Deputy Prime Minister Yigal Allon, speaking the hard line of
the nationalist Left: 'The Government must not yield to American dictation. . . .
Ahdut Ha'avoda . . . cannot support decisions for more retreats. . . . We must . . . not
yield to any pressure.' On that occasion the Government won a decisive majority—
72 to 29. The verbatim record is in Divrei Ha-knesset, xxi, part 2, pp. 1139–88. Allon's
remark is from p. 1147.

[4] Hammarskjöld was responding to Dulles's reported acceptance, on the 25th, o.
Ben Gurion's request for five US assurances: (1) American ships would sail to Eilat;
(2) the US Government would declare that, if Egypt renewed interference with
shipping through the Straits after Israel's withdrawal, Israel would have the right to
act in self-defence; (3) the US would secure a similar announcement by other maritime
powers; (4) Israeli ships would be included in the definition of 'free and innocent
passage'; and (5) a UN naval flotilla would operate in the Gulf if the stationing of a
force at Sharm-e-Sheikh were not possible. A detailed Israeli Minute on Israel's
questions and the Secretary of State's replies was approved by Dulles's aides and prepared for publication on the 26th.

Eban to see Mollet and Pineau, then in Washington for consultations with the President and the Secretary of State.

The French remained Israel's unshakeable ally to the end: they would not put pressure on Israel, said Pineau to Eban and Shiloah at their 4 p.m. meeting on the 26th. The essence of the French diplomats' proposal was that:

Israel would evacuate Gaza on the 'assumption' that the UN accepted full responsibility for its security and administration;

if the 'assumption' were violated, Israel reserved the right of freedom of action; and

the US, France, and other states would confirm in the General Assembly the legitimacy of Israel's 'assumption', thereby providing international sanction for the right to self-defence.

Mollet and Pineau saw the President again at 6 p.m.; and an hour later the French Ambassador told Eban the US agreed to the plan. In fact, the UN role in Gaza was to be 'exclusive'.

Sympathetic French intervention at the highest level eased and, as on 8 November 1956, influenced Israel's response. On 27 February her Cabinet accepted final withdrawal, in principle. But Ben Gurion, who was in strategic control of the political campaign throughout, emphasized to Eban the 'assumption' of Egypt's non-return to Gaza in any form, even if the assurance was secret. He also wanted the UN to authorize Israel to remain in the Strip until a peace settlement, and he insisted that no reference be made to the 'dead' 1949 Armistice Agreement.

The crucial implementing meeting took place at the State Department on the 28th. Eban and Shiloah were joined by Rafael. The US team comprised Phleger, Rountree, Wilcox, de Flemier, Wilkins, and Burgess.[1] Dulles arrived later. 'We went over the document sentence by sentence', wrote Eban, and agreement was unqualified. Moreover, 'an agreed draft of the [Israeli] Foreign Minister's announcement [to the Assembly] emerged. . . .' When the discussion ended Dulles said that Lodge would receive instructions to note favourably the Israeli announcement. Later in the day the Secretary of State lined up support of the plan—via the British, Canadian, and French envoys.

4. *Dénouement: Final Withdrawal and Perceived Injury, 1–19 March 1957*

The Israeli Government approved the Dulles–Eban document and the text of the Foreign Minister's UN statement, at a special meeting on Friday afternoon, 1 March. That evening Meir made the long-awaited announcement to the General Assembly that Israel would

---

[1] Herman Phleger was Legal Counsel, State Department. Francis O. Wilcox was Assistant Secretary of State for United Nations affairs.

withdraw from Gaza and the coastal strip between Eilat and Sharm-e-Sheikh on the basis of certain 'assumptions':

(a) That on its withdrawal the UN forces will be deployed in Gaza and that the take-over of Gaza from the military and civilian control of Israel will be exclusively by the UNEF.

(b) It is, further, Israel's expectation that the UN will be the agency to be utilized for carrying out the functions enumerated by the Secretary-General, namely: '. . . safeguarding the life and property in the area by providing efficient and effective police protection; as well guarantee good civilian administration; as well assure maximum assistance to the UN refugee programme; and as well protect and foster the economic development of the territory and its people.'

(c) It is, further, Israel's expectation that the aforementioned responsibility of the UN in the administration of Gaza will be maintained for a transitory period from the take-over until there is a peace settlement, to be sought as rapidly as possible, or a definitive agreement on the future of the Gaza Strip.

It is the position of Israel, that, if conditions are created in the Gaza Strip which indicate a return to the conditions of deterioration which existed previously, Israel will reserve the freedom to act to defend its rights.[1]

Lodge, who spoke immediately after Meir, caused consternation and anger among Israel's decision-makers. Although he termed her 'assumptions' about the Straits 'not unreasonable',[2] he deviated sharply on Gaza, emphasizing the Armistice Agreement and the UN Secretary-General's primary role.[3] An agitated Ben Gurion summoned the Cabinet to an extraordinary session on 2 March, the only Sabbath meeting of the Government since independence.[4] It was decided to delay the Burns–Dayan meeting, intended to arrange the final withdrawal. And Eban was instructed to secure directly from Dulles a clear announcement of Egypt's non-return to Gaza and an acknowledgement

[1] UN.GAOR, Eleventh Session, 666th Pl. Mtg., pp. 1275–6.

[2] The UNEF Commander at the time noted, without comment: 'This half-hearted phrase ["not unreasonable"] was, so it was said, substituted at the last moment for the word "legitimate".' Burns, p. 256.

[3] Mrs. Meir perceived Krishna Menon's influence on Lodge's speech as malicious. Terming the Indian Permanent Representative at the time anti-Semitic as well as anti-Israeli, she recalled vividly that, as Lodge walked to the podium to deliver his 'revision' speech on 1 March, just after her announcement, Menon followed him, whispering 'words of advice' into his ear. Meir interview, 1966. Menon's remarks to this writer appeared to confirm his role: 'We [India] practically carried the burden of the Egyptian campaign at the UN, and Lodge and I were working there closely together.' Brecher 1968, pp. 68–9.

[4] Following Lodge's speech, the Meir announcement was supported by statements from France, Argentina, Costa Rica, Cuba, Panama, Holland, Norway, Belgium, Australia, New Zealand, Sweden, Britain, Canada, Portugal, Italy, etc. However, the Lodge (US) deviation offset all these expressions of international support for Israel's 'assumptions'. These statements are in GAOR, Eleventh Session, 666th and 667th Pl. Mtgs., pp. 1277–1304.

of Israel's right to self-defence, as promised; both in a document to be dispatched to the Prime Minister.[1]

Dulles responded by assuring Eban and Shiloah they could tell the Prime Minister the United States confirmed and officially recognized the Meir Assembly text. The Secretary of State also offered to spell out in writing US identification with Israeli 'assumptions'.[2] The result was Eisenhower's letter to Ben Gurion on 3 March, the essence of which was: 'I believe it is reasonable to entertain such hopes and expectations . . . and I want you to know that the United States . . . will seek that such hopes prove not to be in vain.'[3]

The French reaffirmed their support during the two-day tension (2 and 3 March) following Lodge's speech. Mollet telephoned Eban from Ottawa urging Israeli withdrawal. Pineau wrote to Dulles on the 3rd, specifying what the US and France had agreed to do: in the French view, he wrote, the UN presence should remain until 'the conclusion of a peace treaty or of a definitive settlement concerning the area' and that 'if the responsibility should be abandoned in whole or in part by the United Nations to Egypt, Israel would have the right to apply the safeguard clause . . . [i.e.] Israel would reserve its freedom to act to defend its rights'.[4] And on the 4th a letter from the French

---

[1] Eban complained to Murphy about Lodge's speech and saw Dulles on Saturday, the 2nd. That evening Meir and Eban talked with French leaders who agreed to support Israel's efforts in Washington to undo the damage caused by Lodge's speech.

[2] On Dulles's role during the political struggle Meir remarked: 'At the end he was very helpful. As time went on, he saw that Israel's case had merit. This was due mainly to Eban's influence.' Interview, 1966. And Pineau had revealed to Meir at a high-level conference in Paris on 30 September 1956 that, when he once raised the idea of Israeli military action against Nasser, the US Secretary of State had approved—on condition that it occurred not before the end of 1956 [because of the impending US presidential elections]. Peres Diary (Evron), p. 84.

Ben Gurion shed further light many years later: 'Only eight months after the US forced us to withdraw from Sinai in 1957, John Foster Dulles *told me that the US had made a mistake.* I'm sure that this opinion came from Eisenhower.' Speech in Jerusalem, *Jerusalem Post,* 7 April 1969. For a harshly critical assessment of Dulles in the Suez–Sinai issue see Finer, *passim.*

[3] The President's reassuring letter followed two telephone calls from Dulles to Eisenhower on the 2nd, during his conversation with Eban and Shiloah. The same day, 2 March, Eisenhower had congratulated Ben Gurion on Israel's 'difficult' decision: 'I was indeed deeply gratified at the decision of your Government to withdraw promptly and fully behind the Armistice lines. . . . I know that this decision was not an easy one. I believe, however, that Israel will have no cause to regret . . .' Eisenhower, p. 189. Another (oral) reassurance from the President was communicated to Shiloah by Bedell-Smith, whom he had approached and who, after telephoning Eisenhower, felt authorized to say that nothing had changed, that the President and the United States Government had undertaken moral obligations to Israel, which would be fulfilled.

[4] Private communication to the author, October 1971. The Secretary-General, too, had assured Eban on 25 February that UNEF would not be withdrawn overnight, peremptorily. And in an important *aide-mémoire* he spelled out the relationship between Egypt, the UN, and UNEF. The salient passage was as follows:

'. . . the procedure in case of a request from Egypt for the withdrawal of UNEF

Foreign Minister to Ben Gurion confirmed France's stand, as well as revealing pressure on Washington to honour its commitments.

There was one final effort to get iron-clad guarantees. Ben Gurion instructed Eban on the 3rd to ask Dulles once more for a *written* recognition of Israel's right to self-defence regarding both the Straits and Gaza. Dulles agreed to exchange letters concerning the former but felt unable to comply about the latter. Alphand, after speaking to the Secretary of State, told Eban that written US undertakings were impossible and that the President's 3 March letter to Ben Gurion, along with Dulles's oral assurances, were the maximum obtainable. Only then did the persistent search for guarantees come to an end. Israel told the Assembly on 4 March that she was implementing her undertaking of the 1st. Total withdrawal from Gaza took place on 6-7 March. A UNEF unit arrived at Sharm-e-Sheikh on the 8th. And on the 12th the *Tzahal* unit withdrew.[1]

The dénouement to the political struggle was disappointment and bitterness in Israel: first, at Lodge's distortion of US pledges, on 1 March; secondly, at the ineffective US response to the return of an Egyptian administration to Gaza, from 13 March onwards;[2] and thirdly, at Hammarskjöld's defence of Egypt's rights in Gaza, as conveyed to Meir once more in a 'bitter and protracted discussion' as late as 19 March 1957. The mood of the nation was most simply expressed by Rabbi Mordekhai Nurock in the *Knesset* on 6 March, the

---

would be as follows. The matter would at once be brought before the General Assembly. If the General Assembly found that the task was completed and Egypt, all the same, maintained its stand and enforced the withdrawal, Egypt would break the agreement with the United Nations. . . . I showed the text to Fawzi at our first talk on 16 November and I discussed practically only this issue with Nasser for seven hours in the evening and night of 17 November. . . . In this final discussion . . . the text I had proposed was approved with some amendments. . . . All further discussion . . . has to start from the text of the agreement. . . . The interpretation of the text must be the one set out above.' Private Memorandum of Secretary-General Hammarskjöld, August 5 1957, as reproduced in Draper, Appendix 3. The quoted passage is from p. 146.

And Eban, reflecting upon the manner in which UNEF was withdrawn in 1967, recalled that Hammarskjöld's assurances in February 1957 had been influential in the final Israeli—implementing decision—withdrawal from Gaza and Sharm-e-Sheikh. Interview, 1968.

[1] For the first UNEF Commander's account see Burns, ch. 17 and 18. See also Higgins, part 2, sections 5, 6, 7, 12, and Frye, ch. III.

[2] Ben Gurion had no illusions, as evidenced in his remark to the *Knesset* on 5 March: '. . . there is no absolute certainty and no clear and authoritative undertaking that the Egyptians will not return or be restored . . . , relying, as it were, on the Armistice Agreement. And my heart is with the border settlements . . . in the South and the Negev, who listened with fear to the evacuation decision.' *Divrei Ha-knesset*, xxii, p. 1240. Dulles reaffirmed to Meir on 18 March that the President's assurances to Prime Minister Ben Gurion on 3 March and other US expectations about Gaza and the Straits remained unchanged. US Department of State, *Release*, 18 March 1957.

day *Tzahal* withdrew from Gaza: 'Now we stand before a *fait accompli*. With a broken heart we face retreat.'[1]

(E) DECISION FLOW

Pre-Decisional Events

1.	27 July 1954	Egypt–UK Agreement for British evacuation of Suez Canal Base within 20 months; formally signed 19 October 1954.
2.	13 August 1954	(Secret) France–Israel Agreement (Catroux–Peres) for sale of Ouragan planes and, later, of tanks, 75mm. guns, radar equipment; modest flow of weapons began in February 1955.
3.	24 February 1955	Formation of Baghdad Pact, initially as Iraqi–Turkish alliance; joined by UK in April, Pakistan in September, and Iran in October.
4.	28 February 1955	Gaza Raid.
5.	May 1955	Ben Gurion letter to French Defence Minister Koenig, expressing desire for French-equipped Israel Air Force and other military aid.
6.	25 August 1955	Beginning of Egyptian Army-directed *feda'iyun* raids from Gaza bases (following April 1955 Egyptian decision to launch guerrilla war).
7.	11/12 December 1955	Kinneret reprisal by Israel, the most important of several responses to *feda'iyun* raids in 1955.

Decisive Inputs to Tactical Decision

8.	12 September 1955	Egypt's blockade of Gulf of Aqaba strengthened and broadened, to include Israel's air link to Africa.

[1] There was no rejoicing, only sadness or anger. *Herut's* Bader termed the decision 'pitiful' and called for new elections. Bernstein accused the Government of placing before the *Knesset* a *fait accompli*. The Progressives' Harari was more sanguine: 'It is better for us to evacuate these areas and achieve guarantees and friendship, which will give us more security in the future than we had before the Sinai Campaign.' Warhaftig of *Ha-po'el Ha-mizrahi*, too, perceived the four-month struggle as an achievement, especially the international declarations on the Straits. His orthodox religious colleague Mintz, from *P. Agudat Yisrael*, was resigned to reality. The harshest criticism came from *Ahdut Ha'avoda's* Galili: 'The decision to retreat was a grave mistake. . . . The Government decided to rely upon American promises and their value is . . . nil.' *Mapam's* Ya'ari echoed this view. To *Maki's* Mikunis, 'the retreat is not a disaster for Israel; the conquest was a disaster'. Three Opposition motions were defeated by large majorities: by *Herut* (no confidence), 25–84; by *Maki* (no confidence), 6 to 104; and by General Zionists (calling for 'an immediate halt to the withdrawal . . .'), 25 to 85. The verbatim record of the 5–7 March debate is in *Divrei Ha-knesset*, xxii, pp. 1233–81. Nurock's remark is from p. 1271. The three motions are on p. 1281.

9. 28 September 1955 — Massive Soviet (Czech)–Egyptian Arms Agreement disclosed by British Foreign Office; announced by Nasser the next day.

10. October 1955 — US decline of Israeli overtures for alliance, which began in spring of 1955.

11. 9 March 1956 — Collapse of Anderson Mission after two months of secret, indirect talks between Egypt and Israel.

12. ... 1956 ... — Escalation of *feda'iyun* raids into Israel from Egyptian-controlled Gaza Strip and from Jordan.

13. 27 June 1956 — Large-scale France–Israel Arms Agreement, following modest agreements of 23 Dec. 1955 and 23 April 1956, provided tangible demonstration of French military support role.

14. early August 1956–mid-September — In light of Egypt's aid to Algerian nationalists (military and propaganda) and, on 26 July 1956, of Suez Canal nationalization, French ministers inquired about Israel's willingness to co-operate with France–UK 'Operation Musketeer' against Egypt.

Tactical Decision

15. 20 September 1956 — Prime Minister–Defence Minister Ben Gurion decided to co-ordinate military and political actions with France, with a view to waging war against Egypt; communicated orally to Bourgès-Manoury by Peres.

Implementation of Tactical Decision

16. 30 September–1 October 1956 — Franco–Israeli secret talks in Paris re implementation of tactical decision (Israeli participants—Dayan, Peres, Meir, Carmel) following Israel Cabinet decision of 25 Sept. to accept French invitation.

17. 2 October 1956 — Dayan issued Early Warning Order to *Tzahal* General Staff to prepare for (estimated three-week) campaign against Egypt, to begin 20 Oct.

18. 3 October 1956 — Ben Gurion–Mangin agreement to set up joint Franco–Israeli planning staff in Paris following French military mission to Israel (1–3 Oct.) to explore three possibilities of joint campaign against Egypt.

19. 15–16 October   Amit discussions with French military leaders in Paris—inconclusive.

Decisive Inputs to Strategic Decision 1

(12 September 1955   As noted, Egypt's blockade of Gulf of Aqaba strengthened and broadened, to include Israel's air link to Africa.)

(28 September 1955   As noted, massive Soviet (Czech)–Egyptian Arms Agreement announced.)

(. . . 1956 . . .   As noted, escalation of *feda'iyun* raids into Israel from Egyptian-controlled Gaza Strip and from Jordan.)

(27 June 1956 . . .   As noted, large-scale France–Israel Arms Agreement and later co-operation provided tangible demonstration of French military support role.)

20. 16 October 1956   UK agreement to certain form of Israeli participation reached at Eden–Lloyd–Mollet–Pineau conference in Paris.

21. 24 October 1956   Tripartite Military Command established by Egypt, Syria, Jordan.

22. 22–24 October 1956   After Mollet's invitation to Ben Gurion to secret talks in Paris (17 October), Franco-Israeli–British conference culminated in signed 'Treaty of Sèvres', setting out details of co-ordinated attack on Egypt.

Strategic Decision 1

23. 25 October 1956   Ben Gurion decided to launch Sinai Campaign to begin on 29 October.

Implementation of Strategic Decision 1

24. 25–28 October 1956   Secret mobilization of *Tzahal* reserves.

25. 27 October 1956   Arrival of two squadrons French planes, trucks, other equipment, and approach of promised French ships to provide naval protection.

26. 28 October 1956   Government meeting authorized Sinai Campaign.

27. 29 October 1956–5 November 1956   Campaign began, all Israeli military objectives reached.

28. 5 November 1956   Israel accepted General Assembly call for cease-fire.

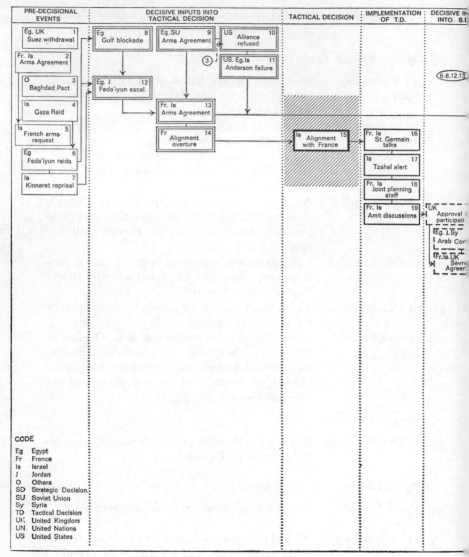

PRE-DECISIONAL EVENTS	DECISIVE INPUTS INTO TACTICAL DECISION		TACTICAL DECISION	IMPLEMENTATION OF T.D.	DECISIVE IN INTO S.D

CODE

Eg	Egypt
Fr	France
Is	Israel
J	Jordan
O	Others
SD	Strategic Decision
SU	Soviet Union
Sy	Syria
TD	Tactical Decision
UK	United Kingdom
UN	United Nations
US	United States

FIGURE II. DECISION FLOW: SINAI CAMPAIGN

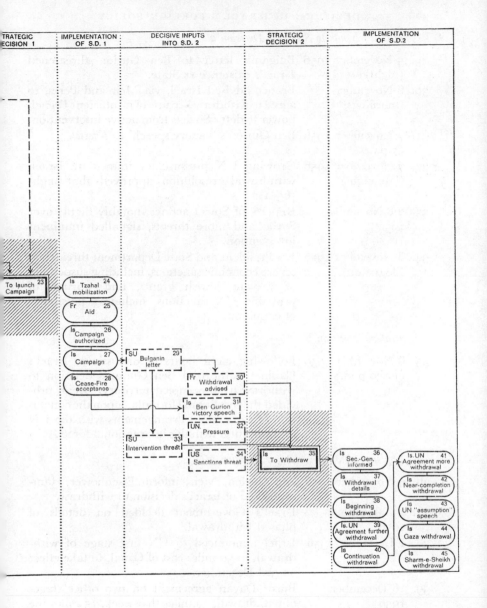

STRATEGIC DECISION 1	IMPLEMENTATION OF S.D. 1	DECISIVE INPUTS INTO S.D. 2	STRATEGIC DECISION 2	IMPLEMENTATION OF S.D.2

To launch 23 Campaign

Is 24 Tzahal mobilization

Fr 25 Aid

Is 26 Campaign authorized

Is 27 Campaign

SU 29 Bulganin letter

Is 28 Cease-Fire acceptance

Fr 30 Withdrawal advised

Is 31 Ben Gurion victory speech

UN. 32 Pressure

SU 33 Intervention threat

US 34 Sanctions threat

Is 35 To Withdraw

Is 36 Sec.-Gen. informed

Is.UN 41 Agreement more withdrawal

Is 37 Withdrawal details

Is 42 Near-completion withdrawal

Is 38 Beginning withdrawal

Is 43 UN "assumption speech

Is.UN 39 Agreement further withdrawal

Is 44 Gaza withdrawal

Is 40 Continuation withdrawal

Is 45 Sharm-e-Sheikh withdrawal

Decisive Inputs to Strategic Decision 2

29. 5 November 1956 (night) — Bulganin letter to Ben Gurion threatened Israel's existence as State.

30. 6 November (morning) — France advised Israel, via Meir and Peres, to agree to withdraw because of insufficient French power to deter Soviets from active intervention.

31. 7 November 1956 (7 p.m.) — Ben Gurion's 'victory speech' to *Knesset*.

32. 7 November 1956 (late night) — Growing UN pressure for immediate Israeli withdrawal—resolution approved that night (65–1).

33. 7/8 November 1956 — Reports of Soviet actions, notably flights over Syria, and more threats, signalled imminent intervention.

34. 8 November 1956 (8.30 a.m.) — US President and State Department threatened severe economic sanctions, including suspension of private Jewish grants, and warned of probable UN sanctions, including possibility of expulsion.

Strategic Decision 2

35. 8 November 1956 (11.30 p.m.) — Following eight hours of discussions, Israel's Cabinet authorized Ben Gurion's decision to withdraw from occupied territory. (Eban provided the conditional formula, 'upon the conclusion of satisfactory arrangements with the UN in connection with this international force . . .'.)

Implementation of Strategic Decision 2

36. 9 November 1956 — Ben Gurion, Meir, inform Eisenhower, Hammarskjöld of Israel's decision to withdraw.

37. 17 November 1956 — Israel's Government decided on details of phased withdrawal.

38. 1 December 1956 — Israel announced to UN first stage of withdrawal, to 30 miles east of Canal, to take effect on 3rd December.

39. 16 December 1956 — Burns–Dayan agreement on two other stages of withdrawal, 30 miles that week, 15 miles the following week.

40. 21 December 1956 — Israel yielded to Hammarskjöld pressure and agreed to complete withdrawal west of El-Arish by first week of January 1957.

41. 4 January 1957 — Burns–Dayan agreement for further withdrawal.

42. 15 January 1957	Execution of Government of Israel's Implementing decision on 13th (conveyed to UN Secretary-General on 14th) to complete withdrawal from Gaza and Sinai, except for coastal strip between Eilat and Sharm-e-Sheikh.
43. 1 March 1957	After prolonged UN and US pressure, the latter especially from 11 to 28 February, Foreign Minister Meir announced to General Assembly that Israel would withdraw from Gaza and Sharm-e-Sheikh, on basis of 'assumptions' about Egypt's non-return and a UN presence, as well as Israel's right of 'innocent passage' in Straits and right to self-defence.
44. 7 March 1957	Following further assurances from Eisenhower to Ben Gurion (3 March), Israeli troops withdrew from Gaza and UNEF established control.
45. 12 March 1957	Evacuation from Sharm-e-Sheikh, after UNEF arrival on 8th.

(F) FEEDBACK

Israel's Sinai decisions had widespread and cumulative consequences —for all the external components of her operational environment, as well as for the military and political aspects of the internal setting. Indeed, the multi-dimensional feedback flow from the Sinai Campaign was greater than from any other foreign-policy decision (or decision cluster) except that pertaining to the Six Day War.[1]

Israel's behaviour in 1956–7 led to increasing isolation and mistrust of her objectives within the universal organization of the global system (G). The 'victory speech' of 7 November and the rejection of five Assembly calls for 'immediate withdrawal' accentuated the UN image of Israel as militantly aggressive and expansionist. Her relations with the Secretary-General, already undermined by the friction of 1955 and 1956, became tense and resentful as a result of the prolonged deadlock over withdrawal. The inability or unwillingness of Hammarskjöld to comprehend Israel's security complex, especially during the implementation of her withdrawal decision (S_2), and the 'oum shmoum' attitude of Ben Gurion widened the gulf. The relationship between Israel and the UN did not improve; in fact, it deteriorated steadily during the following decade and beyond—notwithstanding the contribution of an international force in the Near East Core to separate the warring parties.

[1] Israel's Sinai decisions also had wide-ranging effects upon the foreign policy systems of other actors, but these will not be treated here, for they do not lie within the compass of this analysis.

One strand of DB feedback—Israel's relations with the United States—is pervasive. The strategic decision to withdraw and its implementation created an even greater sense of dependence on that super power than had hitherto existed. The reality of US influence was laid bare throughout the Sinai issue: by sanctions threats (7/8 November and 20 February); by Ben Gurion's admonition to Eban in December 1956 to concentrate on American, not UN, assurances; by the effect of the 11 February *aide-mémoire* and related clarifications; by the surrender to Eisenhower's carrot/stick pressure at the end of February; by considering the implications of Lodge's deviation speech at an unprecedented Sabbath Cabinet session on 2 March; and by the calming effect of the President's letter the following day. The Sinai issue did not transform Israel into a US vassal. But she was on the way to becoming a client state.

For Israel's other DB relationship, the consequences of her Sinai decisions were less striking. Deterioration had set in long before, reaching an initial climax in the diplomatic rupture of 1953. The Soviet arms deal of 1955, combined with continuous active support for the Arab cause, accentuated the rift. The climax was Bulganin's threat of 5 November 1956, which was received with deadly seriousness by Ben Gurion. Hostility was sustained during the decade that followed. And Soviet behaviour in 1967 caused a dramatic and dangerous escalation of the crisis. One direct link to Israeli behaviour in 1967 is evident: the Soviet threat of 1956 led to instinctive caution in Israel's Syria campaign on 10–11 June 1967, affecting both the timing and the limited objectives of the operation. And Soviet partisanship on behalf of the Arabs since the Six Day War has made totally unacceptable any Moscow initiative towards a 'political settlement'. The Sinai experience did not cause this attitude, but made it more likely.

By contrast, the Sinai decisions cemented Israel's tacit alliance with France (B_1) during the next decade. The tactical decision initiated the alignment. It was given quasi-legal form in the 'Treaty of Sèvres' and was tested on the anvil of the Suez–Sinai War and the political siege at the UN. Indeed, the French role of support for Israel throughout the struggle was a vital element in her determination to extract concessions in return for withdrawal to the 1949 Armistice lines.

There was also an improvement in Israel's ties with Britain (B_2). Correct but not cordial since the troubles of 1947–8, the relationship was given a stimulus towards friendliness as a result of the collusive alliance. It was neither as deep nor as long-lasting as with France; and there was no major policy derivative. But it did represent a positive fall-out of Israel's 1956 Sinai decisions.

In terms of the Near East Core (S) the effect of the Sinai Campaign was to stabilize the conflict for a decade. Egypt's defeat, the decimation of her *feda'iyun* bases, and the display of Israel's military prowess altered the balance between the parties—in the direction of Israeli security and Egyptian acquiescence. Other Arab participants in the conflict system abstained from the 1956 'round' and acquired an even greater respect for Israel's capability to survive and prosper. As for Egypt, her long-term goal—the extinction of Israel—yielded to short-term realism. And the presence of UNEF provided Egypt with a face-saving device to accept the new pattern of stability, legitimized, sanctioned, and, in appearance, preserved by the international organization. That Egyptian attitude was conducive to Israel's tolerance of UNEF as a useful transitional buffer.

Stabilization of the Near East Core was accompanied—and perpetuated—by a marked increase in Israel's military capability (M) vis-à-vis her Arab adversaries. The Sinai Campaign had resulted, inter alia, in the capture of a large quantity of Egyptian weapons and equipment. Notable among them were: a destroyer; almost 300 pieces of artillery; 100 tanks, among them 26 of the Soviet T-34 variety and 40 Shermans; 40 anti-tank guns; 60 armoured troop-carriers, and an array of vehicles; millions of rounds of ammunition, etc.[1] That, combined with the demoralization of Egypt's armed forces and the infusion of self-confidence into Tzahal, transformed the military balance in Israel's favour.

In the political realm (PS) the major beneficiary of the Sinai Campaign and the ensuing border tranquillity was Mapai. Ben Gurion's image as guardian of Israel's security was further strengthened by Tzahal's triumph. Withdrawal under pressure did not detract from that symbol. And the reality of 1957–9—few incidents and fewer casualties—redounded to the 'Old Man's' wisdom, and his party's continued pre-eminence in the Coalition Government. Although a causal link to election results cannot be proved, the rise in Mapai's popularity is noteworthy: from 32·2 per cent (40 seats) in 1955 to 38·2 per cent (47 seats) in 1959, the first Knesset election after the Sinai Campaign. It was the largest base of electoral support ever achieved.

How did Israel's leaders perceive the consequences of their Sinai decisions? And what policy acts flowed from those images? The task of analysing the feedback to their psychological environment is made easier by the plethora of published reflections, especially by Ben Gurion, Dayan, and Eban.

To the Zionist General Council in 1959 Ben Gurion noted 'three extremely important results: (a) . . . an inestimable improvement in the security position on the borders . . .; (b) our consolidation of our position in the international scene . . .; and (c) our freedom of shipping in the Straits . . .'.[2] Ben Gurion's most considered reflections

---

[1] Dayan 1966, Appendix 6.
[2] To the Zionist General Council, on 3 May 1959. Made available by the Government Press Office, Jerusalem.

appeared in a lengthy assessment of the Campaign the following year:

Israel is now one of the nations most respected and admired among many of the Asian and African peoples, and the Sinai Campaign . . . made no small contribution to this new attitude [though] in the first months after the Campaign . . . apprehensions seemed to be justified . . . that the Campaign would arouse [their] antagonism. . . .

The expectations of its initiators, in both the security and the economic fields, have been realized. Never . . . has there been such a measure of tranquillity on the borders . . . and never has the inner confidence of the nation and its faith in its army been so profound. . . . We have not only won freedom of navigation in the Straits and the Red Sea. . . . Oil has been flowing from Eilat to Haifa. . . . As for the Jewish people, no action . . . has done so much to intensify its love for Israel and pride in Israel. . . .[1]

Viewed in terms of the psychological environment, Ben Gurion focused on the following components—in sequence, but not in order of importance: 1959–M, G, S; and 1960—SO, M, E, G.

Dayan's perception of the consequences was stated in an epilogue to his Diary:

The military victory in Sinai brought Israel not only direct gains—freedom of navigation, cessation of terrorism—but, more important, a heightened prestige among friends and enemies alike. Israel emerged as a state that would be welcomed as a valued friend and ally, her army was regarded as the strongest in the Middle East. . . . And the sale of arms for her forces ceased to be conditional upon prior agreement among the 'Big Powers'. . . .

The main change . . . however, was manifested among her Arab neighbours. . . . [It] deterred the Arab rulers in the years that followed from renewing their acts of hostility.[2]

All these gains were also noted by Dayan in his tenth-anniversary reflections, that is, S, M, G. However, he distinguished between the Campaign's *purposes*—the elimination of the *feda'iyun* bases and the termination of the Gulf blockade—which were achieved, and further *aims*—the overthrow of Nasser and peace—which remained unfulfilled.[3]

No less revealing was his articulated image fifteen years after the Sinai Campaign, with a direct bearing on the policy challenges of 1972 ff.:

We must learn some lessons from the Sinai Campaign . . . both from what we shouldn't have done and what we should do. One of the negative lessons is that we should not retreat under pressure and we should not agree to a settlement that is temporary and, in our view, without substance. And we should not stop in the middle of our struggle before the true test that awaits us.[4]

[1] Ben Gurion 1960, pp. 54–5. He reaffirmed—in 1965 (Moncrieff, p. 72) and 1971 (interview)—that Israel's main aims were achieved.

[2] Dayan 1966, pp. 206–7.

[3] 'Ten years after the Sinai Campaign', *Jerusalem Post*, 28 Oct. 1966.

[4] Reported in *Ha'aretz* (Tel Aviv), 5 Nov. 1971.

Eban's image of the Sinai feedback is important because of his high-policy position—as Foreign Minister—since the beginning of 1966. On the tenth anniversary he described the Campaign as 'a turning-point in Israel's history' and he specified the following results:

1. Passage in the Tiran Straits: 'This brought about a basic change in Israel's geopolitical status. Now . . . a country on the Red Sea as well as on the Mediterranean. It is significant that our relations with Africa and Asia have developed with intensity since 1957.'
2. Gaza: 'The number of incidents with Egypt in the past Jewish calendar year is exactly nil. Compare this . . . with the nightmare of *feda'iyun* raids in 1954 and 1955. . . . The fact is that since 1956 this has been a quiet border.'

He also cited intangible gains *vis-à-vis* Israel's most formidable adversary: 'Nasser's stature has never fully recovered from Sinai. His army was defeated in the field. And then the victory wrought an important psychological change in Israel itself.' Finally, with respect to one super power, 'the crisis never left a permanent harmful impact on our relations with the US. Quite the opposite. . . . They increased our aid and began to discuss Middle East and world affairs with us with an intimacy that has grown ever since.'[1] Thus for Eban the benefits relate to the SO, S, M, B (Egypt), and DB (United States) components of the environment. In fact, the perceptions by Israel's decision-makers are almost consensual, with marginal differences of emphasis—Ben Gurion and Dayan on Military Capability and Security, Eban on relations with the United States, Ben Gurion and Eban on Africa–Asia.

The most balanced assessment of the Sinai effects was provided by General Amit fifteen years after the Campaign: '. . . The debit side of the ledger would include the following: the transformation of the Egyptian defeat into a [propaganda] victory for them; identification of Israel with the "imperialists"; a final break between Nasser and ourselves.' On the positive side, 'Israel has become an undisputed place on the map. . . . Then there was of course the opening of the Tiran Straits and the subsequent development of Eilat and the Negev; the stop put to the activities of the *fedayeen*; the scattering of the Egyptian Army, destruction or capture of sizeable quantities of arms, and the acquisition by *Zahal* of a near-legendary reputation in the world.'[2]

There were several fundamental policy derivatives of these images, though not all are evident in the passages which have been quoted. The inability to implement the General Assembly's withdrawal resolution heightened Israel's disrespect for the world body. Among the

[1] 'Abba Eban Reviews Diplomatic Results', *Jerusalem Post*, 28 Oct. 1966. See also his remarks in Moncrieff, pp. 74–5.
[2] Amit, 'Sinai 1956', *Jerusalem Post*, 29 Oct. 1971.

inputs of her withdrawal decision UN pressure, as noted, was the least important. And in the final 'surrender' it was United States 'assurances', not United Nations 'guarantees', which determined Israel's behaviour. With the passage of time sceptical tolerance of a UNEF buffer role gave way to modest appreciation. But when, in May 1967, at the first demand of Egypt's President, the UN Secretary-General summarily withdrew the Force and thereby made a tranquil frontier live once more, the image of 'perfidious Thant' became superimposed upon that of a biased Hammarskjöld. Moreover, Israel perceived the United Nations as powerless. The importance of that direct feedback effect can hardly be overestimated. All the (thinly-concealed) suspicion of UN motives came to the fore. The world organization was not only ineffective in a moment of need: it was dangerously lacking in courage and foresight. What value could be attached to UN guarantees and a buffer presence when they vanished at the very outset of a crisis? That, in turn, spilled over into distrust of Security Council Resolution 242 (November 1967) and its appointed implementor, the Secretary-General's Representative Gunnar Jarring, and, most important, to the rejection of all suggestions since 1967 about UN guarantees of an Arab–Israel settlement. In short, UN behaviour in 1956–7 resurrected in an acute form Israel's image of a pro-Arab bias, of weakness, and unreliability. That denigrating image was accentuated by the shattering in May 1967 of Israeli expectations concerning UNEF—which had maintained border peace for a decade. And that, in turn, induced the post-Six Day War disdainful policy line towards the United Nations. The frequent denigration of 'international guarantees', especially by Mrs. Meir, and Israel's behaviour since June 1967 provide abundant evidence of the Sinai feedback in this sphere of perceptions and policy.

Much was expected of Israel's American patron as a result of Washington's role in the 1956–7 crisis. The designation of Israel's assumptions as 'not unreasonable' was perceived by her decision-makers then and later as a firm US commitment. And that, in turn, was the cornerstone of Israel's policy for a decade towards UNEF and freedom of passage in the Straits. As long as relative tranquillity obtained in the Near East Core, Israel did not need to request US action in accord with her 'comprehension of the Gulf as an international waterway'. But after Nasser's proclamation of a blockade of the Tiran Straits, on 22 May 1967, Israel attempted to 'cash in the promissory note'. Indeed, the momentous Israeli internal controversy over the wisdom of the 'Hamtana'—'waiting'—was a direct feedback from the claim by its proponents, led by Eban, that the United States was *obligated* by her 1957 'assurances' to play an active role in breaking the blockade. The link between Israeli decision-makers' perceptions of the 1957 settlement, especially the accompanying US pledge, and the expectations in May 1967, which governed their behaviour throughout the crisis, is stark, real, and direct—and was potentially catastrophic. One cannot dissect the Six Day War decisions other than in the psychological environment shaped by the feedback effects of decisions and consequences a decade earlier. The perception–policy link between Israel's Sinai and Six Day War issues in the case of the 'Soviet factor' was, as noted, essentially marginal: it was confined to caution on the Syrian campaign because of concern over Moscow's likely response.

During the decade 1957–67 the alliance with France permeated Israel's foreign policy. It was the pillar of her 'Europe orientation'. It influenced and eased the accommodation with Germany, including the arms agreements of 1957, 1958, 1960, and then the establishment of diplomatic relations, in 1965. And it provided one path, the most important, to some form of association with the Common Market. In short, the feedback effects of Israel's Sinai decisions had discernible SO (Europe) spillover benefits as well. Thus while de Gaulle's *volte-face* in 1967 and the French embargo did not deter Israel from the Six Day War decisions, it came as a traumatic shock after a decade of close co-operation following the Sinai Campaign.

The role of the Sinai Campaign in achieving Near East stability was not lost on Israel's decision-makers. Their perception of military strength as the *sine que non* to stability gave an added impetus to the policy of broadening Israel's sources of arms—especially from Germany.

Israel's relations with one subordinate system other than her primary region (SO) were influenced directly by her Sinai decisions. As long as the Tiran Straits were blocked, physical contact with Africa was dependent upon the prohibitively expensive round-the-Cape route. The breaking of the blockade in November 1956 paved the way to an Israeli presence in Africa. And the coming of independence to that area of classical colonial rule, beginning soon after the new short route to Africa was open, added a new and significant territorial dimension for Israeli diplomacy, aid, trade, and propaganda, first in Ghana (1957) and then, swiftly, throughout sub-Saharan Africa. What the Sinai Campaign made possible became an impressive foreign policy achievement by the mid-1960s.

Most Israeli high-policy decision-makers in the early 1970s, including Meir, Allon, and Galili, shared Dayan's view of the 'lessons' of Sinai, noted earlier. Indeed, their behaviour since 1967 on the cluster of issues concerning a 'political settlement'—the forum, locale, and manner of negotiations, territorial conditions, type of concluding document, and, most important, the timing of Israel's withdrawal—flows directly from their perceived experience of 1956–7—the Sinai Campaign and its aftermath.

FIGURE 12

FEEDBACK: SINAI CAMPAIGN

Operational Environment	Psychological Environment and Policy Derivatives
External	*External*
G Increased Israel's isolation and negative image within UN; at same time created UNEF buffer (S_2)	Perception of anti-Israel UN bias and UN weakness, along with image of temporary tranquillizing UNEF role: policy derivative was denigration of UN guarantees as path to peace in Middle East and, after 1967 disbandment of UNEF, greater distrust of all UN acts—Resolution 242, Mediator role, etc. (P–D)
DB₁ Demonstrated pervasive influence of United States on Israeli policy (S_2)	Perception of that pre-eminent US role: policy derivative was continuous and sometimes desperate attempt to broaden and deepen relations with Washington—to secure military and economic aid, diplomatic support, etc. (M–S, P–D, E–D)
DB₂ Sharpened rift between Jerusalem and Moscow ($S_{1,2}$)	Image of Soviet hostility and its Arab guardian role greatly strengthened: this led to caution in June 1967 campaign against Syria and added incentive to search for closer links with United States (M–S, P–D)
B₁ Solidified the tacit alliance with France (T, $S_{1,2}$)	Vital role of French support throughout Sinai struggle correctly perceived: policy effects were strengthened French alliance, decision to seek entry into European Common Market, and, more generally, European orientation (M–S, P–D, E–D)
B₂ Improved Israel's relations with UK (S_1)	
S Stabilized Arab–Israel conflict system at very low level of violence (S_1)	Achievement of stability recognized: policy effects were to make UNEF tolerable buffer against renewed war with Egypt and UN role in Middle East conflict more acceptable (M–S, P–D)
SO Freedom of passage through the Straits made possible direct access to East Africa (S_1)	Geopolitical change perceived: policy derivative was creation of Israeli presence in Third World, especially in Africa (P–D, E–D)

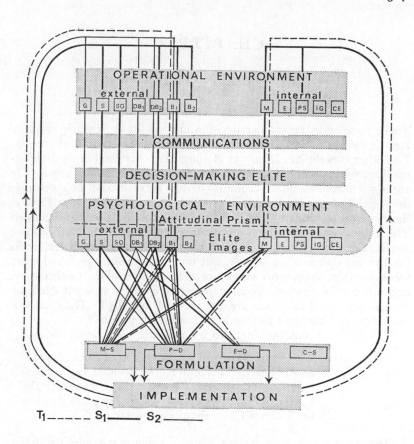

	Internal	*Internal*
M	Transformed military balance in Near East Core to Israel's advantage (T, S_1)	Greater security achieved by military campaign was perceived: policy derivative was to strengthen deep conviction that enhancement of Israel's military capability was key to survival; thus closer ties to France, Germany (M–S, P–D)
PS	Ben Gurion's (*Mapai*'s) role as guardian of Israeli security strengthened in public opinion; consequence was greater popular support in 1959 *Knesset* election (S_1)	

CHAPTER 7

Six Day War[1]

There have been two major decision clusters in the security area of Israel's foreign policy. One was the Sinai Campaign and its aftermath. The other was the Six Day War of 1967. Both involved crisis decision-making, with profound consequences extending into the 1970s. The 1956–7 cluster, as noted, comprised one tactical and two strategic decisions during a period of six months—the alignment with France, the decision to launch the Campaign, and the decision to withdraw. The 1967 cluster was much more concentrated in time, barely three weeks. The level of intensity of crisis was much higher. Moreover, it was unidimensional, leading to war, but not withdrawal—yet. And there were more decisions, more closely integrated, three of the tactical type, and one fateful strategic decision: all were focused on what decision-makers perceived to be the greatest threat since 1948.[2] The issue was presented in Israel and the world as, 'to live or perish'.[3]

The decisions may be identified by a simple operational code.

Mobilization　On the afternoon of 16 May 1967 Prime Minister Eshkol and Chief of Staff Rabin decided upon partial mobilization of *Tzahal* reserves, in response to the widely publicized dispatch of an Egyptian division to Sinai via Cairo the previous day.　　　T$_{1a}$

[1] The author is indebted to Shimon Wainer, a graduate student of the Hebrew University, Jerusalem, for the care and skill with which he assembled much of the data for this chapter; and to Benyamin Geist, a Ph.D. candidate in International Relations at the Hebrew University, for greatly enriching the documentation and the analysis, drawing from his research study of Israeli crisis decision-making in 1967.

[2] The War of Independence was the first of three direct Arab–Israel military confrontations but it is not comparable to the Sinai Campaign and the Six Day War as *a decision cluster in the M-S issue area* of Israel's foreign policy. On the fateful days of 14–15 May 1948 there were no meaningful foreign policy choices: the Arab assault on the morrow of the proclamation of independence created a simple alternative—to fight or die.

[3] The title of Eban's (unpublished) account of the 1967 crisis. A brief published Eban version of the crisis as a whole is to be found in Eban 1973 (1), ch. 10. During the crisis itself a very large part of Israel's population, including most decision-makers, believed the alternative to be so. In 1972, however, dissent from the 'holocaust' perception of the threat in 1967 was expressed by *Mapam* leader Bentov and three *Tzahal* generals of the time: Haim Bar-Lev, who was appointed Deputy Chief of Staff on 28 May; Ezer Weizman, Chief of Operations; and Matityahu Peled, Quartermaster-General. Their views and the rebuttals are discussed in section (B) below.

In the late afternoon of 19 May a large-scale mobilization of reserves was set in motion by Eshkol and
Rabin, following U Thant's agreement the previous
day to Nasser's demand to withdraw UNEF. T_{1b}

Delay   Shortly after noon on 23 May the Ministerial
Committee on Defence decided to postpone a
decision for 48 hours, in response to President
Johnson's advice; later that day Eshkol assented to
Foreign Minister Eban's clarifying mission to Paris
and Washington. T_{2a}

On 28 May the Cabinet decided to continue
Israel's political response to the crisis, following
Johnson's urging against a pre-emptive strike, along
with Kosygin's 'conciliatory' letter and Britain's
apparent flotilla initiative. T_{2b}

Unification   On 1 June a National Unity Government was
formed by bringing in *Gahal* leaders and Dayan, in
response to intense domestic pressures from competing élites and interest groups, and after the
signing of an Egypt–Jordan military pact on 30 May.
T_3

War   On 4 June 1967 the Government of Israel decided
'to take military action in order to liberate Israel
from the stranglehold of aggression which is progressively being tightened around Israel . . .'.[1]   S

That strategic decision was implemented the following morning. At
the conclusion of the Six Day War, on 10 June, Israel was the strongest
and most secure actor in the Near East Core. The goal of peace, however, remained elusive six years later.

(A) OPERATIONAL ENVIRONMENT

The setting for decision was as complex as the events which it
generated. All components, except other subordinate systems (SO),
were relevant, with a striking interaction between external and internal
dimensions of the environment.

The universal actor in the *global system* (G) had been enmeshed in
the Arab–Israel conflict for twenty years, ever since the 'Palestine
Question' had been placed before the UN by the Mandatory Power.
A myriad of resolutions followed: during the 1948 War, culminating
in the Armistice Agreements of 1949; on the Suez Canal, in 1951,

---

[1] From the text of the Government decision, made public on the fifth anniversary
of the Six Day War. *Jerusalem Post*, 5 June 1972.

1954, and 1956; with respect to the Israel–Syria Demilitarized Zone, 1951 ff.; regarding the Sinai–Suez War and its aftermath, from November 1956 to March 1957; the presence of UNEF in the Israel–Egypt borderland for a decade; and intermittent resolutions on *feda'iyun* raids and Israeli reprisals through the 1960s. In the fateful month of May 1967 the Secretary-General's withdrawal of the international force played a catalytic role in the ensuing crisis. At the same time the Security Council debates from 24 May onwards demonstrated the world body's impotence. And the Cease-Fire on 10 June formalized the *de facto* situation on the battlefield, with *Tzahal* in triumph everywhere—in Sinai, Gaza, Jerusalem, the West Bank, and Golan.

During the 1956–7 crisis the General Assembly dominated UN activities. The Security Council's pre-eminence is evident in the aftermath of the June War, through the compromise Resolution 242; but its attempt to prevent that war was paralysed by a basic clash of interests between the super powers. It was, rather, the Secretary-General's actions, especially between 16 and 18 May, and Jerusalem's sharp dissent with respect to the manner and haste of UNEF's departure, which made the world organization relevant and, in negative terms, consequential to Israel's 1967 decisions.[1]

The second G facet which impinged on those decisions was acute Soviet–American rivalry in the Middle East. The Cold War had declined in intensity and a balance of terror had served as an effective deterrent to nuclear war since the Cuba missile crisis of 1962. 'Force in the relationship between the United States and the Soviet Union', as one writer aptly remarked, 'has been "unavailable" in the sense that the effects of nuclear action are considered unacceptable to either side.'[2] This constraint was clearly evident in the 1967 crisis, with both Washington and Moscow, especially the latter, determined to avoid a direct confrontation. Yet it is facile to dismiss their role as 'secondary', even though they were unable to prevent the ultimate resort to war.[3]

Super-power competition as a global system phenomenon and the *DB relationships* are so closely intertwined that they merit interaction analysis. The US and USSR had created a patron relationship with actors in the Near East Core, the former with Israel since independence and with Jordan since the ouster of British hegemony in 1956, Moscow with Egypt and Syria, beginning with the arms agreement of 1955. More specifically, the Soviets contributed to the developing crisis in several ways. First, a steady flow of arms to their clients greatly in-

[1] The UN role in 1967 is discussed at length in Higgins, Part 2; Lall, *passim*; Draper, esp. Appendices 3–8; and *Middle East Record 1967*, pp. 5–91, 192–4. Henceforth the last source will be cited as *MER*, and all references are to the 1967 volume unless otherwise indicated. See also Burns, Cohen, and Tandon.

[2] Herz, p. 20. Of the voluminous literature on this phenomenon the most creative is Wohlstetter.

[3] An untenable and unproved thesis of Laqueur 1968, p. 160.

creased the level of power in the Core, compelling Israel to seek weaponry which would maintain at least the qualitative balance with her adversaries.[1] Moreover, Moscow helped to catalyse the crisis by accusing Israel of massing troops and planning a preventive war against Syria—in a vain effort to activate Egypt and thereby to shore up the Damascus regime. It was not a mere propaganda venture, however. According to a pro-Nasser Middle East expert, Egypt's President sought Moscow's view on a Syrian Intelligence report (to him, personally, on 8 May) that Israel was about to launch a large-scale military operation aimed at toppling the Ba'ath regime: 'When the Soviet information services confirmed that indeed Israel intends to attack Syria, Nasser was convinced that immediately afterwards it would be his turn.'[2] Two British journalists remarked more bluntly: 'It all started with a lie—a Russian lie.'[3] There was, too, strident Soviet support for all Arab claims and deeds during the first two weeks of the crisis. That, in turn, may well have led to an Egyptian expectation of Soviet intervention. And to those acts of commission must be added Moscow's failure to exert a restraining influence on Nasser, though it tried to do so—*after* the crisis had escalated beyond external control.

Ironically, this Soviet role occurred at a time when Israel was attempting to reverse the pattern of deterioration in her less important super-power relationship. In 1966 2,000 Jews had been permitted to migrate from the USSR to Israel, after a long period of near-total denial.[4] In October that year Gromyko reminded Eban at the United Nations of the positive Soviet role in the establishment of Israel.[5] Prime Minister Eshkol wrote in the *Government Year Book* for 1966–7 that Israel 'would not relinquish the hope that our relations with it [the Soviet Union] will be better one day'.[6] And just a few months before the crisis, in February 1967, Eban claimed a measure of success in this Israeli variant of *Ostpolitik*: 'Our diplomatic, commercial and cultural relations with parts of Eastern Europe have been somewhat strengthened during the past year. . . .'[7] The modest success, however,

---

[1] This escalating arms race will be explored below, under Military Capability, in the environment for decision.

[2] Eric Rouleau, in Rouleau, Held, Lacouture, pp. 49–50.

[3] Churchills, p. 28. A former British Ambassador to Egypt asked: 'Why did the Russians warn the Syrians and Egyptians that the Israelis were going to attack Syria, almost certainly incorrect information?' Trevelyan, p. 245. See also Bar-Zohar, p. 13; Yost, p. 308; and, especially, Nasser's 23 July 1967 speech, in *International Documents on Palestine, 1967* (henceforth cited as *Documents on Palestine*), Doc. 393, p. 621.

[4] Foreign Ministry sources.

[5] Eban interview, 1968.

[6] *GYB*, p. 8.

[7] Eban (1). Other evidence of an Israeli 'winds of change' approach to the Soviet Union is in Brecher, pp. 296–7, and Dagan, ch. xvi, xvii. For a synopsis of Soviet–Israel relations during the year preceding the June War see Dagan, ch. xviii, xix; and *MER*, pp. 13–15, 36–7.

did not soften the Soviet political and diplomatic assault on Israel in May–June 1967, culminating in the breaking of relations on 10 June.

The United States role in the crisis was no less significant but it took different forms. Most important was the pressure on Israel for restraint, especially on the 23rd, 26th, and 28th of May, in the midst of crucial discussions among Israel's high-policy decision-makers: on those occasions President Johnson's *démarche* had the desired effect, namely, the postponement of military action. The (unsuccessful) attempt to organize an international naval flotilla to keep the Tiran Straits open to all shipping was another exercise in restraint. But when that failed Washington stood aside. And when, in the early hours of Israel's campaign against Syria, Moscow threatened to intervene momently unless Israel ceased operations, the President deterred the other super power by moving the Sixth Fleet closer to the scene of hostilities.[1] That Washington could perform the function of restraint and then protection was due to a cumulative improvement in relations with Jerusalem during the 1960s. It was marked by arms agreements in 1962 (Hawk missiles), in 1964 (tanks), and in 1966 (Skyhawk planes). In 1962 President Kennedy assured Foreign Minister Meir that the United States and Israel were *de facto* allies. The following year a written assurance from Kennedy to Eshkol contained a virtual guarantee of Israel's territorial integrity. The 'special relationship' was strengthened by Johnson to include machinery for joint consultation at various levels, buttressed by the appearance of personal rapport and trust between the two Heads of Government. And there were American concessions on such vital matters as Jordan Waters and the Arab refugees.[2] In short, the United States was a major actor in the 1967 crisis, as was the Soviet Union, influencing the behaviour of the principal regional actors, though not determining the outcome of the war.

The only *bilateral* relationship (B) worthy of note in the setting for decision is that with France.[3] For a decade it had flourished as a tacit alliance (1956–66) with far-reaching benefits for Israel, from the Sinai Campaign to military aid, to relations with Germany, to association

---

[1] The Hot Line was used three times during the 1967 crisis—on 5, 6, and 10 June. Johnson, pp. 287, 298–9, 301–3. The direct Johnson–Kosygin exchanges were first reported in Velie, ch. 1, and pp. 167–8, 199–200. They tended to be disbelieved at the time (1969).

[2] Foreign Ministry sources. See also Brecher, pp. 43–6; Peres, pp. 103ff. For an informative survey of Israel's DB relationships until 1962 see Safran 1963, ch. xiii–xv. On the super powers in the Middle East conflict see Hurewitz, *passim*; and Safran 1969, pp. 119–37.

[3] The UK and, to a lesser extent, Canada and other middle powers were involved in the attempt to form a naval force, but their role was marginal in *Israel's* environment. It will be noted in section (c) below.

with the European Common Market.[1] French arms continued to flow
to Israel as late as 15 May 1967—in fact, until the end of 1968.[2] Yet
there were clear signs of change in French policy, at first toward
'evenhandedness' in 1964-5, dramatized by the official visit of Field
Marshal Amer to Paris in October 1965, and then to a pro-Arab posture
the following year. French reserve towards Israel became conspicuous:
there was not a single visit to Israel by a French minister in 1966-7
nor an expression of Franco–Israel amity by the French Embassy in
Tel Aviv. The Director-General of the Quai d'Orsay visited Arab
capitals in May 1967, and Arab statements became increasingly pro-
French.[3] But most important was de Gaulle's apparent *volte-face*.
Despite the 1957 commitment by France and other states, the French
President did not affirm the right of free passage through the Straits.
Moreover, he warned Israel, through Eban on 25 May, as the French
Cabinet did publicly on 2 June, not to fire the first shot, terming it in
advance an act of aggression.[4] And he strongly urged a Four-Power-
imposed solution of the conflict.[5] The shock to Israel's attentive and
mass publics—and some decision-makers—was great. It heightened
the national feeling of aloneness, the perception of threat to survival,
and the sense of urgency in the last days of May—to act before it was too
late or the costs of victory became intolerable.

The relevance of the Middle East *subordinate system* (S) does not
require elaboration: it was the source of the crisis and the arena of the
conflict; that is, it was the pervasive component of the operational
environment. Yet two specific factors bear mention: (1) Syria's acute
instability, extremist behaviour, and special client relationship to the
Soviet Union; and (2) the intense rivalries among Core Arab states.
The first was manifested in the escalation of incidents on the Syria–
Israel border during 1966-7 and open support for *feda'iyun* guerrilla

---

[1] For the origins of that alignment and the consequences of their intimate collaboration during the Sinai Campaign see pp. 262-73, 299, 301-2, 310 above.
[2] A special airlift that day is noted in *Le Monde*, 22-28 June 1967, as cited in Safran
1969, p. 443. It is confirmed by a Foreign Ministry source. The embargo, which took
effect on 5 June, applied to heavy weapons only and even then not to spare parts. A
total French arms embargo came into force only after the Beirut Airport reprisal raid
of December 1968.
[3] See *MER*, pp. 62-3.   [4] *Documents on Palestine*, Doc. 49, p. 50.
[5] There is evidence that Nasser perceived this anti-Israel posture; and it is reasonable
to infer that the disappearance of the 'French factor' as an Israeli asset contributed
to Nasser's decision to escalate the crisis, from 28 May onwards. On 26 May Egypt's
President declared before the Central Council of the International Confederation
of Arab Trade Unions: 'Israel today is the United States. The United States is the
chief defender of Israel. As for Britain, I consider it America's lackey. . . .' Draper,
p. 223. France was conspicuously absent from this image of Israel's alleged patrons.
And on 23 July, in reflecting on the war, Nasser remarked at Cairo University:
'. . . the entire world was against the opening of war. French President de Gaulle
was clear when he said that France would adopt its stand on the basis of "who fired
the first shot".' Ibid., p. 240.

warfare from any Arab sanctuary. For the Damascus regime these *external* activities were necessary to sustain its uncertain *internal* basis of power. The second took several forms. The most conspicuous was the taunting of Nasser for 'hiding behind the UNEF skirt', with charges of cowardice, dishonour, and fear unworthy of an Arab leader. Jordan took the lead, but Saudi Arabia, Iraq, Syria, and the Palestinians also engaged in harassing the *Rais*. Moreover, relations between Syria and Jordan were intensely hostile, at times seeming to overshadow the Syria–Israel conflict. And the PLO's Shukeiry, who articulated the most strident verbal attacks on the Jewish state, accused King Hussein of disloyalty to the Arab cause.[1] In short, the intra-Arab dimension of the Middle East environment induced uncertainty of tenure and rash behaviour by Arab rulers. In particular, Egypt's leader became increasingly isolated—and he perceived the expulsion of UNEF as essential to retain his leadership position in the Arab world. That act, on 16 May 1967, triggered the crisis, culminating in the Six Day War.

The balance of *military capability* (M) on the eve of the 1967 War revealed the same pattern as throughout the protracted conflict— Arab quantitative superiority in weapons and manpower, Israeli superiority in training, skill, leadership, and motivation. There is a broad consensus on force levels, with marginal differences in one category or another (see Table 12 opposite).

Israel's countervailing assets were formidable. With respect to geography she possessed an accurate early-warning system, an effective intelligence network, a strategy of offensive defence or interceptive warfare, interior lines of communication, and the physical separation of her adversaries. The population gap was offset by a superior mobilization capability, training, morale, and leadership. *Tzahal* also manifested superiority in the maintenance and use of weapons, and in the optimal investment of funds for defence. The effect of these qualities was summed up at the height of the crisis by an Israeli military commentator: '. . . There is no doubt that the qualitative gap in manpower is still in our favour. This manifests itself in the standard of the Israeli tank driver . . . and certainly . . . of the Israeli pilot. . . . But above all one must remember the important element of "win or lose everything" found in our people.'[2] That pervasive sense of '*ein breira*' was, in fact, the most important Israeli military asset, for the price of defeat was universally held to be extinction. Eban, as often, expressed the mood most poignantly:

---

[1] For a detailed summary of Syria–Israel border incidents and guerrilla raids, and inter-Arab relations, see *MER*, pp. 110–34, 166–78. See also Kerr, *passim*. Quantitative (event data) analyses of the link between Syria's internal instability and her foreign conflict behaviour and of the escalating tension in the Near East Core from 1965 to 1967, are to be found in Burrowes (1) and (2) respectively.

[2] Schiff, in *Ha'aretz*, 25 May 1967. He also noted the quality of Israel's officers, and morale in the army and on the home front.

TABLE 12

ARAB–ISRAEL MILITARY CAPABILITY: MAY 1967

	Forces of Arab States Bordering Israel					Other Arab Forces*	Total Arab Forces	Israel
	Egypt	Syria	Jordan	Lebanon	Total			
Regular Army	190,000	65,000	55,000	11,000	321,000	70,000	391,000	71,000
Effective national guard and reserves	20,000	45,000	20,000	—	85,000	18,000	103,000	205,000–230,000
Other reserves	100,000	—	—	—	100,000	—	100,000	—
Tanks (all types)†	900	400	300	45	1,645	400	2,045	800
Assault guns	400	100	unknown	unknown	500	420	920	250
Planes (approx.)	430	80	18	18	546	250	796	307
Artillery and Mortars (approx.)‡	870	unknown	unknown	unknown	870	unknown	870	unknown

Source: The figures are derived from Safran 1969, Appendix B and pp. 238–42; his data are drawn from a variety of open sources, and his estimates include 'the author's judgement'.[1]

* Refers to Iraq and Saudi Arabia (mid-1965), whose armed forces were only partly involved in the 1967 War.

† Egypt and Syria received Soviet equipment; Israel and Jordan were supplied by the UK, US, and France.

‡ Anti-tank guns and missiles are not included.

[1] Goliath, *passim*; Howard and Hunter, pp. 50–1; see also Churchills, pp. 60–2, 97, 103. For the balance of military capability from 1948 to 1967 see Brecher, ch. 4; Kemp; and Safran 1969, ch. IV, V.

Nobody who lived those days in Israel will ever forget the air of heavy foreboding that hovered over our land. . . . For Israel there would be only one defeat. If the war had ended as those who launched it planned, there would be no discussion now of territories, populations, negotiations. . . . There would be a ghastly sequel, leaving nothing to be discussed—an ending with no renewal and no consolation.[1]

The state of Israel's *economy* (E) on the eve of the Six Day War was profoundly disturbing to her policy-makers and populace alike. The aggregate annual average of more than 10 per cent growth in GNP from 1949 to 1964 had declined, precipitously, to barely 1 per cent in 1966–7. The reason was the policy of *mitun* or artificial slow-down, introduced at the end of 1964 in an effort to combat an overheated economy with full employment, conspicuous inflation, over-consumption, and escalating imports. Restraint was expressed in various measures: reduced governmental spending; credit restriction; subsidies to export industries; freezing of part of the capital import—mainly restitution payments from Germany; attempts to hold the wage–price line; and a curb on building activity. The effects became evident at the beginning of 1966. There was a noticeable improvement in the balance of payments, but the price was the sharp decline in GNP, as noted, and widespread unemployment, variously estimated from 40,000 to 100,000 in 1966–7. There was also a sharp decline in net immigration (of *olim* (immigrants) and temporary residents) from an annual average of 65,000 between 1961 and 1964 to 23,000 in 1965 and about 12,000 each in 1966 and 1967.[2]

Those facts had a depressant effect, as well, on Israeli morale. But it was the spiralling economic cost of mass mobilization of *Tzahal* reserves, from 16 May onwards, which made the E component especially relevant to the setting for decision. The withdrawal of a quarter of a million men from the labour force brought Israel's economy near to a standstill in production. To wait indefinitely for a peaceful resolution of the conflict through external efforts—the naval flotilla, etc.—was imposing an increasingly intolerable burden. And that economic reality loomed even larger in the discussions among her high-policy

[1] Speech to the Jerusalem Economic Conference on 4 April 1968. *Weekly News Bulletin*, 2–8 April 1968.

[2] Discussions of the *mitun* are to be found in Bank of Israel, *Annual Report 1966*, Part I; Horowitz, pp. 181–8; Boehm, M., and Kleiman, E., 'The Price of Mitun', *Banking Quarterly* (in Hebrew), 29, June 1968, pp. 31–42; Halperin, A., 'The *Mitun* and the Recovery of the Economy', *Economic Quarterly* (in Hebrew), 14, 56, Feb. 1968, pp. 287–96; and Ronen, J., 'The *Mitun* from the Long-Range Viewpoint', *Economic Quarterly* (in Hebrew), 13, 52, Feb. 1967. The unemployment rate in the civilian labour force rose from 7·4 per cent in 1966 to 12·4 per cent during the first quarter of 1967. *MER*, p. 387. The immigration data are taken from *CBS:SAI 1968*, no. 19, p. 88, and *1970*, no. 21, p. 110. *MER*, p. 384, gives slightly higher figures—18,510 in 1966, and 18,065 in 1967.

decision-makers during the last week of May, adding one more dimension to the perceived threat.

Israel's *political structure* (PS) in May 1967 was characterized by a stable, Labour-dominated Coalition majority of 75 seats in a *Knesset* of 120: it comprised the Alignment (*Mapai* and *Ahdut Ha'avoda*) (45), *Mapam* (8), NRP (11), Independent Liberals (5), pro-Alignment Arab parties (4), with the usual support of the *Po'alei Agudat Yisrael* (2). That Government took office in January 1966. As in all Israeli coalitions, however, the National Religious Party held a pivotal balance-of-power position. And when its leaders, in the last week of May, joined the vocal demand for a wall-to-wall coalition, including *Gahal*, with 26 MKs, and *Rafi*, with 11 MKs, Prime Minister Eshkol yielded. The NRP threat to resign, along with a revolt within *Mapai*, transformed the political structure by bringing Dayan to the Defence Ministry, and Begin and Y. Saphir to the Cabinet. This structural change symbolized the unity of the nation and became one of the environmental conditions for Israel's strategic decision.

Interest group (IG) pressures of several kinds were also present in the setting for decision. Among institutional groups *Tzahal* was the most important; but its higher officers were not united in their advocacy. The hawks were led by Weizman, Chief of the General Staff Branch, the second-ranking post in *Tzahal*; Yariv, Director of Military Intelligence; and Amit, Director of *Ha-Mosad*. The more moderate group, headed by Rabin, was willing to wait a few more days for a final decision. The Chief of Staff himself reportedly acknowledged this: 'After the closure of the Straits of Tiran it was obvious that war was inevitable. As to exactly how we should act there were different opinions on this, even within the army.'[1] Of Weizman's advocacy one commentator wrote, correctly: 'Ezer is one of the pillars of the school who do not feel they have to apologize for Israel's occupation of territory. As far as he was concerned, 1948 had been a tragedy that must be corrected, a miscarriage of justice that needed redress.'[2] Rabin's attitude was reported thus by a Cabinet minister: '. . . the Chief of Staff never called expressly for war. He pointed out all the possibilities to us, the comparative strength of the forces, and he did say that we could win—but he never put pressure on us to open hostilities.'[3]

Weizman submitted a plan for immediate action on 24 May. There were several meetings between the generals and the politicians, with *Tzahal* pressure reaching its zenith on the evening of 28 May, when the *alufim* warned Eshkol, in the presence of Allon, that further delay might bring grave danger to Israel. Its role in the decision process will be examined later. What is noteworthy in this context is the consensus about intense pressure by the military: '. . . Eshkol encountered strong

[1] As quoted by Golan, p. 13.   [2] Landau, p. 74.
[3] As quoted by Golan, p. 7.

criticism in his meeting with the Israeli generals'; '. . . his tempestuous meeting with the generals . . . '; '. . . terse and difficult'; '. . . a
disastrous talk'; and '. . . the *Tzahal* generals expressed all their bitterness'.[1]

Within *Mapai* an *ad hoc* non-associational group of 'pro-changers'
emerged during the last four days of May. They were mostly *vatikim*,
old comrades of Eshkol, persons like the respected Shaul Avigur, a
major figure in the formative phase of *Hagana*, *Knesset* Speaker Kadish
Luz, Reuven Barkatt, Akiva Govrin, David Hacohen, and Dvora
Netzer, along with some 'young Turks', notably Arye (Lova) Eliav
and Moshe Baram. They spoke for many more silent ones, in their call
for a change at the Ministry of Defence. Some urged Allon; the majority preferred Dayan. And on the evening of 1 June Eshkol yielded to
this intra-governing-party interest group. Its primary focus of concern
was the *management* of Israel's military capability, not the issue of war
or peace. However, its successful pressure for Dayan's entry into the
Government—and to the pivotal Defence portfolio—symbolized and
hastened the escalating mood in the country that war was inevitable and that Dayan in command maximized Israel's potential for
victory.[2]

A more conspicuous interest-group pressure was the daily advocacy
of the three quasi-independent newspapers, which have long performed
an opinion-forming function in Israel's political system, *Ha'aretz*,
Ma'ariv, and *Yedi'ot Aharonot*.[3] As early as 22 May *Yedi'ot* urged the
Government 'to demand the withdrawal of the Egyptian army from
our borders immediately . . . and to act—again without delay—
according to the reply given us'. The next day it wrote: '. . . now the
day of decision has come . . .'; and, within the domestic arena, it called
for the creation of an 'emergency government'. *Ha'aretz* was not as
militant in style. Nevertheless, from 17 to 24 May it warned Syria,
Egypt, and the Soviet Union that Israel would not lose her nerve
under pressure and would not accept the blockade of Eilat. On the 25th
it joined the growing demand for a broader Government 'to strengthen
the power of national decision'. *Ma'ariv* urged the establishment of 'a
war cabinet' on the 24th as 'the order of the hour', rather than diffuse
energies on a 'wall-to-wall emergency government', which would be
unable to act as an efficient decision-making body. By the 28th it, too,
advocated a national unity government, as did *Davar* and the *Jerusalem
Post* the following day. Israeli press advocacy reflected—and helped
to crystallize—an increasingly impatient public opinion, articulating

---

[1] These comments are taken, respectively, from *MER*, p. 200; Eban interview,
1968; Burdett, p. 269; Laqueur 1968, p. 144; and Gilboa, p. 170.

[2] The role of the *Mapai* revolt in the decision process will be explored in section (c)
below.

[3] See p. 59, note 1 for an observation on the general outlook of these newspapers.

their dual demands for a military response to the external threat and for a national coalition. As such it was an influential part of the operational environment.

Competing élites (CE) were vocal advocates during the developing crisis of May 1967. Among the factions within the Coalition two trends are apparent. *Mapam* and the *Ahdut Ha'avoda* wing of the Labour Alignment supported the Eshkol-led Government both within party organs and the *Knesset*. The NRP and Independent Liberals did not dissent from Government policy in the House but urged a broadening of the Coalition during the last week of May. An emergency *Knesset* debate on the 22nd provided a forum for their views and those of Opposition groups.

Mapam's second-ranking leader, Ya'acov Hazan, discerned three sources of the tempestuous situation: the inter-power struggle; the inter-Arab struggle; and the Jewish–Arab conflict—which was exploited by the other two. Israel must be cool and courageous, he emphasized, her position clear, calculated, responsible, and firm towards enemies, friends, world public opinion, and the UN. 'We do not want war', he continued; 'we want peace; but peace is not bought by surrender, by concession on a just stand. . . . Our friends in the world must know that we are on the verge of war.' And he advocated 'a front of friendship and help, of decision and political pressure', along with the full exploitation of UN channels for peace.

Yitzhak Rafael of the NRP criticized U Thant's hurried actions regarding UNEF, doubted the success of his mission to Cairo, accused Nasser of preparing the ground for a return to *feda'iyun* activity, and warned Egypt's leader that 'interference with Israeli navigation is like the incitement to general war . . . . We shall never accept a situation of terrorist actions', he continued. And 'if it becomes clear . . . that [modest] preventive measures are not sufficient, then the Israel Defence Forces will be called upon to secure our lives in ways and by means that will seem to them right and effective. . . . The way will then be opened for a test of forces. . . .' The party newspaper, *Ha-tzofeh*, reflected this line and, from 26 May, advocated the formation of a national unity government.

The *Ahdut Ha'avoda*'s *Lamerhav* declared as late as the 29th: '. . . this is not a time for internal reckoning. *The nation depends on its government and has confidence in it. . . .*' And surprisingly, given that party's militant Left-nationalist line, it wrote, when most people were certain war was inevitable: 'it is too early to prophesy whether confrontation with Egypt has been prevented or delayed'. The Independent Liberals' Harari agreed with Hazan and emphasized Israel's desire for peace. But he insisted that there was a limit to provocative Arab acts and he expressed disappointment with the UN's hasty moves. Speaking for *Agudat Yisrael*, Rabbi Meir Levin advocated extreme caution but warned Israel not to depend on the UN or even the US which, despite her friendship, was hesitant in the crisis.

Rafi did not participate in the *Knesset* debate, but Ben Gurion urged a closed-forum discussion in its Foreign Affairs and Security Committee. *Herut's* Begin countered that 'there are things which must be said from the *Knesset* podium to the people, the people of the world, and the enemy'. Noting that the security situation had worsened, he resorted once more to nationalist rhetoric. He rejected the 'show of force' thesis about Egypt's massing of troops in Sinai. His advocacy was composed of several strands—clear declarations by the Government; an urgent political campaign to mobilize pressure on Egypt to pull back from the border; free passage to and from Eilat; and a warning that Israel will not 'make peace with aggression in the north' because of 'the threat of aggression from the south'.

Among the smaller factions, the Free Centre's Shmuel Tamir advocated the creation of a national security council. The New Communists' (*Rakah's*) Meir Vilner blamed the crisis on the West's attempt to destroy the Syrian regime—with the help of Israel and Jordan. He urged once more Israel's global non-alignment and her recognition of the national and legal rights of the Palestinians. *Maki's* Mikunis termed the prevention of war the primary goal, blaming US and UK imperialism for sharpening the tension. He, too, urged recognition of Palestinian rights, along with an Israeli initiative, namely, a return to the Mixed Armistice Commission's discussions. And Uri Avneri of *Ha'olam Hazeh* blamed the Government for not breaking the vicious war cycle. A political solution was still possible, he urged, through an (unspecified) daring gesture by Israel.[1] Nevertheless, all CE factions except *Rakah* perceived war to be inevitable and urged that, whatever the differences, ranks must now be closed.[2]

The relevant features of the operational environment may now be summarized:

Global System	inability of the universal actor to de-escalate the crisis, and excessive haste by the Secretary-General in withdrawing UNEF;
	declining intensity in the Cold War, accompanied by super-power rivalry and deep penetration of the Middle East as a 'zone of competition';
Subordinate System	instability and extremism of the Syrian regime; fierce rivalry within the Arab camp;

[1] The views of Avneri, as well as of Natan Yellin-Mor and *Maki's* Moshe Sneh, were conveyed to J. F. Held in directly-quoted interviews. See Rouleau, Held, Lacouture, pp. 46–7.

[2] This account of party advocacy, including the quoted passages, is taken from *Divrei Ha-knesset*, xlix, 22 May 1967, pp. 2225–44.

Dominant Bilateral	sharp deterioration in Soviet–Israel relations; conspicuous improvement in United States–Israel relations;
Bilateral	*volte-face* in French policy towards the Arab–Israel conflict;
Military Capability	qualitative Israeli superiority, compensating quantitative inferiority; declining deterrent value of *Tzahal*;
Economic Capability	the *mitun*; the growing burden of mobilizing *Tzahal* reserves;
Political Structure ⎫ Interest Groups ⎬ Competing Élites ⎭	growing pressure for a decision; growing pressure for a national unity government.

In terms of their relative importance, an ordinal scale would suggest the following:

S	10	G	6
PS ⎫		M	5
CE ⎬ 9		E	4
IG ⎭		B	3

Whether or not Israel's decision-makers perceived their environment in these terms will be the focus of the following section.

(B) DECISION-MAKERS AND THEIR IMAGES

The May 1967 tactical decisions were taken by a five-party Coalition Government of 18 ministers which had assumed office on 12 January 1966. The Alignment of *Mapai* and *Ahdut Ha'avoda* held a decisive majority (12); the other participants were the National Religious Party (3), *Mapam* (2), and the Independent Liberals (1). The strategic decision was made by the National Unity Government formed on 1 June 1967 and enlarged to 21 with the addition of 2 members from *Gahal* and 1 from *Rafi*. Its composition was as follows:

Alignment
  Mapai

L. Eshkol	Prime Minister (and Defence Minister to 1 June)
Z. Aranne	Education and Culture
A. Eban	Foreign Affairs
H. Gvati	Agriculture
P. Sapir	Finance
E. Sasson	Police[1]

[1] Of the original January 1966 Cabinet members, Shitreet, Minister of Police since

Y. S. Shapiro	Justice
Z. Sharef	Industry and Commerce
Y. Yeshayahu	Posts

Ahdut Ha'avoda
Y. Allon	Labour
M. Carmel	Transport
Y. Galili	Without Portfolio (in charge of information)

Mapam
| Y. Barzilai | Health |
| M. Bentov | Housing |

National Religious Party
Y. Burg	Welfare
H. M. Shapira	Interior
Z. Warhaftig	Religious Affairs

Independent Liberals
| M. Kol | Tourism and Development |

Rafi (1 June)
| M. Dayan | Defence |

Gahal (1 June)
| M. Begin | Without Portfolio |
| Y. Saphir | Without Portfolio[1] |

On no other issue in Israel's foreign policy was the Cabinet as influential a decision-making body: it met almost daily through the crisis, sometimes around the clock, and was engaged in what one civil servant aptly termed 'an exercise in collective cable reading'.[2] It is germane, therefore, to examine the attitudinal prism of the decision-making group as a whole before exploring in depth the images of the more select decision-making élite.

A major component of that prism was the *historical legacy of 1957*, when the United States compelled Israel to withdraw from Sinai, Sharm-e-Sheikh, and the Gaza Strip. A decade later this perceptual link was manifested in Israel's efforts to clarify the US stand, notably by Eban on 26 May and Amit on 31 May–2 June, and her yielding to Washington's 'advice' on two occasions to delay unilateral action—on 23 and 28 May.

A second dimension of that legacy may be defined as the *Ben Gurion 1956 complex*, which warned that military action by Israel without

---

independence, died at the end of December 1966. Sasson, who held the portfolio of Posts, moved to Police on 1 January 1967 and was succeeded by Yeshayahu.

[1] Saphir joined the Cabinet's deliberations on 2 June after being designated that day by the Liberal Party as its ministerial representative for *Gahal*.

[2] Herzog interview, 1968.

Great Power support was fraught with danger. BG's own 'doveishness' during the 1967 crisis was shaped by this conviction, as is evident in his 29 May press conference. However, its importance went far beyond his individual view: this was the first crisis in the military-security issue-area in which Ben Gurion was not the pre-eminent figure; since he, at the height of his leadership, would not act alone, 'how could we, lacking his decisiveness, act without Great Power backing'. Such was the gnawing fear which deterred some Cabinet ministers from an early response to Nasser's deeds. As Carmel recalled:

It was known that BG opposed taking military action, and that he had expressed the opinion that the general mobilization [19 May] had been a mistake, and that Israel had simply to dig in and await developments. I also think that Ben Gurion did not believe that we were capable of waging this war alone. Members of the Cabinet heard from him that, as long as we did not have any of the Powers on our side, any action taken by us would be a dangerous adventure. He influenced quite a few Ministers; for them he was after all still an authority on military matters.

This was particularly so with the N.R.P. and its leader, the late Haim Moshe Shapira, who was among the most adamant against taking independent action.[1]

Shapira himself vividly recalled to this writer the 'Ben Gurion complex' as a prominent part of the May–June psychological environment among Israel's decision-makers.[2]

Another component of the commonly shared attitudinal prism was the *Holocaust syndrome*, the fear that Israel's survival was threatened. As a prominent technical élite member remarked, simply: 'Israel, including her leaders, felt in mortal danger—no doubt of that.'[3] This was expressed on the eve of the war and in its midst by two high-policy decision-makers:

. . . Only 25 years ago, a third of the Jewish people was cruelly annihilated by the murderous forces of the . . . Nazi enemy. . . . Only 19 years have passed since these survivors won their independence and began reconstructing the ruins of their national existence. . . .

. . . the State thus threatened with collective assassination was itself the last sanctuary of a people which had seen six million of its sons exterminated by a more powerful dictator two decades before.[4]

Five years after the war several senior *Tzahal* officers denigrated the 'Holocaust syndrome' and denied that Israel had been in jeopardy in May–June 1967. Thus the then Deputy Chief of Staff, Haim Bar-Lev, replied to a question: '. . . not a danger of destruction, but a vital problem for its existence. . . . No, there was no danger of destruction on the eve of the Six Day War, and we did not speak or think in such terms.' General Ezer Weizman expressed this view in even sharper

[1] Carmel (2).   [2] Interview, 1968.   [3] Herzog interview, 1968.
[4] The first extract is from Eshkol (6), p. 50; the second is from Eban (5), p. 301.

terms.[1] And General Matityahu Peled wrote: 'I am convinced that the Cabinet never heard from the General Staff that the Egyptian military threat [in 1967] is dangerous for Israel, or that Israel is unable to defeat the Egyptian army, which exposed itself with such incredible shortsightedness to Israel's crushing blows.'[2]

That interpretation was strongly refuted by Moshe Carmel—*Ahdut Ha'avoda* leader and Minister of Transport in May 1967—who had been a general in the War of Independence:

When I recreate before my eyes those fateful days of May–June 1967 and recall the long meetings and many discussions of the Government—in some of which members of the General Staff participated with all their forebodings, hesitations, and soul-searching, I have no doubt that everybody saw the ring enclosing us and the approaching danger to our unstable peace, our security and our existence as a free people. No one may have expressed that fateful phrase, 'danger of destruction'. However, those words were there in the air, even if they were not uttered.

As for the persons who were denigrating the fatefulness of the 1967 crisis, he remarked:

All those people are using the privilege of hindsight in order to justify their present political stand. I can assure you—from personal knowledge—that not one of them said we were not under the threat of annihilation at the end of May 1967—whether it is Aluf (Res.) Matityahu Peled, former Housing Minister Mordechai Bentov or Aluf (Res.) Ezer Weizman. . . . It was a war for the very survival of the State of Israel and for its free existence in the future.[3]

Rabin, who was Chief of Staff at the time, was even blunter in asserting the psychological reality of the 'Holocaust syndrome':

I said at the time: 'We have no alternative but to answer the challenge forced upon us, because the problem is not freedom of navigation, the challenge is the existence of the State of Israel, and this is a war for that very existence.' . . . This feeling that the war was to secure our very existence was shared by all the people in Israel. . . . Above all else, our victory was due to this sense, far removed from the hairsplitting of the leaders and the loquacious generals. . . . For freedom of navigation the people fought thus? Nonsense![4]

Allon and Meir added their support to the view that Israel's choice in May–June 1967 was 'to live or perish'. The former *Palmah* com-

[1] Bar-Lev (1). At the height of the controversy Bar-Lev (2) reaffirmed even more strongly that 'such a danger' ['the destruction of Israel'] did not exist'. And on the eve of Israel's 25th anniversary of independence he replied to a question, 'Was this, in your opinion, or was it not, a war of survival?'—'In my eyes, no! This was not a war of survival! . . . The Egyptians saw this war [in this light]. . . . *Tzahal*, as *Tzahal*, without going into detail . . . did not see the 1967 war as a war of survival.' Bar-Lev (3). A similar view was expressed by Bentov, a *Mapam* Cabinet minister in 1967. *Al Ha-mishmar*, 18 May 1972.   [2] Peled.
[3] The first extract is from Carmel (1); the second is from Carmel (2).
[4] Rabin 1972.

mander and Labour Minister in the 1967 Government declared that, had the Arabs won, they would have committed genocide. 'Had we not struck first in June 1967, our casualties and suffering would have been much greater. We need not try to justify our action. I only regret that some of Zahal's best commanders have mixed the people up and caused confusion on this issue.' And Prime Minister Meir remarked that, despite 'the nonsense uttered by some of our generals', Israel was in danger of annihilation in June 1967.[1]

The pervasive view of the high-policy élite *at the height of the crisis* accorded with that of Eban, Carmel, Rabin, Allon, and Meir. This is evident from the prologue to the Cabinet decision of 4 June 1967: 'After hearing a report on the military and political situation from the Prime Minister, the Foreign Minister, the Defence Minister, the Chief of Staff and the head of military intelligence, *the Government ascertained* that the armies of Egypt, Syria and Jordan are deployed for immediate multi-front aggression, *threatening the very existence of the state.*'[2] This was not mere rhetoric or form. The Holocaust psychology was deeply rooted in Israeli national consciousness, especially among non-*Sabras* of European descent; and that included 16 of the 21 Cabinet members on 4 June 1967.

Still another common feature of the attitudinal prism was the element of *surprise*. As late as the beginning of May, Israel's decision-makers (and her population at large) were psychologically unprepared for an imminent full-scale war with their neighbours. According to Eban,

it seemed unthinkable, in the early days of May 1967, that war would descend upon Israel within a month; the tension was not abnormal; there was no evidence for an imminent Arab threat to attack; the crisis escalated suddenly, swiftly, without warning or foreknowledge. The argument amongst our planning groups was about whether we could count on a continuing respite for five years—or for more.[3]

Dayan's biographer wrote in a similar vein:

. . . it is worth noting the starting point, and that is that, like everybody else' he was surprised by the events which began on May 14th. He thought, as did Chief of Staff Rabin, that war with Egypt was far away. During his visit to the United States in April 1967 he spoke before a group of professors at Harvard University and told them that he did not forecast a war for the next ten years.[4]

Rabin, too, vividly recalled the element of surprise:

We were certain at the beginning of 1967—and this opinion was strengthened

---

[1] As reported in *Jerusalem Post*, 15, 16, June 1972.
[2] From the official text, as published in *Jerusalem Post*, 5 June 1972 (emphasis added).
[3] Eban interview, 1968.   [4] Tevet, p. 560.

in April of that year when in air battle we felled the 6 Syrian Migs—that the Air Force had proved its strength so persuasively that one could not suppose that the Arab states would seriously contemplate challenging Israel. In May 1967 there was no atmosphere of co-operation in the Arab world and it was *impossible to suppose* that in this setting the Arabs would strike against us.[1]

Other ministers, including Allon and NRP leader Haim Moshe Shapira, emphasized this psychological unpreparedness for imminent war.[2] Thus the reaction to Egypt's first step—dispatching troops to eastern Sinai on 14/15 May—was to play down its significance. Even the withdrawal of UNEF (16–18 May) was not perceived as an irrevocable input to war. Israel's decision-makers were predisposed to disbelieve the magnitude of the crisis because of its suddenness and rapid escalation. It required Egypt's closure of the Straits (22/23 May) to restore the link between image and reality. And when that drastic deed was accompanied by a massive build-up of Egyptian power in Sinai, they reacted with seeming suddenness, perceiving only then a grave threat. In short, the unexpected Egyptian action re-awakened the 'Holocaust syndrome'. These three components—the historical legacy (1956–7), the 'Holocaust syndrome', and surprise—were common to the decision-making group as a whole. And the *Hamtana*, the 'waiting period', accentuated day by day the saliency of these prismatic elements.

Of the *formally equal* high-policy decision-makers, four have been selected for image analysis, those persons who shaped the decisions of 1967. Eshkol and Eban occupied pivotal posts and roles throughout the crisis. Dayan joined the decision-making élite on 1 June; in fact, his appointment as Defence Minister was a decisive input into the strategic decision. But throughout the week before he entered the Cabinet he was the focus of personal–political attention; his images are therefore relevant from about 25 May. And Allon was influential from the moment he returned from the Soviet Union (24 May), as one of Eshkol's principal advisers on military issues. Two other ministers are noteworthy. Haim Moshe Shapira was the key figure in the internal political crisis during the last days of May, which generated the National Unity Government and, especially, the coming of Dayan to the Defence Ministry. In that domestic political transformation he was a high-policy decision-maker; but he did not exercise special influence on the strategic decision for war or acquiescence. Carmel was the most consistent—and persistent—of the Cabinet 'hawks', advocating a military response to Egypt's acts from the very outset (16 May). In the end, almost three weeks later, all his colleagues supported this view, but they were persuaded by their own perception of escalating events, not by his advocacy. He is not, therefore, regarded as an inner circle decision-maker.

[1] Rabin 1972 (emphasis added).   [2] Interviews, 1968.

Among the Foreign Service Technical Élite Ya'acov Herzog stands apart. As Director-General of the Prime Minister's Office and trusted adviser, he provided Eshkol with ideas, drafted his cables and speeches, and often crystallized thinking at the Cabinet table. Others of consequence were Ambassador Avraham Harman and Minister Ephraim Evron at the Washington Embassy; Moshe Bitan, Assistant Director-General of the Foreign Ministry in charge of US affairs; and Aviad Yaffe, Head of the Prime Minister's Bureau. From *Tzahal* the assessment and advice of Chief of Staff Yitzhak Rabin and Director of Military Intelligence Aharon Yariv weighed heavily with Eshkol and others. So too did that of Meir Amit, Head of *Ha-Mosad*. And from an earlier *Tzahal* era, Yigael Yadin was consulted several times by the Prime Minister during the days of decision. Only the four designated high-policy decision-makers, however, will be subjected to image analysis, in an attempt to uncover the link between perception and decision. Both qualitative and quantitative data will be used, with a focus on the global system and dominant-bilateral relations, the Middle East subordinate system, military capability, and their advocacy.

Eshkol's view of the G and DB components in May 1967 was marked by realism. As his biographer remarked: 'He never expected the maritime powers to do much and so he was not too sadly disappointed when they did nothing at all. . . .'[1] That reaction was manifested in speeches throughout the crisis, a notable theme being the primacy of Israel's self-reliant military capability, with international commitments of supportive value only. Thus on 17 April, soon after the dramatic air battle over Syria, he said: 'When we ask the United States for arms we are told: "Don't spend your money. We are here. The Sixth Fleet is here!" My reply to this advice is that the Sixth Fleet might not be available fast enough for one reason or another, so Israel must be strong on its own. . . .'[2] This image was reaffirmed in his 28 May broadcast to the nation: '. . . There is no doubt that the mobilization of the Israel Defence Forces and their readiness for any test constituted and continue to constitute a decisive factor in the stimulation of world political activity.'[3]

The global system's responsibility for the maintenance of Middle East stability, along with that of the super powers, was clearly articulated in his address to the *Knesset* on 22 May, just before Nasser's closure of the Straits: '. . . . it is incumbent on UN members, and the big powers in particular, to declare in unmistakable terms their strongest opposition to the acts of sabotage carried out against a member state of the UN and to demand the complete cessation of such acts. . . . What is at stake is a clear and formal international undertaking. . . .'[4] Eshkol's

[1] Prittie, p. 256.   [2] Eshkol (1).   [3] Eshkol (5).
[4] Eshkol (3), pp. 86, 88.

perception of the UN and its Secretary-General was candid and even bitter, especially after the withdrawal of UNEF. One illustration is sufficient. In the same *Knesset* speech he declared: 'I must point out that Israel was a party to this international arrangement, reached in 1957, but the Secretary-General did not see fit to consult Israel before he adopted his hasty decision.'

Eshkol's image of the Soviet Union during the crisis was increasingly negative. 'Particular responsibility', he told Parliament on 22 May, 'rests with the Soviet Union, which has friendly relations in Damascus and in Cairo. . . .' And in his letter to Kosygin on 1 June he stated bluntly: '. . . the USSR has adopted the false claim and accusations of Israel's enemies.'[1] By contrast, the Prime Minister's perception of the United States role was positive, even warm: '. . . .the Government', he told the *Knesset* on 29 May, 'was deeply impressed by the unambiguous stand of the United States in favour of the safeguarding of freedom of passage. . . .'[2] The next day he wrote to Johnson, 'to welcome the assurance that the United States would take any and all measures to open the Straits of Tiran to international shipping . . .'. His perception of the US as a patron and ally is evident in his further remark: 'One of the difficulties that I face is that I must call on my people to meet sacrifices and dangers without being able fully to reveal certain compensatory factors such as the United States commitment and the full scope of your determination on the matter of the Straits of Tiran.'[3] In summary, Eshkol's perception of the G and DB components embraced a hostile Soviet Union, a powerless United Nations and an impulsive, unfriendly Secretary-General, a sympathetic, well-intentioned United States and Britain—and the aloneness of Israel, ultimately dependent upon her self-defence capability. As such it was an accurate image of the operational environment during the last week of May and early days of June 1967.[4]

---

[1] Eshkol (6). Eshkol's biographer shed further light on his disdain for the Soviet attitude, particularly as manifested during Ambassador Chuvakhin's late-night visit to the Prime Minister on 27 May: '. . . The Soviet Ambassador brought him no assurance of the slightest value. An insistent demand for peace [in the face of the blockade and the massing of Egyptian troops] could be regarded only as effrontery.' Prittie, p. 257.

[2] Eshkol (5), p. 100.

[3] Foreign Ministry sources. The letter is also revealing for its realism, emphasizing that, despite US–UK assurances, Israel could not wait much longer in exercising her right of self-defence, as embodied in the declarations of many maritime states on 1 March 1957 to the UN General Assembly.

[4] Eshkol himself later asserted that he knew exactly what the situation was and what he wanted to achieve (Eshkol 11). This estimate was shared by many, including Bitan and Herzog (interviews, 1968). And Prittie wrote: 'Eshkol was a shrewd, thoughtful statesman seeking the right line of action in face of some confused opposition within his own cabinet, a visceral sense of self-preservation among the citizens of Israel, and a complex and unpromising international situation' (p. 264).

The point of departure in Eban's image of the global and dominant-bilateral components was very similar to that of Eshkol: 'There is no doubt that the readiness shown by the big powers to protect the freedom of passage has been influenced . . . by their knowledge that . . . Israel will protect its rights.'[1] Eban evinced a positive perception of public opinion; for example: 'In the history of our generation it is difficult to think of any other hour in which progressive world opinion rallied in such tension and agony of spirit.'[2] The universal actor, however, was perceived with growing disappointment, sarcasm, and anger. On 30 May he declared: 'The United Nations did not emerge from the events of the last two weeks with brilliance and credit. In fact . . . [the] situation . . . in large measure arises from errors of UN judgement.' And the day after the outbreak of war he asked the Security Council: 'What is the use of a United Nations presence if it is, in effect, an umbrella which is taken away as soon as it begins to rain?'[3]

The Eban image of the United States was even warmer than Eshkol's, resting as it did on two pillars: his ambassadorial experience in Washington for almost a decade, which included securing the 1957 US commitment to free passage through the Straits, one of his finest diplomatic achievements;[4] and his perception of a continuous American commitment to the balance of power and the territorial *status quo* in the Middle East. As early as February 1967 he told a press conference: 'I became impressed by the conviction with which President Johnson, Secretary Rusk, and Secretary McNamara uphold the *status quo* and the arms balance in our region. . . .'[5] The US role through the crisis was seen by him as falling into three phases: (1) until 22 May, when Washington did not act fully in terms of declared policy; (2) 22 May–5 June, a period of US perplexity, when she did not find a way to carry out her self-recognized obligations; (3) after 5 June, when firm US support for Israel was perceived.[6]

The Foreign Minister's image of the Soviets began from a cold, negative analytic posture and became increasingly hostile. In his February 1967 news conference he chided Moscow for the 'fallacy' of thinking 'that the road to Arab hearts lies through alienation from Israel. . . . Other Powers have gone through this phase but have grown out of it by experience.' By 30 May he rebuked the Soviet Union: 'It is not necessary for anyone to urge restraint on Israel. . . . The Soviet influence should in our view be applied in Cairo and Damascus.'

[1] Eban (2), p. 28.
[2] Eban (6), p. 313. The same tone is evident in his reference to public opinion at the 30 May news conference; Eban (3).
[3] Eban (5), p. 304.
[4] See ch. 6, (D), above for an analysis of Eban's role in attaining the 1957 US pledge during the political struggle following the Sinai Campaign.
[5] Eban (1).
[6] Eban (7), supported by Foreign Ministry sources.

Before the Security Council on 6 June he called for a balanced Soviet policy. But on the 19th he delivered a scathing attack: '. . . its role in recent Middle Eastern history . . . is a sad and shocking story. . . . A Great Power which professes its devotion to peaceful settlement . . . has for 14 years afflicted the Middle East with a headlong armaments race. . . .' As for Britain and France, he perceived a strong under-current of unembarrassed sympathy from Wilson, which was totally absent from his talks with de Gaulle. In Paris he was an eye-witness to the death of solemn commitments. In short, Eban's image of G and DB was essentially the same as Eshkol's, sharply negative towards the USSR, warmly positive towards the US, and marked disappointment with the UN—as well as with France's behaviour.

Allon has consistently displayed scepticism about the value of alliances, guarantees, and external friendship in the military-security area: it is, undoubtedly, the result of his life-experience—*Ha-kibbutz Ha-me'uhad* and *Palmah*—and of the activist, militant, Left-nationalist philosophy of his party, *Ahdut Ha'avoda*. Typical was his remark in 1970: 'As for dependence on a foreign power for her security: Israel (I urged) must absolutely eschew such a policy. It was, of course, a good thing to have friends . . . especially among the major powers. . . . But . . . Israel must in no circumstances let her existence be militarily dependent on any guarantees from outside. . . .'[1] And more than a decade earlier he wrote: 'In any event, Israel has had, has and will have, but one faithful ally: the Jewish people in its diaspora.'[2]

On the eve of the May 1967 crisis he attributed the lack of peace not only to Arab hostility 'but also to the competition . . . between the big powers to attain influence in the Arab countries. . . .'[3] And in a careful analysis of the crisis, written soon after the Six Day War, he termed the (Eban) policy of *Hamtana*, waiting, for external help in the form of a naval flotilla, 'a serious error'; and all suggestions and advice 'were irrelevant to the seriousness of the situation . . .'.[4]

Allon's perception of the Soviet role was even more harshly expressed than that of Eshkol and Eban: 'The Soviet Union went on perniciously with her anti-Israel argument, through a malicious neglect of the facts, completely and totally.'[5] At the same time he was certain that Moscow would not intervene in an Arab–Israel war.

---

[1] Allon 1970, p. 78.
[2] Allon 1959, p. 113. His general image of the global system is best expressed ibid., pp. 83–165.
[3] Allon (1).
[4] Allon (3), p. 7. It is noteworthy that, in a speech on 2 June 1967, at the height of the crisis, the conflict-resolving efforts of the international community were not even mentioned. The only indirect reference to the global system was the analogy drawn between the blockade of Eilat and a blockade of Marseilles, New York, or London, which Allon perceived as identical in provocation. Allon (2).
[5] Allon (3), p. 7.

First, it was too risky—it could have meant confrontation with the United States;
Secondly, they were too weak in the Middle East militarily to risk war with Israel; it would have meant a military build-up equal to the size of the American build-up in Vietnam;
Thirdly, based on history I concluded they are not inclined to intervene; and
Finally, I counted on a short war, one not long enough to give the Russians time to intervene.[1]

He was no less persuaded of US non-intervention, he continued, 'provided we acted quickly'. Moreover, 'I profoundly believed there was no alternative to war and was prepared to risk American embarrassment.' And 'I knew that it was a US objective interest for us to win; but they might be compelled to act if the war dragged on.' He was not oblivious of France and Britain, but they were 'secondary': 'Even if Eban had reported that France would break diplomatic relations we would have gone to war.' In summary, G was less important in Allon's image of the external environment; the Soviets were hostile but would not intervene; neither would the basically friendly United States; and France, Britain, and the UN were of little consequence.

Dayan, too, was sceptical of the global system's value in the 1967 crisis. As early as 23 May he objected to consultations with external factors, fearing pressure which would limit Israel's freedom of action.[2] On the role of diplomacy and the UN in resolving the conflict he remarked on 3 June: 'I will be happy and *surprised* if they do it.'[3] After the war he referred disdainfully to the UN and UNEF role: 'Yugoslavia and India were awarded the guarding of the Eilat Straits only because Nasser knew they would not oppose his will. Such was the UN control of free navigation in the Straits.' As for the US role: 'I will not detail the attempts—pathetic sometimes—which the United States made for free navigation, without any concrete result.'[4] The other super power, however, was perceived by Dayan as the principal culprit, abetted by other anti-Israel forces in the global system: 'The Russians incited, the Yugoslavs and Indians co-operated in, the French approved of, the closing of the Straits. . . .' There was, in short, a broad consensus in the images of G and DB components held by the four high-policy decision-makers: the unreliability of global system action in the crisis; UN powerlessness; USSR perfidy; and US friendliness, but ineffectiveness. There were, of course, shades of emphasis, notably Dayan's concern about Soviet behaviour, Eban's greater attention to the UN and diplomacy. But a relatively homogeneous group image is apparent from the qualitative data. The content-analysis data,

---

[1] Allon interview, 1968.
[2] Nakdimon, p. 51. In this view, Dayan split with his mentor, Ben Gurion, who perceived foreign support for Israel as imperative. Tevet, pp. 561–2.
[3] Dayan (1).   [4] Dayan 1969, p. 11.

however, do not support these findings, except in regard to awareness of the UN as a factor in the crisis and Eban's perception.[1]

Eshkol's articulated image of tension in the Middle East subordinate system recognized the complexity of causal factors—'the state of inter-Arab relations and the relationship between the Powers—against the background of their global and regional policies. All these . . . are inextricably linked with each other.'[2] His perception of 'the Arabs' was marked by extreme hostility and saturated with the Second *Aliya* emphasis on force and retaliation: 'The firm and persistent stand we have taken on behalf of our rights has strengthened the awareness among our neighbours that they will not be able to prevail against us in open combat. . . .'[3] And after the war he expressed the universal Israeli view during the 1967 crisis: 'If the Arabs had won, Hitler's six million victims of World War II would have been joined by another

[1] For sources see p. 345, n. 4 below.

TABLE 13
Decision-Makers' Images of the Global System and Dominant–Bilateral Relations: May–June 1967

Variable	Eban	Eshkol	Dayan	Allon	Total
UN	97	115	48	18	278
UK	38	8	24	4	74
US	36	14	8	12	70
USSR	36	6	0	18	60
France	34	2	12	4	52
Total	241	145	95	56	534

The overwhelming attention given the universal actor—over half the references—is also reflected in the qualitative data: Israel's decision-makers manifested an acute awareness of the withdrawal of UNEF, the Secretary-General's behaviour, and the Security Council deliberations. And *awareness* is not synonymous with perceived *importance* of the object of attention.

The distribution of Eban's references also conforms with other known data: the near-equal attention to the Four Powers reflects his role in the crisis, as Israel's supreme diplomat-advocate. The gap between UN and all other references in Eshkol's data is not supported by the qualitative data. Nor is Dayan's attention to the UK—and his non-awareness of the USSR. And Allon's greater attention to the Soviet than to the American factor is also surprising. Nor do the DB data correct these blatant deviations:

Variable	Eban	Allon	Eshkol	Dayan	Total
Israel–US	8	0	2	0	10
Israel–USSR	4	4	4	0	12
Arabs–US	0	0	0	0	0
Arabs–USSR	4	8	0	0	12
Total	16	12	6	0	34

The emphasis on the Israel–USSR and Arabs–USSR relationships do not coincide with the qualitative findings. Nor does Dayan's absolute silence on the DB component. Once more, the Eban distribution is closest to his articulated images as quoted above.

[2] Eshkol (3), p. 85.　　　　[3] Eshkol (2), p. 70.

two and a half million victims of the Arab lust for destruction. . . .'[1] The Holocaust psychology, as noted, was a pervasive part of the psychological environment. The Prime Minister's image of the cause of tension focused on Syria during the first stage. 'Syria was at that time [April 1967]', he recalled soon after the war, 'the decisive factor, and by her behaviour she brought the developments of May–June 1967.'[2] From 23 May onwards, however, the focus shifted to Egypt and Nasser—and the related withdrawal of UNEF. Thus, on 22 May: 'The concentrations of Egyptian forces in Sinai have reached proportions which increase the tension in our region and arouse world concern. . . .' And the following day: 'Any interference with freedom of passage in the Gulf and the Strait constitutes . . . an act of aggression against Israel.' As for Nasser's aim, it was 'to attack Israel for the purpose of destroying her . . .'.[3] Jordan's place in Eshkol's image, by contrast, was secondary, as his remark on 7 June 1967 makes clear: 'By its actions, the Government of Jordan, with the agreement of Egypt and *following upon pressure from Cairo*, violated international law, the United Nations Charter, and the neighbourly relations between our two countries.'[4]

Eban's starting point was an oft-expressed perception of a heterogeneous regional system: 'The Middle East was never united nor entirely Arab. There will never be a Middle East without sovereign Israel within it.' And he shared the Ben Gurionist image about bargaining from strength. 'With Israel weak,' he cautioned on 17 May, 'the Arabs will not make peace. With a strong Israel they will be compelled to make peace.'[5] Moreover, the Weizmannist perception of mutual distortions of reality—by Israel and her neighbours—in the form of a mirror-image was replaced by an unequivocal perception of the cause of the 1967 crisis.[6] Nor is there any doubt as to the prime mover of the threat. Referring to Nasser's 28 May speech, Eban declared: 'Here, then, was a systematic, overt, proclaimed design at politicide, the murder of a State.'[7] Among Egypt's provocative acts, the concentration of troops in Sinai heightened tension, but the blockade of the Straits was 'the most electric shock of all'. Indeed, on 30 May he warned Nasser that this was a *casus belli*, terming free passage 'a central and vital national interest . . . the kind of national interest for which a nation stakes all that it has, all its interests, and for which it is ready . . . to undertake every sacrifice'.[8] Despite this emphasis on Egypt, Eban perceived Syria's primary role—in time: 'The first link in the chain was the series of sabotage acts emanating from Syria.' And Jordan, in his image, is a source of dissatisfaction, creating almost a sense of betrayal:

[1] Prittie, p. 263.   [2] Eshkol (11).
[3] Eshkol (3), p. 86, and (4), p. 93.
[4] Eshkol (8), p. 113 (emphasis added).
[5] Eban (2). This view was set out in Eban 1965, p. 626.
[6] See Brecher, pp. 349–53.   [7] Eban (5), p. 301.   [8] Eban (3), p. 28.

'Jordan had been intimidated against its better interests into joining a defence pact', but 'became to our surprise, and still remains, the most intense of all the belligerents.' In particular the shelling of Jerusalem was cited as a cause of his chagrin.[1]

Allon's views in 1967 were consistent with his image of 'the Arabs' and their pre-eminent leader almost a decade earlier.[2] '. . . The blindness of the war situation', he remarked at the outset of the crisis, 'prevents the Arab States from understanding how they have fallen victim to aggressive policy, which is not expressed on the battlefield but . . . in limitless arms, which are expensive to acquire and to maintain.' His respect for Nasser was undiminished, however: 'I am not certain that Nasser, with his standing and prestige, could not permit himself an interim settlement. . . . Those who think [so] belittle his strength and influence. . . . Had he given a signal, I do not think a danger of patriotic competition would have arisen. . . .'[3] However, the prestige capable of making peace also has very strong aspirations: 'The surging ambitions in Nasser overcame the clever statesman and impelled him. . . .'[4] 'I didn't think', he reflected a year later, 'that any rational leader would escalate it to war.'[5]

The causes of the crisis were perceived clearly on 2 June 1967: 'The military collision forced upon us against our will is inevitable; as long as the Arab concentrations of forces do not draw back from their attack positions, as long as the border is not secure against a resumption of terror, and as long as the Eilat Straits are blockaded—the war is inevitable.'[6] The order in which these causes was stated is not by chance, for unlike Eban he did not perceive the Straits as pivotal in the crisis: 'In the situation which was created the problem of freedom of navigation became secondary. The offensive concentrations in Sinai and, at a later stage, Jordan's joining the military pact—these became the central problem.'[7]

Dayan, too, perceived the Sinai troop concentration as catalytic in the escalation of the crisis. According to one of his biographers, he predicted the major steps towards war as early as 16 May at a gathering of former *Tzahal* Chiefs of Staff:

. . . Dayan pointed unerringly at the south as the scene of an impending flare-up. 'Nasser is the real enemy', said Dayan, 'and it is with him we should mainly concern ourselves. He is launching a new round in his struggle to maintain his position as leader of the Arab world, and this will oblige him to pick up any gauntlet his opponents may throw down. As a first step, he is *quite likely* to

---

[1] Eban (5), pp. 300–3, 305.
[2] See Allon 1959, pp. 338–64, and Brecher, pp. 361–6.
[3] Allon (1).   [4] Allon (3), p. 5.   [5] Allon interview, 1968.
[6] Allon (2). This assessment was reiterated in Allon interview, 1968, and in Allon 1970, p. 91.
[7] Allon (3), p. 7.

expel the UN force and his next step *may be* an attempt to blockade the sea lanes to Eilat.'[1]

Dayan himself declared almost a year later that he felt war was unavoidable the moment Nasser closed the Straits, that is 22/23 May.[2] Nasser's role in the process was decisive, in his view: 'The Six Day War broke out because the leadership of Abd-el-Nasser was put to the test. . . . Nasser became more and more infatuated from his own words and those of heads and representatives of other Arab states.' And on another occasion after the war he remarked: '. . . The leaders of Egypt and the commanders of her army were drunk with power, from the great quantities of Mig aircraft and tanks. . . . They intoxicated themselves and were swept away by their enthusiasm.'[3]

The content-analysis data confirm the findings based on qualitative data, except for those noted.[4]

[1] Lau-Lavie, p. 20 (emphasis added).
[2] Interview in *Ma'ariv*, 30 April 1968.   [3] Dayan 1969, pp. 7, 11.

[4] Approximately 10,000 words were analysed for each decision-maker. Where less than 9,500 words were available, or more than 10,500 words were analysed, the raw totals of frequencies were weighted. It is these weighted totals which appear in Tables 13–18. Most speeches analysed antedated the outbreak of fighting on 5 June 1967. Where possible a variety of audiences was selected for each decision-maker. Intercoder reliability was verified at 79 per cent. The speeches and statements subjected to content analysis were:

Allon, Y.,   (a) Interview in *Lamerhav*, 14 May 1967 (Allon (1)).
              (b) Interview in *Lamerhav*, 4 June 1967 (Allon (2)).
              (c) 'The Last Stage in the War of Independence' (Allon (3)).
              (d) 'Active Defence: A Guarantee for Our Existence' (Allon (4)).

Dayan, M.,   (a) Press Conference in Tel Aviv, 3 June 1967, in *Lamerhav*, 4 June 1967 (Dayan (1)).
              (b) Statement to *Tzahal*, 5 June 1967.
              (c) Speech on 6 June 1967.

Eban, A.,   (a) Press Conference in Jerusalem, 30 May 1967, in *Documents on Palestine*, Doc. 41, pp. 28–9 (Eban (3)).
              (b) Press Conference in Tel Aviv, 5 June 1967, ibid., Doc. 60, p. 59 (Eban (4)).
              (c) Address to the Security Council, 6 June 1967, in Eban 1969, pp. 299–312 (Eban (5)).

Eshkol, L., (a) Broadcast on Remembrance Day for Those Who Fell in Defence of Israel, 13 May 1967, in Christman, pp. 69–73 (Eshkol (2)).
              (b) Statement at the Opening of the Summer Session of the *Knesset*, 22 May 1967, ibid., pp. 77–89 (Eshkol (3)).
              (c) Statement in the *Knesset*, 23 May 1967, ibid., pp. 93–4 (Eshkol (4)).
              (d) Statement in the *Knesset*, 29 May 1967, ibid., pp. 97–104 (Eshkol (5)).
              (e) Broadcast to the Nation, 5 June 1967, ibid., pp. 107–10 (Eshkol (7)).
              (f) Address to the Chief Rabbis and Spiritual Leaders of All of Israel's Communities, 7 June 1967, ibid., pp. 113–15 (Eshkol (8)).
              (g) Statement to the *Knesset*, 12 June 1967, ibid., pp. 113–34 (Eshkol (9)).
              (h) Public Statement, 27 June 1967, ibid., pp. 137–40 (Eshkol (10)).

TABLE 14
DECISION-MAKERS' IMAGES OF NEAR-NEIGHBOURS: MAY—JUNE
1967

	(a) Actors Decision-Makers				
Variable	Dayan	Eban	Eshkol	Allon	Total
Egypt	192	91	83	74	440
Jordan	8	34	20	42	104
Syria	8	22	45	12	87
Iraq	8	6	3	4	21
Palestine (community)	0	0	0	10	10
Lebanon	0	3	4	0	7
Total	216	156	155	142	669
	(b) Leaders				
Variable	Dayan	Eban	Eshkol	Allon	Total
Nasser	28	16	35	46	125
Hussein	1	0	0	2	3
Total	29	16	35	48	128

The *primacy of Egypt* in the awareness of *all* the inner-circle decision-makers is stark: it accounted for 89 per cent of Dayan's references to Israel's near-neighbours; the proportion was less for the others but striking nonetheless—58, 54, and 52 per cent respectively, for Eban, Eshkol, and Allon. The only other Arab states that attracted substantial attention—of some decision-makers—were Jordan and Syria: the former accounted for 30 per cent of Allon's and 22 per cent of Eban's references, while Eshkol devoted 35 per cent of his recorded attention to Syria. For the decision-making group as a whole, moreover, the gap between awareness of Egypt and of the others is even greater: 65·8 per cent for one state, 34·2 for the rest of the Near East Core, Jordan receiving 15·5 per cent of the references, Syria 13 per cent. And if the data on leaders are added to those for states, the pre-eminence of Egypt is still more pronounced: Dayan 90 per cent (220 of 245); Allon 63 per cent (120 of 190); Eshkol 62 per cent (118 of 190); and Eban 62 per cent (107 of 172). Thus, while Syria's behaviour evoked expressions of concern in the pre-crisis period, the crisis from 15 May to 4 June 1967 was dominated by Israel's awareness of Egypt and Nasser as the catalyst and the threat. The qualitative and quantitative findings are identical on this crucial point.

There are several other salient themes in the content-analysis data:

1. Dayan's image of the Near East Core is the most actor-oriented, with almost 30 per cent more codable references to states-cum-leaders than any other decision-maker;

2. Dayan reveals the greatest concentration—over 90 per cent on one actor;

3. Eshkol's distribution of references is the most balanced, with Syria accounting for more than half of the number of references to Egypt; Allon, too, reveals a wider scatter, with Jordan occupying an even more prominent place in his image; and Eban, too, focuses on three actors; in short, Dayan has a single-actor focus, while Eshkol, Allon, and Eban have a three-actor focus;

4. Iraq, Palestine, and Lebanon are marginal in the image oι the group as a whole, another important theme of the qualitative data as well; only Allon mentioned Palestine, and only Eshkol and Eban mentioned Lebanon;

5. Nasser is the only Arab leader to attract widespread attention; and

6. Allon's is the most personalized image, with over 25 per cent of his actor references given to individuals, and all but 2 of these to Nasser. Eshkol is second with 18 per cent—and Eban is at the other extreme, with 9 per cent. The *Ahdut* Minister of Labour was the most leader-conscious among Israel's inner-circle decision-makers.[1]

Eshkol contributed much to the strengthening of *Tzahal*'s capability during his four years as Defence Minister. As a former Cabinet colleague from a competing Labour party acknowledged: 'We should never forget that Eshkol as Premier and Defence Minister readied the army

---

[1] Although Rabin was not a high-policy decision-maker, his advisory role as Chief of Staff gives special interest to his images of the Arabs and the Near East Core. These emerge from his interviews on the eve of the outbreak of the crisis:

Arab world—	'... The cardinal change in the pattern of inter-Arab relations is a process of polarization ... between Egypt, Syria and Iraq ... and ... Saudi Arabia, Jordan and to a certain extent Lebanon. For our purposes I remove the Maghreb countries from the game.'
Arab co-operation against Israel—	'... as long as there is no political co-operation among the Arab countries one should not expect any military co-operation against Israel.'
Egypt—	'Today Egypt's weight has not changed in the Arab world.'
Syria—	'Today the immediate conflict is not with Egypt but with Syria, who is organizing and operating the saboteurs against Israel.'
Possibility of War—	'... there is today more a danger of deterioration as a result of Syrian attempts to drag into war states that do not want it.' Rabin (1).

Four months after the war Rabin asserted that on 15–16 May he took into account the possibility of war. When UNEF withdrew he felt war had become unavoidable. The closing of the Straits he had perceived as a declaration of war. Rabin (3).

for the test of the Six Day War.'[1] As one student of the military observed: 'Eshkol's reign [sic!] was characterized by Zahal's most prosperous growth. . . . [He] failed to pull his weight against the aggrandizement of Zahal and complied with General Rabin's requests for expensive new weapons.'[2] Thus, when the crisis of May 1967 erupted, he was sanguine, as the following remarks illustrate:

22 May: . . . The remarkable capacity of our army . . . has reached a high level today. The Israel Defence Forces are capable today of meeting any test . . . and, knowing the facts as I do, I could say even more.[3]

29 May: Today our army is at the zenith of its strength in manpower, skill, fighting spirit, and military equipment. . . . if the necessity arises, they have the strength to defeat the aggressors. . . . You know better than any, how much our strength has increased in recent years.[4]

Eban's perception of Israel's M was positive—about the future. On 17 May he declared: 'The twentieth year of Israel's existence will be a peak year in the renewal of *Tzahal*'s strength in several types of equipment . . . especially . . . aviation, armour, and navy.'[5] Compared with his colleagues, however, he devoted less attention to this component. When he did so it was largely to explain Israel's arms purchases. Moreover, he was more concerned about the military balance, as the quantitative data will reveal.

Allon, as always, was very optimistic about the outcome of an Arab–Israel war, especially because of her mobilization potential: 'The large and quick mobilization [of *Tzahal* reserves]—this is what saved Israel from a surprise attack and a swift invasion by the Egyptian army.' Yet the situation had changed since 1948 and 1956: 'If, however, war is forced upon us, difficult battles await us. . . . The methods of warfare and its scope have fundamentally changed. . . . [Nevertheless,] I have no shadow of a doubt as to the final outcome, nor the outcome at each stage. . . . It is in our power', he concluded on 2 June, 'not only to check the enemy, but to obliterate him.'[6] For him, too, the quantitative data confirm this image.

Dayan's references to military capability during the crisis were brief and, by design, unclear, especially at his 3 June press conference. Nevertheless, to a question about the duration of a war he replied, simply: 'If a war should break out, I know we will win it; that's the main thing.'[7] Rabin's image, also suffused with optimism, is germane here: 'We have it in our power, not just to check aggression, but also to be decisive over the enemy armies in their own land, all this on

---

[1] Carmel (2).
[2] Perlmutter, p. 106. On Eshkol's tenure as Defence Minister see ibid., ch. VIII.
[3] Eshkol (3), p. 87.   [4] Eshkol (5), pp. 101–2, 103.
[5] Eban (2).   [6] Allon (2).   [7] Dayan (1).

condition that we show patience . . . in awareness, readiness and willingness. . . . They [*Tzahal*] will be able to defeat any enemy. . . .'[1]

That confidence is corroborated by the quantitative data on decision-makers' images of military capability, using the notion of relative military balance.

TABLE 15

DECISION-MAKERS' IMAGES OF ISRAEL'S RELATIVE MILITARY
CAPABILITY: MAY–JUNE 1967

Image of	Allon	Eshkol	Dayan	Eban	Total
Increasing*	80	19	16	0	115
Same†	24	27	28	31	110
Decreasing‡	34	9	8	16	67
Total	138	55	52	47	292

* Increasing—'increasing' for Israel's M, 'decreasing' for enemies' M.

† Same—'same' for both Israel's and enemies' M.

‡ Decreasing—'decreasing' for Israel's M, 'increasing' for enemies' M.

The image balance is heavily weighted to optimism: for all but Eban the references to 'increasing' relative military capability exceed those to 'decreasing' M, in the case of Dayan by 2:1, of Eshkol slightly more, and of Allon still higher. The interpretation of references to 'same' as expressing concern would, of course, shift the weight to disquiet or pessimism. However, the data on 'victory', combined with the many quoted passages, do not indicate concern or pessimism about the result: of the 34 references to 'outcome of a war'—by Dayan (28) and Allon (6)—22 predicted victory and 12, all of them by Dayan, indicated uncertainty—a ratio of almost 2:1.

Apart from optimism, tempered by the caution that it would be a 'slow victory', there are other salient themes in the data:

1. Among the four persons coded, the *Ahdut Ha'avoda* decision-maker devoted the most focused attention to this component, conforming with its philosophy of militant activism; Allon accounts for almost 50 per cent of all references to M, with two and a half times as many references as any of the others;

2. Allon was the most optimistic, Eban the least (though the Foreign Minister's ranking was affected by the heavy weight given to his 19 June 1967 speech to the UN Assembly, which was defensive on the matter of Israel's military power);

3. of the two who predicted victory, Dayan was clearly the more cautious;

[1] Rabin (2).

4. the number of references to an unchanged military balance, almost 40 per cent of the total, suggests some doubt, or at least uncertainty, about the military capability of Israel's adversaries; and

5. three of the four decision-makers perceived a 'high' mobilization potential for Israel—Eshkol 5 references, and Allon and Dayan 4 each; only Dayan perceived his adversaries' potential, 4 references to 'medium'; and the frequency ratio of perceived mobilization potential was 3:1 in favour of Israel, a major source of optimism about the outcome of a war.[1]

The external dimension of the psychological environment is also illuminated by the data on *symbols* and *advocacy*, as articulated by Israel's decision-makers. The quantitative materials indicate a wealth of symbolic imagery—1,361 references to 15 symbols. Allon contributed 43 per cent of the total (584), Eban 25 per cent (338), and Dayan and Eshkol the rest, 236 and 203 references respectively. Two of the symbols, Conflict and Peace, account for almost half of the total; and 5 symbols, attracting almost three-fourths of all references, indicate the stimuli to Israel's 1967 decisions: Conflict (482); Peace (171); Free Navigation (140); Aggression (125); and Defence (81).[2]

Notwithstanding the widespread perception of Eshkol's *hesitancy* during the 1967 crisis, his *advocacy* of Israel's objectives was the model of clarity:

22 May: The *status quo* must be restored on both sides of the border;[3]

---

[1] Economic capability was barely perceived by Israel's decision-makers in the 1967 setting for decision—a total of 21 references, of which Allon accounts for 14, Eshkol 5, and Eban 2. In so far as awareness of this component exists, it is the 'Infrastructure of Israel's economy' (12 references) and 'Israel's economic capability' (7), with 1 reference to 'enemies' economic capability'. There is no greater articulated awareness of the IG component—a total of 22 references in the coded speeches divided as follows: 'religious interest groups' (10); 'Arabs in Israel' (9); and 'public opinion' (3).

[2] Only one other symbol attracted more than 50 references—Security (65). The others ranged from Economic Development (50) to Balance of Power, Friendship, and Danger (20 each); the remainder were Terrorism (45); Victory (44); Independence (43); Violence (29); and Destruction of Israel (26).

Allon's and Dayan's were the most concentrated images: almost half of their references were focused on Conflict. The image of Eban was the most evenly distributed: no symbols attracted more than 20 per cent of his attention; only 2 were not mentioned; and 10 of them received 10 or more references. Apart from his preoccupation with Conflict, Allon's image, too, was evenly distributed among 10 other images. Viewed in total symbolic image terms, Dayan's was the narrowest, with no references to 6 symbols, and less than 10 references to 3 other symbols. Eshkol's image, the least frequent, is distributed relatively evenly among 7 symbols. Apart from the six leading symbols for the group as a whole, the only ones to attract attention were: for Allon, Economic Development, Terrorism, Victory, and Balance of Power; for Eban, Independence, Violence, and Destruction of Israel; for Dayan, Victory; and for Eshkol, Economic Development, Terrorism, and Destruction of Israel.

[3] Eshkol (3), p. 86.

29 May: The Israel Government's statement at the United Nations Assembly on March 1, 1957 still expresses our policy with complete accuracy;[1]

1 June:
(letter to Kosygin) This situation cannot be tolerated.[2]

Eban's public advocacy was virtually identical, with emphasis on the Straits and the massing of Egyptian troops in Sinai: 'The Government and People [of Israel] intend to ensure that these two changes are rescinded, and in the shortest possible time. . . . We will have no part of any suggestion or arrangement which implies that all other ships can go through, but not Israeli ships.'[3] Allon's advocacy, by contrast, was consistent with his militant image generally: 'There are no preconditions for the opening of the Straits. . . . They must be opened to every ship, without any difference of flag or cargo. The aggressive forces must be moved away . . . and . . . the terror activities . . . stopped. If all this is not granted, war will be forced upon us. . . .'[4] And, though Dayan did not specify his goals in the speeches and press conference remarks during the crisis, all other evidence points to his shared image of inevitable war.

The *intensity* of attitude by Israel's decision-makers is illuminated by the quantitative data on advocacy statements. All these were ranked on a seven-point scale, with 7 representing the most militant posture and 1 the most conciliatory point.[5] The *advocacy statement scale* which guided the coding was as follows:

7. The survival of Israel is in jeopardy in the light of Egypt's massing of troops in Sinai; we must take action immediately.
6. We must prevent, at all costs, the closing of the Straits of Tiran.
5. The Western Powers will do nothing; we have no one to rely upon but ourselves.
4. The morale of our people is sagging under the pressure of Arab threats; we must try to restore national self-confidence.

[1] Eshkol (5), p. 101. That 1 March 1957 statement read as follows: 'Interference by armed force with ships of the Israel flag, exercising free and innocent passage in the Gulf of Akaba and through the Straits of Tiran, will be regarded by Israel as an attack entitling it to exercise its inherent right of self-defence under Article 51 of the United Nations Charter and to take all such measures as are necessary to ensure the free and innocent passage of its ships in the Gulf and in the Straits.' UN.GAOR XI, 666th Pl. Mtg., 1 March 1957, pp. 1275–9, paras. 1–48; the extract is from para. 13.
[2] Eshkol (6), p. 49.   [3] Eban (3).   [4] Allon (2).
[5] Several alternative scaling procedures were considered. The Q-Sort method was rejected because of its forced distribution, which did not allow for optimal treatment of the data, given the interest in policy positions as well as intensity of advocacy. The pair-comparison method did not permit comparisons *across* decision-makers. Thus we superimposed on the data an external scale, which neither forces distribution nor eliminates comparison. The 7-point scale was developed from the writer's general knowledge of competing advocacies and was pre-tested for sensitivity. The results should not be considered interval data.

3. We should wait another week to give the maritime states time to organize an international flotilla to pass through the Straits of Tiran.

2. We will lose the sympathy of the world if we act before all efforts at peaceful settlement have been exhausted.

1. We should not strike first; only thus will our just cause win support from governments and peoples—and this will be necessary if we have to act alone.

The results are evident in Tables 16 and 17 and Figure 13.

TABLE 16

DISTRIBUTION OF ADVOCACY OF DECISION-MAKERS,[1] FREQUENCY AND INTENSITY: MAY–EARLY JUNE 1967

INTENSITY		FREQUENCY				
	Scale Point	Allon	Dayan	Eshkol	Eban	Total
Maximum Militancy	7	58	16	7	9	90
	6	18	8	4	9	39
	5	76	0	6	3	85
	4	2	0	3	0	5
	3	0	8	2	0	10
	2	36	4	3	4	47
Minimum Militancy	1	0	0	1	0	1
Total		190	36	26	25	277

TABLE 17

MEDIAN VALUE OF ADVOCACY STATEMENTS BY DECISION-MAKERS: MAY–EARLY JUNE 1967

Dayan	6·3
Eban	6·1
Eshkol	5·2
Allon	4·7
Decision-Makers' Median	5·3

The salient points emerging from the advocacy data are as follows:

(a) The *group as a whole* was *militant* in May–June 1967: 77 per cent of their statements fell above the mid-point, that is, at scale-points 7, 6, and 5; only 21 per cent fell below the mid-point;

[1] All advocacy statements were extracted from the text by two coders. Intercoder agreement was 81 per cent. All statements were then placed on separate cards and the names of all countries, places, and leaders were masked. The statements were then scaled on the advocacy scale developed for this purpose. Intercoder agreement was 84 per cent.

other indicators of high militancy are: the comparative frequency
of statements at the two extremes—90 at point 7, only 1 at
point 1; the clusters at points 7 and 5, each almost double the
largest frequency cluster below the mid-point of the scale, at
point 2;

FIGURE 13
ADVOCACY POSITION OF ISRAELI DECISION-MAKERS:
MAY–JUNE 1967

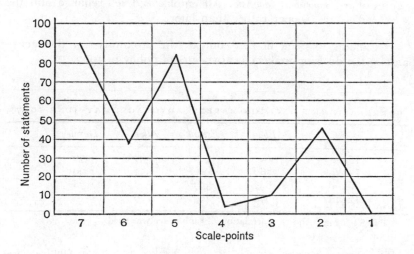

(b) almost one-third of all advocacy statements clustered around point
5, indicating a *self-reliant*, 'Fortress Israel', outlook; it was even
more clustered around the theme of preventive war;

(c) the *only 'doveish' posture* is the call for delay and an exhaustive
search for a peaceful settlement before responding with force—in
order to retain the sympathy of world public opinion (point 2);

(d) *Dayan* was the most militant advocate: two-thirds of his statements
cluster at the upper end of the scale, and he manifests the *highest
militancy* median; however, he made less than one-fifth as many
(recorded) advocacy statements as Allon;

(e) Foreign Minister *Eban* was the second most militant advocate in
1967 but his advocacy is distorted by the heavy reliance on a post-
war UN speech; this does not, however, fundamentally alter the
findings, because his share of the total number of advocacy statements was less than one-tenth;

(*f*) *Eshkol*'s advocacy was the *most evenly distributed*, with statements at all 7 points on the scale, compared with 4 clusters each for Dayan and Eban, and 5 for Allon; and his overall median advocacy was 5·2, well above mid-point;

(*g*) the *Ahdut Ha'avoda* leader, Allon, was *conspicuously the most voluble* advocate during the 1967 crisis, accounting for almost 70 per cent of all advocacy statements; he was also the most moderate, with total concentration at point 2 on the scale, which did not eschew action but only urged the use of all methods of pacific settlement before resorting to war;

(*h*) in short, *none was 'doveish'*. All emphasized self-reliance and the need to act, sooner rather than later.

It remains to note, in this context, the proximity—or distance—among the decision-makers as advocates of policy in 1967.

TABLE 18

CORRELATION OF DECISION-MAKERS' ADVOCACY: MAY–JUNE 1967*

	Eban	*Eshkol*	*Allon*	*Dayan*
Eban	—	·786	·697	·670
Eshkol	·786	—	·357	·429
Allon	·697	·357	—	·170
Dayan	·670	·429	·170	—

* The Spearman Rho (ρ) correlation of rank order was used.

The strongest association is between Eshkol and Eban (·786 correlation and significance at less than the ·05 level), while the weakest is between Allon and Dayan (·170 correlation). Both of these findings conform with other indicators—the mutual respect of Prime Minister and Foreign Minister for each other's role, the rivalry–friction relationship between *Ahdut Ha'avoda* and *Rafi*, and the Allon–Dayan competition within Israel's younger leadership. Eban is the most closely associated with all. The very low correlation between Eshkol and Allon is surprising. The maverick position of Dayan is not: there is *no* significant correlation between his articulated advocacy and that of any other Israeli decision-maker on the 1967 issue.

The combined qualitative and quantitative data suggest the following ranking of image-components in the psychological environment of the four high-policy decision-makers on the 1967 issue:

S   10   the grave threat to Israel posed, first, by the closing of the Tiran Straits and then, even more ominous, by the massing of Egyptian troops in eastern Sinai;

DB	9	pressure for restraint by the US President, combined with US initiative to establish an international naval flotilla to break the blockade; for Dayan only, the other DB relationship, the Soviet Union, was an important image-component;
E	8	the growing strain on the Israel economy as a result of the mobilization of *Tzahal* reserves;
IG	7	the decline of national morale and the increasingly vocal pressure for action by the mass public and pressure groups, notably the Army;
G	6	the swift withdrawal of UNEF by the Secretary-General and the powerless debates in the Security Council, making unilateral action seem inevitable;
B_1	5	the French embargo and de Gaulle's hostility;
B_2	4	British friendliness and apparent willingness to help organize an international flotilla.

An ordinal ranking is misleading: the S and DB components were of overwhelming importance in the decision-makers' images throughout the crisis. The E and IG components became important with the passage of time. All the others were marginal.

(c) and (d) DECISION PROCESS AND IMPLEMENTATION

PRE-DECISIONAL EVENTS

The third Arab–Israel military confrontation began and reached its climax with the suddenness of an elemental force of nature. All actors were surprised by its eruption and velocity. And when that collision was over, on 10 June, most of the preconceived ideas and accepted views about the Near East Core lay in ruins.

The roots of the 1967 crisis are as deep as the Arab–Israel conflict itself, leading to a wide range of speculation about its origins: the beginning of the Zionist idea; the 1957 arrangements following the Sinai Campaign; the 1961 decision of the Arab Defence Council to prevent the completion of Israel's National Water Carrier; and the onset of Soviet patronage for the Syrian regime.[1] All of these are plausible. The *specific* origins of the crisis, however, may be traced to the second half of 1966—to the increasing intransigence of the Syrian *Ba'ath* regime and the escalation of violence on the Syrian and Jordanian borders, directed from Syria and backed by the Soviet Union. As Eban remarked: 'The Six Day War was undoubtedly born in

[1] Respectively Lacouture, Held, Rouleau; Foreign Ministry sources; Gilboa; and Draper. Some of these authors or sources trace the crisis to other periods as well. For a resident diplomat's view of the origins of the 1967 War, see Wilson, ch. vi, esp. pp. 90–8.

Syria.'[1] Yet there were similar situations in the past—even one identical mini-crisis—that passed unnoticed in the outside world.[2]

Several other pre-decisional events contributed to the heightening of tension between Syria and Israel. On 4 November 1966 a Mutual Defence Pact was signed between Syria and Egypt, declaring 'armed aggression against one of them as aggression against both'.[3] The same day the Soviet Union vetoed a mildly-worded Security Council resolution critical of *feda'iyun* infiltration from Syria and the resulting loss of human life.[4] For Syria the Pact ended her isolation in the Arab world, while Soviet support was taken as a permissive signal to escalate activities against Israel. For Israel, on the other hand, the Soviet veto strengthened a feeling of isolation in the world at large:

It was the fifth veto the Russians had cast in Arab–Israeli disputes at the Council, but the double-edged cut of the sword on this occasion was disastrous. If it did not set the course of events for the following months, it at least sharpened their pace. The Syrians took the veto as a green light, a political victory that shielded them from international censure and encouraged them in their Al-Fath warfare. The Israelis saw it as a final demonstration that there was nothing they could hope for from the United Nations. In the absence of international pressure, they would have to rely on their own 'deterrent' of reprisal action.[5]

The reprisal raid of 13 November against the Jordanian village of El-Samū signalled a change in Israeli policy. Planned as a warning to Syria of the danger of continuing to direct *feda'iyun* attacks against Israel via Jordan territory, and to King Hussein to limit guerrilla movement within his domain, it was too effective: internal Jordanian reaction to the inability of the Arab Legion to rebuff the severe *Tzahal* raid endangered Hussein's position and left Syria unscathed. The

---

[1] Interview, 1968.

[2] At the end of 1959 and the beginning of 1960 there was a sharp increase in the exchange of fire on the Syrian–Israeli border, leading to Israeli reprisals. On 1 February 1960 Egypt began to concentrate troops on the Suez Canal: lorry-loads of troops passed through Cairo, reportedly on their way to Sinai. On 15 February Egypt was warned by Soviet intelligence sources that Israel was concentrating a large number of troops on the Syrian border. On the 18th three Egyptian divisions, one armoured, were reported to have been moved into Sinai and to have taken up positions in Gaza, El-Arish, Abu Ageila, and Kutzeima; all troop movements were made, in the only contrast to the situation in May 1967, 'secretly'. After a few days Egypt announced that her troop concentrations had achieved their aim—in deterring Israel from attacking Syria. And on 1 March 1960 Egyptian troops began to return to their bases west of the Suez Canal. This incident appears to have influenced Israeli decision-makers' perceptions during the early days of the 1967 crisis. Gilboa, pp. 22–3; *MER*, 1960, pp. 197–204; and Rabin (4).

[3] Gilboa, p. 72.

[4] *UN Monthly Chronicle*, 3, 11 Dec. 1966, p. 7, Res. S/7575/Rev. 1.

[5] Burdett, p. 174. Ch. 4 of Burdett's book provides an incisive analysis of Russian, Syrian, and Egyptian motives.

subsequent UN censure of Israel on 25 November only encouraged the Syrians to step up border disturbances and *Al Fath* incursions.[1]

Israel's reaction to these incidents was political and diplomatic. On 18 January 1967 she accepted U Thant's invitation to an extraordinary meeting of the Israel–Syria Mixed Armistice Commission (ISMAC), the first in seven years. ISMAC met on 25 and 29 January and on 2 February. A fourth meeting, set for 9 February, was postponed at Syria's request to the 16th; that meeting was postponed, and a new date was never announced. There was serious discussion at the first meeting only; yet it, too, led to no results.[2]

Between 9 January and 2 June 1967 Israel also sent a stream of letters—more than fifteen—to the President of the Security Council, but did not request a Council session.[3] All emphasized the seriousness of the situation. Only one, delivered on 11 May, a few days prior to Independence Day, went further: 'So long as the Syrian Government persists in this policy, the Government of Israel must hold it responsible for all the consequences, and in the face of the continuous Syrian provocation and threats, regards itself as *fully entitled to act in self-defence as circumstances warrant.*'[4] This statement was in line with others by Israeli leaders warning Syria during the period 9–14 May. They followed a resumption of incidents, culminating in the very serious outbreak of 7 April, which escalated from the usual cultivation problem[5] to a major skirmish in which six Syrian Migs were shot down. Syria's reaction to the 7 April incident and the subsequent Israeli warnings was close to panic. Given her instability, it spurred Damascus to further extremism, renewing the call for 'a popular war of liberation' and emphasizing Israel's intention to attack Syria.[6]

---

[1] The Security Council censure motion was passed by 14 to 0; only New Zealand abstained. The resolution mentioned nothing of the *feda'iyun* sabotage incidents and the resulting loss of life which preceded the raid. The operative paragraphs read as follows:

'The Security Council

....

1. *Deplores* the loss of life and heavy damage to property. . . .
2. *Censures* Israel for this large-scale military action in violation of the United Nations Charter and of the General Armistice Agreement between Israel and Jordan;
3. *Emphasizes* to Israel that actions of military reprisal cannot be tolerated and that if they are repeated, the Security Council will have to consider further and more effective steps as envisaged in the Charter to ensure against the repetition of such acts.
4. Requests the Secretary-General to keep the situation under review . . .'
(Resolution S/RES 1228 (1966), November 25 1966).   [2] *MER*, pp. 173–4.

[3] Israel's correspondence may be found in UN.SCOR, 22nd Year, Supplement for 1967.

[4] S/7880—Letter from Permanent Representative of Israel to President of the Security Council (emphasis added). See also note 2, pp. 359–61 below.

[5] For a careful discussion of disputes over cultivation of land in the Israel–Syria Demilitarized Zone from September 1957 to October 1966 see Bar-Yaacov, ch. 6, 9.

[6] Speech of President al-Atassi, 17 April 1967. *Documents on Palestine*, Doc. 301, pp.

Israel's policy in April–May was threefold: to try to persuade the Soviet Union to restrain her client from bellicose actions; to stop infiltration; and to convey verbal warnings to Syria, as a prelude to limited military retaliation. The policy of trying to restrain the Soviet Union, as with Syria, had no practical success. If anything, it had the opposite effect. Russian communiqués to Israel were harsh and menacing in tone.[1] Furthermore, Moscow now put into effect a series of steps, the purpose of which was to stimulate Egyptian militancy and to create a military presence on Israel's southern border, thus easing the pressure on Syria. The first of these acts may have been the sudden and rather mysterious visit of Foreign Minister Gromyko to Cairo from 29 March to 4 April 1967.[2] However, there is no mystery about Soviet warnings of Israeli troop concentrations.[3]

Syria's dramatic defeat in the 7 April encounter compelled Nasser to make some gestures to his allies and to the Arab world. On the 10th the Commander of Egypt's Air Force went to Damascus for five days. On the 17th the Egyptian Prime Minister made the first visit to Syria's capital by a high-ranking Egyptian political leader since 1961. Most important, on the basis of reports of an imminent Israeli attack against Syria, which reached him between 9 and 13 May, Nasser decided to move armour into Sinai. He sent General Fawzi to Damascus to co-ordinate action.

As noted, there was no evidence of Israeli troop concentrations on the Syrian frontier. Yet the *facts* themselves were less important than perception, given the background of tension and Israel's undoubted capacity to organize, at very short notice, a large-scale military reprisal against Syria. What may have triggered Nasser's perception of the threat was a series of public warnings emanating from the highest Israeli sources, including Prime Minister Eshkol. As one high-ranking member of the Israeli élite remarked afterwards, drily: 'There

---

512–16. The instability is evident in the 11 May memorandum of the Syrian *Ba'ath* Party, especially the remarks about Israeli aims:

'4. To smash the morale of the Arab people, especially in Syria, with the object of preventing them from responding to the Syrian revolutionary regime . . .

'8. To cast doubts on the soundness of the Party and its ability, after the liquidation of rightist, hesitant and deviationist pockets from its ranks, to continue its socialist advance and confront the enemies of the nation. This would give rightists, reactionaries and capitalists an opportunity to pounce upon the rising revolutionary regime and to cast suspicion on its principles and strategy.' Ibid., Doc. 308, pp. 527–8.

[1] Foreign Ministry sources.

[2] The mystery of this visit has not yet been cleared up. Most references and comments suggest that its probable purpose was to warn Egypt against further involvements in South Arabia. One source, however, stated that Gromyko would discuss the problems of the UN peacekeeping force in Gaza. *MER*, p. 22. See also Kimche and Bavly, p. 51.

[3] For the ample evidence on this point see p. 321 above, including nn. 2 and 3.

were some who thought that these warnings may have been too frequent and too little co-ordinated. . . . If there had been a little more silence the sum of human wisdom would have remained substantially undiminished.'[1]

There is no doubt that these were part of the usual pattern of Israeli warnings which, if unheeded, would have been followed by reprisal action. And it is reasonable to assume that such a reprisal would have been directed against Syria and would have been on a large scale. Yet at that stage the warnings were intended to deter Syria and her allies from further escalation of tension. And all evidence indicates that, if Syria had heeded them, another period of tension would have passed, as part of the pattern of hostile interaction between Israel and her neighbours.[2]

[1] Eban interview, 1968. As early as 21 May 1967 Ben Gurion and Peres criticized Eshkol and Rabin sharply for their statements, which in the BG–Peres view had awakened the Russian bear from his sleep. Gilboa, p. 124.

[2] *MER* (pp. 179–80, 186–92) is particularly valuable for the empirical data on these warnings, as well as for the evaluation of the context in which they were made in Israel and their effects on the actors concerned. Briefly recapitulated, the Arab (and Soviet) version was that Israel had announced publicly that she would attack Syria with the avowed intent of toppling the Syrian regime. Nasser gave that version in his 22 May speech announcing the closure of the Straits of Tiran, made at an advanced air force base in Sinai (Bir Gafgafa):

'On May 12 the first statement was made. . . . the statement said that the Israeli leaders had announced that they would undertake military operations against Syria to occupy Damascus and bring down the Syrian regime. And on the same day, 12 May, the Prime Minister of Israel, Eshkol, made a very threatening statement against Syria. At the same time the commentators said that Israel thought that Egypt could not make a move because she was tied up in the Yemen.'

Published in *Al-Ahram* (Cairo), on 23 May 1967; the speech was reprinted in *Documents on Palestine*, Doc. 318, p. 538; in Draper, Appendix 9, p. 214; and in Laqueur 1970, Doc. 38, p. 208. A wrong date, 25 May 1967, is given in Laqueur.

'. . . News agencies reported yesterday that these movements [of Egyptian troops into Sinai] must have been the result of a previously well-thought-out plan. I say that it was *the course of events that determined the plan*. We had no plan before May 13 . . .' (emphasis added).

The Syrian version is contained in a statement by a Syrian Foreign Ministry spokesman on the 'Repeated Threats by Israel', on 13 May 1967:

'The representatives in Syria of the countries that are members of the Security Council were summoned to the Foreign Ministry, where it was disclosed to them that imperialist and Zionist circles are engaged in a conspiracy against Syria. . . .'

'The series of threats made by a number of Israelis—Eshkol, Abba Eban, the Israeli Ambassador in Washington, the Israeli representative at the United Nations and certain military men—are intended specifically to prepare world public opinion . . . for the forthcoming Zionist aggression . . . against the Syrian Arab Republic. . . .'

'. . . This conspiracy . . . consists, basically, of a major aggression by Israel on a variety of trumped-up pretexts. . . .'

'The object of the Israeli aggression . . . is the overthrow of the revolutionary regime in this region. This was made perfectly clear in the statements of Rabin. . . .'

The crisis may be divided into five phases:

14–18 May	the period of innocence	(I)
19–22 May	the period of apprehension	(II)
23–28 May	the period of diplomacy	(III)

Published in *Al-Bath* (Damascus), 14 May 1967, reprinted in *Documents on Palestine*, Dec. 309, pp. 529–30.

Valuable sources on the Egyptian version of the origins of the 1967 War and of the three-week crisis as a whole are Heikal, pp. 38–9, 217–34, and Stephens, pp. 436–42, 466ff.

The Soviet understanding of and reaction to Israeli warnings was slightly less extreme. They advanced the curious idea that foreign 'imperialist agents' might be at work to cause trouble between Israel and Syria and they warned Israel not to become an 'imperialist tool' in undermining the Syrian regime. *MER*, p. 180, and Foreign Ministry sources. A quasi-official Soviet interpretation of the 1967 crisis is to be found in Belyayez *et al.*, *passim*. What exactly were the Israeli warnings and threats? The following is a short résumé of statements by Israeli leaders and officials from 9 to 13 May, until which date, according to Nasser, no Egyptian plans had been made.

9 May—'Addressing a meeting of students at the Hebrew University on 9 May, FM Eban warned Syria not to believe that she could send marauders into Israel without risking an Israeli response.' Reported in *Jerusalem Post*, 10 May.

10 May—General Odd Bull was received at the Israeli Foreign Ministry and told that the cultivation of 'controversial' plots of land was no longer the centre of tension; rather, it was *feda'iyun* activity inside Israel. *MER*, p. 179.

'Israeli embassies in the member-states of the Security Council were instructed to draw attention to the gravity of the mounting Syrian attacks.' Ibid. See parallel reaction of Syrian Foreign Ministry above.

'The Israeli Representative at the UN, G. Rafael, met with the Assistant SG of the UN, R. Bunche, and informed him of Israel's attitude towards the worsening situation on the Israeli-Syrian border.' *Ha'aretz*, 12 May; *Jerusalem Post*, 11 May.

11 May—'Addressing a *Mapai* meeting on 11 May, PM Eshkol said that Israel took an extremely grave view of the recent acts of sabotage. ... He warned Syria that Israel might have to take measures "no less drastic than those of 7 April".' BBC, 13 May; *Ha'aretz*, 12 May; *Kol Yisrael*, 11 May.

'Israeli Ambassador to the US, A. Harman, met with the Assistant Secretary of State for the ME, L. Battle [and] ... stressed that Israel could not allow her current situation to continue.' *Ha'aretz*, *Lamerhav*, 14 May.

'The Israeli Representative to the UN, in a letter to the President of the Security Council, stated: "The increasing number and gravity of hostile activities instigated by Syria in recent months demonstrate that the Syrian Government is not prepared to abide by its obligations under the Charter or the General Armistice Agreement. ..."' *MER*, p. 180.

'So long as the Syrian Government persists in this policy, the Government of Israel ... regards itself as fully entitled to act in self-defence as circumstances warrant (S/7880).'

'A briefing was given to foreign military attachés in terms which they understood to augur a major assault in the coming days.' Foreign Ministry sources.

12 May—'The Director-General of the Israeli Foreign Ministry, A. Levavi, met with Soviet Ambassador Chuvakhin at his own request and drew the Ambassador's attention to the situation along the Israeli–Syrian border. Chuvakhin

29 May–4 June   the period of resolution   (IV)

5–10 June   the period of implementation   (V)

A detailed Chronology of Crisis will follow the analysis of each of the first four periods:

(I) *14-18 May: The Period of Innocence*

The Israeli decision process began on 14 May, on the eve of Independence Day: General Yariv, chief of *Tzahal*'s Intelligence Branch,

---

reportedly warned Israel not to be influenced by "Imperialist" policies aimed at weakening the Syrian regime. Levavi stressed that Israel did not concern itself with the nature of the regime in Syria or any other neighbouring country, and was ready to negotiate a settlement of all outstanding differences with any one of them.' *Jerusalem Post, Lamerhav*, 14 May.

'The following UPI dispatch, widely publicized, was probably interpreted as the most serious warning to be issued during the whole period. It was based on a briefing given by an Israeli officer.

"A high Israeli source said today Israel would take limited military action designed to topple the Damascus army regime if Syrian terrorists continue sabotage raids inside Israel. Military observers said such an offensive would fall short of all-out war but would be mounted to deliver a telling blow against the Syrian Government."'

The transcript of the off-the-record briefing shows, according to *MER* (p. 187), that the 'high Israeli source' was neither Eshkol nor Rabin. Furthermore, unlike the UPI version, it does not contain direct threats designed to topple the Syrian regime. But the briefing officer did stress:

(*a*) the connection between the border incidents and the politics of the Damascus regime, whose popular base he described as 'very narrow';

(*b*) his personal opinion that the only sure answer to the problem is a military operation of great size and strength, but he added that not everything that is sure is possible;

(*c*) that Israel needed a warning type of action, but to this there existed alternatives between the extremes of a counter-guerrilla war and 'an all-out invasion of Syria and conquest of Damascus';

(*d*) that the USSR were not going to restrain Syria, and the Western Powers were incapable of doing so; therefore, the Syrians would not change their policy before Israel used force.

13 May—Eshkol in a broadcast and a radio interview, Deputy Minister of Defence Z. Dinstein, and the Minister in charge of Information, Y. Galili, all added their warnings.

The only warning that can be attributed to Chief of Staff Rabin was published in an interview which appeared on the morning of 14 May, in which he compared the Syrian regime unfavourably with the Lebanese and Jordanian governments, which were against sabotage raids, while the Syrians supported them officially. He added: 'Therefore the aim of action against Syria is different from what it ought to be against Jordan and Lebanon.' Rabin later denied the allegation that this was to be a warning for an all-out attack, though an Israeli observer stated later that it could have been interpreted as a warning to overthrow the Syrian regime. Bar-Zohar, p. 24. But all the available evidence indicates that Nasser had made up his mind about the ostentatious move of troops into Sinai by 13 May, as he himself stated on 22 May and repeated again and again in later speeches, if not earlier. Most of the evidence is mentioned in *MER*, pp. 190–1.

informed Rabin of a state of alert in the Egyptian Army. The Chief of
Staff informed Eshkol the next morning, one hour before the *Tzahal*
parade.[1] Eshkol received a further report while attending the annual
Bible Quiz. Then, forgoing a special Independence Day reception
given by Teddy Kollek, the Mayor of Jerusalem, he called Eban,
Herzog, and Rabin to his home for consultations. The first reactive
steps of a routine nature were taken at that meeting. Rabin informed
the group of *Tzahal*'s decision to reinforce its Negev positions with an
armoured brigade—because the Sinai border on 15 May was 'practically naked'.[2] Eban reported that Israel's Washington and London
embassies had confidently been informed that Egypt's moves were
demonstrative only. It was a plausible appraisal and was accepted as
such.

From that consultation came a second routine step: Eban instructed
UN Representative Gideon Rafael to inform Egypt, through the
Secretary-General, that there were no Israeli troop concentrations
threatening Syria and that Syria was plotting to drag Egypt into
hostilities against Israel. 'Israel wants to make it clear to the Government of Egypt that it has no aggressive intentions whatsoever against
any Arab state at all.' Rafael delivered this message immediately to
Under-Secretary Bunche for U Thant and was informed in the
evening that Nasser had received it.[3]

At the end of the first full day of the crisis the Israeli assessment was
that Nasser's manœuvre was political. There was little concern among
the highest decision-makers. Reinforcements were sent to the Sinai
front as a precautionary measure.[4]

At the weekly Cabinet meeting on 16 May Eshkol reported on
Egyptian military movements, while Eban reported on the exchange
between Soviet Ambassador Chuvakhin and the Foreign Ministry a
few days earlier, on 12–13 May.[5] He also noted the appraisal of the
Western Powers that the Egyptian move was demonstrative only and

---

[1] As a conciliatory gesture the 1967 Independence Day parade was, by Cabinet
decision, kept within the limits of armaments in Jerusalem, described by the 1949
Armistice Agreement with Jordan.

[2] Burdett, p. 234. This move is to be distinguished from the partial mobilization,
ordered the next day.

[3] Rafael 1972. He claims he received Eban's message on the morning of 15 May.
The difference in time between New York and Jerusalem in the summer months was
then six hours.

[4] Egyptian troops had crossed into Sinai, with operational orders to be at full alert
there by 6.00 a.m. on 16 May. *MER*, p. 186.

[5] Foreign Ministry sources. The Soviets claimed that the border tension was the
result of problems between Syria and the West. Eban rejected the Soviet allegation
and replied that Israel was convinced the USSR had the power to relieve the tension.
On 12 May the Foreign Ministry had invited Chuvakhin to inspect the northern border
to see for himself that there was no truth to his charge of troop concentrations. He
refused.

that Israel should not panic.[1] The consensus was that Nasser was executing a political stunt, not a military threat. Egypt, with her war in Yemen, 'did not have the capacity of starting a war'; but 'there was always the danger of an unexpected deterioration of the situation';[2] therefore, Israel should prepare for the worst contingency.[3]

After the Cabinet meeting Eshkol and Rabin decided on a partial mobilization of military reserves, effective immediately: it was the first tactical decision in the 1967 crisis.[4] In a sense T_{1a} was a logical result of the Cabinet's consensus to prepare for the worst. However, it was Egyptian troop movements and Rabin's report to Eshkol of the General Staff's 'cautiously-revised estimates'[5] that was the decisive input into the initial tactical decision.

Eshkol's testimony before the *Knesset* Committee on Foreign Affairs and Security referred to the Egyptian troops in Sinai, now about 30,000, with 200 tanks, as more dangerous than a mere demonstrative act. Opposition members demanded direct action against Arab moves. The debate centred on the exact limits of a response.[6] A final internal event during the afternoon of the 16th was a tour by former commanders-in-chief at a *Tzahal* base. There, Moshe Dayan expressed the opinion that the situation was serious and that Nasser would very likely expel the United Nations Emergency Force and close the Straits of Tiran.[7]

At that point external events began to take a serious turn. At 22.00 hours Middle East time, Egyptian Brigadier Mokhtar presented UNEF Commander General Rikhye with a written request (telegram) from the Egyptian Commander-in-Chief that UNEF be withdrawn from its border posts. Orally, he requested withdrawal from the El-Sabha and Sharm-e-Sheikh posts and that UNEF be confined to its camps. Rikhye refused and referred the matter to U Thant.[8]

[1] Nakdimon, p. 20.　　　[2] *MER*, p. 194.　　　[3] Foreign Ministry sources.
[4] All sources (Burdett, p. 235; Draper, p. 75; Gilboa, p. 104; Kimche-Bavly, p. 98; Laqueur 1968, pp. 110–11; *MER*, p. 194; Nakdimon, p. 20) agree that this decision was taken on 16 May. Kimche-Bavly and Laqueur claim it was decided in the morning. Laqueur argues that it was affirmed by the Cabinet. Burdett claims it was taken 'at the end of the day'. Nakdimon contends that it was taken at the meeting between Eshkol and Rabin, which took place between the Cabinet meeting and the *Knesset* Foreign Affairs and Security Committee meeting later in the afternoon. As many people interviewed endorsed Nakdimon's accuracy, his version is accepted. Moreover, the difference in Eshkol's account to the Cabinet and to the *Knesset* Committee later in the day appears to support the Nakdimon version.
[5] This phrase is from Burdett, pp. 234–5.
[6] Eshkol (11); Nakdimon, p. 21.
[7] Lau-Lavie, p. 201; Nakdimon, p. 21. It should be added, however, that Dayan, until that point, shared the prevailing evaluation at the time, that war with Egypt was far away.
[8] Gilboa reported (pp. 108–9) that Nasser sent a liaison officer to General Rikhye the same night to soften the impact of the telegram. The officer explained to Rikhye that Egypt did not actually plan to withdraw the UNEF as a cushioning force

U Thant's extraordinary reaction to the request, decided upon within one hour of its receipt,[1] was to call in Egypt's UN Representative at 18.45 New York time, i.e. 00.45, 17 May, Israel time, and request that Ambassador El-Kony stress to his government that:

If it was the intention of the Government of the United Arab Republic to withdraw the consent which it gave in 1956 for the stationing of UNEF on the territory of the United Arab Republic and in Gaza it was, of course, entitled to do so. . . .

A request by the United Arab Republic authorities for a temporary withdrawal of UNEF from the Armistice Demarcation Line and the International Frontier, or from any parts of them, would be considered by the Secretary-General as tantamount to a request for the complete withdrawal of UNEF from Gaza and Sinai. . . .

On receipt of such a request, the Secretary-General would order the withdrawal of all UNEF troops from Gaza and Sinai, simultaneously informing the General Assembly of what he was doing and why.[2]

U Thant's decision has been widely criticized ever since[3]—for its haste, for the lack of prior consultation with Israel and/or other states involved in the 1956–7 UNEF commitments, and for his over-reaction, that is, *complete* withdrawal, in response to Egypt's request for *partial* withdrawal. It can fairly be stated that, however much he may have been justified in his actions on purely legal–procedural grounds—and serious doubts have been raised about this aspect as well—in substantive terms he could have decided otherwise and more wisely. There is no doubt that his actions contributed to the process of escalation.[4] They were totally unexpected, even by Nasser, and, as some commentators

---

between Israel and Egypt. All it wanted to do, said he, was to stage a modest 'show' before the eyes of the Arab world. Gilboa gives no source, and there is no confirmation from other sources, though most observers felt that the very careful wording of the Egyptian telegram substantiates the 'show' interpretation and that Mokhtar's oral request about the evacuation of Sharm-e-Sheikh was probably unauthorized. Draper, p. 151; *MER*, p. 193; U Thant's 18 May Report; U Thant's 26 June Report.

[1] The one-hour time span for U Thant's decision is given in the timetable of the crisis included in his 26 June report to the General Assembly. He stated that he received Rikhye's cable at 17.30 N.Y.T.; by 18.45 N.Y.T. El-Kony, the Egyptian UN Representative, was in U Thant's office, at the Secretary-General's urgent request, and received from him the above-mentioned communiqué. The report is reprinted in Draper, Appendix 8, pp. 175–213; *Documents on Palestine*, Doc. 226, pp. 211–27; *UN Monthly Chronicle*, IV, 7, July 1967, pp. 135–61.

[2] U Thant's 18 May Report, para. 6, 3. (c).

[3] Besides Brown see Rouleau in Rouleau, Held, Lacouture, pp. 64–8; Wilson, p. 395; Eban in several public statements, including his address to the General Assembly, 19 June 1967. Draper defends U Thant by contending that the fault was in the system, not in the man (pp. 121–9). Laqueur calls his action 'precipitate' but contends that a few more days would have made no difference (Laqueur 1968, p. 104).

[4] Howard and Hunter, pp. 47–9.

note, may have been the catalyst that marked the point of irreversibility of the crisis.[1]

The verdict on U Thant's actions by British Foreign Secretary George Brown sums it up colourfully and to the point:

> To everybody's surprise, and, as I now know, certainly to President Nasser's, the Secretary-General promptly declared the force non-operational preparatory to its removal. I shall never understand how he was advised to come so quickly to this very ill-considered and, I feel absolutely sure, totally unnecessary and unexpected decision. Certainly at that moment, if at no other, the need for a very different character at the head of this vital organization . . . became very apparent. . . . All of this [the need to withdraw] was legalistically true, but wise men, faced with big events whose possible consequences are immeasurable, shouldn't in my view act as though they were working in a solicitor's office conveyancing property.[2]

Nonetheless, by the end of 16 May the idea that Nasser's motives were demonstrative was still accepted by most of Israel's political élite. The Prime Minister and the military were a little more cautious, though still optimistic. The consensus was that Egypt was not in a position to wage war.

Wednesday 17 May marked the beginning of a process of continuous consultations that characterized Israeli behaviour during the crisis. From that day onward there was constant interaction between the Cabinet, its Defence Committee, and the Army chiefs, as well as consultations with the political structure through the *Knesset* Committee on Foreign Affairs and Security. In the external arena, there was a series of reports by Gen. Rikhye to U Thant, at 10.00, 12.30, 14.00 and 15.30 local time: they affirmed that Egyptian forces had reached the Armistice Line between Israel and Egypt. They also told of two demands, from UAR military authorities: for UNEF to withdraw to El-Kuseima camp; and to withdraw the Yugoslav detachment in Sinai within 24 hours, taking up to 48 hours to do so, if necessary.[3]

Internally, there were four meetings that day, interconnected in time and substance. At 11.00 a.m. there was a meeting of the Ministerial Committee on Defence and another immediately afterwards between Eshkol and Rabin. A little later, overlapping with the Ministerial meeting, the *Knesset* Committee on Foreign Affairs and Security went into session. Rabin and Eshkol testified before that body as well. For seven hours thereafter, Rabin, Eshkol and others continued consultations: participating were Eshkol, Eban, and Galili from the Cabinet (Allon was then in the Soviet Union); Herzog and Yaffe from the Prime Minister's Office; Levavi, Bitan, Tekoah, and Lourie from the

---

[1] Draper quotes comments that called the war 'U Thant's War' (p. 127). See also Bar-Zohar, p. 44; Burdett, p. 233.
[2] Brown, p. 136. On the withdrawal of UNEF see also Burns, and Cohen.
[3] Draper, pp. 178–9.

Foreign Ministry; and, from *Tzahal*, apart from Rabin, Weizman and Yariv.[1] No decisions were taken. Militarily, the advice was still tranquil: there was but one Egyptian infantry division on the Negev border, with armoured support in the rear; there was no sign yet of Egyptian preparations for an attack; and Nasser's goals still appeared to be deterrent.[2] Eban asked what help Rabin required from the diplomats. The Chief of Staff replied that he needed time to set up his defence lines in the Negev.[3]

Egypt's request for a *partial* withdrawal of UNEF was also discussed at the meetings of 17 May. Eban referred to Hammarskjöld's commitment in their discussion a decade earlier—on 25 February 1957—when the Secretary-General affirmed that it was UNEF's duty 'to prevent belligerency' in the Straits of Tiran. Moreover, on being asked whether the Force might be withdrawn overnight without giving Israel time to adjust any disturbed military balance, Hammarskjöld was reassuring.[4] Amidst those consultations on 17 May Eban instructed Rafael to bring the Israeli arguments before U Thant. Rafael did so, after learning of the official UN announcement that an Egyptian insistence on UNEF's withdrawal, even partial, would mean pulling out the whole force.[5]

---

[1] Bar-On interview, 1968; Nakdimon, pp. 21–2.

[2] Rabin (3) confirmed this; to him, war was unavoidable only when UNEF evacuated its position, i.e. on 19 May.   [3] Eban interview, 1968.

[4] The Secretary-General's Memorandum also indicated a procedure for the withdrawal of the Force:

'. . . An indicated procedure would be for the Secretary-General to inform the Advisory Committee on the United Nations Emergency Force, which would determine whether the matter should be brought to the attention of the Assembly.'

UN.GAOR (XI), Annexes, Doc. A/3563, submitted by the Secretary-General on 6 Feb. 1957.

The Cabinet was also apprised of a relevant passage in Hammarskjöld's 5 Aug. 1957 private memorandum, as follows:

'. . . Egypt would declare to the United Nations that it would exert all its sovereign rights with regard to the troops on the basis of a good faith interpretation of the tasks of the force. The United Nations should make a reciprocal commitment to maintain the force as long as the task was not completed. If such a dual statement was introduced in an agreement between the parties, it would be obvious that the procedure in case of a request from Egypt for the withdrawal of UNEF would be as follows. The matter would at once be brought before the General Assembly. If the General Assembly found that the task was completed, everything would be all right. If they found that the task was not completed and Egypt, all the same, maintained its stand and enforced the withdrawal, Egypt would break the agreement with the United Nations. . . .'

Draper, Appendix 3, p. 146. Obviously U Thant's statement to El-Kony on 16 May 1967 (p. 364 above) was a serious blunder, of potentially explosive proportions, which was exploited to the full. Those assurances, according to Eban, were important inputs into Israel's decision to withdraw from Sinai in 1957. Interview, 1968.

[5] Rafael's version of the conversation with Bunche emphasized the 1957 commit-

There were two other noteworthy diplomatic events on the 17th. At 16.00 hours New York time U Thant held an informal consultation with representatives of those countries that had UNEF contingents. Opinions were divided. Yugoslavia and India supported U Thant's actions in response to any potential Egyptian request, while Canada and Brazil proposed to bring the matter before the General Assembly. At 17.50 U Thant handed Ambassador El-Kony two *aides-mémoire*. One reaffirmed the UN spokesman's noon announcement and the gist of the 16 May conversation, while the second reminded Egypt of the 'good faith' memorandum in response to the General Assembly's November 1956 resolution regarding UNEF.[1]

Thursday 18 May was hectic, both internally and externally. On the domestic front it began with two meetings. At the first Eshkol met Eban, Yariv, and other *Tzahal* officers at the Prime Minister's Tel Aviv Office.[2] Although the Intelligence assessments had begun to change, the consensus was that war was a possibility but a remote one. Later in the morning Eban called in the Ambassadors of the US, Britain, and France and expressed Israel's objections to the removal of UNEF, emphasizing that this would lead to a change in the *status quo* in the region, which would have serious implications. The Foreign Minister also re-emphasized the 1957 UN commitment.[3]

Externally, UNEF ceased to function, *de facto*. In five messages to U Thant, General Rikhye reported that, in the early morning and at 13.00, 14.10, and 14.20, UNEF troops were forced out of their camps and posts by UAR forces, including the camp and post at Sharm-e-Sheikh and Ras Nasrani. At 17.00 hours New York time U Thant convened the Advisory Committee of UNEF and three other members with contingents in the Force. The differences of opinion still remained, but U Thant informed the Committee of a *fait accompli*: 'that he intended to reply promptly to the United Arab Republic and to report to the General Assembly and to the Security Council on the action he had taken . . .'.[4] About two hours later, at 19.00 hours New York time, 1.00 a.m. on the 19th, Israel time, he handed a letter to the Egyptian Ambassador accepting Cairo's official demand.

In Israel there were three important afternoon meetings on the 18th. Mrs. Meir warned Alignment leaders that 'war might be nearer than expected'. *Mapam*'s Political Committee called for all possible measures to prevent the situation deteriorating into a state of war. And in the evening *Gahal* decided that more information was required in order to

ments, as Eban instructed. Eban also instructed Rafael on 17 May to suggest the idea of U Thant's visit to the region. Foreign Ministry sources. According to his account Rafael did not present the idea—to the US Delegation—until 19 May.

[1] *MER*, p. 193.   [2] Nakdimon, p. 23.   [3] Ibid.; *MER*, p. 194.
[4] 26 June Report; Draper, pp. 183-4. On the withdrawal of UNEF see Burns, and Cohen.

plan strategy for the 22 May opening of the *Knesset*'s summer session. Begin agreed to speak to the Prime Minister.[1] All three meetings revealed increasing concern but, as yet, no alarm. In the late evening Eshkol and Rabin met to review the situation and were alarmed by the report that U Thant was about to order UNEF's withdrawal.

The 18th also witnessed the beginning of the first exchange of letters between Eshkol and President Johnson, another sign of the increasing stress in the perceptions of high-policy decision-makers all over the world. In his 17 May letter, which Eshkol received the following day, Johnson demanded restraint and prior consultations with the US about further Israeli moves:[2] 'I cannot accept any responsibility on behalf of the United States', he wrote, 'for situations which arise as the result of actions on which we are not consulted.' Eshkol's answer, sent the same day, indicated Israel's grave concern about the possible blockade of the Tiran Straits and asked that the US clarify its position in the conflict, in view of the Arab claim that the USSR identifies herself with them.[3] According to some reports Johnson acted upon receipt of this letter and sought urgent contact with Premier Kosygin (19 May) to co-ordinate diplomatic action, before the situation got out of control. In his reply Kosygin declared that the Soviet Union was firmly interested in preserving the peace.[4]

TABLE 19

CHRONOLOGY OF CRISIS: I

The Period of Innocence: 14–18 May 1967

TIME*	EXTERNAL EVENTS	INTERNAL EVENTS
	Sunday 14 May	
14.30	Egyptian Army alert and marching orders. Gen. Fawzi to Damascus	
Evening		Gen. Yariv informs CoS Rabin of Egyptian Army alert.
	Monday 15 May	
Daytime	One Egyptian Division, mostly armour, moves through Cairo to Sinai. Egyptian planes land at Sinai forward bases.	
a.m.		One hour prior to *Tzahal* parade, Rabin informs Eshkol of Egyptian alert and movements.

* Israel time, except when noted otherwise.
[1] Nakdimon, pp. 24–5.   [2] Johnson, p. 290; and Foreign Ministry sources.
[3] Gilboa, p. 145.   [4] *MER*, pp. 194, 196.

TIME	EXTERNAL EVENTS	INTERNAL EVENTS
Early p.m.		Eshkol at Bible Quiz receives further report from Rabin.
Later p.m.		Eshkol holds special consultation at Jerusalem home. Present are Eban, Herzog, CoS Rabin. Decision to send reinforcements to Negev. Eban orders UN Representative Rafael to inform Egypt through U Thant that Israel poses no threat to Syria.
	Tuesday 16 May	
a.m.		Cabinet meeting.
a.m.		Eshkol meets Rabin.
11.00		Partial mobilization order.
p.m.		Tour of former *Tzahal* Chiefs of Staff at airbase. Dayan predicts Nasser will close Straits.
Later p.m.		Meeting of *Knesset* Comm. on For. Aff. and Security. Opposition demand Govt. action. Eshkol perceives serious situation.
22.00	Brig. Mokhtar, Egyptian Army, presents telegram from FM Fawzi to UNEF Commander to withdraw UNEF forces immediately from border posts.	
17.30 (NYT)	U Thant informed by UNEF Commander, Gen Rikhye.	
18.45 (NYT)	U Thant meets UAR Ambassador El-Kony.	
	Wednesday 17 May	
11.00		Meeting of Ministerial Comm. on Def. Eshkol and Rabin meet as well.
12.00 noon		Meeting of *Knesset* Comm. on For. Aff. and Sec.
12.30	UNEF Commander reports Egyptian troops occupy El-Sabha post and UNEF camps	

TABLE 19 (CONT.)

TIME	EXTERNAL EVENTS	INTERNAL EVENTS
	at El-Kuseima and El-Sabha behind UAR positions. UAR Liaison Chief requests UNEF withdrawal to El-Kuseima camp. UNEF replies that authorization of UN Sec. Gen. required.	
p.m.		Eshkol, Rabin, and others hold 7-hour consultation at PM's Tel Aviv Office.
14.00	Fawzi requests Rikhye to withdraw Yugoslav detachment in Sinai within 24 hours, 48 hours if necessary.	
a.m. (NYT)	UN spokesman announces publicly that an Egyptian insistence on UNEF withdrawal, even partial, would lead to pulling out of entire force.	
12.00 noon (NYT)	Rafael hears UN announcement. Immediately sees Bunche, on Eban's instructions.	
16.00 (NYT)	U Thant holds informal consultation with reps. of states having contingents in UNEF.	
17.50 (NYT)	U Thant meets UAR Amb. El-Kony, hands him *aide-mémoire*.	

Thursday 18 May

TIME	EXTERNAL EVENTS	INTERNAL EVENTS
a.m.		Meeting of PM, Eban, Yariv, and other *Tzahal* officers at Eshkol's Tel Aviv Office.
Late a.m.		Eban calls in Western Powers' Ambassadors.
p.m.		Eshkol sends answer to letter of President Johnson, received on that day; asks for public support of Israel.
a.m.	UNEF sentries prevented from entering El-Sabha post by UAR troops. UNEF to withdraw guard.	
13.00–14.20	UAR troops force UNEF out of El-Kuntilla, El-Ams camps.	

TABLE 19 (CONT.)

TIME	EXTERNAL EVENTS	INTERNAL EVENTS
	UAR officers inform UNEF at Sharm-e-Sheikh that they have come to take camp and post at Ras Nasrani.	
12.00 (NYT)	U Thant gives El-Kony formal notification of decision to terminate UNEF presence.	
17.00 (NYT)	U Thant meets with UNEF Advisory Committee, hands it *fait accompli*.	
19.00 (NYT)	U Thant hands El-Kony message agreeing to UNEF withdrawal.	
p.m.		Meeting of Alignment leadership. Mrs. Meir warns that war nearer than expected.
Late evening		Eshkol and Rabin meet to discuss news that U Thant about to order UNEF withdrawal.

(II) *19–22 May: The Period of Apprehension*

Friday 19 May was the day when concern gave way to apprehension about the future: Israel's decision-makers became convinced that the security situation was taking a sharp turn for the worse. The result was the onset of deliberations about suitable action in the face of a perceived threat.

In the morning Eshkol and Rabin reviewed the situation with the Defence Ministry's Department Heads. Plans against air attacks were examined and steps were taken to speed delivery of equipment ordered from Europe. Meanwhile, Israeli Intelligence reported a further build-up of UAR positions: (1) over-flights of Israeli territory by Egyptian Migs for reconnaissance purposes; (2) more than 40,000 Egyptian troops and 500 tanks in Sinai; and (3) an infantry brigade and two armoured battalions at Port Suez, newly arrived from Yemen, immediately dispatched to Sinai. The last was especially disturbing to Eshkol: with UNEF in the process of liquidation it indicated that Nasser had upset the equilibrium of a decade. The renewal of a blockade of the Straits of Tiran had also now become a possibility. This, together with the arrival of troops from Yemen, were the decisive inputs into Tactical Decision 2 (b) taken by Eshkol and Rabin on Friday afternoon,

19 May: a large-scale mobilization of reserves to be implemented immediately.[1]

While Eshkol and Rabin were directing matters at the Defence Ministry, Eban and his aides were at work on the diplomatic front. At a meeting with Soviet Ambassador Chuvakhin, the Foreign Minister pointed out that UAR troops were dug in right up to the Israel border. Even the UN had affirmed that the allegations against Israel were incorrect, he observed; therefore, the Egyptian excuse was without foundation. Israel was confronted with three problems, said Eban: (1) troop concentrations in Sinai; (2) Egypt's expulsion of UNEF; and (3) Syrian incitement to intensify a 'people's war'. He suggested 'a reciprocal de-escalation of troops in the south' and requested Soviet co-operation to this end. 'There will not be war', he declared, 'unless the Egyptians attack our territory or violate our rights of free navigation.' Chuvakhin replied that 'the cause of the present situation lay in the aggressive propaganda of the Government of Israel and especially the speeches of its leaders against Arab States, notably Syria'. He said that 'history would pass judgement on Israel for having played with fire'.[2]

Israel now proceeded to warn the Western Powers about the implications of a renewed Egyptian blockade of the Straits. Eshkol cabled to de Gaulle: 'Israel on her part will not initiate hostile acts: but she is firmly resolved to defend her territory and her international rights. Our decision is that . . . we will not take action against Egyptian forces at Sharm-e-Sheikh—until or unless they close the Straits of Tiran to free navigation by Israel.' At the same time Eban sent a note to French Foreign Minister Couve de Murville, recalling that, 'in previous discussions, the United States and France had confirmed the text' of Meir's 1 March 1957 statement to the General Assembly 'and had identified themselves with it'. He emphasized that Israeli policy remained unchanged and that the 'decision to execute it is solid and unreserved'.[3] He also cabled British Foreign Secretary George Brown, reminding him of Israel's March 1957 statement, adding that Israel would not tolerate the cancellation 'of a decade of free passage' and that 'we will never return to a blockaded position, cut-off from our friends and trading partners in Africa and Asia'. The validity of the March 1957 policy was also communicated to all the maritime states which had endorsed it at the time.[4]

[1] Burdett, pp. 235–7; Draper, p. 75; Foreign Ministry sources; Laqueur 1968, pp. 119–20; Nakdimon, p. 25. The troops from Yemen were also noted by Eshkol as the decisive input, in his 4 Oct. 1967 interview; Eshkol (11).

[2] Foreign Ministry sources. See also Nakdimon, p. 25; and St. John. The author of this biography of Eban states in an author's note that, while the book is not authorized or commissioned, Eban 'did make available his archives and files, without restriction . . .' (p. 413).

[3] Foreign Ministry sources.   [4] Foreign Ministry sources; Nakdimon, p. 25.

Eban also instructed Rafael to explore with U Thant any possibility of salvaging UNEF. Rafael did so at 11.30 a.m. New York time, but without success. One and a half hours before his visit, at 10.00 a.m., i.e. 16.00 Israel time, UNEF wound up its observation posts in Gaza. These were occupied by UAR Palestinian troops.[1] After his meeting with the Secretary-General, Rafael saw US Ambassador Goldberg and suggested the idea of a visit by U Thant to the area. Goldberg passed it on to U Thant who accepted it. The Egyptians asked that he await an invitation.

With the onset of Saturday 20 May the situation was perceived by Israeli decision-makers as increasingly serious: two armies began to face each other directly along Israel's southern border. Eshkol and Rabin toured *Tzahal*'s positions along the southern front. Intelligence reports indicated further Egyptian troop movements in Sinai; and Egyptian paratroopers were dropped at Sharm-e-Sheikh. Egyptian naval units also passed through the Suez Canal en route to Sharm-e-Sheikh. At 7 o'clock, Saturday evening, Dayan telephoned Eshkol's Military Secretary, Yisrael Lior, and requested permission to tour *Tzahal*'s southern units to see things at first hand. The request was granted.[2]

On Sunday 21 May at 7.30 a.m. Eshkol and Rabin met in the Prime Minister's Jerusalem Office for a quick review of the situation. At the Cabinet meeting, immediately afterwards, Rabin reported on Egyptian troop concentrations, which reportedly had reached about 80,000. Prime Minister Eshkol read out the texts of the 19 May Israeli notes to the Western Powers. Both he and Eban expressed optimism that international pressures at that stage would prevent a further deterioration of the situation, i.e. to a blockade of the Straits. A majority of the Cabinet agreed with these assessments, with Carmel a vocal dissenter.[3]

During the week-end the first reactions to Israel's expressions of concern began to arrive, most of them disconcerting. US and British spokesmen urged that the situation be handled within the UN, while their governments seek restraint by all parties. The idea of stationing UN forces on both sides of the border was aired. It was also suggested by London and Washington that Israel should not open hostilities, even after Egyptian troops occupied the entrance posts to the Straits (Ras Nasrani, Sharm-e-Sheikh), but should await a prior act by the UAR. This was accepted by Israel (on the 20th of May, a cargo ship passed through the Straits unmolested). The French Government did not react officially until several days later. Most disquieting were the

---

[1] *MER*, p. 104; Rafael 1972 account.

[2] Nakdimon, p. 27.

[3] Laqueur 1968, p. 121; Nakdimon, p. 28. Most of the people interviewed affirmed Carmel's hawkishness from the beginning.

British and French statements that they no longer felt bound by the Tripartite Declaration of 1950.

The only encouraging sign was contained in a letter from Prime Minister Wilson to Eshkol: 'If it appeared that any attempt to interfere with the passage of ships through the waterway was likely to be made, we should *promote* and support international action through the United Nations to secure free passage.' Wilson never wavered from his open and avowed support of Israel's right to free passage, and the UK became the initiator of an international flotilla to open the Straits. Yet active support for the flotilla evaporated quickly under the pressure of events; by the end of May only Holland was still openly committed to support such a move. Nevertheless, Wilson's sympathy with Israel's plight (in sharp contrast to de Gaulle's cynical disregard of the dangers facing the small state) was of psychological value to some of Israel's decision-makers in their hour of trial.[1]

Monday 22 May centred on the opening of the *Knesset* summer session. Under the influence of Herzog a mild speech was drafted so 'that nothing should be said that might be seen as inflaming Nasser, lest in the future the world hold Israel responsible for overreacting . . .'.[2] Eshkol's address had three basic themes: (1) return to the *status quo* 'on both sides of the border'; (2) 'international influence to ensure continuation of the quiet . . .'; and (3) an assurance to Egypt and Syria that Israel harboured no aggressive designs.[3]

The speech was followed by a *Rafi* motion, moved by Ben Gurion, to transfer the debate to the *Knesset* Committee on Foreign Affairs and Security. A harsh exchange of words followed between Meir and Ben Gurion.[4] With the *Ma'arakh* establishment and *Gahal* both agreeing that the debate should be open, it was resumed before the full house. That day also witnessed the first suggestions for the formation of a national unity government: Rafael of the NRP broached the idea to *Herut*'s Begin and *Rafi*'s Peres in the corridors of the *Knesset*. They

---

[1] The full passage reads as follows:
'I am on public record as saying that the Straits of Tiran constitute an international waterway which should remain open to the ships of all nations. If it appeared that any attempt to interfere with the passage of ships through the waterway was likely to be made, we should promote and support international action through the United Nations to secure free passage. We stand by this statement. We think it important however that attention should be concentrated on free passage and not on the shore positions. If we are to give you the international support we wish, it must be based on your undoubted rights.' Foreign Ministry sources.

[2] Burdett, p. 237.

[3] This speech was analysed in the psychological environment, pp. 337–8 above.

[4] Of the *Ma'arakh*, Eban, Sapir, Aron, Aram, and Fisher were willing to accept BG's motion. On the other hand Meir, Y. S. Shapiro, M. Carmel, Y. Yeshayahu, and MKs Dinstein, Eliav, and Zadok rejected it, fearing BG would use the Committee as a platform to attack Eshkol and the Government. Yitzhak Rafael of the NRP was willing to accept the suggestion only if the coalition partners agreed.

appeared interested and requested a letter inviting them to join the Government's deliberations. Rafael also spoke to *Mapam* leader Hazan, while Y. S. Ben-Meir, also of the NRP, suggested the idea to the Liberals' Yosef Saphir.[1]

In Washington, Ambassador Harman met with Assistant Secretary of State Lucius Battle and told him that the US position was an invitation to Nasser to interfere with free passage in the Straits. A second letter from President Johnson to Eshkol was worded very cautiously and eschewed a public statement in support of Israel's security: it spoke of '*supporting suitable measures* in and outside the United Nations'.[2] In New York Rafael met with U Thant prior to his departure for Cairo and handed him a letter from Eban, which emphasized the seriousness of the situation and the danger to the Straits. Rafael then went to see Goldberg to ascertain what steps the US was taking in the crisis.[3] The day ended with a major escalation. After midnight Cairo Radio broadcast Nasser's Bir Gafgafa speech in which he announced the closure of the Straits of Tiran to Israeli flagships, as well as to passage of all strategic materials.[4]

TABLE 20
CHRONOLOGY OF CRISIS: II
The Period of Apprehension: 19–22 May 1967

TIME	EXTERNAL EVENTS	INTERNAL EVENTS
	Friday 19 May	
8.00		President Shazar leaves for Expo 67 in Montreal.
a.m. and p.m.		Meetings at Min. of Def. between Eshkol, Rabin, and Dept. Heads. $T_1(b)$—Major Mobilization.

[1] Nakdimon, pp. 34–5, 41–2.
[2] Foreign Ministry sources (emphasis added).
[3] Rafael 1972.
[4] The text is in Draper, Appendix 9, pp. 214–20. See also n. 2, p. 359, above. The Egyptian decision appears to have been taken on the 21st, according to the following unpublished report by a knowledgeable source. Nasser's perceptions leading to his decision to close the Straits are laid bare.

'On 21 May Nasser assembled his Vice-Presidents with the Prime Minister, the Foreign Office chiefs, and the military leaders, in order to appraise the situation. Nasser expressed the view that Israel would not fight since she had no allies; was afraid of the Soviet Union; understood that the United States was involved in Vietnam; and that the numbers in the General Assembly and Security Council were in favour of the Arabs. He also noted the internal division and rivalries in Israel. He pointed out that only five per cent of Israel's foreign trade went through Eilat. He also observed the reserved attitude of France towards Israel's interests at Sharm-e-Sheikh.' Foreign Ministry sources.

TABLE 20 (CONT.)

TIME	EXTERNAL EVENTS	INTERNAL EVENTS
Later a.m.		Eban meets Soviet Amb. Also informs maritime powers of implications of UNEF withdrawal and that any blockade of Straits would not be tolerated.
16.00	UNEF operation terminated. Observation posts occupied by UAR Palestinian troops.	
11.30 (NYT)	Rafael meets with U Thant re UNEF withdrawal.	
p.m.	Rafael suggests U Thant Middle East visit to US Amb. Goldberg.	
Saturday 20 May		
a.m.		Eshkol and Rabin tour *Tzahal* units in south.
Daytime	UAR paratroops dropped at Sharm-e-Sheikh. Egyptian naval units pass through Suez Canal en route to Sharm.	
19.00		Dayan 'phones to request permission to tour *Tzahal*'s southern units; request granted.
Sunday 21 May		
7.30 a.m.		Eshkol and Rabin meet in PM's Jerusalem office.
a.m.		Weekly Cabinet session. Rabin reports on UAR troop concentrations; Eshkol gives texts of notes to Powers; Cabinet optimistic.
Monday 22 May		
p.m.		Opening of *Knesset* summer session; Eshkol speech; rejection of BG motion; first spontaneous consultations on national unity government idea.
a.m.–p.m. (NYT)	Harman meets with Assistant Sec. Lucius Battle re US stand.	

TABLE 20 (CONT.)

TIME	EXTERNAL EVENTS	INTERNAL EVENTS
	Letter from Pres. Johnson to Eshkol; wording is cautious. Rafael meets U Thant prior to his departure for Cairo; stresses seriousness of situation. Rafael then meets Amb. Goldberg to ascertain US position.	
After midnight	Nasser's Bir Gafgafa speech announcing blockade of Straits against Israeli shipping.	

(III) *23–28 May: The Period of Diplomacy*

On Tuesday 23 May at 4.30 in the morning Rabin informed Eshkol by telephone of Nasser's blockade speech. By 5.00 Eban was notified. The Prime Minister immediately called Herzog and Yaffe to his home for consultations. An hour later Eban summoned some Foreign Office *Hanhala* (Directorate) members to an emergency meeting; they included Michael Comay, Moshe Bitan, and Moshe Raviv, Head of Eban's Bureau. After preliminary discussions both groups set out for Tel Aviv. En route, Herzog's suggestion to Eshkol that Opposition leaders be called in for consultations was accepted. But Eshkol insisted on the prior approval of Meir, then *Mapai*'s Secretary-General.[1] On arrival in Tel Aviv, David Hacohen, Chairman of the *Knesset*'s Committee on Foreign Affairs and Security, was requested to invite *Gahal* and *Rafi* members of the Committee to the deliberations of the Ministerial Committee on Defence. They were flown to Tel Aviv— Begin, Ben-Eliezer, Landau, Serlin, and Rimalt from *Gahal*, Peres and Almogi of *Rafi*, and Hacohen; and at about 9.00 a.m. they joined the Cabinet ministers and others already in session. Unnoticed at the time, Begin asked Peres if Ben Gurion was willing and able to serve as Prime Minister of a national unity government. Peres replied that BG could do so but was unwilling. The discussion was left open.[2]

Present at the enlarged Ministerial Committee on Defence were: Eshkol, Eban, Galili, Aranne, and Sapir of the *Ma'arakh*; Moshe Haim Shapira and Warhaftig of the NRP (*Mafdal*); Meir and Shaul Avigur

---

[1] Burdett, p. 244; *MER*, p. 196; Nakdimon, pp. 43–6. Parenthetically, the period from 23 May onwards is an excellent example of the participation of various organs of the political structure in a foreign policy decision process: Party Secretariat; Political Committee; Caucus; Central Committee; *Knesset* Committee on Foreign Affairs and Security, etc. For other illustrations of the political structure in foreign policy decision-making see Brecher, ch. 16 (*b*) and (*c*).

[2] Begin (1); Foreign Ministry sources; Nakdimon, p. 47.

of the *Mapai* establishment; Rabin, Weizman, and Yariv of *Tzahal*; Barzilai of *Mapam*; and, as noted, Hacohen and Opposition members of the *Knesset* Committee on Foreign Affairs and Security. The Chief of Staff began by reviewing the military situation. Rabin also pointed out that it was not feasible to expel the Egyptians from Sharm-e-Sheikh alone; such action would be tactically unsound. A possible alternative would be to attack Egypt's air force, occupy the Gaza Strip, and wait. He did not commit himself about the scale of Israeli losses. In reply to Eban's question whether anything would be lost by a few days' delay in military action, there was no negative answer. It is now clear that, at the meeting of 23 May, there was *no military pressure* for immediate action and that accounts reporting this are not well founded.[1] Indeed, Eban carried the day, with his lucid exposition of arguments for diplomatic action, reinforced later in the afternoon by President Johnson's demand for a 48-hour delay and prior consultation with the United States.

Eban contended that Israel should make every effort to secure American understanding and, in any event, to avoid isolation. The Soviets had played an important role in creating the crisis, and their intentions should be explored through the United States. He informed the meeting of American moves—conveyed to Israeli diplomats by Eugene Rostow —in Egypt, Syria and Russia, stressing freedom of navigation in the Straits and urging de-escalation of the crisis. Then he read out a cable from Evron containing a formal request by Johnson to delay any action for the next 48 hours. The President again warned that he would take no responsibility for actions on which he was not consulted. The respite thus granted could be put to good use to test Great Power commitments given in the wake of the Sinai Campaign.[2] These commitments, he noted, were as follows:

[1] For a detailed account by the then Foreign Minister of the events and decisions of 23 May, especially the absence of pressure for immediate military action by Generals Rabin, Weizman, and Yariv, and the decision to delay for 48 hours all decisions about military action, see Eban 1973 (2).

[2] Foreign Ministry sources; Nakdimon, pp. 47–51. Rabin (3) contended that he saw the closure of the Straits as 'a declaration of war'. In Rabin 1972 he reaffirmed this: '. . . from the moment that the blockade was imposed, it was an act of belligerency against Israel and she was compelled to fight'. Yet all observers and participants agree that he did *not* propose war at this or a later stage. His motives may have been a strict constitutional interpretation of the role a Chief of Staff has to play in a democracy, which would fit in with his ideological *Palmah* background. One Cabinet member who participated in the debates of May–June 1967 was, as noted earlier, quoted: 'Why! even the Chief of Staff never called expressly for war! He pointed out all the possibilities to us, the comparative strength of the forces, and he did say that we could win—but he never put pressure on us to open hostilities.' Golan, p. 7. This was reconfirmed by default in Rabin 1972. Others, especially Weizman, were less reticent, as will be noted. Foreign Ministry sources.

MER also mentions nothing of military or Cabinet pressure at that juncture (p. 196). Nakdimon wrote that the *Tzahal* élite agreed to delay as it was still advantageous

(a) The Dulles 11 February 1957 *aide-mémoire*:

'. . . the United States believes that the Gulf comprehends international waters and that no nation has the right to prevent free
and innocent passage in the Gulf and through the Straits giving
access thereto . . .'[1]

(b) Meir's 1 March 1957 withdrawal speech before the United Nations
General Assembly, which was drawn up after assurances of free
passage had been received from the United States, France, Britain,
and Canada. Every word of that speech was concerted in advance
with Dulles.[2]

Eban then summarized his case by giving four reasons for an intensive
political effort: (1) to ensure arms aid when war came; (2) to retain
the fruits of victory; (3) to compel fulfilment of pledges by friendly
states; and (4) to mobilize international opposition to Nasser.[3]

In the informal discussions, there were hints by Opposition members
that they were interested in a 'collective carrying of the burden'. And
Eshkol, in welcoming them to the meeting, said he was interested in
'*breite pleitzes*' (Yiddish for 'broad shoulders'). Some party leaders, like
Aranne, questioned the idea of sending the Foreign Minister to
Washington, as they perceived in him a pro-US bias: he could be
pressed by Johnson, they feared, limiting Israel's freedom of action.
Meir emphasized the need to ascertain France's attitude, for Israel

---

to them (p. 49). On the other hand, Laqueur 1968 stated that the military argued
'that immediate action had become imperative' (p. 124). Draper asserted that 'the
Israeli Government rejected the plea of its military command for immediate action'
(p. 88). Burdett (p. 245) wrote that 'The General Staff was for immediate war—
Rabin; ... Weizman; ... Yariv ... the generals warned against the dangers of
delay ... her military deterrent would lose its credit; indeed the *casus belli* itself would
lose its edge and urgency if it went unresisted and unchallenged.' The Kimche–
Bavly account (p. 101) is closer to Nakdimon. They wrote that 'the mobilization of
reserves was still not complete. The army could well use the additional time.' Gilboa
(p. 127) wrote that '... the Prime Minister, the Chief of Staff and the head of the
operations staff, *Aluf* Ezer Weizman, claimed that there is place to exploit all political
opportunities in order to assure international understanding. ...'
Bitan drew a political and military spectrum, as follows:

    Eban ————————————Carmel
         caution   action
    Rabin————————————Weizman, Yariv
         caution   action

He also stated that the phase of growing army pressure was 24–28 May, not the 23rd.
Interview, 1968. There was a split in army ranks. This is further affirmed by Rabin's
statements to Golan, loc. cit., and in Rabin 1972. In reply to Golan's question, 'Was
the evaluation of these *alufim* [Weizman, Yariv, Bar-Lev] different from yours?'
Rabin replied: 'I prefer that you ask them.'

[1] Draper, Appendix 1, p. 138.
[2] See pp. 299–301, inc. notes, and 372 above; also Eban 1972.
[3] Foreign Ministry sources.

would be fighting with French arms.[1] A suggestion was also circulated that an unofficial envoy, like Meir, be sent: such an envoy could press for clarifications without committing the government officially. Meir rejected this, as did Eban. Dayan, who joined the meeting late from his tour of the south, also expressed himself in favour of acceding to the US request for a short respite, though he warned against an official commitment to the principle of prior consultations. This warning was seconded by Peres.

The diplomatic argument prevailed: a formal decision—Tactical Decision 2 (a)—was approved without dissent. It read:

1. The blockade is an act of aggression against Israel.
2. Any decision on action is postponed for 48 hours, during which time the Foreign Minister will explore the position of the United States.
3. The Prime Minister and Foreign Minister are empowered to decide, should they see fit, on a journey by the Foreign Minister to Washington to meet President Johnson.[2]

After the 23 May Ministerial Defence Committee meeting and further consultations with the General Staff, Rabin was ordered to rest for a few days. He returned 30 hours later.[3] In the late afternoon a cable arrived from Israel's Ambassador to France, Walter Eytan, stating that Eban might be received by de Gaulle the following day. Eshkol consented that Eban pause in Paris, en route to Washington. At 8.00 in the evening the Prime Minister replied to the *Knesset* debate. The blockade was branded 'an act of aggression against Israel' and the Powers were called upon 'to act without delay' to maintain free passage. This,

---

[1] Nakdimon, pp. 50–1. Burdett (p. 247) also mentions that Eban was suspect in the eyes of other ministers.

[2] Foreign Ministry sources; St. John, p. 420. Eban 1972 referred to a Cabinet decision to send the FM to Washington to 'clarify to the American Administration Israel's expectations that the United States honour its commitments of 1957'. Carmel (2) also referred to a decision to dispatch Eban to Washington.

[3] Nakdimon, pp. 52–6. Whether Rabin became really ill (*Le Figaro*, in an article on 19 January 1968, called it 'depression'), or whether he decided to 'take a breather' at that stage because he felt growing pressure on him to advocate immediate action, something he was not prepared to do, became a subject of speculation. Many felt that Rabin's illness was caused by the impossible burden of decision—whether or not to go to war—which was imposed on the Chief of Staff by an indecisive group of political leaders. Whatever the reasons, in the minds of the decision-makers his 'illness' became an added psychological factor in favour of Dayan's appointment as Minister of Defence; they may have regarded it as a sign of weakening under pressure in a man on whom Eshkol had relied mainly for military advice until that day. (See pp. 348 and n. 2, 363, 371–3 above.) Gilboa (p. 129) mentioned that Weizman suggested to Rabin that he be appointed acting CoS. Weizman's version was that, on 23 May, Rabin offered informally to resign and proposed to Weizman that he become Chief of Staff; Weizman declined. Interview, 1971. It is unlikely that such a suggestion would have been accepted by the Government; Weizman was known to be a somewhat impulsive hardliner and politically to the Right, as later events proved.

coupled with the announcement of Eban's trip, notified the world that Israel had decided to wait.[1]

That day President Johnson made a major declaration: 'The United States considers the gulf to be an international waterway and feels that a blockade of Israeli shipping is illegal and potentially disastrous to the cause of peace. . . .'[2] And Evron cabled encouragingly: first, that the US had decided to approach the Security Council because 'it was essential to use the UN platform *before a unilateral position was adopted*'; secondly, 'the Senior Official repeated that we could rely on the President'; and thirdly, 'they confirmed that the President has told Premier Kosygin of United States commitments'.[3]

In Israel pressure to form a national unity government continued. The focus of the lobbying throughout the next week was on three people and their parties: Peres, Begin, and Shapira of *Rafi, Gahal* and the NRP respectively. The first of their consultations was *ad hoc*, on the morning of the 24th. Begin repeated his proposal that Ben Gurion become Prime Minister and Defence Minister of a national unity government, with Eshkol carrying on as his deputy. Shapira demurred but finally acquiesced. Peres would try to convince Ben Gurion. Talks were resumed in an enlarged forum in the *Rafi* Caucus room of the *Knesset* at noon. Peres informed the meeting that Ben Gurion had agreed. And Begin's initiative to speak to Eshkol about the proposal was approved.[4]

Externally, there were several developments on the 24th. U Thant arrived in Cairo. The Security Council was called into session. But most dramatic was the de Gaulle–Eban meeting, which began at 13.00 hours Israel time. Eytan and French Foreign Minister Couve de Murville were also in attendance.[5]

De Gaulle opened the conversation by warning: 'Israel must not make war unless she is attacked by others. It would be catastrophic if Israel were to shoot first. The Four Powers must be left to resolve the dispute. France will influence the Soviet Union towards an attitude favourable to peace.'

[1] Among the motions brought to a vote following the debate was one by Shmuel Tamir of the Free Centre calling for the establishment of a national unity government. It was soundly defeated but was the centre of discussion at a meeting of the *Gahal* and *Rafi* members of the *Knesset* Committee on Foreign Affairs and Security following the debate. There were also consultations between NRP leaders (Shapira, Warhaftig, Burg, Raphael, Ben-Meir) and *Mapam*'s Ya'ari, Hazan, Peled, Arzi, and Rosen on the question of the national unity government. *Mapam* expressed reservations about co-opting *Gahal* and *Rafi*. Peres interview, 1968; Nakdimon, pp. 57–9.

[2] Draper, Appendix 20, p. 264.

[3] Foreign Ministry sources.

[4] Peres interview, 1968. See also Nakdimon, pp. 62–5.

[5] The following account is based primarily on Foreign Ministry sources. Among published accounts the most reliable are Gilboa, pp. 136–40, Nakdimon, pp. 65–8, and St. John, pp. 421–4.

Eban reviewed the problems with Syrian and Egyptian troop concentrations, placing special emphasis on the blockade of the Straits.
It was an aggressive act, he said, which must be rescinded. Should the
choice lie between surrender and resistance, Israel would resist, and
the decision had been made.[1] Eban stressed, however, that action
would not be taken immediately, in order to allow Israel to explore the
attitude of those who had assumed commitments.

De Gaulle emphasized again that Israel should not go to war, at
least, not strike first. Eban countered that hostilities had already been
opened against her by Nasser's blockade and declarations. Any Israeli
action would be reactive. The French President rejected this definition
and maintained that the opening of hostilities meant firing the first
shot. He agreed that the French 1957 declaration on free navigation
was still valid juridically—but 1967 was different from 1957; and their
UN Representative's statement at the time reflected the particular
1957 context. Moreover, the more Israel turned to the West, the less
would the Soviet Union be ready to co-operate. Time must be given
to France to concert Big Four action to enable Israeli ships to sail
through the Straits. The worst fears of Israel regarding the French
position had materialized: de Gaulle had disavowed all previous French
commitments, did not accept Nasser's action as an act of war, and
counselled Israel to acquiesce in Nasser's *fait accompli* for the time being.[2]

The dynamics of a foreign policy crisis often initiate internal political
change. That process, in Israel's 1967 crisis, became evident on 24
May, when the *Rafi–Gahal–Mafdal* meetings led to countless dialogues
and consultations. The first was the Begin–Eshkol meeting at 4.30 that

---

[1] 'Si le choix se pose entre l'abandon et la résistance, Israël va résister. La décision
est prise.' Eban stated later (Eban 1972) that he deliberately chose the word 'résistance', in order to impress de Gaulle by words with evocative memories.

[2] De Gaulle's stance was in accord with his global policies of previous years and was
linked to several strands of that policy: *rapprochement* with the Soviets; re-establishment
of friendly relations with the Arab states; and hatred of the Americans. Israel's well-
being and, possibly, survival was of little consequence in a game with such high stakes.
Harold Wilson quotes him as saying at their meeting on 18 June 1967:

> '... the situation had changed. The Algerian War was over. France's relations with
> the Arab states had improved. She was on reasonably good terms with many of
> them. Given this, there was no reason for France—"or, I would suggest, the United
> Kingdom"—to ruin its relations with the Arabs, merely because public opinion
> felt some "superficial sympathy" (his phrase) for Israel because she was a small
> country with an unhappy history.' Wilson, p. 404.

Yet the Middle East crisis was to prove a great disappointment to de Gaulle's global
policies. The suggestion of Four-Power talks was rejected by the USSR. And during
the Six Day War and its aftermath the Soviet Government practically ignored France
in its efforts to regain through diplomacy what had been lost in the war. Wilson
states: 'The [French] President was more depressed than I had ever seen him. This
was partly, I think, because Mr. Kosygin had virtually bypassed him. . . . General de
Gaulle felt he had been spurned and if this was so it was a sad ending to all his hopes
about Franco-Soviet relations.' Wilson, p. 402.

afternoon. The *Herut* leader suggested tactfully that Ben Gurion be at the head of a national unity government with Eshkol as Deputy Prime Minister. He reminded the Premier of his own bitter rivalry with BG, which he was willing to forgo because of the external danger. Eshkol replied that he would put the suggestion before his colleagues. If they would accept it he would resign from all his posts, as he could not agree to the proposal. He went on: '. . . One of these days I may prove to you what I have done to equip the Army. As to my understanding of military matters, it is not what they have been thinking for many years. I have learned something in the meanwhile. And as to Johnson, I think I can obtain more from him. Believe me, I have the basis to say this.' On working with Ben Gurion, he said: 'These two horses . . . can no longer pull the same cart. This pair can no longer live together. . . .'[1] Begin then asked Eshkol if he would give Ben Gurion the Defence portfolio. Eshkol absolutely refused and reminded the Opposition leader of the troubles this had caused in the past, between Sharett and Ben Gurion.[2] Inter-party consultations continued through the day: between Peres and *Mapai*'s Avigur and, later, with Shraga Netzer and Morde-khai Surkiss, to get them to use their influence on Eshkol to agree to broaden the Government; between Avigur and Ben Gurion; between Warhaftig, the NRP Minister of Religious Affairs, and *Mapai*'s Justice Minister Ya'acov S. Shapiro, who agreed that *Gahal* and *Rafi* be included in the Government, on condition that Eshkol remain Prime Minister; and between *Rafi*'s Almogi and *Mapai*'s Abba Hushi, the two most influential Haifa politicians.[3]

There were three other internal events of note that day. Minister of Labour Yigal Allon returned in the late afternoon from the Soviet Union. He proceeded immediately to General Staff headquarters with Galili and received a two-hour briefing from General Bar-Lev. In retrospect, Allon stated that, at that juncture, he had felt war to be inevitable.[4] Later in the evening Begin, Peres, and Shapira met again. Begin reported on his failure to persuade Eshkol; and the three decided that Shapira should try to convince the Prime Minister that he should offer BG the Defence Ministry.[5] At midnight, when the meeting adjourned, Peres left to report to Ben Gurion, Arye Bahir, and Isser Harel at Ben Gurion's home. It had been a long day for all concerned.

In the meantime Eban arrived in London, at 16.30 GMT on the 24th, and rushed to 10 Downing St. for the meeting with Wilson. The Foreign Minister noted de Gaulle's 'Four Power' idea. Wilson was

---

[1] Begin (2). See also Gilboa, p. 161; Nakdimon, pp. 68–70.
[2] Allon emphasized that Eshkol wanted the Defence portfolio for himself—to show that he could handle a crisis and was competent without BG. Interview, 1968.
[3] Peres interview, 1968, and Nakdimon, pp. 75–6.
[4] Allon interview, 1968.   [5] Peres interview, 1968; Nakdimon, p. 77.

sceptical but agreed to try it. Eban emphasized Israel's choices on the question of the Straits as surrender, fight alone, or fight in concert with maritime powers: she would not accept a blockade of Eilat. Wilson replied that the British Cabinet had agreed that the policy of closing the Straits must be resisted and that Britain would join others in an effort to secure the right of free navigation for all states. Minister of State George Thomson had been sent to Washington to co-ordinate a plan of action with the US. Action through the UN also came up for discussion, and Eban opined that, with the Soviet veto, there was not much to be expected. The British Prime Minister showed a keen interest in Israel's mood. Eban replied that the atmosphere was grave, but Israel would win if she had to fight. Unlike de Gaulle, the British Prime Minister did not counsel Israel on the wisdom or legitimacy of active response to Nasser's moves.[1]

The same day Harman went to Gettysburg to urge Eisenhower to support Johnson in honouring American commitments. The retired President told Israel's Ambassador that, though he usually did not make public statements, if questioned by journalists, his answer would be that the Straits were an international waterway, as stated by him and Dulles in 1957; denial of the rights of free passage would be illegal.[2]

At 8 o'clock in the morning on 25 May Eshkol met with Shapira. The Minister of the Interior suggested that BG be appointed Defence Minister. Eshkol refused, pointing out his achievements and the objection to separating the two portfolios. He agreed only to the addi-tion of *Gahal* and *Rafi* members to the Ministerial Committee on Defence.[3] At the same hour, in the Tel Aviv headquarters of *Ihud Ha-kvutzot Veha-kibbutzim*, the *Mapai*-linked *kibbutz* movement, a majority of *Mapai* and *Rafi* members present demanded that Eshkol remain Prime Minister but supported the co-option of *Gahal* and *Rafi* to the Government; the Defence Ministry should be given either to

---

[1] The Eban–Wilson meeting is based upon Foreign Ministry sources. Their conver-sation is also summarized in several published sources, mentioned above; see, for example, St. John, pp. 424–5. Eban also requested a speed-up of arms deliveries. Patrick Gordon Walker, a member of the Wilson Cabinet, asserted that 'Harold Wilson and his Foreign Secretary were once overruled by the Cabinet on a matter of great importance concerning a proposal to send naval ships to the Gulf of Aqaba in an attempt to forestall the Six Day War between Israel and Egypt.' In the same book he reasserts this with more detail, in the form of a verbatim reproduction of an 'imaginary cabinet meeting'. Gordon Walker, pp. 138–51. Wilson and Brown strongly denied this claim. When a garbled version of the story first appeared in the *Daily Mail* in 1970, a denial was issued by No. 10 Downing St. Wilson stated that he asked the Lord Chancellor to conduct an independent investigation, with access to Cabinet minutes, and he reported that the *Daily Mail* story was 'completely untrue'. See Wilson, pp. 401–2. See also newspaper articles in the British and Israeli press, May 1972.

[2] President Johnson recalled, in his memoirs (p. 291): '. . . I sought his views. . . . General Eisenhower sent me a message stating his view that the Israelis' right of ac-cess to the Gulf of Aqaba was definitely part of the "commitment" we had made to them.'   [3] Gilboa, pp. 159–60; Nakdimon, pp. 78–9.

Ben Gurion or Dayan. Meir was approached by several *Mapai kibbutz* leaders but rejected any change in Eshkol's posts.[1] Soon after, she neither accepted nor rejected a suggestion by Harari of the Independent Liberals to create a small defence committee to work with Eshkol; but she promised to bring it to Eshkol's attention.[2]

While various associational interest groups and competing élites were working for a national unity government (and, at the same time, laying the groundwork for wresting the Defence portfolio from Eshkol), Eshkol toured the southern front with its commanders Gavish, Sharon, Tal, and Yoffe. The meeting with the generals turned into a sharp confrontation: they openly questioned the wisdom of further waiting— in the face of an increasing Egyptian military build-up in the desert, notably the deployment of Egypt's Fourth Armoured Division, and further Mig reconnaissance flights over southern Israel.[3] Sharon was reportedly the bluntest in warning of a sharp escalation of casualties with each passing day of waiting. From that day on there was almost unanimous pressure (Bar-Lev was the exception) from the army commanders on the Prime Minister to go to war.[4]

Upon their return Allon held further consultations with the General Staff, specifically with Bar-Lev, Hod, and Yariv. Allon came to the conclusion that Israel would win if she took the initiative and that the time for waiting was over.[5]

While Allon was in session with Bar-Lev, Air Force Commander Hod, Yariv, the Chief of Staff and Herzog met with Eshkol. They persuaded the Prime Minister to cable Eban, now on his way to Washington, to emphasize that the issue was no longer the Straits and the blockade but the Egyptian troop-concentrations in Sinai and the attack they were about to launch. In Rabin's words, on the fifth anniversary of the crisis:

After the closing of the Straits, in order to test where Israel stood and to what extent she was not to depend completely on herself, the Director-General of the Prime Minister's Office, the late Ya'acov Herzog, in a conversation with me, suggested that we send a telegram to the Foreign Minister, Abba Eban, who was then in Washington, and in it we would say that, according to the information in our hands, there may be the development of an Egyptian offensive initiative against Israel as the events evolve. And Mr. Herzog further suggested to me that we ask Mr. Eban to clarify to what extent the United States is prepared to make good on obligations, given in the past to Israeli leaders for real help in such an event.[6]

---

[1] Peres interview, 1968; Nakdimon, p. 81. [2] Nakdimon, pp. 81–2.
[3] Burdett, p. 252; *MER*, p. 198.
[4] Nakdimon, p. 79; Schiff; and Bar-Lev (4).
[5] Allon interview, 1968. Laqueur's 1968 version (p. 135) contends that the Generals complained to Allon about Eban's mission. Allon argued, in his interview, that he thought Eban's mission was a mistake and said so.
[6] Rabin 1972, confirmed by Foreign Ministry sources. The ploy succeeded only

In the afternoon *Rafi* and NRP consultations continued. The NRP caucus under Raphael, M. Unna, Burg, Warhaftig, Shapira, and Ben-Meir decided officially in favour of a national unity government and so informed *Gahal*. *Gahal* replied that useful results would be attained if the NRP threatened to leave the Cabinet unless *Mapai* agreed to this. The Independent Liberals' caucus also met in the late afternoon; they decided to support the national unity government idea, quietly. The *Ma'arakh* Political Committee and the Secretariats of *Mapai* and *Ahdut Ha'avoda*, on the other hand, reaffirmed the limited Eshkol offer to the Opposition—to join the deliberations of the Ministerial Defence Committee.[1]

Eban arrived in New York in the early afternoon of the 25th and immediately continued to Washington, with Rafael and Evron.[2] There Harman informed him of a strongly-worded speech by Johnson that morning; further, that the President would receive him the next day at the earliest. Suddenly, the ominous cable arrived from Jerusalem. It was signed by Eshkol and it portended the possibility of a surprise Egyptian attack. The Foreign Minister was requested to communicate this most urgently and to inquire whether the US would regard an attack on Israel as an attack on herself. A second cable arrived confirming the urgency of the first one.[3]

At his first meeting with Rusk (Eugene Rostow and Battle were also present), Eban began by reading a verbatim translation of the cables from Jerusalem. Rusk reacted by suggesting that their talks be suspended in order to communicate this report to the President and the Secretary of Defence with all urgency. At 6.00 p.m. Eban, Harman, Rafael, and Evron returned to the State Department for a 'working dinner' with Rostow, Kohler, Battle, and Joseph Sisco, and George Meeker and Hoopes of the Pentagon. The American officials '. . . felt that the proposal being discussed with the British Government was of great importance and offered some hope. An American decision on the

---

marginally. The US Administration, on the advice of the Pentagon, refused to believe that the UAR was about to launch an attack on Israel. It even backfired slightly, for it created a minor 'credibility gap' in Eban's talks with American leaders. But it did lead to an immediate American warning to Cairo not to start hostilities; and that warning, coupled with subsequent Soviet and American advice and warnings to Nasser about restraint, may have played a slight role in holding Nasser's hand from a sudden attack.

[1] Gilboa, pp. 164–5; Nakdimon, pp. 83–6.

[2] The most valuable sources for the following analysis are: Foreign Ministry sources; and the Eban, Herzog, Evron interviews, 1968, 1968, and 1972, respectively. Among the published accounts the most reliable are Burdett, pp. 252–6, and Gilboa, pp. 146–51.

[3] Foreign Ministry sources. The second cable was signed by Herzog, who feared that the first was not clear enough; Gilboa (p. 146). Draper (p. 88) wrote that the message was so urgent that the first meeting with Rusk, set for 5.30 p.m., was requested to be advanced by two hours. It was held at 5.00 p.m.

proposal . . . would require consultations in the Congress and perhaps a joint Resolution of both Houses.' The proposal under discussion had two basic paragraphs:

A) A Declaration by the maritime powers, open to adherence by all, including Israel, laying down the principle of free passage for all States in the Straits of Tiran and the resolve of the signatories to exercise that right;
B) In case this principle is not endorsed by the United Nations . . . a multilateral group of maritime States will defend their position by a naval patrol. It is considered that Egypt will not resist such a patrol, whose presence would have a deterrent effect.

The State Department officials further contended that discussion of the Declaration in the UN Security Council could not be avoided because of public opinion, as well as for political and juridical reasons. It was necessary to prove that all possibilities of action in the UN had been exhausted; this policy of restraint would also strengthen Israel's position. The Israelis stressed the need for speed and warned against any evasion of Israel's rights of free navigation; the Americans were ambiguous on this point.[1]

The Secretary of State, who had just conferred at length with President Johnson, told Eban that the United States did not share the Israeli appraisal that any Arab state was planning an immediate attack on Israel; in fact, Washington 'did not regard the Egyptian order of battle in Sinai as offensive, though it might change its character'. Furthermore, the President would not act without full Congressional approval: a declaration to the effect that 'an attack on Israel shall be considered an attack on the United States' had been introduced only in the NATO Alliance, and even there it had been accepted after a long, heated debate. On the question of rights of navigation, 'the President was convinced that it was essential for him to be able to carry the Congress with him'. In addition, 'the President felt that it was vital that Israel should not take pre-emptive action; such action would create great difficulties for him and would tie his hands. . . . For the President this was a problem of the highest importance. . . . On the other hand, he was taking political and diplomatic action in Cairo and other capitals to clarify the strong stand of the United States.' Eban answered that Israel had to take into account the worst alternatives. In the past two weeks, all optimism had been shattered by reality.[2]

At midnight Harman returned to the State Department to emphasize that Israel expected 'a concrete and precise proposal' about American intentions, which could be submitted to Israel's Cabinet. He was told

[1] Foreign Ministry sources.
[2] Foreign Ministry sources. The political action that Rusk referred to was the warning not to resort to force, handed to the Egyptian Ambassador at 10.30 p.m., N.Y.T., that evening. The Russians were requested the next day by Washington to intervene in Cairo with the same message.

that Eban would hear from the President himself concerning the US determination to ensure freedom of passage through the Straits.

Eban cabled Eshkol at 1.30 a.m. New York time that 'the President is likely to discuss a programme for opening the Straits by the maritime powers led by the United States, Britain and perhaps others'; further, that some in Washington felt the President could pledge that the Straits would be opened even if there was resistance.[1]

Thursday 25 May thus ended on a note of anxious uncertainty. Within Israel the Independent Liberals and the NRP had opted in favour of a national unity government. Both Alignment wings, *Mapai* and *Ahdut Ha'avoda*, had given Eshkol a vote of confidence, though it was clear that elements of the *kibbutz* movement favoured a broader government in the crisis situation. *Rafi*, *Gahal*, and the NRP had decided to continue their efforts, in spite of the *Ma'arakh* decision and limited offer—membership in the Ministerial Defence Committee. The possibility of Ben Gurion's candidacy had become more and more remote. In the United States, Eban was yet to receive a precise US position. And in the Middle East the Egyptian military build-up was approaching its peak.

On Friday morning 26 May, at 8 o'clock, Eshkol received a Haifa delegation led by the influential Abba Hushi, who urged him to bring Dayan and Begin into the Cabinet.[2] This was followed immediately by a brief ministerial consultation, in which Eshkol was advised by close *Ma'arakh* Cabinet colleagues to appoint Allon as Defence Minister or Assistant Defence Minister—to head off the political pressure. At 10.00 *Mapai*'s Secretary-General, Meir, met with *Mapam*'s Hazan, who related to her what Peres had told him and *Mapam* leader Meir Ya'ari in a meeting the previous day. Only Ben Gurion, he argued, would have enough authority to avoid reacting to Nasser's provocation and not go to war immediately. Israel for the moment had to dig in, for *Tzahal* was not ripe for action, its plans were not mature. The *Mapam* leaders did not accept this evaluation, but Hazan did not conceal his concern.[3] He was followed by Reserve Generals Tolkovsky

---

[1] Foreign Ministry sources.   [2] Nakdimon, p. 96.

[3] Nakdimon, pp. 99–100. Gilboa interviewed Ya'ari and Hazan on their meetings with Peres and Ben Gurion on 24 and 25 May respectively. They conveyed a determined, some felt ruthless, attempt by *Rafi*, led by Peres and supported by Ben Gurion, to dislodge Eshkol from the leadership of the country's Defence Establishment. Peres used all the arguments mentioned in the text; he even brought in Rabin's illness to undermine confidence in Eshkol and his advisers. Ben Gurion demanded bluntly 'that we must cause Eshkol's dismissal from the Premiership, not because of security failure and not even because of the Lavon affair, but because of a completely different charge' (Ya'ari, as quoted in Gilboa, p. 163). Ya'ari was not willing to state what this other, serious, charge was. Gilboa stated that it is not difficult to guess, in the light of other evidence, that the charge was the act that caused the deterioration of relationships between France and Israel. Gilboa continued that this charge, with all the relevant documents, was brought before the Cabinet Defence Committee, as well as the

and Harkabi, who urged Meir to support a national unity government.

While the Government was in session, Eshkol's Head of Bureau, Yaffe, asked *Gahal* leaders Begin and Rimalt to accept the Prime Minister's invitation to join the deliberations of the Ministerial Committee. They gave no definite reply but did not conceal their disappointment. The NRP ministers brought up the question of forming a national unity government. The *Ma'arakh* ministers countered with the original proposal to co-opt Opposition leaders to the Ministerial Defence Committee. The NRP replied that this was unacceptable.[1] The Cabinet adjourned, after deciding to postpone all further action until Eban's return.

After the Cabinet meeting Allon convinced the Prime Minister of the necessity of an Israeli military initiative. 'This is one of the great issues in Jewish history,' he told Eshkol; 'I believe you can go down in Jewish history as another King David—if you decide to act now.' Allon suggested that the PM cable Eban to change his line to the President: the issue was no longer the Straits and the anti-blockade armada, but the Egyptian military threat.[2]

During several *Rafi–Gahal* meetings in the afternoon Eshkol's proposal to co-opt the Opposition to the Ministerial Defence Committee was rejected; it was also concluded that the idea of bringing BG into the Government was unacceptable to the *Mapai* leadership; pressure grew to co-opt Dayan into the Government.[3] At 4 o'clock the *Knesset* Committee on Foreign Affairs and Security heard reports from *Tzahal* officers and debated the situation for four hours. At 5.00 Eshkol met *Mapam*'s Ya'ari and Hazan, who expressed their reservations about the co-option of *Gahal* and *Rafi* to the Government and supported Eshkol's original proposal.[4]

In Washington, important events were in progress on Friday the 26th. At 9.30 (NYT) Rusk telephoned Harman and inquired whether Eban would be remaining till Saturday, when the results of U Thant's Cairo visit would be known. Fifteen minutes later Eban informed Rusk that he intended to leave Washington that night. He explained that there was a Cabinet meeting on Sunday in Jerusalem, which might be the most crucial in the history of the nation, and the decision taken

---

Knesset Committee on Foreign Affairs and Security, and not even Ben Gurion's friends saw the slightest evidence to substantiate it. Though the *Mapam* leaders were very upset by what they heard, they did not change their stance towards Eshkol, since, as members of the *Knesset* Committee, they were informed of exactly the opposite evaluation of *Tzahal*'s preparedness. Furthermore, they probably did not trust Peres's motives.

[1] Gilboa, p. 165; Nakdimon, p. 101.
[2] Allon interview, 1968; Gilboa, p. 180; Nakdimon, p. 98.
[3] Peres interview, 1968; Nakdimon, pp. 103–4.
[4] Peres interview, 1968; Nakdimon, pp. 104–6.

there would be based largely on what President Johnson conveyed to him. Eban stressed that U Thant's report was not the decisive factor in Israel's eyes and that, in his view, Israel would face hostilities the next week. There was an act of blockade which would be resisted.[1]

Eban then proceeded to the Pentagon to meet Defence Secretary McNamara, Chairman of the Joint Chiefs of Staff General Wheeler, and others. He was accompanied by Harman and Military Attaché Geva. The conversation had scarcely begun when a cable from Jerusalem arrived: it reiterated in drastic terms the military appraisal or the night before. But the Americans were unconvinced. Israel would succeed, said their military experts, no matter who took the initiative. The passage of time did not aggravate Israel's security problem. To them, the idea that Israel would have to act in a mood of 'now or never' was utterly remote from the facts. Israel's air superiority was, in the Pentagon view, beyond dispute. Later in the morning Walt Rostow, the President's National Security Adviser, telephoned to delay the Johnson–Eban meeting, in order to give the President time to study the Eisenhower–Dulles commitment to Israel in February 1957. Evron found it necessary to stress at this stage that there was no panic in Israel, but that Israeli decision-makers felt the time had come to know where Washington stood on the crisis.[2]

In mid-afternoon another cable arrived from Jerusalem emphasizing that the Foreign Minister must return by Saturday night. Pressure to enlarge the Government was growing; and *Tzahal* commanders were not as sanguine as the Pentagon experts about the military situation. Evron then telephoned Rostow to try to settle the hour of the Eban–Johnson meeting and was invited to the White House at once. He gave the requested assurances that Israel would not 'publish a word of the conversation'.[3] Rostow informed the President that Evron was in his office and had given him assurances that there would be no publicity. The meeting with Eban was set for 7.00 p.m. But Johnson requested that Evron now come to see him. The following is the full report of the conversation that Evron cabled later that night to Jerusalem:[4]

When I entered his room, the President told me that he fully understood the

---

[1] Foreign Ministry sources.   [2] Foreign Ministry sources; Evron interview, 1972.

[3] Evron demurred only on the suggestion by Rostow that Eban tell the press after the meeting that he had paid a 'courtesy call' on the President, saying that no one would believe that Israel's Foreign Minister, in the midst of a grave crisis, had journeyed 7,000 miles for a courtesy call, and that the President's credibility, too, would be undermined. Rostow agreed. Evron interview, 1972.

[4] Foreign Ministry sources. The Evron cable was important in the Cabinet's further deliberations. It was the main source of information for Israel's Government on the American position during the next 24 hours. Eban did not cable before he arrived on Saturday. Herman sent a short cable while Eban was in flight; and by the time Eban arrived, the Cabinet was in secret session, deliberating on the basis of the information supplied by Evron.

gravity of Israel's position. His reaction to the Foreign Minister would be in accordance with what Mr. Eban had heard from Rusk and others that morning, namely, that any American involvement would require Congressional support of the President. Without this there would be no value whatever in the intentions and decisions of the President. The first step would have to be the laying of a Congressional basis for any support of Israel's position. The President emphasized that he was working energetically in that direction. The United States had pledged itself to preserve freedom of passage in the Straits of Tiran; and the United States would carry out that obligation. But anything involving even a possibility of force would be impractical and would boomerang unless the proper Congressional basis were laid in advance. The President agreed that the United Nations in its present composition would not be able to do anything; no result would come from its discussions. Yet those discussions were vital in order to give proper support to the President, in the Congress and the public, as well as in the international domain. The President spoke without confidence about the result of the Secretary-General's mission to Cairo, but said that it would be foolish to ignore the effect of his report. Any action by any member State before the report were published would be received badly in many places. The President spoke optimistically about the possibility of setting up a structure with the active support of Britain and other maritime powers after the conclusion of a quick debate at the United Nations. Here he mentioned several countries who might be willing to co-operate. He had taken counsel with some of his leading advisers. All of them could be described as friends of Israel. They had expressed their support in the following formulation: 'The objective is to open the Straits for navigation by all States including Israel and this objective shall be carried out.' Mr. Johnson made it clear that the appraisal in Jerusalem about an imminent Egyptian surprise attack was not shared by the United States. Israel was a sovereign Government, and if it decided to act alone, it could of course do so; but in that case everything that happened before and afterwards would be upon its responsibility and the United States would have no obligation for any consequences which might ensue. He refused to believe that Israel would carry out unilateral action which was bound to bring her great damage. But, he added, this was Israel's affair. As President of the United States he must carry out American commitments to Israel in a way which seemed to him best, within the framework of American interests. He emphasized several times, that Israel could depend on him. He said that he was not a coward, and did not renege on his promises, but he was not prepared to act in a manner which seemed to him to endanger the security of the United States, or to bring about the intervention of the Soviet Union simply because Israel has decided that Sunday is an ultimate date.

The formal meeting with Eban started a little late, around 7.15 in the evening.[1] Present in the President's Office were: McNamara, Walt

---

[1] *New York Times* (10 July 1967) reported the following amusing incident. Eban and Harman arrived at the wrong gate. A confused period followed, in which the White House and Evron were trying to find Eban. This ended when a guard telephoned and said: 'Some guy out here by the name of Eban says he is supposed to see the President.' Evron confirmed this in a conversation in 1972. He cleared up the cause of the slight mishap: he had previously agreed with Walt Rostow that the Israeli party would enter the White House by a side entrance, so as to lessen publicity;

and Eugene Rostow, George Christian, and Sisco; Eban, Harman, and Evron. Eban opened by giving the President the essence of information which hab reached him the previous day about the possibility of an Egyptian attack. The maritime blockade, he emphasized, was not the core of the crisis. On the Straits of Tiran there had been a solemn pact between the United States and Israel ten years ago, he continued. A mere prospect had now become a legal situation and an economic fact, enshrined in the 1958 Law of the Sea and in the steady flow of commerce. An act of aggression had already been committed by Egypt, and Israel realized she was faced with a choice between surrender and resistance; she would not surrender. However, in accordance with the President's advice the Government thought it desirable to explore international efforts to resolve the conflict and was interested to know whether the US would take the initiative. Israel's power of deterrence was at stake. Israel must know whether the US was determined to carry out her commitment to open the Straits.

Johnson reiterated that he had said publicly an illegal action had occurred and that the Gulf was an international waterway. The question was when and how to act: only if the Congress and the American people felt that Israel had justice on her side could he respond firmly. Moreover, the UN channel must first be exhausted. What he needed was a very short time and British help to develop an effective solution. He suggested that 'it would not be wise at this stage to call Nasser's hand. If your Cabinet decides to do anything immediately and to do it on their own, that is for them. We are not going to do any retreating. We are not back-tracking. I am not forgetting anything I have ever said.' But a statement to the effect that an attack on Israel is an attack on the United States was beyond his prerogatives. 'What you can tell your Cabinet is that the President, the Congress and the country will support a plan to use any or all measures to open the Straits. But we have to go through the Secretary-General and the Security Council and build up support among the nations. . . . Israel will not be alone unless it decides to go alone. . . . If you want our help in whatever ensues, it is absolutely necessary for Israel not to make itself responsible for the institution of hostilities.' At the end of the meeting, the President handed Eban the following *aide-mémoire*:

The United States has its own Constitutional processes, which are basic to its actions on matters involving war and peace. The Secretary-General has not yet reported to the Security Council and the Council has not yet demonstrated what it may or may not be able or willing to do, although the United States will press for prompt action in the United Nations. I have already publicly stated this week our view on the safety of navigation and on the Straits of

but because of his conversation with the President he had no opportunity to inform Eban. So there he was, waiting with McNamara and others at the side entrance for about fifteen minutes, while Eban and Harman arrived at the front gate!

Tiran. Regarding the Straits we plan to pursue vigorously the measures which can be taken by maritime nations to assure that the Straits and the Gulf remain open to free and innocent passage of all nations. I must emphasize the necessity for Israel not to make itself responsible for the initiation of hostilities. Israel will not be alone unless it decides to do it alone. We cannot imagine that Israel will make this decision.[1]

Eban and Harman left immediately for New York, while Evron went back to the Embassy and sent off his report. Harman dispatched a short account of the conversation to Jerusalem with a résumé of Evron's preliminary talk and the assurances given by Rusk about the prospect of support for a proposed multilateral action. In the meantime Eban went to see Goldberg. Security Council proceedings were coming to nought, he was told. And U Thant had been totally unsuccessful in Cairo, except for Nasser's promise not to start an armed assault. Goldberg stressed that Eban should pay particular attention to what the President himself had said: the alternatives open to America were now so fateful that the President's own words were the only decisive ones. As for the international flotilla, he expressed doubts about the practical aspects, especially logistics. Eban returned to the airport and at midnight started for home.

Two inputs that day are noteworthy. Hasanin Heikal, in his influential *Al-Ahram* column, wrote about the inevitability of an armed clash with Israel. More important, Nasser, in a speech before a delegation of Arab trade unionists, now declared that his basic objective was *the destruction of Israel*. The relevant passage from Nasser's speech was as follows: 'The problem today is not only Israel, but those who are behind Israel. If Israel starts any aggressive action against Syria or Egypt, the fight against Israel will be total war. It will not be an engagement restricted to a particular area or the frontiers of Syria or the frontiers of Egypt. It will be total war with the basic object of destroying Israel which we can do.'[2]

On Saturday the 27th of May Israel's Cabinet came close to a decision to go to war. Pressures were building up within the country and abroad to such an extent that any further delay seemed to many

[1] Foreign Ministry sources, based upon Ambassador Harman's record of the minutes of the meeting with the President; and Evron interview, 1972. Johnson's memoirs (pp. 293–4) corroborate, in general, the above account. His pivotal remark to Eban, wrote the President, was as follows: '"The central point, Mr. Minister, is that your nation not be the one to bear the responsibility for any outbreak of war." Then I said very slowly and very positively: "Israel will not be alone unless it decides to go alone."' He repeated this statement, recalled the President. Secondary sources on the Evron–Rostow, Evron–Johnson, Eban–Johnson conversations are: Burdett, pp. 245–6; Draper, pp. 90–1; Nakdimon, pp. 106–8; St. John, pp. 430–4.

[2] Nasser spoke before a delegation of the Arab Workers' Conference which came to inform him of the resolutions of the Arab Workers' Conference held in Damascus on 22–24 May. Speech published in *Al-Ahram*, 27 May 1967. *Documents on Palestine*, Doc. 326, p. 548.

decision-makers fraught with grave danger: it would sap the country's strength, morally as well as materially. To recapitulate briefly:

(a) The nation had been mobilized for more than a week; the country's economy had slowed down; the civilian population, as well as those called up, were anxiously awaiting a decision, any decision.

(b) There was growing dissatisfaction with the country's leadership; Eshkol was being accused, overtly and, more important, in the corridors of power, of inability to handle the crisis.

(c) The army was pressing for a pre-emptive strike; and dire predictions were voiced about the cost in casualties and resources of each day's delay.

(d) The information about Eban's diplomatic efforts had shown that all guarantees given in the past had become worthless.

(e) Nasser was engaged in continuous escalation; units of other Arab forces had begun to arrive on the frontiers, with promise of more to come; the airwaves from Arab countries carried an immense outpouring of hate around the clock, threatening in the most lurid terms the total destruction of Israel; and Arab leaders seemed to have been carried away by the hysteria of their masses.

All this placed an almost unbearable burden on the shoulders of eighteen exhausted men, living with the memories of the greatest tragedy that had ever befallen the Jewish people, the Holocaust.

The day began dramatically at 2.00 a.m., when the First Secretary of the Soviet Embassy, Bikov, telephoned Yaffe and requested an urgent meeting for Ambassador Chuvakhin with Eshkol. The Soviets were insistent, and the Prime Minister agreed. The Director-General of the Foreign Office, Levavi, and Yaffe were present. Chuvakhin and Bikov arrived at 3.00 a.m. The Ambassador delivered a note from Prime Minister Kosygin dated 26 May, which urged restraint on Israel. The operative passages read:

Guided by the interests of peace and the aspiration to avoid bloodshed, the Soviet Government has decided to send you this appeal.

We wish to call upon you to take all measures in order that a military conflict should not be created. . . . We think that whatever the position may be in the border areas . . . and however intricate the problem may be, it is essential to find means to settle the conflict by non-military means. . . .

It was conspicuously moderate in tone. Not once did Kosygin, in this letter, accuse Israel of responsibility for the tense situation. On the contrary, he spoke of forces which were 'pushing Israel over the precipice of war'.[1]

---

[1] The Kosygin letter is reprinted in full in *Documents on Palestine*, Doc. 33, p. 21, and in *Jerusalem Post*, 4 June 1967. Burdett's version (pp. 262–4) recaptures the drama of the hour most vividly. The tone of Kosygin's letters to Eshkol during the 1967 crisis

Eshkol replied that Israel's mobilization was in direct response to Syrian–Egyptian initiatives and that Soviet pressure should have been directed to those governments to reduce tension in the area. Chuvakhin countered that he was concerned with Israel only and asked whether Israel would fire the first shot. Eshkol was evasive. The Ambassador posed the question once, twice, three times; after the fourth, his First Secretary impatiently noted that Eshkol had declined to answer. At that juncture the Prime Minister exclaimed that the Egyptians had blocked the Straits and their planes had been flying over Israel. Weren't these 'first shots'? He then pointed out that 'the function of an ambassador . . . was to promote friendly relations to the best of his ability, with the country to which he was accredited. It did not seem to him that Chuvakhin had cared or tried to do this. Since this was the case, he would be pleased to welcome a Soviet Ambassador who held this conception of his role.' He also reaffirmed his desire to speak to Soviet leaders in the hope of promoting Soviet–Israeli friendship.[1] Eshkol and his colleagues did not attribute significance to Soviet hostility, as is evident in the lengthy delay in his formal, moderate reply to Kosygin's letter. By 1 June, when it was dispatched, Israel's decision process had moved from the stage of diplomacy to resolution.[2]

At 9.00 a.m. Eshkol was briefed on the military situation by Rabin and Yariv. He then met some of his ministers and informed them of his pyjama confrontation with Chuvakhin during the early morning hours; he also informed the *Knesset* Committee on Foreign Affairs and Security, and Mrs. Meir. During their conversation she suggested

---

was qualitatively more moderate than the harsh and dire threats of destruction contained in Bulganin's letter to Ben Gurion on 5 November 1956; see p. 284 above. This contradicts Yigael Yadin's evaluation on the fifth anniversary of the 1967 War:

'It was a blessing for the country that Eshkol was Prime Minister and Dayan Minister of Defence at the time. Contrary to the popular image of Eshkol as a procrastinator and a pacifist, Eshkol stood firm when he received those threatening and crude notes, almost daily, from Soviet Premier Kosygin. Compared to these notes, those received by Mr. Ben Gurion in '56 were love letters.' *Jerusalem Post*, 11 June 1972.

[1] Burdett, p. 263. The personality of the Russian Ambassador to Israel probably played a role in the exacerbation of Soviet–Israel relations. In contrast to other Russian ambassadors Chuvakhin was aggressively hostile, abrasively arrogant, menacing and downright rude in his contacts with Israeli leaders—an 'ugly Russian'. Even in private, off-the-record, contacts with leading members of the Opposition, obviously undertaken to achieve some understanding for Russia's aims, he turned a deaf ear to all views that were contrary to his interpretation of the official Soviet line. He did absolutely nothing to ease the pressure or to achieve some *rapprochement* with Israeli leaders during this crisis period. He displayed the extreme behaviour of a narrow-minded, over-zealous *apparatchik*. Kosygin chose the worst possible channel for his major gesture of conciliation on 27 May. Moreover, Chuvakhin failed in one of his primary duties—reporting reality: he grievously misunderstood Israel's will or capability to fight.

[2] The text is in Dagan, pp. 220–3, and in *Documents on Palestine*, Doc. 48, pp. 49–50.

that Allon be appointed as special assistant for defence matters. The PM refused.[1]

At a meeting in the afternoon *Rafi* and *Gahal* decided to demand Dayan's appointment as Minister of Defence; *Gahal* agreed to initiate the move.[2]

In the evening, at 8.00 p.m., the Cabinet began its longest session during the 1967 crisis. The meeting lasted until 5 o'clock the next morning, when it broke up to allow its members to 'sleep it over'. The debate resumed the following day, Sunday the 28th, from 3.00 in the afternoon and continued until about 8.30 in the evening. Eban joined the session on the 27th at about 10.00 p.m. and left it again after midnight to report on his mission to the *Knesset* Committee on Foreign Affairs and Security, which went into parallel session at the time, until 3.30 in the morning.

By the time Eban arrived there was an emergent division of views within the Cabinet between those who advocated going to war immediately and those who held out for further diplomatic efforts. Eban advocated an extension to the period of waiting—48 hours. The line-up by the end of the session (about 5.00 a.m. on Sunday the 28th) was as follows:

1. For immediate action (9): Eshkol, Allon, Carmel, Galili, Gvati, Sasson, Y. S. Shapiro, Sharef, Yeshayahu.
2. For a further waiting period (9): Aranne, Barzilai, Bentov, Burg, Eban, Kol, Sapir, M. H. Shapira, Warhaftig.

The atmosphere at the all-night meeting, as well as its substantive content, is best recaptured in the reported views or words of some of the principal participants.

Eshkol: The Prime Minister had been convinced by Allon and others that time was running out and that, if Israel took military action now, she could win. However, he would not impose his views on his colleagues, certainly not for such a momentous decision. 'I knew that if I would have pressed them I would have received the support of the majority. . . . had I banged the table and insisted, no one would have resigned from the Government. I did not do that. . . . I do not regret it.' He decided to press the next day for a decision to act, using the time to convince more of his colleagues, to tell them 'the die is cast'; but in the meantime the situation had changed again.[3]

---

[1] Nakdimon, p. 112.

[2] Begin (1) and (2); Nakdimon, pp. 114–17; Peres interview, 1968.

[3] Eshkol (11). See also Gilboa, pp. 154–5; Nakdimon, pp. 119–23. Eshkol claimed that he took a test vote only, which was deadlocked. Draper (p. 39) called it 'an informal poll'. Burdett (p. 266) and Laqueur 1968 (p. 142) mentioned or implied a *formal* vote.

Allon: Three times he tried to persuade his colleagues to opt for action. Eban's mission was termed a mistake. Waiting for the international flotilla would lessen considerably Israel's chances for victory in the coming confrontation. He opposed the sending of a 'test-ship' through the Straits, for that would only signal to Nasser the opening of hostilities and lead to an all-out attack on Israel.[1]

Eban: The Foreign Minister reviewed his Paris and London conversations briefly, those in Washington more extensively, since his colleagues were already well-informed about the first two talks from ambassadorial cables. His position was, essentially, that the Cabinet should wait another 48 hours for further developments and then reassemble and decide. At least one other round of consultations with the Americans was necessary, he declared, because of the actions taken by them on the basis of an Israeli warning about the danger of an immediate Egyptian attack (something that he transmitted very much against his better judgement). If Israel wanted to attack on the 28th it should not have asked the Americans to restrain the Egyptians on the 25th.[2]

Carmel: He never wavered in his advocacy of immediate action: 'There was no prospect whatsoever that the Straits would be reopened. And even if, by some miracle, they were, that would not solve the main problem—the threat of the massed Egyptian troops poised along our southern border. I feared their military initiative.... There was the over-all military–political view of the necessity for us to take our fate in our own hands and to smash the aggressive Egyptian build-up.'[3]

Given the clear and equal division of opinion, Eshkol decided to postpone a decision at dawn on the 28th. The consensus among participants was that he acted wisely: as Prime Minister he was trying to achieve a broad consensus on a fateful issue. The meeting of the *Knesset* Foreign Affairs and Security Committee was no less tense, with constant coming and going between the two conclaves. There, too, opinions were sharply divided. Deliberations ended as inconclusively as in the Cabinet.[4]

Consultations continued on Saturday concerning the broadening

---

[1] Allon interview, 1968; Nakdimon, p. 119.

[2] Foreign Ministry sources; Eban interview, 1968. Eban apparently wanted the Cabinet to hear his version only of the content of his conversation with Johnson. Gilboa (pp. 154–5) reports that Harman was instructed directly by Eshkol to dispatch his own report. There was another information flow—Evron's cable, which had arrived prior to Eban's return to Israel. Burdett, pp. 264–7, and Nakdimon, pp. 119–21.

[3] Carmel (2) and (3). In both, he stated that a vote was taken at the all-night (27–28 May) session.

[4] Nakdimon, pp. 121–3.

of the Government. Sapir and Aranne went to see Eshkol to bring him up to date on the intra- and inter-party discussions, including Sapir's conversation with Begin. Shraga Netzer, another powerful member of the *Mapai* inner circle, met the PM immediately after and urged him not to turn down demands for a national unity government. At about this time an historic *rapprochement* took place at Ben Gurion's Tel Aviv home: BG, Peres, and Almogi received *Gahal*'s Begin, Saphir, Ben-Eliezer, and Rimalt. The two party leaders (Ben Gurion and Begin), who had fought each other in deed as well as in word for years, who had not been on speaking terms for a decade, now buried the hatchet under the pressure of events. The ground had been laid by Begin's magnanimous gesture several days earlier in approaching Eshkol to give way to Ben Gurion. Israel had to act, the conferees agreed, but the limits and timing were debated. Ben Gurion advocated military action against the Straits only; Begin replied that the main problem was Egyptian troop concentrations, not the Tiran blockade. After the meeting at BG's home, Peres, Almogi, and the *Gahal* contingent continued their deliberations at the Yarden Hotel nearby. *Gahal* now firmly stated that Ben Gurion's candidacy was no longer realistic.

The inputs that persuaded Eshkol and all other Cabinet activists —except Carmel—to delay a decision for war were a series of notes received from all the Powers during the morning of 28 May. There was a cable from Johnson, which included the contents of a communication from Kosygin to the US President; a dispatch from Rusk about Eban's discussions with the President and members of the American Administration; a letter from de Gaulle, in reply to Eshkol's letter of 19 May; and a communication from Wilson. Curiously enough, an addendum to Rusk's note, delivered several hours after the dispatch itself, may have been the most decisive input into the decision of 28 May—Tactical Decision 2 (b)—to wait and see whether the international flotilla would indeed become a reality.

All these communications arrived prior to the Cabinet's resumed session on Sunday afternoon the 28th. President Johnson wrote to Eshkol that Moscow claimed to have information about Israeli preparations for military action, to provoke a conflict. According to one version the President also wrote: 'The Soviets state that if Israel starts military action, the Soviet Union will extend help to the attacked States.' The President repeated his concern about the safety and vital interests of Israel and continued: 'As your friend, I repeat even more strongly what I said yesterday to Mr. Eban: Israel just must not take pre-emptive military action and thereby make itself responsible for the initiation of hostilities.'[1]

---

[1] Foreign Ministry sources; Bar-Zohar, p. 147.

President de Gaulle sent the following reply to Eshkol's letter of 19 May:

... For you the matter at issue is the threat which weighs upon your frontiers and the freedom of navigation in the Gulf of Aqaba. Indeed, it is legitimate to fear that the situation, suddenly tense and disturbing, in the region of which Israel is the geographical centre, may deteriorate into an armed conflict. However, there is nothing to indicate that either of the parties at issue has any interest in such a development. It is not necessary for me to say that that is the case with Israel. Your message testifies to this fact in the most authoritative fashion. It seems to me that that is also true for Syria and for Egypt. That is why it is essential in present circumstances that no party should give a pretext for dangerous reactions. ...

As for the question of free navigation in the Gulf of Aqaba. I know the importance which this has for Israel. In this connection, you know how deeply France is attached to the maintenance of the *status quo* which ultimately seems to us to be essential in the Middle East both for Israel and for the other States in the region.

My government has moreover proposed that the four Great Powers, which are members of the Security Council, should co-ordinate their action on the situation in the Middle East. The need is above all to insure that these powers abstain from intervening in order to impose their own solutions; and that none of them undertakes any action or gesture which could be interpreted as taking sides. We hope that this initiative will first of all support a reduction of tension. Thereafter co-operation between these four States should take place for the establishment of peace and the settlement of the more burning questions which arise in the Middle East.

This letter reconfirmed what was perceived already, namely, that France was advising Israel to acquiesce in Nasser's *fait accompli*. Indeed, the last sentence implied even further pressure for, according to the Arabs, the most 'burning question' in the Middle East was the very existence of the State of Israel, termed by Nasser a 19-year-old aggression.[1]

The British Prime Minister was more sympathetic. He said, *inter alia:* 'We understand that you are approaching a moment of fateful decision, and we strongly urge you to continue a policy of restraint, as long as diplomatic efforts are under way to find a satisfactory solution.'[2]

The US Secretary of State first dispatched to Barbour a résumé of Eban's talks in Washington, officially confirming their substance from an American source.[3] To Johnson's letter he instructed Barbour to add

[1] Foreign Ministry sources.   [2] As quoted in Bar-Zohar, p. 147.

[3] The key passages were as follows:

'1. An energetic effort in the Security Council as a political necessity both for the United States and Israel. He [Johnson] shared Israel's views about the Security Council, "but its mystique is a fact to accept".

'2. A public declaration by the maritime powers embodying the ideas of the President of the United States and Prime Minister of Great Britain and asserting an intent to see the law vindicated. ...

'3. An international naval presence in the area of the Gulf to be made operative

the following explanation for Eshkol and Eban:

The British and we are proceeding urgently to prepare the military aspects of the international naval escort plan and other nations are responding vigorously to the idea. The Dutch and Canadians have already joined even before a text was presented to them. With the assurance of international determination to make every effort to keep the Straits open to the flags of all nations, *unilateral action on the part of Israel would be irresponsible and catastrophic.*[1]

Eban reported these developments to the reconvened Cabinet. Eshkol then stated that he had intended to propose a drastic decision but was now prepared to advise the Cabinet to give the United States two more weeks to realize their project. After prolonged discussion only Carmel remained opposed to the idea of further delay. Allon abstained and stated that he reserved the right to ask that the Cabinet be called into immediate session to reconsider the decision if necessary, for he was of the opinion that the decision was basically wrong.[2] Although not formally inscribed as such in the Government minutes, the decision was to wait as long as another *two weeks*. This is evident from Eshkol's cable to Johnson on the 30th: 'the international naval escort should move through the Strait within a week or two.' It is also apparent from remarks to Rostow and Rusk by Israeli diplomats a few days later.[3]

The decisive role of US pressure was confirmed by the Prime Minister some months after the Six Day War:

---

only if the Security Council failed to keep the Straits and the Gulf open to the shipping of all nations as a matter of right. . . . Eban met with Secretary Rusk, McNamara and on Friday had a long visit with the President. The President stated his determination to make the international maritime plan work and his "fealty" to the commitment he and his predecessors had made.'

Secretary Rusk's report to Ambassador Barbour ended: 'During the course of the conversation Eban said: "Can I take it that I can convey to my Prime Minister that you have decided to make every possible effort to assure that the Straits and the Gulf would be open to free and innocent passage?" The President responded "yes".' Only the words 'every possible effort' might be construed as differing from Eban's report to the Cabinet: it was less firm than 'decided to assure that the Straits would be open . . .'. Foreign Ministry sources.

[1] Foreign Ministry sources (emphasis added).   [2] Allon interview, 1968.

[3] On 2 June an Israeli diplomat reportedly told Walt Rostow 'that they [Israelis] had made a commitment to hold steady for about two weeks . . . from the Cabinet meeting last Sunday . . . , that is, the week beginning Sunday, June 11—although he indicated that there was nothing ironclad about the time period being exactly two weeks.' Rostow's report to the President, as quoted by Johnson, p. 294. The same day Harman told Rusk that 'the test in the Gulf should be made during the next week'. Ibid. The role of US pressure in the 28 May decision to delay was noted by Eshkol in a cable to Johnson two days later: Eban's conversation with the President, he observed, had had 'an important influence on our decision to await developments for a further limited period'. Johnson, p. 294. This account of the 28 May Cabinet meeting is based upon Eshkol (11); Foreign Ministry sources; Burdett, pp. 266–7; Draper, pp. 93–4; Gilboa, pp. 155–7, 168; and Nakdimon, pp. 128–9.

Had we not received Johnson's letter and Rusk's message, I would have urged the Government to make the decision to fight; but their communications pointed out not only that unilateral Israeli action would be catastrophic but also that the United States was continuing with its preparations for multilateral action to open the Gulf to shipping of all nations. I could not forget that the letter was signed by the President who had once promised me face-to-face: 'We will carry out whatever I ever promise you.' I did not want him to come afterwards and say, 'I warned you in advance and now you cannot make any claims whatever on the United States and its allies.'[1]

Eban transmitted the Government's decision of 28 May to the *Knesset* Committee on Foreign Affairs and Security. *Gahal* entered a formal reservation that the decision was the Cabinet's alone.

Eshkol's 'time of troubles' was approaching a climax. The Cabinet had decided that the nation and the world must be given a report on the day's events. The Prime Minister undertook to deliver a speech himself. The hour was late: the Cabinet meeting broke up about 8.00 in the evening and the broadcast was scheduled for 8.30. Herzog and Galili drafted the text. When Eshkol read it he was dissatisfied with some passages, and his Political Secretary, Yaffe, typed in some changes. Eshkol arrived at the broadcasting studio and started reading the announcement—live—without examining the revisions. He stopped reading, started again, stopped once more, for the speech was illegible in parts. The most conspicuous feature was the PM's stammer. The effect on public opinion was disastrous. The nation, wound up tight as a spring, now heard its leader delivering an important announcement in a tired, stumbling, insecure manner. In fact, the mode of delivery triggered the final assault on Eshkol's position as Minister of Defence, and the formation of the National Unity Government, Tactical Decision 3. The speech itself gave notice to Israel, the Arabs, and the world that, though she reserved her right in self-defence to reopen the Straits, Israel would continue diplomatic efforts to achieve the speedy abolition of the Egyptian blockade.[2]

Another trial for Eshkol was his stormy meeting with the generals immediately after the broadcast. Since the morning of the 27th the Army High Command had been prepared for an order to go to war: according to one source, Rabin had come to this conclusion as a result

---

[1] Foreign Ministry sources.

[2] Bar-Zohar, pp. 150–1; Gilboa, pp. 168–9. The text of this speech is in *Documents on Palestine*, Doc. 36, p. 23. The worst incident of the delivery was described by Nakdimon thus (p. 130):

'"Furthermore", continues Eshkol, "lines of action were decided for the removal..." Eshkol suddenly stops. His breathing can be heard, picked up well by the sensitive mike, as well as his whisper: "What's this?" The word "removal" does not please him. And thus he includes in his deliberations his listeners who are in a state of high tension. He changes the word to "movement" (of military concentrations on the southern border of Israel).'

of his talk with Eshkol that morning.[1] When the Cabinet opted for further diplomatic activity—and delay—Rabin told Eshkol that, since he was the Defence Minister, he should inform the *Tzahal* General Staff personally of the Government's decision. Eshkol accepted the task. Totally unaware of the effects of his radio speech, Eshkol arrived in good spirits, told the generals of the decision, and then said: 'You can and must tell me everything. Speak, as if you were not in uniform.'[2] The storm that broke out was acrimonious, with dire warnings about the likely effects of further delay on casualties. Some even described the Cabinet decision as catastrophic. Eshkol was very upset but left the meeting with the feeling that the military were exaggerating. Allon and Rabin, who were present, did not defend the Government decision of 28 May.[3]

TABLE 21

CHRONOLOGY OF CRISIS: III

The Period of Diplomacy: 23–28 May 1967

TIME	EXTERNAL EVENTS	INTERNAL EVENTS
	Tuesday 23 May	
4.30 a.m.		Rabin informs Eshkol of Straits blockade.
5.00		Eban informed. Calls meeting of FO *Hanhala*.
6.00		PM's staff leave for Tel Aviv. Herzog suggests Opposition be called in. Eshkol agrees.
7.00		Yaffe gets Mrs. Meir's approval. *Gahal* and *Rafi* members of *Knesset* Committee on For. Aff. and Sec. invited to deliberations.
8.00		Peres–Begin conversation, re BG as PM.
9.00		Opposition group joins Ministerial Defence Committee

[1] Bar-Zohar, p. 140.   [2] Ibid., p. 151.

[3] The 28 May meeting with *Tzahal* commanders is described in varying detail in Eshkol (11); Bar-Zohar, p. 151; Gilboa, p. 170; Nakdimon, pp. 131–2. Some details were further confirmed by Foreign Ministry sources. According to Nakdimon and Bar-Zohar, General Avraham Yoffe exclaimed that if Israel continued her 'shilly-shallying' in Washington and Paris, while Egypt attacks, Israel would be moving towards a catastrophe. General Ariel Sharon was reported to have said that Eshkol's hesitation would cost Israel thousands of 'dead'. See also pp. 327–8, the bibliographical references in note 1, p. 328 above, and p. 418 below.

TIME	EXTERNAL EVENTS	INTERNAL EVENTS
		meeting already in progress. Meeting accepts US request to wait 48 hours and explore US position—T_{2a}. Cabinet decides on FM trip to US.
p.m.		In meeting on economic matter E. Sakharov suggests Dayan be appointed to Cabinet.
Late p.m.		Eban and Raviv arrive at Eshkol's Jerusalem Office. Cable from Eytan arrives, decisive factor in Eshkol decision to authorize Eban to go to Paris.
Later evening		Meetings at *Knesset*: *Gahal* and *Rafi* members of *Knesset* Committee on For. Aff. and Sec.; *Mafdal–Mapam* meeting.
a.m.–p.m.	Israeli officials inform Western Powers of Israel's right to self-defence under Article 51 of UN Charter. Johnson speech re-endorsing free navigation in Straits and condemnation of blockade.	
	Wednesday 24 May	
3.30 a.m.	Eban leaves for Paris, London, Washington.	
Early a.m.		Meeting of *Gahal*, *Rafi*, *Mafdal* in Shapira's office.
12.00 noon		Meeting of *Gahal*, *Rafi*, *Mafdal* in *Rafi*'s *Knesset* room. Consensus that Begin meet Eshkol re broadening of Government.
During day	U Thant arrives in Cairo. UN Security Council meets.	
12.00 (Paris time)	Eban meets de Gaulle. Also present: Eytan, Couve de Murville.	
16.30		Begin–Eshkol meeting.
17.00		Peres meets Reisner, Bahir briefly, then Avigur.

TABLE 21 (CONT.)

TIME	EXTERNAL EVENTS	INTERNAL EVENTS
		Avigur–BG exchange. In Jerusalem Warhaftig meets Y. S. Shapiro.
18.00–19.30		Peres meets Netzer and Surkiss.
17.00 (GMT)	Eban meets PM Harold Wilson.	
a.m.–p.m. (NYT)	Harman meets Eisenhower at Gettysburg. Latter reaffirms US 1957 commitment to Israel.	
20.00		Haifa meeting between Almogi and Hushi. Haifa mayor promises to see Eshkol.
Late afternoon/evening		Allon returns from USSR; meets immediately with Bar-Lev and Galili.
22.00		Meeting of *Rafi, Gahal, Mafdal* trio in M. H. Shapira's room, Tel Aviv Hilton. Decide on Shapira–Eshkol meeting.
24.00–1.30 (25 May)		Meeting of BG, Peres, Bahir, Harel.
	Thursday 25 May	
8.00		Meeting of M. H. Shapira and Eshkol re BG as Def. Minister. Meeting of *Rafi* and *Mapai* members of *Ihud Ha-kibbutzim*; decide for national unity government, but Eshkol remaining as PM.
10.30		*Rafi*'s Netzer, Brenner, Porat, Bahir meet BG, request him to take Defence Ministry
a.m.		Eshkol, Rabin, Bar-Lev, Dinstein, Kashti tour *Tzahal* positions in Negev. Meet with Generals Gavish, Tal, Sharon.
a.m.–p.m.	Fourth Egyptian Armoured Division deployed in Sinai. Further Mig reconnaissance flights over Negev. Egyptian Defence Minister Badran arrives in Moscow. U Thant ends Cairo talks.	

TABLE 21 (CONT.)

TIME	EXTERNAL EVENTS	INTERNAL EVENTS
14.00		*Mafdal* Caucus meets, opts for national unity government.
16.00–18.00		Meeting of *Rafi* Secretariat.
17.15		Meeting of Indep. Liberals. Decide to work for national unity government.
p.m.		Meeting of *Ma'arakh* Political Committee, *Mapai* and *Ahdut Ha'avoda* Secretariats. Vote of confidence in Eshkol. Only Carmel in favour of enlarged Cabinet.
p.m.		Allon meets Bar-Lev, Hod, and Yariv; agree Israel must take initiative. Rabin–Herzog consultation. Suggest to Eshkol telegram to Eban to test US commitment. Eshkol accepts; telegram transmitted. Herzog sends second to make sure Eban gets gist of message.
p.m. (NYT)	Eban and Raviv reach NY. Met by Rafael and Evron. Leave immediately for Washington; met by Harman and Geva. Shortly after arrival, Eshkol and Herzog telegrams arrive.	
20.00–22.00		Meeting of *Mafdal, Gahal, Rafi* leaders; decide to continue efforts.
Evening		Allon meets with Rabin. Both agree on necessity for Israel military initiative, to save lives.
17.00 (NYT)	Eban meets with Secretary of State Rusk.	
18.00 (NYT)	Working dinner at State Dept. with Eban, Harman, Rafael, Evron for Israel; E. Rostow, Kohler, Battle, Sisco, Meeker for State Dept.; and Hoopes from Pentagon.	

TABLE 21 (CONT.)

TIME	EXTERNAL EVENTS	INTERNAL EVENTS
After dinner	Eban returns to Rusk's office for second meeting.	
22.30 (NYT)	Rostow calls in Egyptian Ambassador and warns him against Egyptian resort to force; requests this be forwarded to Cairo immediately.	
24.00 (NYT)	Harman returns to State Department for further talks.	
1.30 a.m. 26 May (NYT)	Eban cables short message to Eshkol about possible US flotilla plans.	
	Friday 26 May	
a.m.	Hasanin Heikal's article on the inevitability of an armed clash with Israel appears in *Al-Ahram*.	
8.00		Haifa delegation meets with Eshkol, presses for co-option of Dayan and Begin to Cabinet.
10.00		Mrs. Meir meets with Hazan of *Mapam*, informed about Peres–Ya'ari meeting. Avigur called in as well.
a.m.		Eshkol, in consultation with some *Ma'arakh* ministers, rejects advice to appoint Allon as Deputy PM or Defence Minister.
a.m.–p.m.		Cabinet meeting. *Mafdal* under Warhaftig calls for national unity government. Y. S. Shapiro suggests Opposition leaders be co-opted as Ministers without Portfolio.
Late a.m.		Eshkol's aide, Yaffe, suggests to Begin and Rimalt that *Gahal* join deliberations of Ministerial Def. Committee. *Gahal* refuses.
12.45		Meeting of *Gahal* and *Rafi* leaders at Hotel Savoy, Tel Aviv, moving to wider forum at Hotel Samuel. *Gahal* con-

TIME	EXTERNAL EVENTS	INTERNAL EVENTS
		tends BG's co-option is now out of the question.
15.00		Eshkol meets Allon, who urges military initiative to save lives; he persuades Eshkol to send telegram to Eban.
9.45 (NYT)	In response to Rusk inquiry whether he will remain until Saturday, Eban informs him that speedy clarification of US position absolutely crucial.	
11.00 (NYT)	Eban, Harman, Geva meet McNamara and Wheeler at Pentagon. Third telegram arrives re Egyptian troop concentrations.	
a.m.	Evron–Rostow 'phone conversation.	
16.00		*Knesset* Committee on Foreign Affairs and Security hears reports from *Tzahal* staff.
17.00		Eshkol meets Ya'ari and Hazan of *Mapam* who reaffirm support for Eshkol's original proposal.
19.00		Prominent citizens see Eshkol re national unity government.
22.30		*Tzahal* chiefs report to Eshkol.
p.m.–evening	Nasser speech to Central Council of Arab Trade Unions defines objective as destruction of Israel.	
18.00 (NYT)	Rostow–Evron meeting.	
18.15 (NYT)	Johnson–Evron talk.	
19.15 (NYT)	Johnson–Eban conversation. Also present: McNamara, Sisco, Christian, Harman, Evron.	
20.40 (NYT)	Eban and Harman leave White House, return immediately to New York.	
Late evening	Eban visits Arthur Goldberg,	

TABLE 21 (CONT.)

TIME	EXTERNAL EVENTS	INTERNAL EVENTS
(NYT)	who stresses that only President's assurances important in grave situation.	

Saturday 27 May

TIME	EXTERNAL EVENTS	INTERNAL EVENTS
3.00 a.m.		Chuvakhin–Eshkol meeting. Russian note of restraint and warning on the 'firing of first shot'.
3.30	Nasser awakened by Soviet Ambassador in Cairo and restrained from war as well.	
9.00		Eshkol meets Rabin, Yariv, then informs some ministers of night's events. Also informs *Knesset* Committee on Foreign Affairs and Meir. Latter suggests Allon as Deputy Defence Minister. Eshkol refuses.
16.00		*Rafi* leadership meets.
19.00		Sapir, Aranne bring Eshkol up to date on inter-party negotiations.
19.30		BG, Peres, Almogi meet with Begin, Ben-Eliezer, Y. Sapir, E. Rimalt.
20.00		Cabinet goes into session.
22.00		Eban joins Cabinet deliberations.
24.00		*Knesset* Committee on Foreign Affairs and Security meets to hear Eban report.

Sunday 28 May

TIME	EXTERNAL EVENTS	INTERNAL EVENTS
3.30 a.m.		*Knesset* Committee on Foreign Affairs and Security adjourns.
5.00 a.m.		Cabinet adjourns; position deadlocked 9:9.
a.m.	US Ambassador Barbour delivers Rusk dispatch to Bitan.	
11.00	Barbour delivers Johnson note (containing also Kosygin	

TIME	EXTERNAL EVENTS	INTERNAL EVENTS
	warning) and Rusk addendum to Yaffe for Eshkol.	
a.m.	Reply of de Gaulle to 19 May Eshkol letter delivered, calls for restraint.	
a.m.	Letter from Wilson delivered, calls for restraint.	
14.00		Dayan–Eshkol meeting. Dayan insists on post with definite duties.
15.00–20.00		Cabinet reconvenes, decides at 8.00 in the evening to continue political–diplomatic line (Tactical Decision 2(b)).
17.30		*Knesset* Committee on Foreign Affairs and Security reconvenes.
p.m.	Nasser press conference takes matter back to the 'core of the problem', Israel, termed the first and biggest aggression.	
20.30		Eshkol reports to the nation by live broadcast. Delivery is disastrous.
20.45		*Knesset* Committee on For. Aff. and Sec. ends deliberations. No objections expressed after Eban conveys Government decision to continue political line.
21.00		Eshkol, Allon, Yaffe meet *Tzahal*'s *Alufim*; intense pressure on Eshkol for action.
Evening		Eshkol meets *Mapai* ministers, again refuses to give Dayan Defence portfolio.

(IV) *29 May–4 June: The Period of Resolution*

The final week of the 1967 decision-making crisis falls into two phases: 29 May–1 June, which was taken up almost completely with internal events; and 2–4 June, which was concerned exclusively with the external environment and the climactic decision.

The first phase was one of relentless pressure on the Eshkol Government from interest groups—institutional (military), associational (*Kibbutzim*), non-associational, and anomic—and from competing élites to co-opt *Gahal* and *Rafi* into a national unity government, united to face a grave external threat. From 29 May all four major Hebrew-language daily newspapers advocated this move, including *Mapai*'s own *Davar*. There were also spontaneous petitions and demonstrations by businessmen, students, and women.[1]

On Monday the 29th the parameters of battle were set. There were four important internal events: *Rafi*'s pre-*Knesset* session Caucus meeting; Ben Gurion's press conference; the *Ma'arakh* Caucus meeting in the evening; and the *Gahal–Mapai* negotiating session. From the first two meetings BG's advocacy emerged clearly. The country, he argued, must have strong leadership to determine proper military decisions at the correct time; but the leader must be strong enough to hold back, to assure Israel's good relations (for arms) with her friends. In his opinion Eshkol was incompetent to provide that leadership, and Dayan was the man of the hour.[2]

The *Ma'arakh* was not prepared to oust Eshkol from the Prime Ministership, but the evening of 29 May saw the first demand within a *Mapai* party forum that Eshkol give up the Defence Portfolio for the sake of national unity. Dov Sadan and M. Zar were the earliest advocates; younger *Mapainiks* Eliav, Yadlin, and G. Cohen met to work out a common strategy. The *Ahdut Ha'avoda* section of the Caucus claimed the Defence post for Allon, if it was to be separated from the Prime Ministership.

Another important meeting was the negotiating session between *Gahal*'s Begin, Saphir, Bader, and Rimalt and *Mapai*'s Meir, Yeshayahu, and Barkatt. The *Mapai* team reaffirmed the invitation to *Gahal* to join the Cabinet with two ministers without portfolio, who would also be members of the Ministerial Defence Committee. *Gahal*, however, insisted on Dayan's accession to the Defence Ministry so that *Rafi*, too, could join a true national unity government. The issue was left open. There was, in short, a growing consensus by the evening of the 29th that a national unity government of some type had to be formed. All the main Opposition parties were agreed that Eshkol must give up the Defence Ministry. And *Mapai*'s Coalition partners, as well as a growing number of influential *Mapai* members, thought likewise; but they had yet to co-ordinate their actions to this end.[3]

The key 'external' events of 29 May were the parliamentary pronouncements by Eshkol and Nasser, and the Egyptian President's press conference the previous evening. Nasser raised the stakes once

---

[1] The account of these developments is based upon the following: Allon and Peres interviews, 1968; Begin (1); Gilboa; Nakdimon.

[2] Nakdimon, pp. 139–41.   [3] *MER*, p. 370; Nakdimon, pp. 145–6.

more by emphasizing, before both forums, the rights of the Palestinian Arabs and the restoration of the pre-1948 situation. At the same time he explicitly stated that Egypt would not initiate overt hostilities and that, while he was unwilling to contemplate any form of coexistence in peace with Israel, the rights of the Palestinians would be restored by themselves. The implication was that, for the time being, he was satisfied with the restoration of the *status quo ante* 29 October 1956, though specific claims to Eilat and El-Auja were also raised by him.[1]

Eshkol's speech firmly reasserted Israel's right to free navigation through the Straits, a position on which there could be no compromise and which was made absolutely clear to the Powers. He then indicated Israel's willingness to await the actions of the maritime states: 'It was our duty first of all to put international undertakings to the test. In the near future it will transpire whether this prospect is being realized.'[2]

Finally, on the 29th the Security Council held one of its five completely futile meetings on the crisis during the last week of May. By that time none of the delegates voiced the 'why this haste, what's the rush' note they had voiced at their first meeting. But no resolutions were submitted that day. The Egyptian delegate declared that his

---

[1] The denial of Israel's right to Eilat was also included in a memorandum on the Gulf of Aqaba circulated the same day by Arab embassies in countries that had diplomatic relations with the UAR; Foreign Ministry sources. Part of the Egyptian plan of battle was to cut off the southern part of Israel from the rest of the country, thus linking Egypt with Jordan; a special task force was assembled and poised on Israel's border to carry out that plan.

Nasser's press conference and speech (excerpts) appear in *Documents on Palestine*, Docs. 328 and 329, pp. 549–65; and in Draper, Appendix 11 (excerpts), and 12 (excerpts), pp. 224–34. Nasser's press conference began with a long policy statement and ended with a question-and-answer period. It was one of his best performances. Eloquent throughout, sometimes moving, at other times sarcastic, he was in full command of his audience at all times. He untiringly hammered home his message, stressing the importance of the occasion.

'. . . the mere existence of Israel is an aggression; . . . the Palestinians were driven out of their country in 1948; they were robbed of their lands, their homes and their fortunes in 1948. . . . The people of Palestine must recover their rights; what happened in 1948 was an aggression. . . . America and certain other great powers —Britain, for example— . . . this week have turned the world upside down just because we have restored the situation to what it was before 1956. . . . As regards time and place, we are at the present time fully prepared for a confrontation, and . . . if Israel attacks any Arab country, we shall not allow her to confine the operation to a limited area: it will be total war.'

In the press conference, as well as in his speech, Nasser stressed that '. . . the issue now at hand is not the Gulf of Aqaba, the Straits of Tiran or the withdrawal of UNEF, but the rights of the Palestinian people'. He stated '. . . the Palestinian people will have to recover their rights for themselves'.

[2] Eshkol's 29 May statement (Eshkol (5)) is from *Divrei Ha-knesset*, xlix, pp. 2283–5. The English version (excerpts) appears in *Documents on Palestine*, Doc. 38, pp. 24–51; and in Christman, pp. 95–104.

country was in 'a state of war' with Israel and therefore had every right to close the Straits.[1]

A major escalation of the crisis occurred on Tuesday 30 May with the signing of a Mutual Defence Pact between the UAR and Jordan. Similar in language to the UAR–Syrian Defence Agreement of November 1966, Article 7 stipulated that 'in the event of military operations starting, the Chief of Staff of the Armed Forces of the United Arab Republic shall assume command of operations in both states'.[2] This was a severe blow to those in Israel who had urged diplomatic action for another two weeks: the nightmare of a concerted Arab assault had become an all-too-real possibility. Moreover, the most acute point of vulnerability to sudden attack was from Jordanian territory. And King Hussein, who several days earlier had been called the 'Hashemite whore' by Radio Cairo and whose offer of help had been contemptuously spurned by Nasser a week before, had now, by his precipitate action, joined his forces with what seemed to him the winning side.[3]

The Pact was another surprise development for Israel and one fraught with great danger. The rationale for further delay had to be re-examined quickly. Eshkol and Eban met and decided to send *Aluf* Meir Amit, then Head of the Counter-Intelligence agency, *Ha-Mosad*, to Washington, to make a clear on-the-spot evaluation of the seriousness of American commitments. That act was reinforced by a cable from Harman, which arrived around noon on the 30th: it stated that a declaration by the maritime powers now being drafted would contain no threat of the use of force. Contacts with several other maritime states—Canada, Denmark, Norway—had also shown that any support

[1] *UN Monthly Chronicle*, iv, 6, June 1967, pp. 5–26.

[2] *Documents on Palestine*, Doc. 332, pp. 568–9.

[3] The profound effect of this external input on the perceptions of Israeli decision-makers is well documented. Rabin reflected on the fifth anniversary: 'In my opinion Israel should have fought on the 30th of May.' Rabin 1972. Eban stated: 'By his journey to Cairo on May 30 Hussein had made it certain that war would break out. . . .' Eban interview, 1968. See also Eshkol (11) and Gilboa, p. 198. As to Nasser's motives, it seems plausible to accept the arguments that he had come to believe Israel would, after all, fight and that, in the face of the strong Israeli concentration of power in the south, he needed all the help he could get. Bar-Zohar, p. 159; *MER*, p. 202.

King Hussein explained his attitude at the time as a 'spontaneous and natural attitude'. Later he reaffirmed this—he could not stand aside. But he added that the Pact was also forced on him by the superiority of the forces opposing him, implying pressures from within as well. In Hussein's book it was stated that he decided on his move upon hearing Nasser's 29 May press conference. Hussein, p. 39. Some observers have speculated that 'Eshkol's statement of 28 May . . . might have convinced the King that the Israelis were losing in their conflict with the UAR'. *MER*, p. 203. And the fact 'of Nasser controlling the Straits on a permanent basis would control Jordan's only port of entry as well; to be accessible to free navigation at Nasser's whim could also not have escaped Hussein's attention.'

for the use of force, if it existed at all, had quickly evaporated. Harman further reported that Israel would be offered economic aid to compensate for the strain of mobilization and waiting.[1]

Two further steps were taken that day to emphasize Israel's resolve not to compromise, and to emphasize the urgency of international action, if the outbreak of war was to be prevented. On Eshkol's instructions, Eban held a press conference in the late morning: he emphasized that free shipping in the Gulf of Aqaba 'is a central and vital national interest that will under no circumstances whatever be surrendered or abandoned . . .'. He likened Israel to a 'coiled spring' and declared that she intended to exercise her right of self-defence and act accordingly, 'if possible with others, if necessary alone'. The period of waiting could be counted in days or weeks, certainly not in months or years.[2]

In the afternoon Eban and Eshkol drafted a letter from the Prime Minister to President Johnson, which was sent off the same day. Eshkol stated that 'a point is being approached at which counsels to Israel will lack any moral or logical basis. I feel that I must make it clear in all candour that the continuation of this position for any considerable time is out of the question.' More specifically, 'it is crucial that the international naval escort should move through the Straits within a week or two.' He reminded the President of the commitments made in 1957 and a few days previously. He stressed that history showed the futility of trying to appease an 'aggressive dictator'. 'President Nasser's rising prestige has already had serious effects in Jordan. . . . The time is ripe for confronting Nasser with a more intense and effective policy of resistance.'[3]

Internally, party and interest-group pressures were approaching a climax. The NRP leader, Shapira, in two meetings with Eshkol, emphasized the need to appoint Dayan as Defence Minister. The Independent Liberals decided formally in favour of a national unity government but again insisted that Eshkol remain Prime Minister.[4] Prior to this, in the morning, *Mapai*'s Meir, Aranne, and Avigur had urged Eshkol to appoint Allon as Defence Minister or Deputy Prime

---

[1] Foreign Ministry sources; *MER*, pp. 200, 202; Yost, p. 316. Harman had already cabled two days earlier that Walt Rostow had told him the President could see no outcome from the crisis. *MER* summarized the situation as follows: 'On 31 May and 1 June, several official American statements made it clear that the US did not have any immediate plans for opening the Straits by force, or even for testing the blockade, but preferred to confine her efforts to the diplomatic level, focussing, to a large extent, on the UN' (p. 202). This is also confirmed by George Brown: '. . . the reluctance of the Americans to support it [the international action]'. He goes on to say: 'Whether, given more time, we could have assembled an international peace-keeping naval force I do not know.' p. 137.

[2] *Documents on Palestine*, Doc. 41, pp. 28–9.

[3] Foreign Ministry sources. The passage about 'a week or two' is cited in Johnson, p. 294.

[4] Nakdimon, pp. 155–7, 170–1.

Minister in charge of Defence. He refused and countered with the idea of a Defence Council composed of Generals Allon, Dayan, Yigael Yadin, and Haim Laskov. By the afternoon Dayan rejected the plan.[1] Yadin, too, pressed for Dayan's co-option as Defence Minister.[2] Eshkol presented his plan for a Defence Council to the *Ma'arakh* Caucus meeting that evening. The reaction was overwhelmingly negative: one member after another pressed him to relinquish the Defence Ministry. It was a rude awakening to the fact that the party majority, including many of his own friends, had lost confidence in him in defence matters, no matter what his record of achievement had been in the past.[3]

Further confirmation of the erosion of the US position on the opening of the Straits came quickly. Upon receipt of Eshkol's letter on 31 May, Walt Rostow called Evron to the White House and told him that the President was disturbed by the Prime Minister's reference to 'the assurances that the United States would take any and all measures to open the Straits of Tiran to international shipping': it did not reflect accurately his talks with Eban, Johnson observed, and such a commitment went beyond presidential prerogative. Evron protested that this sentence was drawn from a verbatim report by Harman on the Johnson–Eban conversation of 26 May; further, that the Harman account, strengthened by the Rusk version, especially his addendum to the President's letter, had been decisive in staying Israel's hand on 28 May.[4]

On the 31st, too, Rusk declared before a Congressional Committee: 'No conclusion whatsoever can be drawn from what the press writes about a military act. These are guesses only. The United States is not at this time planning any separate military activity in the Middle East but only within the framework of the UN and in conjunction with other powers.'[5] No less disquieting were suggestions from the American Administration, in calculated leaks, whose purpose was to

---

[1] Gilboa, p. 178; Nakdimon, pp. 155–6. Eshkol initially proposed Amit instead of Laskov but by evening Laskov's name was mentioned.

[2] Yadin later revealed that 'he had arrived independently at the conclusion that Eshkol had to hand over the Defence Ministry to Moshe Dayan. . . . I felt that the people had lost faith in Eshkol's military leadership.' *Jerusalem Post*, 11 June 1972.

[3] Gilboa, p. 172; Laqueur 1968, pp. 152–3; *MER*, p. 370; Nakdimon, pp. 162–70.

[4] Foreign Ministry sources; Bar-Zohar, pp. 164–5; Gilboa, pp. 197–8. There was, in fact, a considerable discrepancy on this point between the Harman and Rusk versions, though American commitments made earlier were firm and explicit. The Rusk account of the talks, as noted, referred to 'every possible effort' to open the Straits, compared with Eshkol's phrase, 'any and all measures'.

[5] As quoted in Bar-Zohar, p. 165. The same note was struck by Goldberg at the Security Council meeting that day. Introducing the US Delegation's draft resolution, he stated that the measures proposed in the resolution were designed to ensure a cooling-off period without prejudice to the ultimate rights or claims of any party. *UN Monthly Chronicle*, iv, 6, June 1967, p. 23.

test Israel's willingness to compromise with Nasser's *fait accompli*. These included the idea that the Gulf should be opened for an interim period to all ships, except those bearing the Israel flag, or that the issue should be submitted to the International Court of Justice for decision. On all fronts, the Powers were hard at work to gain time in order to defuse the tension and thus create an atmosphere of negotiation *ex post facto*. To Israeli decision-makers one fact at least was crystal-clear: the deferment of the opening of the Straits by diplomacy or the postponement of war meant acquiescence in the closure of the Straits to Israeli shipping with worse to come.[1]

The internal arena dominated 31 May, despite the US erosion. *Mapai*'s Political Committee voted to make Allon Defence Minister and to offer Dayan the Deputy Premiership. Dayan rejected the proposal and insisted that he become Defence Minister or Prime Minister–Defence Minister, or that he be appointed to an active military command. Eshkol, still fighting desperately to retain the Defence Ministry for himself, more important in his eyes than the Premiership, accepted the third suggestion; and by the evening arrangements had been made to appoint Dayan Head of the Southern Command, with General Gavish, the existing commander, as his deputy. It proved to be an abortive ploy however: the pressure to oust Eshkol from the Defence Ministry became irresistible, no less a force than the demand to appoint Dayan.

Interior Minister Shapira rejected the Eshkol solution and requested a special Cabinet meeting to discuss the situation. At the evening Cabinet session Shapira threatened to leave the Government, along with the other NRP ministers, if Eshkol went through with the Dayan appointment to Southern Command. He emphasized that *Rafi* would not join the Government unless Dayan were appointed Defence Minister. Eshkol conciliated the Cabinet by setting up a Ministerial Negotiating Committee composed of himself, Galili, Shapira, Kol, and *Mapam*'s Barzilai. (By that time *Mapam* had finally acquiesced in a national unity government—with *Gahal* and *Rafi*.)

Parallel with the Cabinet meeting there was a stormy session of the *Mapai* Secretariat. The atmosphere was extremely tense, with bitter exchanges, especially between Meir and Dov Joseph. Meir was the key figure behind Allon's candidacy for the Defence Ministry; Joseph was a staunch advocate of a national unity government, including *Rafi*. The Secretariat decided to support Eshkol's efforts to broaden the Government but insisted on being consulted before a final decision.

On 1 June Eshkol capitulated. There was, first, the cumulative effect of pressure during the previous three days. There was also concern for the morale of *Tzahal*'s General Staff, in appointing someone, even as qualified as Dayan, to a critical command post for political

[1] Foreign Ministry sources; Bar Zohar, pp. 165–7.

considerations. The arguments of a *Gahal* delegation under Begin, as well as the advice and threatened resignation of Shapira, added their weight. The *Mapai* Secretariat's pro-Dayan consensus was the final decisive input. Eshkol now took Tactical Decision 3—to broaden the Government by including Dayan as Minister of Defence and two *Gahal* Ministers without Portfolio, all to serve as well on the Ministerial Defence Committee.

By 10.00 p.m. *Gahal* had delegated Begin as one of its ministers (to represent the *Herut* wing); and *Rafi* acceded to Eshkol's request to delegate Dayan. The *Rafi* decision was taken not without a staunch effort by Peres to convince Ben Gurion of its necessity in face of the military situation; BG preferred to oust Eshkol altogether. Begin and Dayan attended the expanded Cabinet's first though unofficial meeting shortly after. (Begin and Saphir, the second *Gahal* minister, who joined the Cabinet the next day, were officially sworn in on 5 June, and Dayan after the war.)[1]

One commentator aptly summed up the internal political struggle: 'The movement for a national unity government was contradictory in character; partly it was born out of a sincere belief that . . . all party differences should be forgotten . . .; partly it was the result of a sudden wave of emotion . . .; people under stress make their decisions not only on the basis of cold calculations; they need psychological reassurance and a symbol. Dayan was a symbol of military strength and confidence, Eshkol was not. . . .'[2]

During 31 May Israeli high-policy decision-makers were preoccupied with the final crucial phase of the internal crisis, culminating in Tactical Decision 3. At the same time the flow of reports about the procrastination of the maritime powers, and especially the US, regarding the opening of the Straits helped to crystallize the growing conviction that nothing was to be gained from further waiting.[3]

---

[1] Gilboa, pp. 174–8; Nakdimon, pp. 184, 191–200.

[2] Laqueur 1968, pp. 151–2.

[3] The previous day Foreign Secretary George Brown referred in Parliament to the Tripartite Declaration of 1950, in words similar to those used by de Gaulle a week earlier in his conversation with Eban: 'The situation has entirely changed since that date. We do not now claim to play any special role in the Arab/Israel dispute.' He went on to say that Britain's policy was to work in and through the UN; but since this may not be sufficient, '. . . we have . . . decided to consult other like-minded nations about the issuing of a clear declaration by the international maritime community that the Gulf of Aqaba is an international waterway into which and through which the vessels of all nations have a right of passage'. He added that Britain was consulting other nations about the situation that would arise if the above initiatives were to fail. Prime Minister Wilson repeated the same three-stage scenario in his concluding remarks to the House of Commons debate. His words on the important third stage were that Britain was consulting now '. . . with those concerned about the situation which would then arise and what action would then be appropriate to ensure that the objective which we have in mind is fulfilled'. *Documents on Palestine*, Docs. 44, 46, pp. 30,

Meir Amit's first report, which arrived that day, served to underline this Israeli view. 'At the end of my first round of talks in Washington', he wrote, 'my conclusions are that we should wait a few days in order to give a chance for the operation of freeing the Straits. . . .' However, he added: 'From hints and scattered facts that I have heard, I get the impression that the maritime force project is running into heavier water every hour.'[1] The same day a report arrived that Rusk, when asked by a journalist whether the Americans were making any efforts to restrain Israel, answered: 'I don't think it is our business to restrain anyone.'[2]

Reviewing these reports, Eban then took what he considered one of his most momentous steps during the crisis. Accompanied by the Director-General of the Foreign Ministry, he met Rabin and Yariv and told them that he withdrew his political inhibitions to a military riposte: the waiting period had achieved its purpose—Israel would not be isolated as in 1956. Nothing was to be gained from further waiting. Subsequent decisions on methods and timing should now be reached on military grounds alone.[3]

The Thursday night meeting of the Cabinet (1 June) started at 9.30 p.m. without the new ministers. Eshkol's formal proposal to appoint Dayan as Defence Minister and to form a national unity government was accepted. At 10 o'clock Begin and Dayan joined the meeting. According to one source, it was decided to transfer the

---

42. On 1 June the State Department spokesman stated that 'the United Nations was the focus of American attempts to solve the crisis' and that the US supported 'the British initiative on a joint declaration of free navigation'. Foreign Ministry sources.

[1] Foreign Ministry sources. Eban revealed five years later that Amit, in his preliminary report, had added: '. . . there is a growing chance for American political backing if we act on our own'. Eban 1972. The American Administration was busy on several fronts. They were in touch with the USSR on ways to control the crisis. They sent two special emissaries to Nasser: UN Representative Charles Yost arrived in Cairo on 19 May but got to see Foreign Minister Mahmud Riad only on 1 June; and the President sent Robert Anderson on a secret personal mission to Nasser. Washington also put into circulation the draft of the resolution by the maritime powers—by the 31st, to 28 of the 80 states which were to be approached by the US. The upshot of these activities was that, on the one hand, the Egyptians and their Soviet patron, while willing to be conciliatory about further moves, were not prepared to budge an inch from their positions as of that date; on the other hand, the maritime nations consulted were clearly in no mind to act hastily, even to the extent of signing a declaration: only five states ultimately signed: US, UK, Australia, Holland, and Israel. Foreign Ministry sources; Bar-Zohar, pp. 173–4, 181; *MER*, pp. 200–4; Wilson, p. 398.

[2] Eban 1972.

[3] Ibid., and Burdett, p. 302. It is curious that Eban notified Rabin directly of this decision, without consulting Eshkol: the PM was staying next door to him; and in fact Eban met him outside his office while returning from his meeting with Rabin and then informed him of what he told Rabin. This circumvention of the Prime Minister would not have happened under Ben Gurion.

discussion of the military situation to the following morning's meeting of the Ministerial Defence Committee.[1]

The meeting of the Cabinet Committee, on Friday morning, 2 June, was attended by most *Tzahal* commanders from the General Staff. A strong plea was made by them, explicitly or by implication, to end the '*Hamtana*' because of the increasing danger of delaying military activities any longer. Begin described the atmosphere thus:

At that moment the Prime Minister requested the commanders to speak before the members of the Ministerial Committee on Defence with complete candour. They spoke not just with characteristic firmness, but also with feeling. Not all answered the question, what to do. There were some among them who gave factual reports, either about our forces, or about the enemy's alignment. Even from the reports a certain conclusion was implied, but the listeners had to reach it themselves.

Other officers not only posed the principal question, but also answered it. From their words there was also heard, sometimes, an echo of another meeting, previously, between themselves and the Prime Minister and his friends, before the National Unity Government was established [28 May]. . . .

The commanders . . . revealed their basic concern that every additional day without a decision would increase our losses when the hour of implementation arrived. They had no doubts of victory. They expressed their belief not only in the strength of the army but also in its ability to rout the enemy. Sometimes *we* received the impression, that we must not depend on *Tzahal*'s ability 'to solve the problem'. *They* did not doubt this ability at all, even raising the possibility that we would have to fight not just on one front.

Begin also paraphrased a sentence by Aluf M. Peled: 'Nasser concentrated all of his army against *Tzahal*. He would not have dared to do so, had he not depended on the hesitancy of the Government of Israel.'[2]

This description illuminates two strands of the psychological atmosphere of the crisis period that were still relevant two days before the strategic decision:

1. *Tzahal*'s view that an early military riposte would save lives; and
2. the rupture in the generals' relationship with Eshkol after the meeting of 28 May. The change in the Government enabled them to put forward their views again, and forcefully; their audience now included Dayan and Begin, both more sympathetic to their advocacy than Eshkol or others.

Begin and Dayan listened and made few comments. Again there was

---

[1] Tevet, p. 569. See also Nakdimon, pp. 264, 266. The Cabinet meeting lasted for 3½ hours. Except for the above proposals, plus exchanges of formal expressions of goodwill, appropriate to the historic character of the meeting, there seems to have been little discussion of substance; it was left for the next day's meeting with its tighter rules of security.

[2] Begin (2) and (3). Rabin 1972 affirmed that he took Yariv and Weizman to the key ministerial meetings. Tevet (p. 569) says that Air Force Commander Hod was present as well and presented a review of the situation.

no decision. But Begin asserted later that, after leaving the meeting, he and Dayan agreed they would leave the Cabinet if a decision were not taken.[1]

Eban's conviction that the time for diplomatic efforts was over was fortified by reports that day. The French announced that the state which began hostilities would receive no support from France; and their official Cabinet statement ominously linked the problem of the Straits with the 'situation' of the Palestinian refugees.[2] Moreover, Harman telephoned announcing his return the next day, after several discussions with Rusk: his preliminary report again stressed the air of caution now prevailing in Washington. As to the Soviets, Eban was convinced that they would not intervene militarily, particularly if the war was of short duration.[3]

In the evening Allon stated in a speech in Tel Aviv that, unless the blockade was ended, troops were pulled back from the border, and *feda'iyun* activities stopped, war was inevitable.[4]

There were three important external events on Saturday 3 June. The first was the arrival of Iraqi and Egyptian forces in Jordan, i.e. the implementation of the 30 May Pact between Hussein and Nasser. Secondly, Ambassador Eytan was informed in Paris of a French arms embargo on shipments to Israel, effective as of 5 June.[5] Thirdly, President Johnson's answer to Eshkol's letter of 30 May was delivered.

The newly appointed Defence Minister gave two press conferences beginning at 4 p.m. that day, one immediately following the other—to foreign correspondents and to Israeli military reporters respectively. Dayan's self-confidence and flair provided an immense boost to morale on the home front. At the same time, according to some observers, the interpretation put on his words created the impression that Israel was not going to initiate hostilities, not yet: Dayan had said, *inter alia*, that 2 June was either too early or too late for action.[6]

In the evening there was a crucial consultation at Eshkol's Jerusalem home.[7] Present were Allon, Dayan, Eban, Rabin, Yadin, Herzog, Amit,

---

[1] Begin (3).

[2] *Documents on Palestine*, Doc. 49, p. 50. The relevant sentence, obviously formulated in majestic de Gaulle style, reads: '. . . l'Etat qui le premier et on que ce soit, employait les armes n'aurait ni son approbation ni, à plus forte raison, son appui.'

[3] Foreign Ministry sources.

[4] Allon (2). *MER* (p. 201) notes one other meeting, at Eshkol's home that evening, where the PM ordered *Tzahal* to be ready for a counter-strike against Egypt, if necessary.

[5] *MER*, p. 203. As noted earlier, the embargo applied then only to complete heavy weaponry.

[6] Summaries or the full text of these press conferences may be found in Gilboa, p. 199; *Jerusalem Post* and *Lamerhav*, 4 June 1967; Nakdimon, p. 275.

[7] The account of this meeting is based upon Foreign Ministry sources, and Nakdimon, p. 276.

and Harman. Harman had earlier reported on his conversations with
Rusk, which had only served to underline the concern that international
action was fading away. He also reported the one concrete result of the
Anderson mission in Cairo on 31 May—the forthcoming exchange of
visits of Vice-Presidents between Egypt and the United States, to take
place on 7 June.

It was decided at the 3 June *ad hoc* meeting to propose to the Cabinet
the next day to go to war. Harman and Amit, both in touch with the
American Administration a day earlier, did not dissent from the
impression that nothing further was to be gained from waiting. Neither
could President Johnson's last letter be interpreted as containing
promises of specific US action to be taken with or without the help of
other maritime powers. In fact, the letter had stressed that the United
States could not act in isolation and urged Israel not to do so either.
The President had written:

I must emphasize the necessity for Israel not to make itself responsible for the
initiation of hostilities. Israel will not be alone, unless it decides to go alone. . . .
I explained to Mr. Eban that I . . . want to protect the territorial integrity
of Israel and the other nations in this area of the world, and will provide as
effective American support *as possible* to preserve the peace and freedom of your
nation and of the area. I stressed, too, the need to act in concert with other
nations. . . .
Our leadership is unanimous that the United States should not move in isolation.[1]

At the same time, the perceived impression was that, if Israel took the
initiative to break the encirclement of Arab armies, the US would
not take an unfriendly view, while the Soviets would not intervene
militarily. More than five years after the strategic decision, Foreign
Minister Eban made a revealing disclosure, in the course of a eulogy
of the late US President: 'After so many days of contact with him, in

---

[1] Foreign Ministry sources (emphasis added). Johnson stated in his memoirs: 'I
was determined to honor President Eisenhower's 1957 pledge on Aqaba. . . . If it
came to a crunch, I believed the American flag would have to sail the waters of
Aqaba alongside Israel's and, we hoped, many other flags as well.' His sincerity was
perceived by all the Israelis in contact with the White House at the time. But the
President and, particularly, other members of the American Administration also
succeeded in convincing the Israeli envoys and decision-makers that, because of the
'no more foreign adventures' atmosphere created by the Vietnam War, there were
grave doubts whether the President would be able to secure Congressional backing for
unilateral US action. Johnson stated that, though he was convinced that he could do so,
it would not have been easy. He also cited a joint Rusk–McNamara memorandum
that '. . . an effort to get a meaningful resolution from the Congress runs the risk of
becoming bogged down in acrimonious dispute'. Johnson, pp. 295, 297. In this sense,
and in this sense only, the speculation, often voiced, that the Israelis felt the Americans
expected them to solve their problems by themselves, and the sooner the better, was
probably true. The American Administration was certainly taken 'off the hook' by
Israel's actions, in a ticklish internal (American) situation.

writing and in speech, we could all well feel that, if Israel took up its own responsibility and emerged intact, it could count on him not to support or even to permit a policy of international intimidation.'[1]

The emphasis at the 3 June meeting now turned to the military dimension. Those present were apprised—some for the first time— of the military plans prepared by the General Staff, with certain changes made by Dayan. 'It was decided to stage for the time being a holding operation against the Syrians in the north, and not to attack Jordan unless Jordan attacked first. . . . The main blow was to be directed against the Egyptians.'[2] There would be a three-pronged thrust into Sinai to destroy the Egyptian Army and open the Straits. This could not be done except by capturing the entire peninsula. The meeting ended with the final plans approved by the group.

On Sunday 4 June Iraq acceded to the Egypt–Syria–Jordan Pacts; the wording was similar to those previous inter-Arab agreements. By this time, however, no further inputs were necessary to Israel's resolve. At a seven-hour meeting, broken up from time to time for group consultations, the Cabinet reviewed the situation once more and then decided to go to war.[3]

The proceedings were opened by Dayan. He reviewed the data on the Arab armies confronting Israel: 100,000 Egyptian troops in Sinai; 60,000 in reserve; 1,000 tanks, mainly of the Soviet T-54 and T-55 types; 400 interceptors and fighter-bombers; 70–80 medium and light bombers. The Syrians had 50,000 men lined up on the border, 200 tanks, 100 aircraft, 32 of which were Mig-21s. Jordan had 50,000–60,000 men, 250 Patton and Centurion tanks, and 24 British Hawker-Hunter fighters. They were reinforced by an Iraqi division, moving to take up positions on the Israeli border (it never got there).[4]

The meeting then heard Eban's final evaluation of the international situation; some of the information, such as the latest letter from President Johnson, was new to most of those present. After reading that letter to the Cabinet the Foreign Minister emphasized that he believed the Americans were now committed, at least to the extent that the 1956 situation would not be repeated; Israel would not be isolated after an armed clash. As for the Soviet Union, Israel could expect her to remain hostile politically; but there was no indication of armed

---

[1] To a memorial meeting for Lyndon Johnson held by the Israel–America Society and the Zionist Organization of America on 25 January 1973, as broadcast by *Kol Yisrael* in English on 27 January 1973.

[2] Laqueur 1968, p. 158. Bar-Lev (2) recalled that the decision to go to war fell on the night of 3 June.

[3] This account of the Cabinet meeting is based on the following sources: Foreign Ministry sources; Gilboa, p. 201; Nakdimon, pp. 276–8. Laqueur surmised (p. 158) that the vote was informal; this is incorrect.

[4] A careful composite estimate of the opposing forces was presented in Table 12 on p. 325 above.

intervention. Eban also told the Cabinet about a meeting between de Gaulle and Eytan the previous day, at which Israel had been notified of the arms embargo. De Gaulle warned Israel again that, should she decide to go to war, it would be disastrous for her, even if she won: she would suffer tremendous losses; enmities would be increased; the Americans would not support her in the long run, because of oil interests; and no arms would be forthcoming. France was pledged to the survival of Israel, he added, but the solution to the present crisis was to be found in Four-Power consultations. Eban concluded by advocating military action, for Egypt had started the war by all known rules of international law.

Interior Minister Shapira declared that he felt it necessary to recapitulate the views of Israel's elder statesman, Ben Gurion: that it was a serious mistake, even very dangerous, to go to war; that Israel was not ready for war; that she would have to fight alone; and that mobilization had been a grievous mistake. Now, the former Prime Minister believed, there was no choice left but to dig in and defend the country, if attacked. Israel would have to hold out, even for several months, until she could find an ally who would stand by her side and enable her to take up arms against the enemy, as in the Sinai Campaign. Shapira concluded by saying that, though he felt it to be his duty to voice this last warning, he would now join, with a heavy heart, those who were for fighting alone, since no other choice was left.

The dire warning was answered by Dayan, who stated that, if Israel waited until somebody found her an ally, it was doubtful whether the country would still exist. Eshkol also reaffirmed his faith in *Tzahal* and added his weight, clearly and unequivocally, to the proposed action.

The *Mapam* Ministers, Barzilai and Bentov, were somewhat taken aback by the change in attitude of colleagues who until then had advocated further diplomatic efforts (Eban and Shapira, among others). Yet they did not dissociate themselves from the general trend. Rather, they reserved their right to consult senior party colleagues, notably Yia'ar and Hazan, regarding a final position.

Eshkol called for a formal vote at the end of the meeting. Nineteen members of the Cabinet voted for the resolution immediately. The two *Mapam* ministers added their assent after consultation, thus making it unanimous. The resolution—the strategic decision of the 1967 crisis—stated:

After hearing a report on the military and political situation from the Prime Minister, the Foreign Minister, the Defence Minister, the Chief of Staff and the head of military intelligence, the Government ascertained that the armies of Egypt, Syria and Jordan are deployed for immediate multifront aggression, threatening the very existence of the State.

The Government resolves to take military action in order to liberate Israel from the stranglehold of aggression which is progressively being tightened around Israel.

The Government authorizes the Prime Minister and the Defence Minister to confirm to the General Staff of the I.D.F. the time for action.

Members of the Cabinet will receive as soon as possible the information concerning the military operation to be carried out.

The Government charges the Foreign Minister with the task of exhausting all possibilities of political action in order to explain Israel's stand to obtain the support of the powers.[1]

The die had been cast.

TABLE 22

CHRONOLOGY OF CRISIS: IV

The Period of Resolution: 29 May–4 June 1967

TIME	EXTERNAL EVENTS	INTERNAL EVENTS
	Monday 29 May	
Morning	Nasser's press conference published in *Al-Ahram*, stresses rights of Palestinian Arabs.	
Early p.m.		BG meets Y. M. Levin, S. Lorincz, M. Porush, S. Y. Gross of *Agudat Yisrael*. H. Laskov meets Begin and Shapira, and presses for Dayan as Defence Minister.
		Rafi Caucus—BG advocates Dayan as Prime Minister–Defence Minister, highly critical of Eshkol.
		PM's Jerusalem residence: Eshkol meets with Eban, Galili, Herzog to finalize *Knesset* speech. Some sentences coordinated in advance with Washington.
17.00		Eshkol addresses *Knesset*. As no debate follows speech, BG calls press conference.
p.m.	Meeting of Security Council, no resolutions.	
p.m.	Nasser speech calling for 'restoring situation of 1948'.	

[1] Published officially by the Government of Israel on the fifth anniversary of the Six Day War. See *Ha'aretz* and *Jerusalem Post*, 5 June 1972.

TABLE 22 (CONT.)

TIME	EXTERNAL EVENTS	INTERNAL EVENTS
Evening		*Ma'arakh* Caucus: reports by Galili, Eban, M. Zar, and D. Sadan call for nat. unity government. Eliav, Yadlin, Cohen oppose Eban's report; meet to map strategy. *Mapam*, at Caucus meeting, objects to broadening of Government. *Gahal's* Begin, Saphir, Bader, Rimalt meet *Mapai's* Meir, Yeshayahu, Barkatt. Agree on *Gahal* minister, but *Gahal* insists on Dayan as Defence Minister.

Tuesday 30 May

TIME	EXTERNAL EVENTS	INTERNAL EVENTS
8.30		Meir, Aranne, Avigur press Eshkol to appoint Allon as Defence Minister or Deputy Defence Minister. Eshkol counters with Defence Council suggestion, orders Herzog to investigate it further: i.e. nomination of Allon, Dayan, Yadin, Laskov, or Amit as members.
a.m.		Eban holds press conference at suggestion of Eshkol; emphasizes that Israel like 'coiled spring'.
a.m.		*Mapai's* Meir, Yeshayahu, Barkatt meet *Rafi's* Peres and Almogi. *Mapai* suggests Dayan be Minister without Portfolio and Member of Ministerial Defence Committee or Eshkol's Defence Council. *Rafi* negotiators decline invitation.
Noon	Cable arrives from Harman in Washington: (1) Maritime Declaration without threat of force; (2) consultations for Joint Resolution of Congress to begin tomorrow.	

TIME	EXTERNAL EVENTS	INTERNAL EVENTS
p.m.	Hussein and Nasser sign five-year Mutual Defence Pact. Jordanian troops under Egyptian command. Troops from other Arab countries on Jordanian soil.	
13.00		NRP's Shapira visits Eshkol, informs him of his support for Dayan as Defence Minister and national unity government.
p.m.		Eshkol works with Eban and advisers on reply to Johnson's 28 May letter.
p.m.		Eshkol and Eban decide to send Amit to US to evaluate US attitude.
16.30		Dayan rejects Eshkol's proposed Defence Council.
Evening		Meeting of *Ma'arakh* Caucus with Eshkol present. Barkatt and Yeshayahu review the internal negotiations. Major revolt against Eshkol. Veteran *Mapai* members, e.g. Kadish Luz, urge national unity government. *Gahal* Caucus meets parallel to *Ma'arakh*; remains firm in stated position. Independent Liberals decide formally on national unity government. Insist that Eshkol remain PM. Inform Eshkol, *Ma'arakh*, Begin of decision. NRP and Ind. Liberals decide to work together for nat. unity govt. Religious front of all the religious parties formed.
Late evening		*Gahal* leaders meet *Mapai*'s Yeshayahu and Barkatt; *Gahal* reaffirms insistence on Dayan for Defence portfolio.

TABLE 22 (CONT.)

TIME	EXTERNAL EVENTS	INTERNAL EVENTS
		Eshkol meets NRP's Shapira for second time during day on Dayan question. Y. S. Shapiro, Sharef, Eliav arrive at PM's home.
Wednesday 31 May		
8.00		Arye Eliav suggests to Eshkol that Allon and Dayan be appointed Special Assistants to the Defence Minister.
9.30		Eshkol meets *Mapai* leaders to discuss the dissension. Nothing decided.
11.00		*Mapai* Political Committee meets. Also present: Meir, Avigur, Luz, Eshkol. Committee votes that Allon be Defence Minister and Dayan be Deputy PM. Y. S. Shapiro suggests that Eban be Dep. PM, Allon Defence Minister, Dayan Foreign Minister. Move rejected inside and out of party.
a.m.		M. H. Shapira, Kol, learn of plan against Eban and agree to work against it.
p.m.		Eban meets Shapira to try and persuade him to accept *Mapai* Pol. Committee decision on Allon's appointment; does not succeed. Allon meets *Aluf* Yariv to get final report on situation. Then meets with BG and advocates immediate military action. 'Phones Yaffe to request Eshkol to summon Cabinet.
16.30		Eshkol–Dayan meeting. Eshkol offers Dep. PM position. Dayan insists on Premiership with Def. post, the Def. Mins. alone, or a *Tzahal* field command. Eshkol

TABLE 22 (CONT.)

TIME	EXTERNAL EVENTS	INTERNAL EVENTS
		requests that Rabin come to the office to fix Dayan's return to *Tzahal*. Eshkol informs *Mapai* Pol. Cttee and also Shapira, who rejects it vehemently: demands Cabinet meeting on subject.
Later p.m.		S. Aloni, Eliav, Aharon Yadlin, Asher Yadlin, M. Ofer, M. Piron visit Y. S. Shapiro upon his return from *Mapai* Pol. Committee. Group demands Dayan's appointment as Defence Min. Shapiro informs group of the arrangement between Eshkol and Dayan.
a.m.–p.m. (NYT)	Evron–W. Rostow conversation on phrasing of Eshkol's 30 May letter.	
19.00		Meeting of *Knesset* Cttee on For. Aff. and Security. Rabin–Eshkol meeting. Rabin accepts suggestion re Dayan.
20.00		*Knesset* FA and Sec. Cttee ends deliberations. Meeting of Rabin–Eshkol–Dayan; agree on Southern Command for Dayan. Gavish, on Bar-Lev's advice, agrees to be Dayan's deputy.
Early evening		Meeting of NRP leadership. Shapira and Burg want to leave Government. *Herut* section of *Gahal* insists they will enter nat. unity govt. only if Dayan is Defence Minister. Liberals undecided. *Mapam* Caucus meets; decides to remain in Govt. if *Rafi* and *Gahal* are co-opted. Meir informs *Mapai* leaders of Pol. Cttee decision and that Eshkol will be unable to attend

TABLE 22 (CONT.)

TIME	EXTERNAL EVENTS	INTERNAL EVENTS
		Secretariat meeting that evening.
21.45		Cabinet meeting: Eshkol informs Cabinet of the changes he wants to make. NRP, under Shapira, rejects proposals and threatens to leave Cabinet. Ind. Libs.' Moshe Kol agrees with NRP position but does not agree to resign. Eshkol sets up Cabinet Negotiation Cttee composed of himself, Galili, H. M. Shapira, Kol, Barzilai.
Evening		Parallel with Cabinet session, *Mapai* Secretariat meets; supports Eshkol's efforts to broaden Govt. but insists that no final decision be taken without Secretariat being able to discuss it.
	Thursday 1 June	
Early a.m.		BG objects to *Rafi* entering Govt. if Eshkol remains PM.
8.15		Peres meets Netzer and other *Mapai* members; emphasizes that *Rafi* would not join Govt. unless Dayan gets Def. Ministry.
10.00–15.00		Meeting of *Mapai* Secretariat. Eshkol gives full résumé of his activities, then leaves for meeting of Cabinet Negotiating Committee. Secretariat continues debate, supports Eshkol's efforts to broaden Govt. and reaches consensus (without vote) of majority for Dayan as Defence Minister.
Late a.m.		After reappraisal of external situation at Foreign Office, Eban and Levavi apprise Rabin and Yariv that the

TIME	EXTERNAL EVENTS	INTERNAL EVENTS
		Foreign Office would no longer object to military action.
a.m.–p.m.	Preliminary report of Meir Amit arrives from US; describes growing public sympathy; states that the US effort is bogged down; advocates waiting a few more days only.	
11.00		Meeting at Begin's home of *Rafi*'s Peres, Tzur, Navon, and *Gahal*'s Begin, Bader, Saphir, Ben-Eliezer, Rimalt; NRP's Raphael and Ben-Meir. Latter inform meeting of religious *Kibbutz* pressure for national unity government. All present agree Dayan must be Defence Minister.
12.00		*Gahal* reps. (as above) meet with Eshkol and Cabinet Negotiating Committee; Y. S. Shapiro present at Eshkol's request. *Gahal* insists on Dayan as Defence Minister.
14.00		H. M. Shapira visits Eshkol re Dayan's appointment.
14.30		Dayan meets Peres, who informs him that it is irresponsible to refuse Defence Ministry, if offered.
15.00		Kol meets Eshkol; supports Dayan's co-option.
15.15		Yadin presses Eshkol to nominate Dayan to Defence Ministry.
15.45		Eshkol under pressure, esp. Meir's 'phone call about *Mapai* Secretariat consensus and *Gahal* visit, decides to call on Dayan to take Defence post. Informs Hazan of *Mapam*.
16.15		Eshkol–Dayan meeting. Dayan invited to take Defence Ministry as rep. of *Rafi* or by himself, if *Rafi* rejects offer.

TABLE 22 (CONT.)

TIME	EXTERNAL EVENTS	INTERNAL EVENTS
Late p.m.		Eshkol informs Caucus leaders personally of his decision. Calls together *Ma'arakh* Political Committee to inform them. Meir and Avigur absent, in protest.
18.00		Peres meets with BG to induce him to change his mind about Dayan entering an Eshkol Government.
19.00		*Aluf* Bar-Lev appointed Deputy Chief of Staff. Eshkol, H. M. Shapira, Barzilai inform *Rafi's* Peres, Almogi, Navon of invitation to Dayan to be Defence Minister. Invitation to *Gahal* to send two representatives as Ministers without Portfolio and full members of Ministerial Committee on Defence.
19.45		*Gahal* meets, decides to send Begin immediately. Liberal section representative to be chosen next day.
20.00		*Rafi* Caucus meets at BG's home. *Rafi* accepts invitation to join.
21.30		Old Government meets to approve establishment of National Unity Government.
22.00		Peres informs Eshkol of *Rafi's* consent.
22.00–22.15		Begin and Dayan arrive to join Cabinet's deliberations. Adjournment at 1.00 a.m., 2 June.
	Friday 2 June	
Early a.m.		Meeting of Herzog and Yadin, at PM's request, to write up new rules of authority between PM's Office and Defence Ministry.

TIME	EXTERNAL EVENTS	INTERNAL EVENTS
a.m.		Meeting of Mins. Def. Cttee. *Alufim* of *Tzahal* call for military action. Meeting of Liberal Party section of *Gahal*; elects Y. Saphir to Cabinet.
Noon	French statement of policy that state resorting to force of arms would lose her support.	
p.m.		Ambassador Harman 'phones and requests that decisions be held up until he arrives from Washington.
Evening		Allon Tel Aviv speech on inevitability of war.
	Saturday 3 June	
a.m.–p.m.	Iraqi and Egyptian troops arrive in Jordan. Eytan informed by de Gaulle of French arms embargo against Israel.	
16.00 Evening		Dayan press conference. Eshkol's home: meeting of Dayan, Eban, Allon, *Tzahal* chiefs, Harman, and Amit. International commitments seen as dead; military plans approved.
	Sunday 4 June	
a.m.–p.m.	Iraq officially signs pact with Egypt similar to those with Jordan and Syria.	
a.m.–p.m.		Seven-hour Cabinet meeting. Strategic decision, unanimously, to take military action.

(V) *5-10 June: The Period of Implementation*

The Six Day War began on the morning of 5 June at 7.45, with a concerted air attack on Egypt's air force and airfields, and came to an end on 10 June at 6.30 p.m., when the cease-fire on the Syrian front went into effect. Altogether it lasted five days, ten hours, and forty-five minutes. During that incredibly short time *Tzahal* overran territory more than three times the size of pre-war Israel and, while doing so, decimated the armed strength of Egypt, Syria, and Jordan. Two-thirds of Egypt's air force and most of its armour and artillery were destroyed or captured. The Syrian air force was mauled and most of its armour and artillery destroyed. The small Jordan air force was completely wiped out and most of its armour eliminated.[1]

Estimated losses were: Egypt—6,000–11,500 soldiers dead or wounded, 338 planes, 800–900 tanks destroyed or captured; Syria—from 200 to 1,000 dead, up to 2,000 wounded, 61 planes, about 100 tanks lost; Jordan—6,094 dead or missing, 762 wounded, 29 planes, 160 tanks put out of action; Iraq—about 23 planes destroyed. Israel's casualties were—759 dead and 2,500 wounded; 40 planes were shot down, half of them during the first day of the fighting, and about 100 tanks were put out of action.[2]

The war with *Egypt* lasted until 8 June: she accepted a cease-fire that day at 21.30 hrs., but firing stopped only in the forenoon the following day. During those four days *Tzahal* captured the Gaza Strip and all of Sinai. The strong points of the Straits—Ras Nasrani and Sharm-e-Sheikh—were occupied, without a fight, on the second day.

The war with *Jordan* began on the 5th at about 11.00, when Jordan opened fire all along the border with a heavy artillery barrage, reaching the outskirts of Tel Aviv, and several small air strikes. The heaviest shelling was directed against Jewish Jerusalem, followed up by the forcible entry into UN headquarters (at 13.00 hrs.), which lay between the lines. Israel held its hand in Jerusalem for about two hours; but when it became clear that the Jordanians were not just putting up a 'show of solidarity', orders were given to counterattack. During three days of fighting all of Jordan west of the river was overrun, including the crown, the Old City, which fell on 7 June at 10.00 o'clock. King Hussein was the first to accept a cease-fire, on the evening of the 7th.

The Syrians, who precipitated the crisis and were the most vociferous in their advocacy of total war, tried to keep out of it. The fighting on the northern front was limited for the first four days to artillery duels and air-strikes. Three or four probing attacks by Syrian ground troops, in company force, were easily stopped. On the fifth day, Friday 9 June, the war became concentrated on the Syrian front after heavy concen-

---

[1] The war itself is sketched here in the utmost brevity—for two reasons: first, it is not central to the focus of this inquiry, namely, the process culminating in the strategic decision of 4 June; and, secondly, the military operations in June 1967 have been exhaustively treated in the literature. See Churchills, ch. 4 and 7; Hashavia, *passim*; Kimche and Bavly, ch. 9, 10; Legler and Liebisch, *passim*; Marshall, *passim*; Segev, ch. 6–17; Young, *passim*.

[2] There are several conflicting estimates of the losses of all sides. The figures given here are from the summary of *MER*, pp. 232–4. See also Ben Gurion 1969, p. 804; and *The Military Balance 1967–1968*, pp. 39–41.

trated attacks from the air, which started at 9.30 in the morning. Israeli troops swung into action at 11.30, headed by armour and engineering units. Their task was to clear through minefields and, in very difficult hilly terrain, to force lines of attack for armour and infantry. During one and a half days of fighting, mostly uphill, *Tzahal* captured the Golan Heights, including the town of Kuneitra. The cease-fire line was established about fifty miles from Damascus.

The geo-strategic situation created by Israel's overwhelming victory transformed all previous political and military calculations in the Near East Core.[1] All of Israel's centres of population and industry were now safely behind the lines; while the capitals of Israel's main adversaries were now within easy striking distance of Israeli air and ground forces.

Israel's 1967 decision-process occurred within a setting which bears the marks of a foreign-policy crisis: the element of surprise; limited time to take decisions; perception of a high threat to basic values; and the possibility of direct confrontation between super-powers. Six themes may be abstracted from the details of the 1967 decision-process. Perhaps the most striking was the progressive escalation of conflict and threat, leading to step-by-step reactive measures. That rapid input-response escalation points to one outstanding aspect of decision-making in 1967: a crisis between non-nuclear states reached a point of irreversibility with astonishing speed, seriously limiting the options available to decision-makers.

A unique feature of the crisis was the intense efforts made by the super-powers to control their client states, and their total failure to do so. Very little hard data exist about Soviet attempts to restrain Nasser from escalating the situation to the brink of military confrontation. It is generally agreed, however, that there was no prior consultation between Cairo and Moscow on the series of steps taken by Egypt from the 16th of May onwards (withdrawal of UNEF; closing of the Straits; setting the aims publicly as 'the destruction of Israel'). The efforts of the US, France, and the UK to defuse the crisis and gain time are fully documented. All three actors perceived another conflagration in the Middle East as portending grave consequences for their global interests. They played on Israel's sensitivity about the future existence of the State, couching their warnings in almost identical terms.

In technique, too, the crisis was noteworthy: its gravity was accentuated by the fact that diplomatic efforts were conducted throughout at the level of Heads of States; regular channels of communication were replaced by summit correspondence, culminating in the use—for the first time—of the 'hot line', three times, between President Johnson and Premier Kosygin.

---

[1] See Rabin's assessment on p. 447 below.

A further aspect of super-power involvement in the Israeli decision-process was the effort to influence her not to be the first to 'start' the war. While France was obsessed with this theme, the US and the Soviet Union also emphasized 'firing the first shot'. Their behaviour bears tribute to the continuing influence of the long and weary discussions about the nature and definition of aggression, in the aftermath of the First World War.

A war is not necessarily 'started' by an overt act of violence. In any event it entails a decision to risk war or to go to war. Actions flowing from such a decision which endanger the most vital interests of another state are 'acts of war'. The decision to close the Straits was clearly perceived by Israel's decision-makers as the 'start' of war, though not one shot had been fired—just as the Soviet decision to supply Cuba with missiles in 1962 was perceived by the US as a threat that must be resisted at all costs. In purely factual terms, there was shooting throughout the crisis period. Yet none of these shooting incidents was considered an 'act of war' or the 'first shot'.

Another significant feature of the Israeli decision-process was the creation of an intense internal political crisis by the external challenge, and the interaction between the two. The decision-makers, like all persons, had only a limited amount of time and energy to concentrate on the components impinging on the decision. The 1967 process reveals the extraordinary extent to which the internal crisis occupied their time and, in some cases, sapped their strength—severely limiting the time and energy devoted to reviewing and reconsidering the external threat. Moreover, the internal crisis, essentially of confidence in the Prime Minister's leadership during a fateful period in the life of the nation, led inevitably to the polarization of decision-making; it also increased the trend to irreversibility. The decision by Eshkol to give up the Defence Ministry and to appoint Dayan meant also a decision to go to war. This is not to say that, with Eshkol continuing as Defence Minister, Israel would not have so decided; rather, that not to do so after 1 June had become impossible.

Noteworthy, too, was the intense interaction among several strata of Israel's decision-making élite: the Cabinet, the party leadership, the *Knesset*, the army, the technical élite. Whether this or other aspects of the 1967 decision-process were unique may be tested by further empirical investigation of decision-making under crisis conditions.

(E) DECISION FLOW

Pre-Decisional Events

1. second half of 1966	Growing number of *feda'iyun* attacks on Israel, openly supported by Syria which, in turn, was backed by USSR.

2. 4 November 1966 — Signing of Egypt–Syria military pact terming an attack on either party an attack on the other.

3. 13 November 1966 — Israeli reprisal against Jordan village of El-Samū; Israel censured by Security Council on 25 November; Nasser sharply criticized by Arab leaders for not intervening.

4. 25, 29 January, 2 February 1967 — Extraordinary meetings of Israel–Syria Mixed Armistice Commission, in response to U Thant call on 15 January.

5. 7 April 1967 — Serious Israel–Syria border clash, culminating in shooting down of 6 Syrian Mig 21s.

6. 18–22 April 1967 — Visit of UAR Prime Minister to Damascus, with public reaffirmation of unity against 'Israeli aggression'.

7. 8, 12, 13 May 1967 — Nasser warned by Syria, Lebanon, USSR about Israeli troop concentrations, with intent to attack Syria in order to undermine Damascus regime.

8. 9, 11, 13, 14 May 1967 — Warnings by Eban, Eshkol, Rabin and others of Israeli retaliation against Syria if border incidents continue.

Decisive Inputs to Tactical Decision 1(a)

9. 14 May 1967—14.30 — Egypt's army placed on alert; Eshkol informed by Rabin next morning.

10. 15 May—daytime — Egyptian division passes through Cairo en route to Sinai; crosses Canal into the Peninsula on 16th, a.m.

Tactical Decision 1(a)

11. 16 May—afternoon — After Cabinet meeting Eshkol and Rabin decide upon calling up of *Tzahal* reserves.

Decisive Input to Tactical Decision 1(b)

12. 18 May—19.00 (New York time) — Secretary-General formally agrees to withdraw UNEF; its duties officially terminated 19 May, afternoon.

Tactical Decision 1(b)

13. 19 May—afternoon — Large-scale mobilization of *Tzahal*

	reserves set in motion by Eshkol and Rabin.

Decisive Inputs to Tactical Decision 2(a)

14. 22 May	Build-up of Egyptian forces in Sinai.
15. 22 May—after midnight	Nasser speech announcing closure of Tiran Straits to Israeli ships.
16. 23 May—morning	Ministerial Defence Committee informed that President Johnson urged Israel to abstain from unilateral action and decisions for 48 hours.

Tactical Decision 2(a)

17. 23 May—noon, afternoon	Ministerial Committee on Defence decide to postpone a decision for 48 hours and empower Foreign Minister to visit Washington in order to secure support in the light of 1957 US commitments; late afternoon, following Eytan cable about probable meeting with de Gaulle next day, Eshkol assents to Eban's journey to Paris and London as well.

Decisive Inputs to Tactical Decision 2(b)

18. 24 May—noon	At meeting with Eban, de Gaulle disavows 1957 and other French commitments and warns that opening of overt military acts would constitute aggression and lead to catastrophe.
19. 24 May—5.00 p.m.	Wilson declaration of UK willingness to organize international flotilla to break blockade of Straits.
20. 27 May—2.00 a.m.	Relatively moderate Kosygin letter delivered to Eshkol, appealing for settlement of conflict by non-military means.
21. 28 May—morning	Eban–Harman–Evron reports of Eban–Evron–Johnson talks, and message from President to Prime Minister advising against pre-emptive military strike, along with Rusk view that unilateral action would be irresponsible.

Tactical Decision 2(b)

22. 28 May—evening	Government decide to continue with

political response to crisis; noteworthy implementing act was dispatch, on 30 May, of Amit, Chief of Intelligence, to Washington to clarify US views.

Decisive Input to Tactical Decision 3

23. 24–31 May

Cumulative pressure for broader Government and for decision about perceived threat—from interest groups, competing élites, and public opinion, culminating in near-revolt among *Mapai* Inner Circle and Coalition partners.

Tactical Decision 3

24. 1 June 1967—evening

Formation of National Unity Government, with 21 ministers, including two from *Gahal*, and Dayan as Defence Minister.

Decisive Inputs to Strategic Decision

25. 26 May—afternoon

U Thant's acknowledgement of failure of his Cairo mission, eliminating Israeli hope of possible UN conflict-resolution role in crisis.

26. 28 May—evening

Confrontation between Eshkol and *Tzahal* senior officers, with some of latter warning of heavier casualties with each passing day of *Hamtana*.

27. 29 May—afternoon

Nasser speech, defining issue as 'rights of Palestine people' and 'aggression in Palestine since 1948'.

28. 30 May

Signing of Egypt–Jordan military alliance, symbolizing, *inter alia*, declining Arab perception of *Tzahal* as effective deterrent.

29. 30 May ff.

Escalating hysteria in Arab world, with signals of mobilization of Arab power, notably stationing of Saudi Arabian brigade in Jordan and Algeria–Morocco decisions to send troops to Egypt; and Iraq adherence to Egypt–Jordan–Syria Pact, on 2 June.

30. 1 June 1967

As noted, formation of National Unity Government. Intensifying pressure

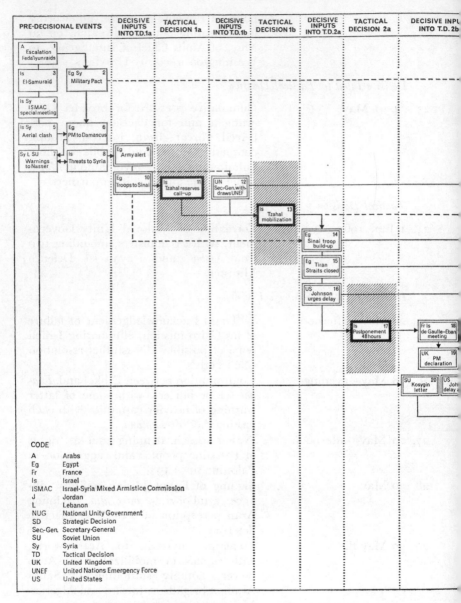

PRE-DECISIONAL EVENTS	DECISIVE INPUTS INTO T.D.1a	TACTICAL DECISION 1a	DECISIVE INPUTS INTO T.D.1b	TACTICAL DECISION 1b	DECISIVE INPUTS INTO T.D.2a	TACTICAL DECISION 2a	DECISIVE INPUTS INTO T.D.2b

Boxes and labels within the figure:

A 1 Escalation Feda'iyun raids
Is 3 El-Samuraid
Eg Sy 2 Military Pact
Is Sy 4 ISMAC special meeting
Is Sy 5 Aerial clash
Eg 6 PM to Damascus
Sy L SU 7 Warnings to Nasser
Is 8 Threats to Syria
Eg 9 Army alert
Eg 10 Troops to Sinai
Is 11 Tzahal reserves call-up
UN 12 Sec-Gen. withdraws UNEF
Is 13 Tzahal mobilization
Eg 14 Sinai troop build-up
Eg 15 Tiran Straits closed
US 16 Johnson urges delay
Is 17 Postponement 48 hours
Fr Is 18 de Gaulle-Eban meeting
UK 19 PM declaration
SU 20 Kosygin letter
US Joh delay

CODE

A	Arabs
Eg	Egypt
Fr	France
Is	Israel
ISMAC	Israel-Syria Mixed Armistice Commission
J	Jordan
L	Lebanon
NUG	National Unity Government
SD	Strategic Decision
Sec-Gen.	Secretary-General
SU	Soviet Union
Sy	Syria
TD	Tactical Decision
UK	United Kingdom
UNEF	United Nations Emergency Force
US	United States

FIGURE 14. DECISION FLOW: SIX DAY WAR

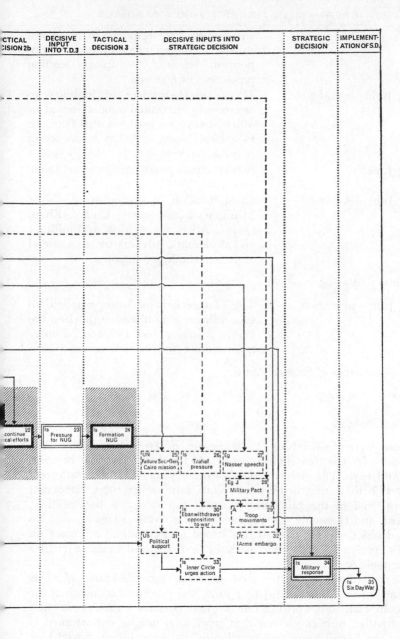

| TACTICAL DECISION 2b | DECISIVE INPUT INTO T.D.3 | TACTICAL DECISION 3 | DECISIVE INPUTS INTO STRATEGIC DECISION | | STRATEGIC DECISION | IMPLEMENT-ATION OF S.D. |

	within Israel for response to perceived threat, including abandonment of opposition to war by Eban, leading proponent of *Hamtana*.
31. 3 June—evening	US acknowledgement of inability to organise international action—naval or other—conveyed by Amit and Harman to Eshkol, along with US assurance of political backing.
32. 3 June	French embargo on arms to Israel made known.
33. 3 June—evening	Crystallization of consensus at Prime Minister's house among Eshkol, Eban, Dayan, Allon, army chiefs, and military and diplomatic advisers to recommend to Cabinet military response.

Strategic Decision

34. 4 June—afternoon	The Government of Israel decided 'to take military action' and authorized the Prime Minister and Defence Minister to determine 'the time for action'.

Implementation of Strategic Decision

35. 5–10 June 1967	Six Day War.

(F) FEEDBACK

There were far-reaching consequences of Israel's Six Day War decisions—for the two environments and for the policy flow between 1967 and 1970. The global and subordinate dimensions were affected, as were both dominant-bilateral relationships, the most important bilateral link of the preceding decade (France), and the military, political, and economic components of the internal environments. No other decision cluster had such a broad and cumulative impact on Israel's Foreign Policy System, with the feedback evident six years after the strategic decision.

The gestation period for that decision, especially the *Hamtana* (waiting) phase from 23 May to 4 June, was perceived by much of the politically conscious world as one of grave peril for Israel. Arab élites and attentive publics viewed that peril as a unique opportunity to destroy the Jewish State and revelled in that expectation. Soviet-bloc élites approved Nasser's deeds—short of war—and his policy goals—except for the destruction of Israel. But most actors in the *global system* (G) observed the escalating tension arising from the withdrawal of UNEF, the closure of the Straits, the massing of Egyptian troops in Sinai, and the mobilization of *Tzahal* reserves, as a 'time of troubles' for Israel; in fact, a real threat to her survival. The result was a wave of sympathy, among non-Jews as well as Jews, not confined to the Western world. It was the peak of pro-Israel sentiment in the history of the State, not excluding the days and weeks following the declaration of independence in May 1948. Fear gave way to a sense of relief when Israel's strategic decision terminated the uncertainty and initiated a sweeping military triumph. Both of these moods—identity with Israel in mortal danger and relief at her victory—created for Israel an extraordinarily positive global setting in the aftermath of the war. For Jewry the weeks of waiting and the war itself had produced a trauma of collective identification with Israel under siege. The outpouring of material aid— half a billion dollars during the three months that followed—was only one indicator of a new consciousness of the national homeland. As for the universal actor, its inability to de-escalate the crisis was laid bare by the Secretary-General's abrupt withdrawal of UNEF, his fruitless mission to Cairo, and the Security Council's failure to reverse or even slow down the road to war. And U Thant's behaviour placed in jeopardy the UN's *bona fides* as a third party in the Arab–Israel conflict.

All of these global-system changes were acutely perceived by Israel's decision-makers, as is amply revealed by the extracts from their speeches. Yet their image-attentiveness was not equally focused on (1) sympathetic world opinion, (2) the rallying of Jewry, and (3) the international organization. The first was welcomed as an additional but marginal support for Israel during and after the crisis. But the behaviour of non-Jewish states or publics is always subconsciously suspect in a pre-eminent Israeli 'two-camp' view of the world. Thus it tended to be perceived as a deviation from the norm of antagonism or indifference to Israel. In any event, public opinion could not alter the geo-strategic or military realities of the Near East Core. And, more pointedly, the decision-makers were so convinced of the righteousness of their cause that it was hard for them to imagine that worldwide sympathy for Israel would ebb away so quickly. The result, in policy terms, was a lack of special efforts—in funds, manpower, ideas— to consolidate this newly acquired external support for Israel and her goals. There was no diminution in the volume of propaganda but there was no recognition of the importance of exploiting a new, unexpected asset; it was allowed to atrophy in the post-June 1967 years and soon did so. In short, low-intensity action was the policy derivative of low-value perception of external opinion about the justice and merits of Israel's case in the protracted conflict. In so far as that unanticipated asset had any causal link to policy, it was to strengthen the HPE predisposition to a hard line on peace terms: since public opinion in the non-Communist world was pro-Israel during the initial post-Six-Day-War period, there was less inducement or pressure to compromise on what the high-policy élite perceived to be basic security interests.

That policy orientation derived largely from the decision-makers' view of the world and their specific images of 'the Arabs' and of the Middle East. An added source of rigidity was the demonstrable fact of UN weakness, its accurate perception, and their corresponding denigration of the world body's—or, indeed, any external—guarantees as a viable path to peace. UN behaviour in May–June 1967 and the total isolation of Israel in her gravest time of troubles demonstrated the illusory quality of the 1957 pledges and guarantees—and created an unshakeable belief among Israel's decision-makers and the nation as a whole that the fruits of victory must not be squandered, as they were after the Sinai Campaign. As an official Israel publication declared, in the context of lessons of the Six Day War: 'Neither the UN, the Security Council nor a UN Force is a reliable guarantee of the security of any State, and certainly not of any small nation. This lesson has been driven home still more pointedly in the sequel of crises that have arisen since 1967 in other regions of the world.'[1] That illuminating reference to events in other subordinate systems was clarified, parenthetically: 'An outstanding example of the ineffectiveness of the Security Council was the India–Pakistan war in 1971.'

A related consequence of the UN's record in the 1967 crisis was renewed distrust of its subsequent proposals and actions. The Secretary-General's pronouncements were, a priori, suspect. His (frequent) public criticism of Israel evoked contempt and/or harsh criticism. Big Four negotiations in a UN context, culminating in Resolution 242 on 22 November 1967, were received coolly. And while Jerusalem did not reject that consensual framework for a settlement, it was not endorsed until July 1970—in the context of a *United States* peace initiative. A further spillover effect was the denigration of the Jarring Mission, designed to implement a Council resolution which Israel perceived as a threat to her newly acquired security. This was expressed in a persistent effort to narrow the UN Representative's terms of reference—virtually to the role of a postal service. All initiative was denied him. That attitude was exacerbated by U Thant's continuous support for Jarring's initiative, until the Secretary-General's retirement at the end of 1971. The feedback from his behaviour in May 1967 was, therefore, marked deterioration in Israel–UN relations. The perceptions of the international organization persisted in a mutual interaction process—UN deeds→ Israeli images of unfriendliness→ Israeli policies toward the UN, its Secretary-General, the Mediator, the Security Council, the General Assembly→ UN critical resolutions regarding Jerusalem, Arabs in occupied territories, etc.

[1] *Menace*, p. 26.

That vicious circle in Israel's global setting is best exemplified by another strand of feedback which spills over both domestic and external components of her operational environment—the nation's commitment to Jerusalem. From 1948 to 1967 Israelis identified with Jerusalem as the Jewish People had done for three thousand years—cradle of their culture, religion, and nation. But the *de facto* compromise of partition between New and Old City gradually became accepted as the basis for coexistence. The Six Day War and its related decisions transformed the nature of the commitment, making a *reunited* Jerusalem the heart of Israel. The collective and individual outpouring of affection for the liberation of 'the Wall' demonstrated the overwhelming power of this identification. Decision-makers perceived this national mood, shared it, and were led to a policy of annexation and a rejection of all suggestions or pressure for compromise on this point. Among all the territories acquired as a result of the Six Day War, Jerusalem stands apart in the psychological environment and policy programme of Israel. Many external actors protested, but none more persistently than the United Nations—in resolutions passed without opposition by the General Assembly and the Security Council in 1967, 1968, 1969, and 1971. The result was an exacerbation of the global setting for Israel's foreign policy in general, even among her traditional supporters at the UN, Latin America.

The response of Jewry exceeded the expectations of most Israeli leaders, even those accustomed to view the Jewish People as Israel's only reliable ally. 'It is a revelation', said Finance Minister Sapir upon returning from an emergency fund-raising mission in June 1967. 'These people are not mere friends or even partners—they are our brothers.'[1] And to the *Knesset* he declared: '. . . we were shown conclusively that Diaspora Jewry—every sector and generation of it—lives by its link with Israel . . .'.[2] Even more dramatic was the qualitative upsurge in militant dissent by Soviet Jewry and their active campaign for the natural right to *aliya*. That reality and its perception led to policy changes directed to strengthening the ties. In the realm of immigration the bureaucratic machine was streamlined and expanded: the Jewish Agency's Immigration, Absorption, and Economic Departments were merged into one; a Ministry of Absorption was created; and a joint Government-Agency Immigration and Absorption Authority was set up. More funds and personnel were invested in *'tsiyonut'*, that is, in trying to translate the manifest identity with Israel's fate into *aliya*. Administrative changes arising from the Six Day War were not exclusively, nor even primarily, responsible for the increase in post-1967 immigration, but they assisted that dimension of growth in Jewry's links with Israel—from about 15,000 each in 1966 and 1967 to

---

[1] *Jerusalem Post*, 20 June 1967.
[2] *Divrei Ha-knesset*, xlix, 19 June 1967, p. 2336.

20,000 in 1968, and 38,000 in 1969.[1] Another strand of feedback was the more active participation of Jewish business and financial circles in Israel's economic development. That policy derivative began with the Jerusalem Economic Conference in April 1968 and was reflected in a wide range of activities: the expansion of Israel's Investment Authority and legislation to encourage the inflow of capital from abroad; the attempt to attract managerial personnel for Israeli enterprises and the purchase of 'second homes' in the national homeland; a second Economic Conference in 1971 on an even larger scale; seeking advice of Jewish entrepreneurs in solving such bottleneck problems as housing; and forging institutional ties between Israeli and Diaspora Jewish firms. Among the effects was reversal of the decline in foreign exchange reserves, which reached a peak of more than $900 million in April 1972.[2] In short, the feedback from Israel's 1967 decisions to her global setting was mixed but important, with consequences for her policy towards the UN, public opinion, Jerusalem, and world Jewry.

The pervasive US influence on Israel's behaviour had been demonstrated often since 1948, especially during the implementation of the withdrawal decision after the Sinai Campaign.[3] It was illuminated once more in the 1967 crisis. No Israeli decision-maker could fail to perceive President Johnson's role during the waiting period and, after the war, his pro-Israeli principles of a just settlement. That image of US power and friendship fortified a predisposition to forge a *de facto*, if not formal, alliance, The policy line was not new—it dates from 1951 —but the Six Day War experience raised it to a new dimension of centrality. Indeed, this objective has dominated Israel's foreign policy from the June War onwards: Prime Minister Eshkol's visit to the USA in January 1968, leading to the first Phantom deal; the close co-operation between Jerusalem and Washington on all facets of the Arab–Israel conflict; the enormous investment of Israeli energies and funds in winning the support of American élites and attentive and mass publics; the successful requests for economic aid; the annual pilgrimages of Prime Minister Meir to the White House, in 1969, 1970, and 1971, either to break deadlocks or to elicit US military, economic, and political support—all these pointed to a *de facto* alliance between a super power and a small state. In short, the feedback from Israel's May–June 1967 decisions was all-encompassing and was reflected in her massive persistent pressure for multiple forms of American aid. As a result, Israel's foreign policy options were narrowed—because of her decision-makers' perception that only the United States could

---

[1] CBS *SAI*, 1970, no. 21, p. 112.

[2] Bank of Israel, *Monthly Balance Sheet for the 30th April, 1972*. At the same time there was considerable controversy over the economic consequences of these Diaspora Jewry-oriented economic policies.

[3] See ch. 6 (D) above.

counteract the menacing Soviet presence in Egypt and Syria. The degree to which Israel's policy had become dominated by the 'American Factor' was to become evident during the decision process on Rogers 'B' in June–July 1970.[1]

The 1967 crisis deepened the hostility between Israel and the Soviet Union, her other *DB relationship*. The diplomatic rupture, both a product and a symbol of the conflict, remained a barrier to a *modus vivendi* six years after the June War. A more important obstacle was the escalating flow of support to Israel's adversaries—arms, economic aid, and diplomatic backing. In this component, too, predisposition was strengthened, namely, the deep-rooted image of Soviet animus towards Zionism, Israel, and Jewry. The policy effects were to treat the USSR as an active participant in the Near East conflict and to contribute an additional thrust to the search for an alliance with the United States. The 'winds of change' attitude to the Soviet Union in 1965 and 1966 became a victim of the Six Day War, accentuated by the reawakening of kinship with Israel on the part of Russian Jewry; and the patron–client relationship between the super powers and the leading Near East Core actors became crystallized in a virtual dual alliance balance-of-power system—though all bilateral relationships were of the mixed-motive genre: that is, the super powers had shared, as well as antagonistic, interests in the Arab–Israel conflict; and even the core actors had certain minimal common interests. The following graphic representation portrays the salient hostile and (broken line) shared-interest links in all four bilateral relationships; the Egypt–US hostility is less intense than that between Israel and the USSR.

FIGURE 15

POST-JUNE 1967 DUAL ALLIANCE SYSTEM

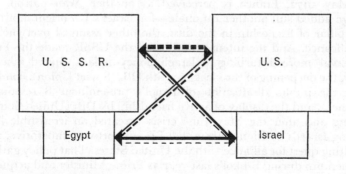

—— Conflictful interests
--- Shared interests

[1] To be discussed in the following chapter.

This pattern, which continued into the early 1970s, had been given a decisive thrust by the Six Day War. But that cataclysmic event and its preceding decisions had even more far-reaching effects on the place of the super powers in the Arab–Israel conflict. Just as the Cuban missile crisis (1962) was a striking precedent for their withdrawal from the brink of direct nuclear war, so the 1967 crisis demonstrated the process of neutralizing each other's role in a subordinate system conflict: the limits of intervention by Moscow and Washington in a 'local war' were henceforth defined as the avoidance of direct confrontation at all costs. The deterrence of direct Soviet military intervention in the Near East Core by the United States had, in short, several feedback effects: (a) it provided the underpinning of stability to the dual alliance system; (b) it thereby intensified Israel's dependence on Washington (and Egypt's on Moscow); (c) in substance, it influenced the images of Israeli leaders in the direction of greater security; and (d) in technique, it strengthened Israel's policy predisposition to 'bargain from strength'.

For more than a decade (1955–66) Israel's foreign policy was built on two pillars—a tacit alliance with France (B) and multi-dimensional friendship with the United States. The former gradually became undermined, following the French–Algerian settlement in 1962, and in May–June 1967 it was ruptured by de Gaulle's arms embargo and harsh anti-Israel stance. Thereafter the relationship deteriorated to an equilibrium of (usually) correct civility. France's interpretation of UN Resolution 242, especially her demand for Israeli withdrawal from *all* occupied territories, caused barely concealed antagonism. Her attempt to mobilize the European Common Market states behind her pro-Arab policy deepened the dismay among Jerusalem decision-makers. And, despite occasional efforts to restore cordiality, such as 'French Week' in May 1972, France is perceived as another Arab patron. That image added still another rationale—for Israel's US orientation: with one pillar of friendship in the dust, the other assumed overwhelming significance. And the intense hostility of the USSR made the French 'betrayal' more disturbing to Israeli policy-makers. Stated schematically, the deepening of the cleavage with DB_2 (Soviet Union), combined with the public disaffection of Israel's pre-eminent B relationship (France), and the display of active friendship by DB_1 (United States)— during and after the May–June crisis—created an irresistible image among Israel's decision-makers that US support was imperative, and a resulting quest for alliance with the United States. That policy gathered momentum during Eshkol's last year as Prime Minister and acquired a quickening pace during Meir's tenure.

For a brief period the Six Day War re-stabilized the *Arab–Israel conflict system* (S) at a low level of overt violence. However, in marked contrast to the decade of tranquillity following the Sinai Campaign, there was a recrudescence of escalating violence culminating in Egypt's launching of the War of Attrition in March 1969. Even more than the second round of warfare, the third established Israel as the pre-eminent actor in the Near East Core. That fundamental fact about Middle East reality was accurately perceived by all decision-makers and was nowhere more lucidly stated than by Rabin in a post-mortem on the war:

The present borders run along natural barriers: Egypt—the Canal; Jordan—the Jordan River, a less impressive barrier than the Suez Canal but nevertheless a barrier; and with Syria, there will no longer be a need to climb up mountains. The distance from the Egyptian border to Tel Aviv was once 130 kilometres and only 80 kilometres from the Gaza Strip. But the distance from our border on the Canal today to Cairo is only 130 kilometres. The distance from our border to Cairo was once something over 400 kilometres. Today the distance from the Egyptian border on the Canal to Tel Aviv is 400 kilometres.[1]

The general effect on policy was to reaffirm the Ben Gurionist 'bargaining from strength' approach to all proposals for a settlement. In terms of territory, that image gave rise to the Labour Party's *Tora shebe'al peh* ('Oral Law') formula under which Israel would retain East Jerusalem, the Golan Heights, Sharm-e-Sheikh, with a Sinai coastal strip linking it to Eilat, and a *Tzahal* 'presence' along the Jordan River; and Gaza would not be returned to Egypt. Closely related was the perception of the uselessness of external guarantees, even those by Great Powers. Both of these *image-cum-policy* consequences of the Six Day War were given repeated expression by Israel's decision-makers. The direct link between them, reflecting their collective view, was presented by a Foreign Ministry publication five years later:

Egypt was tempted to close the Tiran Straits because it was there, on the spot. It was tempted to plan an operation that would cut off the Southern Negev and seize Eilat because its army was at a distance of one to three hours from those targets.

Jordan was tempted to open war in Jerusalem and to bomb Tel Aviv because those two cities were within the operational range of its units.

Syria attacked the Israeli villages in the Jordan Valley because they were within the range of its guns.

The Lesson—The boundaries of Israel, which will be determined in negotiations with the Arab States, must be secure and defensible. Secure boundaries are such as will not again expose Israel to temptations of Arab aggression or give an Arab aggressor decisive advantage in various sectors.

In the test of the 1967 crisis, the Tripartite Declaration of 1950 and the promises made by the USA in 1957 were shown to be futile.

The Lesson—Guarantees may perhaps come after the determination of secure and defensible borders, but can certainly not supplant them. Such guarantees must be the result of agreement between the parties.

[1] Rabin (4).

The Sinai Peninsula and the Gaza Strip—Three times in nineteen years the Sinai desert and the Gaza Strip have served as the area of concentration of Egyptian forces preparing to invade Israel.

The Lesson—Israel will not agree to Egyptian forces returning to Sinai. Egypt will not return to the Gaza Strip. That part of Sinai that would be restored to Egypt under an agreement with Israel will have to be demilitarized. Demilitarization can be assured by a mixed Israel–Egyptian force.

Sharm-el-Sheikh—Twice in nineteen years Egypt has exploited its presence in Sharm-el-Sheikh for the purpose of imposing a maritime blockade on Israel's southern approaches. It has no other use for Sharm-el-Sheikh.

The Lesson—Sharm-el-Sheikh must continue to remain in Israel's hands so as to deny Egypt the temptation to exploit it once more to close the Straits. In order that Sharm-el-Sheikh remain in Israel's hands, there must be territorial continuity between it and Israel.

The West Bank—Twice in nineteen years this has been used as an area for the concentration of Arab forces meant to attack Israel. Practically all the populated areas of Israel were within the range of the Arab artillery emplacements on the West Bank.

The Lesson—The River Jordan will no longer be open to crossing by Arab troops. To assure that, Israel must have a foothold in the Jordan Valley.

As Regards Jerusalem—Twice in nineteen years the city has been the objective of a war launched by Jordan. It was Jordan's aggression that led to the city being split in two.

The Lesson—Jerusalem will remain unified as part of Israel and its capital.

The Golan Heights—These have served Syria as a base for attack upon the Jewish villages in the Jordan Valley.

The Lesson—Israel must stay on the Golan Heights that command the valley.

These are the lessons derived by Israel from the period when it stood alone facing a coalition of Arab Governments which had decided that Israel should be destroyed.

The lessons constitute Israel's positions. . . .[1]

These themes had crystallized rapidly into a near-consensus on Israel's demands for a settlement: both the perceptions and the policy goals were direct feedback effects of the decisions culminating in the Six Day War.

At the same time there has been a conspicuous change in the nature of Israel's relationship with Jordan. In part, the tacit friendliness was a direct result of Israel's most creative initiative since the 1967 War— the 'open bridges' policy, which paved the way for a flourishing commerce between Jordan, the West Bank, and Israel. In part it derived from a natural shared interest in opposition to the *feda'iyun* movement, and King Hussein's awareness that Israel would not stand idle if his regime were in danger of collapse. Not without reason were there well-founded reports of secret discussions for a settlement between Hussein and Israeli leaders from 1969 onwards.

[1] *Menace*, pp. 25–7.

The *military balance* (M), too, was transformed to Israel's great advantage; far more so, indeed, than after the Sinai Campaign. The armed forces of Egypt, Jordan, and Syria were mauled by *Tzahal* between 5 and 10 June 1967, with the major changes being wrought in air power and armour, much of the latter abandoned on the battle-field. Jordan lost 160 of her 250 tanks and all 21 fighter planes. Egypt lost between 800 and 900 tanks, of which Israel acquired 100 intact, 340 planes, and a large quantity of other heavy equipment. And Syria lost 61 planes. To this was added Israeli control over territory more than three times the size of the State when the war began and, with it, a marked improvement in defensible frontiers, as noted—the Canal, the River, and the Heights. The result was a striking disparity in M, quickly corrected, in quantitative terms, by the USSR. The security achieved by a unilateral military campaign and strategically advantageous borders became embedded in Israeli images from 10 June 1967 onwards. It could not be otherwise, for the change in Israel's security position was drastic—and dramatic. All this intensified a policy directed to the maintenance of a superior military capability.

The policy took different forms, but with an identical objective. There was the continuous effort to persuade Washington that Israel needed more—and better—weapons in order to preserve a positive balance in her favour, with the goal of thwarting a fourth round of full-scale war. On the whole that line was successful, as is evident in the Phantom agreements of January 1968 and October 1971, and the frequent Israeli statements of absolute satisfaction with the flow of arms. Another form of expression was a tough negotiating position *vis-à-vis* UN and US proposals, whether for a complete or partial settlement, whether under Jarring or Rogers–Sisco auspices. Anything which might undermine Israel's military–strategic pre-eminence in the Near East Core was rejected; and all manifestations of third-party intervention were suspect.

The E component, as well, was the recipient of feedback in three discernible strands. The most immediate consequence was to terminate the *mitun*, Israel's recession of the preceding two and a half years. Secondly, during the *Hamtana* the economic burden of large-scale mobilization was marked and cumulative. That strain was perceived by Israel's leaders and, as noted, created a further inducement to decision and action towards the end of May. Moreover, it strengthened the conviction that Israel must not, in the future, allow her resources to be drained by an enemy imposing a siege over a protracted period. Offsetting this effect was the reality of Israel's ability to absorb the economic challenge of the May 1967 crisis and still achieve a resounding military triumph. This, too, penetrated the images of her decision-makers, with a consequent easing of concern about the economic dimension of Israel's foreign policy capability.

FIGURE 16
FEEDBACK: SIX DAY WAR

Operational Environment	*Psychological Environment and Policy Derivatives*
External	*External*
G Israel's peril and decisions to delay created widespread sympathy; and outcome of S decision produced (short-lived) sense of relief, combined with awe of *Tzahal*; extraordinary identification of world Jewry with Israel's fate; emotional trauma of Jerusalem regained, alienating many global system actors; and powerlessness of UN laid bare (T_2, S)	Perception of favourable world public opinion and, especially, awakening of Jewry—as well as of weak UN and hostile Secretary-General; policy derivatives of post-strategic-decision images were hard line on peace terms; strengthening of 'two-camp' thesis and corresponding links to Jewry; indifference to UN and other external pressures to compromise on Jerusalem; and denigration of UN guarantees as path to peace in Middle East, as well as distrust of all UN actions and proposals (P–D, C–S, M–S)
DB₁ Demonstrated once more pervasive influence of United States on Israeli policy (T_2, S)	That pre-eminent role clearly perceived; policy derivative of post-strategic-decision images was persistent attempts to forge *de facto* alliance, through US military and economic aid, diplomatic support, etc. (M–S, P–D, E–D)
DB₂ Deepened conflict between Israel and Soviet Union, including break in diplomatic relations and massive support —military, economic, political, and diplomatic—for Arab adversaries.	Image of Soviet animus and patron role *vis-à-vis* Arabs greatly strengthened; policy derivative was to seek even closer relations with US and to view USSR as active participant in Middle East conflict
Neutralized super powers' military intervention in Arab–Israel conflict (S)	That process, correctly perceived, increased self-confidence and disposition to 'bargain from strength' (P–D, M–S)
B Tacit alliance with France sundered and replaced by her pro-Arab line (S)	This change perceived at last; policy effect was to enhance Israel's dependence on US for military and political support, and setback for Israel's search for association with 'Europe' (M–S, P–D)

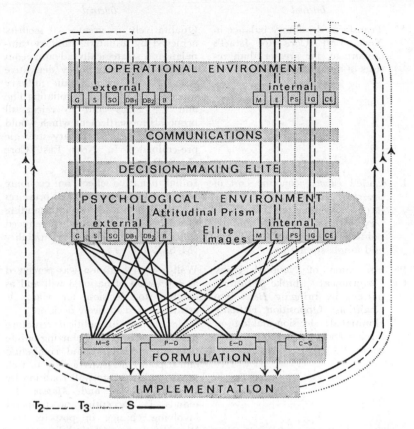

S   Israel's position as pre-eminent actor firmly established; tacit friendship with Jordan (S)

Basic change in Middle East system as a result of Six Day War perceived; policy derivatives were triumph of Ben Gurionist 'bargaining from strength' approach to all proposals for settlement; shared interest with King Hussein re *feda'iyun* recognized and led to support of Amman regime in continuing civil war (P–D)

	Internal	*Internal*
M	Transformed military balance in Near East Core to Israel's advantage, far greater than results of Sinai Campaign (S)	Qualitatively greater security achieved by unilateral military campaign and strategically advantageous borders perceived; policy derivative was to seek to maintain military superiority—by hard negotiating line and US arms—and to reject all proposals for settlement which would undermine Israel's military–strategic pre-eminence in Near East Core (M–S, P–D)
E	Ended *mitun*; economic cost of diverting large part of labour force severe in short run; military triumph, notwithstanding, pointed to economy's resiliency and ample strength (T$_2$, S)	Initial negative effect on economy was perceived, strengthened pressures for decision; success in withstanding protracted Arab pressure reduced concern about economic capability (M–S, E–D)
PS CE	Formation of National Unity Government broke historic pattern by bringing *Herut* into Coalition; Opposition virtually eliminated; decision-making on foreign and security policy paralysed (T$_3$)	Wall-to-wall coalition was perceived as expression of national will and as catalyst to decision for war; its creation eased strategic decision Basic change in political structure perceived, along with blurring of line between incumbent and competing élites; policy derivatives were to seek to maintain wall-to-wall coalition by satisfying *Gahal* and *Mapam* demands, i.e. accepting no proposal involving change in post-Six Day War borders, and indifference to external opposition to unification of Jerusalem (M–S, P–D, C–S)
IG	Decision to delay activated *Tzahal* pressure (T$_2$)	*Tzahal* pressure perceived by decision-makers and contributed to strategic decision (M–S)
	Created Left (*Matzpen, Siah*) and Right (Greater Israel Movement) and reactivated Goldmann's dissent from government peace policy (S)	Dissent perceived; Greater Israel Movement strengthened pressure for *status quo* in government; other groups influenced acceptance of Rogers 'B', July 1970 (P–D)

There was also feedback to Israel's *political structure* (PS) and *competing élites* (CE). The May 1967 crisis had generated a wall-to-wall coalition, the first in Israel's history. And that national unity government had broken the historic pattern by bringing *Herut* into power, sharing responsibility for public policy especially in the security field. As a result, parliamentary opposition virtually ceased—18 of 120 *Knesset* members; and even they were fractured into half a dozen factions. More important was the paralysis in decision-making on foreign and security policy: a Coalition including both *Herut* and *Mapam* could not depart from the minimal *Tora shebe'al peh* territorial formula and remain intact.

In long-run terms perhaps the most important legacy of the Six Day War decisions to PS was the hastening of the formal (January 1968) and actual unification of the three Labour factions into the Israel Labour Party. Noteworthy, but without short-run foreign policy implications, was the embryonic involvement, within Israel's political system, of Arabs from the occupied territories: a heavy voter participation in the Jerusalem municipal elections of 1968, and the West Bank municipal elections of 1972.

The reality of fundamental structural change was accurately perceived. So, too, was the narrowing of the policy gap between incumbent and competing élites; that is, between the Labour Alignment and *Gahal*. Both benefited from their post-May 1967 co-operative relationship and both placed a high value on the Coalition's survival. In policy terms this led to conduct and content which would prevent the dissolution of the National Unity Government—and that meant satisfying the two extremes of the spectrum, *Mapam* and *Herut*. Because of their strong, ideologically-linked, views on peace and security, the Israel Government, in effect, decided to reject any proposal unacceptable to either of those parties. The upshot was non-decisions or a rigid *status quo* policy based on the conditions arising from the Six Day War. It required the protracted and pointed intervention of Israel's pre-eminent external component, the United States, in June–July 1970, to compel a positive decision (on Rogers 'B') and with it the demise of that structural abnormality in Israel's political system.

The Six Day War also spawned several *interest groups* (IG) with an explicit foreign policy advocacy: an anti-Zionist *Matzpen* on the far Left calling for a Trotskyist solution to the conflict and Israel's merger into a revolutionary socialist Middle East Federation; a pro-Zionist, student-initiated, splinter from *Mapam* known as *Siah*, which called for the creation of a Palestinian state and the forging of links with this national entity; an expansionist Greater Israel Movement on the far Right, which advocated the retention of all territory occupied as a result of the war; and a reactivation of the vocal dissent from government policy by Dr. Nahum Goldmann. All of these pressures were perceived. The Greater Israel Movement strengthened the forces within the wall-to-wall coalition in favour of the territorial *status quo*. Dissenting groups were to influence decision-makers in the crisis leading to the acceptance of Rogers 'B' in July 1970.

CHAPTER 8

Rogers Proposals[1]

A period of tranquillity followed the Six Day War. Then in March 1969 Nasser launched a 'war of attrition' to compel Israel's withdrawal from the Sinai Peninsula.[2] It was in the midst of that fourth round of the protracted conflict that her foreign policy was confronted with a major challenge, in the form of several United States initiatives to

[1] The problem of sources is acute in foreign policy research as recent as Israel's decisions relating to the Rogers Proposals. Minutes of Government meetings are unavailable. Only one book-length account has been written thus far: D. Margalit, *Sheder Meha-bay'it Ha-lavan* (Dispatch From the White House), 1971. *Knesset* debates provide insight into decision-makers' images, as do their speeches elsewhere during 1969–70. The decision process and implementation are based upon the detailed coverage in the daily Israeli press, notably in *Ha'aretz, Ma'ariv, Yedi'ot Aharonot*, and the *Jerusalem Post*. These have been supplemented by interviews with high-policy decision-makers and civil servants who participated in the decision process.

On the quality of newspaper reports two views from the inside are noteworthy:

'The Israeli press is an excellent and useful source on the course of events relating to the Rogers Plans although it is clear that the press does not include all the details.' Herzog interview, 1970.

'Generally speaking it can be said that the Israeli press during the months July–August 1970 provided reliable and detailed material, though not complete, on Rogers Plan "B". I would note in particular the political reporters for *Ma'ariv* and *Yedi'ot Aharonot*. Nevertheless, I would also use interviews with senior foreign policy decision-makers, as well as articles and speeches on foreign policy by Cabinet ministers of that time.' Allon interview, 1970.

Others concurred, with reference to the earlier stages of the decision process as well—Rogers 'A', Yost Document, etc.

Where no specific source is cited in the notes the data are drawn from one or more of the daily newspapers mentioned above. Similarly, unless otherwise specified, quoted passages or summaries of remarks identified in the text with an individual are based upon direct interview material written up shortly after the interview.

[2] According to official Israeli doctrine the period June 1967–August 1970 was designated the 'thousand day war', with the following phases:

   (a) 12 June–Sept. 1967: The Aftermath of Victory
   (b) Sept. 1967–July 1968: The Struggle with Terrorists
   (c) Aug. 1968–Feb. 1969: The Bar-Lev Line
   (d) 8 March–20 July 1969: The Limited War of Attrition along the Canal
   (e) 20 July–Dec. 1969: The Developing War of Attrition along the Canal
   (f) January–8 Aug. 1970: Full War of Attrition.

A Thousand Days, p. 1.

A measure of the severity of the War of Attrition is indicated by the casualties during the one year preceding the cease-fire: 319 killed and 1,131 injured. This was more than a third of the total casualties for the five-year period after the June 1967 War: 817 killed and 3,119 wounded. *Ha'aretz*, 6 June 1972.

break the deadlock. The result was a cluster of tactical and strategic Israeli decisions:

on 10 December 1969   the Government of Israel rejected Secretary of State Rogers's Plan 'A', which advocated in essence a return to the 'international border between Israel and Egypt'; (T_{1a})

on 22 December 1969   Israel's Government reiterated its rejection of US proposals, *inter alia*, the Yost Document, which provided for a return to the Israel–Jordan *status quo ante* the June War, apart from insubstantial changes;[1] (T_{1b})

on 21 June 1970   the Israeli Cabinet rejected Rogers 'B', which called for a restoration of a limited cease-fire and negotiations under the auspices of UN Representative Jarring to carry out all the provisions of Security Council Resolution 242: more specifically, to reach agreement on 'a just and lasting peace', based upon 'mutual acknowledgement . . . of sovereignty, territorial integrity and political independence, and Israeli withdrawal from territories occupied in the 1967 conflict'; (T_2) and

on 31 July 1970   the Government of Israel decided to accept Rogers Plan 'B'. (S)[2]

That strategic decision caused the collapse of the National Unity Government, which had been formed on the eve of the Six Day War.[3] It also led to a (self-)controlled conflict (with minimal violence) even more pronounced than during the quiet decade, 1957–67. And the new phase of tranquillity, beginning with the Cease-Fire of 7 August 1970, was sustained until 6 October 1973 despite the deadlock over Jarring's Memorandum of 8 February 1971 and persistent Egyptian threats to resume hostilities, especially in 1971, termed by Sadat 'the year of decision'.

[1] Charles Yost was then United States Representative to the United Nations.

[2] There was a third stage of this decision cluster, in the on-going process of struggle and negotiations for a 'political settlement': Rogers 'C' and its related Israeli decisions are discussed briefly in the Feedback section to this chapter. The main thrust of the analysis, however, is the decision process culminating in Rogers Plan 'B' and the cease-fire with Egypt.

[3] This was one of the three occasions since independence when an Israeli Coalition Government fell or was ruptured because of a foreign policy issue. For an analysis of the other two cases, both concerning relations with Germany (1957–8, 1959), see Brecher, ch. 16 (*b*), (*c*).

(A) OPERATIONAL ENVIRONMENT

Most environmental components were relevant to Israel's decisions on the Rogers Proposals. At the *global* level (G), a transitional phase of super-power *détente* was perceptible in the year 1969–70. The SALT talks on limitation of nuclear arms was one indicator. Another was continuing Soviet restraint in the Vietnam War. A third was the beginning of a dialogue between the two Germanys. But the most important symptom for Israel's decision-makers was active co-operation between the US and the USSR on the Arab–Israel conflict. Horizontal rapport was evident in the Two Power and Four Power Talks from March–April 1969 onwards; the vertical form was reflected in parallel moderating pressure on their respective clients, through withholding, control, or limitation of assistance—military, economic, and political. The objective was to prevent a regional war from escalating into direct super-power confrontation. And the convergence of their plans for a 'political solution' between October 1969 and the summer of 1970 expressed the intensity of that mutual interest. The UN, by contrast, was of marginal relevance. Secretary-General U Thant had long been *persona non grata* with Israel. And the Jarring Mission was in abeyance after the first round of indirect talks in 1968. The world organization provided only a forum for Big Four discussions on the Middle East.

The 'American factor' (DB_1) was pervasive in the setting for Israel's decisions, from incipient 'more even-handedness', shortly before Nixon became President, through the Two Power Talks, Rogers Plan 'A' and the Yost Document, to Rogers Plan 'B' and Nixon's letter of 23 July 1970 to Meir, leading to Israel's acceptance of the United States peace initiative. There was tension and mutual suspicion. Israel was shocked by what she perceived as the pro-Arab territorial proposals of December 1969. The US termed rigid Israel's abrupt rejection of Rogers Plan 'A' and the Yost Document. The American announcement of March 1970 delaying the further supply of Phantom aircraft deepened Israel's concern. In short, there was a conspicuous downswing in the pattern of (mis)trust between Jerusalem and Washington. The other *dominant bilateral* relationship reached its nadir in the early months of 1970, primarily because of the growing Soviet military presence in Egypt. For the first time the possibility existed of a direct military confrontation between *Tzahal* and Soviet forces. Indeed, sporadic incidents occurred from April to July, a warning signal which both heeded.

The Middle East *subordinate system* (S) and Israel's two principal *bilateral* relationships within it—with Egypt and Jordan (B_1, B_2)—were characterized by very high tension in 1969–70. The 'war of attrition' caused a conspicuous increase in Israeli casualties at the Suez Canal, approaching the level of intolerability by the spring of 1970.[1] Israel's

[1] The 'level of (in)tolerability' is a social-psychological concept designating the

deep penetration raids, starting in January, seemed to herald the resumption of full-scale war. That was avoided; but Israel's mastery of Egypt's airspace provided a pretext and/or inducement for increasing Soviet intervention in Egypt's air defence. More generally, 1969–70 witnessed the greater military and economic dependence of the protagonists upon the super powers and, correspondingly, the latter's deeper penetration into the Near East Core. A second source of regional tension was the sharpening conflict between Palestinian guerrilla organizations and Hussein's regime. The King's writ extended to ever smaller parts of Jordan. *Al-Fath* and other underground armies established *de facto* rule in sections of Amman itself and were bolstered by prestige and material support within the Arab world. At the time of Israel's strategic decision (July 1970), when Hussein too accepted Rogers 'B', it was uncertain who would rule in Amman during the ensuing months. And in the wider context of the Middle East system there was a dramatic split between radical Arab republican regimes and conservative Arab monarchies, dramatized at the Rabat summit conference of December 1969. The perennial search for unity received a sharp setback, as did the Palestinian guerrilla movement's appeal for aid in funds and weapons. All these facets of systemic tension impinged upon the environment for Israel's decisions.

Military capability (M) was the most salient internal component, given the demands on resources for the 'war of attrition'. The weaponry of Arab armies, especially that of Egypt, was not restored to its pre-Six Day War strength until late 1968, though Soviet arms shipments began almost immediately after that war. And Israel retained her superiority, primarily because of the US decision, announced in December 1968, to sell her 50 Phantom and 80 Skyhawk planes.[1] Nevertheless, that fact pointed up Israel's virtually total dependence upon the United States for heavy weapons, notably planes and tanks. That condition, a result of France's embargo from early June 1967 onwards, was to have a profound effect upon Israeli decision-makers' perceptions and their consequent decision to accept Rogers Plan 'B'—the peace initiative. It was not until the spring of 1970, however, that the M component assumed importance: the catalyst was the flow of Soviet missiles, planes, pilots, and advisers into Egypt, primarily to bolster her defence capability against Israeli air raids. The build-up was swift and formidable (Table 23):

---

perception by an attentive public of actions affecting their society or polity whose intensity has exceeded, or has not yet approached, societal 'acceptability'. That level is measured by societal response—through voting, articulation of support or protest, public opinion polls, etc. In Israel, the approach of intolerability was manifested by an upsurge of interest group and general public advocacy during the spring of 1970, aimed at ending the 'war of attrition' and the stalemate on negotiations.

[1] For a discussion of the arms race during 1967–8 and the Near East Core military balance in July 1968 see Brecher, pp. 87–9 and Table 8.

TABLE 23

SOVIET MILITARY AID AND PRESENCE IN EGYPT: JANUARY–JUNE 1970

	Pilots	Troops	Others	Total Personnel	SAM Missiles	Planes	Air Bases
1 January 1970	0	0	2,500–4,000	2,500– 4,000	0	0	0
31 March 1970	60– 80	4,000	2,500–4,000	6,560– 8,080	22 SAM-3s	0	1 ?
30 June 1970	100–150	8,000	2,500–4,000	10,600–12,150	45–55 SAM-3s	120 Mig 21Js	6

Source: *Strategic Survey 1970*, p. 47.

It was a super-power presence with which Israel had to contend. And tangible Soviet military power in Egypt continued to grow during the months after the cease-fire.[1] Another dimension of that challenge to Israel's military capability was the economic burden of defence expenditures: imports for defence purposes in 1968 amounted to $249 million; this grew to $334 million in 1969, and to $624 million in 1970; the increase from 1969 to 1970, compared with other imports, was 86·8 per cent compared to 8·3 per cent.[2]

The *political structure* (PS) of Israel in the period of her Rogers decisions was unique: a multi-party system was transformed into a two-plus system, following the seventh *Knesset* elections in October 1969. The parties of the Left—*Mapai, Ahdut Ha'avoda*, and *Rafi*—had already reunited into the Israel Labour Party at the beginning of 1968; together with *Mapam* they had secured 56 seats; the four associated Arab MKs gave the Labour–*Mapam* Alignment, formed in January 1968, exactly half of the total parliamentary members. The Right-wing bloc of *Herut* and the Liberals—*Gahal*—had emerged even more emphatically as the principal opposition group, with 26 seats. The only other party with more than marginal representation in the *Knesset* was the NRP (12).[3] It was thus now theoretically possible to form a Left-of-Centre secular coalition, with the participation of the Independent Liberals. The Alignment, however, chose to reconstitute the National Unity Government, a 'wall-to-wall' coalition, including two perennial partners, the Independent Liberals and the NRP, and the historic opposition, *Herut*. The coincidence of Rogers 'A' with this important domestic development was striking: forty-two days of negotiations had failed to persuade *Herut*'s Begin to rejoin the Government;

[1] By 30 September the estimated number of Soviet pilots had increased to 150, troops to 10,000–13,000, SAM-3s to 70–80, and Mig 21 Js to 150. Changes by the end of December 1970 were 200 pilots, 12,000–15,000 troops, 4,000 others, and 75–85 SAM-3s. *Strategic Survey 1970*, p. 47. In July 1972 most of the Soviet personnel and some of its military equipment were withdrawn from Egypt.

[2] The military imports data are as follows (in million dollars):

TABLE 24
ISRAEL'S MILITARY IMPORTS: 1968–1970

	1968	1969	1970	Percentage increase 1968–9	1969–70
Total Imports	1,812	2,188	2,631	20·7	20·2
Total Defence Imports	249	334	624	34·1	86·8
Total Imports other than Defence Purposes	1,563	1,854	2,007	18·6	8·3

Bank of Israel, *Annual Report* 1970, pp. 26–7.

[3] The other 22 seats in a House of 120 were scattered from Right to Left, in foreign policy terms, as follows: the Free Centre (2); the State List (4); *Agudat Yisrael* (4); *Po'alei Agudat Yisrael* (2); Independent Liberals (4); *Maki* (1); *Ha'olam Hazeh* (2); *Rakah* (3). For a detailed analysis of Israel's multi-party political structure from 1948 to 1968 see Brecher, ch. 6.

within hours of the Secretary of State's proposed territorial settlement
the deadlock in inter-party negotiations was broken; Israel's political
factions had closed ranks.[1] The result was a Government (Cabinet) of
unprecedented size, 24 members, a massive *Knesset* majority, 102 out of
120 seats, and full participation of *Gahal* in the Coalition, with corresponding acceptance of collective responsibility.[2]

One consequence was the overwhelming national consensus inherent
in any decision taken by the National Unity Government. Another,
a direct structural by-product, was the difficulty of arriving at a decision on the fundamental foreign policy issue of the post-Six Day War
period—Israel's conditions for a peace settlement. And that, in turn,
derived from the programmatic and ideological disunity within the
Government, for it contained the two extremes of the *competing élites*
(CE) spectrum—*Herut* and *Mapam*. The Israel Labour Party had
formulated a self-binding *Tora Shebe'al Peh* ('Oral Law') in its 1969
election platform, indicating the territories Israel would insist upon
retaining: sovereignty over reunited Jerusalem; control over the Gaza
Strip, the Golan Heights, and Sharm-e-Sheikh, with a corridor linking
it to Israel. Moreover, the Jordan River was to be Israel's 'security
frontier'; that is, no Arab army would be permitted on the West
Bank.[3]

The nationalist Right termed this insufficient, while the Left-
socialists urged far-reaching concessions for a genuine peace agreement.
And within the Labour Party the Allon and Dayan 'Plans' competed
for support.[4] These diverse maps on conditions of peace may be compared in schematic form. (See the back endpaper maps in this volume.)

Jerusalem: All insisted upon Israeli sovereignty
                               over the reunited city. The Labour
                               Alignment,   including   *Mapam,*

---

[1] The deadlock was over domestic issues, notably health insurance and arbitration
in labour disputes. The role of Rogers 'A' as a catalyst in Israel's political system is
emphasized in Margalit, pp. 11–16. Begin denied the causal link. Interview, 1971.

[2] *Gahal* was represented in the National Unity Government from May 1967 until
December 1969 by the *Herut* and Liberal leaders only—among 21 ministers; and both
Begin and Saphir were, at their own insistence, Ministers without Portfolio. It did not
subscribe to—and was not bound by—the 'Basic Principles of the Government
Programme', approved after the 1965 elections. Only with the new coalition of
December 1969 and the new 'Basic Principles' did *Gahal* become a full partner, with
6 of 24 ministers.

[3] The tense debate within Israel's Labour Party preceding the adoption of the
'Oral Law' was reported at length in the Israeli press, 31 July–6 August 1969.

[4] For an authoritative statement of Allon's views six years after the Six Day War,
see Allon (3). A detailed map and exposition of the Allon Plan is to be found in
Ben Porat (1). A clear statement of Dayan's views is found in his BBC TV interview
with Alan Hirt on 14 May 1973; text is in *Jerusalem Post*, 15 May 1973. *Mapam*'s
official stand on border issues can be found in 'Mapam's Plan for Peace—1972',
New Outlook, 16, 3 (140), March–April 1973, pp. 75–8.

would accept exercise of control over the Holy Places by the governing bodies of the respective religious communities

Gaza Strip: 'Oral Law';

Dayan; *Gahal*   —Israeli control

Allon Plan   —Israeli control, with transportation rights, but not a territorial corridor, between Jordan and the West Bank and Gaza city, including the use of port facilities

Mapam   —no return to Egypt, status to be determined

Golan Heights: 'Oral Law'   —Israeli control, border unspecified

Allon Plan   —border to pass through Heights, west of Kuneitra

Dayan   —Israeli control over most of Heights

Gahal   —the slopes under Israeli control, the rest to be discussed

Mapam   —Israel–Syria border to pass through Heights, remaining area to be demilitarized

West Bank or Judea and Samaria: 'Oral Law'   —the Jordan River to be Israel's 'security frontier'

Allon Plan   —an 'Arab solution'; the Hussein idea of a Jordan–Palestine federation, but not its territorial extent on the West Bank, plausible and acceptable; by implication, an autonomous or independent West Bank Palestinian state not ruled out; and, most important, a 'security belt' along the Jordan River, from 15 to 22 kilometres in width, controlled by Israel through a series of *Nahal* posts; this security zone includes the Judean Desert, with its boundary adjacent to Hebron; a Jericho Corridor, between the north and south sections of this zone, would provide a direct land link between the Kingdom of Jordan east of the River and the West Bank

	Dayan	—to be returned to Jordan's control, with minor border changes in heights overlooking Jordan River; the Jordan River to be Israel's 'security frontier'; the right of Israelis to settle anywhere on the West Bank; and four or five Jewish towns to be established— next to Hebron, Ramallah, and Nablus, and between Nablus and Jenin
	Gahal	—Israeli annexation
	Mapam	—demilitarized, with minor border adjustments; to be returned to Jordan's control; the Jordan River to be Israel's 'security frontier'
Sinai Peninsula and Sharm-e-Sheikh:	'Oral Law'	—Sharm-e-Sheikh under Israeli control, with a corridor along the east coast of Sinai linking it to Eilat
	Allon Plan	—ditto, except that corridor to continue north of Eilat through Sinai; border unspecified
	Dayan	—Israeli control over Sharm-e-Sheikh and some changes all along the old Egypt–Israel border
	Gahal	—Israeli control over Sharm-e-Sheikh and the eastern part of Sinai
	Mapam	—the entire peninsula to be returned to Egypt and demilitarized; some form of Israeli presence at Sharm-e-Sheikh

The differences were substantial, centring on the West Bank— Israeli control or return to the Arabs (Palestine entity) or Jordan, and Sinai—Israeli control of part of the peninsula or demilitarization. Anything less than the 'Oral Law'—or even giving it formal Government sanction—would have led to *Gahal*'s withdrawal from the Government (as it did on 4 August 1970). Anything more than the 'Oral Law' —or even an attempt to make it formal Government policy—would have meant *Mapam*'s resignation. The result was a paralysis in decision-making on this issue between June 1967 and July 1970.

Internal pressures were not entirely absent or without influence. Indeed, *interest group* advocacy (IG) during the spring and early summer of 1970 created an atmosphere conducive to concessions by Israel's Government. Notable was the role of Nahum Goldmann, who pressed his 'doveish' views in a series of speeches, as well as through articles in the Israeli and foreign press. That *non-associational* form of advocacy activated some marginal *associational* interest groups on the Left— *Siah* and *Matzpen*, the former urging concessions of the *Mapam* genre, the latter of the anti-Zionist Trotskyite persuasion.[1] He also articulated a widespread mood within the academic and student community. It was a mood of fatigue, of demoralization, and of doubt about the Government's will for peace. In other words, the 'Goldmann Affair' brought to the surface *anomic* interest group pressures. They included such disturbing signals as letters to the Prime Minister from high school students, including sons of impeccable Establishment figures like the founder of *Palmah*, questioning the wisdom of military service in view of the Government's rigid line on peace terms. One example will suffice:

We, a group of high school students who are about to enter military service in *Tzahal*, protest against the Government's policy in the Goldmann–Nasser talks affair. Until now we believed that we were going to fight and to serve our country for years because there is no alternative. This affair proved that, when there was an alternative, even the slightest one, it was ignored. In the light of this we and many others wonder whether to fight a permanent and endless war while our Government directs its policy in such a way that the chances of peace are missed. We call upon the Government to exploit every opportunity and every chance for peace.[2]

It caused widespread shock among decision-makers and society as a whole.[3] Moreover, wide publicity abroad was given to Israeli criticism of government policy in a *Newsweek* symposium in April 1970 by half a dozen academics and other intellectuals. Among other interest groups, *Ha-tenu'a Lema'an Eretz Yisrael Ha-shlema*, the 'Greater Israel' (or Land of Israel) Movement, acted as a supportive pressure for the

[1] Views similar to those of *Siah* had been advocated by an electoral interest group, the Peace List, in the October 1969 *Knesset* elections; it failed to secure a single seat. The views of Goldmann and of the interest groups noted in this summary of IG pressures are analysed in Brecher, ch. 7, esp. pp. 134–7, 140–1, 154–6, and 159.

[2] Letter of 58 twelfth-grade students to the Prime Minister, April 1970; the text is in *Ha'olam Hazeh*, 17 June 1970.

[3] One *Herut* minister at the time acknowledged the anomic interest articulation thus: 'The Egyptians finally succeeded in wearing out the spirit of Israel's public and, in particular, of Israeli fighting youth, due to the war of attrition. Signs of refusal to serve in *Tzahal*, growing depression among soldiers, and even sarcastic jokes among new recruits such as "we'll meet on the memorial board", were frequent during 1970, whereas they never appeared in 1948, 1956, and 1967. In my view this had an enormous influence upon Cabinet members and especially upon the Prime Minister—as a woman.' Weizman interview, 1971.

The effects of the 'Goldmann Affair' were discussed in, *inter alia*, *Ma'ariv*, 24 April 1970, and *Yedi'ot Aharonot*, 8, 9, 22, 30 April, and 10 July 1970. A classification of *Knesset* members into 'hawks' and 'doves' at the time is to be found in *Ha'olam Hazeh*, 15 April 1970.

hard-line nationalist programme espoused by *Gahal* and sections of other parties, including the NRP and the Labour Party.[1] The Israel Defence Forces, normally the most influential *institutional* interest group in Israel's foreign policy, were inactive in the Rogers decision process.[2] In short, internal environmental conditions, notably M and IG, were receptive to change, but powerful external inputs were required to compel a decision.

(B) DECISION-MAKERS AND THEIR IMAGES

The tactical and strategic decisions relating to the Rogers Proposals were made by the largest government in Israel's history. The Alignment, comprising the Israel Labour Party and *Mapam*, held a majority of 14 among 24, distributed as follows: former *Mapai* (FM)—8; former *Ahdut Ha'avoda* (AH)—2; former *Rafi* (R)—2; and *Mapam*—2. *Gahal* provided 6 ministers, equally divided between its two components, *Herut* and the Liberals. There were 3 from the National Religious Party; and 1 from the Independent Liberals.

Alignment

Israel Labour Party

Golda Meir (FM)	Prime Minister
Yigal Allon (AH)	Deputy Prime Minister, Education and Culture
Yosef Almogi (FM)	Labour
Moshe Dayan (R)	Defence
Abba Eban (FM)	Foreign Affairs
Yisrael Galili (AH)	Without Portfolio
Haim Gvati (FM)	Agriculture
Shlomo Hillel (FM)	Police
Shimon Peres (R)	Without Portfolio
Pinhas Sapir (FM)	Finance
Ya'acov Shimshon Shapiro (FM)	Justice
Ze'ev Sharef (FM)	Housing

---

[1] On the programme and leadership of the 'shlema' movement see Brecher, pp. 155–6.

[2] Weizman, a new Cabinet minister with active service in *Tzahal* from its creation, noted this with chagrin (interview, 1971): '*Tzahal* had great influence on decision-making in foreign affairs throughout, and especially since 1967. However, in July 1970 it was not active as an interest group in this field. I have no doubt that, if the higher officers of *Tzahal* had opposed the acceptance of Rogers Plan 'B' and had put pressure on Cabinet members, the Government would ultimately have refused to accept the Plan.' And Herzog noted (interview, December 1970): 'Senior *Tzahal* officers took no part in key meetings on Rogers Plan "B". *Tzahal* was not at all a pressure group on the Government regarding this subject.'

Mapam

Natan Peled	Without Portfolio
Victor Shemtov	Without Portfolio[1]

Gahal

Herut

Menahem Begin	Without Portfolio
Haim Landau	Development
Ezer Weizman	Transport

Liberals

Arye Dulzin	Without Portfolio
Elimeleh Rimalt	Posts
Yosef Saphir	Commerce and Industry

National Religious Party

Yosef Burg	Social Welfare
Haim Moshe Shapira	Interior
Zerah Warhaftig	Religious Affairs

Independent Liberals

Moshe Kol	Tourism

As always, all ministers were formally equal decision-makers, but in reality some were 'more equal than others'. By consensus, on issues requiring Government sanctions, the high-policy élite at the time on foreign and security policy consisted of five persons—Meir, Dayan, Galili, Allon, and Eban.[2]

The Prime Minister makes decisions quickly, a personality trait which was evident in her immediate rejection of Rogers 'B', when the US Ambassador presented it to her on 19 June 1970, and her *volte-face* within a day of receiving President Nixon's letter on 24 July.[3] Dayan was the most pragmatic—and inconsistent—among the principal decision-makers. In June he was the staunchest opponent of Rogers 'B', reportedly threatening to resign if it were accepted. At the informal meeting on 25 July, where the US initiative was approved, Dayan did not express a view. The following day there were reports once more

[1] *Mapam* was assigned the Ministries of Absorption and Health but refused them because of intra-Coalition conflicts. Peled and Shemtov assumed those posts—at higher *Mapam* directive—after the departure of *Gahal* from the National Unity Government on 3 August 1970.

[2] Finance Minister Sapir carried immense influence within the Labour Party and the Cabinet, then and later; but he was rarely active in foreign policy discussions, except those pertaining to economic affairs. He was inactive during the 1969–70 decision process on Rogers Plan 'A' and 'B'. For the high-policy élite in these issue-areas from 1948 to 1968 see Brecher, ch. 10, esp. (*a*) and Table 21.

[3] A point noted in Allon and Weizman interviews, 1971, and in Begin 1970.

of his threat to resign if the Government accepted the US peace initiative. The same day, however, he declined Begin's suggestion that he announce his dissent. Dayan voted for acceptance at the Cabinet meeting on the 31st, but on 2 August he proposed a qualified formula.[1] Yet that inconsistency did not diminish his prestige among many Cabinet colleagues, 'who voted for Dayan's proposals regularly because they accepted him as *the* authority in security matters'.[2] Galili, least known among the five in Israel and abroad, derived his influence largely from the esteem in which he was held by the Prime Minister. He was, throughout the period of decision, the closest political adviser to Meir in the foreign policy–security field, as well as chief drafter of Government decisions. Allon and Eban were members of the high-policy élite by virtue of their formal position and their long experience in this area of public policy. It was the images of these five persons which shaped Israel's decisions on the Rogers Proposals. To uncover their salient psychological environment we shall use both qualitative and quantitative data and methods of analysis.

The pre-eminent components for Meir were, clearly, relations with the United States (DB_1) and military capability (M), the two being inextricably intertwined in her perception. There is abundant evidence to support this ranking. Thus, on 24 June 1970, just three days after the Cabinet unanimously rejected Rogers 'B', the Prime Minister remarked:

I do not wish [us] to delude ourselves that differences of opinion do not exist between us and the United States and that these differences might increase. . . . At the same time we must not treat lightly the friendship and good relations between us and the US. . . . Even if we have to face a sharp and grave disagreement with [them], let us not forget the importance of preserving the friendship between us and the US.[3]

Two months earlier Meir stated the decision problem without frills: 'It is difficult, not simple, to say "no" to the Americans; who else remains to supply us with arms?'[4] And in her address to the *Knesset* on 4 August, while explaining the strategic decision to accept Rogers 'B', the Prime Minister declared: 'In this resolution, moreover, we kept in mind our duty to ensure the continued strengthening of the Israel Defence Forces as well as to continue to nurture the friendly relations between Israel and the United States, its people and its government.'[5]

---

[1] This summary of Dayan's changing attitude in July–August is based, respectively, upon *Ma'ariv*, 30 June 1970; Allon interview, 1971; *Ma'ariv* and *Yedi'ot Aharonot*, 26 July 1970; Harif interview, 1971; and *Ma'ariv*, 14 Aug. 1970, *Ha'olam Hazeh*, 19 Aug. 1970, and Margalit, p. 176.   [2] Weizman interview, 1971.

[3] *Ha'aretz*, 25 June 1970.   [4] *Ma'ariv*, 20 April 1970.

[5] *Divrei Ha-knesset*, lviii, 99th Sitting, 7th *Knesset*, 4 Aug. 1970, p. 2757 (English version issued by the Ministry for Foreign Affairs, Information Division, Meir (2), p. 5). The other DB relationship was of no consequence in Meir's articulated image.

Meir was also conscious of the regional environment (S), but it was of distinctly less importance, for she did not perceive any change in Arab attitudes to peace, despite their acceptance of the US proposal. Nonetheless, she acknowledged that the façade of an Arab will to peace could not go unchallenged:

Since the publication of the American peace initiative, and even after their announcement of its acceptance, we have heard and continue to hear authoritative pronouncements by the Heads of Arab States . . . which clearly indicate that they aim at war and not peace . . . at the continuation of the conflict and not its liquidation. . . . Even so . . . we have felt duty-bound carefully to examine every prospect, be it ever so slim, which could lead us to peace. . . .[1]

Meir confessed that the growing evidence of dissatisfaction among Israeli youth (IG) disturbed her, for among the critics were the hope of Israel's future.[2] The fact that Rogers 'B' included a cease-fire, even if temporary, which meant a respite in the roll of casualties, made the proposal more attractive to her. Finally, in her rejection of Rogers 'A', the Jewish component of Meir's attitudinal prism was crucial—along with M. 'Each of the American proposals, about borders and the return of [Arab] refugees, would cause grave harm to the security of Israel and to . . . her survival [as a Jewish state]. It would be a return to the geography of 1967 and to the demography of 1947.'[3]

In Dayan's perception Israel's relations with the super powers (DB) was overwhelming. Three illustrations point up its intensity, one in April 1970, another in June, and the last just three days before the strategic decision at the end of July.

I do not belong to those who say—'I don't care, Russians or no Russians'; I care very much. I prefer not to have Russians. . . . I wish . . . that Russians will not try to shoot down our planes [and that] . . . we should never have to kill at all, but least of all, Russians.[4]

[As for America,] let us not adopt the over-simple formula, according to which there is nothing to worry about, for if the Russians want to increase their presence or their military activities here . . . the Americans will prevent them. I wish it were so. But I take into consideration that United States policy is

---

Thus on 5 May 1970 she observed: 'We are not at war with the Soviet Union, but if they send pilots to Egypt and if they compel us to fight against them, we shall do so. We will have no other choice. We do not aspire to this, but it if happens we will not run away.' Meir (1).

[1] *Divrei Ha-knesset*, loc. cit., p. 2756; Meir (2), p. 11.

[2] In a political report to the Secretariat of the Israel Labour Party. *Ma'ariv*, 8 May 1970.

[3] *Divrei Ha-knesset*, lvi, 29 Dec. 1969, p. 312.

[4] It was this kind of remark which led many to attribute to Dayan fear of the Soviet Union. Weizman (interview 1971) offered an extreme interpretation: 'Dayan has developed a complex of Sovietphobia. He even decided on his own, without a clear decision of the Government, to stop the deep raids into Egypt, after Soviet pilots began to embarrass our pilots.'

influenced first and foremost by American public opinion—it is not to get involved, as much as possible, in remote disputes that do not have definite and decisive implications for the United States.[1]

The 'Russian factor' was emphasized again in mid-June: 'To avoid as much as possible contact with the Soviets, this is the key. . . .'[2] And to a convention of high-school students in Tel Aviv he declared in the midst of the decision-making process on Rogers 'B':

We are strong enough so as . . . to be able not to be compelled to accept directives, neither from enemies nor from friends. We are strong enough to maintain our position . . . but we are not strong enough to allow ourselves to give up allies, even if, to attain allies, we have to compromise. Compromises are necessary in order not to lose allies who are ready to march a long way together with us. It is not good to be isolated.[3]

As Defence Minister, Dayan was of course not impervious to the military component (M); but it was less important than for Meir. The above extract and others point to Dayan's confidence in Israel's military capability *vis-à-vis the Arabs*. His concern was, rather, to avoid military confrontation with the Soviets. And in that context his aim was not so much direct US arms aid as Washington's willingness to neutralize Soviet military intervention in the Arab–Israel conflict. Dayan was also aware of dissatisfaction with government policy, the urge to peace, and the desire to put an end to the undermining 'war of attrition' (IG). He acknowledged this in his candid remarks to high-school students on 28 July.

Galili, a veteran leader of *Ahdut Ha'avoda*, was among the most hawkish of Israeli decision-makers. Like the Prime Minister, his psychological environment during the Rogers period was dominated by relations with the United States (DB$_1$) and Israel's military capability (M). These were emphasized by him in explaining the Government's decision to accept Rogers 'B':

We preferred not to provide a pretext for charging us with responsibility for obstructing the US Government's initiative. We preferred taking a calculated risk in terms of the Jarring Talks and to avoid the risk related to a negative reply to the United States. We had in mind not only the hope for peace, deeply-rooted in our nation, but also the necessary conditions to assure a firm capability for *Tzahal* along the Cease-Fire lines.

An irresponsible policy might bring political isolation and increase our difficulties in acquiring all that Israel needs to face a war in which a Great Power is involved to an increasing extent, both militarily and politically, allied to our enemies.[4]

The loss of five Israeli Phantoms over Egypt in June and July had a profound effect on Galili's perception; a negative reply to the US, at a

---

[1] *Ma'ariv*, 10 April 1970.   [2] Ibid., 18 June 1970.
[3] Dayan (1).   [4] Galili (3).

time of escalating Soviet intervention, would have g⟩⟨470⟩
Israel's security.[1]

Allon's image, like that of Eban, was much broa⟩
logical setting for the other decision-makers: it e⟩
five components—S, DB$_1$, M, IG, and G. More⟩
in perceiving the regional environment, especially ⟩
positive Arab response to Rogers 'B', as a significant deve⟩
Shortly after the strategic decision he referred with respect to Egyp⟩
new policy of realism: 'Nasser took a risk by accepting the American
initiative. I do not believe there is Soviet coercion here. . . . I do not
believe the Egyptian President has already become a Russian satellite
and I believe he still wants to see Egypt independent and developed—
and he is still not too late.'[2]

On Jerusalem's relationship with Washington he remarked: 'By
accepting the American initiative, we proved goodwill and can face the
problem, while postponing the confrontation with the United States
to a later date; but the rejection of the American initiative would have
brought the confrontation immediately.'[3] Allon was also acutely
conscious of the image of Israel's rigidity in the Western world and its
adverse effect on public opinion: 'We will not miss this opportunity.
Either it will lead us to peace or if, alas, the Arab states shatter the
chances for peace, we will not bear the responsibility. . . .'[4]

A year later the Deputy Prime Minister articulated his image with
striking consistency, though he added two components:

Five factors affected my calculations in accepting the American initiative in
July 1970:

1) I believed that in Egypt's acceptance there was something essentially new
   in her posture towards the Arab–Israel conflict and that there exists an
   aspiration for peace among the régime and the people of Egypt;

2) I was conscious of the fact that the people of Israel, including our soldiers,
   wanted peace. Unless we had accepted the Rogers plan, there would have
   arisen doubt, in particular among the young generation, as to whether
   the Government really wanted peace at all;

3) Non-acceptance of the American initiative would have created an immediate confrontation with the United States, which would have been very
   dangerous for Israel;

4) We wanted to increase our military strength . . . by obtaining military and

---

[1] Weizman, not an entirely 'objective' source, recalled (interview, 1971): 'He was
under an emotional shock when the Phantoms were shot down. At one time he asked
me: "Can we continue this way? What will happen if we do not get the Shrike
missiles from the United States to overcome the dense Soviet missile system in the
Canal region?" I think he contributed more than anyone else to anxiety among
Government members, which was already great anyhow.' Galili's views on the 'Russian
factor' were also expressed in Galili (1) and (2).

[2] Allon (1).

[3] Allon (2). By contrast with Dayan, he minimized the danger of Soviet intervention.

[4] *Ma'ariv*, 6 Aug. 1970.

.onomic aid from the United States. It was clear that to reject the initiative
would have narrowed our prospects [of receiving] arms—and vice-versa;
[and]

5) Israel had to accept the peace initiative to gain the support of world public
opinion, and especially not to let down American Jewry. Otherwise the
Government would have undergone a total political defeat in the global
sphere.[1]

The Foreign Minister was primarily concerned with Israel's DB_1
relationship. 'There were three possibilities', observed Eban the day
after the strategic decision:

to reject the American proposal, but we could not imagine doing so; to accept
the proposal without any further clarification, but that was impossible after
Nasser and Riad falsified the real meaning of the American proposal and the
Security Council decision. We therefore preferred the third way—of strengthening mutual understanding between the United States and Israel. [At the
same time,] it was Nasser who helped us more than any other factor [S] to
accept the American proposal because Nasser said that he had accepted [it]
without giving up anything in his policy. According to the law of mutuality,
what is permissible and acceptable from Nasser is permissible and acceptable
from Israel.[2]

There were many more image-components in Eban's approach to
Rogers 'B'. These were contained in a succinct chiding of Begin's
attitude, towards the end of August:

If not for this vote Israel's situation at present would have been much more
difficult and serious than it is. We would have been at war against Egypt [S],
and in increasing danger of a confrontation with the Soviet Union [DB_2],
involving increased casualties and corrosion of air power [M] vital to a supreme
strategic objective—Israel's existence. A negative vote would have weakened
United States support for our defence [DB_1 and M] and would have caused
us to seem indifferent to the opportunity to halt bloodshed, in the eyes of our
people [IG] and the world [G]. A negative vote would have weakened our
defence, our international position, our internal unity, and our moral prestige.[3]

From these and other qualitative data there emerges the following
ordinal ranking of perceptions for the five high-policy decision-makers
on Rogers 'B':

Meir	DB_1, M (both 10); IG (8)
Dayan	DB_2 (10); DB_1 (9); M (8); IG (7)
Galili	DB_1, M (both 10)
Allon	S (10); DB_1, M (both 9); IG (7); G (6)
Eban	DB_1, M (both 10); G (8); S (7); IG (6).

In summary, all decision-makers attached importance to Israel's

[1] Interview, 1971.
[2] Interview on Israel's television network, 1 Aug. 1970, published in *Ma'ariv*,
2 Aug. 1970.   [3] Eban (1).

relations with the United States and to military capability; for all but Dayan DB_1 and M were inextricably intertwined, and for the Defence Minister they were closely linked. These two image-components ranked first in the psychological environment of Meir, Galili, and Eban, and second for Allon. In the case of the Prime Minister and her closest confidant they were pervasive or nearly so. Allon and Eban articulated the broadest images, Galili the narrowest. Allon was unique in his emphasis on the Middle East–Arab setting, though Eban noted it. Dayan, as so often, was the maverick: the 'Soviet factor' was pre-eminent in his image alone; it was virtually non-existent for the others, though Eban and Galili mentioned it marginally. Four of the five persons indicated an awareness of internal dissent and pressure, resulting from the 'war of attrition' and given a focus by the 'Goldmann Affair'; but IG ranked relatively low in all perceptions. And anticipated reaction abroad was mentioned only by Eban and Allon: concern by Israel's decision-makers about the external world was confined to the United States.

Four of the principal findings are confirmed by content-analysis data on the Rogers Proposals:

(1) greater concern about Israel's relations with the United States than with the other super power—by all except Dayan (Table 25);
(2) acute awareness of the Arab–Israel military balance and greater concern by Allon and Galili (Table 26);
(3) the Defence Minister's maverick position among the high-policy decision-makers (Tables 28–30); and
(4) pragmatic moderation in response to Rogers 'B'—change from June to July 1970 (Table 28).

There are other insights as well, especially into the moderate–extremism spectrum of advocacy and objectives, and the symbol foci of perception.[1]

[1] Approximately 10,000 words were analysed for each decision-maker. Where fewer than 9,500 words were available, or more than 10,500 words were analysed, the raw totals of frequencies were weighted. It is these weighted totals that appear in Tables 25–30. Of the 16 selections which were content-analysed, six preceded the strategic decision, seven were within the following month (August 1970), and three were delivered in September. The articulated images *prior to* the decision were not sufficient in volume to constitute the total word count for analysis. A wide variety of audiences was drawn upon. The sources were:

Meir	(1)	Interview on *Galei Tzahal*	5 May	(Meir (1))
	(2)	Address to the *Knesset*	4 Aug.	(Meir (2))
	(3)	Interview on 'Face the Nation'	28 Aug.	
Allon	(4)	Statement on missiles	14 Aug.	
	(5)	Statement to Information Personnel	17 Aug.	(Allon (1))
Dayan	(6)	Policy statement	10 May	
	(7)	Address to Tel Aviv students	28 July	(Dayan (1))

TABLE 25
DECISION-MAKERS' IMAGES OF DOMINANT-BILATERAL RELATIONS:
APRIL–SEPTEMBER 1970

Variable	Meir	Allon	Galili	Eban	Dayan	Total
Israel–US	43	10	22	5	0	80
Israel–USSR	0	0	0	0	8	8
Arabs–US	4	0	6	2	5	17
Arabs–USSR	1	30	0	7	0	38
Total	48	40	28	14	13	143

The ratio of overall $DB_1:DB_2$ references was 10:1; and only Dayan mentioned the Israeli–Soviet Union relationship. Perception of the Arab link to the super powers accounted for 38 per cent of all DB references but it is a significant dimension only for Allon and Eban. A focus on the Arab–Soviet relationship is complementary to awareness of the Israel–US tie, just as references to Israel–USSR and Arab–US links are complementary. Thus the combined data support the qualitative evidence even more emphatically: Meir (44-4), Allon (40-0), Galili (22-6), and Eban (12-2) articulated a much greater awareness of the DB_1 (United States) relationship. Only Dayan was preoccupied with the DB_2 (Soviet Union) association (0-13).[1]

References to Israel's military capability numbered 164, those to the M of her adversaries, 196, making a total of 360. Dayan and Allon devoted the most attention to this component: the Defence Minister

---

Eban	(8)	Announcement in *Knesset*	7 April	
	(9)	Press conference	17 Aug.	
	(10)	TV speech in Arabic	28 Aug.	
	(11)	Remarks at Labour Party session	29 Aug.	(Eban (1))
	(12)	Israeli TV interview	4 Sept.	
	(13)	Address to UN	28 Sept.	
Galili	(14)	Interview in *Jerusalem Post*	17 April	(Galili (1))
	(15)	Interview on *Galei Tzahal*	5 June	(Galili (2))
	(16)	Interview in *Jerusalem Post*	4 Sept	

Inter-coder reliability was verified at 83 per cent.

[1] There was also a very high overall frequency count for the US and USSR *per se*, 438 and 450 respectively. These, however, do not amend the DB ratios noted above. Rather, they indicate an acute awareness of the super powers, apart from their direct relationship to the Middle East conflicting parties. The significance of that awareness is at the global system level: the references to the US and USSR account for two-thirds of all G references. The only other variable at that level to attract substantial attention was the United Nations—230 references, of which 126 were made by the Foreign Minister. The Cold War and the Jewish People were conspicuously marginal in the decision-makers' articulated perceptions relating to the Rogers Proposals—49 each, that is, 4 per cent each of the G references. And the three other state actors coded were even more marginal, China (30—all by Allon), and Britain and France (10 each—all by Meir and Eban).

noted Israel's capability 85 times, that of the Arabs an equal number, that is, a total of 170; for the Deputy Prime Minister the corresponding figures were 40 and 80, a total of 120. More significant is the pronounced *image of concern about* the Arab–Israel *military balance*: this is derived from a combination of references to Israel's increasing M and her enemies' decreasing M on the one hand, and references to Israel's decreasing M and her enemies' increasing M, on the other.

TABLE 26

DECISION-MAKERS' IMAGES OF ISRAEL'S RELATIVE MILITARY
CAPABILITY: APRIL–SEPTEMBER 1970

Image of	Dayan	Allon	Galili	Eban	Meir	Total
Increasing	50	10	8	9	6	83
Same	60	20	6	9	10	105
Decreasing	60	90	14	7	1	172
Total	170	120	28	25	17	360

The image of concern is very striking for Allon, with a 9:1 ratio of perceived *decreasing* Israeli M, and for the group as a whole, with more than twice as many references to decreasing Israeli capability. Dayan's overall image was of an essentially unchanged military balance, corresponding to his sanguine view of M in the qualitative data. Eban's perception, too, was of a static condition. The data for Galili reveal greater concern, as did the extracts from his interviews. Meir was the most optimistic, a deviation from the qualitative evidence. But the two overall indicators, high volume and its distribution, point up intense awareness and concern by the high-policy group as a whole.

The frequency count data also confirm Allon's primacy in attention to Israel's near-neighbours.

TABLE 27

DECISION-MAKERS' IMAGES OF NEAR-NEIGHBOURS:
APRIL–SEPTEMBER 1970

	(a) Actors					
Variable	Allon	Eban	Dayan	Meir	Galili	Total
Egypt	270	109	85	48	42	554
Palestine (community)	0	31	65	73	0	169
Jordan	0	65	30	37	4	136
Lebanon	0	7	20	34	0	61
Syria	0	10	5	5	0	20
Iraq	0	1	0	1	0	2
Total	270	223	205	198	46	942

Other aspects of Israeli élite perceptions of their Arab neighbours are illuminated by these data: (1) the primacy of Egypt for the group as a whole—59 per cent of all references—and for Allon, Eban, and Galili; (2) the prominence of Palestine Arabs, first rank for Meir, second for Dayan—and for the group as a whole; (3) combined with references to Jordan, Israel's eastern neighbours account for a third of the total; they are also a very marked first rank in the Prime Minister's image of Israel's neighbours, as well as a somewhat less pronounced first rank for Dayan, and a very close second to Egypt in Eban's image. Striking is the paucity of attention to Syria and the non-awareness of Iraq. Noteworthy, too, is the non-attention of Allon and Galili to all actors in the Near East Core except Egypt.

The pre-eminence of Egypt, as well as the attention given to Palestine Arabs and Jordan, are given added weight by the data on Arab leaders:

TABLE 27

Variable	Allon	Eban	(b) Leaders Dayan	Meir	Galili	Total
Nasser	60	17	75	30	14	196
Hussein	0	0	5	11	0	16
Arafat	0	2	0	3	2	7
Habash	0	2	0	0	0	2
Total	60	21	80	44	16	221

Egypt's President received almost 90 per cent of all references to individual Arabs; Jordan's King and the two best-known Palestinian guerrilla leaders received the rest. Only the Prime Minister and Defence Minister mentioned Hussein. If the gross data for Middle East entities and leaders are combined, Egypt's proportion of the frequency count rises from 59 to 64 per cent; and the Palestine–Jordan complex declines from 32 to 28 per cent. All other regional actors are minuscule in Israeli decision-makers' images. Two other observations are relevant: (1) Nasser was the only Arab leader to command the attention of Israel's decision-makers; and (2) the awareness of Israel's neighbours to the east is overwhelmingly in state/community, not personality terms.

Awareness of interest group pressures (IG), so conspicuous in the qualitative data, is not evident in the content analysis: rather, it is competing élites (CE) which receive some attention, a total of 84 references, 66 by Galili, and 9 each by Meir and Eban. By contrast, there is an intense articulation of symbols, with a concentration similar to élite perceptions relating to the Sinai Campaign and the Six Day War. Among the 13 coded symbols 5 account for almost 90 per cent of the 1,591 references: Peace (562), Conflict (402), Security (184),

Terrorism (119), and Independence (109); the first two, which may be viewed as a cluster, represent no less than 60 per cent of all symbol references.[1] Dayan is unique in this context, too, with much greater attention to Conflict than to Peace (180–70); all other decision-makers reverse the order. In terms of range of attention, Allon's and Galili's are the narrowest symbolic images, with no references to 7 of the 13 symbols; for Meir and Eban there are references to fewer than 6 symbols, and for Dayan, to 4 symbols. In short, a small cluster of symbol awareness is pervasive.

The content analysis of advocacy statements reveals *pragmatic moderation* for the group as a whole. A total of 228 such assertions, urging, recommending, demanding, pressing for, a particular line of policy was uncovered and classified according to a nine-point *advocacy statement scale*, ranging from extremism (hawkishness) to moderation (doveishness):[2]

9. We are better off to renew war than to have peace without security.
8. We must be vigilant in the defence of our interests, for our security is at stake.
7. We must insist on direct negotiations with our Arab neighbours; only this way will a permanent peace be established with secure and recognized borders.
6. In return for concessions, Israel must have secure and recognized borders.
5. The Rogers Plan, though risky, is worth accepting in the interests of peace.
4. The United Nations mediator should be encouraged; his role is important in the achievement of a peaceful settlement.
3. We must show greater tactical flexibility, for we are isolated in the world because of our hard line.
2. We must be prepared to engage in mutual dialogue and try to understand our neighbours in the interests of peace.
1. We must make concessions to achieve peace; security cannot be attained simply by more defensible borders.

The salient points emerging from the advocacy data are as follows:

(a) For the group as a whole the evidence indicates acute concern with *security*: the largest number of advocacy statements cluster around

---

[1] The other symbols, which range from 4 to 1 per cent in frequency, are Aggression (61); Economic Development (37); Destruction of Israel (29); Defence (25); Equality (18); and Unity, Friendship, and Zionism (15 each). Only Allon accords considerable attention to any of these—30 each for Aggression and Economic Development.

[2] See p. 249, n. 2. above for the rationale of this nine-point scale. Inter-coder agreement on the extraction of advocacy statements was 81 per cent. It was 86 per cent on the masked scaling of the statements along the nine-point scale.

point 8 of the scale; and those on the extremist part above the mid-point (5) are 80 per cent more than statements of moderation, 110 to 62. Yet the mid-point stand of *calculated risk* attracted one-fourth of all statements. And the frequency of emphasis on *secure and recognized*

TABLE 28

DISTRIBUTION OF ADVOCACY OF DECISION-MAKERS,
FREQUENCY AND INTENSITY: APRIL–SEPTEMBER 1970

INTENSITY				FREQUENCY			
	Scale Point	Allon	Dayan	Eban	Meir	Galili	Total
Maximum							
Militancy	9.	0	10	1	1	2	14
	8.	30	15	5	5	2	57
	7.	0	0	4	1	0	5
	6.	10	5	5	8	6	34
	5.	30	0	4	12	10	56
	4.	0	0	3	1	0	4
	3.	10	15	0	0	0	25
	2.	0	20	7	1	2	30
Minimum							
Militancy	1.	0	0	2	1	0	3
Total		80	65	31	30	22	228

TABLE 29

MEDIAN VALUE OF ADVOCACY STATEMENTS BY
DECISION-MAKERS: APRIL–SEPTEMBER 1970*

Allon	5·5
Galili	5·5
Meir	5·3
Eban	5·0
Dayan	2·6
Decision-Makers' Median	5·4

* The distribution of these advocacy statements may also be portrayed in graphic terms—to point up sharp scalar fluctuations.

boundaries is more than offset by references to the need for *flexibility and mutual dialogue*. In short, the collective advocacy of Israel's high-policy élite on Rogers Plan B was pragmatic, with two competing tendencies— to security and to predisposition to risk in the interests of peace.

(*b*) Allon was the most voluble among the five persons, accounting or 35 per cent of all 228 advocacy statements. Dayan ranked second,

FIGURE 17
ADVOCACY POSITION OF ISRAELI DECISION-MAKERS:
APRIL–SEPTEMBER 1970

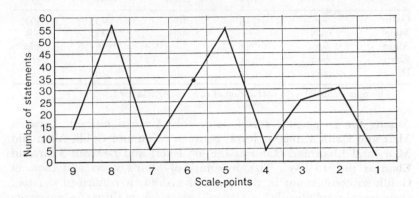

with almost 30 per cent of those statements. Galili spoke least about Israeli objectives, though the gap between him, Prime Minister Meir, and Foreign Minister Eban was marginal. Indeed, their statements combined barely exceeded those of the Deputy Prime Minister alone.

(*c*) Dayan's statements cluster near the two extremes of the scale, more so at the moderation end—25 at points 9 and 8, 35 at points 2 and 3.

(*d*) Eban's advocacy was the most evenly distributed, with the largest single group at point 2—moderation.

(*e*) The views of Meir and Galili were heavily concentrated at the mid-point—40 per cent for the former, almost half for the latter; and for both the second point of emphasis was the relatively moderate secure and recognized borders; together, points 5 and 6 account for two-thirds and 70 per cent of Meir and Galili statements respectively.

(*f*) Deputy Prime Minister Allon, too, has a large cluster of midpoint statements but he made four times as many hard-line statements as moderate ones.

(*g*) Allon and Galili emerge as the most extreme advocates, with Dayan the most moderate. The group average lies mid-way between calculated risk (point 5) and secure and recognized borders (point 6).

Finally, the data indicate that all decision-makers strongly perceived as compatible the objectives of peace and secure borders.

The distance between pairs of Israel's decision-makers on the Rogers Proposals is apparent from the following data:

TABLE 30
CORRELATION OF DECISION-MAKERS' ADVOCACY:
APRIL–SEPTEMBER 1970*

	Galili	Meir	Allon	Eban	Dayan
Galili	—	·745	·670	·603	·397
Meir	·745	—	·633	·524	− ·081
Allon	·670	·633	—	·339	·382
Eban	·603	·524	·339	—	·319
Dayan	·397	− ·081	·382	·319	—

* The Spearman Rho (ρ) correlation of rank order was used.

Among the 20 possible correlations, only 4 are significant: between Meir and Galili at the ·02 level; between Allon and Galili, Allon and Meir, and Eban and Galili at the ·05 level; and between Meir and Eban at the ·10 level. The proximity of Meir's views and those of Galili, so conspicuous in the qualitative data, is confirmed. So too, even more emphatically, is Dayan's maverick position: in advocacy terms he correlates with no one. Moreover, particularly striking is the negative correlation between Dayan and Meir. This would seem to confirm the thesis that beneath the appearance of harmony between the PM and Defence Minister lay a cleavage on the conditions of settlement with the Arabs.

(c) DECISION PROCESS

Israel's acceptance of Rogers 'B' and the accompanying cease-fire was the result of US initiative (presentation of the Plan on 19 June 1970), of waiting and not anticipating Egypt's response (21 June–22 July), and of President Nixon's assurances (23 July). But the high-policy decision, made on 31 July, was preceded by more than a year of pre-decisional events, decisive inputs, and two important tactical decisions.

The process began on 23 March 1969 with the inauguration of two sets of talks on the Arab–Israel conflict: one between US Assistant Secretary of State Sisco and Soviet Ambassador Dobrynin in Washington; and the other, ten days later, among the UN Representatives of the Big Four in New York. Four Power Talks had been proposed by de Gaulle on the eve of the Six Day War: their acceptance, because of Nixon's desire to cultivate the French President, was a further sign of the desire for a *détente* and, in particular, of the emergent super-power interest in avoiding a direct confrontation in the Near East Core. The inclusion of France and Britain was designed to broaden the consensus, as a bridge to Security Council authorization of a political settlement. While those talks were 'official' and received wide publicity, the informal Big Two dialogue was the far more important forum for external penetration of the Arab–Israel conflict.[1]

Disturbing indicators of super-power co-operation in the Middle East became apparent during the second half of 1969. Secretary of State Rogers announced on 5 June that the US and USSR had reached an understanding on the need for a final and all-inclusive political settlement within the framework of a package deal; the Sisco–Dobrynin talks, he added, were encouraging and mutually satisfactory.[2] Then, on 28 October, Washington presented to Moscow a (secret) plan for a political settlement. Its contents were made known to Israeli decision-makers and, within a week, appeared in the Israeli press.[3] Rogers Plan 'A', as it came to be known, was formally disclosed by the Secretary of State in a New York address on 9 December. The *timing*—but *not* the *substance*—was unanticipated and caused dismay in Jerusalem.[4]

Rogers Plan 'A' flowed from the recently acquired American posture of 'more even-handedness'. In Rogers's own words:

Our policy is and will continue to be a balanced one.

We have friendly ties with both Arabs and Israelis. To call for Israel withdrawal as envisaged in the U.N. resolution without achieving agreement on peace would be partisan toward the Arabs. To call on the Arabs to accept peace without Israel withdrawal would be partisan toward Israel. Therefore, our policy is to encourage the Arabs to accept a permanent peace based on a binding agreement and to urge the Israelis to withdraw from occupied territory when their territorial integrity is assured as envisaged by the Security Council resolution.

Apart from 'emphasizing the key issues of peace, security, withdrawal and territory', Rogers addressed himself to two special problems—the Arab refugees and Jerusalem. He was vague about the former: 'There can be no lasting peace without a just settlement of the [Palestine refugee] problem. . . .' He offered further generous US aid and noted the need to 'take into account the desires and aspirations of the refugees and the legitimate concerns of the Governments in the area'. On Jerusalem, however, he was much more precise:

We have made clear repeatedly in the past two-and-one-half years that we cannot accept unilateral actions by any party to decide the final status of the City. We believe its status can be determined only through the agreement of

---

[1] The parallel talks were noted at once in the Israeli press; see *Lamerhav* and *Yedi'o Aharonot*, 4 April 1969. Israel was regularly informed of the contents of Big Two discussions, as Rogers revealed in making known his Plan 'A' on 9 Dec. 1969.

[2] *New York Times*, 6 June 1969.

[3] All of its salient provisions were published by *Ma'ariv* on 5 Nov. 1969.

[4] Israeli decision-makers acknowledged—in interviews—that they did not expect the Plan to be announced as official United States policy, certainly not so quickly; furthermore, that they were chagrined by Washington's action, without any advance warning.

the parties concerned, which in practical terms means primarily the governments of Israel and Jordan, taking into account the interests of other countries in the area and the international community.

He also set out certain principles regarding Jerusalem:

Specifically, we believe Jerusalem should be a unified city within which there would no longer be restrictions on the movement of persons and goods. There should be open access to the unified city for persons of all faiths and nationalities. Arrangements for the administration of the unified city should take into account the interests of all its inhabitants and of the Jewish, Islamic and Christian Communities. And there should be roles for both Israel and Jordan in the civic, economic and religious life of the City.

Rogers referred to the eight months of discussions with the Soviets and, in that context, he indicated the 'three principal elements' of an overall Israel–Egypt settlement:

First, there should be a binding commitment by Israel and the U.A.R. to peace with each other, with all the specific obligations of peace spelled out, including the obligation to prevent hostile acts originating from their respective territories.

Second, the detailed provisions of peace relating to security safeguards on the ground should be worked out between the parties under Ambassador Jarring's auspices, utilizing the procedures followed in negotiating the Armistice Agreements under Ralph Bunche in 1949 at Rhodes. This formula has been previously used with success in negotiations between the parties on Middle Eastern problems. A principal objective of the Four-Power talks, we believe, should be to help Ambassador Jarring engage the parties in a negotiating process under the Rhodes formula.

So far as a settlement between Israel and the U.A.R. goes, these safeguards relate primarily to the area of Sharm-e-Sheikh controlling access to the Gulf of Akaba, the need for demilitarized zones as foreseen in the Security Council resolution, and final arrangements in the Gaza Strip.

Third, in the context of peace and agreement on specific security safeguards, withdrawal of Israeli forces from Egyptian territory would be required. Such an approach directly addresses the principal national concerns of both Israel and the U.A.R. It would require withdrawal of Israeli armed forces from U.A.R. territory to the international border between Israel and Egypt which has been in existence over half a century. It would also require the parties themselves to negotiate the practical security arrangements to safeguard the peace.[1]

The contents of Rogers Plan 'A' were widely at variance with the five pillars of Israel's policy towards the Arabs, laid down in Prime Minister Eshkol's speech of 1 December 1967: 'permanent peace'; 'direct negotiations' and 'peace treaties between Israel and her neighbours'; free navigation for Israeli shipping through the Canal and the Straits; the determination of 'agreed and secure borders', to be incorporated

---

[1] The full text is in *New York Times*, 10 Dec. 1969, and *Jerusalem Post*, 11 Dec. 1969.

into a peace treaty; and 'a settlement of the refugee problem within a regional and international context'—after the establishment of peace.[1]

The extent of disagreement, which explains in large part the chagrin of Israel's decision-makers, is apparent from Table 31.

The official announcement of Rogers 'A' created a sense of crisis within the Israel Government: all three preconditions of 'crisis' were present—surprise, a perceived threat to high values, and the absence of time for leisurely response.[2] News of the Secretary of State's Tuesday night speech reached Jerusalem on Wednesday morning, the 10th. The Cabinet was summoned to an emergency session which culminated in an unqualified rejection of the US Plan.[3] The Government Statement, issued at 1.00 a.m. on the 11th, declared:

The Israel Government discussed in special session the political situation in the region and the latest speech of the U.S. Secretary of State on the Middle East.

The Government states that the tension in the Middle East referred to by Mr. Rogers derives from the *aggressive* policy of the Arab governments: the absolute refusal to make peace with Israel and the unqualified support of the Soviet Union for the Arab aggressive stand.

Israel is of the opinion that the only way to terminate the tension and the state of war in the region is by perpetual striving for a durable peace among the nations of the region, based on a peace treaty reached through direct negotiations which will take place without any prior conditions by any party. The agreed, secure and recognized boundaries will be fixed in the peace treaty. This is the permanent and stated peace policy of Israel and is in accordance with accepted international rules and procedures.

The Six Day War, or the situation created in its wake, cannot be spoken of in terms of expansion or conquest. Israel cried out against aggression which threatened its very existence, and used its natural right of national self-defence.

In his speech, Mr. Rogers said that states outside the region cannot fix peace terms; only states in the region are authorized to establish peace by agreement among themselves. The Government states regretfully that this principle does not tally with the detailed reference in the speech to peace

[1] A partial text is in *The Israel Digest*, lx, 25, 15 Dec. 1967.

[2] Begin, Herzog, Peres, Weizman, Foreign Ministry officials' interviews, 1970–1.

[3] The Government which made the first tactical decision was a caretaker one, in office since the seventh *Knesset* elections on 28 October. It was, in fact, the Cabinet formed by Mrs. Meir, who succeeded Levi Eshkol as Prime Minister on 17 March 1969. Its membership, when the decision was taken to reject Rogers 'A', comprised:

Allon, Almogi, *Aranne*,* *Carmel*, Dayan, Eban, Galili, Gvati, Meir, Sapir, *Sasson*, Y. S. Shapiro, Sharef, *Yeshayahu* (Israel Labour Party)

Barzilai, Bentov (*Mapam*)

Begin, Saphir (*Gahal*)

Burg, *H.M. Shapira*, Warhaftig (NRP)

Kol (Independent Liberals)

* Persons in italics were not members of the Government which made the strategic decision on 31 July 1970. Barzilai died in June 1970 and was succeeded by Peled; H. M. Shapira died a week before that decision; and the others were not included in the post-*Knesset* election Government formed on 15 December 1969.

TABLE 31

POLICY OF UNITED STATES AND ISRAEL ON SETTLEMENT OF ARAB–ISRAEL CONFLICT, 1969–73

Issue	Rogers Plan 'A'	Government of Israel
1. *Peace*	'... our policy is to encourage the Arabs to accept a permanent peace based on a binding agreement....'	Formal peace treaty
2. *Boundaries*	Minor changes in the 1949–67 Armistice lines: 'should not reflect the weight of conquest and should be confined to insubstantial alterations required for mutual security'	'Secure, agreed and recognized boundaries', reached by direct negotiations; not identical to Armistice lines (4 June 1967) nor to Cease-Fire lines (10 June 1967). According to semi-official *Tora Shebe'al Peh* ('Oral Law') of Israel Labour Party, Israel would retain united Jerusalem, Gaza Strip, Golan Heights, Sharm-e-Sheikh, and linking coastal strip in Sinai Peninsula to Eilat
3. *Refugees*	Call for 'just settlement' of problem, based upon their aspirations and legitimate concerns of Near East governments	Solution lies in resettlement of refugees in Arab lands; problem can be solved only after peace
4. *Jerusalem*	Status must not be determined by unilateral acts but by agreement between Israel and Jordan; should remain united city; administrative arrangements should reflect interests of the three religious communities	United Jerusalem must remain capital of Israel and wholly integrated into Israel, while meeting universal religious interests in Holy City
5. *Method of Negotiation*	Indirect negotiations—'a negotiating process under the Rhodes [1949] formula'	Direct negotiations between the parties without prior conditions
6. *Sharm-e-Sheikh*	Assurance of free navigation for Israeli ships, with international guarantees	Retention of Israeli rule over Sharm-e-Sheikh

terms, including territorial and other basic questions, among them Jerusalem. Jerusalem was divided following the conquest of part of the city by the Jordanian Army in 1948. Only now, after the unification of the city under Israel administration, does there exist freedom of access for members of all faiths to their holy places in the city.

The position of Israel is: the negotiations for peace must be free from prior conditions and external influences and pressures. The prospects for peace will be seriously marred if states outside the region continue to raise territorial proposals and suggestions on other subjects that cannot further peace and security.

When the Four Power talks began, the Government of Israel expressed its view on the harmful consequences involved in this move in its statement of March 27, 1969. The fears expressed then were confirmed.

Peace was not promoted. Arab governments were encouraged by the illusion that an arrangement could be reached by the exertion of external influences and pressures with no negotiations between the parties. In this period Egyptian policy reached the most extreme expressions, especially in President Nasser's speech in which he spoke of rivers flowing with blood and skies lit by fire. In this period, the region has not become tranquil. In an incessant violation of the cease-fire arrangement, fixed by the Security Council and accepted by all sides unconditionally and with no time limit, the Egyptians have intensified their attempts to disturb the cease-fire lines. Conveniently, Arab aggression in other sectors continued and terrorist acts, explicitly encouraged by Arab governments, were intensified. Even the Jarring mission to promote an agreement between the parties was paralysed.

The focus of the problem as stated by Mr. Rogers lies in the basic intentions and positions of the governments of the region to the principle of peaceful coexistence. The lack of intention of the Arab governments to move towards peace with Israel is expressed daily in proclamations and deeds. The positions and intentions of the parties towards peace cannot be tested unless they agree to conduct negotiations as among states desiring peace. Only when there is a basic change in the Arab position, which denies the principle of negotiations for the signing of peace, will it be possible to replace the state of war by durable peace. This remains the central aim of the policy of Israel.[1]

The rebuke to Rogers is unmistakable, especially because he did not adhere to his own principle that states outside the region were neither authorized nor able to solve the Arab–Israel conflict. So too is the rejection of his territorial proposals and his strictures on Jerusalem. At the same time Israel's T_{1a} decision was cautiously formulated: the principal reason was to avoid a confrontation on the eve of the Foreign Minister's departure for Washington to discuss the US proposal.

The eruption of tension was not calmed. Nor was the crisis dissolved by the State Department's refusal to forewarn Eban—or any other Israeli official—of a second American initiative on the Middle East then in process. On 18 December the United States Representative to

---

[1] An English translation of the text is in *Jerusalem Post*, 12 Dec. 1969, under the heading 'Israel Rejects Territorial Settlement By Outsiders'.

the UN presented a plan for an Israel–Jordan settlement at the Four Power Talks. Israel's Ambassador to Washington, Yitzhak Rabin, received a copy of the Yost Document the same day. Essentially it was an extension of the principles of Rogers 'A' to the Jordan–Israel dimension of the conflict, particularly the call for a 'state of peace', Israel's withdrawal to the Armistice lines, apart from marginal territorial changes, and a 'just settlement' of the refugee problem. It also reiterated the formula for Jerusalem by the Secretary of State.

An authoritative *New York Times* version of the 'secret plan', published on the 22nd, noted twelve points:

1. The parties would determine procedures and a timetable with the use of a map for the withdrawal of Israeli troops from substantially all of the West Bank.
2. Each country will accept the obligations of a state of peace between them, including the prohibition of any acts of violence from its territory against the other.
3. The two countries would agree upon a permanent frontier between them, 'approximating' [to] the armistice demarcation line that existed before the 1967 war, but allowing for alterations based on practical security requirements and 'administrative or economic convenience'.
4. Israel and Jordan together would settle the problem of ultimate control over Jerusalem, recognizing that the city should be unified, with free traffic through all parts of it, and with both countries sharing in civic and economic responsibilities of city government. The language of this point repeats almost word-for-word a proposal made publicly by Secretary of State Rogers on December 9 and subsequently denounced by Israeli officials.
5. Jordan and Israel would participate in working out final arrangements for the administration of the Gaza Strip, on the basis of a parallel accord to be reached by Israel and Egypt.
6. The two countries would negotiate security arrangements, including the delineation of demilitarized zones on the West Bank, to take effect with the Israeli withdrawal.
7. Jordan would affirm that the Straits of Tiran and the Gulf of Akaba are international waterways, open to shipping of all countries, specifically including Israel.
8. This point explains the refugee settlement and notes that Ambassador Jarring could establish an international commission to determine the choice of each refugee on returning to Israel. Since the procedures would be lengthy, the proposal states that the rest of the package could go into effect before the refugee procedures were carried out.
9. The two countries would enter a mutual agreement, formally recognizing each other's sovereignty, territorial integrity, political independence and the right to live in peace.
10. The total accord would be recorded in a signed document to be deposited with the United Nations. Any breach in any provision could entitle the other country to suspend its obligations until the situation had been corrected.

11. The complete accord would be 'endorsed' by the U.N. Security Council. And the Big Four Powers would 'concert their future efforts' to help all parties abide by the provisions of the peace.

12. The American proposal notes that an Israeli–Jordanian peace would take effect only with a simultaneous accord between Israel and Egypt, a point stressed by U.S. officials to rebut Arab charges that the plan seeks to divide the Arabs.[1]

The Yost Document intensified the atmosphere of crisis in Israel–US relations for two reasons: first, because the proposal for virtually complete withdrawal from the West Bank clashed with the historic and religious associations of Judea and Samaria as part of the Land of Israel; and secondly, because of the concealment of its contents— from Eban, during his meeting with Rogers and Sisco on the 16th, and from Rabin, until the last moment; it was a marked departure from the pattern of close consultation on matters relating to the Middle East conflict.

Jerusalem showed its concern by summoning Eban and Rabin home at once. On the 21st an informal meeting of senior Alignment ministers was held at the Prime Minister's home: present were Allon, Barzilai, Dayan, Peres, Sapir, and Shapiro.[2] The following day the Cabinet reaffirmed its rejection of US proposals, including the Yost Document, in blunt terms:

The Cabinet rejects these American proposals, in that they prejudice the chances of establishing peace; disregard the essential need to determine secure and agreed borders through the signing of peace treaties by direct negotiations; affect Israel's sovereign rights and security in the drafting of the resolution concerning refugees and the status of Jerusalem, and contain no actual obligations of the Arab states to put a stop to the hostile activities of the sabotage and terror organizations. If these proposals were to be carried out, Israel's security and peace would be in very grave danger. Israel would not be satisfied by any power or inter-power policy, and will reject any attempt to impose a forced solution upon her. . . . The proposals submitted by the US cannot but be construed by the aggressive Arab rulers as an attempt to appease them, at Israel's expense.[3]

The same day Prime Minister Meir conveyed the decision-makers' consensus view to a *New York Times* correspondent, namely, that any Israeli Government which accepted the Yost Document would be guilty of betrayal.[4] The *Knesset* seemed to concur: on 29 December it rejected by 57 to 3, with 2 abstentions, both Rogers Plan 'A' and the

[1] As reproduced in *Jerusalem Post*, 23 December 1969.

[2] Galili's absence was due to an automobile accident but he was consulted then and later, while in hospital.

[3] The text is in *Jerusalem Post*, 23 Dec. 1969. According to the *Ha'aretz* account the same day, the decision was drafted by an *ad hoc* Cabinet committee consisting of Meir, Allon, Barzilai, Begin, Eban, Peres, and Warhaftig.

[4] Reported in *Ma'ariv*, 23 Dec. 1969.

Yost Document, thereby adding the legislature's support to Government decisions.[1]

The first half of 1970 was a tense and difficult period for Israel. Relations with the United States deteriorated. And Soviet involvement in the Middle East conflict became more ominous. The widely publicized request for more Phantoms dominated the Jerusalem–Washington dialogue for three months and was ultimately rebuffed. On 29 January the President announced that he would make a decision within thirty days. It was delayed almost another month. Finally on 23 March Rogers announced that Nixon had 'decided to hold in abeyance for now a decision with respect to Israel's request for additional aircraft', on the grounds that 'Israel air capacity is sufficient to meet its needs for the time being'.[2]

Political support was perceived by Israel in Nixon's hard line during his exchange of letters with Kosygin on 30 January and 4 February. The Soviet Premier warned of the 'grave danger' of Israel's deep penetration air raids into Egypt—which had begun on 7 January, in response to the continuing 'war of attrition'—and he announced further Soviet aid to Egypt. He did not, however, threaten military intervention if Israel persisted with her raids. The President rejected the warning and charged Soviet behaviour with responsibility for escalation of Middle East tension, especially her dispatch of huge arms supplies to the front-line Arab states. He proposed a joint limitation on super-power arms to the Near East Core—and emphasized that the US would preserve the balance of military power between Israel and her adversaries.[3] Nixon's remarks on the Middle East in his 'State of the World' speech on 18 February were in a similar vein.[4] Sisco visited the Near East Core in mid-April to signal that the United States would resume her initiative for a political settlement. He also tried to secure concessions in the spirit of Rogers 'A', but both Israel and Egypt were adamant. And his visit to Jordan was cancelled because of large-scale anti-American riots in Amman.

---

[1] *Divrei Ha-knesset*, lvi, pp. 344–5. In favour were all Coalition factions, *Agudat Yisrael*, *Po'alei Agudat Yisrael*, and the State List. Opposed were *Ha'olam Hazeh* and *Rakah*. The Free Centre and *Maki* abstained.

[2] The text is in *New York Times*, 24 March 1970. Israel was told informally about the negative reply on 14 March. See Margalit, p. 75, and *Yedi'ot Aharonot*, 20 March 1970.

[3] The letters were not officially published; but an authentic version of their contents was leaked through the Associated Press in London and appeared in, *inter alia*, *Ma'ariv* and *Jerusalem Post*, 5 Feb. 1970.

[4] The President said: '. . . we believe a settlement can only be achieved through the give and take of negotiation by those involved. . . . the United States would view any effort by the Soviet Union to seek predominance in the Middle East as a matter of grave concern. . . . I now reaffirm our stated intention to maintain careful watch on the balance of military forces and to provide arms to friendly states as the need arises . . .' Nixon, pp. 78, 80, 81.

Even more alarming to Israel's decision-makers was the growth of Soviet military intervention in the conflict, a direct response to Israel's air raids into the heart of Egypt. 'The decision to bomb deep into Egypt', observed one minister, 'was urged by the General Staff and supported by Dayan. The aim was to weaken Egypt's army and to compel Cairo to stop the war of attrition which had caused us heavy casualties.'[1] At Egypt's request, Moscow began to supply SAM-2 missiles and, as noted, to increase substantially the number of Soviet troops. In scope of aid to a non-Communist state, it was without precedent—an estimated $4·5 billion by 1970.

Israel requested additional US arms assistance, arguing that the new dimension of Soviet military presence was a fundamental change in the balance of power. Washington demurred, through a Nixon statement on 21 March; the desired American warning to Moscow was not forthcoming. Concern about Soviet intervention increased with the discovery on 18 April that Soviet pilots were flying operational missions over Egypt.[2] Israel expressed grave anxiety and sought both US planes and an American formal declaration, to deter Moscow.[3] At the same time her total dependence on the United States led to several conciliatory statements.

On 1 May Eban announced that Israel would be prepared, for the sake of peace, to make concessions that would surprise the world. More important, the Prime Minister declared before Parliament on the 26th that Israel accepted the Security Council's Resolution 242 of 22 November 1967:

There are those who argue—and the Arabs among them—that we did not accept the UN [Security Council] Resolution of 22 November 1967, while they did. In fact, the Arabs accepted the UN Resolution with *their* interpretation, which is biased and garbled. . . .

. . . Israel announced on 1 May 1968, through her Ambassador to the UN. . . . 'The Government of Israel . . . accepts the Resolution of the Security Council for the promotion of an agreement to establish a just and lasting peace.' I am authorized to reaffirm that we are prepared to reach an agreement with every Arab state on all matters included in the Resolution.[4]

Meir's formal announcement on 26 May 1970 and the *Knesset*'s approval

[1] Weizman interview, 1971. During the first four months of 1970 Israel's Air Force made an estimated 3,300 strikes into Egypt and dropped 8,000 tons of bombs. *Strategic Survey*, 1970, p. 46.

[2] That development was first disclosed by the *New York Times* and was quoted by the Israeli press, for example, in *Ma'ariv*, on 29 April. Because of rigid military censorship regulations, Israeli newspapers were prohibited from reporting the incident immediately after its occurrence.

[3] The text is in *Ma'ariv*, 29 April 1970.

[4] *Divrei Ha-knesset*, lvii, 26 May 1970, p. 1864. The text of Resolution 242 is in UN.S/, p. 8.

the following day was a significant policy innovation.[1] As one knowledgeable civil servant remarked, 'Israel did not reject the 242 Resolution but, during almost 3 years, she manoeuvred in various ways not to
come out and state clearly she accepted the Resolution and the commitment to withdrawal'.[2] The National Unity Coalition survived
through the device of permission to *Gahal* to abstain on Meir's announcement. Another indicator of change was the Prime Minister's statement, during her 26 May speech, that Israel was willing to accept
something akin to the Rhodes formula of indirect-cum-direct negotiations.[3] As with Resolution 242, this statement was not entirely new—

[1] To some the Prime Minister's statement was merely a reaffirmation of an announcement by Israel's UN Representative on 1 May 1968: 'For example, when Jarring
asked in April 1969 whether Israel was willing to accept the paragraph on withdrawal in Resolution 242, the Government, in its reply, avoided reference to the word
"withdrawal" or its acceptance of the resolution.' Begin interview, *New York Times*,
2 May 1968. However, while Tekoa's declaration was not nullified by the Government, neither was it approved or confirmed, largely because of *Gahal*'s pressure from
within the Cabinet. Thereafter the nationalist Right asserted that, since the Government had never formally approved Resolution 242, Tekoa's view was not binding—
even though he was Israel's official representative. There are several versions concerning the authoritative source for Tekoa's announcement in the UN. The most convincing
attributes it to Foreign Minister Eban. Foreign Ministry officials' interviews, 1970–1,
and Margalit, p. 117.

[2] The Government of Israel's refusal to use the abhorrent word 'withdrawal' was
illuminated by *Gahal*'s leader the day the Rogers-initiated cease-fire went into effect.

'During two-and-a-half years, that is, from December 1967 until now, the Government refused to use this word in all the documents exchanged between us and Dr.
Jarring, between us and other governments. The proof is that Dr. Jarring demanded
that we use the word "withdrawal"; we did not. The Americans demanded that
we say, plainly, the word "withdrawal"; we did not accept their advice. What did
we do? It is true that we sought formulas which could facilitate the continued
existence of the National Unity Government while bearing in mind that there were
basic differences of opinion among its members. . . . At one of the Cabinet meetings
the late Levi Eshkol decided the matter. When, at that session, we were asked to
use the word "withdrawal", and I opposed it, I suggested the term "deployment of
forces" . . . not "redeployment", but "deployment of forces". Eshkol was asked by
one Cabinet member what was the difference between "withdrawal" and "deployment of forces", and he replied in his characteristic manner: "If we say 'withdrawal',
we are then committed to it. If we say 'deployment of forces', then Eban will
interpret it as he thinks correct, and Begin will interpret it as he thinks correct."
When we decided not to use the word "withdrawal", both interpretations were
possible.'

After an exchange between Begin and Eban at the same Cabinet meeting over the
choice between 'position' and 'disposition' of forces, the latter was accepted. There
was also pressure to use the word 'redeployment' if 'withdrawal' were too strong.
'The Government discussed it', Begin continued, 'and everyone understood the prefix "re". But the Government in good conscience rejected the additional prefix. . . .
After all these semantic difficulties we used, during the two years, only the nice word
"disposition of forces". . . . There is a crucial difference between "disposition" and
"withdrawal". "Withdrawal" means moving backwards, while there is no notion of
movement in the word "disposition".' Begin 1970.

[3] *Divrei Ha-knesset*, lvii, pp. 1911–13, 1863. There was also a basic disagreement

she had made the gesture during her September 1969 visit to the United States: reiteration in the *Knesset* gave it the stamp of authority. All these conciliatory moves, however, were in large part the result of internal pressures already noted—students' dissent, expressions of fatigue, and the desire to terminate the 'war of attrition', dramatized by the 'Goldmann Affair'. These, along with concern about the possible loss of United States political and military support (DB_1 and M), induced the signs of Israeli flexibility.

The month of May and the first half of June 1970 was a gestation period for Rogers Plan 'B' within the US Administration, following Nasser's tacit signal in his May Day speech that Egypt would accept a limited cease-fire. On the 20th of May Eban met with Rogers and the next day with Nixon. The President assured Israel's Foreign Minister that the flow of arms would continue—quietly; moreover, that the United States was planning a new initiative to solve the Middle East conflict, and that there would be prior consultation. Prime Minister Meir's statement to the *Knesset* five days later concerning Resolution 242 and the Rhodes formula was, objectively, and perhaps subjectively as well, Jerusalem's *quid pro quo*.

When Ambassador Barbour presented the US 'peace initiative' (Rogers 'B') to the Prime Minister on Friday afternoon, 19 June, it came as a surprise. The reason appears to have been Rabin's refusal to heed at least three requests from the Foreign Ministry to clarify Washington's intent, following the Secretary of State's TV announcement on 7 June that the United States would undertake a new Middle East initiative within a fortnight.[1] The result was unnecessary tension—both at the Jerusalem meeting on the night of 19 June (Meir, Eban, Foreign Ministry DG Rafael, and Political Adviser to the Prime Minister Dinitz, with Barbour and Zurhellen, US Counsellor), and during the Rabin–Rogers conversation in Washington the same afternoon. 'We were very bitter and reacted violently.'

within the Cabinet on the Rhodes formula. *Gahal* interpreted it as *indirect* talks and therefore a violation of the principle of 'direct negotiation' adopted by the National Unity Government. All other coalition members did not perceive a violation: to them the Rhodes talks began on an indirect basis with a UN mediator and later became *direct* negotiations between Israeli and Arab representatives. Parenthetically, the decision to carry out Resolution 242 in all its parts was taken by the Government only in the strategic decision two months later to accept Rogers 'B'.

[1] *Ma'ariv*, 8 June 1970. The relations between Rabin and the Foreign Ministry were disharmonious from the outset of his tenure in Washington, February 1968ff. On this occasion he complained to the Prime Minister about Foreign Office pressure for consultations, and it ceased. Further evidence of the continuing friction appeared in May 1972 when the Ambassador openly criticized the Foreign Ministry and its methods of work, in newspapers and radio interviews, and claimed that he and his staff (February 1968ff.) were responsible for Israel's good relations with the United States. Foreign Minister Eban rebutted that claim and chided Rabin for his emphasis on personal contributions. *Jerusalem Post*, 18 and 19 May 1972.

The US Ambassador urged Israeli leaders not to decide at once but, rather, to let the Arabs respond to the initiative first. Meir was not persuaded and stated her unqualified opposition to the Plan. The atmosphere was not eased by Barbour's reported remark that, if progress were made towards a cease-fire, there might not be a need for further US arms aid to Israel. The Prime Minister was aghast; an assurance came on Sunday morning, the 21st, that Israel would continue to receive arms regardless of the outcome on Rogers 'B'.

That morning the Government of Israel decided to reject the US initiative—Tactical Decision 2. According to one minister,

The Prime Minister informed us that she had said to Barbour, 'I am convinced the Government will reject your suggestions.' After discussion in the Cabinet it was decided unanimously to support the negative replies of both the Prime Minister and the Foreign Minister to the American Ambassador. . . . In other words . . . the American proposals were actually rejected even before the discussion at the Cabinet meeting, by the Prime Minister and the Foreign Minister, while on Sunday the matter was discussed and concluded with a unanimous decision.[1]

The Deputy Prime Minister concurred: 'The decision was taken unanimously, without a vote. This was because, when there is unanimity of opinion within the Government a decision is made by general consent, not by a vote.' It was also decided to communicate that negative decision on Rogers 'B' directly to the President, in the form of a special dispatch.

The US peace initiative, or Rogers 'B', was a brief document presented to Israel, Egypt, and Jordan:

. . . The United States puts forward the following proposal for consideration: (a) That both Israel and the U.A.R. subscribe to a restoration of the cease-fire for at least a limited period; (b) that Israel and the U.A.R. (as well as Israel and Jordan) subscribe to the following statement which would be in the form of a report from Ambassador Jarring to the Secretary-General, U Thant: The U.A.R. (Jordan) and Israel advise me that they agree:

(a) That having accepted and indicated their willingness to carry out Resolution 242 in all its parts, they will designate representatives to discussions to be held under my auspices, according to such procedure, and at such places and times as I may recommend, taking into account as appropriate each side's preference as to method of procedure and previous experience between the parties;

(b) That the purpose of the aforementioned discussions is to reach agreement on the establishment of a just and lasting peace between them based on (1) mutual acknowledgement by the U.A.R. (Jordan) and Israel of each other's sovereignty, territorial integrity and political independence, and (2) Israeli withdrawal from territories occupied in the 1967 conflict, both in accordance with Resolution 242;

[1] Begin 1970.

(c) That, to facilitate my task of promoting agreement as set forth in Resolution 242, the parties will strictly observe, effective July 1 until (at least) October 1, the cease-fire resolutions of the Security Council.[1]

A statement by the Secretary of State on 25 June referred to the 'political initiative . . . which we have launched directly with the parties and with other interested powers', but he declined to disclose details or to discuss publicly military assistance to Israel.[2]

In the meantime Israel's decision to reject Rogers 'B' was frozen—by direct intervention of her Ambassador to Washington. The Cabinet was informed on 25 June that Rabin objected to the tone of the message to Nixon and did not communicate it to the White House! Summoned to Jerusalem to explain his behaviour, Rabin persuaded the Government at its meeting on the 28th to soften the tone—but not the substance —of a revised letter to the President.[3] The Deputy Prime Minister justified that intervention thus: 'I remember the incident. Nevertheless, I think that Rabin, as Ambassador, was within his rights to withhold the dispatch and to seek further clarifications.' Parenthetically, 'the explicit request of the United States was that we should not be the first to reject the new initiative.'

A waiting period followed Israel's Tactical Decision 2, from 21 June until 22 July: the Arab reply was yet to come. In the interim there were two authoritative pro-Israel American statements: first, a 'background' remark on 26 June by the President's Adviser on National Security Affairs at San Clemente to a group of journalists—that the United States would 'expel' the Soviets from the Middle East; and secondly, Nixon's assertion at a TV press conference on 1 July that Syria was aggressive and wanted to 'throw Israel into the sea', and that Israel was entitled to 'defensible', not just 'secure' borders.[4] Both of these remarks, especially the latter, influenced the softer tone of Jerusalem's revised dispatch to the President, which was sent at the beginning of July.[5]

Then the unanticipated occurred: on 22 July Egypt's Foreign Minister, Mahmoud Riad, wrote to Rogers that Cairo accepted his formula, with qualifications indicated in a separate letter.[6] The follow-

---

[1] The text is in *Jerusalem Post*, 31 July 1970. It also appears in 'Note to the Secretary-General on the Jarring Mission for the Information of the Security Council'. UN.SC. S/9902, 7 Aug. 1970.

[2] *Jerusalem Post*, 26 June 1970.

[3] *Yedi'ot Aharonot*, 1 July 1970; *Ma'ariv*, 2 July 1970; and Margalit, p. 135.

[4] *New York Times*, 27 June, 2 July 1970.

[5] *Ma'ariv* and *Yedi'ot Aharonot*, 5 July 1970. On 29 June, *before* the Nixon statement, Meir clearly implied to the *Knesset* that Israel would reject the US initiative; she later confirmed that Jerusalem had done so. *Yedi'ot Aharonot*, 17 July 1970.

[6] The Riad reply to Rogers's letter is illuminating, particularly on the extensive reservations to Egypt's acceptance of the US initiative, which are ignored, overlooked

ing day Nasser announced it in an address to the nation: he had just
returned from a fortnight in the Soviet Union, with prolonged talks
in Moscow followed by medical treatment. The Israeli Establishment
view on the reason for Egypt's acceptance of Rogers 'B' was expressed
by Air Force Commander Mordekhai Hod two years later: 'The deep
penetration bombings during the war of attrition hurt Egypt and caused
Cairo to agree to a cease-fire and to keep it.'[1]

A signal that Egypt would reply favourably was apparent from a
detailed Soviet plan for a political settlement, published on 11 July: in
spirit and content it was very similar to Rogers 'A'.[2] Israel's decision-
makers did not absorb the hint. Despite the reservations, Egypt's
response became a decisive input into Israel's strategic decision, for it
compelled a reconsideration of her 21 June rejection of Rogers 'B'.
That process began on 24 July and dominated Israel's political life
for eight days.

---

or unknown by large segments of the international attentive public. The salient
passages of the Foreign Minister's letter are:

'Cairo, July 22, 1970

'Dear Mr. Secretary of State,
'I have received your message of June 19, 1970 . . .
'The withdrawal of Israel from all the Arab territories occupied as a result of its
aggression of June 5, 1967 is fundamental to the achievement of peace in the area.
The liberation of Arab territories is not only a natural right but a national duty. . . .
'Israeli leaders openly declared that they waged the war for the purpose of expansion. To this day, their stated intention to annex Arab lands is reiterated in their
successive declarations. . . .
'I am confident that you realize that to continue to ignore the rights of the Palestinian people who were expelled by Israel from their homeland can in no way
contribute to the achievement of peace in the area, and that to establish peace in
the Middle East it is necessary to recognize the legitimate rights of the Palestinian
people in accordance with the United Nations resolutions. . . .
'Israel's rejection of that resolution impeded the realization of peace and conse-
quently war continued. . . .
'As for the resolution adopted by the Security Council in June 1967 calling for the
cease-fire, it is to be noted that we respected it from the outset. Yet Israel never
respected this resolution at any time and continued its aggression on the Suez
Canal area, bombarded its cities and destroyed the economic installations. . . .
'We also believe that for Ambassador Jarring to be able to achieve quick progress
in the first stage of his work, the four powers should provide him with specific
directives with regard to the implementation of the articles of the Security Council
resolution and in particular the withdrawal of Israeli forces and the guarantees
for peace. . . .
'We believe that the correct procedure with which this could be started is to draw
a time-table for the withdrawal of the Israeli forces from the occupied territories. . . .
/s/ Mahmoud Riad'
Text was published by UAR Ministry for Foreign Affairs on 7 Aug. 1970.

[1] Television interview, commemorating Air Force Day. Reported in *Jerusalem
Post*, 16 July 1972. The same interpretation was conveyed to this writer soon after
the cease-fire. Elizur interview, 1972.

[2] It appeared in the bulletin of the USSR Embassy in London, *The Soviet Weekly*,
on 11 July 1970. *Ma'ariv* carried its contents a day earlier.

Egypt's acceptance was followed at once by US pressure—and assurances—to secure a positive Israeli response. The most decisive input took the form of a special dispatch from Nixon to Meir, delivered by Ambassador Barbour on the afternoon of the 24th: it was clearly designed to influence the outcome of the tense debate just beginning within the National Unity Government. Although not officially published, its contents were disclosed by the Israeli press. The salient points were:

(1) US recognition of the need to preserve the Jewishness of Israel;
(2) US acknowledgement that Israel's borders would not be the same as those of 4 June 1967;
(3) an assurance that the US would not be a party to an imposed solution;
(4) support for a peace settlement upon secure and recognized boundaries, as the outcome of negotiations between the parties to the conflict;
(5) agreement that Israeli troops would remain on the cease-fire lines until a contractual peace agreement was signed;
(6) a pledge to maintain the balance of military power in the Near East Core and to continue the supply of arms to Israel; and
(7) a promise of continuing large-scale American economic aid.

Nixon concluded with a request that Israel respond affirmatively to Rogers 'B'.[1]

It was difficult to reject the President's *démarche*. On the spirit and form of US inducements there is a diversity of perception. Three Cabinet ministers observed thus:

Allon: The Americans did not use pressure on us, as they did in 1948–9 and 1956; they tried to develop among us a feeling of being partners and of a dialogue with friends.

Peres: As to the question of US pressure on us to accept their programme, I would say they handled us more with a carrot than with a stick; in any event they never threatened us with sanctions.

Weizman: It is clear that pressures were imposed upon us by the US with the receipt of an affirmative reply from Egypt; the pressures were not spelled out but it was clear to everyone in the Government that it meant military, political and economic pressures at the same time; there was no need for them to use public pressures or threats as long as they had more pleasant methods.

The catalytic role of Nixon's dispatch in the process leading to Israel's strategic decision was admirably summed up by one Foreign Office expert:

The Nixon dispatch was the turning point: it altered the Government's

[1] *Ma'ariv*, 26 July 1970, and *Davar*, 2 Aug. 1970. The accuracy of this summary was confirmed by Israeli officials with access to the Nixon letter.

negative stand on Rogers Plan 'B'. In June 1970 the Government thought that Rogers Plan 'B' was meant to introduce Rogers Plan 'A' through the back door. That is why she rejected it. By contrast, the Government saw in Nixon's dispatch a fundamental change from Rogers Plan 'A' and thus decided to accept the new plan.

And he added: 'The Government erred in exaggerating the meaning of Nixon's dispatch. That dispatch did not contradict at all Rogers Plan "A" and was not intended to nullify it.'

The strategic decision process extended over an entire week of intensive deliberations, from 25 to 31 July 1970. The principal forums for debate were the Labour Party's ministerial élite, the Cabinet, and the Leadership Bureaux of all coalition parties, especially of the *Herut* and Liberal allies in *Gahal*, the 'opposition' group within the National Unity Government. It began with a meeting of Labour's Inner Circle at Prime Minister Meir's home on Saturday evening, the 25th: present were Allon, Dayan, Eban, Galili, and Shapiro. The Deputy Prime Minister called for acceptance of Rogers 'B' on the basis of the new constellation—Egypt's positive reaction and Nixon's assurances. All but Dayan were openly in favour; the Defence Minister did not express a view. A decision could have been taken at the regular weekly Cabinet session on Sunday morning, 26 July, for a clear majority was assured. There were, however, three mutually-reinforcing stimuli to delay: (*a*) the attempt to persuade *Gahal* not to leave the National Unity Government; (*b*) disagreement over the wording of acceptance of Rogers 'B'; and (*c*) the perceived need for clarifications from the US Government.

Acceptance of the American initiative was advocated with varying degrees of enthusiasm at the Government meeting on the 26th—by all factions except *Gahal*. *Herut* leaders in particular pressed for a reaffirmation of the 21 June negative decision and served a warning that they would withdraw from the Coalition if Rogers 'B' were accepted. The issue was complicated by disagreement within *Gahal*: the Liberals, too, opposed the US Plan but they did not share Begin's seeming penchant to return to the Opposition. And the Prime Minister had provided them with a self-satisfying rationalization, namely, that acceptance of Rogers 'B' did not, *ipso facto*, mean Israel's withdrawal from the cease-fire lines. Meir offered two reasons: first, Rogers 'B' did not incorporate the territorial provisions of Rogers 'A', which the Government of Israel had formally rejected in December 1969 and continued to reject; indeed, she and many others claimed that Rogers 'B' was a distinct (pro-Israel) advance, for it avoided substantive proposals on borders, Jerusalem, refugees, *et al.* and was confined to a cease-fire and the *procedure* for *negotiating* a settlement; secondly, Nixon's letter had firmly supported Israel's insistence on no withdrawal whatsoever until after a peace agreement was signed. The Liberal Party was convinced, and urged *Herut* not to press for dissolution of the National Unity Government, but in vain; Begin's ideological imperatives triumphed. However, the outcome was uncertain until after the Government made the strategic decision and a special *Gahal* session endorsed the Begin view against that of Liberal leaders Saphir, Rimalt, and Dulzin.[1] Only the *Mapam* ministers and Eban did not conceal their dissent from the sustained Labour Party attempt to keep *Gahal* in the Cabinet—or their pleasure at the dissolution of the National Unity Government.

The second obstacle to a quick decision was the refusal of several ministers, led by Dayan, to accept the *form* of Rogers 'B' as proposed by the US Secretary of State. Their negative response of 21 June was unchanged, but circumstances now dictated acquiescence in the *substance* of that proposal. How to reply in the affirmative without risking a loss of credibility because of the *volte-face* within six weeks—this was the dilemma of would-be dissenters. Their solution was, formally, to ignore Rogers 'B', i.e. to retain their earlier rejection intact and to reply directly to the President's letter of 24 July. The specious reasoning was summed up by one official with disdain: 'The Nixon letter, for Meir, Galili, Dayan and others, turned Rogers "B" into a *US peace initiative*, a less unpalatable proposition; this is the semantic hocus-pocus we indulge in.' Indirect response was also designed to placate *Herut* and keep *Gahal* within the Government. To Begin, however, it was disingenuous: it did not alter the basic fact of acceptance of Rogers 'B' and the principle of withdrawal, no matter the form.[2] Peres explained the indirect form of acceptance thus: 'We did not want to give a simple reply, "yes" or "no", because any such definite answer would have ultimately harmed us. We therefore chose to avoid the problem and to reply with our own version.' Dayan's formula, including the incorporation of Israel's reservations into the dispatch to Nixon, triumphed in the end.

As so often in the permanent dialogue with the United States, Israel sought 'clarifications' and further 'assurances' from Washington—that

(1) more Phantoms and new Shrike rockets would be provided to *Tzahal*;
(2) Nixon's dispatch constituted US Government policy towards Israel and the Arab–Israel conflict;
(3) Rogers Plan 'A' would be withdrawn; and that
(4) the US would veto any anti-Israel resolution concerning the

---

[1] Some of Begin's *Herut* colleagues, including Weizman, were also reportedly opposed to his view. This dimension of the decision-making process was covered at length by the Israeli press from 27 July to 7 Aug. 1970.

[2] The *Herut* leader wrote soon after the strategic decision: 'I sometimes wonder how intelligent persons believed that a governmental policy to redivide the Land of Israel could be framed and I would continue to assume responsibility for such a policy. . . . The basis of our participation in the Government has been destroyed.' Begin 1970.

terms or procedures for a settlement which would otherwise be approved by the Security Council.

Washington gave assurances on point 1 and reaffirmed point 2; but it refused to yield on Rogers 'A' or to offer an unqualified pledge to invoke a veto in the Security Council.

Satisfaction on the first two demands made the US initiative more palatable. In any event it was the maximum concession to be extracted. Thus at the end of a long week of intra-Coalition and inter-State bargaining the Government of Israel took the strategic decision to accept Rogers 'B': the vote was 17 in favour (Labour–*Mapam* Alignment, NRP, and Independent Liberals) to 6 against (*Gahal*); the 24th minister, H. M. Shapira, had died a few days earlier. The decision as announced by the Government Secretary was as follows:

Having considered the appeals of the President of the U.S., and without abandoning its commitment to its basic policy guidelines and authorized statements, the Cabinet has decided to endorse the latest peace initiative of the U.S. Government and to appoint, at the appropriate time, a representative for peace negotiations without prior conditions, under the auspices of Ambassador Jarring, within the framework of Security Council Resolution 242 and with the aim of reaching a binding contractual peace agreement between the parties.

Israel's position in respect of a cease-fire on all sectors, including the Egyptian front, on a basis of reciprocity, in accordance with the resolution of the Security Council, remains in force. Taking into account the clarifications provided by the Government of the U.S., Israel is prepared to subscribe to the proposal of the U.S. concerning a cease-fire, for three months at least, on the Egyptian front.

A ministerial committee will draft proposals as to the precise language of the reply of the Government of Israel to the Government of the U.S.[1]

At *Gahal*'s insistence two votes were taken; on the second, the cease-fire, the Government was unanimous. According to Allon, *Gahal* wanted to prove that the cease-fire proposal was not connected at all with the American initiative, whereas it was an integral part of the US Plan.

(D) IMPLEMENTATION

The strategic decision was authorized four days later, on 4 August, first by the Government and then by the *Knesset*. The interim was devoted to drafting a reply—to Nixon's dispatch, not to Rogers 'B'—by a committee chaired by Meir and consisting of Allon, Dayan, Eban, Galili, Kol, Peled, Shapiro, and Warhaftig.[2] *Gahal* refused an invitation

---

[1] English translation of the text in *Jerusalem Post*, 2 Aug. 1970. A slightly different English version is to be found in Meir's policy statement to the *Knesset* on 4 Aug.: Meir (2), p. 3. The convoluted phrasing, designed, it would appear, to confuse and to obscure the obvious, was attributed to Galili. *Lamerhav*, 2 Aug. 1970.

[2] Its composition was announced by the Government Secretary on 31 July at the press conference following the strategic decision. As often, every faction in the Government was represented on the committee.

to participate; in fact, it withdrew from the Government on 4 August. The previous day the draft, prepared largely by Galili and submitted to the committee on the 1st, had been approved informally by the Prime Minister and Defence Minister, the two crucial decision-makers at this juncture.

The formula, as read to the *Knesset* by Meir on 4 August, began with the two operative paragraphs of the 31 July Cabinet decision and continued:

Having considered President Nixon's message of 24 July 1970, basing itself on its contents and in strict adherence to its policy principles and authoritative statements, the Government of Israel has decided to reply affirmatively to the latest U.S. peace initiative, and to inform the U.S. that it may convey to Ambassador Jarring that:

1. Israel is prepared in due time to designate a representative to discussions to be held under Ambassador Jarring's auspices with the U.A.R. (Jordan), according to such procedure and at such places and times as he may recommend, taking into account each side's attitudes as to method of procedure and previous experience of discussions between the parties.

2. Israel's position in favour of a cease-fire on a basis of reciprocity on all fronts, including the Egyptian front, in accordance with the Security Council's cease-fire Resolution, remains unchanged. On the basis of clarifications given to the U.S. Government in this matter, Israel is prepared to reply affirmatively to the U.S. proposal for a cease-fire (for at least three months) on the Egyptian front.

3. The discussions under Ambassador Jarring's auspices shall be held within the framework of the Security Council Resolution (242) on the basis of the expression of readiness by the parties to carry out the Security Council Resolution (242) in all its parts, in order to achieve an agreed and binding contractual peace agreement between the parties which will ensure:

    a) Termination by Egypt (Jordan) and Israel of all claims or states of belligerency and respect and acknowledgement of the sovereignty, territorial integrity and political independence of each other and their right to live in peace within secure and recognized boundaries free from threats or acts of force. Each of the parties will be responsible within its territory for the prevention of all hostile acts by regular military forces or paramilitary forces, including irregular forces, against the armed forces or against civilians living in the territory of the other party.

    b) Withdrawal of Israeli armed forces from territories occupied in the 1967 conflict to secure, recognized and agreed boundaries to be determined in the peace agreements.

4. Israel will participate in these discussions without any prior conditions. Israel will not claim the prior acceptance by the other party of her positions, as Israel does not accept in advance the positions of the other parties as communicated publicly or otherwise. Each party will be free to present its proposals on the matters under discussion.[1]

[1] *Divrei Ha-knesset*, lviii, 4 Aug. 1970, pp. 2755–6; Meir (2), pp. 3–4.

The text of this reply to the US Government was approved by 66 to 28, with 9 abstentions. In favour were the Alignment; the NRP, except for Hammer and Shaki, who abstained; the Independent Liberals; *Maki*; and *Ha'olam Hazeh*. Opposed were *Gahal*; the Free Centre; and the State List, except Avizohar, who abstained. Other abstainers were the MKs from *Agudat Yisrael, Po'alei Agudat Yisrael*, and *Rakah*.[1]

There were several illuminating retrospective comments on the Government's formula for accepting Rogers 'B'—both the process of arriving at the draft and its meaning:

Begin: My governmental colleagues thought that they had achieved a great deed by adding, after the words committing us to 'Israeli withdrawal from territories conquered in 1967', the sentence, 'to recognized and secure borders which will be fixed in a peace agreement'. .... [However,] in these announcements [accompanying the dispatch of Israel's reply] there is a mockery to logic. The document [Rogers 'B'] exists. Even though we didn't sign it, our signature is on it.[2]

Allon: The formula of Israel's reply to the American plan was a grave mistake. There was no chance that it would be accepted seriously by the United States Government or by any government. Israel should not have made the slightest change in the original text of the American plan and she should have inserted her reservations in a separate document, as Egypt did. I strongly opposed this move by the Government since I saw in it a serious tactical error, but my view was not accepted.[3]

Weizman: I think the principal factor which caused the Government to reply as it did to the American plan was Dayan. The Alignment members were very concerned about the possibility that, if Dayan would be left in a minority he wouldn't hesitate to leave the Government. A situation in which both *Gahal* and Dayan would be out of the Government scared them. Therefore they did almost everything in order to appease Dayan.[4]

Civil Servant: I participated in the Cabinet meeting where the reply to the new American plan was discussed. Dayan announced that he would only agree to insert into the body of the text of the American initiative Israel's reservations. During the Cabinet session he was very excited and didn't abstain from shouting. It seemed that this issue was very important to him. Finally, his view prevailed.

The US peace initiative had explicitly linked a (90-day) cease-fire with the parties' acceptance of indirect negotiations under Jarring's auspices, on the basis of the principles enunciated in UN Resolution

---

[1] *Divrei Ha-knesset*, lviii, p. 2798. The Alignment *Knesset* faction voted 14 to 12 against permitting Mordekhai Surkiss, a vocal hawk, from abstaining; he acquiesced. The NRP allowed Hammer and Shaki to abstain. A third member from that religious party, Rabbi Neriya, was permitted by the NRP to absent himself from the *Knesset* session that day. And a fourth, Rabbi Ben-Meir, walked out of the House—without permission—just before the vote. *Yedi'ot Aharonot*, 5 Aug. 1970.
[2] *Ma'ariv*, 28 Aug. 1970.   [3] Interview, 1971.   [4] Interview, 1971.

242. Yet, ironically, when Israel made her strategic decision to accept Rogers Plan 'B', on 31 July, and even as late as 4 August, when the *Knesset* approved the decision and *Gahal* left the National Unity Government, it was uncertain that a cease-fire would go into effect. Rogers 'B' could have remained stillborn, for the emphasis in the parallel bilateral negotiations (US–Egypt, US–Israel) thus far, and Egypt's (qualified) acceptance of Rogers 'B', related almost exclusively to Resolution 242 and indirect negotiations. It was only on 6 August, when Barbour informed Israel's Foreign Office that he wished *now* to discuss the terms of a cease-fire, that this crucial provision in the US peace initiative was arranged; until the 6th Egypt had not signified her acceptance of a cease-fire of any duration.[1]

The terms were agreed upon quickly, and the cease-fire went into effect on 7 August.[2] It was violated at once by Egypt, who moved SAM-2s and SAM-3s closer to the Suez Canal, acts that delayed, *inter alia*, the implementation of Israel's strategic decision.[3] The cease-fire was followed by another implementing act on 23 August, when the Government authorized Eban and Tekoa to conduct talks with the UN Representative. Two days later Israel's Ambassador to the UN met Jarring, the first official meeting in months. It proved to be an abortive resumption of negotiations, however: Israel suspended the talks on 6 September because of Egypt's violation of the cease-fire. Under US pressure she returned once more, early in January 1971. Jarring's controversial Memorandum of 8 February 1971 led to a

---

[1] Communicated by a Foreign Ministry official.

[2] Its salient terms were noted by Dayan as follows:

'A. Israel and the U.A.R. will observe cease-fire effective at 22.00 G.M.T. Friday, August 7.

'B. Both sides will stop all incursions and all firing, on the ground and in the air, across the cease-fire line(s).

'C. Both sides will refrain from changing the military *status quo* within zones extending 50 kilometres to the east and the west of the cease-fire line. Neither side will introduce or construct any new military installations in these zones. Activities within the zones will be limited to the maintenance of existing installations and their present sites and positions and to the rotation and supply of forces presently within the zones.

'D. For purposes of verifying observance of the cease-fire, each side will rely on its own national means, including reconnaissance aircraft, which will be free to operate without interference up to 10 kilometres from the cease-fire line on its own side of that line.

'E. Each side will avail itself as appropriate of all U.N. machinery in reporting alleged violations to each other of the cease-fire and of the military standstill.

'F. Both sides will abide by the Geneva Convention of 1949 relative to the treatment of prisoners of war and will accept the assistance of the I.C.R.C. (International Committee of the Red Cross) in carrying out their obligations under that convention.'

English translation in *Jerusalem Post*, 14 Aug. 1970.

[3] After the initial violations of August 1970, the cease-fire was maintained through 1970, 1971, 1972, until 6 October 1973, with a very small number of incidents.

further lengthy break in the negotiations because of Israel's categorical refusal to give a 'positive' reply to the UN Mediator's request that she undertake to withdraw her forces to the traditional 'international boundary' with Egypt. The impasse remained unbroken in the spring of 1973, when Israel celebrated the twenty-fifth anniversary of independence. Nevertheless, the cease-fire had been approved by the Government of Israel and was being implemented effectively.

It remains to note the reasons for Israel's *volte-face* on Rogers 'B'. Meir, in her 4 August Statement to the *Knesset*, observed that 'important clarifications [from the US] on most essential subjects . . . made it easier for the Government of Israel to reply affirmatively. . . .'[1] Galili remarked simply, 'the highly valuable message from President Nixon'.[2] And one official summed it up with the pithy remark: 'The convergence of the positive elements of Nixon's letter and the negative element of Arab acceptance made Israel's rejection impossible.'

(E) DECISION FLOW

Pre-Decisional Events

1. March 1969	Beginning of Egypt's 'war of attrition'.
2. 23 March 1969	Opening of Two-Power Talks (US–USSR, Sisco–Dobrynin) on political settlement of Arab–Israel conflict.
3. 3 April 1969	Opening of Four-Power Talks (US, USSR, UK, France) on Arab–Israel conflict.
4. 5 June 1969	Rogers announcement of progress in Two-Power Talks towards political settlement based upon 'package deal'.

Decisive Inputs into Tactical Decision 1 (re Rogers 'A' and Yost Document)

5. 28 October 1969	United States presented to Soviet Union comprehensive plan for Middle East political settlement.
6. 9 December 1969	Publication of Rogers 'A', focusing on Israel–Egypt territorial settlement, Jerusalem, refugees, peace.
7. 18 December 1969	United States presented Yost Document, focusing on Israel–Jordan territorial settlement, Jerusalem, refugees, peace, to Four-Power Talks and, on same day, to Israel.

Tactical Decision 1 (a,b)

8. 10 December 1969	Government of Israel rejected Rogers 'A'.

[1] Meir (2), pp. 2–3.   [2] Galili (3).

9. 22 December 1969   Government of Israel rejected US proposals, including Yost Document (both decisions approved by *Knesset* on 29 December).

Pre-Decisional Events for Tactical Decision 2 and Strategic Decision (re Rogers 'B')

10. 7 January 1970   Beginning of Israeli deep penetration air raids into Egypt—in response to Egypt's 'war of attrition'.

11. 30 Jan.–4 Feb. 1970   Nixon–Kosygin exchange of letters on Middle East conflict.

12. February 1970 ff.   Escalation of Soviet presence in Egypt.

13. 23 March 1970   Rogers announcement of US decision not to supply Israel with more planes 'for the time being'. (Followed 29 January announcement by Nixon of intent to make decision on planes within 30 days.)

14. 31 March 1970   Cessation of Israel's deep air raids into Egypt.

15. 12–24 April 1970   Sisco visit to Egypt, Israel, Lebanon, Saudi Arabia, Iran.

16. 18 April 1970   Discovery by Israel that Soviet pilots were flying operational missions over Egypt.

Decisive Inputs into Tactical Decision 2 (re Rogers 'B')

17. 1 May 1970   Nasser signalled to US his willingness to accept cease-fire.

18. 19 June 1970   United States presented Rogers 'B' to Egypt, Israel, and Jordan—after six weeks of gestation within United States Administration.

Tactical Decision 2

19. 21 June 1970   Israel's Cabinet rejected Rogers 'B'.

Decisive Inputs into Strategic Decision

20. 22 July 1970   Following Nasser's fortnight's visit to USSR and publication of Soviet peace plan on 11 July, very similar to Rogers 'A', Egypt conveyed her acceptance of Rogers 'B' to United States.

21. 24 July 1970   Nixon's dispatch on assurances reached Meir.

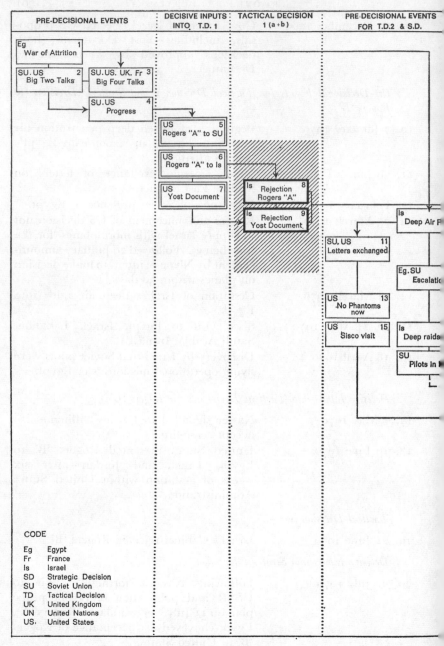

PRE-DECISIONAL EVENTS	DECISIVE INPUTS INTO T.D. 1	TACTICAL DECISION 1 (a + b)	PRE-DECISIONAL EVENTS FOR T.D.2 & S.D.

Eg 1
War of Attrition

SU.US 2
Big Two Talks

SU.US.UK.Fr 3
Big Four Talks

SU.US 4
Progress

US 5
Rogers "A" to SU

US 6
Rogers "A" to Is

US 7
Yost Document

Is Rejection 8
Rogers "A"

Is Rejection 9
Yost Document

SU, US 11
Letters exchanged

US 13
No Phantoms now

US 15
Sisco visit

Is
Deep Air F

Eg.SU
Escalatio

Is
Deep raids

SU
Pilots in

CODE

Eg   Egypt
Fr   France
Is   Israel
SD   Strategic Decision
SU   Soviet Union
TD   Tactical Decision
UK   United Kingdom
UN   United Nations
US.   United States

FIGURE 18. DECISION FLOW: ROGERS PROPOSALS

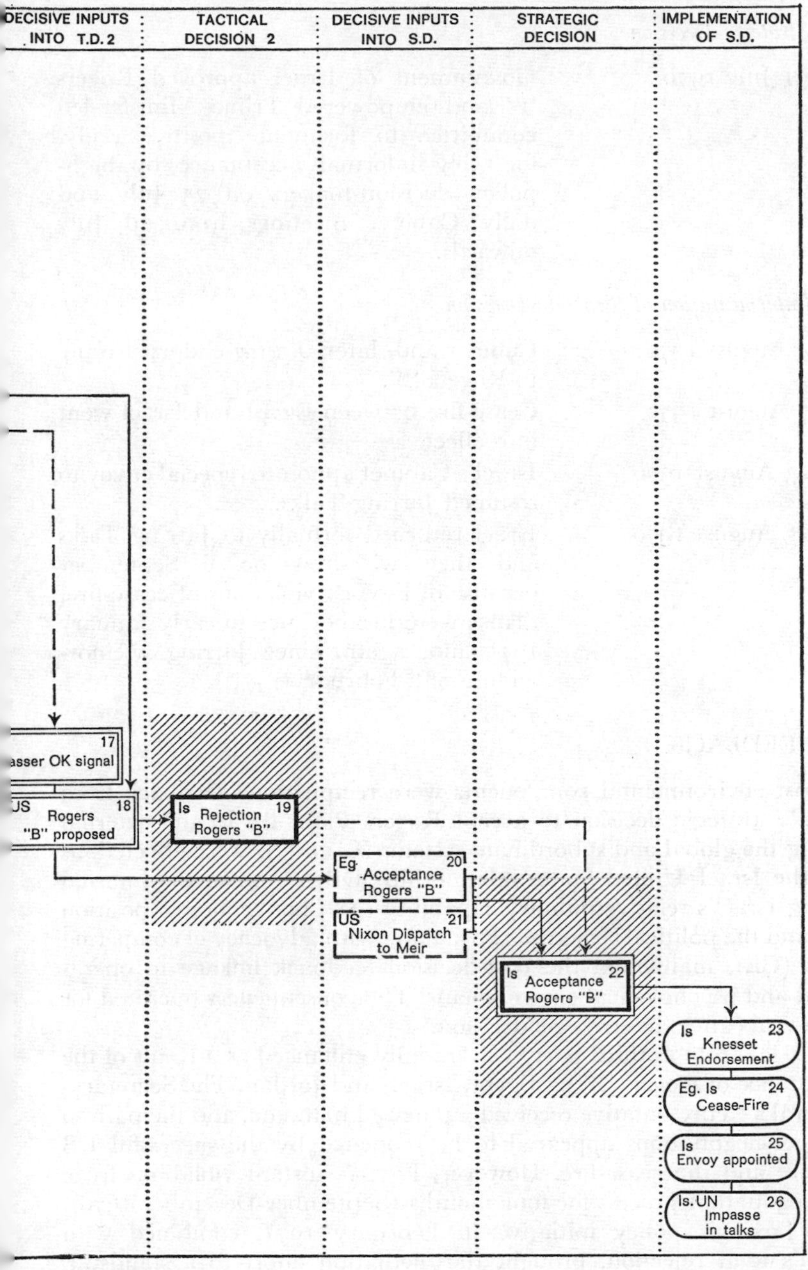

DECISIVE INPUTS INTO T.D. 2	TACTICAL DECISION 2	DECISIVE INPUTS INTO S.D.	STRATEGIC DECISION	IMPLEMENTATION OF S.D.

17 asser OK signal

18 US Rogers "B" proposed

19 Is Rejection Rogers "B"

20 Eg. Acceptance Rogers "B"

21 US Nixon Dispatch to Meir

22 Is Acceptance Rogers "B"

23 Is Knesset Endorsement

24 Eg. Is Cease-Fire

25 Is Envoy appointed

26 Is. UN Impasse in talks

Strategic Decision

22. 31 July 1970   Government of Israel approved Rogers
                           'B' and empowered Prime Minister-led
                           committee to formulate positive reply,
                           following informal acceptance by high-
                           policy decision-makers on 25 July and
                           daily Cabinet meetings from 26 July
                           onwards.

Implementation of Strategic Decision

23. 4 August 1970   Cabinet and, later, *Knesset* endorsed reply
                           to Rogers 'B'.

24. 7 August 1970   Cease-fire between Egypt and Israel went
                           into effect.

25. 23 August 1970   Israel's Cabinet appointed special envoy to
                           resumed Jarring Talks.

26. 25 August 1970   Israel returned formally to Jarring Talks
                           and then withdrew on 6 September
                           because of Egypt's violations of cease-fire.
                           (Talks were in abeyance to early January
                           1971 and, again, since Jarring Memor-
                           andum of 8 February 1971.)

(F) FEEDBACK

Most environmental components were recipients of feedback from
Israel's strategic decision to accept Rogers Plan 'B'. In the external
setting the global and subordinate systems (G and S) were affected, as
was the Israel–United States relationship (DB$_1$). And in the internal
setting Israel's relative military capability (M), her economic position
(E), and the political structure (PS), along with advocacy of competing
élites (CE), manifested the post-decision feedback linkage to operational and psychological environments. The consequences operated for
three years after the strategic decision.

The UN role as third party was initially enhanced as a result of the
acceptance of Rogers 'B' by Egypt, Israel, and Jordan. The Secretary-
General's Representative received a renewed mandate, and the path to
indirect negotiations appeared to be reopened by the successful US
venture and the cease-fire. However, Egypt's instant violations froze
the negotiation process for four months (September–December 1970).
And Jarring's policy initiative in February 1971, combined with
Israel's total rejection, brought the mediation effort to a standstill.
In the perception of Israel's high-policy decision-makers the world
organization fell into disrepute once more. In essence, the Jarring

Memorandum of 8 February 1971 sought from Egypt a declaration of readiness to sign a peace agreement with Israel, and from Israel a prior commitment to withdraw to the traditional international boundary between Palestine and Egypt. Cairo responded affirmatively, though with reservations. Israel charged the UN Representative with exceeding his authority and, more important, with excluding the border issue from negotiations by demanding an advance commitment to total withdrawal. The result was deadlock, until October 1973. Israel steadfastly refused to give Jarring a 'positive' reply to his withdrawal question of 8 February 1971. And he, in turn, stubbornly refused to withdraw his demand or to regard Israel's answer to his Memorandum, dated 26 February, as a sufficient basis for resuming his mission.[1]

Other forms of global system penetration into the Arab–Israel conflict, such as the Four-Power Talks, were treated with no less disdain than was the United Nations. The decline of the G component was partly a function of the 1970 cease-fire and partly the result of a more active United States role. The reality of UN insignificance was correctly perceived by Israel's decision-makers—and was emphasized by Israel's behaviour. In fact, from February 1971 onwards the UN occupied a minuscule and wholly negative position in her psychological environment. This in turn spilled over to Israel's UN policy, which was to ignore Jarring and all General Assembly resolutions on the conflict—relating to Jerusalem, Resolution 242, Arab refugees, the rights of Arabs in the occupied territories, etc.—and to concentrate on a 'partial', Suez Canal, settlement under American auspices.

The basic conflict within the Near East Core (S) was tranquillized by Israel's (and Egypt's) decision to accept Rogers 'B'. Hostility and mistrust remained unchanged, but the overt manifestations of the conflict declined markedly: they were confined largely to threats by Sadat and other Egyptian leaders to resume full-scale military operations. These reached a peak during the last months of 1971, which had been designated by Sadat the 'year of decision'. Thereafter threats were spasmodic and less vitriolic. The lesser intensity of Arab–Israel conflict was due partly to a growing perception in Cairo that the Sinai Peninsula could not be regained on the battlefield. More important, perhaps, was the internal struggle for power following Nasser's death in September 1970. That preoccupation left Sadat, even after his

---

[1] Jarring's demand and Israel's negative reply derive from conflicting interpretations of Resolution 242 and Rogers 'B'. The UN Representative assumed that Israel's acceptance of Rogers 'B' constituted an undertaking to withdraw from the territories occupied in the 1967 War—because of the inclusion of the Resolution in the Rogers 'B' formula and clear admonition in the Security Council resolution against the acquisition of territory by conquest. In short, to request Israel to commit herself to withdraw to the international frontier with Egypt was, for Jarring, to articulate an implicit commitment.

domestic triumph, with less assurance and expendable resources for the battle against Israel. Fratricidal strife was an even greater deterrent to Jordan's resumption of hostilities. And even after Hussein's victory over the Palestine guerrillas in the civil war of September 1970, his realistic appreciation of the balance of forces, as well as his own interests, precluded open war against Israel. All of these catalysts to relaxation of Near East tension were strengthened by the US peace initiative.

The de-escalation of the conflict after August 1970 was accurately perceived by Israel's decision-makers. So too was the internal strife in Egypt and Jordan, the reassuring military balance, and Israel's capacity to withstand a direct assault from Arab armies against the strategically advantageous frontiers arising from the Six Day War. All of these specific images strengthened the perception that 'peace *with* security' was a feasible policy goal, with a minimum of concessions to an adversary in disarray. At the same time Sadat's persistent verbal belligerence appeared to confirm the fundamental Israeli image of distrust of the Arabs. Self-confidence and rooted mistrust led to a policy of negativeness, accompanied by an articulated disbelief in Arab declarations of willingness. Thus the reduction of tension, with virtually no casualties, had made the sub-system more ready for a formalized *modus vivendi*; but it had also strengthened Israel's resolve to extract maximal concessions for peace, notably 'secure and recognized borders', involving basic territorial revisions of the 4 June *status quo*.

Israel's relationship with the United States (DB_1) has always been vital to the setting for her decisions. The consequence of her strategic decision on Rogers 'B' was to make 'the American factor' even more significant in Israel's foreign policy. For one thing, Washington became the most active mediator in the Arab–Israel conflict. For another, the dictates of third-party intervention led to US efforts at a diplomatic *rapprochement* with Cairo. Thirdly, Israel's acceptance of Rogers 'B' made it possible for the United States to press for even larger concessions. This pressure culminated in Rogers 'C', a set of six points proposed on 4 October 1971 by the Secretary of State as a basis for a 'partial' or 'interim' Suez Canal settlement.[1] Their distance from Israel's bargaining posture brought her DB_1 relationship to its most acrimonious and mistrustful level since before the 1967 War.

Rogers 'C' was received with harsh comments by Israel's high-policy decision-makers. As Mrs. Meir told a press conference on 6 October: 'I feel obliged to say that it seems to me this speech, to our great regret, did not advance the special partial arrangement for reopening the Suez Canal. Moreover, this speech might be interpreted by the Egyptian rulers as an encouragement to carry on their rigid

[1] The text is in *New York Times*, 5 Oct. 1971.

TABLE 32

ROGERS 'C' AND THE CONFLICTING PARTIES' STAND: OCTOBER 1971-3

Topic	Israel's Stand	Egypt's Stand	US (Rogers 'C') Stand
1. Relationship of Suez Canal and overall settlements	'Partial' and overall settlements are independent of each other	'Interim' settlement on Suez Canal is integral part of overall settlement	'Interim' settlement as step towards overall settlement
2. Duration of cease-fire	Unlimited	Six months	Vague—not too short, not too long
3. Extent of Israeli withdrawal during partial or interim settlement	Approximately 10 kilometres from Suez Canal	To El-Arish	Not precisely indicated
4. Supervision over evacuated territory in Sinai Peninsula	Bar-Lev line to remain under *Tzahal*'s control	Evacuated territory to be restored to Egypt's control	Not clearly indicated
5. Issue of Egyptian personnel on east bank of Canal	Only Egyptian civilians and technicians to be permitted to cross, in order to prepare Canal for navigation	Egyptian troops to cross Canal and to take possession of all evacuated territory	Not indicated; later, US efforts to find acceptable formula based on limited number of uniformed Egyptian police, lightly armed
6. Free passage through Canal	Immediate application of the principle of free navigation for *all* states, with explicit inclusion of Israel	Free navigation to be granted to Israeli shipping through the Canal *after* a final peace settlement and a solution to the Arab refugee problem	Free navigation for all shipping should be acknowledged in principle; the date for its application to Israeli shipping should be arranged by agreement between Israel and Egypt

stand.'[1] Within hours of the Secretary of State's speech, Eban conveyed to him personally Israel's strong opposition. The formal rejection of Rogers 'C', however, came on the 12th following a special three-hour Cabinet meeting: 'The Government once again reiterated unanimously its stand favouring a partial agreement to reopen the Canal as defined by the Prime Minister in her speech of October 6 after . . . Rogers's address at the UN General Assembly.'[2] Eban informed Rogers of the decision on the 14th; the result was one of the stormiest exchanges in the history of US–Israel relations.

In essence the six points rekindled Israel's fears of a 'sell-out'—the sacrifice of her interests by Washington in an attempt to curry favour with the Arabs. It was a fear rooted in the Holocaust psychology of the Jewish State and periodically confirmed by Great-Power behaviour. United States attitudes during the missiles affair of August 1970 was a disturbing omen: she was slow to acknowledge Egypt's violations of the cease-fire; she minimized their gravity even after confirming Israel's charges; and she pressed Israel to return to the Jarring Talks nonetheless. The Rogers 'C' proposal, following upon Jarring's Memorandum of 8 February 1971, which was ascribed by Israel to US initiative, created a profound gloom about the reliability of Israel's bastion relationship with the super power of the West. US firmness in support of the pro-Arab territorial provisions of Rogers 'A' deepened Jerusalem's suspicion to the point of near-crisis on the eve of Prime Minister Meir's supplicant mission to the White House in December 1971.

That mission was successful in securing a presidential commitment to the resumption of the flow of aircraft, especially Phantoms, to Israel. Moreover, the scope and nature of US good offices in her proposed 'proximity talks' were clarified to Israel's partial satisfaction during discussions in December and January. As with Rogers 'B', Nixon's assurances and US clarifications led to an Israeli decision rescinding her earlier rejection of an American initiative. On 6 February 1972 the Cabinet decided to accept the US invitation to 'close proximity' talks, with a US official acting as the indirect link between Egyptian and Israeli representatives.[3]

The various proposals associated with the United States Secretary of State do not constitute a straight-line progression of interlinked ideas and plans.

Rogers 'A' was a comprehensive US outline of, if not blueprint for, a general Arab–Israel settlement. It was articulated in public after lengthy discussions with the Soviets, against the background of the

---

[1] *Ma'ariv*, 7 Oct. 1971.

[2] The text is in *Jerusalem Post*, 13 Oct. 1971. There was no formal vote. The formula of the Cabinet decision was drafted by Meir, Galili, and Assistant Government Secretary Dr. Nir. *Ha'aretz*, 13 Oct. 1971.

[3] The text is in *Jerusalem Post*, 7 Feb. 1972.

'war of attrition' and with an eye to the forthcoming Arab summit in Rabat. The US Government knew that on some important points no agreement had been reached with the USSR but it felt that there was a meeting of minds regarding many others.

Rogers 'B' shunned the substantive issues that had been postulated in Rogers 'A'. It confined itself to proposing procedures for negotiations between the parties under Jarring's auspices, reverting to the deliberately vague language of Security Council Resolution 242 on the purpose of the discussions. Moreover, its immediate, overriding, goal was to stop the fighting along the Suez Canal.

Rogers 'C' abandoned the attempt to reach a comprehensive 'overall' settlement in accordance with 242 and under Jarring's auspices, since the latter's Memorandum of 8 February 1971 (which excluded the border question from the scope of the negotiations by asking Israel to pre-pledge herself to total withdrawal) had been rejected by Israel. Rogers 'C', therefore, addressed itself to a defined, partial issue on the assumption and in the hope that tackling it would alleviate tension, would pave the way for further agreements, and would keep away from the presently insoluble 'theological' questions of an ultimate settlement.

In summary, Rogers 'A' was conceived as reflecting a US–Soviet consensus and was thus thought capable of securing acceptance by Arabs and Israelis. Rogers 'B' sought to utilize American leverage to activate an internationally (that is, Soviet) recognized mechanism for Arab–Israel negotiations, building on the convergence of interest in a cease-fire. And Rogers 'C' cut loose from the UN moorings. Except for the cease-fire, all initiatives remained a dead letter; but the launching of each filled a certain diplomatic void.[1]

Israel's *strategic* decision generated positive and negative feedback to three external components. The perception of those consequences and their environmental sources was pervasively negative: renewed disdain for the United Nations and mistrust of Jarring's intentions (G); *a priori* rejection of Arab statements affirming a willingness to make peace (S), in view of simultaneous statements to the contrary; and a broadening fear of abandonment by the United States (DB_1). All this flowed from Rogers 'B' despite the substantial benefits to the military and economic capability (M and E) components of Israel's operational environment.

Large-scale military aid was promised by the United States in the autumn of 1970, including 18 Phantoms, 115 Skyhawks, and 200

---

[1] The Israeli decisions relating to Rogers 'C' are not included in the testing of hypotheses and consequent findings—in chapter 9 below. That segment of the analysis of Israel's Foreign Policy System in action concludes with the decision to accept Rogers 'B' and the resultant cease-fire, in August 1970.

Patton tanks.[1] Foreign Minister Eban confirmed this by-product of the strategic decision: 'The years 1970–71 were the golden age in military supplies from the United States.'[2] In the economic sphere, too, the effect was marked—massive loans to finance Israel's military purchases, among others, and food supplies, totaling £1703 million in the period 1969–71, most of it following Rogers 'B' and the cease-fire. This was vital because Israel's defence budget reached its peak in 1971—£15·2 billion, comprising 40 per cent of total government expenditures and a staggering 26 per cent of GNP.[3] This dual strengthening of Israel's material capability led to an infusion of confidence, reflected in the articulated images of Israeli leaders. The flow of arms and aid persuaded them that Israel could successfully face a new military confrontation with her adversaries as well as absorb political pressures from the global system and DB relationships. Dayan summed this up on 15 October 1971 with the remark: 'I do not say we cannot be subject to pressures but I do say we cannot be squeezed ["like an orange" —Sadat's phrase] and forced to accept unacceptable things. Certainly not in 1971.'[4]

The political structure (PS) and the party system (CE), too, were affected by Israel's strategic decision—in both operational and psychological terms. The wall-to-wall Coalition was dissolved and the anomaly of a democratic polity without an Opposition came to an end. The NRP reacquired its balance-of-power role, with disproportionate influence in domestic affairs—in a Government comprising the Labour–*Mapam* Alignment, the Independent Liberals, and itself, with a majority of 76 seats in a *Knesset* of 120 members. Moreover, the struggle between incumbent and competing élites (Alignment and *Gahal*) was transferred from the Cabinet to the *Knesset*, thereby restoring the traditional polarization between the dominant *Mapai* wing of the Labour Party and *Herut* over foreign and security policy. However, the clash was much less sharp than over the issues of Germany—reparations (1951–2), arms (1957–8, 1959, 1960), and diplomatic relations (1965):[5] three years of association in the National Unity Government had softened the personal and policy antagonism, with Labour moving closer to the *Herut* hard line. A further consequence was greater manœuvrability in the conduct of Israel's foreign policy after three years of paralysis in decision-making in this issue-area.

The reality that an Israel Government could survive, even flourish, without *Gahal*, affected decision-makers' perceptions, too. It created

---

[1] Margalit, p. 114, based upon reports in the *Washington Post* and *New York Times* in October 1970, none of which was denied by US Government spokesmen.

[2] Interview on Israel's TV network, 13 Dec. 1971.

[3] *GBY 5732*, 1971–2 (Hebrew edition), pp. 48 and 66.

[4] To the Engineers' Club in Tel Aviv, *Jerusalem Post*, 17 Oct. 1971.

[5] See Brecher, ch. 16 (*b*) and (*c*), and ch. 3 above.

greater self-confidence among those in power and a potential for more flexibility in foreign policy initiatives. At the same time, the revival of a vociferous Opposition, in the form of *Gahal*'s strident criticism of the 'government of national disaster',[1] created a high-policy élite image of concern that flexibility might be interpreted in Israel as a concession to external pressure; and that, in turn, would reduce the Government's credibility in the eyes of the mass public. In addition to that restraining factor, many members of the Coalition had been persuaded that a hard line was just and sound.

Feedback from the strategic decision to interest groups (IG) may also be detected. The influence of all groups articulating foreign policy demands declined, notably that of the 'Greater Israel Movement' but also of the Left pressure groups such as *Matzpen*, *Siah*, and the Movement for Peace and Security. A brief flurry of interest in the protest of 35 Israeli 'doveish' academics and former civil servants, in late December 1971 and early January 1972, had no discernible effect on Israel's policy.[2] More generally, public opinion and pressure-group activity shifted dramatically and overwhelmingly from foreign to internal economic and social policy, a result of institutionalized tranquillity during the two years which followed the Rogers-initiated cease-fire. The influence of foreign-policy interest groups, never high, was reduced, as Israel's decision-makers perceived a declining concern with security matters: they could now ignore—even more confidently than usual—dissenting voices from Left and Right.

Several noteworthy shortcomings in Israel's decision-making process emerge from this inquiry. One is the lack of long-range—or, in fact, any—planning in foreign policy; and related to it is the insufficient recourse to expertise in decision-formulation and implementation. Thus on 31 July 1970 the Cabinet adopted a decision which went directly counter to a decision made by the Government on the identical issue six weeks earlier. In both cases improvisation was the dominant trait; planning was eschewed. The possibility that Egypt might accept Rogers 'B' was not seriously explored, for it violated deep-rooted perceptions and expectations. The result was unnecessary crisis. As Peres remarked: 'It is difficult to say that there was any planning in the Government on the subject of the US initiative. We didn't confer every day and we didn't plan long-run actions. We acted according to the needs of the situation.' A senior official observed: 'There has never been long-run policy planning in the Israel Government, and it is clear that the decision regarding Rogers Plan "B" was not unusual in this respect.' Equally conspicuous was the absence of preparatory and

[1] Begin's phrase the day the *Knesset* approved the decision to accept Rogers 'B'. *Yedi'ot Aharonot*, 5 Aug. 1970.

[2] The exchange of letters between Prof. Patinkin and Prime Minister Meir is to be found in *New Outlook*, 15, 1(129), Jan. 1972, pp. 4–7.

FIGURE 19

FEEDBACK: ROGERS PROPOSALS

Operational Environment	*Psychological Environment and Policy Derivatives*
External	*External*
G After brief enhancement of UN Representative's status, a sharp deterioration in Israel's relations with Jarring and UN generally and their consequent declining role as mediator in Arab–Israel conflict (S)	Deep-rooted mistrust of UN revived; its hostility perceived, especially in Jarring Memo of February 1971; policy consequence was to adopt negative posture to all efforts at 'overall' settlement in favour of 'partial' settlement (P–D)
S Cease-fire and consequent de-escalation of military conflict, and shift to political–diplomatic area, accompanied by wider fissure in Arab camp and intense vocal Egyptian threats of resumed war (S)	All real changes perceived, but persistent Arab threats given primacy in Israeli images, predisposed to mistrust Arab intent; policy derivative was continued hard line on terms of settlement, with PR emphasis on Arab threats (P–D, M–S)
DB Rejection of Rogers 'A' and, initially, of Rogers 'B' increased tension in Israel–US relationship, including calculated Washington delay in supply of military aid in first half of 1971 (T$_1$, T$_2$)	Tension and adverse effects perceived; policy derivative was to respond favourably to Nixon's assurances on military aid and his request for Israeli acceptance of Rogers 'B' (P–D, M–S)
US became principal active mediator in Arab–Israel conflict; continuing pressure on Israel to make concessions, slow Washington response to missiles affair (August 1970) and Rogers 'C's' six points led to recriminations	US role perceived as 'even-handed', with potential sellout of Israel; policy derivative was to make no concessions which might weaken Israel's advantages from strategically defensible boundaries arising from Six Day War, especially in light of apparent shift of US policy, in search of better relations with the Arabs (P–D, M–S)
Internal	*Internal*
M Qualitative strengthening of Israel's military capability from autumn 1970 onwards (S)	Flow of US arms strengthened self-assurance in ability to withstand external pressures—and corresponding policy of non-departure from Israel's conditions of peace (P–D, M–S)
E Large-scale United States economic aid eased Israel's balance-of-	Improved economic capability correctly perceived, resulting in added

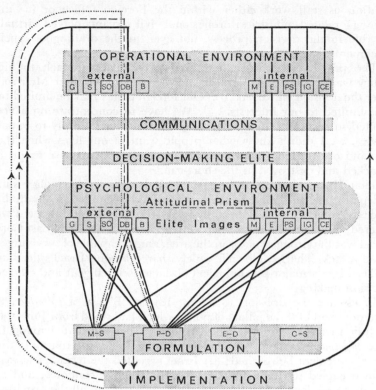

T_1 .... T_2 – – – – S ———

payments and general financial burden, caused by spiral of defence costs (S)	support for inflexible negotiating stance regarding 'partial' and 'overall' settlements (E–D)
PS Dissolution of National Unity Government, leading to normalization —*Gahal* in Opposition, smaller *Knesset* majority, and pivotal role of NRP in Coalition (S)	Image of need for wall-to-wall Coalition dispelled, leading to potential for greater flexibility and, in general, easier process of decision-making in foreign policy (P–D)
IG Influence of all interest groups advocating foreign policy demands declined, as attention shifted to internal social and economic problems (S)	Perception of change in interest-group focus of attention gave Government greater flexibility of manœuvre in foreign policy–security issue-areas (P–D)
CE Transfer of foreign policy disagreements to *Knesset* with result of increasing polarization between Alignment and *Gahal*, the incumbent and competing élites (S)	Policy consequence of perceived increase in polarization was less readiness for concessions, to avoid Opposition charge of betrayal (P–D)

continuous staff work either within the Foreign Office or in—and among—related ministries: professional civil servants played virtually no role in the decision process, not even in the drafting of crucial documents.

The pragmatic, short-sighted, purely reactive approach to high policy was acknowledged and defended by Prime Minister Meir soon after the decision on Rogers 'B': 'Our foreign policy may be limited but it is limited to our interests. . . . We have to concentrate on a very limited subject, according to all of us—in the worry simply to remain alive. . . . I didn't know what people want of our lives when they demand of us a long-run view when, at the same time, we might be attacked and destroyed in the short-run.'[1]

That Holocaust fixation has pervaded Israel's foreign policy since independence. Justifiable in the early years, it began to lose credibility after the Sinai Campaign; and in 1970, when the Meir statement was uttered, it was remote from the reality of power in the Near East Core; Israel was the strongest actor in the area, amply capable of surviving an Arab attack. The Meir belief, widely shared among Israel's decision-makers, was a major psychological obstacle to intelligent and efficient decision-making.

In essence the decision to accept Rogers 'B' was a *volte-face*, an abandonment of three pillars of policy which had stood from June 1967 to July 1970: (1) Israel reversed course on her insistent demand for *direct negotiations*, though her leaders continue to declare that only thus can a settlement be reached; (2) Israel accepted the term '*withdrawal*' from occupied territories and everything which it connotes; and (3) Israel agreed, for the first time, officially, to carry out all the provisions of Security Council *Resolution 242*, with its admonition, among others, against acquisition of territory by conquest. As such, Rogers 'B' challenged the bases of Israel's post-Six Day War policy. By deciding to accept it Israel decided to change her policy—a strategic decision of profound significance, with multiple feedback effects as noted. Yet the decision-makers rationalized the decision as marginal and consistent with past policy.

Meir told Parliament: 'These resolutions of the Government of Israel [regarding Rogers 'B'] are predicated on the principles of our policy over the years and conform to what has been the policy of the Government ever since the [1967] Cease-Fire. . . .'[2]

She also informed the Labour Party *Knesset* Caucus on 29 July 1970 that acceptance of the US proposal did not involve any concessions, for Israel would be bound only by her letter to Nixon which would specify Israel's reservations.[3]

---

[1] *Yedi'ot Aharonot*, 20 April 1970.
[2] *Divrei Ha-knesset*, lviii, 4 Aug. 1970, p. 2756; Meir (2), p. 5.
[3] *Yedi'ot Aharonot*, 30 July 1970.

Dayan perceived only procedural changes as a result of the strategic decision; and these he designated as acceptance of indirect negotiations and the term 'withdrawal'. They were of no practical importance because, as Meir asserted, Israel was bound only by her reservations in the letter to Nixon.[1]

Almost a year later the Defence Minister opined that Israel had never announced her readiness to withdraw.[2]

Galili, too, echoed Meir's view, that Israel's acceptance of Rogers 'B' was linked indissolubly to the reservations in her formal reply (though neither the US nor the UN nor any other party accepted the notion of qualified acceptance, a Talmudist rejection of the unpleasant reality of fundamental change in Israel's foreign policy).[3]

Eban remarked a month after the strategic decision: 'The Government's policy did not change. It is only exposed now in a clear and revealing way. . . . She did not decide, by accepting Rogers' initiative, to change her policy but to clarify it.'[4]

Allon replied to a question on the meaning of the decision: 'Israel did not betray her policy line since 1967; she only changed a move but in essence she did not change the line.'[5]

Objectively this may be termed collective self-delusion. Rogers Plan 'B' was merely Resolution 242 in a new garb. By accepting it Israel abandoned her (concealed) opposition to the UN formula for a settlement. If the reply to the US had been drafted properly, Israel's reservations would have constituted a separate and valid restraint on demands against her, notably by Jarring.

Two years after the Rogers-initiated cease-fire went into effect, the long-smouldering dispute over the conditions of peace erupted in Israel once more. The principal forum was a continuous debate within the Secretariat of Israel's multi-faction Labour Party. Finance Minister Sapir, leader of the doves, reportedly declared that he believed more strongly than ever before in his warning of 18 June 1967 that retention of the occupied territories and their inhabitants would lead to the strangulation of Israel. He spoke of the danger of 'the flooding of the labour market' by Arab workers—from the social, political, moral, and security aspects. Apart from the economic burden, he referred to the political implications: 'I disagree with those naive enough to think that higher living standards can compensate for national aspirations.'

[1] *Ma'ariv*, 9 Aug. 1970.   [2] Ibid., 18 June 1971.
[3] Interview on Israeli TV, 4 Sept. 1970, published in *Yedi'ot Aharonot*, 5 Sept. 1970.   [4] Eban (1)   [5] Interview, 1971.

'Is this the Jewish State we dreamed of and spilled blood for?', he asked, referring to a population projection of 1998, Israel's 50th anniversary—nine million persons, nearly half Arabs.

The other extreme within Israel's Labour Party leadership, Defence Minister Dayan's emphasis on 'establishing facts' in the territories until a peace settlement is reached, was pungently defended by Transport Minister Peres: 'If it's such a catastrophe, why are we still in the territories. . . . But if we are going to remain, then what are we going to do until the day of withdrawal?' And in support of Dayan's policy he declared: 'Neither we nor the Arabs have the same view of each other as before 1967.' Prime Minister Meir shared the hawkish Dayan view within the Labour Establishment. Her *éminence grise*, Galili, adopted a posture far more unyielding, which placed him close to the Greater Israel adherence.

Deputy Prime Minister Allon took a middle position: 'I believe in a peace settlement that will ensure us free access to the territories without our being directly in control.' Moreover, he expressed support, with reservations, for King Hussein's plan for a federation of Jordan and the West Bank.

Foreign Minister Eban urged that all options be left open. He reaffirmed most of Sapir's arguments, especially on the demographic threat to a Jewish Israel and, in that context, supported the Allon Plan, 'because it omits the heavily-populated areas in the West Bank'.[1]

Histadrut Secretary-General Yitzhak Ben-Aharon startled his colleagues by advocating unilateral withdrawal from an unspecified part of the occupied territories—'without receiving any kind of signature as a *quid pro quo* . . . [for] a kind of peace already exists though no signature of the other side confirms it'. His primary concern was a return to Jewish labour, which had built the Jewish state, and the eschewing of 'the exploitation of others or the expropriation of the national or political rights of others'. Like former Labour Party Secretary-General Lova Eliav, he advocated the creation of an independent Palestinian Arab state.[2]

The sharp division within the Labour Party, on the eve of Israel's twenty-fifth anniversary, was part of a national spectrum of political opinion on borders and related issues. Thus, for example, the second largest party in the coalition Government, the NRP, adopted a maxi-

---

[1] *Jerusalem Post*, 10, 24 Nov. 1972.

[2] The text of Ben-Aharon's speech, delivered on 1 Feb. 1973, is in *Jerusalem Post*, 14 Feb. 1973. Eliav's views are set out at length in *Eretz Ha-tzvi* (The Land of the Deer), Am Oved, 1972. The 'great debate', extending over 6 months and involving 80 speakers in 180 hours, ended on 12 April 1973 with the decision to make no formal departure from the Labour Party's 'Oral Law' of 1969. See *Jerusalem Post*, 13 April 1973. The sharp divisions between the 'doves', led by Sapir and Eban, and the 'hawks', led by Dayan and Galili, continued to reverberate through the mass media and at party meetings, with increasing intensity in the spring and summer of 1973.

malist position at its fourth national convention in March 1973: 'The
National Religious Party will be unable to share Government responsibility if a peace programme is tabled involving the sacrifice of parts of
the Land of Israel which is our ancestral heritage.'[1]

There were several shades within this policy spectrum, as evidenced
in Figure 20.[2]

FIGURE 20

POLICY SPECTRUM ON CONDITIONS FOR PEACE: SPRING 1973

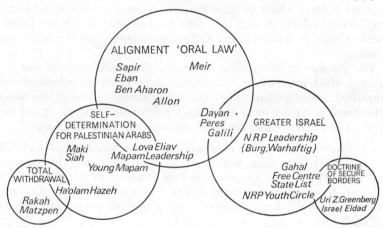

Essentially the division extended from the overwhelmingly Arab New
Communists (*Rakah*) and the revolutionary anti-Zionist *Matzpen*, who
called for complete Israeli withdrawal to the borders of 4 June 1967, to
extreme adherents of the Land of Israel Movement, who advocated
the retention of all territory acquired as a result of the Six Day War.
A few, like poet Uri Zvi Greenberg and former *Lehi* commander Israel
Eldad, went even further. These highly vocal competing advocacies
were prominently present in the setting for Israel's post-Rogers policy
towards a peace settlement.

[1] *Jerusalem Post*, 2 March 1973.
[2] This form of demarcating the competing views is set out in Ben Porat (2), p. 11

CHAPTER 9

Theory-Building and Research Findings

Intellectual inquiry has traditionally followed two basic paths. One is abstract theory, which disdains empirical research. The other is pure empiricism, which decries generalization or the search for pattern. Neither has been fruitful in the study of state behaviour in international systems.

The purpose of this book is theory-building. An approach has been created which attempts to combine the assets of theory orientation and empirical investigation. The synthesis, *structured empiricism*, is the refinement of earlier incursions into foreign policy theory. It has been applied in the preceding chapters, through the following stages:

(1) a framework capable of organizing, integrating, and analysing foreign policy data was used to illuminate one international actor's behaviour in seven diverse issues embracing twenty-one important decisions during a period of more than two decades;

(2) a viable multi-dimensional method of analysis was operationalized; and

(3) a large quantity of data which can be used to test hypotheses was systematically assembled.

The objective of hypothesis-testing is generalization or theory-building. We seek to discover, affirm, or confirm a relationship, that is, one which obtains for a number of non-identical occurrences, phenomena, processes, etc., which are artificially grouped for research purposes. The critical criterion of the *internal* validity of a hypothesis—did X have the effect?—is its capacity to predict in probabilistic terms. With respect to *external* validity, that is, to what else is the effect generalizable, the test is ability to predict *new* occurrences, phenomena, processes, etc. Thus, in foreign policy analysis it must be possible to predict the probable outcome of decision processes which have been investigated (internal validity) and those not yet investigated (external validity) but which clearly fall within the scope of definition of the given universe of data, i.e. foreign policy decisions. In short, the method used here requires that hypotheses tested with Israeli data be applied to comparable decisions—strategic or tactical—of other states. Only then can any of these hypotheses be regarded as valid building blocks for a theory of state behaviour. This inductive approach to theory is arduous but perhaps more potentially creative than pure model-building or atomic empiricism, so rampant in the international relations field.

There is an inherent subjective bias in such an enterprise and it is well to clarify one's predispositions. The very choice of strategic and tactical foreign policy decisions reflects the author's intellectual concerns—to describe, explain, and, within the limits already noted, to predict probable behaviour by decision-makers in foreign policy. That, in turn, derives from an assumption that knowledge about patterns of state behaviour would theoretically make possible a modest contribution to greater rationality by international actors in the pursuit of objectives; and that this would reduce the strain on the International System's capacity to manage and absorb conflict. In short, this book is marked by a subjective orientation to peace research.

There is another dimension to the subjectivity problem which must be aired. Evaluation of the results of hypothesis-testing is, frequently, interpretative; that is to say, it is often accompanied by explanation and reasoning of the non-mathematical type. The data are not always amenable to exact measurement; and assessment therefore contains, inevitably, an element of subjectivity, large or small. In the social sciences especially there are sharp differences of opinion as to the significance of empirical findings. This is not, however, a serious obstacle to the progression of empirically-based scientific propositions. A 'biased' evaluation can be challenged—and corrected—by peer-critics, those engaged in similar research. More important, interpretation of evidence can—and should—lead to supplementary or alternative hypotheses which give rise to a new round of empirical investigation and, ultimately, to modifications of theory. This conception of ceaseless interaction between research, hypothesis-generation, hypothesis-testing, and theory-building, the very essence of science, provides the rationale for the approach to the decision studies in this book. Along with its companion work, *The Foreign Policy System of Israel*, it was designed to demonstrate the vitality and potential of theory-oriented empirical research, that is, of structured empiricism, one type of empirical theory. This approach can be extended to the behaviour of any contemporary international actor and, if data are available, to actors in any historical international system.

The seven case studies revealed the presence of twenty-one strategic and tactical decisions; four of these are pairs. They may be recapitulated as follows:

Issue	Type of Decision	Symbol	Date	Decision
Jerusalem	1. Strategic	(S/Jer)	11 Dec. 1949	To make Jerusalem the seat of

Issue	Type of Decision	Symbol	Date	Decision
				Government (the official capital)
	2. Tactical	(T/Jer)	18 June 1967	To annex East Jerusalem and surrounding areas
German Reparations	3. Strategic	(S/GR)	3 Jan. 1951	To seek and to accept reparations for Jewish property plundered by the Nazi regime
	4. Tactical	(T/GR)	30 Dec. 1951	To recommend to the *Knesset* that Israel enter into direct negotiations with West Germany for reparations
Korean War –China	5. Tactical 1	(T$_1$/ K-C)	9 Jan. 1950	To accord *de jure* recognition to People's Republic of China
	6. Strategic 1	(S$_1$/ K-C)	2 July 1950	To support UN resolutions and actions taken in response to the outbreak of the Korean War
	7. Tactical 2	(T$_2$/ K-C)	(a) 25 May 1954	To postpone active pursuit of diplomatic relations with China until after Geneva Conference on Indo-China
			(b) 14 Nov. 1954	To dispatch an official trade

Issue	*Type of Decision*	*Symbol*	*Date*	*Decision*
				delegation to China
	8. Strategic 2 (S_2/ K-C)		28 Mar. 1955	To decline Peking's overtures for diplomatic relations at that time
Jordan Waters	9. Tactical 1 (T_1/ JW)		late July 1953	To begin work on diversion canal at Gesher B'not Ya'acov, in Israel–Syria Demilitarized Zone
	10. Strategic	(S/JW)	22 Feb. 1955	To accept Revised Unified Plan
	11. Tactical 2 (T_2/ JW)		post-18 Nov. 1959	To shift diversion point from Gesher B'not Ya'acov to Eshed Kinrot, at north-west corner of Lake Tiberias
Sinai Campaign	12. Tactical	(T/SC)	20 Sept. 1956	To co-ordinate military and political actions with France, with a view to waging war against Egypt
	13. Strategic 1 (S_1/SC)		25 Oct. 1956	To launch Sinai Campaign, to begin on 29 October
	14. Strategic 2 (S_2/SC)		8 Nov. 1956	To withdraw from occupied territory

Issue	Type of Decision	Symbol	Date	Decision
Six Day War	15. Tactical 1	(T₁/ SDW)	(a) 16 May 1967	To call up Tzahal reserves
			(b) 19 May 1967	To order large-scale mobilization of Tzahal reserves
	16. Tactical 2	(T₂/ SDW)	(a) 23 May 1967	To postpone a decision for 48 hours and to empower Foreign Minister to visit Washington
			(b) 28 May 1967	To continue with political response to crisis
	17. Tactical 3	(T₃/ SDW)	1 June 1967	To form National Unity Government
	18. Strategic	(S/ SDW)	4 June 1967	To take military action to terminate Arab 'stranglehold of aggression'
Rogers Proposals	19. Tactical 1	(T₁/RP)	(a) 10 Dec. 1969	To reject Rogers 'A'
			(b) 22 Dec. 1969	To reject Yost Document
	20. Tactical 2	(T₂/RP)	21 June 1970	To reject Rogers 'B'
	21. Strategic	(S/RP)	31 July 1970	To approve Rogers 'B'

All of the hypotheses were tested against the evidence of Israel's behaviour in the 21 decisions—where relevant. Where propositions were not relevant, these are noted. The results provide the basis for comparisons and for ranking along a scale of validity, with related clustering of hypotheses and decisions. Reliability tests were made by subjecting the findings to the independent reading of two colleagues, Professors Steinberg and Stein of McGill University. Reliability scores were 85 per cent and 80 per cent, respectively.

One interpretation of the conclusions of case studies, like those undertaken in this volume, is that they are based solely upon the behaviour of one among 130 state actors in the global system in 1973, or one among 55 in 1950, for a period of twenty years. Yet the prominence of that actor, Israel, as a focus of events, decisions by other actors, and conflict, as well as efforts at conflict-management, gives to her behaviour analytic value disproportionate to her size as a small, though economically developed, state of less than three million people —less than two million at the time most of these decisions were made. An alternative interpretation is that Israel is a member of a numerically large type of international actor, namely, a *new, middle power* in the global system, along the scale: super power, great power, middle power, small power.[1] As such, the findings from research on Israel's foreign policy behaviour have wide potential generalizability—perhaps to twenty-five states.[2]

From the myriad of propositions which have been generated in the recent literature of international relations, about 50 will be tested in the pages that follow.[3] They fall into two broad types. First and foremost is a set of hypotheses relating to images and foreign policy, including (a) the flexibility and intensity of images; (b) information and images; and (c) images and behaviour (decision-making). The other relates to state behaviour under crisis conditions; but that, too, includes frequent reference to the role of images in conflict situations. These categories of hypotheses are not mutually exclusive; in fact, they combine interactively. The rationale for the emphasis on images, it may be noted, is the fact that central to the framework of research in this volume, and the model within it, is the thesis that decision-makers' images constitute the causal link to foreign policy choices. And many of the hypotheses to be tested—18 of the 23 on general behaviour by actors—derive from the framework and its on-going application to decision analysis.

[1] In the contemporary international system states can be plotted along a continuum of capacity to influence the behaviour of other actors and the dynamics of the system as a whole. There are four broad categories: super powers, great powers, middle powers, and small powers. The place of any state in the power scale depends upon a combination of four components—size, population, military capability, and economic capability, the last two especially at the point in time of status designation. The super powers (US and USSR) possess all four components in such quality and quantity as to give them a unique veto over the survival of the system and all its members. The great powers (UK, France, Germany, China, and Japan) possess any three of the four so as to give their foreign policy decisions a far-reaching but less than total territorial impact. Small powers possess such a limited quantity of the four components that the effects of their foreign policy decisions are confined to their near-neighbours. All other states, whose foreign policy decisions influence either their own subordinate system as a whole or some facet of the global system, may be termed middle powers.

[2] This would also be so if one used the three Rosenau criteria for classifying international actors: size (large or small); type of polity (open or closed); type of economy (developed or underdeveloped). Rosenau, pp. 90–1.

[3] A continuing inventory of hypotheses exceeds 200, apart from the 311 noted in Hermann 1972, Appendix, containing a collection of studies of crisis behaviour.

A more significant classification of these hypotheses would be the universal and the particular. The first three sub-types apply to *the totality of foreign policy behaviour.* The last type refers to a specific, limited —and very important—arena of international relations decision-making, namely, state behaviour in the crisis phase of conflict situations.

The framework of research used in this study has built within it an embryonic model, with explicit parameters and conditions:

FIGURE 21
FOREIGN POLICY ANALYTIC MODEL[1]

Throughout, the hypotheses will be tested in terms of these parameters and conditions. Given a model with the parameters and conditions as specified above, one would expect that of the two broad types of propositions being examined with the evidence from Israel's foreign policy behaviour, those relating to *image and decision* would be largely supported.[2] Hypotheses unconcerned with image and decision

---

[1] Operational definitions of the parameters and conditions in this model are set out in Brecher 1974b.

[2] Image (or perception) comprises three interrelated aspects of psychological behaviour: recognition, that is, notice of incoming information; accurate (or inaccurate) absorption of messages, i.e. definition of the situation; and response to inputs in terms of stating actor goals. Image and perception have been used synonymously throughout. My term, 'image-component', is identical to Ole Holsti's term, 'image'. His broader designation, 'belief system', which seems to be the equivalent

have no theoretical grounds for one to expect that they should be valid in this study.[1]

A. HYPOTHESIS-TESTING

I. *General Foreign Policy Behaviour*

(a) *Flexibility and Intensity of Images*

Hypothesis (H) 1: 'The flexibility of an image seems to be an inverse function of the level of intensity.'[2]

Jerusalem
    Strategic decision: Supported
    Tactical decision: Supported

(**S and T/Jer**) Israel's decision-makers felt intensely about Jerusalem throughout; and their image of all external proposals and acts relating to that issue revealed marked rigidity. That image, in turn, predisposed them to inflexible decisions—in 1949 and 1967—in response to perceived threats or challenges, from the UN, super and great powers, the Vatican, in fact from the global system as a whole.

German Reparations
    Strategic decision: Not supported
    Tactical decision: Not supported

(**S and T/GR**) In 1950–2 Israel's high-policy élite evinced an intensely hostile image of Germany and the Germans, because of the unparalleled atrocities committed by them against European Jewry. 'Let not the murderers of our people be their inheritors as well', said Ben Gurion. Sharett, Meir, Joseph and others were no less forceful in articulating their negative image of Germany at the time. Yet in subsequent years most of these decision-makers manifested a striking flexibility in perception—Ben Gurion more than any other, but not excluding the most intensely hostile, Mrs. Meir.

Korean War–China
    Tactical decision 1: Supported
    Strategic decision 1: Supported
    Tactical decision 2 (a) and (b): Supported
    Strategic decision 2: Supported

(**T₁/K-C**) The image of China's Civil War held by Israel's decision-makers was almost one of indifference. This was accompanied by

---

of Kenneth Boulding's term, 'image', I have referred to, in this study and elsewhere, as 'view of the world'. These macro concepts have not been operationalized thus far.

[1] A quantitative assessment of the relative potency of external and internal inputs into Israeli decisions in the three principal conflict situations—Sinai Campaign, the Six Day War, and the War of Attrition—is to be found in Brecher 1974.

[2] Hypothesis 1 is from Pruitt, p. 411.

flexibility in image and response—to a regime with a hostile ideology: Israel accorded recognition to Peking as soon as it was possible for a then non-aligned state to do so.

(S_1/K-C) Israeli decision-makers did not manifest an intense image of the Korean War. And, while they subscribed to the US–UN interpretation of the origins of the war, Sharett and Eban displayed, for the most part, moderation and flexibility on that issue during the summer of 1950 to the spring of 1951, with a notable, though unsuccessful, initiative in mediation.

(T_2 and S_2/K-C) The image of China in 1954–5 held by Sharett and most other decision-makers was distant and tranquil, almost indifferent. This trait was accompanied by flexibility and uncertainty in their perception of China and her intentions.

Jordan Waters
    Tactical decision 1: Supported
    Strategic decision: Supported
    Tactical decision 2: Supported

(T_1, S and T_2/JW) The decision-makers' image of the Jordan Waters issue, including the Arab Plan and Arab attitudes, and of Johnston's role, was at a low level of intensity, though with continuous involvement and concern about water. It was also very flexible at most stages of the lengthy decision process. And that combined image—low intensity and high flexibility—led to moderation and compromise in the acceptance of the Revised Unified Plan and in the earlier and later decisions concerning the diversion point, all for pragmatic reasons.

Sinai Campaign
    Tactical decision: Not relevant[1]
    Strategic decision 1: Supported
    Strategic decision 2: Supported

(S_1/SC) Israeli images of Nasser, Egypt, and 'the Arabs' were very intense: they perceived them as determined to destroy Israel at the earliest feasible opportunity. That high level of intensity was accompanied by extreme rigidity of outlook. In the case of Ben Gurion an intense mistrust of British *bona fides* also correlated with extreme rigidity throughout the decision process leading to the Sinai Campaign, and even beyond.

(S_2/SC) The image of Soviet and US determination (5–8 November 1956) to compel Israel's withdrawal—by military intervention and economic sanctions respectively—was intensely held, especially by Ben

---

[1] The decision to align with France did not involve the dimensions of intensity or flexibility of image. Non-relevance of hypotheses to specific decisions may be due to several factors. The reasons for each designation, 'Not relevant', are not specified in this report on research findings.

Gurion. And that perception was accompanied by an unshakeable conviction that Israel must agree to withdraw, though he was willing to attempt to secure their acceptance of *conditional* withdrawal; and Israel did so.

Six Day War
    Tactical decision 1 (a) and (b): Supported
    Tactical decision 2 (a) and (b): Supported
    Tactical decision 3: Not relevant
    Strategic decision: Supported

(T_1, T_2 and S/SDW) The three-week crisis of 1967 reveals an increasingly intense decision-makers' image of Nasser and 'the Arabs' and, at the same time, a correlative rise in rigidity of perception. During the early days (14–18 May) they perceived a 'show of force' by Nasser, which did not constitute a serious threat to Israel's vital interests: their image was neither intense nor rigid. Change was apparent between 18 and 22/3 May, but even then their perception was one of controlled apprehension and relative flexibility. After the closure of the Straits a steady change took place in the intensity and rigidity of their images of Nasser's intentions: the 'Holocaust syndrome' became more and more conspicuous in the policy-makers' psychological environment, and with it a declining flexibility in response.

Rogers Proposals
    Tactical decision 1 (a) and (b): Supported
    Tactical decision 2: Supported
    Strategic decision: Supported

(T_1 and T_2/RP) Israel's decision-makers felt very intensely about Rogers 'A', the Yost Document, and Rogers 'B' (December 1969, June–July 1970). Their corresponding images were inflexible and their first two decisions were inflexible as well.

(S/RP) The acceptance of Rogers 'B' in July 1970 does not invalidate this assessment. The intensity level remained high, as did the inflexibility of image; but a perception of declining capability to withstand US pressure overcame high intensity and inflexibility and led to acquiescence.

H2: 'The rigidity of the image of the decision-making élite and the time lag will be greater than in the case of the attentive and mass publics.'[1]

Jerusalem
    Strategic decision: Not supported
    Tactical decision: Not supported

(S and T/Jer) Both the decision-makers and Israeli publics manifested

---

[1] Hypothesis 2 is from Brecher 1967, p. 91.

a consistently hostile and distrustful image of all external acts and resolutions directed to the Jerusalem issue from 1948 onwards. There was no evidence of flexibility by the decision-making élite or by any public, either during the strategic or tactical decision processes, in 1948–9 and 1967 respectively—or, in fact, at any time since independence.

German Reparations
    Strategic decision: Not relevant
    Tactical decision: Not supported
(T/GR) Ben Gurion, Sharett, and other high-policy decision-makers adapted much more quickly to the challenge posed by a Bonn offer of reparations in the autumn of 1951. Some sections of Israel's attentive and mass publics did so as well, but more haltingly, less decisively, and largely in response to the flexibility displayed by her political leadership. The hostile image of Germany, then and later, was retained more rigidly by the public than by the high-policy élite.

Korean War–China
    Not relevant

Jordan Waters
    Not relevant

Sinai Campaign
    Tactical decision: Not relevant
    Strategic decision 1: Not relevant
    Strategic decision 2: Not supported
(S₂/SC) Israeli attentive and mass publics shared the essential rigidity of the élite image of the Arabs: there is no discernible difference in flexibility during the prolonged implementation of the decision to withdraw—November 1956–March 1957.

Six Day War
    Tactical decision 1 (a) and (b): Not relevant
    Tactical decision 2 (a) and (b): Not supported
    Tactical decision 3: Not supported
    Strategic decision: Not supported
(T₂, T₃ and S/SDW) The image of the 1967 crisis held by Israeli attentive and mass publics was markedly more rigid than that of the decision-makers throughout. They expressed their dissatisfaction with the *Hamtana* (waiting) policy of the high-policy decision-makers and pressed for decisive action, especially during the period 27 May ff., after Eban returned from Paris, London, and Washington and after it had become increasingly apparent that: (a) external efforts were of no avail; and (b) the Arab threat was becoming more and more grave. They also contributed to the growing pressure for a National

Unity Government. They were, in short, less calm in their perception of the danger confronting Israel and more demanding in advocacy.

Rogers Proposals

Tactical decision 1 (a) and (b): Not relevant
Tactical decision 2: Supported (for Attentive Public)
Strategic decision: Supported (for Attentive Public)

(**T₂ and S/RP**) By the spring of 1970 highly vocal publics had made known their dissent from the Government's rigid stand on the terms of a peace settlement. Their demands for concessions in order to end the 'war of attrition' penetrated the consciousness of Israel's decision-makers and influenced their behaviour. The *mass* public, according to opinion polls, supported the Government's unchanging rigid policy. However, the image and advocacy of segments of the *attentive* public were far more flexible: they responded more *quickly* to changes in the operational environment. In fact, their role in the strategic decision was catalytic: the decision-makers responded to the critical Israeli attentive public, as well as to the United States.

(b) *Information and Images*

H3: 'The evidence from both psychology and history overwhelmingly supports the view that decision-makers tend to fit incoming information into their existing theories, and images. . . . In other words, actors tend to perceive what they expect.'[1]

Jerusalem

Strategic decision: Supported
Tactical decision: Not relevant

(**S/Jer**) Prime Minister Ben Gurion and most of his colleagues absorbed into their images the cumulative flow of information about the attitudes of UN, the super powers, the Vatican, and other actors towards the Jerusalem issue in 1948 and 1949. They expected hostility to Israel's establishment of the seat of government in Jerusalem—and they perceived hostility.

German Reparations

Strategic decision: Not relevant
Tactical decision: Supported

(**T/GR**) Ben Gurion absorbed the cumulative flow of information about West Germany's willingness to pay reparations (from April 1951 onward) into his images of: Israel's rightful claim; Germany's historic obligation; the demands of the 'Six Million'; Israel's economic

---

[1] Hypothesis 3 is from Jervis, p. 455. Complete validation or invalidation of H3 requires a negative test as well, namely, what information was rejected and its relationship to Israeli decision-makers' pre-existing images. This negative dimension of the information flow is unknown in the cases tested.

compulsions; and the primacy of Israel's security needs. The last two of these image-components were so vital to Ben Gurion as to enable him to submerge the competing image-components of Germany as 'the devil' nation and to respond flexibly to this information, as noted in H2. The other key decision-makers, Sharett and Kaplan, engaged in the same image response to information about Germany's attitude.

Korean War–China

    Tactical decision 1: Not relevant
    Strategic decision 1: Supported
    Tactical decision 2 (a) and (b): Supported
    Strategic decision 2: Supported

(S_1/K-C) For both Ben Gurion and Sharett the inflow of information about North Korea's attack on South Korea, as interpreted by the UN Security Council, was absorbed into an essentially Western, anti-communist view of the world. They expected 'aggression' from the communist North and perceived it. Moreover, Ben Gurion and Sharett perceived US pressure on Israel to 'stand up and be counted' when the Korean War broke out and the Security Council asked all UN member-states to furnish aid to the UN action. The information flow conformed to their existing image of US concern about the outcome in Korea. And Israel's response was profoundly influenced by their perception of Washington's commitment to the Seoul regime.

(T_2 and S_2/K-C) Both in 1954 and 1955 Sharett absorbed the flow of information from Israel's Washington embassy into his two-tiered image: (*a*) the United States would really regard Israel's establishment of diplomatic relations with the PRC as an unfriendly act, regardless of the disclaimer by the Under-Secretary of State; and (*b*) the US would respond with sanctions, if Israel proceeded. Similarly, the flow of information from Hacohen, Israel's Minister to Burma, was absorbed into an image of the Peking regime as not really wanting diplomatic relations with Israel. In short, basic mistrust led to a perception of ambiguity about Peking's intentions. This, in turn, created scepticism in Sharett's mind and a consequent high value on China's reciprocity—a mission to Israel—before he would make a decision on diplomatic relations.

Jordan Waters

    Tactical decision 1: Supported
    Strategic decision 1: Supported
    Tactical decision 2: Supported

(T_1 and S/JW) In the setting for both decisions, Israeli decision-makers expected Arab concessions and willingness to co-operate in a regional water plan, and they perceived an Arab move towards accommodation. Even the League's *de facto* rejection of the Revised Unified Plan was not seen, initially, as a final rejection: they expected differently and they so perceived, until after the spring of 1956. Ben Gurion was the most sceptical about Arab *bona fides* but he, too, advised acceptance of the Plan, expecting that it would lead to a breakthrough in the conflict as a whole.

(T_2/JW) When these expectations fell through, Israeli decision-makers perceived the situation correctly and decided to activate the National Water Carrier project (with the diversion point at Eshed Kinrot), in accordance with Israel's water allocation in the Revised Unified Plan.

Sinai Campaign
  Tactical decision: Supported
  Strategic decision 1: Supported
  Strategic decision 2: Supported

(T/SC) Israeli high-policy decision-makers on the Sinai issue, especially Peres, perceived France as friend, ally, trustworthy; and they incorporated the flow of information about and from France into their predispositional images.

(S_1/SC) Ben Gurion displayed this tendency in an acute form with regard to Britain and, particularly, to Eden's behaviour.

(S_2/SC) Ben Gurion's expectation of brutal behaviour by the Soviet Union governed his interpretation of the Bulganin letter and related acts, 5–8 November 1956. And, in his response to Eisenhower's communications during February–March 1957, Ben Gurion fitted information about the President's demands and assurances into his image of the United States as Israel's friend and patron.

Six Day War
  Tactical decision 1 (a) and (b): Supported
  Tactical decision 2 (a) and (b): Supported
  Tactical decision 3: Not relevant
  Strategic decision: Supported

(T_1/SDW) News of the Egyptian Army alert and the dispatch of troops to Sinai was absorbed into an image of demonstrative Arab behaviour, as in 1960. Israel's decision-makers expected this from past experience and, initially, perceived it as such.

(T_2 **and** S/SDW) The high-policy decision-makers perceived the US as a friend and absorbed all information about President Johnson's attitude in this light. Their expectations about UN ineffectiveness and the Secretary-General's hostility permeated their interpretation of all information about U Thant and the Security Council. The same pattern of information-flow into pre-existing images is apparent *vis-à-vis* Soviet and Arab behaviour. They had long expected from Moscow a nefarious role in escalating the crisis, along with its avoidance of direct military intervention, and they read the signals accordingly. Along with the short-term image of the 1960 scenario, they had always mistrusted Nasser's long-term intentions; stated differently, they had persistently expected an Arab assault at the first militarily possible opportunity; and, from the closure of the Straits onward, they interpreted all information about Arab actions as leading inevitably to war.

Rogers Proposals

Tactical decision 1 (a) and (b): Not relevant
Tactical decision 2: Not relevant
Strategic decision: Supported

(**S/RP**) High-policy decision-makers absorbed the news about Cairo's acceptance of Rogers 'B' as disingenuous, concealing the Arabs' pathological inability to arrive at a peace settlement with Israel. It was disbelieved, and Egypt's reservations were emphasized, her acceptance doubted. Secondly, the demand that Israel reply directly to the UN Representative (Jarring) conflicted with her prevailing image of the world body as pro-Arab; this, in turn, contributed to the decision to send Israel's acceptance of Rogers 'B' directly to the US Secretary of State. And thirdly, Israel attached special importance to Nixon's dispatch of 23 July 1970 because of her prevailing image of a friendly United States Chief Executive.

(c) *Images and Behaviour Patterns*

i. *Military-Security Issue-Area*

H4: 'There is no pre-eminent component in this issue-area. Rather, there are four key variables—military capability, interest groups, subordinate, and bilateral; and for developed states it comprises as well global and dominant-bilateral.'[1]

Sinai Campaign

Tactical decision: Not supported
Strategic decision 1: Supported
Strategic decision 2: Supported

(**T/SC**) Ben Gurion's decision to align with France was dominated by the perceived imbalance of military capability resulting from the Soviet arms flow to Egypt and Syria: M was the pre-eminent component.

(**S₁/SC**) The decision to launch the Sinai Campaign was the outcome of diverse inputs, all of them within an attitudinal prism dominated by a rigid image of Nasser as Israel's enemy, as noted in relation to H1: M—a perceived shift in the balance of weaponry in the Arabs' favour; S—escalating border violence; B—the tacit alliance with France as a pre-condition to action; G—the UN's failure to tranquillize

---

[1] Hypotheses 4–20 are from Brecher, Steinberg and Stein, pp. 91–3.

the conflict; and IG—public opinion pressure at home to end the *feda'iyun* raids.

(S₂/SC) The American and Soviet factors (DB) were the most decisive inputs into the decision of 8 November 1956 to agree to withdraw. But there were others: M—the known inability to deter massive Soviet bombing of Israel's cities; B—French advice to yield because of that military weakness; G—United Nations and global-system pressure; and even the urging of Jewish leaders in the United States.

Six Day War
    Tactical decision 1 (a) and (b): Not relevant   ᴹ
    Tactical decision 2 (a) and (b): Not relevant
    Tactical decision 3: Not relevant
    Strategic decision: Supported

(S/SDW) The decision of 4 June to go to war was the result of diverse inputs: S—destabilization of the Near East Core through Egypt's (Soviet) military build-up and, especially, Moscow's goading of Egypt into militant behaviour, intra-Arab rivalries, escalating *feda'iyun* raids, etc.; B—Nasser's direct challenge to the 1957 UN settlement, symbolized by the presence of UNEF in the Gaza Strip, Sinai, and Sharm-e-Sheikh; G—the UN's failure to de-escalate the crisis, to provide a face-saving formula for Egypt's withdrawal from the brink, or to prevent the threat from exploding into war; DB—the vital role of the 'American factor' throughout the period 23 May–4 June; IG—the pressure of *Tzahal* officers for a decision; and M—the military balance, which created concern, though not alarm. None of these components was pre-eminent; all operated in both operational and psychological environments to influence the strategic decision.

    All other decision clusters: Not relevant   ᴹⁱˡ

H5: 'Élites of developed states have a sharp awareness of the global system and of dominant-bilateral relationships.'[1]

Sinai Campaign
    Tactical decision: Not relevant
    Strategic decision 1: Supported
    Strategic decision 2: Supported

(S₁/SC) In the decision process leading to the Sinai Campaign Ben Gurion revealed an acute perception of what harm the Soviet Union could do if she dispatched 'volunteers' to assist Egypt.

(S₂/SC) The UN factor was marginal, but the dominant-bilateral pressures—inducements and threats from Washington, along with

---

[1] Support for this hypothesis does not *ipso facto* constitute validation of the reverse, namely, that *developing state's* élites are *not* sharply aware of the global system and dominant-bilateral relationships. More generally, support for Hypotheses 5, 9, 10, 14, 16 refers only to *positive* linkages between development and other image variables.

threats from Moscow—weighed very heavily in the decision to agree to withdraw.

Six Day War

    Tactical decision 1 (a) and (b): Not relevant
    Tactical decision 2 (a) and (b): Not relevant
    Tactical decision 3: Not relevant
    Strategic decision: Supported

(S/SDW) Israel's decision-makers were acutely aware of global-system behaviour, through the United Nations—the withdrawal of UNEF, the Secretary-General's mission to Cairo, the Security Council debates at the end of May and in early June 1967. They were even more conscious of the 'American factor', especially the President's role, from 23 May onwards. And concern about the extent and forms of the other super-power's intervention was widespread in Israel's high-policy and technical élites, among ministers like Dayan, Aranne, and Sapir, the Foreign Office Director-General, Levavi, and others.

    All other decision clusters: Not relevant

H6: 'In most cases, the pre-eminent interest group is the armed forces establishment.'

Sinai Campaign

    Tactical decision: Supported
    Strategic decision 1: Supported
    Strategic decision 2: Not relevant[1]

(T/SC) It was Peres and the Defence Ministry Establishment which took the initiative in 1954–5 towards a tacit alliance with France.

(S_1/SC) It was Peres and Dayan, the latter representing the higher officer corps interest group of *Tzahal*, who urged, recommended, and pressed Ben Gurion in the direction of the decision to launch the Sinai Campaign.

Six Day War

    Tactical decision 1 (a) and (b): Supported
    Tactical decision 2 (a) and (b): Supported
    Tactical decision 3: Not relevant
    Strategic decision: Supported

(T_1, T_2 and S/SDW) Pressure by *Tzahal* officers was brought to bear

---

[1] The S_2 decision was made within 30 hours and, as H34 will amplify, interest-group influence was minimal. During the lengthy implementation of S_2 (November 1956–March 1957) several groups were opposed to actual withdrawal, notably *Herut*, *Ahdut Ha'avoda*, and, with respect to Gaza, *Mapam*. However, the interest group whose advocacy was perceived by Ben Gurion as most relevant was that of a group of army officers in March 1957, headed by *Aluf* Laskov—further verification of H34. This case illustrates the complementary relationship of time and issue-area as variables affecting the influence of interest groups in foreign-policy decisions.

directly on the decision-makers—by reports at Government meetings on the strategic situation, by conversations with individual ministers and politicians, and, especially, by their confrontation with the Prime Minister on 28 May. The mobilization decisions (T_{1a} and T_{1b}) were directly influenced by *Tzahal* advice. The first *Hamtana* decision (T_{2a}) on 23 May—to delay for 48 hours—was influenced by the advice of Rabin and other officers that nothing would be lost by waiting. Public opinion was also gravely concerned as the crisis continued, but army officers were certainly the pre-eminent *organized interest group* in the setting and the process for decision, as distinct from competing élites (political parties) or the mass public.

All other decision clusters: Not relevant

H7: 'Decision-makers perceive their own subordinate system as the level of the international system most directly impinging on vital questions of security.'

Sinai Campaign
    Tactical decision: Supported
    Strategic decision 1: Supported
    Strategic decision 2: Supported
(T, S_1 and S_2/SC) While more or less emphasis was placed on Egypt or Jordan, it is the Near East Core, that is, the subordinate system as a whole, which was perceived during the Sinai issue as the primary level concerning Israel's security.

Six Day War
    Tactical decision 1 (a) and (b): Supported
    Tactical decision 2 (a) and (b): Supported
    Tactical decision 3: Supported
    Strategic decision: Supported
(T_1, T_2, T_3 and S/SDW) Throughout the 1967 crisis Israel's decision-makers perceived the Near East Core as central to their environment, with its grave, escalating threat to Israel's vital interests. The global level was distinctly marginal. And bilateral relationships, including those with super powers, were important as impinging upon the conflict *within* the Middle East *subordinate system*, raising or tranquillizing tensions, stabilizing or destabilizing the arms balance, etc. It was the behaviour of Israel's Arab neighbours within the Core of that system which constituted the decisive input into all her decisions from 16 May to 4 June 1967.

All other decision clusters: Not relevant

H8: 'Awareness of economic capability and concern with its enhancement do not impinge significantly on élite perceptions in the military-security issue-area.'

Sinai Campaign
   Tactical decision: Supported
   Strategic decision 1: Supported
   Strategic decision 2: Supported
(**T/SC**) Israel's alignment with France in 1956 was not induced at all by economic considerations.

(**S₁/SC**) There is some evidence of a Ben Gurion perception that freedom of passage through the Tiran Straits would facilitate oil imports from Iran and, indirectly, bring economic benefits to Israel through growing relations with the countries of Asia and Africa. But this was not a significant component in his image. And it was not articulated by Meir or Peres. Dayan mentioned it, marginally, in his analysis of the significance of freedom of navigation through the Straits.

(**S₂/SC**) The US threat of economic sanctions was clearly perceived as of more than marginal relevance—but it did not determine the crisis decision of 8 November 1956 to agree to withdraw from conquered territory.

Six Day War
   Tactical decision 1 (a) and (b): Not relevant
   Tactical decision 2 (a) and (b): Not relevant
   Tactical decision 3: Not relevant
   Strategic decision: Not supported
(**S/SDW**) Élite perceptions during the 1967 crisis were not overtly concerned with the *enhancement* of economic capability. At the same time, decision-makers perceived the economic *cost* of drawing a large segment of Israel's labour force into military service from 18 May onwards. During the last phase of the crisis, as the economic drain mounted, that component became more salient in decision-makers' images—affecting the sense of urgency and the *timing* of Israel's strategic decision.
   All other decision clusters: Not relevant

ii. *Political-Diplomatic Issue-Area*

H9: 'Developed states' élites have a much sharper awareness of dominant-bilateral relations than of their regional system characteristics and pressures.'

Korean War–China
   Tactical decision 1: Supported
   Strategic decision 1: Not supported
   Tactical decision 2 (a) and (b): Supported
   Strategic decision 2: Supported
(**T₁/K-C**) The decision to recognize the Peking regime in 1950 was based primarily on global system considerations—non-alignment, China's importance in world politics, the principle of recognizing

political reality everywhere. Nonetheless, there was an awareness of opposition from Washington, a DB relationship. The decision was not made in terms of Middle East system pressures.

(S_1/K-C) Ben Gurion and Sharett were acutely conscious of the implications—both as precedent and as spillover—of the Korean War for the Arab–Israeli conflict; that is, regional system pressures were decisive in the support given by Israel to US–UN actions *vis-à-vis* Korea in 1950–1. Their desire not to alienate the US was a function of their security goal in a regional system of protracted conflict.

(T_2 and S_2/K-C) The decline of Peking's overtures was due primarily to Sharett's perception of the 'American factor' (DB). In concrete terms this meant fear of possible US sanctions, in the form of less economic aid and political support for Israel in the persistent conflict with her adversaries. There were other components in the psychological environment, but the perceived impact of possible US alienation on Israel's vital interests, not the Middle East system *per se*, was decisive in his choice.

Rogers Proposals
    Tactical decision 1 (a) and (b): Supported
    Tactical decision 2: Supported
    Strategic decision: Supported

(T_1 and T_2/RP) Israeli decision-makers accorded the highest rank to the DB relationship—Meir, Galili and Eban to the United States, Dayan to the Soviet Union; and for Allon and Dayan the US relationship ranked second.

(S/RP) Only Allon, among the high-policy decision-makers, attached significance to the subordinate system dimension, perceiving Egypt's and Jordan's acceptance of Rogers 'B' in July 1970 as a symbol of fundamental change in their attitudes to peace with Israel. For all the other decision-makers the relationship with a super power (DB_1) and concern about the possible decline of military support (M) were paramount. And even in the Deputy Prime Minister's image those two linked components ranked very high.

    All other decision clusters: Not relevant

H10: 'To the extent that decision-makers of developed states perceive their internal environment, they attach greatest importance to the advocacy by competing élites and interest groups.'

Korean War–China
    Tactical decision 1: Supported
    Strategic decision 1: Supported
    Tactical decision 2 (a) and (b): Supported
    Strategic decision 2: Supported

(T_1/K-C) Israel's leftist parties, *Mapam* and *Maki*, were active pressure groups on the China issue in the autumn of 1949, the only internal component that her decision-makers perceived in the process of deciding to recognize the People's Republic of China.

(S_1/K-C) In the 1950 Korean War case the internal environmental component which was most visibly relevant to the decision was, once more, CE advocacy (which incorporated all leftist non-organized interest group advocacy as well).

(T_2 and S_2/K-C) The same is true of the China decisions in 1954–5. Competing élite advocacy did not shape any of these decisions but it was perceived as pertinent.

Rogers Proposals
  Tactical decision 1 (a) and (b): Not relevant
  Tactical decision 2: Not relevant
  Strategic decision: Not supported

(S/RP) The probable effect on military capability (M) ranked highest among internal variables in the decision of July 1970 to accept Rogers 'B'. The advocacy by *Gahal* and the 'Greater Israel Movement', on the one hand, and by *Mapam* and the Left interest groups calling for compromise, on the other, were recognized by decision-makers and helped to shape their behaviour on Rogers 'B', but they were less important than M.

  All other decision clusters: Not relevant

H11: 'Foreign policy élites in both developed and developing states attach marginal weight to four variables in this issue-area: other subordinate systems, political structure, economic capability, and military capability.'

Korean War–China
  Tactical decision 1: Supported
  Strategic decision 1: Supported
  Tactical decision 2 (a) and (b): Not supported
  Strategic decision 2: Not supported

(T_1/K-C) None of these components is apparent in the calculus of Israeli decision-makers relating to the decision to recognize Peking in 1950.

(S_1/K-C) In the 1950 Korean War case Israel's decision-makers were concerned about the possible adverse effect of continued non-identification on US economic aid; but it was not decisive; and the other three components were irrelevant.

(T_2 and S_2/K-C) In the China decisions of 1954–5, Sharett was influenced during the early stage by warnings from the embassy in Washington of serious damage to Israel's economic capability if she pursued the path to diplomatic relations with Peking. He was also influenced by the uncertain consequence for the stability of his coalition Government of opposition within his own *Mapai* party and from the General Zionists.

Rogers Proposals

   Tactical decision 1 (a) and (b): Supported
   Tactical decision 2: Supported
   Strategic decision: Not supported

(T_1 and T_2/RP) Only one of these components, the perceived adverse effect on Israel's security, that is, her military capability, was relevant to the decisions to reject Rogers 'A' and, initially, Rogers 'B'.

(S/RP) In their July 1970 approach to Rogers 'B' Israel's decision-makers were conspicuously concerned with the adverse effect of renewed rejection on Israel's political structure and on her military and economic capability. The second of these was important and the other two were more than marginal.

   All other decision clusters: Not relevant

iii. *Economic-Developmental Issue-Area*

H12: 'The economic variable is pre-eminent for both developed and developing states.'

German Reparations

   Strategic decision: Supported
   Tactical decision: Supported

(S and T/GR) For Ben Gurion, Sharett, Kaplan and others, Israel's grave economic condition in 1950–1 was the pre-eminent *short-term* image-component: it shaped both decisions—to seek and accept German reparations and to negotiate directly with the Bonn regime.

Jordan Waters

   Tactical decision 1: Supported
   Strategic decision: Not supported
   Tactical decision 2: Not supported

(T_1/JW) The decision to divert Jordan water at Gesher B'not Ya'acov (1953) was taken solely on economic grounds—lesser cost and greater purity of water than at other possible diversion points.

(S/JW) Eshkol, Sharett, and Ben Gurion, especially the first, attached great importance to increasing Israel's water supply. However, both Sharett and BG were much more conscious of the political implications of an Arab–Israel agreement on water. They were, in fact, willing to make what they perceived to be 'sacrifices'—acceptance of the Revised Unified Plan (1955)—in order to achieve an accommodation with hostile neighbour states.

(T_2/JW) The decision to shift the diversion point to Eshed Kinrot, outside the Demilitarized Zone, was made solely on political grounds, with the full knowledge of higher costs to be incurred.

All other decision clusters: Not relevant

H13: 'There is one notable disparity in élite images within this issue-area: decision-makers of developed states are acutely conscious of interest-group demands; decision-makers of developing states are not.'[1]

German Reparations

Strategic decision: Not relevant
Tactical decision: Supported

(**T/GR**) In the decision process on reparations Ben Gurion, Sharett, and other high-policy élite members acknowledged both the legitimacy and the genuineness of demands articulated by interest groups, especially those opposing direct talks with West Germany—even though they did not acquiesce in their demands. Sharett's speech to the *Knesset* on 9 January 1952 devoted special attention to these interest-group views.

Jordan Waters

Tactical decision 1: Supported
Strategic decision: Supported
Tactical decision 2: Not relevant

(**T₁ and S/JW**) Eshkol and Sapir in particular, but all decision-makers on the Jordan Waters issue, were the object of demands by *kibbutzim* and *moshavim*. This advocacy was regarded as legitimate; and the articulated needs of agricultural settlements weighed heavily in their calculations.

All other decision clusters: Not relevant

H14: 'Decision-makers of developed states are more aware of pressure from interest groups than from competing élites.'

German Reparations

Strategic decision: Not relevant
Tactical decision: Not supported

(**T/GR**) The distinction between these two institutional types of advocacy was blurred in the reparations case: parties and pressure groups of both persuasions united into two coalitions struggling for majority support.

Jordan Waters

Tactical decision 1: Not relevant
Strategic decision: Supported
Tactical decision 2: Not relevant

---

[1] The second part of this hypothesis is not tested here; but other evidence, based upon the author's research into developing areas, tends to support it.

(S/JW) Parties, especially *Herut* and *Mapam*, periodically expressed strong criticism of Israel's posture during the Johnston talks—1953-5. Little, if any, attention, however, was given to this advocacy, in contrast to the effective though quiet transmission of demands by water-conscious agricultural settlements, the principal interest group on Jordan Waters.

All other decision clusters: Not relevant

H15: 'Four environmental variables are marginal or non-existent in élite images within this issue-area: political structure, subordinate other, military capability, and bilateral.'

German Reparations
    Strategic decision: Not supported
    Tactical decision: Not supported
(S and T/GR) All but the second of those four components were highly salient in the images of Ben Gurion, Sharett, *et al.* during the decision process of 1950-2.

Jordan Waters
    Tactical decision 1: Supported
    Strategic decision: Supported
    Tactical decision 2: Supported
(T_1, S and T_2/JW) None of these variables was salient to Israel's decisions on Jordan Waters—in 1953, 1955, or 1959.
    All other decision clusters: Not relevant

iv. *Cultural-Status Issue-Area*

H16: 'Élites in developed states attach greater weight to the external environment than to internal variables.'

Jerusalem
    Strategic decision: Supported
    Tactical decision: Not supported
(S/Jer) External pressures, from all components of the environment, shaped Israeli élite images in 1948-9 and the consequent decision to make Jerusalem the seat of government. To the extent that internal advocacy was relevant, it came from competing élites, notably *Herut*, and the Jerusalem Jewish community as an interest group. However, it required an external (UN) challenge to induce the decision.

(T/Jer) The incumbent élite perceived the intense activity not only of interest groups, but also of competing élites and public opinion. In fact, the nation as a whole pressed for, and/or enthusiastically supported, the integration of East and West Jerusalem in June 1967.
    All other decision clusters: Not relevant

v. Cross-Issue-Area

H17: 'The distinction between articulation and aggregation is far less meaningful in a foreign policy system than in a domestic policy system. "Advocacy" in a foreign policy system is performed without functional differentiation by interest groups and competing élites.'

Jerusalem

Strategic decision: Supported
Tactical decision: Not relevant

(S/Jer) Pressure in 1948–9 to make Jerusalem the seat of government came primarily from two sources—*Herut*, a competing élite, and Jerusalem Jewry, an institutional interest group. Other political parties, as well as independent newspapers (associational interest groups), also pressed for the decision. There was no differentiation in performance of the advocacy function on that issue. (The unification decision of June 1967 was not accompanied by distinctive group advocacy; it was based on a national consensus.)

German Reparations

Strategic decision: Not relevant
Tactical decision: Supported

(T/GR) In 1951–2 there was passionate advocacy against direct Israeli negotiations with Germany—by competing élites, notably *Herut, Mapam*, and *Maki*, and by associational interest groups, especially the partisan and ghetto-fighter organizations. These institutional carriers of group demands coalesced on the reparations issue and performed an identical advocacy function—to reject Germany's offer of compensation.

Korean War–China

Tactical decision 1: Not supported
Strategic decision 1: Not supported
Tactical decision 2 (a) and (b): Not supported
Strategic decision 2: Not supported

(T_1, S_1, T_2 and S_2/K-C) There was occasional advocacy by Left parties: to recognize Peking in the autumn of 1949; to remain aloof on the Korean War; to establish diplomatic relations with Peking, in 1954–5. There was, however, no autonomous interest-group activity: it was all subsumed in the aggregating function of the Left parties.

Jordan Waters

Tactical decision 1: Not relevant
Strategic decision: Supported
Tactical decision 2: Not relevant

(S/JW) Both interest groups, notably agricultural settlements, and political parties, advocated demands for more water and the safeguarding of Israel's sovereignty, during the period of the Johnston negotiations (1953–5). There was no distinction in the nature of their role; parties did not aggregate interest-group demands.

Sinai Campaign

 Tactical decision: Not relevant
 Strategic decision 1: Not relevant
 Strategic decision 2: Not supported

(S_2/SC) During the lengthy process of implementation, November 1956–March 1957, many of Israel's political parties advocated retention of territory acquired as a result of the Sinai Campaign. The only interest group to convey pressure, quietly, was *Tzahal* officers, led by Laskov. It displayed functional differentiation both in performance and perception.

Six Day War

 Tactical decision 1 (a) and (b): Not relevant
 Tactical decision 2 (a) and (b): Not relevant
 Tactical decision 3: Supported
 Strategic decision: Supported

(T_3/SDW) Pressure to form a National Unity Government (24 May–1 June 1967) was mounted by a wide spectrum of societal groups: political parties—*Rafi*, NRP, *Gahal*; politicians within the largest Coalition party, *Mapai*; economic interest groups; associational interest groups (newspapers); and public opinion. To some extent parties aggregated diverse, more specific, channels of interest articulation. For the most part, however, parties and interest groups engaged in autonomous, complementary advocacy of a wall-to-wall coalition Government.

(S/SDW) The pressure for a military response to Nasser's closing of the Tiran Straits emanated from diverse parties and interest groups, including, among the latter, senior *Tzahal* officers. The same pattern as with T_3 is evident, that is, a political party aggregation function, in small part, along with autonomous, complementary streams of advocacy by competing élites and interest groups.

Rogers Proposals

 Tactical decision 1 (a) and (b): Not relevant
 Tactical decision 2: Not relevant
 Strategic decision: Supported

(S/RP) Pressure to accept Rogers 'B' in June–July 1970—after its initial immediate rejection by the Government—came from interest groups like *Siah*, *Matzpen*, university teachers, and Dr. Goldmann, and from parties like *Mapam*, the Independent Liberals, *Maki*, and *Rakah*. These were complementary channels of advocacy, not aggregated demands by parties. Among those who advocated rejection, it was a specialized interest group, the 'Land of Israel Movement', not a political party, *Herut*, which performed the function of aggregating demands.

H18: 'The role of military or economic capability in the image of middle-power foreign policy élites will be marginal except in those decisions that are specifically military or economic in content.'[1]

Jerusalem

Strategic decision: Supported

Tactical decision: Supported

(**S and T/Jer**) There is no evidence that Israeli decision-makers, in 1949 or 1967, perceived military or economic capability as relevant to their decisions—to make Jerusalem the seat of government, and to unify East and West Jerusalem. If anything, they perceived these acts as economic liabilities, which were merited on other grounds.

Korean War–China

Tactical decision 1: Supported

Strategic decision 1: Not supported

Tactical decision 2 (a) and (b): Not supported

Strategic decision 2: Not supported

(**T_1/K-C**) Israel's military and/or economic capability were not part of the operational image leading to the January 1950 recognition of the PRC.

(**S_1, T_2 and S_2/K-C**) The decision to support the UN–US response to the Korean War, and the decisions not to pursue, actively, diplomatic relations with Peking, were all profoundly influenced by the 'American factor'; in particular, by the image of diminution of US military and economic aid, if contrary choices in policy were made.

All other decision clusters: Not relevant, German Reparations and Jordan Waters because they were economic in content, Sinai Campaign, Six Day War, and Rogers Proposals because they were military/ security in content.

H19: 'Decision-makers of middle powers will be marginally influenced in their decisional choice by their own political structure.'

Jerusalem

Strategic decision: Supported

Tactical decision: Supported

(**S and T/Jer**) Israel's political structure provided a supportive element in the 1949 and 1967 decision processes; but it was not central to decision-makers' images.

[1] As with H3, a complete validation of H18 would require a negative test, that is, to determine whether the marginality of these components is unique or applies as well to super, great, and/or small powers.

German Reparations
Strategic decision: Not supported
Tactical decision: Not supported
(**S and T/GR**) Israel's high-policy decision-makers were acutely conscious of the *Knesset*'s importance on the reparations issue—in the light of the anticipated (1950) and actual (1951) massive division of opinion in the nation. The consequences of proportional representation made such awareness inevitable.

Korean War–China
Tactical decision 1: Supported
Strategic decision 1: Supported
Tactical decision 2 (a) and (b): Supported
Strategic decision 2: Supported
(T_1, S_1, T_2 and S_2/K-C) There is some evidence that Sharett's 1954–5 decisions not to proceed actively in pursuit of diplomatic relations with Peking were influenced by the character of the Coalition, particularly the presence of a strong anti-communist General Zionist element. At the same time it had a marginal effect on his images and decisions.

Jordan Waters
Tactical decision 1: Supported
Strategic decision: Supported
Tactical decision 2: Supported
(T_1, S and T_2/JW) The political structure had no influence in the decisions to divert at Gesher B'not Ya'acov, to accept the Revised Unified Plan, and to shift the diversion point for the National Water Carrier.

Sinai Campaign
Tactical decision: Supported
Strategic decision 1: Supported
Strategic decision 2: Supported
(**T and S_1/SC**) In making both decisions Ben Gurion totally ignored Israel's political structure. In fact, the decisions were maintained in utter secrecy until authorization became necessary; then the Government was informed.
(S_2/SC) Nor did the political structure as such influence the decision to withdraw, though the Cabinet role on 8 November was more important than in the earlier decisions.

Six Day War
Tactical decision 1 (a) and (b): Not relevant
Tactical decision 2 (a) and (b): Not supported
Tactical decision 3: Not supported
Strategic decision: Not supported
(T_2, T_3 and S/SDW) The political structure, in the form of a split

coalition Cabinet, was important in the decisions to delay and to form a National Unity Government. It became a decisive input into the strategic decision. The growing demand for a wall-to-wall Coalition, including *Rafi* and *Gahal*, from 24 May onward, was a focus for the more fundamental debate within the decision-making élite—and the nation at large—over the correct form of response to Nasser's threat. The victory of the 'pro-changers' and the consequent formation of a National Unity Government on 1 June was a manifestation of the influence of the political structure in the 1967 decision-making process as a whole.

Rogers Proposals
    Tactical decision 1 (a) and (b): Supported
    Tactical decision 2: Supported
    Strategic decision: Not supported
(T_1 and T_2/RP) The PS component was not present in the images pertaining to these instantaneous decisions.
(S/RP) There was great concern about the effect of a break-up of the National Unity Government on Israel's political stability. Although that perceptual component did not prevent the affirmative decision on Rogers 'B' in July 1970, the character of Israel's political structure was influential in the decision-making process—both its duration and its intensity.

H20: 'The much publicized view that the maximization of power, defined as military and economic capability, is the chief motivating factor in state behaviour is invalid for middle powers.'

Jerusalem
    Strategic decision: Supported
    Tactical decision: Supported
(T and S/Jer) The maximization of power was wholly irrelevant to Israeli decision-makers' images and to the Jerusalem decisions of 1949 and 1967. On the contrary: the consequences were recognized to be a power liability as a result of alienating international actors, including the world organization, the two super powers, and many other states. The decisions were dominated by a pervasive attitudinal prism of Jewishness and the historic-religious-national links of Jerusalem to the Jewish People.

German Reparations
    Strategic decision: Not supported
    Tactical decision: Not supported
(S and T/GR) Israel's decision-makers perceived reparations in the short run as a means of easing grave economic problems: their decisions were dominated by: (a) the prism of Jewishness, that is, the sense of

Israel as territorial legatee of the Jewish People; and (*b*) the recognition that economic growth was a pre-condition to national security.

Korean War–China
    Tactical decision 1: Supported
    Strategic decision 1: Not supported
    Tactical decision 2 (a) and (b): Not supported
    Strategic decision 2: Not supported

(T_1/K-C) The decision to recognize Communist China, in the face of known opposition by Washington, was in no sense a product of the goal of power maximization.

(S_1, T_2 and S_2/K-C) All of these decisions were influenced by considerations of military and economic capability; in particular, to elicit continued US aid—by supporting her on Korea and by not alienating her on diplomatic relations with China. In the case of S_1, United Nations aid against an Arab attack was another power-maximizing objective.

Jordan Waters
    Tactical decision 1: Not relevant
    Strategic decision: Supported
    Tactical decision 2: Supported

(S and T_2/JW) Israel's decision-makers wanted to maximize the quantity of water available to her for purposes of economic development; but they agreed to accept less water in the Revised Unified Plan (1955), in the interest of a larger political objective—accommodation with Arab states. And they decided to shift the diversion point, in order to reduce political friction with neighbouring states. Power maximization was not the principal motivation.

Sinai Campaign
    Tactical decision: Not supported
    Strategic decision 1: Not supported
    Strategic decision 2: Not supported

(T, S_1 and S_2/SC) The primary goal of Ben Gurion and his aides in the Sinai issue of 1956–7 was to overcome a shift in the military balance, which had begun to tilt in the Arabs' favour in 1955 and which was perceived as a threat to Israel's survival. Similarly, in the struggle for concessions in return for withdrawal (S_2), greater military security was Israel's objective and rationale.

Six Day War
    Tactical decision 1 (a) and (b): Supported
    Tactical decision 2 (a) and (b): Supported
    Tactical decision 3: Not relevant
    Strategic decision: Supported

(T_1, T_2 and S/SDW) Israel's high-policy decision-makers, like the entire nation, did not perceive the 1967 crisis in terms of the increase of power, but rather in terms of avoiding a grave adverse shift in the balance of survival capability. Israel's behaviour was responsive throughout, unlike that in the Sinai Campaign—partial mobilization on 16 May, large-scale mobilization on the 18th, and military action on 5 June. The maximization of military and economic capability are nowhere evident in élite images as analysed. The chief motivating factor was security in its most elemental sense—survival against a perceived assault by powerful adversaries, with a self-declared aim of expunging the Jewish State by war.   *intro.*

Rogers Proposals

Tactical decision 1 (a) and (b): Not supported
Tactical decision 2: Not supported
Strategic decision: Not supported

$(T_1, T_2$ and S/RP) Israel's decisions on both Rogers 'A' (and the Yost Document) and Rogers 'B' were shaped by preoccupations with military capability. Her rejection of the first was due to an immediate consensus view that the territorial provisions of Rogers 'A' would, if accepted, jeopardize Israel's security and defensibility. Moreover, the affirmative response to the United States peace initiative—Rogers 'B'— in July 1970 was largely due to the conviction that only thus would the continued flow of arms from America be assured.

H21: 'The former colonial power will occupy a disproportionately important position in the foreign policy image of decision-makers of new states.'[1]

Jerusalem

Strategic decision: Not supported
Tactical decision: Not supported

(S and T/Jer) Neither in 1949 nor in 1967 did Israeli decision-makers attach special significance to the attitudes of the UK. Rather, it was the United Nations, the Vatican, and Latin America that were perceived as highly salient to the decision to make Jerusalem the seat of government. In the images pertaining to the unification decision no external actor was perceived as significant.

German Reparations

Strategic decision: Not supported
Tactical decision: Not supported

(S/GR) Israel did approach the UK, along with the other Occupying Powers, in her Notes of January and March 1951. However, no special significance was attached to London's response. In fact, the United States was perceived as far more important in the indirect quest for reparations.

[1] Hypothesis 21 is from Stein.

(T/GR) It was the unwillingness of the three Western Powers to approach Bonn on behalf of Israel that led her to decide in favour of direct negotiations. Once more, the US loomed much larger in Israeli images. And, during the protracted negotiations, Washington's links with Bonn were regarded as the most important path to a satisfactory agreement.

Korean War–China

Tactical decision 1: Supported
Strategic decision 1: Not supported
Tactical decision 2 (a) and (b): Not supported
Strategic decision 2: Not supported

(T_1/K-C) The most decisive input into the timing of Israel's decision to recognize Peking was the recognition accorded by several non-Communist states during the preceding two weeks, especially by the UK.

(S_1, T_2 and S_2/K-C) Israel's response to the outbreak of war in Korea and to Peking's overtures for diplomatic relations were greatly influenced by the 'American factor', not by the UK. It was concern about undermining the economic and military ties with Washington which guided Israel's decision-makers in those cases.

Jordan Waters

Tactical decision 1: Not relevant
Strategic decision: Not supported
Tactical decision 2: Not relevant

(S/JW) The decision to accept Johnston's Revised Unified Plan in 1955 was influenced in large measure by the US presence. The UK played no role in this foreign policy issue.

Sinai Campaign

Tactical decision: Not relevant
Strategic decision 1: Supported
Strategic decision 2: Not supported

(S_1/SC) Ben Gurion's mistrust of Britain, rooted in the Mandate experience, occupied a key place in his articulated image of the environment during September and October 1956. As late as the Sèvres Conference, the behaviour of 'perfidious Albion' seemed to Israel's Prime Minister uncertain and potentially dangerous. His refusal to agree to a military campaign without British participation, or at least acquiescence, clearly supports this hypothesis.

(S_2/SC) The crisis decision to withdraw (8 November 1956) was shaped by several factors—American, Soviet, French, UN, and Jewish. The former Mandatory Power played no role in that decision.

Six Day War
    Tactical decision 1 (a) and (b): Not relevant
    Tactical decision 2 (a) and (b): Not supported
    Tactical decision 3: Not relevant
    Strategic decision: Not supported

(**T₂ and S/SDW**) Many external actors provided inputs into the foreign policy system, which generated the decisions of 23 and 28 May, and of 4 June 1967: the US, and especially President Johnson; Egypt, and especially Nasser; de Gaulle; Harold Wilson's UK Government; King Hussein; the Syrian regime; U Thant; etc. The UK role was marginal. Notes were sent by Eshkol and Eban to London, among other capitals. Eban paused in London between his two important encounters—with de Gaulle and Johnson. Only on one occasion was UK behaviour a decisive input: her role in helping to organize a naval flotilla was a factor in the Israel Government's decision of 28 May to delay further a military response to the perceived threat. For the 1967 crisis as a whole the former colonial power was not a crucial element in Israeli decision-makers' images or related behaviour.

Rogers Proposals
    Tactical decision 1 (a) and (b): Not supported
    Tactical decision 2: Not supported
    Strategic decision: Not supported

(**T₁, T₂ and S/RP**) Israel's responses to the challenges posed by Rogers 'A' and 'B' were not affected by an image of the 'British factor'. The UK was involved in the Four-Power Talks but her attitude to a Middle East settlement, while not totally ignored, was treated as marginal for Israel's position in the conflict, in world public opinion, or in her relations with the United States, the overpowering element in the calculus of Israel's decision-makers.

II. *Crisis Behaviour*

    The most numerous type of hypothesis in foreign policy analysis relates to state behaviour in the crisis phase of conflict situations. Many were generated from research on the outbreak of the First World War (the Stanford group—North *et al.*, Holsti, North and Brody, Zinnes, etc.). Others arose from studies of United States crisis decisions: her response to the outbreak of the Korean War (Paige, Hermann, Robinson); the Cuban Missile crisis (Hermann, Holsti *et al.*, Paige); the Bay of Pigs misadventure (Lentner); and Quemoy and Berlin (McClelland). Hypotheses have also been formulated by individuals without specific reference to a crisis—Pruitt, Snyder, Milburn, Verba, and Milbrath. Some are important and worth testing against the behaviour of diverse states. They will be explored here with the data drawn from three Israeli strategic crisis decisions of great importance in the foreign policy of that *new, developed, middle* power: (1) to agree, in principle, to withdraw from territory acquired during the Sinai Campaign, 8 November 1956; (2) to go to war against Egypt, 4 June 1967; and, for the first dozen of these hypotheses, (3) to accept the US peace initiative—Rogers 'B', 31 July 1970.

H22: '. . . in times of "national stress", when national aspirations seem threatened, decision-makers are likely (*a*) to be less aware of the complexity of their environment, (*b*) to consider fewer alternatives, and (*c*) to choose among alternatives more impulsively with less adequate review of their consequences.'[1]

This hypothesis is closely related to two others, as follows:

'The higher the tension, the stronger the tendency for élite perceptions of the crisis to coalesce around a few simplified stereotypes and a limited range of alternatives'; and 'The higher the tension, the stronger the tendency to make decisions on the basis of affective feelings rather than cognitive calculations.'[2]

Sinai Campaign

(*a*) Not supported

(*b*) Supported

(*c*) Supported

(*a*) During the 30-hour crisis Prime Minister Ben Gurion and his Cabinet colleagues were acutely aware of the complexity of their environment—Soviet and US threats, UN pressure, French advice to yield, and similar fraternal advice by American Jewry.

(*b*) For much of the discussion on 8 November the alternatives were perceived as: to accept or to reject the multiple demands for withdrawal. A third alternative—conditional withdrawal—was injected into the debate from outside (Ambassador Eban) and was seriously considered very late in the day, after the decision had been taken to withdraw in principle and after it was proposed by an adviser, Herzog.

(*c*) While there was a review of the consequences, concern and fear played a large role in the choice among alternatives *discussed*; and they curtailed the search for other alternatives—for example, agreement to withdraw after a peace settlement or after Egypt's declaration of intent to recognize Israel, etc.

Six Day War

(*a*) Not supported

(*b*) Not supported

(*c*) Not supported

---

[1] Hypothesis 22 is from Pruitt. See H40 for a complementary proposition about stress and the consideration of alternatives, stated in *dynamic* terms.

[2] A very similar earlier formation is found in two hypotheses by North *et al.*, pp. 163, 169.

(*a*) Eshkol, Eban, Dayan, and Allon, in fact the 1967 Israeli decision-making group as a whole, were acutely aware of the complexity of their environment: Nasser's bravado; intra-Arab rivalries; Soviet mischief in misleading their clients; the limited capability of Western Powers in organizing a naval flotilla; de Gaulle's criticism of Israeli claims *vis-à-vis* the Straits; U Thant's panic response to Cairo's demand to withdraw UNEF; the deterioration in Israeli morale; the economic cost of waiting, etc.

(*b*) Several alternatives were carefully considered during the 1967 crisis: (1) an early preventive strike, from the closure of the Canal on 22/23 May; (2) a limited delay to permit organized international naval action; (3) mobilization of *Tzahal* reserves and waiting for an Arab military attack; (4) a limited military riposte, etc.

(*c*) Israel's decision-makers did not act impulsively in the May–June crisis. They were engaged in a prolonged dialogue, which included a careful review of the likely consequences of their decisions.

Rogers Proposals
  (*a*) Not supported
  (*b*) Supported
  (*c*) Supported

(*a*) There was ample awareness of the environment—external and internal—in formulating the positive decision on Rogers 'B', along with a tendency to stereotyped 'two-camp' thinking about the setting: a hostile non-Jewish world—Arabs, Muslims, Communist bloc, France, Third World—and a friendly United States, which must be assuaged lest she too join the enemy camp, leaving Israel and world Jewry—the 'Jewish camp'—at bay.

(*b*) In July 1970 acceptance of the United States peace initiative was assumed to be inevitable from the moment the crisis began; that is, when Egypt accepted the proposal on the 22nd. The only choice under discussion was the form and wording of Israel's reply.

(*c*) The decision on Rogers 'B' was immediate: it was made, *de facto*, on 25 July, a day after the receipt of President Nixon's reassuring dispatch to Prime Minister Meir.

H23: 'As stress increases in a crisis situation: (*a*) time will be perceived as an increasingly salient factor in decision-making; (*b*)decision-makers will become increasingly concerned with the immediate rather than the distant future.'[1]

---

[1] Hypothesis 23 is from Holsti 1965, p. 226. A similar proposition on the greater salience of time and of the immediate future is to be found in North *et al.*, p. 165. The other three Holsti hypotheses used to test actor behaviour in the 1914 crisis are not relevant to Israeli behaviour except his H4 (*c*). See the observations on p. 574 below. Concern with the *immediate* future does not, *ipso facto*, preclude simultaneous concern with the *distant* future: the former may be an instrument to satisfaction of

Sinai Campaign

    (*a*) Supported

    (*b*) Supported

    (*a*) From 8.30 a.m. on 8 November 1956, when the Eisenhower letter and Hoover's oral threat of sanctions reached the Israeli decision-makers, throughout the course of the day, the sense of urgency escalated and influenced the discussions. From Washington Eban had emphasized that morning the need for a withdrawal statement within 24 hours. Reports of imminent Soviet intervention, particularly the 'news' of a Soviet plan to 'flatten' Israel the following day—these and other indicators of stress all had the effect of making *time* more salient in decision-makers' perceptions.

    (*b*) The greater saliency of time, in turn, led to greater emphasis on the present than on the distant future. The crisis was perceived as preventing Soviet intervention *the next day*, not in terms of long-term conditions for Israeli security; similarly, how to avoid severe US economic sanctions, not in terms of winning American support in the long run. At a late stage, however, a focus on the intermediate or relatively short-term goal of concessions was intruded, as an adjunct to immediate objectives.

Six Day War

    (*a*) Supported

    (*b*) Supported

    (*a*) From 15 to 22 May 1967, when stress increased moderately, Israeli decision-makers did not perceive Nasser's actions as pointing to war: the time dimension was not central to the process. However, with the qualitative rise in stress following the closure of the Straits (22/23 May), they became increasingly preoccupied with time and, in particular, with the danger to Israel's vital interests if they waited more than some days. The saliency of time became more and more evident from 27 May, when Eban returned with the knowledge of de Gaulle's hostility and of the Western Powers' ineffectiveness. Stress reached its high point on the 30th, when Jordan and Egypt concluded a defence pact; from that date decision-making was dominated by the time dimension.

    (*b*) Israel's decision-makers were primarily oriented to the immediate challenge posed by Nasser's actions—a challenge which had to be met within days or weeks, not longer. There was also a double link to the distant future: (1) through the 'Holocaust syndrome', a possible second Holocaust which would terminate the reality of a Jewish national homeland; and (2) the danger of Israel's inaction undermining the credibility of her deterrence strategy in the eyes of the Arabs, the

---

the latter. Decision-makers may or may not be aware of the link between the two dimensions of time.

Soviets, the US, and the world at large. The main focus of attention, however, was the perceived immediate threat of Egypt's military build-up in Sinai.

Rogers Proposals
    (*a*) Supported
    (*b*) Supported
    (*a*) The time factor was crucial in Israeli deliberations on Rogers 'B', following the news of Egypt's acceptance and the arrival of Nixon's assurances to Meir, 23 and 24 July 1970 respectively. Awareness of time was pervasively evident, even though the decision process lasted a week. But for the desire to maintain the National Unity Government intact, the affirmative decision, which was reached *de facto* within a day, would have been announced before 31 July.

    (*b*) Confirmation is even more striking. Attention was riveted on the probable consequences of acceptance or rejection for Israel's friendship with the United States and the related flow of arms in the *immediate future*. Long-range implications of 'withdrawal', 'direct negotiations', etc., do not appear to have been weighed. The pattern of short-term calculus, so pronounced in Israel's foreign policy decisions since 1948, was replicated in the strategic decision on Rogers 'B'.

H24: 'The higher the tension, the stronger the tendency for rumour to be transmitted as fact.'[1]

Sinai Campaign
    Supported
A flurry of reports on the night of 7 November 1956, continuing through the 8th, came to be believed by Israel's decision-makers: rumour was readily transformed to 'fact' under the impact of escalating tension. Thus the fact of the shooting down of a British Canberra by jet planes led to the rumours that they were Migs, and that the incident was detected by radar based in Syria, which must have been operated by Russians. So too with the CIA-leaked rumour about Soviet 'plans' to bomb Israel on the 9th—and a series of 'unconfirmed reports'. The tendency of Israeli decision-makers was to treat all of these as 'facts'. And that, in turn, led to the strategic decision to agree to withdraw, made on the 8th.

Six Day War
    Not supported
The input flow of facts into Israel's decision-making system was unencumbered with rumour. The behaviour of the Powers was known through an efficient communications network—diplomatic cables, press, radio, TV. There were *threats* of Soviet intervention, notably

[1] Hypothesis 24 is from North *et al.*, p. 165. See also p. 174.

on 10 June at the beginning of Israel's campaign against Syria, as conveyed to Johnson by Kosygin on the 'Hot Line'. There were also fears of possible Soviet action. They were accurate perceptions of the operational environment and of the USSR as hostile and threatening. That image of Soviet intent was not based on rumours, but on past experience.

Rogers Proposals
    Not supported
Tension mounted during the week beginning 23 July 1970, with Egypt's formal acceptance of Rogers 'B'. The need for Israel to respond—quickly—was recognized. But there is no evidence that rumour became influential in the deliberations. The crucial problems were how to reply affirmatively without undermining Israel's bargaining position and, if possible, to provide a face-saving formula for *Gahal* to remain in the National Unity Government.

H25: 'Crisis decisions tend to be reached by *ad hoc* decisional units.'[1]
Sinai Campaign
    Not supported
The decision to withdraw from occupied territory was taken at night on 8 November 1956 by the full plenum of Israel's Government—which authorized the *de facto* decision by Prime Minister–Defence Minister Ben Gurion.

Six Day War
    Not supported
The decision to take military action was made by the full Cabinet on 4 June 1967. There was no *ad hoc* decisional unit in Israel's 1967 crisis, though some decision-makers were more influential than others.

Rogers Proposals
    Not supported
The strategic decision relating to the Rogers Proposals was made in the full Cabinet, though preliminary discussions were held by an inner group of Alignment ministers—as in June 1967. It was at most a *pre*-decisional unit: the institutionalized executive organ of the political system, the Cabinet, was the formal and actual decision-making body.

H26: 'The more technical the problems of decision implementation, the greater the role of the appropriate specialists in the decisional unit.'
Sinai Campaign
    Supported
It was a specialist, Ambassador Eban, who devised the formula for

---

[1] Hypotheses 25–32 are from Paige, pp. 281–312.

conditional withdrawal, on 8 November 1956. And it was a group of specialists, headed by Eban in Washington and New York (Shiloah, Rafael, Kidron) and Herzog in Jerusalem, who played the crucial role in implementing the withdrawal decision—from 9 November 1956 to 12 March 1957.

Six Day War
Supported

Eban, though Foreign Minister, was the outstanding Israeli diplomatic specialist—and he played a crucial role in implementing the delay decisions of 23 and 28 May 1967. Dayan, the acknowledged outstanding military specialist in the Cabinet, played a pivotal role in implementing the strategic decision of 4 June.

Rogers Proposals
Not supported

The Cabinet did not use Israel's professional civil servants to draft the affirmative response to Rogers 'B'. It was, in fact, badly formulated, one of the reasons for the controversy over the violation of the cease-fire on 7 August 1970 ff. Minister without Portfolio Galili's reputation for drafting and, in general, the high-policy decision-makers' assumption of technical knowledge relating to foreign policy, as often in the past, caused implementing problems following Israel's acceptance of Rogers 'B'.

H27: 'The greater the crisis, the greater the felt need for face-to-face proximity among decision-makers.'

Sinai Campaign
Supported

Cabinet sessions from 28 October 1956, when the decision to launch the Campaign was authorized, to 7 November, when the text of Ben Gurion's 'victory speech' was approved, were of near-normal duration. On 8 November, however, the day of crisis, the Government was in almost continuous session—for eight hours. Ministers, including Ben Gurion, it may be deduced, felt the need for face-to-face contact while the making of what they perceived as a fateful decision was in process.

Six Day War
Supported

The Cabinet met frequently during the three-week crisis, more frequently and for longer periods from 23 May than during the first week. Moreover, the sessions became longer, for example almost around the clock on 27–28 May. And, apart from formal Government meetings, there was a myriad of discussions among the inner circle, all indicating a greater felt need for face-to-face contact among the decision-makers. They were in close consultation to a far greater extent than in non-crisis situations, when Israel's Cabinet meets weekly.

Rogers Proposals
Supported
Israel's decision-makers met in Cabinet session five times during the period 26–31 July 1970, apart from many informal discussions among smaller groups of ministers. There is clearly evident a high correlation between perceived crisis and the felt need for face-to-face proximity.

H28: 'The greater the crisis, the greater the acceptance of responsibility for action by the leader and the more the follower expectation and acceptance of the leader's responsibility.'

Sinai Campaign
Supported
Israeli ministers looked to Prime Minister Ben Gurion for guidance throughout the crisis of 7–8 November 1956. In fact, the Government decision was 'to leave the decision to Ben Gurion': in essence, it authorized his decision to withdraw. His followers expected and accepted his leadership in a momentous decision with far-reaching consequences.

Six Day War
Not supported
At no time during the 1967 crisis did Israelis or Israeli ministers expect or accept Eshkol's special responsibility for decision-making. Nor did the Prime Minister himself assume greater responsibility. Moreover, as time passed, there was a decline in expectation of inspired leadership— especially after Eshkol's disastrous radio broadcast on 28 May. It culminated in the *Mapai* revolt, a vote of no-confidence in his capacity to lead the nation during a grave crisis.

Rogers Proposals
Not supported
There was no special deference to Prime Minister Meir during the decision-making process relating to Rogers 'B'. The leader–follower pattern of decision-making, so conspicuous in the Sinai case, 1956–7, was not replicated in 1970. Other ministers, notably Dayan, Galili, Eban, and Allon, occupied important leadership (decision-making) roles with regard to the Rogers Proposals.

H29: 'The greater the crisis, the more the leader's solicitation of subordinate advice.'

Sinai Campaign
Supported
At the height of the Sinai crisis, on the evening of 8 November 1956, Ben Gurion accepted Herzog's suggestion and sought Eban's advice on the issue of conditional withdrawal—was it or was it not acceptable to US leaders and, therefore, feasible. Moreover, he appeared to rely

heavily on Eban's reply: he announced the formula of conditional withdrawal soon after the Ambassador telephoned his assessment. The intensity of consultations was much greater than at earlier stages of the 30-hour crisis.

Six Day War
Supported

The advice of Rabin, the Chief of Staff, was sought from the outset. However, the intensity of consultation grew. Other senior *Tzahal* officers were invited to Cabinet meetings after 23 May. Most conspicuously, General Meir Amit, then Head of *Ha-mosad*, the premier intelligence agency, was dispatched urgently to Washington on 30 May to secure information about US Government intentions. And Ambassador Harman was called to Jerusalem for the inner circle meeting on 3 June to advise the Cabinet on Washington's mood and attitude to the crisis.

Rogers Proposals
Not supported

During the decision process Israel's high-policy decision-makers did not solicit advice from their aides any more than usual. Ambassador Rabin took the initiative and offered advice throughout but it was not, for the most part, solicited by Israeli leaders. And Foreign Ministry personnel, though invited to participate in high-policy discussions, played a marginal role: their expertise was rarely sought.

H30: 'The greater the crisis, the greater the felt need for information.'

Sinai Campaign
Supported

On the evening of 8 November 1956, as the deadline for decision drew nearer, Ben Gurion sought information from Eban about the mood of US leaders regarding conditional withdrawal; that information was regarded by him as essential: the Prime Minister would not decide upon a course of action without it. And on the morning of 8 November, when the crisis erupted, he sought information from Eban by telephone about the feasibility of an immediate summit meeting with Eisenhower. On both occasions the information was perceived by the pre-eminent decision-maker as crucial.

Six Day War
Supported

In addition to the Amit and Harman data, to be noted in H34, Eban was sent urgently to Paris, London, and Washington (25–27 May) to secure information about the Western Powers' intentions—as well as to influence their behaviour. Moreover, the cable and telephone media between Jerusalem and Israel's Washington embassy were utilized to a much greater extent than in non-crisis situations—and especially so following Evron's cable of the 27th concerning his and Eban's talks with President Johnson that evening. Intense communication continued until the strategic decision was taken on 4 June.

Rogers Proposals
Supported

The crisis attending Rogers 'B' in July 1970 heightened the felt need for 'clarifications' by a decision-making group which was not keen to accept the proposal. Thus, after the Cabinet meeting on 26 July, the Government sought information from Washington about the meaning of the US initiative and the nature of her future commitments to Israel. That search for 'clarifications' continued until the 30th.

H31: 'The greater the crisis, the greater the propensity for decision-makers to supplement information about the objective state of affairs with information drawn from their own past experience.'

Sinai Campaign
Supported

The hard data available to Israeli decision-makers on the day of crisis, 8 November 1956, were very limited. Unconfirmed reports were more plentiful. Decision-makers tended to supplement information, particularly reports about Soviet intentions, with their own past experience and their images of the Communist regime and its ideology. The result was to give reports of imminent saturation bombing by the USSR greater credibility than they deserved. And those scare reports constituted a decisive input into the withdrawal decision that day.

Six Day War
Supported

As the 1967 crisis became more intense, Israel's decision-makers supplemented their information about Arab acts—the ouster of UNEF, closure of the Straits, and the massing of troops in Sinai—with 'information' based upon their past experience with the Arab states. The objective threat became exacerbated by Israeli images of the protracted conflict, in particular of Arab determination to engage in politicide, if not genocide. The information flow portrayed a stark challenge to Israel's vital interests. Past experience accentuated the gravity of the situation for her decision-makers.

Rogers Proposals
Supported

Israel's decision-makers, notably Prime Minister Meir, frequently invoked the experience of 1956–7 and 1967 in expressing their views on the US initiative of 1970. In particular, the emphasis on 'secure and recognized boundaries' is a projection from their reading of: US and

UN commitments after Israel withdrew from Sinai and Gaza in March 1957; the abrupt Egyptian expulsion of UNEF in May 1967; the attitude of the Powers and the world organization in May–June 1967; and the three rounds of Arab–Israel warfare, with exposed Israeli frontiers during the first nineteen years of independence.

H32: 'The greater the crisis, the greater the efforts to withhold details of response execution strategies from inimical external-setting elements.'[1]

Sinai Campaign
Supported
On 9 November 1956 Kidron was evasive on the question, '*when* would Israel withdraw?', posed by a Soviet UN delegate. And at every stage, from the announcement of the conditional withdrawal formula to final withdrawal on the ground, in March 1957, Israel concealed her strategy of execution from the UN and USSR, inimical external-setting elements, as well as from a friendly US.

Six Day War
Supported
Israel's behaviour during the last 72 hours of the 1967 crisis revealed this trait. Dayan's press conference on 3 June was effectively uninformative about the impending strategic decision. In fact, it was sufficiently diversionary to persuade some foreign correspondents to leave Israel that weekend and others to believe that no action would occur in the near future. Remarks by Allon and Galili the previous day were no more communicative about Israel's strategy of military response.

Rogers Proposals
Not supported
Throughout the crisis culminating in acceptance of Rogers 'B' there was no discernible effort to conceal Israel's response from the Arabs or the Soviets: her strategy of response execution was openly discussed.

H33: 'The greater the [emotional] involvement of an individual in a situation, the greater will be the effect of . . . predispositional influence.'[2]

Sinai Campaign
Supported
All high-policy decision-makers were deeply involved in the Sinai Campaign. Yet their attitude to the crisis issue of withdrawal was not identical. Dayan and Peres did not yield to Soviet pressure from 5 to 8 November 1956, and they opposed the decision to withdraw. Ben

---

[1] The reader's attention is drawn to the evidence relating to H16, which deals with foreign policy in general; a comparison can then be made between crisis and non-crisis behaviour.

[2] Hypothesis 33 is from Verba, p. 99.

Gurion, however, reacted much more in terms of his predispositional image of the Soviets, based upon past experience and rooted perception, rather than on the flimsy and unreliable evidence of an imminent Soviet assault. The proposition is thus supported for the key decision-maker in the Sinai crisis decision.

Six Day War
Not supported
The decision to go to war (4 June) was made after lengthy and careful deliberations, based upon all known data. It was calculated—not predispositional. The end of the *Hamtana* was presaged by the withdrawal of a US-imposed restraint on Israeli military action. Despite deep involvement, Israel's decision-makers displayed rational choice. That is to say, the highest estimate of cost for delay between 28 May and 4 June was 200 additional casualties per day, and the benefit of delay was twofold: continued direct US support for Israeli claims *vis-à-vis* the Straits and a steady escalation of support for Israel in distress by world public opinion and other states. Once Washington's restraint was withdrawn, the cost element of the equation was perceived as far greater than any benefit from continued delay. Hence the decision to take military action, a rational conclusion from a cost-benefit analysis.

Rogers Proposals
Not supported
As for the *volte-face*, acceptance of Rogers 'B' at the end of July 1970, Israel's decision-makers were deeply involved in the 'war of attrition', in which disquieting developments converged during the spring and summer: the trauma caused by the shooting down of five Israeli Phantoms over Egypt in June and July; the 'letter of the twelfth-graders', questioning whether they should accept military service; and cumulative evidence of societal dissent from Government policy. These coincided with the increase of casualties at the Suez front to a point approaching intolerability. In the week-long decision process leading to acceptance of Rogers 'B' they entered a conscious or, for some, subconscious cost-benefit analysis. The cost part of the equation increased qualitatively by the conviction that continued rejection of the US peace initiative would alienate the United States, in particular President Nixon; undermine Israel's military capability; and thirdly, offend the acute sensitivities of large segments of Israel's population. It is true that there was a predisposition not to alienate, undermine, and offend—even a sense of '*ein breira*', no alternative, to acceptance, among the decision-makers. Nevertheless, there was a calculus, however primitive and unstructured. Predispositions coincided with, but did not determine, the decision. Thus the hypothesis is not supported.

H34: 'Decisions allowed to gestate over a period of several months are more open to [interest] group influence than decisions that must be made in a few days.'[1]

Sinai Campaign
Supported

The decision to withdraw—in principle—was made in a day. The challenge, in the form of simultaneous pressures from several external sources, notably the Soviet Union, the US, and the UN, was known to interest groups. There is no evidence, however, of group influence in the making of that crisis decision, not even from *Tzahal*. Dissent from army officers came later during the implementation of that decision.

Six Day War
Supported

All of the group pressures from 24 May, including an increasingly dissatisfied public opinion, made it impossible for the high-policy élite, even if its members were so inclined, to avoid—or even delay much longer—the strategic decision to go to war. In short, once a few days had passed, latent group pressures in the political system became manifest and became one of the decisive variables in Israel's 1967 crisis decision-making.

Rogers Proposals
Supported

Although the strategic decision to accept Rogers 'B' was made in a week, the gestation period extended from 19 June to 31 July, that is, a month and a half. And the influence of interest groups was conspicuously greater than in the earlier Rogers decisions.

A recent volume containing ten studies in crisis behaviour has generated a large number of hypotheses (311).[2] Five types of evidence were used: illustrations; simulation; events data; content analysis; and interviews/questionnaires. Although most are empirically testable, only the most significant, analytically, will be noted briefly, to supplement our findings. They will be tested with the data from the Sinai Campaign and Six Day War decisions, those in which *threat, hostility, time, expression,* and *coercive acts* were all present. (The first two and the last of these traits were absent in the Rogers case.) To avoid repetition, the explanatory comments will be confined to the essential minimum.

H35: 'In a crisis situation, the search for alternatives constitutes a substantial portion of decision-making time.'[3]

---

[1] Hypothesis 34 is from Milbrath, p. 150.   [2] Hermann.
[3] Hypothesis 35 is from Robinson, in Hermann, Hypothesis 4, p. 304, elaboration on p. 26.

Sinai Campaign
Supported
Virtually all of 8 November 1956 was devoted to the search for alternatives—eight hours of Cabinet discussions, telephone calls and cable
communication with Eban in Washington, consultations with opposition parties.

Six Day War
Supported
From the closing of the Straits (22/23 May) to the strategic decision for
war (4 June), Israel's decision-makers were preoccupied with the
alternative to war—the Ministerial Defence Committee's meeting on
the 23rd; Eban's mission to Paris, London, and Washington, 25–27
May, with the Cabinet dependent upon its outcome; the Cabinet
sessions on 27–28 May and thereafter; the Meir Amit mission to
Washington, etc.

H36: 'The greater the crisis, the more information about it tends to be
elevated to the top of the organizational hierarchy.'[1]

Sinai Campaign
Supported
During non-crisis situations the cable flow of information into Israel
is channelled to a few ministers only, apart from senior Foreign Office
personnel. On the night of 7 November and throughout the 8th the
information-consuming public became broader and included the entire
formal high-policy élite, that is, the whole Cabinet.

Six Day War
Supported
This phenomenon was even more striking in 1967, especially in the
Cabinet sessions, from 27 May to 4 June. Decision-making took place
following a 'collective reading of cables'.

H37: 'The longer the decision time, the greater the consultation with
persons outside the core decisional unit.'

Sinai Campaign and Six Day War
Supported
There was some discussion with Opposition leaders on 8 June 1956, but
the range of consultation was much narrower than in the 1967 crisis.
From 23 May onward a wider and wider spectrum of Israel's political
élite was consulted by the core decisional unit, the 10-member Ministerial Defence Committee. On the 23rd its session was enlarged to include

[1] Hypotheses 36–9 are from Paige, in Hermann, Hypotheses 14, 25, 28, 31, pp.
305–6, elaborations on pp. 47, 52.

Opposition leaders, *Mapai* Establishment persons, and others. Thereafter, the consultation process extended horizontally—across the party system, and vertically—within the dominant party.

H38: 'The longer the decision time, the greater the inputs of written versus oral information and interpretation.'[1]

Sinai Campaign and Six Day War

  Supported

The November 1956 withdrawal decision—with very short decision time—was based overwhelmingly on oral information, notably about Soviet threats to bomb Israel and US threats of sanctions. In 1967, while oral information abounded, there were many more written appreciations and correspondence between Eshkol and Eban on the one hand, and foreign leaders on the other—throughout the crisis.

H39: 'The longer the decision time, the greater the efforts to communicate with allies on a face-to-face basis.'

Sinai Campaign and Six Day War

  Not supported

At the very outset of the 1956 crisis, upon receiving an Eisenhower threat at 8.30 a.m. on 8 November, Ben Gurion telephoned Eban to try to arrange a summit conference in Washington that day. During the 1967 crisis there were only two special face-to-face communications—Eban with Johnson on 27 May, and Amit with lower levels of the US hierarchy, 31 May–2 June.

H40: 'As stress increases, decision-makers will perceive the range of alternatives open to themselves to become narrower.'[2]

Sinai Campaign

  Supported

As the hours of a crisis day (8 November) passed, Ben Gurion and his Cabinet colleagues experienced mounting stress, perceiving as they did that the super powers were impatiently waiting for Israel's decision. In that context of stress there seemed only one possible choice—withdrawal, though at the last moment a condition was attached.

Six Day War

  Supported

Stress increased steadily from 23 May. The pressure from within

---

[1] This hypothesis complements and supports similar hypotheses, 26 and 29 above.

[2] Hypotheses 40–1 are from Holsti, O.R., in Hermann, Hypotheses 51, 57, p. 307, elaborations on pp. 70, 75. H40 posits a relationship between stress and the perceived range of alternatives in *dynamic* terms, thereby complementing the *static* formulation in H22. Moreover, it provides the logical link between the three variables, namely, stress, saliency of time, and search for alternatives, in both static and dynamic dimensions.

Israel's political system and society grew in intensity. And by 30 May it reached a peak with the Egypt–Jordan treaty of alliance. Combined with the failure of the flotilla project, it led to a perception that Israel now had one choice only—to respond with large-scale military action.

H41: 'The higher the stress in a crisis situation, the greater the tendency to rely upon extraordinary or improvised channels of communication.'

Sinai Campaign
  Supported
On 8 November 1956 Ben Gurion was in telephonic communication with Eban, via Herzog, several times: stress led to his inquiry about a possible meeting with Eisenhower; and, later in the evening, about the feasibility of conditional withdrawal.

Six Day War
  Supported
Foreign Ministers' visits are normally arranged months or weeks in advance: the dispatch of Eban to Paris and Washington (25–27 May), at a moment's notice, was the use of an extraordinary channel of communication. So too was the Amit mission to Washington, 31 May–2 June, and the summoning of Ambassador Harman to Jerusalem to report to the Cabinet.

H42: 'In a crisis as opposed to a non-crisis situation, decision-making becomes increasingly centralized.'[1]

Sinai Campaign
  Not supported
The first strategic decision on that issue—to launch the Campaign—was not of the crisis type and was among the most centralized in Israel's foreign policy: it was made by Ben Gurion alone. The crisis decision of 8 November—to withdraw—was made by the Cabinet as a whole, though BG's pre-eminent role was acknowledged by his colleagues.

Six Day War
  Not supported
As the crisis escalated, decision-making became more decentralized, with the active involvement of all 18 Cabinet members and, for the strategic decision of 4 June, of all 21 ministers.[2]

---

[1] Hypothesis 42 is from Lentner, in Hermann, Hypothesis 84, p. 309, elaboration on p. 130.

[2] The reason for this is that predispositional influence grows with the intensity of the crisis phase: in conflict conditions internal stimuli are more important and, therefore, the perceived need by decision-makers to broaden the base of national consensus —as on 8 November 1956 and from 23 May to 4 June 1967.

This hypothesis is assessed as not supported in terms of the *number of decision-makers*. However, in terms of *hierarchy of levels of decision-making*, the process became centralized

H43: 'There is a positive relationship between x's expression of hostility to y and y's perception of threat.'[1]

Six Day War
Supported
There is evident a direct correlation between Nasser's increasingly blunt expressions of hostility to Israel and Israel's perception of threat. The 'period of innocence' (14–18 May) corresponds to the absence of hostile Nasser words—and deeds—relative to later phases of the crisis. But the escalation of verbal hostility by Egypt's President (23 May, announcing the blockade; 27 May, declaring Egypt's goal as the destruction of Israel; 28 May, indicating Egypt's readiness for war) led to a corresponding increase in Israel's perception of a threat to basic values.[2]

H44: 'As threat increases, the number of participants in a decision tends to increase.'[3]

Sinai Campaign
Supported
As the Soviet threat increased, and with it US economic pressure, on 7–8 November 1956, the number of participants in the Israeli decision-making unit concerning withdrawal grew from Ben Gurion and his immediate aides—Dayan, Peres, Meir—to the entire Cabinet and even Opposition leaders.

Six Day War
Supported
As the perceived threat increased, from 22/23 May 1967 onwards, the number of participants in Israel's decisions grew—from the Prime

---

that is, in the Cabinet as distinct from other structures. The evidence from H37 and H42 combined leads to the conclusion that, in crisis conditions, the longer the decision time the more decentralized will be the process of decision-making, in terms of size of group. This new proposition can readily be tested in other crisis situations.

[1] Hypothesis 43 is from Schwartz, in Hermann, Hypothesis 106, p. 310, elaboration on p. 169.

[2] This finding is consistent with the underlying theoretical exposition within the framework used throughout our study of Israel's foreign policy as a system of action; namely, that misperception is not relevant to the *making* of decisions (choice), though it is relevant to the *consequence* of decisions (feedback). In other words, decision-makers act in terms of what they perceive—whether or not their image is accurate.
At first glance the support for this hypothesis would appear to contradict the evidence in support of H1 dealing with flexibility and intensity of an image. However, the perception of threat is only one part of a decision-maker's image: it is possible that the former is rigid, while the remaining components of the image are flexible, and vice versa.

[3] Hypotheses 44–6 are from Hermann, in Hermann, Hypotheses 134, 135, 153, pp. 311–12, elaborations on pp. 197, 202.

Minister and Chief of Staff, to an enlarged Ministerial Defence Committee, to the Cabinet.[1]

H45: 'As time decreases, the number of participants in a decision tends to decrease.'

Sinai Campaign
    Not supported
As time decreased, on 8 November 1956, the number of participants in Israel's decision to withdraw increased, rather than the reverse.

Six Day War
    Not supported
There was no discernible change in the number of participants in the 1967 crisis decisions from 23 May onwards: they included all Cabinet ministers and some advisers—senior *Tzahal* officers, *Mapai* Establishment persons, etc.

H46: 'In crises the rate of communication by a nation's decision-makers to international actors outside their country will increase.'

Sinai Campaign
    Supported
On 8 November 1956 Ben Gurion attempted to contact Eisenhower, for a summit meeting, and Dulles, for reaction to the idea of conditional withdrawal.

Six Day War
    Supported
Communication between Israel's Prime Minister and Foreign Minister and external actors grew markedly during the 1967 crisis: Eshkol's several letters to Johnson, along with letters to de Gaulle and Wilson, and others, from 18 May until the climax of the decision process. They were designed partly to explain (to elicit understanding) and partly to secure support from Western Powers.

H47: 'If an extreme amount of coercive pressure is applied to an adversary, the adversary will then tend to assume that the only way he can achieve his ends is through coercive means of his own.'[2]

Sinai Campaign and Six Day War
    Supported
Egypt applied extreme coercive pressure against Israel in the autumn

---

[1] Whereas the inferred proposition from the combined evidence of H37 and H42 used *time* as the independent variable in a dynamic equation, H44 uses *threat* as the dynamic independent variable.

[2] Hypothesis 47 is from Snyder, in Hermann, Hypothesis 250, p. 317, elaboration on p. 253.

of 1956 and again in the latter half of May 1967: *feda'iyun* raids, the blockade of the Tiran Straits, and the Tripartite Pact in 1956; and in 1967, the abrupt expulsion of UNEF, blockade of the Straits, concentration of forces in Sinai, threatening speeches, and a military pact with Jordan. By October 1956 and again on 30 May 1967 Israel felt that counter-coercion was the only way to ensure survival.[1]

H48: 'As stress increases in a crisis situation, performance generally worsens.'[2]

Sinai Campaign
Supported
As the hours of crisis continued, and stress mounted, Ben Gurion and his colleagues manifested a declining capability to assess the accuracy of rumours and leaks about imminent Soviet bombing. It was that misjudgement, under stress, which led them to agree to withdraw—the same day.

Six Day War
Supported
The prolonged 1967 crisis and long hours of deliberations led to a marked deterioration in performance. Rabin became ill in the midst of the crisis. Eshkol delivered his speech to the nation on 28 May with a catastrophic stammer. The Cabinet could not decide anything—except to delay. Fatigue—and stress—took their toll.[3]

B. SUMMARY OF FINDINGS: GENERAL BEHAVIOUR

This analysis focuses on one dimension—the degree of support for a set of 48 propositions which were tested across the spectrum of 21 Israeli decisions. The hypotheses were selected from approximately 400 which the literature of international relations generated in a frenetic period of theorizing and research since the late 1950s. The criteria were: first, *substantive value*—as perceived by this researcher, that is, their *a priori* meaningfulness about some facet of state behaviour; and secondly, their *potential* as building-blocks for *foreign policy theory*. The choice was not conspicuously influenced by their possible relevance to the decisions under inquiry.

---

[1] This hypothesis is applicable: (1) to conditions of conventional coercion—which is operative in the Arab–Israel conflict; and (2) when perceived vital interests are at stake. By way of explanation: when a qualitative gap in nuclear technologies exists, and rational adversaries are threatened by nuclear coercion, they will yield rather than respond with coercive means of their own; secondly, in situations of asymmetrical balances of vital interests, the party with less vital interests will yield rather than respond coercively.

[2] Hypothesis 48 is from Milburn, in Hermann, Hypothesis 263, p. 318, elaboration on p. 264.

[3] 'Performance', as operationalized here, includes both the *content* and *conduct* of foreign-policy decisions.

The composite data derived from the seven case studies of Israel's foreign policy are presented in Table 33. They are classified by: decision cluster; specific decision; types of hypothesis about state behaviour; individual propositions; and grouping by issue-area. A comparison of strategic and tactical decisions is made possible, along with a scale of validity.

TABLE 33

HYPOTHESIS-TESTING OF ISRAELI FOREIGN POLICY DECISIONS: GENERAL BEHAVIOUR

Hypothesis no.	Intensity of Images		Information and Images	Images and Behaviour Issue–Areas												C–S	Cross-issue				
				M–S					P–D			E–D									
	1	2	3	4	5	6	7	8	9	10	11	12	13	14	15	16	17	18	19	20	21
Decision Clusters																					
1. (S/JER)	S	NS	S	NR	NR	NR	NR	NR	NR	NR	NR	NR	NR	NR	NR	S	S	S	S	S	NS
2. (T/JER)	S	NS	NR	NR	NR	NR	NR	NR	NR	NR	NR	NR	NR	NR	NR	NS	NR	S	S	S	NS
3. (S/GR)	NS	NR	NR	NR	NR	NR	NR	NR	NR	NR	NR	S	NR	NR	NR	NR	NR	NR	NS	NS	NS
4. (T/GR)	NS	NS	S	NR	NR	NR	NR	NR	NR	NR	NR	S	S	NS	NS	NR	S	NR	NS	NS	NS
5. (T₁/K–C)	S	NR	NR	NR	NR	NR	NR	NR	S	S	S	NR	NR	NR	S	NR	NS	S	S	S	S
6. (S₁/K–C)	S	NR	S	NR	NR	NR	NR	NR	NS	S	S	NR	NR	NR	S	NR	NS	NS	S	S	NS
7. (T₂/K–C)	S	NR	S	NR	NR	NR	NR	NR	S	S	NS	NR	NR	NR	NR	NR	NS	NS	NS	NS	NS
8. (S₂/K–C)	S	NR	S	NR	NR	NR	NR	NR	S	S	NS	NR	NR	NR	NR	NR	NS	S	S	NS	NS
9. (T₁/JW)	S	NR	S	NR	NR	NR	NR	NR	NR	NR	NR	S	S	NR	S	NR	NR	NR	NR	NR	NR
10. (S/JW)	S	NR	S	NR	NR	NR	NR	NR	NR	NR	NR	NS	S	S	S	NR	S	NR	S	S	NS
11. (T₂/JW)	S	NR	S	NR	NR	NR	NR	NR	NR	NR	NR	NS	NR	S	S	NR	NR	NR	S	S	NR
12. (T/SC)	NR	NR	S	NS	NR	S	S	S	NR	NR	NR	NR	NR	NR	NR	NR	NR	NR	NS	NS	NR
13. (S₁/SC)	S	NR	S	S	S	S	S	S	NR	NR	NR	NR	NR	NR	NR	NR	NR	NR	S	S	S
14. (S₂/SC)	S	NS	S	S	S	NR	S	S	NR	NR	NR	NR	NR	NR	NR	NR	NS	S	S	S	NS
15. (T₁/SDW)	S	NR	S	NR	NR	S	S	NR	NR	NR	NR	NR	NR	NR	NR	NR	NR	NR	S	NR	NR
16. (T₂/SDW)	S	NS	S	NR	NR	S	S	NR	NR	NR	NR	NR	NR	NR	NR	NR	NR	NR	S	NS	NS
17. (T₃/SDW)	NR	NS	NR	NR	NR	NR	S	NR	NR	NR	NR	NR	NR	NR	NR	NR	NR	NR	NS	NR	NR
18. (S/SDW)	S	NS	S	S	S	S	S	NS	NR	NR	NR	NR	NR	NR	NR	NR	NR	NR	NS	S	NR
19. (T₁/RP)	S	NR	NR	NR	NR	NR	NR	NR	S	NR	S	NR	NR	NR	NR	NR	S	NR	NS	NS	NS
20. (T₂/RP)	S	S	NR	NR	NR	NR	NR	NR	S	NR	S	NR	NR	NR	NR	NR	NR	NR	NS	NS	NS
21. (S/RP)	S	S	S	NR	NR	NR	NR	NR	S	NS	NS	NR	NR	NR	NR	NR	S	NS	NS	NS	NS

NR = Not Relevant   NS = Not Supported   S = Supported

TABLE 34

SUPPORT FOR SELECTED HYPOTHESES APPLIED TO ISRAELI FOREIGN POLICY DECISIONS: GENERAL BEHAVIOUR

BY HYPOTHESIS NUMBER

Type of Hypothesis	Hypothesis Number	No. of Decisions Supporting Hy	Total Number of Relevant Decisions	Degree of Support	Support*
Intensity of Images	1	17	19	0·89	High
	2	2	9	0·22	Low
Information and Images	3	15	15	1·00	High
	4	3	4	0·75	High
	5	3	3	1·00	High
	6	5	5	1·00	High
Military-Security Issue-Area	7	7	7	1·00	High
	8	3	4	0·75	High
Political-Diplomatic Issue-Area	9	6	7	0·86	High
	10	4	5	0·80	High
	11	4	7	0·57	Low
Economic-Development Issue-Area	12	3	5	0·60	Low
	13	3	3	1·00	High
	14	1	2	0·50	Low
	15	3	5	0·60	Low
Cultural-Status Issue-Area	16	1	2	0·50	Low
Cross Issue-Area	17	6	11	0·55	Low
	18	3	6	0·50	Low
	19	14	20	0·70	High
	20	8	19	0·42	Low
	21	2	16	0·13	Low

BY RANKED DEGREE OF SUPPORT

Hypothesis Number	Degree of Support	
3	1·00	
5	1·00	
6	1·00	
7	1·00	
13	1·00	
1	0·89	High Support
9	0·86	
10	0·80	
4	0·75	
8	0·75	
19	0·70	
12	0·60	
15	0·60	
11	0·57	
17	0·55	
14	0·50	
16	0·50	Low Support
18	0·50	
20	0·42	
2	0·22	
21	0·13	

* 'High' indicates a degree above 0·66, that is, a number of supporting decisions at least twice the number of non-supporting decisions. 'Low' indicates a degree less than 0·67.

FIGURE 22

DEGREE OF SUPPORT FOR SELECTED HYPOTHESES APPLIED
TO ISRAELI FOREIGN POLICY DECISIONS: GENERAL BEHAVIOUR

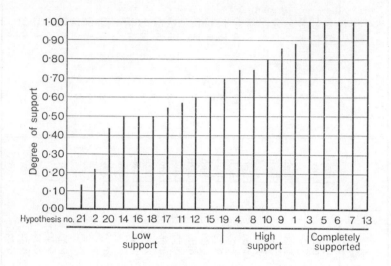

The degree of support for an hypothesis (Hy) may be defined thus:

$$DS\ (Hy) = \frac{\text{Number of Decisions Supporting Hy}}{\text{total Number of Relevant Decisions}}$$

Table 34 and Figure 22 present the composite data on support of hypotheses drawn from an analysis of Israel's foreign policy decisions.

The findings on degree of support for hypotheses about general state behaviour may now be summarized.

1. A majority (11 of 21) have a high score for support, 70 per cent and higher. Of these, five hypotheses register total support. Only two propositions, H2 and H21, rank very low, 22 and 13 per cent of support, respectively. Another seven hypotheses fall in the low verging on medium score, 50 to 60 per cent.

2. Among the total support group, four propositions (5, 6, 7, 13) relate to the specific issue-area type, as defined by Brecher, Steinberg, Stein.

3. Most of the specific issue-area hypotheses have a high degree of support; for three M-S decisions and one E-D decision the support is total.

4. There are conspicuous differences in the degree of support for strategic and tactical decisions:
H4 and H5, relevant to four and three military-security decisions

respectively, and H14, H16, each relevant to two decisions, economic-developmental for the former, cultural-status for the latter, are supported by the evidence of strategic decisions but are not supported by the evidence of tactical decisions.

5. Most striking, the evidence suggests that, while it is valid to define issue-areas objectively, that is, by the content of the decision, the analytically significant dimension of the issue-area concept for understanding the behaviour of states is not that *reality* definition but, rather, the way decision-makers *perceive* the issue.

   Stated differently, there is strong evidence in favour of the thesis underlying this book and its companion volume, *The Foreign Policy System of Israel*, namely, that the key to dissecting state behaviour is the analysis of images and advocacy of decision-makers.

6. If any of the eleven propositions revealing a high score for support from Israel's behaviour are supported by evidence drawn from other international actors, they can serve as building blocks for foreign policy theory.

C. SUMMARY OF FINDINGS: CRISIS BEHAVIOUR

Thirty hypotheses on crisis behaviour were tested with Israeli data: H22–H34, for three decisions—to agree in principle to withdraw from Sinai and Gaza (8 November 1956), to go to war (4 June 1967), and to accept the Rogers peace initiative (31 July 1970); H35–H48, except for H43, for the first two of these decisions. The only dimension explored was the degree of support.

The quantitative findings on Israeli crisis behaviour are presented in Tables 35 and 36 and Figure 23. The most important results are as follows:

1. More than 70 per cent of the hypotheses (22 of 30) score a high degree of support. And seventeen propositions are fully supported, that is, they seem to be valid for Israeli strategic crisis decisions.

2. Eight hypotheses reveal a low degree of support; and five of these are not supported at all, that is, are invalid.

3. The invalid propositions relate to: H22a, H25, H39, H42, and H45.

4. The two military-security area crisis decisions—Sinai Campaign and Six Day War—reveal identical contrasting evidence for Hypotheses 22b, 24, 28: the 1956 decision provides supporting evidence for all of them, the 1967 decision the contrary evidence.

5. Crisis behaviour hypotheses as a group reveal polar contrasts: most of them are either valid (seventeen hypotheses) or invalid (five hypotheses). The general behaviour hypotheses as a group manifest larger variation in the degree of support, partly due to the much larger sample of decisions.

The propositions which are supported by Israel's experience were derived primarily from three other conflict situations: (a) the multi-power crisis in July-August 1914, leading to the First World War; (b) United States behaviour at the outset of the Korean War (June 1950); and (c) US actions during the Cuban Missile Crisis (October 1962). These hypotheses concentrate on several significant facets: the impact of *stress*; the consequences of *time*; *interaction* among decision-makers; the scope of *consultation*; the link between expressions of *hostility* and perceptions of *threat*, etc.

Israeli behaviour in 1956, 1967, and 1970 offers strong support to the four Ole Holsti theses about the effects of an increase in stress in a crisis situation: (1) time will be perceived as more salient; (2) decision-makers will become more concerned with the immediate future; (3) they will perceive the range of alternatives open to themselves to be narrower; and (4) they will tend to rely more on extraordinary methods of communication.[1] All of these are based upon the 1914 crisis. The similarity of data is striking and potentially significant: behaviour by actors (great and small powers) in a multi-state two-coalition crisis within a balance-of-power system at the beginning of the twentieth century was replicated by a middle power in an essentially two-actor subordinate system conflict, within a global system characterized by nuclear technology and super-power penetration of lesser conflicts. Moreover, (5) the positive relationship between x's expression of hostility to y and y's perception of threat, posited by Zinnes, Schwartz, and others, is clearly supported by Israeli data drawn from the 1967 crisis.

That behaviour pattern in another era and international system by a state with a different culture, historical legacy, national identity, attitudinal prism and images, etc., suggests that these hypotheses (and the Stanford project, which spawned them) may be important building-blocks for foreign policy theory. By contrast, the Israeli data tend to refute the (static) Pruitt proposition that in time of national stress decision-makers are likely to be less aware of the complexity of their environment.

Several hypotheses derived from United States behaviour during the Korean and Cuban conflict situations are also clearly supported by Israel's experience. As in the case of a super power, Israeli decision-makers (6) felt the need for greater face-to-face proximity—in 1956,

---

[1] It should be emphasized that the concept of 'stress' as used in this study, and the findings relating thereto (Hypotheses 24–6, 29–34, 40, 41, 44), differ from those to be found in the work of Holsti and the Stanford studies on conflict, generally. For them, stress is derived from a content indicator—perception of threat; stress itself is not directly measured. In research on Israel's foreign-policy behaviour, however, stress was coded directly; for example, Prime Minister Eshkol's stuttering radio speech to the nation on the evening of 28 May 1967, after twenty hours of continuous pressure from external and internal demands—with serious consequences for the decision-making process.

TABLE 35

HYPOTHESIS-TESTING OF ISRAELI FOREIGN POLICY DECISIONS: CRISIS BEHAVIOUR

Decision	*Hypothesis Number*																													
	22* a	22 b	22 c	23† a	23 b	24	25	26	27	28	29	30	31	32	33	34	35	36	37	38	39	40	41	42	43	44	45	46	47	48
S_2/SC	NS	S	S	S	S	S	NS	S	S	S	S	S	S	S	S	S	S	S	S	S	S	NS	S	S	NS	—	S	NS	S	S	S
S/SDW	NS	NS	NS	S	NS	S	NS	S	S	NS	S	S	NS	S	S	NS	S	S	S	S	NS	S	S	NS	S	S	NS	S	S	S
S/RP	NS	S	S	S	S	NS	NS	NS	S	NS	NS	S	NS	S	NS	NS	S													

NS = Not Supported   S = Supported

* Hypothesis 22 comprises three propositions and will be treated as three separate hypotheses.

† Hypothesis 23 comprises two propositions and will be treated as two separate hypotheses.

TABLE 36

SUPPORT FOR SELECTED HYPOTHESES APPLIED TO ISRAELI FOREIGN POLICY DECISIONS: CRISIS BEHAVIOUR

Hypothesis Number	Number of Supporting Decisions	Total Number of Relevant Decisions	Degree of Support	Support*
22a	0	3	0.00	Low
22b	2	3	0.67	High
22c	2	3	0.67	High
23a	3	3	1.00	High
23b	3	3	1.00	High
24	1	3	0.33	Low
25	0	3	0.00	Low
26	2	3	0.67	High
27	3	3	1.00	High
28	1	3	0.33	Low
29	2	3	0.67	High
30	3	3	1.00	High
31	3	3	1.00	High

Hypothesis Number	Degree of Support	
23a	1.00	
23b	1.00	
27	1.00	
30	1.00	
31	1.00	
34	1.00	
35	1.00	Complete Support
36	1.00	
37	1.00	
38	1.00	
40	1.00	
41	1.00	
43	1.00	High Support

34	3	3	1·00	High		
35	2	2	1·00	High		
36	2	2	1·00	High		
37	2	2	1·00	High		
38	2	2	1·00	High		
39	0	0	0·00	Low		
40	2	2	1·00	High		
41	2	2	1·00	High		
42	0	0	0·00	Low		
43	1	1	1·00	High		
44	2	2	1·00	High		
45	0	0	0·00	Low		
46	2	2	1·00	High		
47	2	2	1·00	High		
48	2	2	1·00	High		

22b	0·67	Lower Limit of High Support
22c	0·67	
26	0·67	
29	0·67	
32	0·67	
24	0·33	Low Support
28	0·33	
33	0·33	
22a	0·00	
25	0·00	
39	0·00	Invalid Hypotheses
42	0·00	
45	0·00	

* 'High' support means a degree above 0·66, that is, the number of supporting decisions is at least twice that of non-supporting decisions; 'Low' indicates a degree less than 0·67.

1967, and 1970; (7) they also felt the need for more information before reaching a strategic decision; (8) most important in this context is the overwhelming support for the Paige thesis about the greater propensity of decision-makers to draw 'information' from their own past experience.

Israeli data also support three lesser Paige propositions: (9) that, in a crisis, information tends to be elevated to the top of the organizational hierarchy; (10) that the longer the decision time the wider will be consultation with persons outside the core decisional unit; and (11) that more written information will enter into the policy machine. Thus, in the crisis phase of five conflict situations of the military-security type, two involving a super power and three a middle power in a protracted conflict relationship, the pattern was the same in all of these facets of behaviour.

FIGURE 23

DEGREE OF SUPPORT FOR SELECTED HYPOTHESES
APPLIED TO ISRAELI FOREIGN POLICY DECISIONS:
CRISIS BEHAVIOUR

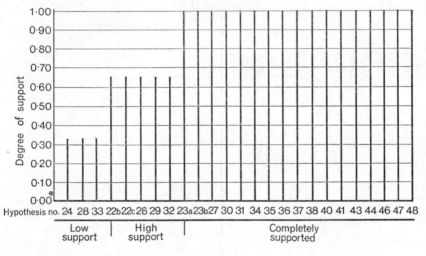

* 5 hypotheses—22a, 25, 39, 42, 45—should be located at the zero point on the 'degree of support' axis.

By contrast, a widely-accepted Paige hypothesis, derived solely from US behaviour, is categorically rejected by the Israeli data: Israel's decisions were *not* made by *ad hoc* decisional units but by the institutionalized executive organ of her political system. In this respect, it would appear, super-power and middle-power decision-making processes differ. Moreover, the US Korean and Cuban crisis experience concerning follower expectation and acceptance of a leader's responsibility is apparent only in the Sinai Campaign decision.

The proposition—by Robinson and others—(12) that the search for alternatives occupies a substantial part of decision-making time, is supported by Israeli experience in both the 1956 and 1967 crisis situations. So too are the Hermann hypotheses in which increasing threat is the independent variable: (13) the number of participants in a decision increases; and (14) the rate of communication with other international actors increases.

The (expected) result of the use of extreme coercive power, as posited by Snyder, namely, (15) that the adversary will tend to assume that the only way out is through counter-pressure, is strongly supported by Israel's Six Day War decision. That also confirms Milburn's proposition (16) that, as stress increases, performance by decision-makers worsens.

In short, a group of sixteen hypotheses, with stress, time, hostile expression, and coercive acts serving as independent variables, have been totally supported by Israeli behaviour in the crisis phase of three conflict situations. Further evidence—from other actors' behaviour —is necessary, however, before any of these propositions can be assessed as valid.

One final observation is appropriate in this qualitative summary of findings. Specific issue-area hypotheses and those relating to crisis behaviour manifest a much higher degree of support than propositions of a more general nature. This suggests that *narrow-gauge theory-building, deriving from specific situations, is more promising than grand design (general) theory.*

D. CONCLUDING REMARKS

The testing of hypotheses is but the first, necessary, stage on the path to foreign policy theory of the kind advocated here. Another dimension, no less important, is decision analysis. A construct has been devised which aims at demarcating a typology of foreign policy decisions along a scale of complexity. Three key indicators—stimulus (input), process, and the scope of consequences (output)—are being used to differentiate decisions along such a scale. Quantitative research, based on the findings from Israel's foreign policy, is now in progress in the search for precision and a universal typology of decisions.

A further stage of empirically-oriented theory-building is the formulation of new hypotheses about state behaviour. This task will be undertaken when a parallel systemic study of India's foreign policy, now in motion, has been completed. The combined data and insights into behaviour by two active producers and consumers of international events, two actors with different cultural, historical, and national characteristics, as well as different levels of economic, political, and social development, will provide a basis for fresh hypotheses about foreign policy. These will explore (a) relationships between the content of images and decisions; (b) the relative potency of external and internal environmental inputs into decisions for war and peace;[1] (c) the role of information inputs in decision-making; and (d) patterns of feedback from decisions for a state's future behaviour.

In the on-going quest for knowledge and theory several crucial research tasks may be indicated.

1. The approach of structured empiricism should be applied to select foreign-policy decisions by actors representing the widest possible range of types of states, in terms of:

> level of power—super, great, middle, and small;
>
> level of development—from the post-industrial states, such as the US and Japan, to the most underdeveloped states in the contemporary international system;
>
> cultural differentiation—Western and non-Western, etc; and
>
> old and new states.

Any confirmed findings from systemic empirical research into decisions would then serve as valid building-blocks for a comprehensive theory of foreign policy. The reason for the choice of these four criteria is that they constitute the essential conditions under which perceived stimuli from the external environment are processed for decision. They represent the main conditions affecting choice.

The extent to which this study is externally valid depends upon the degree to which Israel is representative of one aspect of each of the four conditions specified: and, myths about her uniqueness notwithstanding, Israel is a *middle* power, at an *industrial* level of development, with a basically *Western* cultural milieu, and a *new* state of the post-Second World War era.

2. It is imperative to expand the scope of direct field investigation into state behaviour; this has been neglected in favour of the less demanding, less creative, and somewhat simplistic attempts to extrapolate real behaviour from *a priori* assumptions about expected behaviour.[2]

---

[1] A first attempt in this direction has been made in Brecher 1974a. Thirteen hypo-theses were derived from an analysis of two foreign-policy system linkages: between environmental stimuli and decisions relating to the Sinai Campaign, the Six Day War, and the Rogers Proposals (Linkage A); and the feedback effects of decisions in these cases on the environment for subsequent Israeli war-peace decisions (Linkage B).

[2] In this context, another difference between the approach of the Stanford group and that employed here may be noted. Holsti, North *et al.* discovered *higher* stress in the period *following* the outbreak of the First World War. Stress was indicated by the frequency and intensity of articulated perceptions of threat before and after the outbreak of war. When stress is indicated by observable attributes, documents, and

3. It is time to bring intellectual order into the proliferating chaos of theorizing about foreign policy. We should consolidate what we know before generating another wave of models and constructs, many of which are not subjected to the rigorous test of operational utility and therefore impede the growth of a disciplined study of state behaviour—able to describe, explain, and predict.

4. Some of the recently devised techniques of analysis, which are creatively original, should be harnessed to the task of illuminating this aspect of human behaviour—but directed to more germane questions than so often posed in this field. At the same time the insights of traditional methods should be used as a basis for further inquiry. In the study of Israel's foreign policy a conscious attempt has been made to combine quantitative and qualitative methods of analysis.

5. Perhaps most important, progress in this field will remain limited and distorted as long as the prevalent fallacy of universalizing from the experience of one actor (the US) continues. A research design is necessary, which recognizes the pluralism of international actors and of patterns of behaviour. Generalization from the evidence of one state is inherently faulty—and it has been eschewed in this project. If the base of generalization is a super power, the danger of error is likely to be greater; that is to say, Israel is more typical of more international actors than is the United States. The international system analysis of the 1950s required a corrective, in the form of the concept of subordinate system and its empirical application. Similarly, foreign policy analysis required a fundamental change of emphasis. The surest path to a valid theory of state behaviour is a multi-dimensional attack, designed to uncover findings from a broad typology of actors. The patterns of behaviour which are likely to emerge from such an inquiry would enrich our descriptive, explanatory, and predictive capability much more than *a priori* theorizing.

---

interview data, as in the Israel study, stress *declined* sharply with the outbreak of the June 1967 War. Thus the general approach used in this study may be more valid because it uses multiple streams of evidence. These are derived from a combination of content analysis of the Stanford type with intensive field observation of decision-making processes, drawing upon written and oral sources directly relating to the decision-makers.

APPENDIX

Ministers of the Governments of Israel
May 1948—May 1973[1]

ALLON, Yigal	born 1918, Israel	Ahdut
	Labour, November 1961–July 1968	Ha'avoda
	Deputy Prime Minister July 1968–	ILP[2]
	Immigration and Absorption, July 1968–December 1969	
	Education and Culture, December 1969–	
ALMOGI, Yoseph Aaron	born 1910, Poland	Mapai
	Without Portfolio, November 1961–September 1962	Rafi
	Development and Housing, September 1962–May 1965	ILP
	Labour, July 1968–	
ARANNE, Zalman	1899–1970, Russia	Mapai
	Without Portfolio, January 1954–June 1954	ILP
	Transport, June–November 1955	
	Education and Culture, November 1955–May 1960 and June 1963–December 1969	
BAR-LEV, Haim	born 1924, Austria	ILP
	Commerce and Industry, March 1972–	
BAR YEHUDA, Yisrael	1895–1965, Russia	Ahdut
	Interior, November 1955–December 1959	Ha'avoda
	Transport, May 1962–May 1965	

[1] An open-ended date indicates that, as of May 1973, the minister held the specified portfolio.
[2] Israel Labour Party.

BARZILAI, Yisrael	1913–70, Poland Health, November 1955– November 1961 and January 1966–December 1969 (Also Posts, November 1958– December 1959) Without Portfolio, December 1969–June 1970	Mapam
BEGIN, Menahem	born 1913, Poland Without Portfolio, June 1967– August 1970	Herut Gahal
BEN AHARON, Yitzhak	born 1906, Roumania Transport, December 1959– May 1962	Ahdut Ha'avoda
BEN GURION, David	1886–1973, Poland Prime Minister and Defence Minister, May 1948–January 1954 Defence Minister, February– November 1955 Prime Minister and Defence Minister, November 1955– June 1963	Mapai Rafi State List
BENTOV, Mordekhai	born 1900, Poland Labour and Construction, May 1948–March 1949 Development, November 1955– November 1961 Housing, January 1966–December 1969	Mapam
BERNSTEIN, Peretz	1890–1971, Germany Commerce, Industry and Supply, May 1948–March 1949 Commerce and Industry, December 1952–June 1953	General Zionist
BURG, S. Yoseph	born 1909, Germany Health, October 1951–October 1953 Posts, December 1952–June 1958 Social Welfare, December 1959– August 1970 Interior, September 1970–	Ha-po'el Ha-mizrahi NRP[1]

[1] National Religious Party.

CARMEL, Moshe	born 1911, Poland
	Transport, November 1955–
	    December 1959 and May
	    1965–December 1969
		Ahdut
		    Ha'avoda
		ILP

COHN, Haim	born 1911, Germany Justice, June–December 1952	non-party
DAYAN, Moshe	born 1915, Israel Agriculture, December 1959– October 1964 Defence, June 1967–	Mapai Rafi ILP
DINUR, Ben Zion	1884–1973, Russia Education and Culture, October 1951–November 1955	Mapai

DULTZIN, Arye	born 1913, Russia
	Without Portfolio, December
	    1969–August 1970
		General
		    Zionist
		Gahal

EBAN, Abba	born 1915, South Africa
	Without Portfolio, December
	    1959–August 1960
	Education and Culture, August
	    1960–June 1963
	Deputy Prime Minister, June
	    1963–January 1966
	Foreign Affairs, January 1966–
		Mapai
		ILP

ESHKOL, Levi	1895–1969, Russia
	Agriculture and Development,
	    October 1951–June 1952
	Finance, June 1952–June 1963
	Prime Minister and Defence
	    Minister, June 1963–June
	    1967
	Prime Minister, June 1967–
	    March 1969
		Mapai
		ILP

GALILI, Yisrael	born 1911, Poland
	Without Portfolio, January
	    1966–
		Ahdut
		    Ha'avoda
		ILP

GERI, Jack Myer	born 1901, Lithuania
	Commerce and Industry,
	    November 1950–October
	    1951
		non-party

GOVRIN, Akiva	born 1902, Russia Without Portfolio, December 1963–December 1964	Mapai

	Tourism, December 1964– January 1966	
GRUENBAUM, Yitzhak	1879–1970, Poland Interior, May 1948–March 1949	General Zionist
GVATI, Haim	born 1901, Poland Agriculture, November 1964– (Also Health, December 1969– July 1970) (Also Development, September 1970–)	Mapai ILP
HAZANI, Michael	born 1913, Poland Welfare, September 1970–	Ha-po'el Ha-mizrahi NRP
HILLEL, Shlomo	born 1923, Iraq Police, December 1969–	Mapai ILP
JOSEPH, Dov	born 1899, Canada Supply, Rationing and Agriculture, March 1949–November 1950 Transport, November 1950– October 1951 Commerce and Industry, October 1951–December 1952 (Also Justice, October 1951– June 1952) Without Portfolio, December 1952–June 1953 Development, June 1953– November 1955 (Also Health, June–November 1955) Justice, November 1961– January 1966	Mapai
JOSEPHTHAL, Giora	1912–62, Germany Labour, December 1959– November 1961 Development and Housing, November 1961–August 1962	Mapai
KAPLAN, Eliezer	1891–1952, Poland Finance, May 1948–June 1952 (Also Commerce and Industry, March 1949–November 1950) Deputy Prime Minister, June– July 1952	Mapai

KOL, Moshe	born 1911, Poland Development and Tourism, January 1966–December 1969 Tourism, December 1969–	Progressive (Independent dent Liberal)
LANDAU, Haim	born 1916, Poland Development, December 1969– August 1970	Herut Gahal
LAVON, Pinhas	born 1904, Poland Agriculture, November 1950– October 1951 Without Portfolio, August 1952– January 1954 Defence, January 1954– February 1955	Mapai
LEVIN, Rabbi Yitzhak Meir	1894–1971, Poland Welfare, May 1948–September 1952	Agudat Yisrael
LUZ, Kadish	1895–1972, Russia Agriculture, November 1955– December 1959	Mapai
MAIMON, Rabbi Yehuda Leib	1875–1962, Russia Religious Affairs and War Veterans, May 1948–October 1951	Mizrahi NRP
MEIR, Golda	born 1898, Russia Labour and National Insurance, March 1949–June 1956 Foreign Affairs, June 1956– January 1966 Prime Minister, March 1969– (Also Justice, July–September 1972)	Mapai ILP
MINTZ, Benyamin	1903–61, Poland Posts, July 1960–May 1961	Po'alei Agudat Yisrael
NAFTALI, Peretz	1888–1961, Germany Without Portfolio, October 1951–June 1952 Agriculture, June 1952–November 1955 (Also Commerce and Industry, June–November 1955) Without Portfolio, November 1955–January 1959	Mapai

NAMIR, Mordekhai	born 1897, Russia Labour, June 1956–December 1959	Mapai
NUROCK, Rabbi Mordekhai	1884–1963, Latvia Posts, November–December 1952	Mizrahi NRP
PELED, Natan	born 1913, Russia Immigration and Absorption, 1970–	Mapam
PERES, Shimon	born 1923, Poland Without Portfolio, December 1969–August 1970 (In charge of Immigration and Absorption, December 1969–July 1970) Posts (Communications) and Transport, September 1970–	Mapai Rafi ILP
PINHAS, David Zvi	1895–1952, Hungary Transport, October 1951–August 1952	Mizrahi NRP
REMEZ, David	1886–1951, Russia Transport and Communications, May 1948 November 1950 Education and Culture, November 1950–May 1951	Mapai
RIMALT, Elimeleh	born 1907, Poland Posts, December 1969–August 1970	General Zionist Gahal
ROKAH, Yisrael	1896–1959, Israel Interior, December 1952–June 1955	General Zionist
ROSEN, Pinhas	born 1887, Germany Justice, May 1948–October 1951 and December 1952–November 1961	Progressive (Independent Liberal)
SAPHIR, Yoseph	1902–71, Israel Transport, December 1952–June 1955 Without Portfolio, June 1967–December 1969 Commerce and Industry, December 1969–August 1970	General Zionist Gahal

SAPIR, Pinhas	born 1909, Poland	Mapai
	Commerce and Industry, November 1955–May 1965 and August 1970–March 1972	ILP
	Finance, June 1963–August 1968 and December 1969–	
	Without Portfolio, August 1968–December 1969	
SASSON, Eliahu	born 1902, Syria	Mapai
	Posts, November 1961–January 1967	ILP
	Police, January 1967–December 1969	
SERLIN, Yoseph	1906–74, Poland	General
	Health, September 1953–June 1955	Zionist
SHAPIRA, Haim Moshe	1902–70, Poland	Ha-po'el
	Immigration and Health, May 1948–October 1951	Ha-mizrahi
	Religious Affairs, October 1951–June 1958	NRP
	(Also Interior, March 1949–December 1952 and June–November 1955)	
	(Also Welfare, December 1952–June 1958)	
	Interior, December 1959–July 1970 (Also Health, November 1961–January 1966)	
SHAPIRO, Ya'acov Shimshon	born 1902, Russia	Mapai
	Justice, January 1966–July 1972 and September 1972–	ILP
SHAREF, Ze'ev	born 1906, Roumania	Mapai
	Commerce and Industry, November 1966–December 1969	ILP
	(Also Finance, August 1968–December 1969)	
	Housing, December 1969–	
SHARETT, Moshe	1894–1965, Russia	Mapai
	Foreign Affairs, May 1948–January 1954	
	Prime Minister and Foreign Affairs, January 1954–November 1955	

Foreign Affairs, November 1955–
June 1956

SHAZAR, Zalman   born 1889, Russia   Mapai
Education and Culture, March
1949–November 1950

SHEMTOV, Victor   born 1915, Bulgaria   Mapam
Without Portfolio, December
1969–July 1970
Health, 1970–

SHITREET, Behor-
Shalom   1895–1966, Israel   Sepharadim
Police, May 1948–December   Mapai
1966

TOLEDANO, Rabbi
Ya'acov Moshe   1880–1965, Israel   non-party
Religious Affairs, November
1958–October 1960

WARHAFTIG,
Zerah   born 1906, Poland   Ha-po'el
Religious Affairs, November   Ha-mizrahi
1961–   NRP

WEIZMAN, Ezer   born 1924, Israel   Herut
Transport, December 1969–   Gahal
August 1970

YESHAYAHU,
(Sharabi)
Yisrael   born 1910, Yemen   Mapai
Posts, January 1967–December   ILP
1969

ZADOK, Haim
Yoseph   born 1913, Poland   Mapai
Commerce and Industry, May
1965–November 1966
(Also Development, May 1965–
January 1966)

ZISLING, Aaron   1901–65, Russia   Ahdut
Agriculture, May 1948–March   Ha'avoda
1949

Bibliography

WIDELY-USED SOURCES (NOT LISTED IN CHAPTER BIBLIOGRAPHIES)

Brecher, M., *The Foreign Policy System of Israel*, Oxford University Press, London, and Yale University Press, New Haven, 1972 (Brecher)

Eban, A., *Voice of Israel*, Horizon Press, New York, 2nd ed. 1969 (Eban 1969)

Eytan, W., *The First Ten Years: A Diplomatic History of Israel*, Simon & Schuster, New York, 1958 (Eytan)

Government of Israel, Press Office, *Editorials in the Hebrew Press*, 1948–73

Interviews (I): Interviews conducted by the author are indicated in the chapter bibliographies by (I). In the notes they are cited as person—interview—date, for example, Ben Gurion interview, 1966. The position held by persons interviewed at the time of the decision for which they were a primary source, and the decision itself, are indicated in the chapter bibliographies beside the name of the person.

Israel and the United Nations, Manhattan Publishing Co., New York, 1956 (Israel and the United Nations)

Newspapers (daily except the weeklies *Bemahane*, *Ha'olam Hazeh*, *Ha-po'el Ha-tza'ir*, the fortnightly *Israel Digest*, and the monthly *New Outlook*):

Al Ha-mishmar	(Tel Aviv)
Bemahane	(Tel Aviv)
Davar	(Tel Aviv)
Ha'aretz	(Tel Aviv)
Ha-boker	(Tel Aviv)
Ha-dor	(Tel Aviv)
Ha-mashkif	(Tel Aviv)
Ha'olam Hazeh	(Tel Aviv)
Ha-po'el Ha-tza'ir	(Tel Aviv)
Ha-tzofeh	(Tel Aviv)
Herut	(Tel Aviv)
Israel Digest	(Jerusalem)
Jerusalem Post	(Jerusalem)
Kol Ha'am	(Tel Aviv)
Lamerhav	(Tel Aviv)
New Outlook	(Tel Aviv)
New York Times	(New York)

Weekly News Bulletin (Jerusalem)
Yedi'ot Aharonot (Tel Aviv)
Private communications to the author
State of Israel, *Divrei Ha-knesset* (Official Records of the *Knesset*, in Hebrew), Government Printer, Jerusalem, Tel Aviv, 1949–71 (*Divrei Ha-knesset*)
— *Government Year-Book*, Information Services, Government Printer, Jerusalem, 1949–72 (GYB)
— *Sefer Ha-hukkim* (Laws of the State of Israel), Government Printer, Jerusalem (*Sefer Ha-hukkim*)
United Nations, Documents (Doc.)
— General Assembly Documents (UN. A/)
— General Assembly Official Records (UN.GAOR)
— General Assembly Resolutions (UN.GARes.)
— Security Council Documents (UN.S/)
— Security Council Official Records (UN.SCOR)
— Trusteeship Council Official Records (UN.TCOR)
— Treaty Series (UN Treaty Series)

BIBLIOGRAPHY ON INTRODUCTION (CH. 1)

Brecher, M., Steinberg, B., and Stein, J., 'A Framework for Research on Foreign Policy Behavior', *The Journal of Conflict Resolution*, xiii, 1, March 1969, pp. 75–101 (Brecher, Steinberg, Stein)
Deutsch, K. W., *The Nerves of Government*, The Free Press, New York, 1963 (Deutsch)

BIBLIOGRAPHY ON JERUSALEM (CH. 2)

PRIMARY SOURCES AND INTERVIEWS (I)[1]

Ben Gurion, D., *Medinat Yisrael Ha-mehudeshet*, Am Oved, Tel Aviv, 1969 (Ben Gurion 1969)
An English translation appeared as *Israel: A Personal History*, Funk & Wagnalls, New York, 1971 (Ben Gurion 1971)
— 'War Diary', *Ma'ariv*, 6 May 1973 (Ben Gurion 1973)
— (I) June 1966, Prime Minister and Minister of Defence
— (I) May 1971
Eban, A., (I) Dec. 1965, Permanent Representative to the UN
Eytan, W., (I) Jan. 1971, Director-General, Foreign Ministry

---

[1] The formal post indicated beside persons interviewed refers to the 1949 strategic decision.

Government of Israel, Office of Information, *The Peace of Jerusalem*, New York, 1950 (*The Peace of Jerusalem*)
— *Jerusalem and the United Nations*, New York, 2nd ed. 1955
Government of Palestine, Supplement to a *Survey of Palestine*, Government Printer, Jerusalem, 1947 (Government of Palestine)
Herzog, Y., (I) April 1966, Adviser on Jerusalem Affairs to the Foreign Ministry
Horowitz, D., (I) Dec. 1965, Director-General, Finance Ministry
Joseph, D., *The Faithful City*, Simon & Schuster, New York, 1960 (Joseph)
— (I) July 1960, Minister of Supply and Rationing
— (I) June 1971
Meir, G., (I) Aug. 1966, Minister of Labour
Navon, Y., (I) May 1966, (later) Political Secretary to the Prime Minister
Rosen, P., (I) Feb. 1971, Minister of Justice
Shapira, H. M., (I) Aug. 1968, Minister of Immigration and Health
Sharef, Z., *Three Days*, W. H. Allen, London, 1962 (Sharef)
— (I) March 1966, Secretary to the Government
— (I) Feb. 1971
State of Israel, *Records of the Provisional State Council* (in Hebrew), Government Printer, Tel Aviv/Jerusalem, 1948–9 (RPSC)

OTHER SOURCES

Benvenisti, M., *Jerusalem: The Torn City*, Weidenfeld & Nicolson, Jerusalem, 1973 (Benvenisti)
Bernadotte, F. E., *To Jerusalem*, Hodder & Stoughton, London, 1951 (Bernadotte)
Bilby, K. W., *New Star in the Near East*, Doubleday, New York, 1950 (Bilby)
Bovis, H. E., *The Jerusalem Question, 1917–1968*, Hoover Institution Press, Stanford, California, 1971 (Bovis)
Churchill, R. S. and Churchill, W. S., *The Six Day War*, Heinemann, London, 1967 (Churchills)
Collins, L., and Lapierre, D., *O Jerusalem*, Weidenfeld & Nicolson, Jerusalem, 1972 (Collins & Lapierre)
Halpern, B., *The Idea of The Jewish State*, Harvard University Press, Cambridge, Mass., 1961 (Halpern)
Harel, Y., and Gur, M. (eds.), *Sha'ar Ha'arayot* (Lions' Gate), Ma'arakhot, Tel Aviv, 1972 (Harel and Gur)
Horowitz, D., *State in the Making*, Knopf, New York, 1953 (Horowitz)
Hurewitz, J. C., *The Struggle for Palestine*, Norton, New York, 1950 (Hurewitz)

Kurzman, D., *Genesis 1948: The First Arab–Israeli War*, World Publishing Co., Cleveland & New York, 1970 (Kurzman)

Lauterpacht, E., *Jerusalem and the Holy Places*, Geerings, London, 1971 (Lauterpacht)

Lorch, N., *The Edge of the Sword: Israel's War of Independence 1947–1949*, Putnam, New York, 1961 (Lorch)

McDonald, J. G., *My Mission in Israel 1948–1951*, Simon & Schuster, New York, 1951 (McDonald)

Mohn, P., 'Jerusalem and the United Nations', *International Conciliation* No. 464, October 1950, New York (Mohn)

Nakdimon, S., 'Behi'a Ledorot' (A Tragedy for Generations), *Yedi'ot Aharonot*, 16 Oct. 1970 (Nakdimon)

Narkiss, U., 'The Breakthrough to the Old City through Zion Gate', *Yedi'ot Aharonot*, 6 May 1973 (Narkiss)

Pfaff, R. H., *Jerusalem: Keystone of an Arab-Israeli Settlement*, American Enterprise Institute for Public Policy Research, New York, 1969 (Pfaff)

Rabinovich, A., *The Battle for Jerusalem June 5–7, 1967*, Jewish Publication Society, Philadelphia, 1972 (Rabinovich)

Rosenne, S., *Israel's Armistice Agreements with the Arab States*, Blumstein's Bookstore, Tel Aviv, 1951 (Rosenne)

Schechtman, J. B., *The United States and the Jewish State Movement*, Herzl Press, Yoseloff, New York, 1966 (Schechtman)

Schleifer, S. A., *The Fall of Jerusalem*, Monthly Review Press, New York, 1972 (Schleifer)

Wilson, E. M., *Jerusalem: Key to Peace*, Middle East Institute, Washington, 1970 (Wilson)

Zander, W., *Israel and the Holy Places of Christendom*, Weidenfeld & Nicolson, London, 1971 (Zander)

BIBLIOGRAPHY ON GERMAN REPARATIONS (CH. 3)

PRIMARY SOURCES AND INTERVIEWS (I)

Adenauer, K., *Erinnerungen, 1953–1955*, Deutsche Verlags-Anstalt, Stuttgart, 1966, ch. III (Adenauer)

Avner, G., (I) July 1968, Head, Western Europe Department, Foreign Ministry (S, T)
— Member, Israel Delegation to the Wassenaar Conference

Barou, N., 'The Origin of the German Agreement', *Congress Weekly* (New York), 19, 24, 13 Oct. 1952, pp. 6–8 (Barou)

Bartur, M., (I) April 1966, Assistant Head, Economic Department, Foreign Ministry (S, T)

Ben Gurion, D., *Medinat Yisrael Ha-mehudeshet*, Am Oved, Tel Aviv, 1969 (Ben Gurion 1969)
   An English translation appeared as *Israel: A Personal History*, Funk & Wagnalls, New York, 1971 (Ben Gurion 1971)
— (I) June 1966, Prime Minister and Minister of Defence (S, T)
— (I) May 1971
Blaustein, J., *A Dramatic Era in History*, American Jewish Committee, New York, 1966 (Blaustein)
Eytan, W., (I) Jan. 1971, Director-General, Foreign Ministry (S, T)
Goldmann, N., *The Autobiography of Nahum Goldmann: Sixty Years of Jewish Life*, Holt, Rinehart and Winston, New York, 1969, ch. 22 (Goldmann 1969)
— (I) April 1966, President, Conference of Jewish Material Claims Against Germany (T)
Halpern, B., and Wurm, S. (eds.), *The Responsible Attitude: Life and Opinions of Giora Josephthal*, Schocken, New York, 1966 (Josephthal)
Horowitz, D., (I) March 1966, Director-General, Finance Ministry (S, T)
— (I) Feb. 1971
Joseph, D., (I) July 1960, Minister of Transport (S)
— (I) Feb. 1971, Minister of Commerce and Industry, and Justice (T)
Meir, G., (I) Aug. 1966, Minister of Labour (S, T)
Navon, Y., (I) Dec. 1965, Private Secretary to the Foreign Minister (S, T)
Pearlman, M., *Ben Gurion Looks Back in Talks with Moshe Pearlman*, Weidenfeld and Nicolson, London, 1965, ch. 13 (Ben Gurion 1965)
Peres, S., (I) July 1960, later, 1953–9, Director-General, Defence Ministry
Rosen, P., (I) Feb. 1971, Minister of Justice (S)
Shapira, H. M., (I) Aug. 1968, Minister of Immigration and Health, and Interior (S)
— Minister of Religious Affairs (T)
Sharef, Z., (I) March 1966, Secretary to the Government (S, T)
— (I) Feb. 1971
Sharett, M., *Problems of the State: German Reparations*, Government Information Services, Jerusalem, 1952 (Sharett)
Shinnar, F. A., *Be'ol Kora Ouregashot: Yahasei Yisrael-Germania, 1951–1966*, Schocken, Tel Aviv, 1967 (Shinnar 1967)
— Letter to the author, 24 January 1966 (Shinnar 1966)
— (I) Dec. 1965, Adviser to Foreign Ministry on Reparations (T)
   Later Co-Head, Israel Delegation to the Wassenaar Conference
State of Israel, Ministry for Foreign Affairs, *Documents Relating to the Agreement Between the Government of Israel and the Government of the*

Federal Republic of Germany, Government Printer, Jerusalem, 1953 (*Documents* . . .)
— *Yedi'ot Le-Netziguyot* (News to Representatives), no. 473, 14 March 1952 (Y.L.)
Yahil, H., (I) April 1966, Consul of Israel in Munich (pre-S)
— (I) Feb. 1971

OTHER SOURCES

Balabkins, N., *West German Reparations to Israel*, Rutgers University Press, New Brunswick, N.J., 1971 (Balabkins)

Deutschkron, I., *Israel und die Deutschen: Zwischen Ressentiment und Ratio*, Verlag Wissenschaft und Politik, Köln, 1970 (Deutschkron)

Giniewski, P., 'Germany and Israel: The Reparations Treaty of September 10, 1952', *World Affairs Quarterly*, xxx, 1959–60, pp. 169–85 (Giniewski)

Grossmann, K. R., *Germany's Moral Debt: The German–Israel Agreement*, Public Affairs Press, Washington, 1954 (Grossmann)

Halevi, N., and Klinov-Malul, R., *The Economic Development of Israel*, Praeger, New York, 1968 (Halevi & Klinov-Malul)

Honig, F., 'The Reparations Agreement Between Israel and the Federal Republic of Germany', *American Journal of International Law*, 48, 1954, pp. 564–78 (Honig)

Infield, M. F. (ed.), *Essays in Jewish Sociology, Labor and Cooperation in Memory of Dr. Noah Barou, 1889–1955*, Yoseloff, London, 1962 (Infield)

Landauer, G., *Der Zionismus in Wandel Dreier Jahrzeiten*, Bitaon Verlag, Tel Aviv, 1957 (Landauer)

Moses, S., *Die Jüdischen Nachkriegsforderungen*, Bitaon Verlag, Tel Aviv, 1944 (Moses)

Patinkin, D., *The Israel Economy: The First Decade*, Falk Project for Economic Research in Israel, Jerusalem Post Press, Jerusalem, 1960 (Patinkin)

Prittie, T., *Konrad Adenauer 1876–1967*, Tom Stacey, London, 1972 (Prittie)

Vogel, R. (ed.), *The German Path to Israel*, Oswald Wolff, London, 1969 (Vogel)

BIBLIOGRAPHY ON KOREAN WAR AND CHINA (CH. 4)

PRIMARY SOURCES AND INTERVIEWS (I)

Ben Gurion, D., (I) July 1966, Prime Minister and Defence Minister (T₁, S₁)

— (I) May 1971, Defence Minister (S₂)

Eban, A., (I) Dec. 1965, Permanent Representative to United Nations (T₁, S₁, T₂, S₂)

— Communication to the author, Aug. 1971

Eytan, W., (I) Jan. 1971, Director-General, Ministry for Foreign Affairs (T₁, S₁, T₂, S₂)

Gazit, M., (I) Feb. 1966, Chargé d'Affaires, Rangoon (post-S₂)

Government of Israel, Ministry for Foreign Affairs, *Cables, Letters, Communications*

— *Yedi'ot Le-Netziguyot* (News to Representatives) (Y. L.)

Hacohen, D., *Yoman Burma* (Burma Diary), Am Oved, Tel Aviv, 1963 (Hacohen)

— 'Behind the Scenes of Negotiations Between Israel and China', *New Outlook*, 6, 7 (58), Nov.–Dec. 1963, pp. 29–44 (Hacohen (2))

— 'Thus We Missed Out on the Establishment of Relations with China', *Yedi'ot Aharonot*, 6 May 1973 (Hacohen (3))

— 'Chou En-lai Announced that He Expects Negotiations on Relations Between China and Israel', *Ma'ariv*, 6 May 1973 (Hacohen (4))

— (I) March 1966, Minister to Burma 1953–55, and Head, Israel Delegation to China, 1955 (T₂, S₂)

— (I) July 1971

Herzog, Y., (I) April 1966, Head, United States Department, Ministry for Foreign Affairs (T₂, S₂)

Israel Labour Party (*Mapai*), Archives (T₁, S₁)

Joseph, D., (I) June 1971, Minister of Supply and Rationing and of Agriculture (T₁, S₁)

— Minister of Development (T₂, S₂)

Kidron, M. R., (I) May 1966, Counsellor, Israel's Delegation to UN (T₂, S₂)

Levavi, A., (I) Feb. 1966, Counsellor, Legation to the Soviet Union, (T₁, S₁)

— Assistant Director-General, Ministry for Foreign Affairs (T₂, S₂)

Lewin, D., (I) Dec. 1965, Head, Asian Department, Ministry for Foreign Affairs, and Member, Israel Delegation to China, 1955 (T₂, S₂)

Lourie, A., (I) Nov. 1965, Deputy Permanent Representative to UN

(T_1, S_1); Assistant Director-General, Ministry for Foreign Affairs (T_2, S_2)

Namir, M., *Shlihut BeMoskva* (Mission in Moscow), Am Oved, Tel Aviv, 1971 (Namir)

Rosen, P., (I) Feb. 1971, Minister of Justice (T_1, S_1, T_2, S_2)

Schneerson, M., (I) Aug. 1971, Head, Asian Department, Ministry for Foreign Affairs (post-decisions)

Sharef, Z., (I) March 1966, Secretary to the Government (T_1, S_1, T_2, S_2)

— (I) Feb. 1971

Sharett, M., Letter to David Hacohen, 19 Jan. 1955

Shek, Z., (I) July 1965, Head, Foreign Minister's Bureau (T_2, S_2)

Shimoni, Y., Letter to the author, Oct. 1966 (Shimoni letter)

— 'Peking and Jerusalem', *Jerusalem Post*, 18 Feb. 1972 (Shimoni 1972)

— Communication to the author, July 1972 (Shimoni communication 1972)

— (I) Aug. 1960, Head, Asian Department, Ministry for Foreign Affairs (T_1, S_1)

— (I) Dec. 1969

World Zionist Organization, Archives

Yuval, M., (I) July 1972, On Special Assignment in Shanghai (Pre-T)

— 'No Chance for Ties with China' (interview with Meir de Shalit, Member, Israel Delegation to China, 1955), *Jerusalem Post*, 22 Aug. 1971

OTHER SOURCES

Brecher, M., *Israel, the Korean War and China*, Academic Press, Jerusalem, 1974 (Brecher 1974)

Chou En-lai, *Report of the Work of the Government Made at the First Session of the First National People's Congress of the People's Republic of China, September 23 1954*, Foreign Languages Press, Peking, 1954 (Chou En-lai Report)

Eyal, E., 'Israeli Ping-Pong with Peking', *Ma'ariv*, 23 April 1971 (Eyal)

Halpern, A. M. (ed.), *Policies Toward China: Views from Six Continents*, McGraw-Hill, New York, 1965 (Halpern)

Lie, T., *In the Cause of Peace*, Macmillan, New York, 1954 (Lie)

Medzini, M., 'Israel and China—A Missed Opportunity?', *Wiener Library Bulletin*, xxv, no. 1–2, Autumn 1971, pp. 33–42. A more elaborate version is in *Keshet* (Tel Aviv), 54, Feb. 1972, pp. 5–22 (in Hebrew) (Medzini)

New China News Agency, Reports

Paige, G. D., *The Korean Decision*, Free Press, New York, 1968 (Paige)

Rivlin, M., 'Taking Full Responsibility', *Jerusalem Post*, 24 June 1966 (Rivlin)

Israel and the United Nations (Report of a Study Group at the Hebrew University), Manhattan Publishing Co., New York, 1956

BIBLIOGRAPHY ON JORDAN WATERS (CH. 5)

PRIMARY SOURCES AND INTERVIEWS (I)

American Friends of the Middle East, *The Jordan Water Problem: An Analysis and Summary of Available Documents*, Washington, 1964 (AFME)

Arnon, Y., (I) Dec. 1971, Director of the Budget, Finance Ministry (T_1, S_1)
— Director-General, Finance Ministry (T_2)

Baker, M., Jr., and Harza Engineering Co., *Yarmuk-Jordan Valley Project, Master Plan Report*, Rochester, Pa., 1955 (Baker–Harza)

Ben Gurion, D., 'Israel's Security and Her International Position Before and After the Sinai Campaign', in *Government Year-Book 5720*, 1959/60, Jerusalem, 1960, pp. 9–87 (Ben Gurion)
— (I) June 1966, Prime Minister and Defence Minister (T_1)
— In 'retirement' (S_1)
— Prime Minister and Defence Minister (T_2)

Blass, S., *Water in Strife and Action*, Massada, Ramat Gan, 1973 (Blass)
— Letter to the author, June 1972 (Blass letter)
— (I) Nov. 1971, Director, *Tahal*, and engineering adviser to Israel Delegation to Johnston talks, 1955 (T_1, S)

Bunger, M. E., 'Prospectus: Yarmuk-Jordan Valley Project', n.d. (Bunger (1))
— 'Information on the Yarmuk River Watershed (Proposed Dam at Maqarin)', n.d. (Bunger (2))

Eshkol, L., (I) July 1966, Minister of Finance (T_1, S, T_2)

Gazit, M.,[1] (I) Nov. 1965, First Secretary, Embassy to UK (T_1, S)

Government of Israel, Ministry of Finance, 'Ten Year Water Plan Completed', *Israel Digest*, vii, 7, 17 Feb. 1956 (*Israel Digest*)
— 'Seven Year Plan', *Data and Plans Submitted to the Jerusalem Conference*, Jerusalem, Oct. 1953 (National Water Plan 1953)

Government of Israel, Ministry for Foreign Affairs: Rosenne, S., *Some Legal Aspects of Israel's Lake Kinneret–Negev Water Project*, Jerusalem, 1964 (Rosenne)
— 'Talks on Regional Water Projects Concluded', *Political Affairs*, 30, 28 June 1954 (MFA 1954)

[1] See note on p. 600.

— 'The Israel Water Plan', *Background Notes on Current Themes*, no. 35, Dec. 1959 (MFA 1959)

— 'Israel's Water Project', *Topics*, nos. 10, 11, Jan. 1964 (MFA 1964 (1), MFA 1964 (2))

Government of Israel, Office of Information: Cotton, J. S., *The Cotton Plan for the Development and Utilization of the Water Resources of the Jordan and Litani River Basins*, Israel Office of Information, New York, June 1954 (Cotton)

— Eban, A. 'Israel's Position on the Jordan Canal Project' (speech to UN Security Council, 30 Oct. 1953), Israel Office of Information, New York, 1953 (Eban)

Hays, J. B., *T.V.A. on the Jordan: Proposals for Irrigation and Hydro-Electric Development in Palestine*, Public Affairs Press, Washington, 1948 (Hays)

Herzog, Y., (I) March 1966, Head, US Department, Foreign Ministry (S)

— Minister (No. 2) to United States (T_2)

Ionides, M. G., *Report on the Water Resources of Transjordan and their Development*, Incorporating a Report on Geology, Soils, Minerals and Hydro-Electric Correlations by G. S. Black, London, March 1939 (Ionides (1))

— 'Jordan Valley Irrigation in Transjordan', *Engineering*, 162, 13 Sept. 1946, pp. 241–3 (Ionides (2))

Johnston, E., 'Mission to the Middle East' (Address to the Second Annual Conference of the American Friends of the Middle East), New York, 28 Jan. 1954 (Johnston (1))

— 'Formula for a Mideast Settlement', *New York Times Magazine*, 10 Aug. 1958 (Johnston (2))

— 'A Key to the Future of the Mideast', *New York Times Magazine*, 19 Oct. 1958 (Johnston (3))

League of Arab States, *The Arab Plan for Development of Water Resources in the Jordan Valley*, Cairo, March 1954 (English text in *Egyptian Economic and Political Science Review*, Cairo, Oct. 1955, pp. 42–4) (*EEPSR*)

Lowdermilk, W. C., *Palestine, Land of Promise*, Harper & Bros., New York and London, 1944, ch. xi (Lowdermilk)

MacDonald, Sir M., *et al.*, *Report on the Proposed Extension of Irrigation in the Jordan Valley*, London, March 1951 (MacDonald *et al.*)

Prushansky, Y., 'Water Development', Fourth (Revised) Edition, *Israel Today*, no. 11, Jerusalem, Dec. 1964 (Prushansky)

Sapir, P., 'The Development of Israel', *Israel and the Middle East*, New York, iv, 24 Dec. 1952 (Sapir)

Sharef, Z., (I) Feb. 1971, Secretary to the Government (T_1, S)

Shimoni, Y., 'The Water of the Jordan', letter to *Middle East Journal*, 7, 4, Autumn 1953, pp. 568–9 (Shimoni)

— (I) Sept. 1971, (Political) Counsellor, Embassy to US (T₁, S)

United Nations: Main, C. T., Inc., *The Unified Development of the Water Resources of the Jordan Valley Region* (prepared at the request of the United Nations under the direction of the Tennessee Valley Authority, Boston, 1953) (Main)

United Nations Conciliation Commission for Palestine, *Final Report of the United Nations Economic Survey Mission for the Middle East,* *(A/AC, 25/6) Part I, 1949* (UN.CCP, Final Report of UNESMME)

United States, Department of State, *Bulletin*, 2 Nov. 1953 (USSD)

— *US Participation in the UN—Report by the President to the Congress for the Year 1955*, Department of State Publication no. 6318, Washington, 1956 (Report by the President for 1955)

— 'Statement by President Eisenhower on Eric Johnston's Mission to the Middle East, Oct. 16, 1953', *Middle Eastern Affairs*, iv, 12, Dec. 1953, p. 413 (Eisenhower)

UNRWA: Clapp, G., 'Letter to the Director, UNRWA', in AFME, op. cit.

— 'Bulletin on Economic Development', no. 14, *Special Reports on Jordan*, July 1956, pp. 81–118 (UNRWA)

Wiener, A., (I) Nov. 1971, Engineering adviser to Israel Delegation to Johnston talks, 1955 (T₁, S, T₂)

Wiener, A., and Wolman, A., 'Formulation of National Water Resources Policy in Israel', *Journal, American Water Works Association*, 54, 3, March 1962, pp. 257–63 (Wiener & Wolman)

Yahil, H.,[1] (I) Aug. 1966, Ambassador to Sweden (T₁, S, T₂)

— 'What Happened to Eric Johnston?', *Jewish Observer and Middle East Review*, xi, 18, 4 May 1962 (*JOMER*)

OTHER SOURCES

American Jewish Committee, 'Water and Politics in the Middle East', New York, Dec. 1964 (AJC)

Bar-Yaacov, N., *The Israel–Syrian Armistice*, Magnes Press, Jerusalem, 1967 (Bar-Yaacov)

Barnes, G., '$200 Million For What?', *The Reporter*, New York, 7 Feb. 1957, pp. 24–6 (Barnes)

Berger, E., *The Covenant and the Sword*, Routledge and Kegan Paul, London, 1965 (Berger)

Bowman, W. G., 'Israel is Banking on Her New Immigrants', *Engineering News Record*, 22 March 1951, pp. 26–30 (Bowman)

---

[1] Gazit and Yahil were actively involved in the implementation stage, 1960ff., the former as Minister (no. 2) to the United States, the latter as DG, Foreign Ministry.

Burns, E. L. M., *Between Arab and Israeli*, Clarke, Irwin and Co., Toronto, 1962 (Burns)

Copeland, M., *The Game of Nations*, Weidenfeld & Nicolson, London, 1969 (Copeland)

Dees, J. L., 'Jordan's East Ghor Canal Project', *Middle East Journal*, 13, 4, Autumn 1959, pp. 357–71 (Dees)

Doherty, K. B., *Jordan Waters Conflict*, International Conciliation, no. 553, New York, May 1965 (Doherty)

Douglas-Home, C., *The Arabs and Israel*, The Bodley Head, London, 1968 (Douglas-Home)

Flapan, S., 'Dispute Over the Jordan', *New Outlook*, iii, 4 (26), Feb. 1960, pp. 3–7 (Flapan)

Frischwasser-Ra'anan, J. F., *The Frontiers of a Nation*, The Batchworth Press, London, 1955 (Ra'anan)

Garbell, M. A., 'The Jordan Valley Plan', *Scientific American* (New York), 212, 3, March 1965, pp. 23–31 (Garbell)

Geyelin, P., 'Preventive Diplomacy—U.S. Hopes It Will Avert Clash Over Jordan River', *The Wall Street Journal*, New York, 10 Jan. 1969 (Geyelin)

Ghobashy, O. Z., *The Development of the Jordan River*, Information Paper No. 18, Arab Information Center, New York, Nov. 1961 (Ghobashy)

Glueck, N., *The River Jordan*, The Westminster Press, Philadelphia, 1946 (Glueck)

Hirsch, A. M., 'From the Indus to the Jordan: Characteristics of Middle East International River Disputes', *Political Science Quarterly* (New York), lxxi, 2, June 1956, pp. 203–22 (Hirsch)

Ionides, M. G., 'The Disputed Waters of the Jordan', *Middle East Journal*, 7, 2, Spring 1953, pp. 153–64 (Ionides (3))

Lowenthal, M. (ed.), *The Diaries of Theodor Herzl*, Victor Gollancz, London, 1958 (Herzl)

Mehdi, M., 'The Arab Summit', *Middle East Forum* (Beirut), May 1964, pp. 25–8 (Mehdi)

Middle East Journal, Chronology, Oct. 1953–Oct. 1955, vols. 8, 9, 10, Washington (*MEJ*)

Middle Eastern Affairs, Chronology, Oct. 1953–Oct. 1955, vols. iv, v, vi, New York (*MEA*)

Nijim, B. K., 'The Jordan Basin and International Riparian Disputes: A Search for Pattern' (paper delivered to Middle East Studies Association, 1970) (Nijim)

Nimrod, Y., 'The Unquiet Waters', *New Outlook*, 8, 4 (71), June 1965, pp. 38–49 (Nimrod (1))

— 'The Jordan's Angry Waters', ibid., 8, 5 (72), July–August 1965, pp. 19–33, 60 (Nimrod (2))

Nimrod, Y., 'Conflict over the Jordan—Last Stage', ibid., 8, 6 (73), Sept. 1965, pp. 5–18 (Nimrod (3))

— Angry Waters: Dispute over the Jordan Waters, Center for Arab and Afro-Asian Studies, Givat Haviva, 1966 (in Hebrew) (Nimrod (4))

Peretz, D., 'Development of the Jordan Valley Waters', Middle East Journal, 9, 4, Autumn 1955, pp. 397–412 (Peretz 1955)

— 'River Schemes and Their Effect on Economic Development in Jordan, Syria and Lebanon', Middle East Journal, 18, 3, Summer 1964, pp. 293–305 (Peretz 1964)

Prittie, T., Israel: Miracle in the Desert, Praeger, New York, rev. ed. 1968, ch. 4 (Prittie)

Rizk, E. A., The River Jordan, Information Paper No. 23, Arab Information Center, New York, 1963 (Rizk)

Schiff, Z., 'Israel Looks for Water', New Outlook, 5, 4 (44), May 1962, pp. 27–31 (Schiff)

Schmidt, D. A., 'Prospects for a Solution of the Jordan River Valley Dispute', Middle Eastern Affairs, vi, 1, Jan. 1955, pp. 1–12 (Schmidt)

Stevens, G. G., The Jordan River Valley, International Conciliation, no. 506, New York, Jan. 1956 (Stevens 1956)

— Jordan River Partition, Hoover Institution Studies 6, Stanford University, Stanford, Cal., 1965 (Stevens 1965)

BIBLIOGRAPHY ON SINAI CAMPAIGN (CH. 6)

SOURCES

There is a large body of literature on the Suez–Sinai issue. Most of it however, focuses on non-Israeli actors except for details of the military campaign. By way of illustration:

British policy and behaviour:	Eden, Macmillan, Nutting, H. Thomas
French policy and behaviour:	Azeau, Bar-Zohar 1964, Bromberger, Tourneaux
United Nations role:	Burns, Fry, Higgins
United States policy and behaviour	Eisenhower, Finer
Military campaign:	Barker, Beaufre, Henriques, Keightley, Marshall, O'Ballance. Stockwell
Canadian role:	Robertson
Commonwealth role:	Eayrs
Egyption policy and behaviour:	Heikal, Love

Several books deal with many aspects of the crisis, notably Azeau, Finer, love, Robertson, Stock, and Thomas.

Emphasis on the Israeli dimension, by contrast, is found in a small number of memoirs or diaries by Israeli decision-makers: Ben Gurion's 'Israel's Security and Her International Position Before and After the Sinai Campaign' (1960) and *Israel: A Personal History* (1971); Dayan's *Diary of the Sinai Campaign* (1966); and Peres' *David's Sling* (1970). Extracts from Ben Gurion's papers were also used by Bar-Zohar (1966) and (1968). Evron contains invaluable selections from Peres' diary. And Tsur published his *Paris Diary*.

PRIMARY SOURCES AND INTERVIEWS (I)

Adams, S., *First Hand Report*, Harper & Bros., New York, 1961 (Adams)

Aldrich, W. W., 'The Suez Crisis: A Footnote to History', *Foreign Affairs* (New York), xlv, 3, April 1967, pp. 541–52 (Aldrich)

Amit, M., 'Sinai 1956', *Jerusalem Post*, 29 Oct. 1971 (Amit)

Bar-On, M., 'With Golda Meir and Moshe Dayan in the St. Germain Mission', *Ma'ariv*, 5, 6 June 1973 (Bar-On)

Bar-Zohar, M., Instalments from biography of Ben Gurion (Hebrew version), in translation, *Jerusalem Post*, Oct. 1966 (Ben Gurion Documents Bar-Zohar 1966)

— *Ben Gurion: The Armed Prophet*, Prentice-Hall, Englewood Cliffs, N.J., 1968 (Ben Gurion Documents Bar-Zohar 1968)

Beaufre, Gen. A., *The Suez Expedition 1956*, Faber & Faber, London, 1969 (Beaufre)

Ben Gurion, D., Address to the Histadrut Convention 18 March 1956 (Ben Gurion 1956 (1))

— Address on Independence Day 15 April 1956 (Ben Gurion 1956 (2))

— Address to the *Knesset* 15 October 1956, *Divrei Ha-knesset*, xxi, Part 1, pp. 57–65 (Ben Gurion 1956 (3))

— Address to the *Knesset* 7 November 1956, *Divrei Ha-knesset*, xxi, Part 1, pp. 197–200 (Ben Gurion 1956 (4))

— Address to the Nation on *Kol Yisrael*, 8 Nov. 1956 (Ben Gurion 1956 (5))

— Address to the *Knesset* 23 January 1957, *Divrei Ha-knesset*, xxii, pp. 826–9 (Ben Gurion 1957 (1))

— Address to the *Knesset* 5 March 1957, *Divrei Ha-knesset*, xxii, pp. 1233–43 (Ben Gurion 1957 (2))

— *Ma'arekhet Sinai*, Am Oved, Tel Aviv, 1959 (Ben Gurion 1959)

— 'Israel's Security and Her International Position Before and After the Sinai Campaign', *Government Year Book 1959/60, 5720*, Jerusalem, pp. 9–87 (Ben Gurion 1960)

— *Israel: Years of Challenge*, Holt, Rinehart & Winston, New York, 1963 (Ben Gurion 1963)

Ben Gurion, D., A series of articles in *Davar* (Ben Gurion 1966)
— *Medinat Yisrael Hamehudeshet* (The State of Israel Reborn), Am Oved, Tel Aviv, 1969; English translation appeared as Ben-Gurion, D., *Israel: A Personal History*, Funk & Wagnalls, New York, 1971 (Ben Gurion 1971)
— 'The Secret Negotiations Between Israel and Egypt', *Ma'ariv*, 2, 9, 16, 23 July 1971 (Ben Gurion 1971 (2))
— (I) July 1966, Prime Minister and Defence Minister (T, S_1, S_2)
— (I) May 1971
Burns, Lt.-Gen. E. L. M., *Between Arab and Israeli*, Geo. G. Harrap & Co., London, 1962 (Burns)
Dayan, M., 'Israel's Border and Security Problems', *Foreign Affairs* (New York), 33, 2, Jan. 1955, pp. 250–67 (Dayan 1955 (1))
— 'Why Israel Strikes Back', in Robinson, D. (ed.), *Under Fire: Israel's 20-year Struggle for Survival*, Norton & Co., New York, 1968, pp. 120–31 (Dayan 1955 (2))
— 'Security before Sinai', *Jerusalem Post*, 24 April 1964 (Dayan 1964)
— *Diary of the Sinai Campaign*, Weidenfeld & Nicolson, London, 1966 (Dayan 1966)
— 'Ten Years after the Sinai Campaign', *Jerusalem Post*, 28 Oct. 1966
Eban, A., 'The Political Struggle in the United Nations and the United States resulting from the Sinai Campaign, October 1956– March 1957' (unpublished) (Eban 1957)
—'Abba Eban Reviews Diplomatic Results', *Jerusalem Post*, 28 Oct. 1966
— (I) Dec. 1965, Permanent Representative to the UN and Ambassador to US (T, S_1, S_2)
Eden, Sir A. (Earl of Avon), *Full Circle: The Memoirs of Anthony Eden*, Cassell, London, 1960 (Eden)
Eisenhower, D. D., *Waging Peace: 1956–1961*, Doubleday, Garden City, New York, 1965 (Eisenhower)
Evron, Y., *B'Yom Sagrir: Suez Me'ahorei Ha-klayim* (In Stormy Days: Suez Behind the Scenes), Otpaz, Tel Aviv, 1968 (Peres Diary (Evron))
Goldmann, N., (I) April 1966, President, World Zionist Organization
Heikal, M. H., *The Cairo Documents*, Doubleday, New York, 1973
Harkabi, Y., Communication to the author, 1972
— Director of Military Intelligence (T, S_1, S_2)
Herzog, Y. (in conversation with S. Tevet), 'The Political Side of the Sinai Operation', *Ha'aretz*, 28 Oct. 1966 (Herzog 1966)
— (I) March, April 1966, Head, US Department, Foreign Ministry, (T, S_1), seconded to Prime Minister (S_2)
— 'Nasser Was Not Ready to Arrive at a Peace Agreement with Israel', *Ma'ariv*, 6 Aug. 1971 (Herzog 1971)

Higgins, R., *United Nations Peacekeeping 1946–1967: Documents and Commentary: The Middle East*, Oxford University Press (for the R.I.I.A.), London, 1969 (Higgins)

Keightley, Gen. Sir C. F., 'Operations in Egypt—November to December 1956', *Supplement to London Gazette*, 10 Sept. 1957, HMSO, London, 12 Sept. 1957 (Keightley)

Kidron, M. R., (I) April 1966, Counsellor, Israel Delegation to the UN (T, S_1, S_2)

Kollek, T., (I) Aug. 1960, Director-General, Prime Minister's Office (T, S_1, S_2)

Macmillan, H., *Riding the Storm 1956–1959*, Macmillan, London, 1971 (Macmillan)

Meir, G., Address to Jerusalem Press Club, 2 July 1956
— United Nations Day Address to Jerusalem Rotary Club, 24 Oct. 1956
— Address to the Emergency Session of the General Assembly on 5 Dec. 1956
— Address to the 11th Session of the General Assembly on 11 Dec. 1956
— (I) Aug. 1966, Foreign Minister (T, S_1, S_2)

Moncrieff, A. (ed.), *Suez: Ten Years After*, Pantheon, New York, 1967 (Moncrieff)

Murphy, R. D., *Diplomat Among Warriors*, Doubleday, Garden City, New York, 1964 (Murphy)

Navon, Y., (I) Dec. 1965, Political Secretary to Prime Minister (T, S_1, S_2)

Nissan, E., 'An Hour With Abba Eban', *Davar*, 29 Oct. 1965 (Nissan)

Nutting, A., *No End of a Lesson*, Constable, London, 1967 (Nutting)

Peres, S., Lecture to Representatives of American Jewry, May 1956
— Address to *Mapai* Party Workers, Tel Aviv, 21 Aug. 1956
— *Ha-Shlav Ha-ba* (The Next Stage), Am Hasefer (Tel Aviv), 1965 (Peres 1965)
— 'We Avoided Destroying the Egyptian Army', *Ha'aretz*, 28 Oct. 1966 (Peres 1966)
— *David's Sling*, Weidenfeld & Nicolson, London, 1970 (Peres 1970)
— (I) March, April, July 1966, Director-General, Defence Ministry (T, S_1, S_2)

Pineau, C., 'Si j'avais à refaire l'opération de Suez', *Le Monde* (Paris), 4 Nov. 1966 (Pineau)

Rafael, G., (I) Aug. 1966, Adviser on UN Affairs, Foreign Ministry (T, S_1, S_2)

Robertson, T., *Crisis: The Inside Story of the Suez Conspiracy*, Atheneum, New York, 1965 (Robertson)

Rosen, P., (I) Feb. 1971, Minister of Justice (T, S_1, S_2)

Sharef, Z., (I) March 1965, Feb. 1971, Secretary to the Government (T, S₁, S₂)

Sharett, M., (I) July 1960, ex-Foreign Minister

Stockwell, Gen. Sir H., 'Suez from the Inside', *Sunday Telegraph* (London), 30 Oct., 6 and 13 Nov. 1966 (Stockwell)

Talbott, S. (ed.), *Khrushchev Remembers*, Little, Brown & Co., Boston, 1970 (Khrushchev)

Tsur, Y., *Yoman Paris* (Paris Diary), Am Oved, Tel Aviv, 1968 (Tsur)

United States, Department of State, *United States Policy in the Middle East: September 1956–June 1957*, Department of State Publication 6505, G.P.O., Washington, Aug. 1957

— *The Suez Canal Problem, July 26–September 22, 1956: A Documentary Publication*, G.P.O., Publication No. 6392, Washington, 1956

OTHER SOURCES

Allon, Y., 'Israel at Bay', *Midstream* (New York), ii, Spring 1956, pp. 5–11 (Allon)

Azar, E. E., 'Conflict Escalation and Conflict Reduction in an International Crisis: Suez, 1956', in the *Journal of Conflict Resolution*, xvi, 2, June 1972, pp. 183–201 (Azar)

Azeau, H., *Le Piège de Suez*, Laffont, Paris, 1964 (Azeau)

Barker, A. J., *Suez, The Six Day War*, Faber & Faber, London, 1969 (Barker)

Barraclough, G., *Survey of International Affairs 1956–58*, Oxford University Press (for the R.I.I.A.), London, 1962

Barraclough, G., and Wall, F., *Survey of International Affairs 1955–1956*, Oxford University Press (for the R.I.I.A.), London, 1960

Bar-Zohar, M., *Suez: Ultra-Secret*, Fayard, Paris, 1964 (Bar-Zohar 1964)

— *Ha-Memuneh* (The Boss), Weidenfeld & Nicolson, Jerusalem, 1971 (Bar-Zohar 1971)

Beal, J. R., *John Foster Dulles*, Harper & Bros., New York, 1957 (Beal)

Berding, A. H., *Dulles on Diplomacy*, Van Nostrand, Princeton, N.J., 1965 (Berding)

Berger, E., *The Covenant and the Sword*, Routledge and Kegan Paul, London, 1965 (Berger)

Blechman, B. M., *The Consequences of the Israeli Reprisals: An Assessment* (unpub. Ph.D. diss.), 1971 (Blechman 1971)

— 'The Impact of Israel's Reprisals on Behavior of the Bordering Arab Nations Directed against Israel', in the *Journal of Conflict Resolution*, xvi, 2, June 1972, pp. 155–81 (Blechman 1972)

Bloomfield, L. M., *Egypt, Israel and the Gulf of Aqaba in International Law*, Carswell, Toronto, 1957 (Bloomfield)

Brilliant, M., 'Israel's Policy of Reprisals', *Harper's Magazine*, March 1955 (Brilliant)

Bromberger, M. & S., *Les Secrets de Suez*, Édition des 4 fils Aymon, Paris, 1957 (Bromberger)

Campbell, J. C., *Defence of the Middle East*, Praeger, New York, rev. ed., 1960 (Campbell)

Childers, E. B., *The Road to Suez*, MacGibbon & Kee, London, 1962 (Childers)

Copeland, M., *The Game of Nations*, Weidenfeld & Nicolson, London, 1969 (Copeland)

Dagan, A., *Moscow and Jerusalem*, Abelard-Schuman, New York, 1970 (Dagan)

Dan, U., 'French Intelligence Man Reveals Secrets', *Ha'aretz*, 3 March 1972 (Dan)

Dinitz, S., 'The Legal Aspects of the Egyptian Blockade of the Suez Canal', *Georgetown Law Journal*, xlv, Winter 1956–1957, pp. 169–99 (Dinitz)

Eayrs, J. (ed.), *The Commonwealth and Suez: A Documentary Survey*, Oxford University Press, London, 1964 (Eayrs)

Epstein, L. D., 'Partisan Foreign Policy: Britain in the Suez Crisis', *World Politics*, xii, 1960, pp. 201–14 (Epstein)

Finer, H., *Dulles Over Suez: The Theory and Practice of his Diplomacy*, Quadrangle Books, Chicago, 1964 (Finer)

Finkelstone, Y., 'Maurice Auerbach Acted Thus in Conducting Talks in Cairo', *Ma'ariv*, 22 Nov. 1971 (Finkelstone)

Fontaine, A., 'Il y a dix ans la Guerre de Suez', *Le Monde* (Paris), 30, 31 Oct., 1 Nov. 1966 (Fontaine)

Foot, M., & Jones, M., *Guilty Men*, Rinehart & Co., New York, 1957 (Foot)

Frankland, N. (ed.), *Documents on International Affairs 1956*, Oxford University Press (for the R.I.I.A.), London, 1959 (Frankland)

Frye, W. R., *A United Nations Peace Force*, Stevens & Sons Ltd., London, 1957 (Frye)

Gee, J., *Mirage—Warplane in the Israel Air Force*, Macdonald, London, 1971 (Gee)

Glubb, Sir J. B., 'Violence on the Jordan-Israel Border: A Jordanian View', *Foreign Affairs*, 34, 4, July 1954, pp. 552–62 (Glubb)

Hayter, W., *The Kremlin and the Embassy*, Hodder, London, 1966 (Hayter)

Henriques, R., *A Hundred Hours to Suez*, Viking, New York, 1957 (Henriques)

Hourani, A. H., 'The Middle East and the Crisis of 1956', *Middle*

Eastern Affairs, St. Antony's Papers No. 1, Chatto & Windus, London, 1958 (Hourani)

Howard, H., 'Post-Mortems on the Suez Conflict of 1956', *ORBIS*, xi, 3, Fall 1967, pp. 903–7 (Howard)

Jackson, R., *The Israeli Air Force Story*, Tom Stacey, London, 1970 (Jackson)

Johnson, P., *The Suez War*, MacGibbon & Kee, London, 1957 (Johnson)

Love, K., *Suez: The Twice Fought War*, McGraw-Hill, New York, 1969 (Love)

Marshall, S. L. A., *Sinai Victory*, Morrow, New York, 1958 (Marshall)

Menzies, Sir Robert, *Afternoon Light*, Cassell, London, 1967 (Menzies)

Monroe, E., *Britain's Moment in the Middle East 1914–56*, Chatto, London, 1963 (Monroe)

Nahumi, M., 'Ten Years after Suez', *New Outlook*, 9, 9 (84), Dec. 1966, pp. 4–10 (Nahumi)

O'Ballance, E., *The Sinai Campaign 1956*, Faber & Faber, London, 1959 (O'Ballance)

Ra'anan, U., *The USSR Arms the Third World*, MIT Press, Cambridge, Mass., 1969 (Ra'anan)

Safran, N., *The United States and Israel*, Cambridge, Mass., 1963 (Safran 1963)

— *From War to War*, Pegasus, New York, 1969 (Safran 1969)

Schmidt, D. A., 'The Little War of the Borders', *New York Times Magazine*, 14 June 1953, pp. 111–15 (Schmidt)

Seale, P., *The Struggle for Syria*, Oxford University Press (for the R.I.I.A.), London, 1965 (Seale)

Siverson, R. M., *The Evaluation of Self, Allies, Enemies and a Mediator in an International Conflict* (Part of Contract No. 225 (82), Project NR117254), Office of Naval Research, Washington, 1969, published in part as 'The Evaluation of Self, Allies, and Enemies in the 1956 Suez Crisis', in the *Journal of Conflict Resolution*, xvi, 2, June 1972, pp. 203–10 (Siverson 1969)

— 'International Conflict and Perceptions of Injury: The Case of the Suez Crisis', *International Studies Quarterly*, 14, 2, June 1970, pp. 157–65 (Siverson 1970)

Smolansky, O. M., 'Moscow and the Suez Crisis 1956: A Reappraisal', *Political Science Quarterly*, 80, 4, Dec. 1965, pp. 581–605 (Smolansky)

Stephens, R., *Nasser: A Political Biography*, Allen Lane, London, 1971 (Stephens)

Stock, E., *Israel on the Road to Sinai 1949–1956*, Cornell University Press, Ithaca, New York, 1967 (Stock)

Tevet, S., *Moshe Dayan: A Biography*, Schocken, Tel Aviv, 1972 (in Hebrew) (Tevet)

Thomas, H., *The Suez Affair*, Penguin Books, London (rev. ed.), 1970 (H. Thomas)

Tournoux, J. R., *Secrets d'État*, Librairie Plon, Paris, 1960, Part II, ch. v–vii (Tournoux)

Trevelyan, H., *The Middle East in Revolution*, Macmillan, London, 1970 (Trevelyan)

Wint, G., and Calvocoressi, P., *The Middle East Crisis*, Penguin Books, London, 1957 (Wint)

BIBLIOGRAPHY ON SIX DAY WAR (CH. 7)

PRIMARY SOURCES AND INTERVIEWS (I)[1]

Allon, Y., *Masakh Shel Hol (Curtain of Sand)*, Ha-kibbutz Ha-me'uhad Publishing Co., Tel Aviv, 1959 (Allon 1959)
— Interview in *Lamerhav*, 14 May 1967 (Allon (1))
— Interview in *Lamerhav*, 4 June 1967 (Allon (2))
— 'The Last Stage of the War of Independence', *Ot* (Tel Aviv), 3–4, Nov. 1967, pp. 5–14 (Allon (3))
— 'Active Defence': A Guarantee for Our Existence', *Molad*, i, 2(212), July–Aug. 1967, pp. 137–43 (Allon (4))
— (I) July 1968, Deputy Prime Minister and Minister of Education
— *The Making of Israel's Army*, Vallentine, Mitchell & Co., London, 1970 (Allon 1970)

Bank of Israel, *Annual Report 1966*, Jerusalem (Bank of Israel)

Bar-Lev, H., Interview with Dov Goldstein, *Ma'ariv*, 18 April 1972 (Bar-Lev (1))
— Interview in *Yedi'ot Aharonot*, 2 June 1972 (Bar-Lev (2))
— Interview with Dov Goldstein, in *Ma'ariv*, 16 May 1973 (Bar-Lev (3))
— Interview with Nakdimon, in *Yedi'ot Aharonot*, 5 June 1973 (Bar-Lev (4))

Bar-On, H., (I) Aug. 1968, Spokesman, Ministry for Foreign Affairs

Begin, M., 'A Chapter from a Book to be Written in the Future', *Ma'ariv*, 18 June and 2 July 1971 (Begin (1) and (2))
— 'Ha-pgisha Beshtayim Beyuni 1967' (The Meeting of 2 June 1967), *Ma'ariv*, 2 June 1972 (Begin (3))

Ben Gurion, D., *Medinat Yisrael Ha-mehudeshet* (The Restored State of Israel), 2 vols., Am Oved, Tel Aviv, 1969 (Ben Gurion 1969)

---

[1] The formal post indicated beside persons interviewed refers to all tactical and strategic decisions leading to the Six Day War.

Bitan, M., (I) Aug. 1968, Assistant Director-General, Foreign Ministry, in charge of North America

Burns, E. L. M., 'The Withdrawal of UNEF and the Future of Peace-keeping', *International Journal*, xxiii, 1, Winter 1967–8, pp. 1–12 (Burns)

Carmel, M., 'Nevertheless We Were Faced with the Danger of Destruction', *Ma'ariv*, 21 April 1972 (Carmel (1))
— 'Matter of Survival', *Jerusalem Post*, 2 June 1972 (Carmel (2))
— 'Milkhama al Ha-kiyum—Ma'avak al Ha-shalom' (Fighting for Survival—Struggling for Peace), *Davar*, 2 June 1972 (Carmel (3))

Christman, H. M. (ed.), *The State Papers of Levi Eshkol*, Funk & Wagnalls, New York, 1969 (Christman)

Dayan, M., *Mappa Hadasha—Yahasim Aherim* (New Map—Other Relations), Shikmona, Haifa, 1969 (Dayan)
— Press Conference in Tel Aviv, 3 June 1967, in *Lamerhav*, 4 June 1967 (Dayan (1))
— Statement to *Tzahal*, 5 June 1967 (Dayan (2))
— Speech on 6 June 1967 (Dayan (3))

Draper, T., *Israel and World Politics—The Roots of the Third Arab-Israeli War*, Viking Press, New York, 1968 (Draper)

Eban, A., (I) Aug. 1968, Foreign Minister
— 'Reality and Vision in the Middle East', *Foreign Affairs* (New York), 43, July 1965, pp. 626–38 (Eban 1965)
— Interview in *Jewish Observer and Middle East Review*, 17 Feb. 1967, in *Documents on Palestine*, Doc. 6, pp. 2–3 (Eban (1))
— Speech in Rehovot, 17 May 1967, in *Ma'ariv*, 18 May 1967 (Eban (2))
— Press Conference in Jerusalem, 30 May 1967, in *Documents on Palestine*, Doc. 41, pp. 28–9 (Eban (3))
— Press Conference in Tel Aviv, 5 June 1967, ibid., Doc. 60, p. 59 (Eban (4))
— Address to the Security Council, 6 June 1967, in Eban 1969, pp. 299–312 (Eban (5))
— Address to the General Assembly, 19 June 1967, ibid., pp. 313–38 (Eban (6))
— Interview in *Ma'ariv*, 1 Dec. 1967 (Eban (7))
— Speech to the Jerusalem Economic Conference, 4 April 1968, *Weekly News Bulletin*, 2–8 April 1968 (Eban 1968)
— Interview in *Ma'ariv*, 2 June 1972 (Eban 1972 (1))
— 'Yamim Yafim Mul Iy-Nahat' ('Nice Days as Against Uneasiness'), *Ha'aretz*, 2 June 1972 (Eban 1972 (2))
— *My Country: The Story of Modern Israel*, Weidenfeld & Nicolson, London and Jerusalem, 1973 (Eban 1973 (1))

—'From What Our Commanders Said [on 23 May], It Seemed that the Struggle Might Be Long', *Ma'ariv*, 6 May 1973 (Eban 1973 (2))

Eshkol, L., Interview in *U.S. News and World Report*, 17 April 1967, reprinted in *Documents on Palestine*, Doc. 12, pp. 4–5 (Eshkol (1))

— Broadcast on Remembrance Day for Those Who Fell in Defence of Israel, 13 May 1967, in Christman, pp. 69–73 (Eshkol (2))

— Statement at the Opening of the Summer Session of the *Knesset*, 22 May 1967, ibid., pp. 77–89 (Eshkol (3))

— Statement in the *Knesset*, 23 May 1967, ibid., pp. 93–4 (Eshkol (4))

— Statement in the *Knesset*, 29 May 1967, ibid., pp. 97–104 (Eshkol (5))

— Letter to the USSR Premier Kosygin on 1 June 1967 in Reply to the Soviet Note of 26 May 1967, in *Documents on Palestine*, Doc. 48, pp. 49–50 (Eshkol (6))

— Broadcast to the Nation, 5 June 1967, in Christman, pp. 107–10 (Eshkol (7))

— Address to the Chief Rabbis and Spiritual Leaders of all of Israel's Communities, 7 June 1967, ibid., pp. 113–15 (Eshkol (8))

— Statement in the *Knesset*, 12 June 1967, ibid., pp. 113–34 (Eshkol (9))

— Public Statement, 27 June 1967, ibid., pp. 137–40 (Eshkol (10))

— Interview in *Ma'ariv*, 4 Oct. 1967 (Eshkol (11))

Evron, E., (I) March 1972, Minister (No. 2), Embassy to the US Government of Israel, Ministry for Foreign Affairs, Cables and Communications (Foreign Ministry Sources)

Heikal, M. H., *The Cairo Documents*, Doubleday, New York, 1973 (Heikal)

Herzog, Y., (I) Aug. 1968, Director-General, Prime Minister's Office

Higgins, R., *United Nations Peace Keeping 1946–1967: Documents and Commentary, Vol. 1—The Middle East*, Oxford University Press (for the R.I.I.A.), London, 1969 (Higgins)

Institute for Strategic Studies, *The Military Balance 1966–7*, London, 1967 (*Military Balance 1966–7*)

Jabber, F. A. (ed.), *International Documents on Palestine 1967*, The Institute for Palestine Studies, Beirut, 1970 (*Documents on Palestine*)

Johnson, L. B., *The Vantage Point: Perspectives of the Presidency 1963–9*, Holt, Rinehart and Winston, New York, 1971 (Johnson)

Ministry for Foreign Affairs, Information Services, *Menace: the Events that Led up to the Six Day War and their Lessons*, Jerusalem, 1972 (*Menace*)

Nakdimon, S., *Likrat Sha'at Ha'efes: Ha-drama She'Kadma L'Milhemet Sheshet Hayamim* (Towards the Zero Hour—the Drama that Preceded the Six Day War), Ramdor, Tel Aviv, 1968 (Nakdimon)

Peled, M., 'Tivan Shel Sakanot' (The Character of Danger), *Ma'ariv*, 24 March 1972 (Peled)

Peres, S., (I) July 1968, Secretary-General of *Rafi*
— *David's Sling*, Weidenfeld & Nicolson, Tel Aviv, 1970 (Peres 1970)

Rabin, Y., Interview in *Ma'ariv*, 14 May 1967 (Rabin (1))
— Interview in *Lamerhav*, 1 June 1967 (Rabin (2))
— Interview in *Ma'ariv*, 4 Oct. 1967 (Rabin (3))
— 'How We Won the War', *Jerusalem Post Weekly*, 4 Oct. 1967 (Rabin (4))
— 'Shisha Yamim Ve'od Hamesh Shanim' (Six Days and Five More Years), *Ma'ariv*, 2 June 1972 (Rabin 1972)

Rafael, G., '1967—Dokh Ishi' (1967—Personal Report), *Ma'ariv*, 18 April 1972 (Rafael)

Shapira, H. M., (I) July 1968, Minister of the Interior

United Nations, *Monthly Chronicle* (UN Monthly Chronicle)

Weizman, E., (I) Nov. 1971, Chief, General Staff Branch, *Tzahal*

Wilson, H., *The Labour Government: A Personal Record, 1964–70*, Weidenfeld & Nicolson, London, 1971 (Wilson)

Yadin, Y., Interview in *Jerusalem Post*, 11 June 1972 (Yadin)

OTHER SOURCES

Abu-Lughod, I. (ed.), *The Arab-Israeli Confrontation of June 1967: An Arab Perspective*, Northwestern University Press, Evanston, Ill., 1970 (Abu-Lughod)

Bar-Yaacov, N., *The Israel-Syrian Armistice*, Magnes Press, Jerusalem, 1967 (Bar-Yaacov)

Bar-Zohar, M., *Hahodesh Ha'arokh Be'yoter, 2 May–10 June 1967* (The Longest Month, 2 May–10 June 1967), Levin-Epstein, Tel Aviv, 1968 (Bar-Zohar)

Belyayez, I., Kolesnichenko, T., and Primakov, Y., *The Dove Has Been Released* (English translation in) Joint Publication Research Service, Washington, D.C., 1968 (Belyayez *et al.*)

Brown, Lord George-, *In My Way: the Political Memoirs of Lord George-Brown*, Victor Gollancz, London, 1971 (Brown)

Burdett, W., *Encounter with the Middle East: An Intimate Report on What Lies Behind the Arab-Israeli Conflict*, Atheneum, New York, 1969 (Burdett)

Burrowes, R., and Spector, B., 'The Strength and Direction of Relationships Between Domestic and External Conflict and Cooperation: Syria 1961–7', in Wilkenfeld, J. (ed.), *Conflict Behavior and Linkage Politics*, McKay, New York, 1973, pp. 294–321 (Burrowes (1))

Burrowes, R., and Muzzio, D., 'The Road to the Six Day War: Aspects of an Enumerative History of Four Arab States and Israel,

1965–7', *Journal of Conflict Resolution*, xvi, 2, June 1972, pp. 211–26 (Burrowes (2))

Cohen, M., 'The Demise of UNEF', *International Journal*, xxiii, 1, Winter 1967–8, pp. 18–51 (Cohen)

Dagan, A., *Moscow and Jerusalem*, Abelard-Schuman, London, 1970 (Dagan)

Douglas-Home, C., *The Arabs and Israel*, Bodley Head, London, 1968 (Douglas-Home)

Gilboa, M., *Shesh Shanim Shisha Yamin: Mekoroteha Vekoroteha Shel Milkhemet Sheshet Ha'yamim* (Six Years, Six Days: The Origins and History of the Six Day War), Am Oved, Tel Aviv, 1968 (Gilboa)

Golan, A., *The Commanders, Victors of 1967: 25 Profiles of Israel's Senior Officers*, A. Mozis Publications, Tel Aviv, 1968 (Golan)

Hashavia, A., *A History of the Six Day War*, Ledori Publishing House, Tel Aviv, 1968 (Hashavia)

Herz, J. H., 'The Territorial State Revisited: Reflections on the Future of the Nation-State', *Polity*, i (Fall 1968), pp. 12–34 (Herz)

Howard, M., and Hunter, R., *Israel and the Arab World: The Crisis of 1967*, Institute for Strategic Studies, Adelphi Papers, no. 41, London, Oct. 1967 (Howard & Hunter)

Hurewitz, J. C. (ed.), *The Soviet-American Rivalry in the Middle East*, Academy of Political Science, Columbia University, New York, 1969 (Hurewitz)

Kemp, G., 'Strategy and Arms Levels, 1945–67', in Hurewitz, op. cit., pp. 21–36 (Kemp)

Kerr, M. H., *The Arab Cold War 1958–67*, Oxford University Press (for the R.I.I.A.), London, 2nd ed., 1967 (Kerr)

Kimche, D., and Bavly, D., *The Sandstorm: the Arab-Israeli War of June 1967, Prelude and Aftermath*, Secker & Warburg, London, 1968 (Kimche & Bavly)

Lall, A., *The United Nations and the Middle East Crisis*, Columbia University Press, New York, 1968 (Lall)

Laqueur, W. Z., *The Road to War*, Macmillan, London, 1968 (Laqueur 1968)

— *The Israel-Arab Reader, a Documentary History of the Middle East Conflict*, Weidenfeld & Nicolson, London, rev. ed., 1970 (Laqueur 1970)

Lau-Lavie, N., *Moshe Dayan: A Biography*, Mitchell, London, 1968 (Lau-Lavie)

Legler, A., and Liebisch, W., *Militärische Ereignisse im Nahen Osten, Juni 1967: Eine Dokumentation*, Bibliothek für Zeitgeschichte (Weltbriegsbucherei, Stuttgart), 39 (1967), pp. 321–95 (Legler & Liebisch)

Marshall, Brig.-Gen. S. L. A., *Swift Sword*, American Heritage Publishing Co., New York, 1967 (Marshall)

Middle East Record 1960, Weidenfeld & Nicolson, London, n.d. (*MER* 1960)

Middle East Record 1967, Israel Universities Press, Jerusalem, 1971 (MER 1967)

Perlmutter, A., *Military and Politics in Israel*, Frank Cass, London, 1969 (Perlmutter)

Prittie, T., *Eshkol, the Man and the Nation*, Pitman, New York, 1969 (Prittie)

Rouleau, E., Held, J. F., and Lacouture, J. S., *Israel et les Arabes, le 3ᵉ Combat*, Éditions du Seuil, Paris, 1967 (Rouleau, Held, Lacouture)

Safran, N., *The United States and Israel*, Harvard University Press, Cambridge, Mass., 1963 (Safran 1963)
— *From War to War: The Arab-Israeli Confrontation 1948–67*, Pegasus, New York, 1969 (Safran 1969)

St. John, R., *Eban*, Doubleday, Garden City, New York, 1972 (St. John)

Sam'o, E. (ed.), *The June 1967 Arab-Israeli War: Miscalculation or Conspiracy?*, Medina University Press, International, 1971 (Sam'o)

Schiff, Z., 'The Three Weeks that Preceded the War', *Ha'aretz*, 4 Oct. 1967 (Schiff)

Segev, S., *Sadin Adom* (Red Sheet), Tversky, Tel Aviv, 1967 (Segev)

Stephens, R., *Nasser: A Political Biography*, Allen Lane, London, 1971 (Stephens)

Talmon, J. L., *Israel Among the Nations*, Weidenfeld & Nicolson, London, 1970

Tandon, Y., 'UNEF, the Secretary-General, and International Diplomacy in the Third Arab-Israeli War', *International Organization*, xxii, 2, Spring 1968, pp. 529–56

Tevet, S., *Moshe Dayan: A Biography*, Shocken, Tel Aviv, 1972 (in Hebrew), (Tevet)

Trevelyan, Lord, 'Problems of the Middle East', *Australian Outlook*, 25, 3, Dec. 1971, pp. 243–58 (Trevelyan)

Vance, V., and Laver, P., *Hussein of Jordan: My War With Israel*, William Morrow, New York, 1969 (Vance & Laver)

Velie, L., *Countdown in the Holyland*, Funk & Wagnalls, New York, 1969 (Velie)

Walker, F. P., *The Cabinet*, Fontana/Collins, London, rev. ed., 1972 (Walker)

Wohlstetter, A., 'The Delicate Balance of Terror', *Foreign Affairs* (New York), 37, 2, Jan. 1959, pp. 211–34 (Wohlstetter)

Yost, C. W., 'How it Began', *Foreign Affairs* (New York), 46, 2, Jan. 1968, pp. 304–20 (Yost)

Young, Brig. P., *The Israeli Campaign, 1967*, W. Kimber, London, 1967 (Young)

BIBLIOGRAPHY ON ROGERS PROPOSALS (CH. 8)

PRIMARY SOURCES AND INTERVIEWS (I)

*Allon, Y., Statement on Missiles, 14 Aug. 1970, *Lamerhav*, 15 Aug. 1970
— Statement to Information Personnel, 17 Aug. 1970, *Ma'ariv*, 18 Aug. 1970 (Allon (1))
— Interview in *Ha'aretz*, 4 Sept. 1970 (Allon (2))
— 'Strategy of Peace', Address to Eshkol Institute Symposium on changes since the Six Day War, 3 June 1973 (Allon (3))
— (I) Nov. 1971, Deputy Prime Minister and Minister of Absorption (T_1)

Bank of Israel, *Annual Report 1970*, Jerusalem, 1971

Begin, M., 'The Right to a Homeland, and the Right to Security', interview in *Yedi'ot Aharonot*, 7 Aug. 1970 (Begin 1970)
— (I) Oct. 1971, Minister without Portfolio (T_1, T_2, S)

*Dayan, M., Policy Statement, Address to Tel Aviv students, 29 July 1970, *Yedi'ot Aharonot*, 29 July 1970 (Dayan (1))

*Eban, A., Announcement in *Knesset*, 7 April 1970
— Press Conference, 17 Aug. 1970
— TV Speech in Arabic, 28 Aug. 1970
— Remarks at Labour Party Session, 29 Aug. 1970, in *Press Bulletin*, 29 Aug. 1970 (Eban (1))
— Israeli TV Interview, 4 Sept. 1970
— Address to UN, 28 Sept. 1970

Eliav, A. (Lova), *Eretz Ha-tzvi* (The Land of the Deer), Am Oved, Tel Aviv, 1972 (Eliav)

Elizur, M., (I) Oct. 1970, Head, North American Department, Foreign Ministry (T_1, T_2, S)

*Galili, Y., Interview in *Jerusalem Post*, 17 April 1970 (Galili (1))
— Interview on *Galei Tzahal*, 5 June 1970, *Press Bulletin*, 5 June 1970 (Galili (2))
— Interview in *Yedi'ot Aharonot*, 7 Aug. 1970 (Galili (3))
— Interview in *Jerusalem Post*, 4 Sept. 1970

Gazit, M., (I) Oct. 1970, Oct. 1971, Assistant Director-General, Foreign Ministry, in charge of North America (T_1, T_2, S)

* See note on p. 616.

Harif, Y., (I) Nov. 1971, political correspondent, *Ma'ariv*

Herzog, Y., (I) Nov. 1970, Director-General, Prime Minister's Office (T_1, T_2, S)

*Meir, G., Interview on *Galei Tzahal*, 5 May 1970, in *Yedi'ot Aharonot*, 6 May 1970 (Meir (1))

— *Israel Policy Statements*: Address to the *Knesset*, 4 Aug. 1970, Jerusalem, 1970 (Meir (2))

— Interview on 'Face the Nation', New York, 28 Aug. 1970

Ministry of Defence, *A Thousand Days*, ed. Y. Arad, Tel Aviv, 1971 (in Hebrew) (*A Thousand Days*)

Peres, S., (I) Oct. 1971, Minister without Portfolio (T_1, T_2, S)

United Nations, *Resolutions and Decisions of the Security Council*, New York, 1968 (UN. SCD)

United States, *U.S. Foreign Policy for the 1970s: A New Strategy For Peace. A Report to the Congress by Richard Nixon, President of the United States, Feb. 18, 1970*, G.P.O., Washington, 1970 (Nixon)

Weizman, E., (I) Oct. 1971, Nov. 1971, Minister of Transport (T_2, S)

'Mapam's Plan for Peace—1972', *New Outlook*, 16, 3 (140), March–April 1973, pp. 75–8

OTHER SOURCES

Ben Porat, Y., 'The Allon Map—From Theory to Reality', *Yedi'ot Aharonot*, 6 May 1973 (Ben Porat (1))

— 'Future of the Territories', *New Middle East*, 51, Dec. 1972, pp. 11–14 (translated from an article in *Yedi'ot Aharonot*) (Ben Porat (2))

Institute for Strategic Studies, *Strategic Survey 1969, 1970, 1971*, London, 1970–2 (*Strategic Survey*)

Margalit, D., *Sheder Me-Ba'yit Ha-Lavan* (*Dispatch from the White House*), Otpaz, Tel Aviv, 1971 (Margalit)

Schiff, Z., 'Everything About Withdrawal and Peace Maps', *Ha'aretz*, 2 June 1972 (Schiff)

BIBLIOGRAPHY ON THEORY-BUILDING AND RESEARCH
FINDINGS (CH. 9)

Brecher, M., 'Elite Images and Foreign Policy Choices: Krishna Menon's View of the World', *Pacific Affairs*, xl, 1–2, Spring–Summer 1967, pp. 60–92 (Brecher 1967)

* The sources for the five decision-makers listed above are those which were content-analysed. They made many other statements used in this study, which were reproduced or summarized in the Israeli press.

— 'Inputs into Decisions for War and Peace: The Israel Experience', in *International Studies Quarterly*, 18, 2, June 1974 (Brecher 1974a)

— 'Research Findings and Theory-Building on Foreign Policy Behavior', in *Sage International Yearbook of Foreign Policy Studies*, II, Beverly Hills and London, 1974 (forthcoming) (Brecher 1974b)

Brecher, M., Steinberg, B., and Stein, J., 'A Framework for Research on Foreign Policy Behavior', *The Journal of Conflict Resolution*, xiii, 1, March 1969, pp. 75–101 (Brecher, Steinberg, Stein)

Hermann, C. F. (ed.), *International Crises: Insights from Behavioral Research*, The Free Press, New York, 1972 (Hermann)

Holsti, O. R., 'The 1914 Crisis', *American Political Science Review*, lix, 2, June 1965, pp. 365–78 (Holsti)

Jervis, R., 'Hypotheses on Misperception', *World Politics*, xx, 3, April 1968, pp. 454–79 (Jervis)

Milbrath, L. W., 'Interest Groups and Foreign Policy', in Rosenau, J. N. (ed.), *Domestic Sources of Foreign Policy*, The Free Press, New York, 1967, ch. 8 (Milbrath)

North, R. C., Holsti, O. R., Zaninovich, M. G., and Zinnes, D. A., *Content Analysis: A Handbook for the Study of International Crisis*, Northwestern University Press, Evanston, Ill., 1963 (North *et al.*)

Paige, G. D., *The Korean Decision*, The Free Press, New York, 1968 (Paige)

Pruitt, D. G., 'Definition of the Situation as a Determinant of International Action', in Kelman, H. C. (ed.), *International Behavior*, Holt, Rinehart and Winston, New York, 1966, ch. 11 (Pruitt)

Rosenau, J. N., 'Pre-Theories and Theories of Foreign Policy', in Farrell, R. B. (ed.), *Approaches to Comparative and International Politics*, Northwestern University Press, Evanston, Illinois, 1966, pp. 27–92 (Rosenau)

Shilbaya, Muhammad Abu, 'Jerusalem Before and After June 1967: An Arab View', *New Middle East*, nos. 42 and 43, March/April 1972, pp. 43–5

Stein, J., *Elite Images and Foreign Policy: Nehru, Menon and India's Policies* (unpublished Ph.D. thesis), McGill University, 1969 (Stein)

Verba, S., 'Assumptions of Rationality and Non-Rationality in Models of the International System', *World Politics*, xiv, 1, Oct. 1961, pp. 93–117 (Verba)

Glossary

Agudat Yisrael	ultra-orthodox, anti-Zionist movement; its branch in Israel is a political party
Ahdut Ha'avoda	Unity of Labour Party; formed as a coalition of *Po'alei Zion* (*Tziyon*) and other minor Socialist-Zionist parties in *Eretz Yisrael* in 1919. Merged with *Ha-po'el Ha-tza'ir* in 1929/30 to form the *Mapai* party. Faction B, which split from *Mapai* in 1942, assumed the old name *Ahdut Ha'avoda*. In 1954, when it split from *Mapam*, this group assumed the name *Ha-Tenu'a Le'Ahdut Ha'avoda* (The Movement for the Unity of Labour)
Al-Fath	inverted initials of (Arabic) 'Movement for the Liberation of Palestine'; also Arabic for 'The Conquest', the largest Palestinian guerrilla organization, founded in 1965, based mainly in Jordan
Al Ha-mishmar	'On Guard', daily newspaper of *Mapam*
Aliya (pl. *Aliyot*)	immigration
Aluffim (sing. *aluf*)	Generals, includes ranks from Brigadier-General (*Tat-Aluf*) to Lieutenant-General (*Rav-Aluf*)
Am Yisrael	People of Israel
Bank Le'umi Le-Yisrael	The National Bank of Israel (not the state Bank of Israel), the largest private bank in the country
Behi'a Ledorot	'a tragedy for generations'
Bemahane	'In Camp', weekly of Israel Defence Forces
Davar	'Word', daily newspaper of the *Histadrut*
Divrei Ha-knesset	Official Records of the *Knesset*
Ee-hizdahut	Non-Identification, Hebrew Israeli term for Non-Alignment
Eesh meshek	a practical man, down to earth
Ein breira	no alternative
Eretz Yisrael	Land of Israel, Palestine
Etzel	abbr. for *Irgun Tzva'i Le'umi* (also IZL); see *Irgun Tzva'i Le'umi*
Feda'iyun	Arabic for 'self-sacrificer for cause', i.e. commando suicide-squad; first organized by Egyptian army in 1955, later used for

	all Arab guerrillas
Gahal	abbr. for *Gush Herut Liberali*, *Herut*-Liberal bloc, formed by merger of *Herut* and Liberal (formerly General Zionist) parties in 1965
Galei Tzahal	'Waves of *Tzahal*', Army Broadcasting Service
Galut	exile
Ha'aretz	'The Land', influential independent daily newspaper
Ha-boker	'The Morning', daily newspaper of General Zionist, later Liberal, Party, defunct since 1969
Ha-dor	'The Generation', daily newspaper of *Mapai* from 1948–55
Hagana	Defence, principal underground military self-defence organization of Palestine Jews, founded in 1921
Ha-Kibbutz Ha'artzi	The National Kibbutz; *kibbutz* movement of *Ha-shomer Ha-tza'ir*, established in 1927
Ha-Kibbutz Ha-me'uhad	The United Kibbutz; *kibbutz* movement— officially non-party, *de facto* mainly of *Ahdut Ha'avoda*, established in 1927; also a publishing house
Ha-Kirya	the quarter housing government offices
Ha-mashkif	'The Observer', daily organ of the Revisionist Movement from 1938 to 1948
Hamtana	lit. waiting; refers to the policy adopted by the Government of Israel from 23 May to 4 June 1967
Ha-Mosad	The Institute, which deals with all Israeli intelligence activities abroad
Ha'olam Hazeh	small Left-wing party which grew out of weekly magazine of same name
Ha-po'el Ha-mizrahi	workers' branch of *Mizrahi* Party; separate political party in Israel
Ha-po'el Ha-tza'ir	The Young Labourer, a Zionist-Socialist (non-Marxist) party, founded in 1905; merged with *Ahdut Ha'avoda* in 1929/30 to form *Mapai*; also a weekly by the same name, defunct since 1970
Ha-shomer Ha-tza'ir	The Young Guard, a Zionist Left-socialist movement, which established *Ha-Kibbutz Ha'artzi* and became from 1948 onwards the basis of *Mapam*

Ha-Tenu'a Lema'an Eretz Yisrael Ha-shlema	the 'Land of Israel Movement', which arose after 1967 War, advocating Jewish rule over the entire territory included in Mandatory Palestine
Ha-tzofeh	'The Scout', daily newspaper of National Religious Party (NRP)
Herut	Freedom Party, formed by Revisionists as legal successor to *Etzel* in 1948; merged with Liberal Party in 1965 to form *Gahal*
Histadrut	lit. organization; The General Federation of Jewish Labour in Eretz Yisrael, founded in 1920
Ihud Ha-Kibbutzim Veha-kvutzot	lit. Union of the *Kibbutzim*, one of three federations of communal settlements, affiliated with *Mapai*
Irgun Tzva'i Le'umi	National Military Organization, an underground force under Revisionist command, which seceded from *Hagana* in 1938 because of IZL's advocacy of extremist methods
Kadesh	lit. biblical name of town in the Sinai Peninsula; the code name for the Sinai Campaign 1956
Kedem	lit. east; the code name of the military operation to liberate the Old City of Jerusalem in July 1948
Kibbutz Galuyot	'Ingathering of the Exiles', the immigration and absorption of Diaspora Jews and their merger into one nation
Kibbutzim (sing. *Kibbutz*)	collective or communal settlements based primarily on agriculture, in recent years diversifying into industry as well
Knesset	the Israel Parliament
Kol Ha'am	'Voice of the People', daily, later weekly, newspaper of the Israel Communist Party (*Maki*)
Lamerhav	'Into the Open', daily newspaper of *Ahdut Ha'avoda*, merged with *Davar* in 1971
Lehi or LHI	abbr. for *Lohamei Herut Yisrael*, Fighters for the Freedom of Israel, an underground Revisionist movement, which advocated and practised individual terrorism; founded in 1940 by Avraham Stern (thus also known as Stern Group), it was dissolved in 1951
Ma'arakh	'The Alignment', an electoral alliance formed by *Mapai* and *Ahdut Ha'avoda* in

	1965 on eve of Sixth Elections; similar Alignment, in 1969, of Israel Labour Party and *Mapam* on eve of Seventh Elections
Ma'ariv	'Evening News', independent newspaper with widest circulation in Israel
Mafdal	*Miflaga Ha-datit Ha-le'umit*, the National Religious Party, formed in 1956 from a fusion of *Mizrahi* and *Ha-po'el Ha-mizrahi*
Maki	abbr. for *Miflaga Kommunistit Yisraelit*, the Israel Communist Party
Mapai	abbr. for *Mifleget Po'alei Eretz Yisrael*, the (social-democratic) Israel Workers Party, largest party in Israel since its foundation; formed in 1929/30 by a union of *Ha-po'el Ha-tza'ir* and *Ahdut Ha'avoda*; it merged with a revived *Ahdut Ha'avoda* and *Rafi* to form the Israel Labour Party in 1968
Mapainik	colloquial for member of *Mapai*
Mapam	abbr. for *Mifleget Po'alim Me'uhedet*, the (Zionist-Marxist) United Workers Party, formed in 1948 by a union of *Ha-shomer Ha-tza'ir* and *Ahdut Ha'avoda*; the latter split off in 1954; *Mapam* joined an Alignment with the Israel Labour Party in 1969
Matzpen	'Compass', organ of the Israeli Socialist Organization, a small revolutionary group which advocates the de-Zionization of Israel and her integration into a socialist Middle East
Mekorot	lit. sources; Water Planning for Israel, a public corporation concerned with the distribution of Israel's water resources and water construction projects
Minhelelt Ha'am	lit. The National Council; the pre-independence executive body of the *Yishuv*, April-May 1948
Misrad	Office
Mitun	turning down, recession (economic), usually referring to Israel's economic policy 1964–7
Mizrahi	Orthodox group within the Zionist Movement; in Israel it is the larger of two components of the National Religious Party (NRP or *Mafdal*)
Moshav (pl. *moshavim*)	co-operative settlement of smallholders
Olim (sing. *oleh*)	immigrants

'Oum Shmoum'	In Yiddish and, from this, now in the Hebrew spoken by East European Jews, the addition of 'shm', or some words formed from these letters, has a derogatory, even rude inference. 'Oum' is Hebrew for UNO
Palmah	abbr. for *Plugot Mahatz*, literally, striking platoons or shock troops; the élite unit of *Hagana* and its only formation permanently mobilized. *Palmah* was founded in 1941 and dissolved in 1949 when it was merged into *Tzahal*
Po'alei Agudat Yisrael	the religious party representing ultra-orthodox workers
Rafi	abbr. for *Reshimat Po'alei Yisrael*, the Israel Workers List, a *Mapai* splinter group formed by Ben Gurion and Peres in 1965; it merged with *Mapai* and *Ahdut Ha'avoda* in 1968 to form the Israel Labour Party
Rakah	abbr. for *Reshimat Kommunistit Hadasha*, New Communist List, anti-Zionist party which split from *Maki* in 1965; Moscow-oriented, it is composed mainly of Arabs
Reshimat Po'alei Yisrael	*Rafi*
Sabra (pl. *sabres*)	lit. prickly pear; name for Israelis born in Israel
Sepharadim	lit. Spaniards; refers to Jews of Spanish descent, more generally used to designate all Jews other than *Ashkenazim*
Siah	abbr. for *Smol Israeli Hadash*, the Israeli New Left, a small group formed at the end of 1967; it advocates two independent states in historic Palestine, one Jewish, one Arab
Solel Boneh	large, *Histadrut*-owned contracting, construction, and industrial complex
Tahal	*Tikhnun Ha-mayim Le-Yisrael*, the Water Planning Authority of Israel, the firm of consultants on water matters in Israel
Tora Shebe'al Peh	'Oral Law', unwritten formulation by the Israel Labour Party in August 1969, which specified the party's attitude to the ultimate disposition of the territories occupied by Israel as a result of the Six Day War
Tsiyonut	the aspiration and the movement to return to Zion

Tzahal   abbr. for *Tzva Ha-Hagana Le'Yisrael*, the Defence Forces of Israel, or Israel Defence Forces; established under the Defence Service Act of 1949

Vatikim   lit. veterans; used to designate 'old-timers', for example, in an occupation, long-established settlers, etc.

Yedi'ot Aharonot   'Latest News', independent, daily evening newspaper

Yishuv   lit. Community; refers to Palestine Jewry during the British Mandate 1920–48

NAME INDEX

Abdullah, King, 26, 27n., 244
Abramov, Z., 35n.
Abs, H., 81n., 92, 93, 93n., 94ff., 94n., 102
Abu Shilbaya, M., 49n.
Acheson, D., 78n.
Adams, S., 277ff., 297n., 298n.
Adenauer, K., 57, 62, 73, 73n., 74, 74n., 77, 78ff., 89ff., 94ff., 98ff., 103ff., 118, 284n.
al-Atassi, N., 357n.
Alessandrini, F., 50
Allon, Y., 37, 38, 166, 298n., 315, 328, 332, 334, 335, 336, 340ff., 365, 383, 383n., 385, 385n., 388, 389, 389n., 396, 397, 397n., 400, 400n., 402, 404ff., 419, 419n., 424, 426, 431, 440, 454n., 460n., 461, 462, 464ff., 469ff., 485, 485n., 493, 494, 496, 498, 515, 516, 537, 552, 557, 560; see also Subject Index
Almogi, Y., 424, 430, 464
Aloni, S., 427
Alphand, H., 284n.
Alterman, N., 248n.
Altmaier, J., 74, 74n., 80n., 98
Altman, A., 118
Amer, A. H., 323
Amit, M., 264, 267, 291n., 305, 313, 313n., 327, 337, 412, 414n., 417, 424, 425, 429, 437, 440, 558, 564
Anderson, R., 259ff., 259n., 417n., 420
Arafat, Y., 474
Aranne, Z., 32n., 37, 38, 87, 123, 124, 126, 140, 142, 145, 146, 146n., 160, 181, 233, 259, 287ff., 331, 374n., 377, 379, 396, 413, 424, 534
Argov, M., 58n., 87n.
Argov, N., 234, 234n., 270
Arnon, Y., 202n., 205n., 210
Auerbach, M., 261n.
Avidar, Y., 153
Avigur, S., 328, 377, 403ff., 413, 424, 430
Avizohar, M., 498
Avner, G., 62, 62n., 66n., 71, 71n., 89n., 90, 91n., 94n.
Azeau, H., 268n.

Bader, Y., 86, 116n., 303n., 410, 424, 429
Badran, S., 404
Bahir, A., 383, 403, 404

Balaban, B., 298n.
Balabkins, N., 60n., 73n., 75n., 81n., 91n., 95n., 96n., 97n., 109n.
Baram, M., 328
Barbour, W., 399, 400n., 408, 489, 490, 493, 499
Barjot, Admiral P., 264
Barkatt, R., 328, 410, 424, 425
Barker, A. J., 230n., 275n.
Bar-Lev, H., 318n., 333, 379n., 383n., 385, 385n., 404ff., 421n., 427, 430
Barnes, G., 194n., 198, 200, 206n., 207n.
Bar-On, M., 366n.
Barou, N., 73n., 74, 80, 80n., 81n., 82n., 94n., 95, 98
Barraclough, G., 227n.
Bartur, M., 71, 71n., 89n.
Bar-Ya'acov, N., 189n., 213n., 357n.
Bar-Yehuda, Y., 87, 233, 275
Barzilai, Y., 38, 233, 259, 332, 378, 396, 415, 422, 427
Bar-Zohar, M., 230n., 240n., 256, 256n., 261n., 268n., 269n., 290, 321n., 365n., 399n., 401n., 402n., 412n., 414n., 415n., 417n.
Bashore, H. W., 197n.
Battle, L., 375, 376, 386, 405
Beaufre, A., 269n., 275n.
Beba, C., 87n.
Begin, M., 11n., 26, 32, 32n., 38, 58n., 62, 70, 84, 85, 86, 87, 87n., 89n., 105, 179, 180, 231n., 275n., 294n., 327, 330, 374, 377, 377n., 381ff., 388ff., 396n., 402ff., 410ff., 429, 430, 459, 460n., 465, 466, 488n., 490n., 494ff., 511n.
Bejarano, M., 147
Ben Aharon, Y., 116n., 179, 294n., 516, 516n.
Ben-Dak, J., 152n.
Ben-Eliezer, A., 39, 88n.
Ben-Gal, E., 155
Ben Gurion, D., 5, 11, 11n., 12, 13, 13n., 14, 14n., 16, 17, 17n., 18, 19, 22, 22n., 23n., 24, 24n., 25ff., 41, 42, 43, 46, 61ff., 70n., 75, 76n., 80, 81n., 84, 86, 88n., 89, 89n., 94, 97n., 103ff., 106, 110, 113n., 118ff., 125n., 126ff., 130, 130n., 134, 135n., 137n., 138n., 166, 166n., 178n., 181ff., 189, 190ff., 201ff., 206, 208, 208n., 209, 210, 211, 215, 218, 225, 228, 229n., 231ff., 255ff., 263ff.,

281ff., 284n., 285ff., 308ff., 330, 332, 333, 341n., 359n., 374, 374n., 376, 377, 383ff., 389n., 395n., 402, 404, 407, 408, 410, 416, 417n., 422, 423, 426, 428, 430, 525ff., 536ff., 545, 547, 549, 551, 555ff., 561, 564ff.; *see also* Subject Index
Ben Meir, Y.S., 375
Bennike, General V., 191
Ben-Porat, Y., 460n., 517n.
Bentov, M., 24n., 38, 233, 258, 318n., 332, 396, 422
Benvenisti, M., 40n.
Ben Zvi, E., 136, 136n.
Ben-Zvi, Y., 11n., 35n., 79, 287
Berger, H., 87n., 180n., 229n.
Berlin, M., 11n.
Bernadotte, F., 22, 23, 23n., 42
Bernstein, P., 24n., 26n., 116n., 124, 181, 231n., 303n.
Bikov, V., 394
Bilby, K., 18, 18n.
Bitan, M., 337, 338n., 377, 379n., 408
Blankenhorn, H., 73, 74n., 78, 80n., 93, 95, 95n., 98
Blass, S., 182ff., 186n., 188n., 189, 190ff., 195n., 197n., 198, 198n., 201ff., 204, 204n., 214; *see also* Subject Index
Blaustein, J., 82n., 92, 92n.
Boger, H., 87n.
Bohlen, C., 285, 285n.
Bohm, F., 90, 93, 93n., 94, 94n.
Boissevain, G. W., 35n.
Boulding, K., 525n.
Bourgès-Manoury, M., 242n., 263ff., 268n., 270, 271, 272n., 273, 280n., 285, 304
Bovis, H. E., 21n., 22n., 23n., 28n., 34n., 35n., 40n.
Bowles, C., 293, 293n.
Bowman, W. G., 191n.
Brandeis, J., 253n.
Brandt, W., 81n.
Braunschvig, J., 82n.
Brecher, M., 3n., 17n., 85n., 106n., 126n., 127n., 135n., 183n., 185n., 196n., 232n., 234n., 258n., 283, 300n., 321n., 322n., 325n., 344, 377n., 455n., 457n., 459n., 463n., 464n., 465n., 510n., 525n., 527n., 532n., 572, 580n.
Brentano, H. von, 79n.
Brody, R., 550n.
Bromberger, M. & S., 268n.
Bronfman, S., 82n.
Brown, G., 364n., 365, 365n., 372, 384n., 413n., 416n.
Bruce, D., 105n.
Bulganin, N., 284ff., 290, 308, 310, 395n., 531
Bull, O., 35, 360n.
Bunche, R., 15n., 291n., 293ff., 362n., 366n., 370, 480

Bunger, M. E., 189, 189n., 196
Burdett, W., 328n., 356n., 362n., 372n., 379n., 380n., 385n., 386n., 393n., 394n., 397n.
Burg, Y., 32n., 38, 124, 182, 233, 259, 275, 287, 332, 396, 417n., 427, 465
Burns, E. L. M., 229n., 255, 256n., 258n., 293ff., 300n., 302n., 308, 365n., 367n.
Byroade, H., 78n.

Callman, R., 82n.
Calvocoressi, P., 227n.
Campbell, J., 229n., 255n., 258n.
Carmel, M., 37, 38, 231n., 233, 233n., 275, 288, 304, 332ff., 348n., 373, 373n., 374n., 379n., 380n., 396, 397, 397n., 400, 404ff.
Carver, L., 193n.
Catroux, L., 262, 263
Challe, M., 266, 266n., 267, 270, 273
Chang Han-fu, 148
Chen Chia-kang, 150, 152
Chiao Kuan-hue, 155
Childers, E. B., 255, 256n., 275n.
Chou En-lai, 123, 127, 143, 145, 145n., 148, 151, 152, 152n., 153, 153n., 155, 156, 159, 161, 169, 257
Christian, G., 392, 407
Churchill, W. S., 35n., 325n.
Chuvakhin, A., 338n., 360n., 362, 362n., 372, 394, 395, 395n., 408
Clay, L., 294, 295n.
Cohen, C., 410
Cohen, H., 76n.
Cohen, I., 294n., 365n., 367n., 424
Cohen, M. R., 72n.
Collins, L., 23n.
Comay, M., 377
Copeland, M., 256n., 258n., 259n., 260n.
Cordier, A., 291n.
Cotton, J.C., 197n.

Dagan, A., 227n., 321n., 395n.
Dam, H. van, 78
Davis, K., 203n.
Dayan, M., 23n., 35, 38, 41n., 190, 211, 229n., 230, 230n., 232ff., 257ff., 262n., 263ff., 265n., 266, 267n., 268ff., 270, 270n., 272ff., 284n., 293ff., 304, 308, 311ff., 315, 319, 327, 328, 332, 335, 336, 341ff., 369, 373, 376, 380, 380n., 385, 388, 395n., 403, 406, 409, 410, 414ff., 434, 437, 440, 460n., 461, 462, 464ff., 470ff., 485, 487, 494ff., 510, 515, 516, 516n., 534, 536, 537, 552, 556, 557, 560, 566; *see also* Subject Index
Dean, A., 293, 293n., 294
Dean, P., 272, 273
de Gaulle, C., 315, 323, 323n., 340, 372, 374, 380ff., 398, 399, 403, 409, 416n., 419n., 422, 431, 436, 446, 478, 550, 552, 553, 567

de Murville, C., 372, 381
de Shalit, M., 146, 147, 148
Deutschkron, I., 73n., 74n., 91n., 93n., 94n.
Dewey, T. E., 295, 295n.
Dillon, D., 285
Dinitz, S., 489
Dinstein, Z., 361n., 374n., 404
Dinur, B. Z., 123, 181
Dixon, Sir P., 294
Dobrynin, A., 478, 479, 500
Doherty, K. B., 175n., 187n., 188n., 189n., 191n., 196n., 197n., 199n., 207n.
Douglas, P., 296n.
Dulles, J. F., 116, 180, 205, 210, 215, 240, 255, 260, 263n., 270n., 279ff., 286, 293, 293n., 294ff., 567
Dulzin, A., 465, 495
Dvorjhetsky, A., 83

Easterman, A. L., 75n.
Eban, A., 10n., 15, 15n., 22n., 25, 27, 29, 29n., 32n., 33, 33n., 34n., 38, 39, 40, 40n., 83n., 120, 120n., 123, 123n., 130, 130n., 131, 133, 133n., 134, 135n., 136n., 137ff., 151, 159, 161, 167, 167n., 189n., 191, 192n., 202n., 204, 234ff., 240, 240n., 245n., 252n., 255n., 256n., 267n., 270n., 277n., 278ff., 285n., 286ff., 308, 310ff., 313, 314, 318n., 319, 321, 321n., 323, 324, 328n., 331, 332, 333n., 335, 335n., 336, 338ff., 365ff., 372, 372ff., 396ff., 412ff., 416n., 417ff., 431, 435ff., 440, 464ff., 469ff., 483, 485, 487, 488n., 489, 494, 495, 496, 499, 508, 510, 515, 515n., 516, 516n., 528, 537, 550ff., 555ff., 563ff.; see also Subject Index
Eden, A., 228, 229n., 242ff., 265, 267ff., 271, 273, 285n., 305, 549
Eisenhower, D., 116, 191n., 192, 200, 206, 215, 228, 239, 240, 259, 260n., 270n., 271, 277ff., 284, 286ff., 295, 296n., 297ff., 308, 310, 384n., 531, 553, 558, 564, 565, 567
Elath, E., 130, 130n.
Eldad, Y., 517n.
El-Ghazzi, S., 207n.
Eliav, A., 328, 374n., 424ff.
Eliav, L., 516, 516n.
Elizur, M., 26n., 492n.
El-Kony, M., 364n., 366n., 367, 369, 370, 371
Eren, M., 87n.
Eshkol, L., 5, 37, 38, 65, 83, 123, 155, 166, 180, 181ff., 190, 191, 191n., 198, 200ff., 208, 208n., 214, 218, 233, 233n., 254n., 268, 270, 275, 288, 290, 318ff., 321, 322, 327ff., 331, 333n., 336, 337, 337n., 365ff., 388, 389, 389n., 394ff., 435ff., 440, 444, 480, 488n., 539, 540,

550, 552, 557, 564, 567, 574n.; see also Subject Index
Evans, H., 21
Evatt, H., 26
Evron, E., 239n., 246n., 247n., 248n., 337, 378, 381, 386, 386n., 390, 390n., 391n., 393, 393n., 407, 414, 427, 436, 559
Eyal, E., 24n., 167n., 168n.
Eytan, W., 15n., 18, 27n., 30n., 33n., 34, 34n., 35n., 62n., 66n., 71, 71n., 76, 76n., 103n., 105n., 120, 120n., 123, 123n., 124, 127, 127n., 128, 128n., 130, 130n., 132, 132n., 137, 140, 141, 146, 167, 167n., 290, 380, 403, 419, 436

Fall, B., 275n.
Farouk, King, 244
Fawzi, M., 237n., 302n., 358, 368, 369, 370
Feisal, King, 244
Finer, H., 256n., 268n., 280n., 285n., 291n., 296n., 297n., 298n., 301n.
Fisher, M., 78, 374n.
Fleming, D. F., 227n.
Franco, Generalísimo, 105
Frowein, A., 95
Frye, W. R., 302n.

Gaitskell, H., 269n.
Galili, Y., 38, 229n., 231n., 258n., 275, 275n., 303n., 315, 332, 361n., 365, 377, 383, 396, 401, 404ff., 415, 424, 428, 464n., 494ff., 500, 500n., 508n., 515, 516, 516n., 537, 556, 557, 560; see also Subject Index
Garbell, M. A., 175n.
Gardia, S., 87n.
Gardiner, A., 198, 201
Gavish, Y., 385, 415, 427
Gazit, M., 154, 191n., 209n., 210n., 267
Geist, B., 318n.
Genihouski, M., 88n.
Geri, J. M., 61, 76n., 83
Geva, Y., 405, 407
Geyelin, P., 210n.
Ghobashy, O. Z., 210n.
Gilboa, M., 328n., 355n., 356n., 363n., 368n., 380n., 381n., 383n., 384n., 386n., 388n., 389n., 397n., 400n., 401n., 402n., 412n., 414n., 416n., 419n., 421n.
Giniewski, P., 96n.
Globke, H., 105n.
Glueck, N., 178n.
Golan, D., 327n., 378n.
Goldberg, A., 373, 375, 376, 407, 414n.
Goldman, F., 82n.
Goldmann, N., 62, 62n., 71, 71n., 72, 72n., 73n., 74n., 79ff., 89ff., 102ff., 287, 296n., 453, 462, 463n., 543; see also Subject Index

Goldstein, I., 82n.
Govrin, A., 328
Granat, N., 26n.
Granofsky, A., 11n.
Gromyko, A., 321, 358, 358n., 359n.
Gross, S. Y., 423
Grosmann, K. G., 75n., 79n., 81n., 82n., 95n., 96n., 97n.
Gruenbaum, Y., 26n.
Gvati, H , 38, 331, 464

Habash, G., 474
Hacohen, D., 79n., 88n., 124, 125, 125n., 126, 135ff., 142ff., 158ff., 167, 168, 328, 377, 378, 530; see also Subject Index
Halevi, N., 60n.
Halle, L. J., 227n.
Hallstein, W., 95
Halpern, B., 12n., 15n., 129n., 152n.
Hammarskjöld, D., 226, 235, 237, 237n., 280ff., 289, 291, 291n., 292n., 302, 302n., 308ff., 314, 366
Hammer, Z., 498, 498n.
Han, Y., 87n.
Harari, I., 32n., 58n., 87, 88n., 179, 231, 231n., 275, 275n., 329
Harel, A., 155
Harel, I., 259n., 277, 383, 404
Hareland, G., 35n.
Harkabi, Y., 389
Harman, A., 337, 360n., 375, 376, 384, 386, 387, 389ff., 397n., 400n., 404ff., 411ff., 419ff., 431, 436, 440, 558, 565
Hashavia, A., 432n.
Hatta, M., 127n.
Hays, J. B., 187, 188n., 194, 197n.
Hayter, W., 291n.
Hazan, Y., 26n., 70, 85, 86, 231n., 329, 375, 388, 388n., 389, 406, 407, 422, 429
Hazani, M., 41n., 87
Head, A., 267
Heikal, H., 256n., 269n., 360n., 393, 406
Held, A., 82n., 355n., 363n., 364n.
Henderson, L., 75n.
Henriques, R. D., 230n., 267, 267n., 275n.
Hermann, C., 287n., 550, 562n., 563n., 564n., 565n., 566n., 567n., 568n., 579
Herzfeld, A., 26n.
Herzl, T., 29, 185n.
Herzog, Y., 11n., 15n., 26, 26n., 29, 29n., 33, 33n., 137, 146, 146n., 167n., 182, 182n., 198, 201n., 202n., 209n., 210n., 234, 234n., 237, 237n., 241n., 247n., 255n., 260, 260n., 263n., 282ff., 288ff., 337, 338n., 362n., 365, 369, 374, 377, 385, 401, 402, 405ff., 430, 454n., 464n., 551, 556, 557, 565
Heuss, T., 78
Higgins, R., 302n.
Hillel, S., 464
Hirt, A., 460n.

Hitler, A., 64, 65, 95n., 104, 242n., 342
Hod, M., 385, 405, 418n., 492
Hoffman, P., 293, 293n.
Holsti, O., 524n., 550, 552n., 564n., 574, 574n., 580n.
Honig, F., 96n.
Hoover, H., 192n., 286, 286n., 294n., 297, 553
Horowitz, D., 15n., 22n., 62, 62n., 66n., 68, 68n., 71, 71n., 74n., 75ff., 89n.; see also Subject Index
Humphrey, U., 297
Hurewitz, J. C., 322n.
Hushi, A., 388, 404
Hussein, King, 35, 37, 243, 244, 324, 356, 412, 412n., 419, 425, 448, 457, 461, 474, 506, 550

Ionides, M. G., 187n., 196

Jackson, R., 231n.
Janner, B., 82n.
Jarring, G., 314, 442, 449, 455, 468, 480, 484, 488n., 490n., 491n., 492n., 496ff., 504, 505, 505n., 508, 509, 515
Jervis, R., 529n.
Johnson, L. B., 39, 297, 319, 322, 322n., 338, 339, 368, 368n., 370, 375, 377ff., 390ff., 397n., 398ff., 407, 413ff., 419ff., 436, 444, 531, 550, 555, 559
Johnston, E., 116, 194, 195, 196, 198ff., 203, 203n., 205ff., 215, 218, 549
Joseph, D., 11, 11n., 12, 13, 14, 14n., 15n., 17n., 19, 20, 21n., 22, 22n., 23, 23n., 24n., 29, 29n., 30, 30n., 31, 33, 33n., 42, 61, 62, 69, 70n., 75, 75n., 76, 77n., 118, 123, 124, 126, 126n., 181, 195, 235n., 415, 525; see also Subject Index
Josephthal, G., 89, 89n., 90ff.

Kagan, S., 82n.
Kahana, K., 88n.
Kaplan, E., 12, 13, 24, 24n., 30, 61, 62, 65, 68, 74, 75, 75n., 76n., 82, 89n., 94, 94n., 118, 183, 530, 539; see also Subject Index
Karlebach, E., 85
Kashti, M., 404
Katz, Z., 152n.
Katznelson, B., 11n.
Kemp, G., 325n.
Kempner, R. M. W., 75
Kennedy, J. F., 210, 224, 322
Keren, M., 92
Kerr, M. H., 152n., 324n.
Kessah, Y., 87n.
Khalili, J. E., 152n.
Khrushchev, N. S., 290, 291n.
Kidron, M. R., 234, 234n., 237n., 556, 560
Kidron, R., 122, 122n., 167, 283n., 288ff.

Kimche, J., 358n., 363n., 379n., 432n.
Klausner, J., 85
Klebanoff, Y., 79n.
Klinov-Malul, R., 60n.
Knowland, W., 296n., 297, 297n.
Koenig, P., 263, 303
Kohler, F., 386, 405
Kohn, L., 76, 76n.
Kol, M., 38, 332, 396, 426, 428ff., 465
Kollek, T., 137, 139, 182, 198, 202, 235n., 260, 362n.
Kosygin, A., 338, 368, 381, 382n., 394, 394n., 395, 395n., 408, 433, 436, 486, 501, 555
Kublanov, Y., 208
Kurzman, D., 23n.
Kuster, O., 90, 91n., 93, 93n.

Lacqueur, W., 359n., 363n., 373n., 416n.
La Feber, L. J., 227n.
Landau, H., 116n., 179, 327n., 465
Landauer, G., 72, 72n., 82, 89n.
Lange, N., 292
Lapierre, D., 23n.
Laskov, H., 232, 414, 414n., 423, 424, 534
Lau-Lavie, N., 345, 363n.
Lauterpacht, E., 39n.
Lavon, P., 26n., 58n., 61, 76n., 83, 86, 123, 124, 126, 140, 142, 145, 146, 146n., 160, 178n., 181, 195, 388n.
Lawson, E. B., 270n., 293
Leavitt, A. M., 82n.
Legler, A., 432n.
Lenin, V. I., 168
Lentner, H. H., 550, 565n.
Levavi, A., 128, 129, 129n., 146, 167, 167n., 360n., 361n., 365, 394, 428, 534
Levin, D., 124, 132n., 137, 137n., 143
Levin Y. M., 12, 24n., 30n., 88n., 118, 329, 423
Lewin, I., 82n., 145, 146n., 147, 148, 150, 150n., 151, 151n., 152, 154, 167, 231n.
Li Jen-min, 147
Lie, T., 130, 134n.
Liebisch, W., 432n.
Lior, Y., 373
Livneh, E., 74, 74n., 98
Lloyd, S., 241, 267ff., 269n., 272, 273, 292ff., 305
Lodge, H. C., 279, 292, 295, 297, 299ff., 310
Loren, N., 23n.
Lourle, A., 365
Love, K., 255, 255n., 256n., 258n., 261n., 262n., 267n., 268n., 285n.
Lowdermilk, W. C., 176, 187, 187n., 188n., 194, 197, 214
Lowenstein, T., 26n.
Lukacs, J., 227n.
Luns, J., 292

Luz, K., 233, 259, 328, 425ff.

McCarthy, G., 120
McCloy, J. J., 93n., 94, 295, 295n.
McDonald, J. G., 17, 17n., 26n., 27n.
MacDonald, M., 189n., 196
McMahon, Mgr., 26, 26n., 42
Macmillan, H., 229n., 269n., 280n., 285n.
McNamara, R., 339, 390, 391, 392n., 407, 420
Maimon, Rabbi Y. L., 11, 13, 19, 24n., 30, 31, 61, 62, 76, 83, 119
Main, C. T., 192, 194n.
Mangin, L., 266, 266n., 267, 270, 273, 304
Mao Tse-tung, 168
Marcus, Y., 264n.
Margalit, D., 454n., 466n., 486n., 488n., 491n., 510n.
Marshall, G., 138n., 275n., 432n.
Marzouk, M., 255
Masannat, G. A., 152n.
Medzini, M., 141, 152n.
Meeker, G., 386, 405
Mehdi, M., 211n.
Meir, G., 12, 15, 15n., 29, 30n., 33, 33n., 50, 61, 62, 62n., 68, 69n., 75n., 76n., 83, 83n., 87, 89, 89n., 118, 123, 155, 156, 166, 181, 208n., 232, 233ff., 249ff., 254n., 255n., 266, 268, 270, 270n., 275ff., 278n., 280, 283ff., 287ff., 300ff., 304, 308ff., 314ff., 322, 334, 335, 367, 371, 372, 374, 374n., 377, 379ff., 388, 395, 402, 406, 410, 413, 415, 424, 427, 429, 430, 444, 446, 456, 464ff., 470ff., 485, 485n., 487ff., 493ff., 500, 500n., 501, 506, 508, 508n., 511n., 514, 514n., 515, 516, 536, 537, 552, 554, 557, 559, 566; see also Subject Index
Meir, L.Y., 61
Menken, J., 230n.
Menzies, R., 261n., 269n.
Meron, G., 76n.
Meyer, F. W., 91n.
Mikunis, S., 26n., 32n., 86, 116n., 117, 294n., 303n., 330
Milbrath, L.W., 258n.
Milburn, T., 550, 560n., 579
Mintz, B., 88n., 303n.
Mokhtar, A., 363n., 369
Mollet, G., 228, 242n., 263ff., 266, 268, 268n., 270, 271, 272n., 273ff., 284ff., 299, 301, 305
Moncrieff, A., 232n., 264n., 268n., 269n., 282n., 312n.
Monroe, E., 258n.
Murphy, R., 142, 142n., 292, 295, 301n.

Naftali, P., 26n., 83, 89n., 123, 181, 190, 191n., 194n., 196n., 197n., 199n., 208, 208n., 214, 233

Nahmias, Y., 262, 265
Nahumi, M., 152n.
Nakdimon, S., 341n., 363n., 366n., 367n., 368n., 372n., 373n., 375n., 377n., 378n., 380n., 381n., 383n., 384n., 385n., 386n., 388n., 389n., 393n., 396n., 397n., 400n., 402n., 413n., 414n., 416n., 418n., 419n., 421n.
Nakkache, A., 187
Namir, M., 87n., 128, 128n., 129n., 167, 167n., 233
Narkiss, U., 23n.
Nasser, G. A., 126, 207n., 226, 228, 238n., 239ff., 242n., 249n., 253ff., 257n., 260, 260n., 262, 263n., 265ff., 268n., 271, 302n., 312ff., 314, 319, 321, 321n., 323n., 324, 329, 337, 341, 343ff., 358, 360n., 361n., 362ff., 369, 371, 374ff., 388, 392ff., 397, 407, 408ff., 417n., 418ff., 425, 433, 435ff., 440, 454, 469, 470, 474, 483, 489, 492, 501, 505, 526, 527, 532, 533, 543, 546, 550, 552, 553, 566
Nathan, E., 76n., 89n.
Navon, Y., 33, 63n., 65n., 234, 234n., 235n., 238n., 255n., 261n., 262n., 275n., 279n., 290, 429, 430
Neguib, General M., 179, 254
Nehru, J., 279n.
Nenni, P., 156
Neriya, Y., 498n.
Netzer, D., 328
Netzer, S., 383, 404
Nimrod, Y., 189n., 194n., 196n., 197n., 198n., 199n., 202n., 206n., 207n., 213n.
Nir, N., 508n.
Nissan, E., 245n.
Nixon, R., 297n., 456, 465, 478, 486, 486n., 487, 489, 491, 491n., 493ff., 500, 501, 514, 515, 552, 554, 561
North, R. C., 550, 551n., 552n., 554n., 581n.
Nurock, M., 26n., 58n., 84, 87, 88n., 302, 303n.
Nutting, A., 256n., 268n., 269n., 285n.

O'Ballance, E., 275n.

Paige, G. D., 129n., 550, 555n., 563n., 578
Parodi, A., 78n.
Patinkin, D., 60, 60n., 511n.
Pearson, L. B., 134, 281ff., 292, 295
Peled, M., 318n., 334, 418
Peled, N., 465, 465n.
Percy, S., 294
Peres, S., 63n., 104, 229n., 232ff., 248n., 249ff., 255n., 256ff., 259, 262ff., 270, 271n., 273, 273n., 274n., 277, 280, 283ff., 290, 304, 322n., 359n., 377, 380, 381, 381n., 383, 383n., 385n.,

388, 388n., 389n., 396n., 402ff., 416, 424, 428ff., 464, 485, 485n., 493, 531, 534, 536, 560; see also Subject Index
Perlmutter, A., 348
Pfaff, R. H., 34n.
Phleger, H., 299, 299n.
Pineau, C., 228, 242ff., 264n., 265ff., 268ff., 270ff., 284ff., 292, 293n., 294ff., 299, 301, 301n., 305
Pinkas, D. Z., 83, 83n., 87, 89n.
Polier, S., 82n.
Porush, M., 423
Prittie, T., 96n., 105n., 184n., 337n., 338n., 343n.
Pruitt, D. G., 525n., 550, 551n., 574
Prushansky, Y., 176n.

Ra'anan, U., 185n., 186n., 230n., 257n.
Rabin, Y., 211, 318, 319, 327, 334, 334n., 335, 336n., 337, 347ff., 365ff., 388n., 395, 401, 402, 404ff., 412n., 417, 417n., 418n., 427ff., 433n., 435ff., 447, 447n., 484, 485, 489, 489n., 491, 535, 558, 568; see also Subject Index
Rabinovich, A., 35n.
Rafael, G., 234, 234n., 288, 288n., 291, 299, 360n., 362, 362n., 366, 366n., 367n., 369, 373ff., 405, 489, 556
Rafael, Y., 87n., 180n., 231n., 294n., 329, 374n.
Raviv, M., 377, 403, 405
Reisner, M., 403
Remez, D., 12, 24, 24n., 30, 61, 83, 118
Riad, M., 211n., 417n., 470, 491, 492n.
Riftin, Y., 32n., 87n., 116n., 117, 124, 179, 180n., 294n.
Rikhye, General I. J., 363, 363n., 364n., 365, 367, 369, 370
Riley, Major-General W. E., 189n.
Rimalt, E., 85, 377, 406, 424, 465, 495
Rivlin, M., 146, 146n.
Rizk, M., 196n., 211n.
Robertson, T., 229n., 231n., 237n., 256n., 262n., 264n., 268n., 271n., 272n., 273n., 280n., 282n.
Robinson, J., 89n., 96n., 550, 562n., 579
Robinson, N., 72, 72n.
Rogers, W., 479ff., 489, 491, 500
Rokah, Y., 87n., 124, 181
Roosevelt, K., 259n.
Rophe, W., 91n.
Rosen, P., 12, 24n., 61, 63, 63n., 65, 65n., 66n., 68n., 70, 70n., 75n., 76n., 83, 86, 118, 124, 126, 126n., 182, 233, 235n., 259, 275, 287ff.
Rosenne, S., 10n., 25n., 175n., 209n.
Rosenzaft, Y., 75n.
Rostow, E., 378, 386, 392, 405ff.
Rostow, W., 390, 390n., 391n., 393n., 400, 400n., 414, 427
Rouleau, E., 355n., 363n., 364n.

Rountree, W., 279, 286, 286n., 294n., 299
Roy, Y., 227n.
Rubin, H., 117
Rusk, D., 339, 386, 386n., 389, 391, 393, 398, 400, 400n., 401, 405, 407ff., 417, 419ff., 436
Rutenberg, P., 186, 186n.

Sadan, D., 410, 424
Sadat, A., 505, 506, 510
Safran, N., 228n., 230n., 322n., 323n.
St. John, R., 380n., 393n.
Sakharov, E., 403
Salim, M., 196n.
Saphir, Y., 32, 32n., 38, 87 88, 124, 182, 327, 332, 332n., 375, 431, 460n., 465, 495
Sapir, P., 38, 182, 190, 198, 202n., 214, 218, 233, 258, 270, 270n., 287ff., 331, 374n., 396, 410, 464, 515, 516, 516n., 534, 540
Sasson, B. S., 88n.
Sasson, E., 38, 285, 331
Saud, King, 244
Savage, J. L., 187, 197n.
Schaffer, K., 91n., 93n., 97n.
Schechtman, J. B., 22n.
Schiff, Z., 176n., 324n., 385n.
Schleifer, S. A., 35n.
Schmidt, C., 79, 79n., 194n., 197n.
Schwartz, D. C., 566n., 574
Seale, P., 255n.
Serlin, Y., 86, 116n., 124, 182, 377
Shaki, A., 498, 498n.
Shaltiel, D., 23n.
Shapilov, D., 257
Shapira, Haim Moshe, 12, 18, 24n., 31, 38, 61, 70, 70n., 119, 124, 182, 233, 259, 275, 287ff., 332, 336, 377, 396, 403ff., 465, 496; see also Subject Index
Shapira, Moshe, later Haim Moshe, q.v.
Shapiro, Y. S., 32n., 38, 332, 374n., 404, 429, 464, 494ff.
Sharef, Z., 14n., 15, 17n., 22n., 29, 29n., 30n., 38, 76n., 121, 121n., 182n., 233n., 332, 426, 464
Sharett, M., 5, 12, 13, 14, 17, 17n., 18, 19, 24, 24n., 27, 30, 30n., 32, 32n., 33, 39, 42, 43, 58n., 61, 62, 67, 67n., 68, 68n., 74, 75, 76n., 77ff., 84, 87, 87n., 89n., 90ff., 94, 96, 102, 110, 113, 115n., 116ff., 130ff., 137ff., 143ff., 149ff., 153n., 156, 157, 159ff., 166, 178n., 181, 182, 184, 185, 190, 194, 195, 198, 200ff., 204, 215, 218, 232, 235n., 240n., 245n., 258ff., 261n., 262ff., 279n., 383, 525, 526, 528, 530, 537, 545; see also Subject Index
Sharon, A., 385, 402n., 404
Shazar, Z., 12, 30n., 76n., 83, 118, 375

Shek, Z., 124
Shemtov, V., 465, 465n.
Shiloah, R., 137, 138, 139, 140, 141, 142, 142n., 159, 192n., 202, 234, 234n., 279ff., 286ff., 294ff., 556
Shimoni, Y., 120ff., 127, 127n., 128n., 150, 152n., 154, 154n., 167, 167n., 192n., 202, 209n.
Shinnar, F. A., 62, 66n., 68n., 71, 71n., 72n., 76n., 78ff., 89ff., 102ff., 107
Shishakly, A., 190
Shitreet, B. S., 12, 13, 24n., 31, 61, 118, 123, 181, 233, 288, 331n.
Siegfried, M., 72, 72n.
Silver, Rabbi A. H., 14, 277
Sisco, J., 386, 392, 405, 407, 449, 478, 479, 486, 500, 501
Siverson, R. H., 238n., 244n.
Smith, W. Bedell, 139, 140, 141, 159, 293, 297n., 298n., 301n.
Smolansky, O. M., 291n.
Sneh, M., 85n., 116n., 180, 330n.
Snyder, G., 567n.
Sobolev, A., 289
Spaak, P. H., 292
Spellman, Cardinal, 26
Sprinzak, Y., 82
Stalin, J., 116, 168
Stein, J., 3n., 532n., 548n., 572
Steinberg, B., 3n., 532n., 572
Stephens, R., 256n., 360n.
Stevens, G., 175n., 187n., 188n., 193n., 195n., 196n., 199n., 206n., 207n., 210n.
Stock, E., 229n.
Surkiss, M., 383, 404

Tal, Y., 385, 404
Tamir, S., 330
Tekoa, Y., 488n., 499
Tevet, S., 269n., 335n., 418n.
Thomas, H., 256n., 264n., 266, 267n., 268ff., 269n., 272n., 273n., 285n.
Thomson, G., 384
Tillmann, R., 79n.
Tourneaux, J. R., 268n.
Trevelyan, H., 257n., 321n.
Troxell, O., 198
Truman, H. S., 92, 129, 157, 270
Tsur, Y., 255n., 262, 262n., 263, 279n.
Tzur, Z., 429

U Thant, 314, 364, 364n., 365, 441, 442, 456, 490, 531, 552
Unna, M., 386

Verba, S., 550, 560n.
Vogel, R., 75n., 97n., 107n., 110n.

Walker, F. P., 384n.
Wall, R. F., 227n., 332
Walman, A., 197n.
Walner, S., 318n.

Warhaftig, Z., 11n., 26n., 38, 88n., 303n., 332, 377, 396, 465
Wartman, E., 138n.
Weizman, E., 318n., 327, 333, 334, 366, 378n., 379n., 380n., 418n., 463n., 464n., 465, 465n., 466n., 467n., 469n., 487n., 493, 495n., 498
Weizmann, C., 24, 35n., 42, 72, 73n., 74n.
Wiener, A., 182, 182n., 183n., 191n., 195n., 196, 197n., 198, 198n., 199, 202, 202n., 206n., 207, 208n.
Wilcox, F.O., 299, 299n.
Wilenska, E., 86, 87n., 231n.
Wiley, J., 227n.
Wilkins, F., 299
Williams, W. A., 227n.
Wilner, M., 11n., 28n., 86, 116n., 124, 330
Wilson, H., 34n., 35n., 49n., 340, 355n., 364n., 374, 382n., 383ff., 404, 416n., 417n., 436, 550, 567
Wohlstetter, A., 320n.
Wu Te-shen, 120n.

Ya'ari, M., 116n., 303n., 388, 388n., 389, 406, 422

Yadin, Y., 23n., 337, 395n., 414, 414n., 424, 429, 430
Yadlin, A., 424, 427
Yaffe, A., 365, 394, 402, 406, 409, 426
Yahil, H., 65, 65n., 66n., 74n., 95n., 96n., 105n., 202n., 209n., 210, 210n.
Yao Chung-ming, 135, 136, 143, 145
Yariv, A., 327, 337, 361n., 366, 367, 368, 370, 378, 378n., 379n., 385, 395, 405, 408, 417, 418n., 426, 428
Yellin-Mor, N., 26n., 330n.
Yeshayahu, Y., 332, 374n., 410, 424, 425
Yisrael, Y., 38
Yisraeli, R., 152n.
Yoffe, A., 385, 402n.
Yost, C., 413n., 417n., 454n., 455n.
Yuval, M., 119n.

Zadok, H., 374n.
Zander, W., 26n., 49n., 50n.
Zar, M., 410, 424
Zarchin, J., 147
Zinnes, D., 550n., 574
Zisling, A., 11n., 24n., 180n.
Zurhellen, O., 489

SUBJECT INDEX

Advocacy Statements:
  regarding the Sinai Campaign, 249–54
    scale of, 249
  regarding Six Day War, 328, 350–5
    scale of, 351–2
  regarding Roger Proposals, 475–8
    scale of, 475
Africa:
  policy toward Jerusalem, 35
  Israel's presence in, 315
Agudat Yisrael:
  policy regarding Jerusalem, 11
Ahdut Ha'avoda:
  policy regarding German Reparations, 106
  on Jordan waters, 179
  role in Sinai Campaign, 231ff., 294n.
Al-Fath, 168, 357, 457
Allon, Y.:
  role in Six Day War, 335, 340–1, 344, 347, 348, 352ff., 385, 389, 397
  and 'Allon Plan', 460–3
  images relevant to Rogers Proposals, 469ff., 515
Anderson Mission, the, 259ff.
Anglo-Egyptian Agreement (1954), 254–255
Aqaba, Gulf of, 253, 259, 295, 296, 480
Arab Higher Committee, 21
Arab-Israel conflict system, 446–7
Arab League, 204ff., 207, 224
  debates methods to obstruct Israel's Water Carrier Project, 211
Arab Legion, 16, 17, 23
Arab Plan, the, 196–7, 204
Arab States, 59
  rejection of UN Partition Resolution, 9
  and the Jerusalem question, 26
  pressure on West Germany, 105
  recognize Taiwan, 137
  reaction to the Draft Memorandum of Understanding, 205–6
  plan diversion of the Yarmuk, 211
  Israeli image of, 224
  and Nasser's leadership, 229
  rivalries among, 323–4
Arab Summit Conference(s):
  first, 211
  second, 211
Arms:
  to Egypt, 208, 229–31, 255, 257–8

to Israel, 262–3, 509–10
Asia, East, 111, 113, 118
Attitudinal prism, 66, 71

Bandung Conference, 151, 151n.–152n. 169
Ben Gurion, D:
  on Jerusalem, 11, 13–14, 16–17, 18, 22, 25, 27–8, 29, 31
  and the Latrun operation, 24
  relations with Sharett, 33, 61
  on German reparations, 62, 63–7
  relations with Begin, 62, 105
  perception of West Germany, 107
  on the Korean/China issue, 120, 121ff., 166
  attitude towards UN role in Jordan Waters issue, 209
  image related to Sinai Campaign, 234ff., 249–54
    regarding the UN, 235–6
    regarding the global setting, 238–43
    regarding the Near East core, 243–246
  on military capability, 246ff., 258
  and the Anderson Mission, 259–60
  and French arms, 264
  role in the Sèvres Conference, 268ff.
  decides to launch the Sinai Campaign, 273–4
  decides to withdraw from Sinai, 288–289, 290
  1956 complex of, 332–3
Bipolarity, 10, 57, 112, 116, 226
Blass, S.:
  role in decisions on Jordan Waters, 185ff.
Bundestag, 58, 74, 87, 93, 97
Burma, 135, 169

Cabinet's Economic Affairs Committee, 65
China (PRC):
  Israeli decisions regarding, 111ff.
  a Communist power, 112
  role in Asia, 124–5
  cable to Sharett, 128
  gestures toward Israel, 135–7, 143, 145
    receives Israeli trade mission, 147–9
    and Jewish property in Shanghai, 148

supports Arab states, 151
policy toward Israel since May 1955, 153–6, 168
Claims Conference, the, 90, 95, 96
Cold War, the, 112, 116, 238ff., 320
Competing élites, activities:
regarding Jerusalem, 11
role regarding German Reparations, 58
and the Sinai Campaign, 231, 275–7
role in the Six Day War, 329–30, 381ff.
Cotton Plan, the, 197, 203–4, 220
Crisis, in foreign policy, 287
and hypothesis testing, 550–79

Davar, 258
advocacy concerning the Six Day War, 328
Dayan, M.:
role in decisions on Jordan Waters, 190
images related to Sinai Campaign, 236, 242, 244, 247, 249ff., 312
as Chief of Staff, 264–5, 266–7, 275
images relevant to Six Day War, 341, 344–5, 346–7, 348–9, 352ff.
tours *Tzahal*'s positions, 373
as Defence Minister, 419, 421, 422
and 'Dayan Plan', 460–3
images relevant to Rogers Proposals, 478ff., 515
stand on Rogers Plan 'B', 495
favours 'establishing facts', 516
Decision makers, in Israel, 5, 12–19, 52, 53, 105, 110, 114, 118ff., 136ff., 166ff., 181ff., 219ff., 234ff., 285ff., 331ff., 44off., 464ff.
Decisions in foreign policy:
defined, 1–2
classification of, 2
strategic, 2, 8, 9, 28, 98, 103, 456ff.
tactical, 2, 8, 9, 37, 99, 156ff.
implementation, 2, 8, 9, 99, 102, 156ff.
as a process through time, 5
and predecisional events, 8
systemic phases in, 5–8
flow of, 8
typology of, 579
Demilitarized Zone, 126, 174, 179, 188ff., 208

East Asia, 111, 113, 118
Eban, A.:
on Jerusalem, 15, 29
on Korean/China issue, 119, 123, 133, 138, 140–2, 143, 151
role in Sinai Campaign, 277–81, 286–7, 288, 313
images relevant to Six Day War, 339–340, 343–4, 347, 348, 351, 352ff.
meets Chuvakhin, 372
stand in Six Day War deliberations, 378–9, 397, 417

meets with de Gaulle, 381–2
deliberations in Washington, 386–8, 389–90, 391–3
images relevant to Rogers Proposals, 470ff., 515
Economic Affairs Committee, 65
Economic capability:
effect on decisions regarding German Reparations, 59–60, 65, 66, 70–1, 106–7
effect on decisions regarding Jordan Waters, 176–8, 221
effect on decisions regarding the Sinai Campaign, 248–9
on the eve of the Six Day War, 326–7
post-1967, 449, 510
Ee-hizdahut, policy of, 10, 113n.
abandonment of, 57, 131, 165
and the question of China, 113, 119, 127, 132
Egypt, 10, 116, 136
military capability of, 59, 271
role in Jordan Waters issue, 196, 213
and Czech arms deal, 208, 229–31, 257, 257n.
focus of Israeli images, 243
and the Gaza Raid, 255–6, 256n.
effects of Sinai Campaign on, 313
receives information on Israel's intentions *v.* Syria, 321
and the Six Day War, 326, 363–5, 371, 431ff.
signs Mutual Defence Pact with Syria, 356
blocks the Straits of Tiran, 375
threatens the destruction of Israel, 393
launches a 'war of attrition', 454
Soviet military presence in, 458, 487
accepts Rogers Plan 'B' 491–2, 492n.
violates the cease-fire agreement, 499
Eilat, 300
'*Ein Breira*', 324
Eshed Kinrot, 173, 208
Eshkol, L.:
role in decisions regarding the Jordan Waters, 182ff., 201–2, 212
linked to image held by, 183–4
deals with pressures from *Tzahal*, 327–328, 401–2
images relevant to Six Day War, 337–338, 342–3, 347–8, 350–1, 352ff.
decides on partial mobilization, 363
exchanges letters with President Johnson, 368, 413
decides on large-scale mobilization, 372
pressures on, to hand over defence portfolio, 382ff., 410ff.
meets with Chuvakhin, 394–5
postpones a decision on war, 396–7, 398
de Gaulle's letter to, 399

Eshkol, L. (*cont.*):
  addresses the nation, 401
Etzel, 105–6
Europe, West, 103
European Common Market:
  Israeli efforts to attain entry into, 103

Feda'iyun, 226, 229, 249, 253, 256, 261, 270, 275, 313
Feedback, 4, 8
  and Israel's decisions regarding Jerusalem, 47–55
  and Israel's decisions regarding German Reparations, 102–10
  from Israeli decisions on the Korean/China issue, 164–72
  from Israeli decisions on Jordan Waters, 219–24
  from Israeli decisions on the Sinai Campaign, 309–17
  from Israeli decisions on Six Day War, 440–53
  from Israeli decisions on Rogers Proposals, 504–17
Foreign Affairs and Security Committee, 32, 83
  role in German Reparations debate, 88–9, 92
  and the Six Day War, 363, 365–6, 395, 396, 401
Foreign Office, 33, 124, 127
  moves to Jerusalem, 34
  role in forming relations with China, 127ff., 142, 144
Foreign Service Technical Élite:
  image of Korea/China issue, 121–2
  role in Sinai Campaign, 234, 291
  role in Six Day War, 337, 377
Framework of analysis, 3
  systems approach, components of, 3, 5
  dynamic interaction, components of, 4
France, 103
  policy regarding question of Jerusalem, 50
  Israel's ally, 228, 262ff., 299
  negotiations with UN regarding the Sinai Campaign, 268
  and the Sèvres Conference, 268–73
  reaction to Soviet threats toward Israel, 284–5
  attitudes toward Six Day War, 322–3, 381–2, 382n., 399, 419

Gahal:
  and the Six Day War, 367–8
  stand on Resolution 242, 488
  and Rogers Plan 'B', 494–5
  leaves the Government, 496–7
Galili, Y.:
  regarding role in Rogers Proposals, 468ff., 515

Gaza Strip, 226ff., 255ff., 265, 275, 291, 293, 296ff., 313, 448, 480
General Zionists:
  policy regarding Jerusalem, 32
  on the Korean War, 114, 115, 126
  on Jordan Waters, 179–81
German Reparations, decisions regarding, 1
  strategic *v.* tactical, 56
  operational environment of, 56–60, 108
  indirect arrangements, 62
  decision process, 71–89
    and Weizmann's letter, 72–3
    pre-decisional events, 97–8
  Israeli cabinet debates, 76, 83
    sends notes to the Powers, 76–7
    Adenauer's declaration, 80, 87
  implementation of decisions, 89–97, 98, 99, 102
  negotiations concerning, 90ff.
  and the Reparation Agreement, 96–97
  flow of, 97–102
  feedback from, 102–10
  and hypothesis testing, 525ff.
Germany, West, 56ff.
  Adenauer on reparations from, 73, 73n., 74, 77ff., 93–5, 95n.–96n.
  Blankenhorn influence on, 73–4, 78, 93ff.
  Israeli delegation to, 89n.
  arms from and to, 103
  as a bilateral component of Israel's foreign policy system, 103
  role in Israel's entry into EEC, 103–4
Gesher B'not Ya'acov, 173, 175, 190, 207, 208, 220
Golan Heights, the, 448
Goldman, N.:
  role in German reparations, 62, 72, 80–1, 92ff.
'Greater Israel' Movement, the, 463–4

Ha'aretz:
  on German reparations, 59
  advocacy concerning Six Day War, 328–9
Hacohen, D.:
  role in Chinese-Israeli relations, 135ff.
Ha-Kibbutz Ha-artzi, 180
Ha-Kibbutz Ha-me'uhad, 180
Ha-Kirya, 30, 130, 134
Hamtana, the, 336, 340, 418, 440
Ha-tzofeh, 329
Hays Plan, the, 187–8, 188n.
Herut:
  policy regarding Jerusalem, 11, 26, 32
  policy regarding German reparations, 58, 59, 84ff., 105–6
  on the Korean War, 115ff.
  on Jordan Waters, 179–81
  role in Sinai Campaign, 231ff., 294n.

Holland, 103
Holocaust, the, 56, 65
Holocaust Syndrome, the, 333-4, 508, 514
Horowitz, D.:
role in German reparations, 75, 78, 78n., 79
Huleh Valley, 175ff.
Hypothesis testing:
objectives of, 518
problems of subjectivity in, 519
on Israeli case studies, 519-22, 525-79
classification of, 523-4

Ihud Ha-kvutzot, 180
Images, 5
of Israeli decision makers:
regarding Jerusalem, 12-19
regarding West Germany, 61-71, 104
regarding China and the Korean War, 119ff., 166
regarding Jordan Waters, 181-5
regarding the Sinai Campaign, 232-254
regarding the Six Day War, 331-355
regarding the Rogers Proposals, 464-478
and hypothesis testing relevant to, 523-4, 525-50
and information, 529-32
and behaviour patterns, 532-50
the Military-Security Issue Area, 532-6
the Political-Diplomatic Issue Area, 536-9
the Economic-Development Issue Area, 539-41
the Cultural-Status Issue Area, 541
the Arms Issue Area, 542-50
India, 125, 127, 134, 135, 300n.
Interest groups:
regarding the question of Jerusalem, 10-11
regarding German Reparations, 58-9
the Kibbutz-Moshav complex as, 180-181, 184, 220
Tzahal as, 232
role in Six Day War, 410
associational v. non-associational in post-1967 period, 463-4
International System:
classification of states in, 523n.
pluralism in, 581
Iraq, 208, 255, 421
Israel Labour Party, 459
debates conditions of peace, 515-17
Israel's Foreign Policy System:
inputs into, 28, 29, 43, 46, 98, 99, 118ff., 129

feedback effects on, 47, 102-3, 166ff., 219ff., 229
global setting of, 47-8, 51, 56-7, 112, 164, 238-43, 330, 440-3, 504-5
subordinate systems in, 48-9, 51, 57, 168, 330, 505-6
issue areas affected by decisions regarding Jerusalem, 53

Jerusalem, decisions regarding, 1, 5
the Yishuv concession, 9, 14, 20
the seat of Israel's Government, 9, 12, 28, 29-30
annexation of East Jerusalem (from 1967 on), 1, 9, 37
related operational environment, 9-12, 49-51, 52
appointment of Military Governor to, 11, 24
relevant images of Israeli decision makers, 12-19, 51-3
decision process, 19-31
UN corpus separatum resolution, 20-1, 23-24, 25, 26n.
predecisional events, 21-31, 41-3
Special Commissioner for, 21
population of, 21n.
Latin American pressure on, 26
implementation of decisions, 31-41, 43-6, 47
flow of, 41-7
feedback from, 47-55
and hypothesis testing, 525ff.
Jerusalem Post:
on German Reparations, 59
advocacy concerning Six Day War, 328
Jewish Agency, the, 14, 21
Jewish prism, the, 64, 66, 67, 71
Johnston Mission, the, 175, 192, 194ff.
Jordan, 10
behaviour regarding Jerusalem, 10
signs a General Armistice Agreement, 25
attacks on 5 June 1967, 35
and the Bunger Plan, 189
negotiates with Israel on Jordan Waters, 197-8, 221
Israeli reprisal against, 356
signs a Mutual Defence Pact with Egypt, 412
in the Six Day War, 432ff.
and Rogers Plan 'A', 484-5
Jordan Valley Authority, 187
Jordan Waters, decisions regarding, 1, 5
strategic v. tactical decisions, 173-4, 214-19
relevant operational environment, 174-181, 222
psychological environment of, 181-5, 222
decision process, 185-207

Jordan Waters (*cont.*):
    predecisional events, 185–90, 213–14
    role of Blass in, 185ff.
    and the diversion plan, 190–3
    and the Seven Year Plan, 194
    reacting to the Arab Plan, 196–7
    and Johnston's proposals, 198ff.
    implementation of decisions, 207–13
    adoption of a Ten Year Plan, 207–8
    US backing sought, 210–12
    flow of, 213–19
    feedback from, 219–24
    and hypothesis testing, 525ff.
Joseph, D.:
    on Jerusalem, 13, 14, 20, 29
    on German Reparations, 69–70, 84

Kadesh, Operation, 233, 275
Kaplan, E.:
    on German reparations, 68
Kinneret, Lake, 190ff., 208
Knesset, the, 11
    the First, 24
    Legislative Committee of, 26
    debates the question of Jerusalem
        (1949), 26–7, 31–2
    and annexation of East Jerusalem, 39
    and the question of German repar-
        ations, 58, 63n., 64, 84ff.
    debates the Korean War, 115–16, 117–
        118, 124, 125, 131
    and the Jordan Waters question, 178,
        178n., 179–81
    on *Tzahal*'s withdrawal from Sinai,
        303n.
    debates related to Six Day War, 374–5
    debates Rogers Plan 'B', 497–8
Korea, North, 114, 115, 123, 129, 132
Korea, South, 115, 129
    offered Israeli medical aid, 131
Korean Armistice Agreement, 138
Korean War, the 111, 112, 113–14, 129–
    130, 165ff.
Korean War and China, decisions re-
    garding, 1
    strategic, tactical and implementing,
        111–12, 156ff.
    operational environment relevant to,
        112–18, 170
    debates within Israel's Cabinet, 113–
        114, 129, 152n.–154n.
        backing for UN resolutions, 110,
            114, 130ff.
        regarding Hacohen negotiations,
            135–7
        influenced by Israel's Washington
            Embassy, 140–1
    sends trade mission to China, 145–50
    seeks full diplomatic relations with
        China, 152
    psychological environment related to,
        118–27, 170

    decision process and implementation
        of, 127–56
        initiative regarding cease-fire, 134,
            135n.
        vote in UN, 143–5, 155
        contacts after May 1955 with, 153–
            156
    flow of, 156–63
    feedback from, 164–72
    and hypothesis testing, 525ff.

Lake Tiberias, 173, 174ff.
Lamerhav, 329
Latin America:
    policy toward Jerusalem, 26, 35, 49
Lavon Affair, the, 178
Lebanon, 10, 175ff., 208
Luxemburg Agreements, 65, 96–7, 105

Ma'ariv:
    on German Reparations, 59, 85
    advocacy concerning Six Day War,
        328
Main Plan, the, 192–3, 194, 203, 204
Maki:
    policy regarding Jerusalem, 11, 52
    policy regarding German Repara-
        tions, 58
    policy regarding China, 112–13, 115ff.
    on Jordan Waters, 180
    role in Sinai Campaign, 231ff., 294n.
Mapai:
    policy regarding Jerusalem, 13
    and the Big Three, 361
    debates German Reparations, 82–3,
        83n. 106
    policy regarding Korean War and
        China, 113, 126, 142
    inner divisions concerning Six Day
        War, 328
Mapam:
    policy regarding Jerusalem, 11, 32
    policy regarding German Reparations,
        58, 59, 84, 85, 106
    policy regarding China, 112–13, 115ff.
    on Jordan Waters, 179–81
    role in Sinai Campaign, 231ff., 294n.
    and Six Day War, 367, 422
Meir, G.:
    on Jerusalem, 15
    on German Reparations, 68–9
    images related to Sinai Campaign,
        237, 244, 246, 249ff.
    images relevant to Rogers Proposals,
        465ff., 514
Middle East:
    core of, 10, 174
    subordinate system, 48
        affected by Israel's policy toward
            China, 168
        inputs into Israel's foreign policy
            system, 229

Israeli images of, 243–6
  affected by the Sinai Campaign,
    310–11
Military capability:
  effect on decisions regarding German
    Reparations, 59, 66, 68, 107–10
  effect on decisions regarding Sinai
    Campaign, 229–30
    Israeli images of, 246–8
    post-Sinai Campaign, 311
  on the eve of Six Day War, 324–5
  post-1967, 449, 457, 510
Minhalat Ha'am:
  considers truce proposals for Jerusalem,
    22
Ministerial Committee on Defence, 365
  debates the Six Day War, 377–80,
    418
Ministerial Committee on Foreign Affairs
  and Defence, 111
  deliberates relations with China, 140
Mitla Pass, the, 272, 274
Mitun, 326, 449
Mizrahi:
  policy regarding Jerusalem, 11
  policy regarding German Reparations,
    84
  on the Korean War, 114, 115

National Unity Government (of Israel),
  106
  acting on the question of Jerusalem,
    37–8
  pressure to form, 381ff., 398ff., 410
  post-1967 tensions within, 460–1
  and Rogers Plan 'B', 494–5
National Water Carrier Project, 174, 176,
  207, 209ff.
NATO, 112
Near East Core, see Arab States
Negev, the, 207, 209, 213

Operational environment, 4
  regarding decisions about Jerusalem,
    9–12, 54–5
  regarding decisions about German
    Reparations, 56–60, 108–9
  regarding decisions about the Korean
    War and China, 112–18, 170–1
  regarding decisions on Jordan Waters,
    174–81, 222–3
  regarding decisions on Sinai Campaign,
    226–32, 316–17
  regarding decisions on Six Day War,
    319–31, 450–2
  regarding decisions on Rogers Pro-
    posals, 454–64, 512–13

Palestine, Economic Union of, 20
Palestine Arab refugees, 260
Palestine Conciliation Committee, 23, 25
Peel Commission, 15

Peres, S.:
  images linked to Sinai Campaign, 237,
    241, 244, 247, 249ff.
  and French arms deal, 263–4
  negotiates with French Government,
    264ff.
Political structure:
  effect on Jerusalem question, 52
  effect on German Reparations, 59, 106
  effect on Korea/China issue, 118–19,
    123–4, 165
  effect on decisions about the Jordan
    Waters, 181–2
  effect on decisions about the Sinai
    Campaign, 233
  effect of Sinai Campaign on, 311–12
  effect on Six Day War decisions, 327,
    331–2
  effect of Six Day War on, 453
  in post-1967 period, 459–60
  and the Rogers Proposals, 464–5,
    510–11
Proclamation of Independence, 22
Progressive Party, the:
  policy toward German Reparations,
    70
  on the Korean War, 114–15
Provisional State Council, 11, 16, 22
Psychological environment, 5
  qualitative and quantitative analysis
    of, 5
  regarding the Jerusalem question, 12–
    19, 54–5
  regarding German Reparations, 108–
    109
  regarding the Korean War and China,
    118–27, 170
  regarding decisions on Jordan Waters,
    181–5, 222–3
  regarding decisions on Sinai Campaign,
    232–54, 316-17
  regarding decisions on Six Day War,
    331–55, 450–2
  regarding decisions on Rogers Pro-
    posals, 464–78, 512–13

Rabin, Y.:
  as Chief of Staff, 319, 327, 334, 347n.,
    348, 362, 371, 378, 378n., 385
  as Ambassador to the US, 489, 491
Revised Unified Plan, the, 198ff., 210,
  211, 220–1
Rogers Proposals, decisions regarding, 1
  strategic, tactical and implementation,
    455, 500–4
  operational environment of, 456–64,
    512
  psychological environment of, 464–78,
    512
    content analysis of, 471–8
  decision process, 478–96
    and the Four Power talks, 478–9

Rogers Proposals (cont.):
  and Plan 'A', 479–83
    Cabinet's debate regarding, 485
  acceptance of Resolution 242, 487–
    488, 488n.
  and Plan 'B', 489–96
    Cabinet's debate regarding, 490,
    496
  and Nixon's dispatch, 493–4
  flow of, 500–4
  feedback from, 504–17
    and Rogers 'C', 506–8
    and lack of long-range planning,
    511, 514
  and hypothesis testing, 525ff.

St. Germain Conference, the, 266
Security Council, the, 40, 114, 129, 188,
    191, 226
  debates the Sinai Campaign, 278ff.
  Resolution 242, 316, 442, 487, 497
  condemns Israeli reprisals, 357n.
  and Six Day War, 411–12
Sèvres Conference, 228, 253, 268
Shapira, H. M.:
  on Jerusalem, 18
  role in Six Day War, 336, 422
Sharett, M.:
  on Jerusalem, 14, 17, 18–19, 33
  resigns, 30
  relations with BG, 33, 61
  on German Reparations, 62, 67–8, 77,
    87
  perception of Korea/China issue, 120ff.,
    132, 137ff.
    focuses on India, 125
    cables Chou En-lai, 127–8
    on a cease-fire in Korea, 134
    role in decision to send trade mis-
      sion to China, 145–7, 149–50
    decides to seek full diplomatic
      relations with, 152, 152n.–154n.
  on Jordan Waters, 182–3, 184–5, 194–
    195, 198
  effect of his resignation on Sinai Cam-
    paign, 261–2
Sharm-e-Sheikh, 226, 281, 293, 300,
    363, 378, 480
Sinai Campaign, decisions regarding, 1
  strategic, tactical and implementation,
    225–6, 303–9
  operational environment of, 226–32,
    316–17
  psychological environment of, 232–54,
    316–17
    advocacy statements, 249–54
  decision process and implementation
    of, 254–302
    predecisional events, 254–64, 303
    co-operation with France, 285ff.
    and Sèvres Conference 268–72
    the attack, 274–5

UN role in, 276ff., 295–6
  World Jewry reaction, 287
  and withdrawal from Sinai, 288–9
    conditions for, 293
    US guarantees sought, 296–9, 300–
    302
  flow of, 303–9
  feedback from, 309–17
  and hypothesis testing, 525ff.
Sinai Peninsula, 253, 259, 265, 275, 293,
    448
Six Day War, decisions regarding, 1, 5
  effects of Sinai Campaign on, 314–15
  tactical, strategic and implementation,
    318–19, 434–40
  operational environment of, 319–31
    and superpower competition, 320–1
  psychological environment of, 331–55
    and the Holocaust Syndrome, 333–5
    and the effect of surprise on, 335–6
    content analysis of, 345–7, 349–50
  decision process and implementation
    of, 355–440
    predecisional events, 355–61
    the Period of Innocence, 361–71
      chronology of, 368–71
    the Period of Apprehension, 371–7
      chronology of, 375–7
    the Period of Diplomacy, 377–409
      Cabinet's deliberations during,
      396–7, 398–402
      chronology of, 402–9
    the Period of Resolution, 409–31
      Cabinet's deliberations during,
      417–18, 421–3
      chronology of, 423–31
    the Period of Implementation, 431–
    434
  flow of, 434–40
  feedback from, 440–53
    effect on Jewish immigration to
      Israel, 443–4
  and hypothesis testing, 525ff.
Soviet Union:
  policy toward Jerusalem, 10, 33, 48
  policy regarding German Reparations,
    77
  deterioration of Israel's relations with,
    116–17, 166
  presses Israel to respond to China's
    gestures, 136
  penetrates into the Middle East, 226,
    257
  role in Sinai Campaign, 227, 284–5,
    310
  role in Six Day War, 320–1, 356, 358,
    394–5, 445
  military presence in Egypt, 458, 487
Spain, 105
Structural empiricism:
  defined, 4, 4n.
  operational steps in, 4–8, 518, 580

Suez Canal, 136, 226ff., 253, 262, 272, 281, 293, 506
Syria, 10, 116, 175ff.
  protests to Security Council concerning Jordan Waters, 188, 191
  effect of domestic instability on policies of, 323-4
  responsibility for the Six Day War, 355-6, 357, 432
  Israeli warnings to, 359, 359n.-361n.

Tahal, 195, 208, 210
Taiwan, 119ff., 129, 137, 164
Theory building, 8, 518ff.
  and comparative research, 518
  and problems of subjectivity, 519
Third World, the:
  image of Israel in, 165, 169
Tiran Straits, 136, 253, 258, 265, 274, 291, 313, 338
  blockade of, as a casus belli, 343, 372
Tora shebe'al peh, 447-8, 453, 460-2
Tripartite Declaration, 227
Trusteeship Council, the, 20, 21, 28, 31
Tzahal, 10, 33, 47
  launches Operation Kedem, 22-3, 23n.
  at the end of 1950, 59
  proposal to dispatch contingent of, to Korea, 122
  an interest group, 232, 237
  prepares for the Sinai Campaign, 264-5, 266-7, 274-5
  withdraws from Sinai, 294, 302
  superiority of, 324
  stand on Six Day War, 378n.-379n., 385, 401-2, 418

UNEF, 281, 300, 314, 338, 341, 355
  withdraws from Sinai, 363-5
United Kingdom:
  policy toward Jerusalem, 34
  policy regarding German Reparations, 77
  policy toward China, 127, 134
  on Jordan Waters issue, 212n.
  role in Sinai Campaign, 228-9, 266-8, 268n.-269n., 270-3, 292
  role in Six Day War, 374, 384, 399, 416n.
United Nations, 5
  resolutions regarding Jerusalem, 9, 10, 12, 20, 22, 25, 27-8, 28n., 33-34
  Partition Resolution, 9, 15

post-1967 policy toward Jerusalem, 39-41, 48
Israeli backing for role in Korean War, 110, 114, 120ff., 130ff.
Israeli vote on China issue in, 143, 149n., 155-6
resolutions concerning Jordan Waters, 174, 219-20
role in Sinai Campaign, 226, 278ff., 295
  Israeli images of, 235-8, 314
  and Israel's withdrawal from, 300
Israeli images of, in 1967, 338ff.
and the Jarring Mission, 499-500, 504-5
United States:
  policy toward Jerusalem, 10, 34, 48
  policy regarding German Reparations, 77, 92
  a pre-eminent bilateral factor, 112, 120ff., 130ff., 164, 166
  policy regarding Jordan Waters 175-6, 191-2, 195ff., 219ff.
  and the Draft Memorandum of Understanding, 202-3, 204
  grant to Jordan, 210
  role in Sinai Campaign, 227-8, 276ff., 285-6, 314
  guarantees sought by Israel, 296-299, 300-2
  role in Six Day War, 322, 378-9, 381, 386-8, 389-93, 399, 399n.-400n., 400-1, 414-15, 417, 417n., 420, 444-5
  post-1967 policy, 456, 486
  initiates the Rogers Proposals, 479ff., 508-9
UNRWA, 189, 192
USSR, see Soviet Union

Vatican:
  policy toward Jerusalem, 10, 14, 25, 33n., 50-1

War of Attrition, the, 454, 456, 486
West Bank, the, 448, 462
White Paper (1939), 14
World Jewish Congress, 73

Yarmuk River, 175ff.
Yedi'ot Aharonot:
  on German Reparations, 59, 85
  advocacy concerning Six Day War, 328
Yost Document, the, 484-6